OXFORD STUDIES IN ANCIENT DOCUMENTS

General Editors
Alan Bowman   Alison Cooley

OXFORD STUDIES IN ANCIENT DOCUMENTS

This innovative new series offers unique perspectives on the political, cultural, social, and economic history of the ancient world. Exploiting the latest technological advances in imaging, decipherment, and interpretation, the volumes cover a wide range of documentary sources, including inscriptions, papyri, and wooden tablets.

The Greek Theatre and Festivals

Documentary Studies

Edited by
PETER WILSON

OXFORD
UNIVERSITY PRESS

OXFORD

UNIVERSITY PRESS

Great Clarendon Street, Oxford OX2 6DP

Oxford University Press is a department of the University of Oxford.
It furthers the University's objective of excellence in research, scholarship,
and education by publishing worldwide in

Oxford New York

Auckland Cape Town Dar es Salaam Hong Kong Karachi
Kuala Lumpur Madrid Melbourne Mexico City Nairobi
New Delhi Shanghai Taipei Toronto

With offices in

Argentina Austria Brazil Chile Czech Republic France Greece
Guatemala Hungary Italy Japan Poland Portugal Singapore
South Korea Switzerland Thailand Turkey Ukraine Vietnam

Oxford is a registered trade mark of Oxford University Press
in the UK and in certain other countries

Published in the United States
by Oxford University Press Inc., New York

British Library Cataloguing in Publication Data
Data available

Library of Congress Cataloging in Publication Data
Data available

Typeset by RefineCatch Limited, Bungay, Suffolk
Printed in Great Britain
on acid-free paper by
Biddles Ltd, King's Lynn, Norfolk

ISBN 978–0–19–927747–6

1 3 5 7 9 10 8 6 4 2

Preface

I should like to express my warm thanks to the following institutions and individuals for their support of the colloquium, held in Oxford on 14–15 July 2003, that give rise to this volume: The Faculty of Classics, Oxford University; the Centre for the Study of Ancient Documents, Oxford and its Director, Alan Bowman and its Administrator, Maggie Sasanow; New College, Oxford; the British Academy; the Hellenic Society, London; St Catherine's College, Oxford. Above all, that occasion and this book benefited enormously from the enthusiastic, convivial and learned contribution of all the participants, for which I am very grateful. Eric Csapo and Richard Hunter were especially encouraging and supportive in the earliest stages of planning.

Further thanks are due to Oxford University Press and to the series editors of Oxford Studies in Ancient Documents, Alan Bowman and Alison Cooley, for accepting this book for the series; and to Alison in particular for valuable editorial advice at a critical moment. The Epigraphical Museum, Athens and its Director, Charalambos Kritzas, the School of Philosophical and Historical Inquiry in the Faculty of Arts, the University of Sydney, and the Australian Research Council all provided assistance in various forms in the production of this book. Thanks too to Andrew Hartwig, Tim Buckley, and in particular to Nancy-Jane Rucker, for their fine editorial assistance; and to Kathleen McLaughlin for overseeing the production of the book at the Press.

Rather than imposing a standard form, contributors' preferred spellings of Greek names have on the whole been retained throughout.

Contents

PART III. BEYOND ATHENS

Contributors

Sophia Aneziri, Department of History, University of Athens.

Paola Ceccarelli, Leverhulme Reader in Greek Cultural Studies at Durham University.

Angelos Chaniotis, Senior Research Fellow for Classical Studies, All Souls College, Oxford.

Charles Crowther, Assistant Director, Centre for the Study of Ancient Documents, University of Oxford.

Eric Csapo, Professor of Classics at the University of Sydney.

Hans Rupprecht Goette, Professor of Classical Archaeology at the German Archaeological Institute (Berlin) and at the University of Giessen.

Brigitte Le Guen, Professeur d'Histoire grecque à l'Université de Paris 8.

David Jordan, Senior Associate Member, the American School of Classical Studies at Athens.

John Ma, Fellow and Tutor in Ancient History, Corpus Christi College and Lecturer in Ancient History, Oxford University.

Silvia Milanezi, Professeur d'Histoire grecque à l'Université de Nantes.

Ian Rutherford, Professor of Classics at the University of Reading, (UK) and at Florida State University (USA)

William Slater, Professor Emeritus, McMaster University.

Peter Wilson, William Ritchie Professor of Classics at the University of Sydney.

Illustrations

Abbreviations

AE	*L'Année épigraphique: revue des publications épigraphiques.* Paris, 1889– .
APF	J. K. Davies, *Athenian Propertied Families, 600–300 BC.* Oxford, 1971.
BE	'Bulletin épigraphique', annually in *Revue des études grecques (REG).* 1938–84, by J. and L. Robert, since 1987 under the direction of P. Gauthier.
BMC	*A catalogue of the Greek coins in the British Museum.* London, 1873– .
BTCG	*Bibliografia topografica della colonizzazione greca in Italia e nelle isole tirreniche.* Directed by G. Nenci and G. Vallet. Pisa and Rome, 1977– .
CAH	*Cambridge Ancient History,* 2nd edn. Cambridge, 1961– .
CIA App.	*Inscriptiones Atticae. Supplementum Inscriptionum Atticarum I.* ed. A. Oikonomides. Chicago, 1976. (= *IG* I², II/III² *Paraleipomena et Addenda*).
CID IV.	*Corpus des Inscriptions de Delphes.* Paris, 1978– .
CIG	*Corpus Inscriptionum Graecarum.* ed. A. Boeckh, J. Franz, E. Curtius and A. Kirchhoff. Berlin, 1828–77.
Corinth VIII.3	*Corinth VIII.3. The Inscriptions 1926–1950.* ed. J. H. Kent. Princeton, 1966.
DTWü.	*Defixionum tabellae.* ed. R. Wünsch (= *IG* III³. Berlin, 1897).
EA	*Epigraphica Anatolica.* Österreichische Akademie der Wissenschaften, Rheinisch-Westfälische Akademie der Wissenschaften, Türk Tarih Kurumu. Bonn, 1983– .
EB	'Epigraphical Bulletin', annually in *Kernos.*
EV	Abbreviation used by M. Segré (1993) *Iscrizioni di Cos,* for votive inscriptions and other texts relating to public or private cult.
ED	Abbreviation used by M. Segré (1993) *Iscrizioni di Cos,* for decrees and other documents of a public, administrative, or juridical nature.

I.Mylasa	*Die Inschriften von Mylasa*, 2 vols. (*IGSK* 34–5), ed. W. Blümel. Bonn, 1988.
I.Olympia	*Die Inschriften von Olympia*, ed. W. Dittenberger and K. Purgold. Berlin, 1896.
I.Pergamon	*Die Inschriften von Pergamon*, ed. M. Fränkel (with E. Fabricius and C. Schuchhardt) (*Altertümer von Pergamon 8*), 2 vols. Berlin, 1890, 1895.
I.Perge	*Die Inschriften von Perge. Teil I. Vorrömische Zeit, frühe und hohe Kaiserzeit.* (*IGSK* 54.1), ed. S. Sahin. Bonn, 1999.
I.Priene	*Inschriften von Priene*, ed. F. Hiller von Gaertringen. Berlin, 1906.
I.Side	*Side im Altertum. Geschichte und Zeugnisse. Band II* (*IGSK* 44.2), ed. J. Nollé. Bonn, 2001.
I.Smyrna	*Die Inschriften von Smyrna* (*IGSK* 23 and 24, 1–2), ed. G. Petzl. Bonn, 1982–90.
Inventory	*An Inventory of Archaic and Classical Poleis: An Investigation Conducted by the Copenhagen Polis Centre for the Danish National Research Foundation*, ed. M. Hansen and T. Heine Nielsen. Oxford, 2004.
I.Tralles	*Die Inschriften von Tralleis und Nysa* (*IGSK* 36), ed. F. Poljakov. Bonn, 1989.
LB–W	P. Le Bas and W.-H. Waddington, *Voyage archéologique en Grèce et en Asie Mineure*, 3 vols. Paris, 1851–70.
LCS	A. D. Trendall, *The Red-Figured Vases of Lucania, Campania and Sicily*. Oxford, 1967.
LGPN I	P. Fraser and E. Matthews, *A Lexicon of Greek Personal Names*, vol. I: *The Aegean Islands, Cyprus, Cyrenaica*. Oxford, 1987.
LGPN II	M. Osborne and S. Byrne, *A Lexicon of Greek Personal Names*, vol. II: *Attica*. Oxford, 1994.
LGPN IIIA	P. Fraser and E. Matthews, *A Lexicon of Greek Personal Names*, vol. IIIA: *The Peloponnese, Western Greece, Sicily and Magna Graecia*. Oxford, 1997.
LIMC	*Lexicon iconographicum mythologiae classicae*, 18 vols. Zurich, 1981–99.
LSAM	F. Sokolowski, *Lois sacrées de l'Asie Mineure*. Paris, 1955.
LSCG	F. Sokolowski, *Lois sacrées des cités grecques*. Paris, 1969.

LSSel	M. Jameson, D. Jordan and R. Kotansky, *A lex sacra from Selinous.* Durham, N.C., 1993.
MAMA	*Monumenta Asiae Minoris Antiqua.* London, 1928–93.
Michel	C. Michel, *Recueil d'inscriptions grecques,* with preface by B. Haussoullier. Paris, 1900.
Milet	*Milet. Ergebnisse der Ausgrabungen und Untersuchungen seit dem Jahr 1899.* General editor V. von Graeve. Band 6, 1–3: *Die Inschriften von Milet,* ed. A. Rehm, P. Herrmann, W. Günther, and N. Ehrhardt. Berlin, 1997–2006.
Moretti, *ISE*	*Iscrizioni storiche ellenistiche. Testo critico, traduzione e commento,* ed. L. Moretti, 3 vols. Vol. I: *Attica, Peloponneso, Beozia;* vol. II: *Grecia centrale e settentrionale;* vol. III: *Supplemento e indici,* ed. F. C. de Rossi. Florence, 1967–2001.
NGCT	D. Jordan, 'New Greek curse tablets (1985–2000)', *GRBS* 41 (2000) 5–46.
Nouveau Choix	L'Institut Fernand-Courby, *Nouveau Choix d'inscriptions grecques: textes, traductions, commentaires.* Paris, 1971.
OGIS	*Orientis Graeci inscriptiones selectae. Supplementum sylloges inscriptionum Graecarum,* ed. W. Dittenberger, 2 vols. Leipzig, 1903–05 (unchanged reprint, Hildesheim, 1960).
Olympionikai	L. Moretti, *I vincitori negli antichi agoni olimpici. Atti della Academia Nazionale dei Lincei, Classe di Scienze morali, storiche e filologiche, Memorie,* ser. 8, vol. 8, fasc. 2. Rome, 1957.
OMS	L. Robert, *Opera Minora Selecta: Epigraphie et antiquités grecques,* 7 vols. Amsterdam, 1969–90.
PAA	J. Traill, *Persons of Ancient Athens.* Toronto, 1994– .
Paton-Hicks	W. R. Paton and E. L. Hicks, *The Inscriptions of Cos.* Oxford, 1891; repr. Hildesheim, 1990.
PCG	*Poetae Comici Graeci,* ed. R. Kassel and C. Austin. Berlin, 1983– .
PHal	*Halle Papyri.* Berlin, 1913.
PMich	*University of Michigan Papyri.*
RC	C. B. Welles, *Royal Correspondence in the Hellenistic Period. A Study in Greek Epigraphy.* New Haven, 1934.
Rhodes–Osborne	*Greek Historical Inscriptions 404–323 BC,* ed. P. Rhodes and R. Osborne. Oxford, 2003.

SECir   *Supplemento epigrafico cirenaico*, ed. G. Oliverio, G. Pugliese
         Carratelli, and D. Morelli, *Annuario della Scuola Archeologica
         di Atene* 39–49. Athens, 1961–62 (1963).

SEG   *Supplementum epigraphicum graecum*. Leiden, 1923– .

SGD   D. Jordan, 'A survey of Greek *defixiones* not included in the
         special corpora', *GRBS* 26 (1985) 151–97.

SH   *Supplementum Hellenisticum*, ed. H. Lloyd-Jones and
         P. Parsons. Oxford, 1983.

Syll.³   *Sylloge Inscriptionum Graecarum*, ed. W. Dittenberger, 3rd
         edn., 4 vols. Leipzig, 1915–24 (unchanged reprint, Chicago,
         1974).

Tod II   *A Selection of Greek Historical Inscriptions to the End of the
         Fifth Century BC*, vol. II: *From 403 to 323 BC*, ed. M. Tod.
         Oxford, 1948.

TrGF I   *Tragicorum Graecorum Fragmenta* I, ed. B. Snell and
         R. Kannicht, 2nd edn. Göttingen, 1986.

Introduction: From the Ground Up

Peter Wilson

The Greek—and above all, the Attic—theatre is probably the single most intensively studied institution from the ancient world. And, over the last thirty years in particular, research into Classical drama as an institution of the city-state has enjoyed a spectacular regeneration and efflorescence through the application of a range of fruitful new approaches. The once largely text-centred study of traditional philology and New Criticism has given way to a series of new methodologies that seek to understand dramatic texts within their many original ancient contexts. From the late 1970s performance-analysis and reconstruction pioneered by Oliver Taplin led the way,[1] teaching us to see Classical tragedy and comedy as works for the stage rather than the study, designed for a very real live performance under the alien conditions and conventions of ancient Greek open-air, communal, religious theatre. In the 1980s and beyond the paradigm shifted to more broadly political and social contexts, largely under the influence of the so-called 'Paris School' of Vernant and Vidal-Naquet, with its many successors.[2] This approach has for instance revealed how the theatre was a sounding-board for the deepest and most intractable issues of Athenian political and

---

[1] Taplin (1977); cf. Russo (1984(1962)); Wiles (1997); Rehm (2002).
[2] Vernant and Vidal-Naquet (1988(1972, 1986)); Goldhill (1986), (1987); Hall (1989); Meier (1993(1988)); Seaford (1994); Winkler and Zeitlin (1990); Easterling (1997). Witness the exponential growth of output in the 1980s and 1990s documented by Green (1998).

social life, a site in which to grapple with the tensions and conflicts generated by the meteoric rate of growth of the imperial city-state— for instance, the deep conflicts that rapid social change generated between the genders and generations; or the obligations and perils of wielding huge power, and the consequent emergence of entirely new notions of personal agency. More recently, a further development within this approach has placed the emphasis on the ideological dynamics of tragedy (and to a lesser extent, of comedy) both within and beyond the city-state—serving as a medium of mutual mystifica- tion between the social groups of élite and mass that structured the democratic polity;[3] and as a means of Athenian cultural hegemony in the wider Greek world through the dramatic appropriation of the mythic heritage and heroes of her 'friends' abroad.[4]

A common feature of all these works is that they have sought to ground themselves, more explicitly than their narrowly literary or philological forebears, in the historical moment of the theatre and its instituting societies.[5] A new and welcome value has been attached to the evidence for the operation of the theatre within its original context, or rather within its many original contexts. This sophisti- cated move to historicise drama represents a genuine paradigm-shift of enormous richness. Yet in some cases, the influence of the dichot- omising habits of structuralism has tended to privilege powerful, abstract polarities, particularly in terms of the ideological construc- tion of Athenian identity—which has been the subject of greatest scholarly interest in this development. While the Greek mentality was certainly infused and formed by polarities, there is a danger that excessive attachment to them in interpretation can result, para- doxically, in the elision and homogenisation of the very historical specificity, desire for which motivated the historical turn in the first place.[6]

The approach collectively exemplified in this volume advocates

---

[3] Griffith (1995).   [4] Kowalzig (2006).

[5] 'Historical moment' is the phrase of Vernant and Vidal-Naquet, from the title of their important article of (originally) 1968: see Vernant and Vidal-Naquet (1988 (1972, 1986) 23–8, 417).

[6] For further discussion of these issues see the contributions to Goff (1995) and Pelling (1997).

recognition of the specificity and complexity of the material conditions of dramatic production as they varied over time and place;
and the recognition of the importance of close contact with the
raw data relating to the organisation and operation of theatre and
festivals. Attention to such information need not represent a retreat
to naïve empiricism. Analysed with the appropriate care and sophistication, the documentary evidence can become a more eloquent
testimony to the ideological and historical complexity of its societies.
Interpretation arrives at an apprehension of such complexity
through a 'bottom-up' approach, from the evidence for material
conditions, rather than via the 'top-down' method of some of the
more abstract forms of structuralism and post-structuralism.

Despite the marked interest in the historical and social dimensions
of drama, the documentary base on which all this recent work rests
has itself received little systematic attention for decades. Hundreds
of these interpretative studies blithely refer to the relevant pages
of Pickard-Cambridge's *The Dramatic Festivals of Athens*[2] and
Dithyramb, Tragedy, Comedy and take all that is said in them on trust.
While a number of recent contributions have updated some aspects
of these fundamental works, or presented elements of the material
with significant new analysis, there remains a real need to energise
the study of the documentary base of the Greek theatre—and the
same is true of the performance culture of Greek festivals more
broadly—'from the ground up'. This volume is a first step in such a
project.

To this end, the parts into which this book is divided represent a
three-pronged approach. The first—'Festivals and Performers: Some
New Perspectives'—recognises the need for venturing broad over-
views on some of the big-picture questions. The second—'Festivals
of Athens and Attica'—constitutes a call to reinvigorate the study of
the familiar material from the metropolis of theatre by asking new
questions of it, by recombining its elements in unfamiliar and productive ways, and by integrating less well-known evidence into the
mainstream of discussion. The third part—'Beyond Athens'—moves
away from that metropolis to the wide, enormously rich and still
under-studied world beyond.

William Slater's opening salvo tackles the big picture by refus-
ing to shy away from the sheer bulk and unpredictability of the

epigraphic material at hand for the theatrical and festival culture of Greece. Much of the evidence he presents is largely 'unprocessed' by historians of Greek festival culture, let alone by mainstream historians. For it is a recurrent theme of this volume, and an aspiration for future work, that the evidence of Greek communities' festival life has important ramifications for the more traditional questions of politics, of inter-state relations and the shifting balance of powers in the Mediterranean.

Slater also alerts us to some of the peculiar problems that beset all our evidence: for instance the uncomfortable fit, or entire absence of any observable fit, between epigraphic and numismatic sources for festivals; and the particular variability of the 'epigraphical habit' in relation to festivals across time and place. His survey suggests the need for posing afresh some basic questions in response to the pattern of evidence, such as why certain groups or individuals chose to record their festival arrangements in a permanent manner while others did not.

One boundary that has recently, and very productively, undergone erosion in ancient theatre studies, largely under the influence of developments in anthropology and social anthropology, is that between 'the play' itself and the ensemble of other events—ritual, political, disruptive—that framed and interfered with drama, or any ancient performance: the procession that brought the god and his offerings to the sanctuary; the announcement by heralds of honours awarded to civic benefactors; the presentation of Athens' orphaned boys of the year's war-dead on reaching manhood, or of the Classical empire's tribute, deposited talant-by-talant in the orchestra; or the unscheduled but equally entertaining brawls that broke out between rich and honour-hungry sponsors in front of the assembled audience.[7] The epigraphic dossier is particularly rich in evidence for

---

[7] Goldhill (1987) was a seminal study of the Great Dionysia in this respect; cf. also Sourvinou-Inwood (1994); contributors to Winkler and Zeitlin (1990) and Dougherty and Kurke (1993), (2003). Goldhill and Osborne (1999) refines and extends the approach to other areas of Athenian culture: Kavoulaki (1999) on processions, building on the important article of Connor (1987); cf. also Cole (1993); Maurizio (1998). Wilson (1991) and (2000) 144–97 on khoregic performance and disruption.

the (attempted, desiderated) management of such activities, and a pioneer of its comprehensive analysis, Angelos Chaniotis,[8] gives us here a survey and typology of these activities that ranges very widely in time and place. He shows, among other things, that theatres were 'engines of honour'—sites where the very act of conferring honour on individuals or groups was a performative event that made that honour real. As such, theatres were also the pre-eminent site for communication between men and gods, between the constitutive elements of a city-state and, with increasing importance in the Hellenistic period, between city-states and the succession of powerful forces outside them that so determined their fate: Macedonian overlords, kings, and Roman emperors. These 'stage directions in stone' only became abundant in the Hellenistic period, but we can with some confidence say that their appearance in the epigraphic record should not be correlated with their appearance in practice, for Greek political society had long been a performance culture in which the paradramatic was deeply inscribed, both in the very basic rituals of its religious practice such as sacrifice and procession and in the (alleged or imagined) actions of leaders like Peisistratos and Solon—the former said to have carefully stage-managed his return to power by costuming an especially tall local girl as Athena and putting her in the front of his chariot as though a divine escort; the latter perhaps having 'played mad' in a striking appearance in the agora of Athens designed to persuade his city to war.[9] If the (apparently) endlessly repetitive character of the Hellenistic honorific decrees and similar documents has hitherto encouraged historians to regard (and more often to ignore) them as empty formulae, Chaniotis demonstrates that these formulae, like those of Homer, operate within a tight economy in which subtle variation is all-important.

The single most significant development (and an extraordinarily complex development at that) in the post-Classical history of the Greek theatre is the rise and spread of the powerful organisations known as the Artists ('Craftsmen' might be a better word: I shall use

---

[8] See esp. Chaniotis (1997).
[9] Peisistratos' return: Connor (1987); Cawkwell (1995); Solon plays mad: Plu. *Sol.* 8; D.L. 1.2; Higbie (1997).

the transliteration *Tekhnitai* throughout) of Dionysos (οἱ περὶ τὸν Διόνυσον τεχνῖται). These Guilds or Associations (*koina, synodoi*) were born of the vast and rapid spread of the theatre from Attica in the late Classical period, and more particularly, of the steep escalation in demand for its experts, and so too in its economic force. They provided—to individuals, cities, or the various organising bodies of particular festivals across and beyond Greece—a specially tailored array of the necessary performers of all kinds (including musicians, actors, and poets) as well as production teams (costume makers, trainers) 'publicity' (heralds), even the entire paraphernalia needed to launch new divine or quasi-divine cults. And they negotiated the financial and other terms of labour for their members, providing in turn for the power-brokers of the age the forms of commemoration, propaganda, and honorific publicity that they needed, all the while operating as virtually autonomous political entities issuing their own decrees, electing their own magistrates, and sending ambassadors to all corners of the Greek world.

Our (fragmentary) knowledge of their extraordinary range of activities is based overwhelmingly on epigraphy.[10] We are very fortunate to have two full-scale recent studies devoted to this difficult material. Their authors—Brigitte Le Guen and Sophia Aneziri—both contribute to this volume. The two major works of these scholars—which include authoritative editions and commentary on the entire documentary corpus—have rescued the *Tekhnitai* from nearly a century of effective neglect and built the framework for a new generation of study, and for future discoveries (which are entirely likely, as Ma's contribution here shows).[11] In this volume, Aneziri provides a broad survey of the range of organisational services and participation offered by the *Tekhnitai* in musical contests in the Hellenistic period. This is the sort of big picture issue that has been markedly absent in the study of the *Tekhnitai* for so long. Aneziri

---

[10] In very approximate terms, epigraphical sources for their activities are some 500 percent more abundant than literary (Le Guen 2001a: I.22)—another instance of a striking evidential distribution that merits further consideration.

[11] Aneziri (2003); Le Guen (2001a) I and II. Another valuable contribution to this revival of interest is the introductory essay of Lightfoot (2002). See also the most important items in translation, with synthetic overview, in Csapo and Slater (1994) 239–55.

presents the answers available on the current evidence to such central questions as whether the *Tekhnitai* enforced a members-only policy for participation (and remuneration) in the contests organised, or co-organised, by them.[12]

Metropolis of theatre, the city of Athens also merits the title of metropolis of the epigraphic habit. Important advances, large and small, are currently being made in the ample region where these two spheres overlap: the completion of the third edition of the monumental work of epigraphical scholarship that is *Inscriptiones Graecae* I and II is not far distant; a number of interpretative studies heavily dependent on the relevant elements of it have recently appeared, and new finds continue to be made.[13]

The contributors to the second part of this volume all treat Athenian material in new ways. Eric Csapo assembles for the first time the dossier of epigraphic and other evidence for the neglected figure of the theatre-lessee, and makes a bold and compelling case that, prior to the construction of the first stone theatre of Dionysos in the last third of the fourth century, the Athenian polis had the seating of that theatre rebuilt in wood each year under a contract that saw private, entrepreneurial interests make a handsome profit from takings. The consequences of this argument (based in large part on close analysis of the important but neglected lease for the Peiraieus theatre, *Agora* 19 (1991) L13) are enormous. No Classical drama was

---

[12] For a full discussion of these issues as they relate to actors in particular in the Hellenistic period see also Le Guen (2004).

[13] Examples of recent editions of and studies based heavily on Attic theatre-inscriptions: Mette (1977); Csapo and Slater (1994); Le Guen (2001a); Aneziri (2003); Csapo (2004b); Makres (1994) and Wilson (2000) on khoregic and related inscriptions; Stephanis (1988), a full prosopography of the festival community in and beyond Athens. Jones' study of rural Attic theatre (2004: ch. 4) should also be mentioned. Some important smaller-scale contributions and new finds: Lambert (1998) on the *genos* Bakkhiadai and (2003) on the first Athenian *agonothetai* (further work is promised on decrees honouring members of the theatre-community at Assembly meetings held in the theatre after the Dionysia); Palles (2003); Latini (2003); Summa (2003a), (2003b), (2004). Summa, who is engaged on the *IG* II³ project, also promises work on the deme material. Wilson and Csapo have embarked on a project (funded by the Australian Research Council) to write a new social and economic history of the Classical theatre, on the basis of a complete overhaul of the documentary evidence.

staged at its debut in an urban theatre with permanent seating; the capacity of the fifth-century theatre is much closer to seven than to Plato's 'thirty thousand'; we must recognise the existence of a vigorous theatrical economy at work at a much earlier date than has hitherto been supposed.

In discussion following Csapo's paper at the colloquium which gave rise to this volume, it emerged that Hans Goette's work-in-progress on the archaeology and architecture of the theatre of Dionysos had reached strikingly similar conclusions to Csapo's from its very different angle on the matter of the seating capacity of the Classical theatre. He has accordingly provided a well-illustrated appendix to Csapo's chapter that presents the best available current evidence for the little that we know about the Classical *theatron*, thereby correcting a good deal of entirely misguided and extremely influential discussion of the subject that still fills handbooks of the theatre. His own chapter that follows is also fundamentally archaeological in orientation, and it serves to exemplify an important principle of all epigraphic work: that while inscriptions are indeed texts, they are most importantly—like all texts—texts in contexts. The most immediate material context for the many khoregic inscriptions from the Athenian theatre is that of their monumental setting, the physical structures on which these records of theatrical success were inscribed. Goette presents a comprehensive survey of these, introducing material hitherto overlooked in this connection, based on his extensive work in Athens and his access to the collections of the city's museums. His survey perfectly illustrates the importance of assessing the epigraphic corpus in and against architectural environment. For while the epigraphic formulae of the khoregic inscriptions show relatively limited variation, their monumental settings are spectacularly varied. Important conclusions follow for the politics of display within a (changing) democratic context.

My own chapter looks at a major urban festival of Athens, the Thargelia in honour of Apollo, which has been sidelined in the recent proliferation of integrated studies of festivals like the Panathenaia and Dionysia that have shown very fruitfully how the various constituent elements and the dynamic structures of these festivals—including their prominent agonistic performances—were vital to the formation and development of Athenian collective and group identities.[14] The Thargelia has suffered from the glamour of its siblings, and probably too from the fact that drama was never, apparently, introduced to it (as it was eventually even at the Panathenaia.)[15] Yet musical performance was central to Apollo's festival, in the form of the 'circular choruses' organised according to the Attic tribes that are so prominent on the Athenian festival scene, and well represented in the epigraphic record. Within the context of a general assessment of these performances held at the Thargelia, largely on the basis of the epigraphic dossier, I attempt to initiate a more integrated approach to this festival.

Close study of this urban festival of Athens opens paths beyond Athens and Attica—to Delos in particular and to the cities of the Classical maritime empire, whose performances for Apollo on Delos were significantly moulded, I argue, by Athenian practice in the *Pythion* at home. Those paths beyond Athens are followed much further afield in Part Three, which ranges widely in the vast, growing and (increasingly) well-edited array of rich epigraphic and archaeological material from outside Attica which is, as yet, largely under-exploited.[16]

A further bridge between Parts Two and Three is provided by the elusive but long-lived and widespread performance category of dithyramb. The surviving khoregic monuments discussed by Goette

---

[14] On the Panathenaia: Neils (1992), (1994), (1996); Wohl (1996); Maurizio (1998); Shear (2001); on the Dionysia: Goldhill (1986); Easterling (1997), with further bibliography.

[15] See Tracey and Habicht (1991); D.L. 3.56; *IG* II² 3157 (first century AD).

[16] A few recent contributions to the study of theatrical culture (broadly understood) through epigraphy outside Attica (purely *exempli gratia*): the major re-edition and analysis of the documents relating to the *Tekhnitai* of Dionysos by Le Guen (2001a) and Aneziri (2003); Le Guen (2001b) on theatre in the islands; Ceccarelli (1995) on the Koan Dionysia, to which the ongoing publications of Parker and Obbink (cf. 2000, 2001a, 20001b) will add further material. Important studies of the spread of theatre: Easterling (1994); Dearden (1999); Le Guen (1995); Taplin (1999); Allan (2001); Revermann (1999–2000); Csapo (2004b). Another recent sign of growing interest in the *Realien* of the post-Classical theatre is the collection edited by Martina (2003). This includes a study by Nicolucci (2003) of the role of satyr-drama at the court of Attalos I that can profitably be read alongside the chapters by Le Guen and Ma in this volume.

are overwhelmingly associated with dithyramb,[17] while the circular choruses of the Thargelia are routinely, if (in my opinion) problematically, equated with dithyramb by a scholarly tradition that stretches back at least to late antiquity. Just as this volume seeks to move the centre of attention away from Athens and away from the Classical period, so too it cumulatively makes the case for studying the history of the dramatic genres alongside those with which they shared their theatres, and often their festivals—in particular the dithyramb, but also other musical performances such as song to the *kithara*, instrumental *kithara*-playing and the various crafts (*tekhnai*) for the ubiquitous double-pipe (*aulos*).[18] This is far from being a revolutionary suggestion. Pickard-Cambridge not only devoted a book to the full 'triad' of theatrical genres (*Dithyramb, Tragedy, Comedy* (1927)); his magisterial study of the theatre through all its documented remains (*Dramatic Festivals of Athens* (1988)) also deals with dithyramb, though in a somewhat perfunctory manner. Like so much other scholarly discussion of the form, this is heavily antiquarian in its orientation or simply a modern rewriting of the ancient critical tradition's dismissive history of decline. For dithyramb has always been the ugly sister among the Dionysian genres, and its post-Classical material and performative dimensions in particular are very poorly represented in modern scholarship.[19] Yet this was the most widespread and long-lasting form of choral performance in the ancient world, with a securely dateable history

---

[17] For an exploration of the question as to why the remains of Athenian khoregic monuments are so skewed away from the dramatic forms and towards dithyramb see Wilson (1997a) and (2000), esp. 236–44.

[18] Moretti (2001) is a fine example of an advanced general introduction that includes musical contests (*mousikoi agones*) alongside theatre. For the ubiquity of the *aulos* see the works cited by Le Guen below p. 251, and Wilson (1999).

[19] Some promising recent developments include: Zimmermann's general survey (1992); the collection of testimonia of Ieranò (1997); new editions and commentaries on the surviving texts by Lavecchia (2000) of Pindar (another by d'Alessio is eagerly awaited); and Maehler (1997) for Bakkhylides. Cf. also Wilson (2000) and (2003); Csapo (2004b) on the prominence of dithyramb within the 'New Musical revolution'; Fearn (2003), forthcoming as a monograph. A volume on dithyramb and social change arising from a colloquium held in Oxford in July 2004 edited by Barbara Kowalzig and myself will appear in due course. Among others it includes important contributions on Hellenistic dithyramb (Ceccarelli), the later (imperial) Athenian dithyrambic monuments (Shear) and the changing name of the form (d'Alesssio).

from the early Archaic age well into the late Hellenistic period. It thus offers a rich terrain for the study of changing cultural forms, and in particular of the shifting relationship between drama and dithyramb.

In Part Three the spotlight is twice focussed on dithyrambic performance in widely separated centres of the Greek world—Cyrene and Teos. Paola Ceccarelli and Silvia Milanezi analyse two intriguing items of epigraphical evidence for the performance of dithyramb—as well as tragedy—in the culturally flourishing centre of fourth-century Cyrene (where excavations continue to uncover theatres). The first was published some six years after the appearance of Pickard-Cambridge's authoritative survey of 1927, and as a result has never made it into the mainstream of theatre- or literary-historical discussion. The other was only published in 1998. Their exemplary presentation of and commentary on this difficult material remedies a significant omission in the current works of reference and illustrates nicely how much our knowledge of the big picture of performance history depends on the careful analysis of nugatory finds whose appearance is so unpredictable.

The Cyrenean documents reveal to us civic and religious authorities concerned to account for (among many other things) the expenses that accrued to them from the performance of tragedy and dithyramb at one of their major festivals—principally, it seems, in the form of the 'traditional' beast associated with dithyramb, the ox, which had probably been awarded as the prize for victors in contests of both tragedy and dithyramb. By contrast, the new inscription from Teos published here for the first time by John Ma fits into the well-known category of the victor-list, a permanent record in stone of the successful contenders in a range of competitive events erected by the organising authority of the events. Discovered by Ma with the help of some Turkish schoolchildren—literally unearthed from the soil of their playground—this becomes the fourth inscription testifying to energetic contention in dithyramb and satyr-play in the late third and second centuries. He places his discussion of the new find within a valuable survey of the region, history and epigraphy of Teos. And he attempts to resolve in this specific case the issue addressed in the round by Aneziri in Part One, as to what degree of organisational involvement an Association of *Tekhnitai* (in this instance, that of

Ionia and the Hellespont, based in Teos at the time) had in the festival whose events these lists record.

As a contribution to the history of dithyramb, Ma has given us the title of a new Hellenistic dithyramb—the *Horse*—with all the intriguing possibilities that a performance named thus after the great Trojan exploit may have had in the context of shifting power-relations in second-century western Anatolia. And the document presents a number of other tantalising clues about the development, and regional variation, in the form. For these Tean records, like the Cyrenean, use the specific Greek word διθυραμβός (*dithyrambos*) of their performances in a manner that the much more abundant material from the Classical Athenian Dionysia never does. We have to wait for the inclusion, in a personal list of the agonistic successes won by a famous kitharode, Nikokles son of Aristokles, of a victory 'with a dithyramb at the Lenaia' (Λήναια διθυράμβωι) for anything comparable from Athens. Given that this is dated to the third century, we may, as Ma suggests, be looking at growing evidence for a 'revival' of sorts in dithyramb at that time, but now interpreted or reinvented by great singers and instrumentalists on the *kithara* rather than sung by a civic chorus with an aulos-player.[20] We may also, I suggest, be looking at a deliberately archaising gesture in these Tean and Cyrenean, as well as the third-century Athenian, contexts.

Few musical artists (actors, poets, or instrumentalists) from the Archaic or Classical Greek world are known to us as individuals with any degree of detail or historical credibility. Paradoxically, while we know so little about the content of Hellenistic public performances (Menander aside), the vigour of the epigraphic habit in the period has bequeathed a rich prosopography of performers—admirably documented by Stephanis (1988)—which does permit, in a limited number of cases, the possibility of putting a little flesh on otherwise rather bare bones. Much more needs to be done in this area. For instance, Stephanis' prosopography would make it possible to map all known performers (whose ethnics inscriptions by their nature often record) to the festivals and other sites of their activity, and

---

[20] Nikokles, son of Aristokles: see Stephanis (1988) no. 1839. The identification is based on a combination of *IG* II² 3779 (the list of victories of Nikokles son of Aristokles) with Paus. 1.37.2; cf. Wilson (2000) 391 n. 155.

so give us a sense of the patterns of movement of individuals and groups.[21] And there is a need for a more nuanced sociology of musical performers in particular (kitharodes, kitharists, auletes and the like) that gathers and compares all the evidence for remuneration, reward and other signs of status as they are distributed across the various musical *tekhnai*.[22] Brigitte Le Guen gives us a fine idea of what can be done here, in her detailed study of Kraton the *aulos*-player, probably the one musician from the ancient Greek world about whom we are best informed—and the information is provided entirely by epigraphy. What results from this meticulous assessment of the dossier is an individual who almost certainly rose in society on the back of his musical talent; who energetically served his profession at the highest level for decades, in the course of which he grew close to those in power—especially the Pergamene monarchy, for whose glorification he founded a special new artistic association; and who in later life became a substantial benefactor honoured by (among other things) a painted portrait, public eulogy, and a number of statues, beside at least one of which incense was to be burnt on important occasions. The complex mesh of networks traced by Le Guen between the various artistic associations and centres of power through which Kraton conducted his career make of his dossier an ideal illustration of the extremely close and symbiotic relationship between cultural and political power in this period.

One of the regions in which Kraton spent a good part of his professional career was the city studied by Ma in his chapter, Teos. Indeed, Kraton's career overlaps substantially with the period documented by the Tean victor-lists and he is altogether likely to have attended, perhaps even participated in, such performances at some time.[23] Another of Kraton's haunts was the Karian city of Iasos, where for instance we find him providing two days of musical performance

[21] Aneziri (2003) has made important progress in this direction: in addition to her chapter here, see e.g. her invaluable tables (422–62) tracking Hellenistic performers, including one (no. 8) with the *ethnika* of all known *tekhnitai* at contests.

[22] On *aulos*-players cf. Scheithauer (1997); Wilson (2002); cf. Nordquist (1994) on cultic players; on *kithara*-players: Bélis (1995).

[23] The lists do not record the participation of *aulos*-players, although the satyr-play (in *LB–W* 91 = Le Guen 2001a: no. 46 A, *LB–W* 93 = Le Guen 2001a: no. 46 D and the new document) is likely to have required one, as is tragedy and/or comedy, proposed as possibilities for the same context by Ma.

in the theatre.[24] The cultural and political life of this city, as expressed through its theatre and theatrical community, forms the subject of the chapters by Rutherford and Crowther.[25]

Ian Rutherford looks at a talented native of Iasos, the tragic poet Dymas. Not only does he rescue Dymas from unwarranted obscurity (few even among keen readers of *Tragicorum Graecorum Fragmenta* volume I—*Tragici Minores*—have lingered long over the page devoted to him); Rutherford's analysis of the two surviving decrees passed by the authorities in Samothrace in his honour also shows how, in the high Hellenistic period, newly composed tragedy could, through its *content* and not simply by virtue of the genre's accumu-lated cultural capital,[26] play a significant role in relations between states and sanctuaries, and in the energetic fabrication of myth-histories that oiled the wheels of such relations. Like other contri-butions to this volume, Rutherford's discussion reveals intriguing continuities of practice between Archaic–Classical and Hellenistic pragmatic poetics. The role of Dymas the tragic poet, moving between his home city and major panhellenic or regional sanctuaries with the products of his craft like the tragedy *Dardanos*, forging poetic and political ties between both sites and the far greater powers in the world beyond (in this case, Rome in particular)—all of this bears telling resemblance to the actions of more familiar figures like Pindar or Stesikhoros centuries earlier, crossing the Greek world as honoured purveyors of poetic products for the mighty, mortal, and immortal. The principle is the same; only the songs have changed.[27]

Charles Crowther's chapter is a valuable complement to Ruther-ford's, as it provides a more systematic study of the operation of the Dionysia at Iasos, where Dymas spent at least some of his career as both poet and patron.

Crowther presents a fully integrated study of the artistic life of this city as it is revealed through epigraphy. He incorporates recent

[24] *I.Iasos* 163, ll. 9–10. See Crowther below, p. 310; Le Guen below, p. 251.
[25] For recent historical and archaeological studies of Iasos see Caputo (2004).
[26] On which see e.g. Perrin (1997); Le Guen (1995).
[27] Numerous aspects of this continuity emerged in a conference organised by Richard Hunter and Ian Rutherford and held in the Faculty of Classics, Cambridge, in April 2005 on the subject of '*Poeti vaganti*'. A resultant volume of studies is in preparation.

discoveries, regenerates long-standing questions and provides some substantial new readings of well-known documents. His work high-lights the distinctive quality of Iasos in documentary terms. Here, in a city that was not a major player on the international scene, epigraphy is unusually informative (one wonders whether there is some relation between these two facts). Crowther's study also demonstrates the importance of a full knowledge of the transmission history of epigraphic texts: the accounts of early travellers, the dis-persal patterns of stones, as well as what might well be viewed as the misappropriation of items by visitors that results in the eventual rescue of valuable knowledge—the importance of all these matters is nicely illustrated in the Iasian case.

Here, perhaps uniquely, we are able to observe with some precision the relationship between the texts of a series of theatre-inscriptions, their original architectural settings, and the institutional and social life of the theatre itself. The development of that relation-ship can, moreover, be tracked in some detail over an extended period of the second century. This material also gives us another good example to add to Chaniotis' typology of theatrical and para-theatrical rituals. For at some moment during the programme of the Iasian Dionysia, benefactors were given the opportunity to signify by a highly public and visual act—'giving the nod' (ἐπινεύειν)—that they intended to sponsor a future performance at the festival. This public performance of their own generosity, and all it implied about their role in the community, is uniquely preserved in stone—and Dymas the tragedian is among those recorded as having made such a gesture. (In his contribution, Ian Rutherford makes the interesting observation that Dymas, poet of tragedy, was honoured in Iasos for having funded the sibling—and in many ways, rival—genre of comedy.)

In the opening chapter Slater draws attention to one particular paradox of the epigraphic record: namely, that the Latin festival tradition has left us considerably more abundant evidence of its existence than the western Greek tradition in Italy and Sicily which was, all the same, doubtless extremely full and active.[28] An important and little-known testimony to that tradition is the subject of the last

---

[28] See further Todisco (2002); Burnett (1988).

two chapters, by David Jordan and myself. The fact that this is an incised lead tablet and not an inscription on stone is itself an interesting corollary of the phenomenon observed by Slater. Previous publication of this document is partial and not easily accessible. Jordan's discussion is a full technical presentation with new readings that will, it is hoped, help feed this difficult and intriguing evidence into the mainstream of Greek festival studies.

This tablet takes us back to the early or mid-fifth century. Its author is a man named Apellis, probably a citizen of Gela in Sicily, and clearly—as his role as a guarantor of the financial transaction on the other side of this tablet suggests—a person of substance and standing in his community. In the curse—or prayer—of side B that concerns the subject of this book, Apellis activates chthonic powers through a familiar form of ritual to 'mark down' a group of *khoragoi*, along with all their male relatives, in favour of one Eunikos, who is probably a competing *khoragos* himself. Apellis' principal aim in assisting Eunikos in this way is, it seems, to secure admiration for Eunikos among his audience and his affection for himself.

This document is a quite unique and extraordinary glimmer within a great darkness. It opens a window—very much 'from below', and with a rarely personalised perspective—onto the mechanics of a Greek festival in the West which included choral contests.[29] It comes from a time and a place where the greatest practitioners of both 'old' choral forms (like the *epinikion*), and the newest (tragedy) were active. As Jordan argues, the *khoragoi* in this document are very probably performers, participating leaders of choruses, rather than leitourgical financiers, as we are familiar with the term in its (dominant) Athenian environment.

My own chapter on 'Sicilian choruses' tries to fill out a little more of the possible cultural context from which this intriguing document emerges, drawing some parallels from other choral contexts to illuminate it. In writing this, I was struck by the desirability of a broader history of the theatre seen 'through western eyes', so far as that is possible. This would be a valuable corrective to our

---

[29] The known epigraphic sources relating to Gela—which lacked a supply of good stone—are decidedly uninformative ('poco numerose e di non rilevantissimo interesse': *BTCG* 8.9).

overwhelmingly—if understandably—Athenocentric view of the institution's history. This book offers much material through which that wider project of 'decentring' Athens in theatrical terms might take place, though such a move should not be impelled by the pendulum of revisionist zeal alone. And there are other trajectories along which study could profitably reorient itself on the basis of a fresh and full examination of the documentary evidence. A study of the theatre (Attic or other) that identifies and analyses its economic dimensions fully is a major desideratum, for instance. But there are many others. It is hoped that this volume might encourage some to find and follow them.[30]

---

[30] For a preliminary attempt at a view of Greek theatre history 'through western eyes' see now Bosher (2006). My thanks to Eric Csapo for improving criticism of this Introduction.

Part I

Festivals and Performers:
Some New Perspectives

1

Deconstructing Festivals*

William Slater

A Seleukid king tells his bureaucrats to ensure that a cult of Artemis is established on an island in the Persian Gulf, and that there should be gymnic competitions; the surviving inscriptions testify to the footdragging that this insensitive missive produced for those on the spot.[1] Cultural intrusions into the Gulf are no new thing, but this example serves to remind us that the Greek world, unlike ours, was a militant festival culture.[2] A composite picture of a festival can certainly be drawn.[3] A recent inscription from Kos tells us usefully that a festival comprised *thusia* (sacrifice), *panegyris*, *theorodokia* (festival ambassadors), and competitions.[4] But some Hellenistic festivals did not have a real *panegyris*, if that means a market fair as well as a festival,[5] let alone an expensive *theorodokia*,[6] which we could translate as a marketing strategy. At Didyma we find Hellenistic *hestiasis* (feasting) and *thusia* for a festival for Eumenes II, with the

---

* This is a greatly altered and shortened version of the original paper in Oxford. My thanks to Giambattista D'Alessio for bibliographic help.

[1] *SEG* 35, 1476.

[2] There is a large bibliography on *Festwesen*: Auffarth (1991) 24ff.

[3] E.g. Chaniotis (1995).

[4] Parker and Obbink (2001b) 254; more examples: *SEG* 47, 388 (first century BC): *proxenoi*, *agon*, *thusia*; *Syll.*³ 390: *thusia*, *theoroi*, *agon*. *I. Ilion* 2, 43: sacrifice, *agon*, *panegyris*. Chaniotis (2003) 6 suggests that a *heorte* consists of *agon*, *thusia*, and *pompe*; Mikalson (1982).

[5] Strabo 10.5.4 on Delos, with Débord (1982) 24 and 310; Chandezon (2000).

[6] Hennig (1997) gives a good historical overview of how this worked. Perlman (2000) is more specialised.

added attraction of a procession and arming of the ephebes.[7] At Ilium, procession and sacrifice are specified,[8] but this means banqueting and still later regrettably rowdiness, as policemen with batons are deemed necessary. Such variations are normal, but more importantly a festival might not have competitions at all or even spectacles and shows, *theoriai* and *theai, akroamata* and *theamata* and the like. That leaves *thusia*, killing things, which of course might well occur as the lowest common denominator in all festivals, but the methods of killing varied, and everyone did not necessarily get to eat the results; and they certainly did not all get the same quantity and quality, or maybe anything at all.[9] Greek festivals not only are defined differently: they are different. Drama, even religious performance, was in fact mostly a minor aspect of one part of some Greek festivals.

At Olympia itself the great festival had fallen on hard times till Herod of Judaea decided to give it back its stature;[10] how? buildings, prizes, perhaps, an aqueduct like his later namesake? No, by giving the Eleans a foundation to pay for the sacrifices, more things to kill, i.e. so that more people would come and—to put it bluntly—join in the barbeque. Josephus, an outsider after all, says that Herod, like many a euergete,[11] thereby made the *panegyris* more *semnos*, which my dictionary tells me means 'revered, august, holy'. The provision of a McDonald's product does not to our thinking lead to any improvement in the religious atmosphere; for us Olympia is synonymous with competition not feasting. We are reminded again of the gulf between us and ancient thinking; but we have at least advanced from the time when a leading scholar felt wearily obliged to insist on the connection between sacrifice, banquet, and merrymaking, something I think we now accept as self-evident for a festival.[12] Sometimes therefore translation into a modern culture may be the problem; an

---

[7] *I.Didyma* 488.

[8] *LSAM* 9, the foundation of Hermias; *I.Ilion* 52.

[9] *SEG* 33, 147 = *EB* 1999, 106: 'it seems that the participating unity decided to sell (the meat) as soon as the ritual had been completed rather than struggle with the problem of who was to receive it'.

[10] *OMS* V 382 following A. Wilhelm, citing Joseph. *AJ* 16.149.

[11] Cf. *Hellenica* IX 18 on the 'promise' of a *munerarius* to make the festival more 'brilliant', with the consequent financial implications.

[12] Scheid (1985).

imperial euergete of Kibyra gives 54,000 drachmas for the Kaisareia—
for the '*Fest*' says the German;[13] but the Greek says specifically for
the *euochia*, the merriment, i.e. entertainment, wine and sacrificial
food.[14] Perhaps, as the ancient authors affirm, a festival does raise
the religious fervour, perhaps it does make for economic growth;
but the availability of food—'to enjoy themselves at the altar'—is
fundamental.[15] Notable is an official protest shoved through the
assembly of Miletus against the new habit by some magistrates of
early imperial times who had taken to diverting money intended for
traditional 'religious' *euochia* into general cash funds;[16] I suppose,
technically speaking, *hiera chremata* (sacred monies), which come
first in a budget and support festivals, are finessed by a ledger entry
into general revenue, *adiatakta* (unclassified) and *symmeikta* (con-
solidated).[17] This cleverly worded complaint alleges that the new
accounting procedure shows disrespect for emperors and gods and
tradition, but it takes care not to dwell on the woes of magistrates,
now bereft of their traditional festive dinners.[18] Likewise, a priest of
Men at Sardis in AD 188/9 can complain to the governor that his
civic funding for sacrifices (i.e. *euochia*)[19] has been cut off, and he
neatly points out that the funding is for sacrifices and libations for
the wellbeing of the emperor as well as the god.[20] One can assume
that it was politically unwise to seem to cut off funding for imperial
celebrations, and equally wise to integrate one's religious obligations
with imperial cult, for the readiness of authorities at any level to
confiscate and divert publicly managed funds designed for spectacles

---

[13] *I.Kibyra* 41.

[14] Finer distinctions are sometimes made in inscriptions, e.g. Heberdey (1912)
112 no. 20, the Nikomedes foundation: '*Euochia*, die eigentliche Festfeier, ist hier und
im folgende stets vom *deipnon*, der Mahlzeit der Vorabende, geschieden …'. For good
remarks see Bowersock (1999).

[15] Phld. *Piet.* 27 Ob.; Dio Prus. *Or.* 35.15–16; *IG Epiri* X 2, 347.

[16] *Delphinion* 134, 18–20; cf. Malay (1999) no. 127 and parallels in *EB* 1999, 148.

[17] See *Hellenica* IX 16 on *Delphinion* 147, 19–20.

[18] Cf. the elegant formulation for this kind of thing in Philo Judaeus, *in Flaccum*
42: κατασοφίζοντες τὸ Καίσαρος ὄνομα προκάλυμμα ποιησάμενοι.

[19] In essence a donation ἐπὶ θυσίαν καὶ εὐωχίαν (*I.Kyme* 13, 40ff.) is a hendyades,
equivalent to *ex sacrificio epulari* in the Arval Acts, 65.5 (Scheid) whose equation of
sacrifice and banquet is approved by Rüpke (2002) 53. All these terms have of course
been studied at length, esp. by L. Robert, *Hellenica* X 197ff.

[20] *SEG* 49, 1676 = Malay (1999) 131, with more parallels.

—or banquets—was an old problem, as is clear from Cicero's account of the money that Tralles put together to celebrate the Flacceia.[21] Likewise funds for shows or for banqueting are easily and legitimately diverted into waterworks.[22] Even merrymaking and festival continuity can be curtailed by water shortage.

All of this is meant to put drama into its place; but my aim here is to discuss the variety of festivals rather than the complexity of performance at festivals. Thankfully epigraphers tend to work bottoms-up in their profession, while philologists can start with the grand generalities and work down. So, for example, the idea that festivals were distinguished by a Greek *egalité* is attractive—to Plutarch and many ancients also;[23] and this idea has been exploited in discussions of ancient drama; but it is unjustified; epigraphy shows that some people were invited to a sacrifice—and even that they were given different amounts, and treated differently—and others were not.[24] Rather, when we start looking at festivals on the basis of the epigraphic evidence—the worm's eye view—we will be unwilling to accept that 'all festivals shared in a kind of homogeneous common Greek festival structure which appears to have changed very little over the centuries'.[25] They are all inconveniently different; they changed a great deal and, in what follows, I try to illustrate this.

[21] Cic. *Pro Flacco* 55–9, though one can argue about the honesty of that account; Erkelenz (1999) 43–57.

[22] Reynolds (2000) 16–19 = *AE* 2000, 1441; *SEG* 49, 1556 with commentary.

[23] The idea of Dionysus = Dionysiac festival = democracy seems to have started with Gernet (1932), and has a long ideological development in French scholarship. For criticism of modern developments, see Rhodes (2003), and Jacottet (2003) I.19. I shall deal elsewhere with the related Greek claim of a 'common table' and its problems.

[24] The public ideology of banqueting equality is modified by the different γέρη (prerogatives); cf. Müller and Wörrle (2002) 206, especially the technical term προσφωνεῖν; Robert (1945) 48–9 says of division by weight of sacrifical meat: 'c'était le meilleur moyen d'éviter des contestations sur la façon dont était taillé le morceau'; cf. also Zimmermann (2000) 475. But equality depends on quality not just weight. In addition some people were given *proedria* in public banquets, and invited to lie down, while others sat or stood: Malay (1999) 135. But the most probative and overlooked passage is Plautus, *Trinummus* 468–73.

[25] Van Nijf (2001) 310. I do not mention here the many recent useful surveys of local festivals, e.g. Spawforth (1989) for imperial Achaia and Leschorn for Macedonia = *SEG* 48, 695, all of which continue to modify our picture.

There is much we do not know. The guild of the performing artists never tells us what their fee structure was, though we know exactly what it cost a non-performer to join the Egyptian guild in later antiquity, and how much the athletic guild paid to register as sacred victors in Ephesus.[26] Numismatists have painstakingly shown that there is not nearly the overlap that we should expect between epigraphy of festivals and coins.[27] The epigraphic gaps are startling: the goddess Rome was worshipped at Smyrna from nearly 200 BC, but the Romaia festival of Smyrna only appears once, on an inscribed list of the victories of an *aulos*-player at Delphi, and the date is c. AD 200, more than a century after Romaia have disappeared from other places.[28] Stratonikeia has many inscriptions, and Laumonier could say that there was no drama there, since drama is not mentioned in the inscriptions.[29] But of course there was drama, because there is a Hellenistic theatre. More generally, we might be forgiven for thinking that the Latin West was festally impoverished. But this too would be an error, refuted by the hundreds of theatres that survive. Contrast the sixty members of the drama executive on an inscription from little Bovillae in the time of Marcus Aurelius;[30] the festival industry in Italy really was thriving, yet oddly we have no inscription like this from any Greek area. We need to ask ourselves why this should be; it certainly was not because there was no Greek festival industry. The gaps in our evidence are not easy to locate.

A festival could change its name, its status, and its purpose. The penteteric Delia at Delos vanished with the Athenians in 314 BC, but when they returned in 166 BC, it is restored as annual, and the Delian Apollonia became the Apollonia and Athenaia.[31] The fourteen

---

[26] Frisch (1986) 37; *I.Ephesos* 14 + *Add.* p. 1; Pleket (1973) 200 refers by error to the Sebasta Artemisia, and then denies any meaning to the exception made for *hieronikai* (sacred victors) of the Sebasta Epheseia. Amelotti (1955) is important.

[27] Leschorn (1998), (2002); Ziegler (1985); Wallner (1997). The summary of Burrell (2003) 335–42 reaches the same conclusion and emphasises the confusing evidence.

[28] *FD* III 1, 550.

[29] Laumonier (1958) 303; I hope to have justified my criticism in greater detail in a forthcoming paper for a conference in Tours.

[30] *CIL* XIV 2408; a close relative of the honorand has now appeared in a shrine of Anna Perenna in Rome as a victorious mime: Piranomonte (2002) 26, 30.

[31] Bruneau (1970) 80; the point is made best in the important article of Pleket (1975).

changes of name of the Asclepieia of Pergamum in imperial times are documented.[32] But the start of this trend was the Heraia Lysandreia—the first renaming known—and the most notorious the short-lived Dionysia Demetrieia at Athens.[33] The Nesiotic league started a new festival for Demetrius in Delos, which economically was to alternate year about with an Antigoneia, but the inscription frankly admits that they have no idea where the money is to come from for the next celebration.[34] What is quickly created is quickly ended, and the Erythreans had no difficulty in putting an end to their Seleukeia, which they had added to their Dionysia, when Seleukid overlordship ceased.[35] The city of Kolophon was equally speedy in divesting itself of its Antiocheia when it welcomed Rome in 190 BC;[36] but, to our surprise, Delos is still celebrating Eumeneia two generations after the death of Eumenes II.[37] Kyme around 280 BC has no problems in celebrating its Dionysia and Antiocheia at the same time as Soteria and Philetaireia.[38] Old festivals were hastily renamed, like the Romaia Theophaneia at Chios from 188 BC, and soon Romanising Athenians speed off as ambassadors to the Erotideia Romaia of Thespiae.[39] All of this Darwinian adaption would eventually take its toll; for the history of drama, we can note for example that the many important Dionysia of Hellenistic Asia disappear almost totally from the epigraphic record in imperial times, presumably because Dionysiac performance and civic dithyramb were no longer of such public importance as gymnasium school dancing and imperial ceremonial.

There are of course private festivals, even Dionysia, and no-name festivals like the *epitaphioi agones* (funeral contests) with a victor list at Termessos.[40] Egypt has a festival called simply the sacred penteteric competition, which was popular in imperial times, but it probably

---

[32] Slater (1995).
[33] Plu. *Lys.* 18.4. On these grafted-on festivals, see Ma (1999) 224 n. 133, citing Habicht (1970) 50–5, 76–8.
[34] *IG* XI 4, 1036 = Durrbach (1923) no. 13.
[35] Ma (1999) 48.
[36] Ma (1999) 246.
[37] Byrne (1995) 60, citing Habicht.
[38] *SEG* 50, 42, 28.
[39] Medeios Medeiou *c.* 100 BC: Byrne (1995).
[40] Herodes Atticus' festival in Spawforth (1989) 196; *SEG* 47, 1773; cf. *BE* 2002, 438; 1993, 586.

existed already as a no-name festival in the third century BC.[41] The Kaisareia of Asia which Kleanax of Kyme organised about 2 BC seems to have been limited to sacrificial food and drink, much like his new-fangled penteteric Dionysiac mysteries, but he introduced his prytany with expensive, albeit no-name, shows, which may or may not have consisted of formal drama.[42] When the people of Ephesus decided that their prosperity was due to Antoninus Pius, they piously seized yet another chance to vote to have a new festival to be held every year for ever on his birthday.[43] But what the good citizens had proposed was also five days of fun, *theai*, shows, and it has no name, though one could call it *sebastai hemerai*, 'imperial holidays' or something equally vague; it was noisily proclaimed and silently vanishes. One could of course refer to an old festival by several names simultaneously, and Aspis and Heraia mean the same for hundreds of years at Argos, but then seem to have been also the Hekatombeia.[44] Even the Isthmia and Nemea alter their names and places according to political circumstances. We often cannot tell whether Hadrianeia or Olympia or *koina Asias* are the same or different. People evidently stopped caring about names. . . .

I underline, like L. Robert, but modify, one of the reasons for change.[45] Contests with claims to international status had to be run according to specific rules and so it had to be known which rules were being followed, e.g. regarding age groupings (*helikiai*), or honours (*timai*). The easiest way to do this was to call one's festival *isolympic* or *isopythic*, or in shorthand, Olympia or Pythia, since most contestants knew those rules, as the Delphic Soteria is to be recognised as isopythic in music, but isonemeic in gymnic and hippic contests, in age categories and *timai*.[46] They might tell you

---

[41] See Moretti (1953) 176, 183, 186: (*hieron*) *penteterikon* with *Aktiakoi paides*. Kayser (2000) says that Aktia in Alexandria were celebrated in 27 BC with gladiators! But there is no evidence for these gladiators tacked on to Aktia, and he misreads the term amphitheatre. *PHal.* 1, 260–5 as supplemented suggests that this penteteric contest is earlier, probably third-century BC; see Aneziri (2003) 117 n. 534.

[42] *SEG* 32, 1243.

[43] *I.Ephesos* 21 from AD 138: *OGIS* II 493; cf. *Milet* VI 2, 944 fr. i for celebration on that emperor's *dies imperii* after AD 195.

[44] Strasser (2002) 99; Caldelli (1998) 232 n. 24; *BE* 2000, 49; *AE* 1994, 1612.

[45] *Hellenica* V 61.

[46] *Syll.*³ 402, 10.

how many strings your lyre had to have or for how long you had to
play, or how many actors you were allowed, or how old you had to be
to fit in an athletic category; such regulations are lost but existed,
perhaps in many an agonothetic law.[47] Festivals copied their original,
but not in detail.[48] The sacred *eiselastic* Olympia at Ephesus had a
chequered history, and just like the Pisan Olympia had no musical or
drama competitions, and it did have *hellanodikai* and *alytarchs*, and
even honorary female visitors,[49] as did Pisa, but all this was largely
funded by an endowment by Ti. Cl. Nusios, in the time of Domitian,
so that it was in that respect not really like the original Olympia.
But it also had no hippic competitions, which Olympia obviously
had. However, on the contrary, the Olympia in Smyrna did have
musical and dramatic competitions, which Olympia in Pisa did not;
and when Ptolemy Philadelphos founded his Ptolemaia in honour
of his father,[50] he specified that it would be *isolympic*, but there was
no thymelic or dramatic contest at Olympia as there was at the
Ptolemaia.[51] Likewise, we only have one certain reference to the
Ephesian Hadriana with the epithet Olympia, but it is for a choral
pipeplayer, a prize category, however, that is only allowed in imperial
times.[52] So we may have antiquarian imitation of details but exact
symmetry should never be assumed. One can also suggest why epithets like Olympia appear and disappear. The Dionysia Herakleia of
Thebes were an amalgam of the very old local musical Agrionia and
gymnic Iolaeia Herakleia, and they last into late antiquity as e.g.
Dionysia Herakleia Kommodeia. But around AD 170–200 we find
them also referred to as not just Herakleia but also as Herakleia
Olympia. This is understandable from the point of view of a gymnic
contestant, who did not care about the Dionysiac elements, including
now pantomime, in the festival, but did care about the Olympic rules

---

[47] *PMich.* inv. 4682 gives rules for a *kuklios auletes*: Pearl (1978); Stephanis (1981)
397–9. Cf. rules on finger-breaking at Olympia *BE* 2000, 349.

[48] E.g. Pleket (1975) 61 even says 'identical', which is impossible.

[49] *OMS* VI 669.

[50] *IGRR* IV, 1432; *OMS* VI 709ff., and on the date *SEG* 49, 113; *Syll.*[3] 390.

[51] Artists do claim to win at Olympia, but it seems always in the herald category.

[52] Roueché (1993) no. 67, and possibly *I.Ephesos* 1083 [*Hadria*]*neia Olympia*;
Strasser (2002) 133 unsurprisingly wants two festivals. The Pythia Hadrianeia of
Lämmer (1967) 47 is a misreading of *I.Ephesos* 2073.

under which he personally was operating, and so they were for him personally, if not officially, *isolympic*, because he personally fought according to Olympic rules.[53] Likewise the pankratist Menander at Aphrodisias can refer to the Capetolia Olympia at Rome.[54] In later times we find anomalous terms like Aktia Olympia,[55] and it comes then as no surprise to find *Pythikoi paides* at the Soteria Kapetolia isokapetolia at Laodicea in Syria.[56] One imitated the great festivals with a certain flair.

Presumably people knew what an *Isthmiakos pais* designation meant, as at the games at Klaros, or a *Pythikos pais*;[57] but what was a Ptolemaic *pais* outside of Egypt, or the *Artemisiake krisis*—the 'selection process' introduced for the Ephesian Artemisia in 163?[58] Then there is the *Sebaste krisis* of Naples, with its Klaudianic *paides* there,[59] and who would know the rules for almost nonexistent Klaudianeia? A victor in Ephesus carefully distinguishes his career as a *pais* from his victories as a Pythic *pais*.[60] One can have Pythic and Isthmic gymnic contests at the same festival.[61] In age categories and honours, the Aitolian Soteria at Delphi is isopythic in music but unexpectedly isonemeic in athletics and horseracing.[62] Age categories at the Athenian Theseia depend on whether or not one is a citizen.[63] Gymnasium games especially distinguish even finer groups of *paides* and can be held monthly.[64] These highly specialised rules and regulations, unknown to us, had to be known and broadcast—marketing strategy again—so that a competitor could be allowed to register formally in the proper *krisis*; and failure to do so properly was sometimes heavily fined and could even result in flogging as at the Naples Sebasta. One can be lauded in inscriptions as at Ephesus for having presided successfully over the *krisis*; there was plenty of chance for

---

[53] *FD* III 1, 555; Roesch (1975).   [54] Roueché (1993) no. 91b, 28.

[55] Leschorn (1998) 40; on Pythic boys see on *I.Tralles* 1, no. 121.

[56] *Hellenica* XI 12 from a Rhodian inscription of the second century; *IGLS* IV 1265, 9; cf. Caldelli (1993) 117.

[57] Robert (1989) 52.   [58] *I.Ephesos* 24C 11.

[59] Caldelli (1993) 86 n. 164.   [60] *I.Ephesos* 2702.

[61] *IG* VII 1769 (early imperial Thespiae); or regularly at the Hellenistic Asklepieia at Kos.

[62] *Syll.³* 402, 9–10.   [63] Kennel (1999).

[64] *SEG* 49, 1146 from Samos. Most of our information comes from Egypt: Legras (1999) with *SEG* 49, 2105.

making enemies there.[65] Just how stringent or stressful a *krisis* could be we cannot guess; but the gymnasium in Leontopolis eliminated those who were too small or too big by visual inspection only.[66] Rules for selection obviously varied, and our evidence for dramatic and musical festival rules is almost nonexistent. Even some terms for competitions we cannot understand, and the meaning of the imperial *dia panton* or the *tagma* or the comedic *kleros en plasmati* in Naples or the *nea kataloge* at Larissa and other local categories still defeats us.[67] Even in the very similar inscriptions from Boeotia the actual terminology to describe the different drama competitions changes. *Tragodos* in one place equals *hypokrites* in another,[68] but the '*tragodos* of old tragedy' which occurs once at Thespiae is bizarre, since *tragodos* by itself is always the lead actor of a re-performed tragedy.[69] Standardisation was not achieved.

We know that festivals could change their place, like the moveable Alexandreia of the *koinon* (association) of the Ionians. Can festivals change their times? The idiosyncrasies of Greek polis calendars meant that their festivals were in a state of perpetual temporal movement. The first we hear of the *koinon* of the Greeks of Asia is precisely in organising festivals *c.* 100 BC.[70] Any 'travelling' performer needed to know where and when festivals were held and what festivals would provide a chance to enter, about prizes and qualifications, and of course other rules, for example, that one had to appear so many days in advance, provide guarantors, that there were second prizes, or *siteresia* (expense allowances) and, for drama, that one had to bring one's own *skeuaria* (equipment), etc. The Chalkis decree of the Artists soon after 300 BC shows us that this problem was already of fundamental concern to cities and performers in a highly mobile festival industry.[71] After Caesar's calendar reforms, the Naples Sebasta, Aktia, and later Capetolia are clearly meant to be fitted in with each other and the other major games in a special festival calendar of top games. But the clearest notice of a concern for organised timing is an inscription from Aphrodisias[72] showing that the Roman authorities

---

[65] *I.Ephesos* 24C.   [66] *SEG* 40, 1568, 50–1.
[67] *IG* IX 2, 531.   [68] Also O'Connor (1908) 13 on Delos and Athens.
[69] *IG* VII 1773.   [70] Ferrary (2001) 27–8.   [71] Le Guen (2001a) no. 1.
[72] Rouché (1993) 46 and no. 51.

were finding slots for local minor festivals there, and notably they refer the issue to the association of the Dionysiac Artists, who had been presumably always the driving force in instigating efficient temporal organisation.

The periodicity can change; most festivals would have been annual originally, but might become prestigiously but also precariously penteteric. The sudden appearance of the 517th penteteric Ephesia in second-century Ephesus deserves scepticism.[73] The Ephesian Olympia was also traced back to Mycenaean times, clearly a work of the same local academic industry, but we had heard nothing of it till Domitian.[74] As a contrast, the Hadrianic penteteric Panathenais is well attested, even reaching the twenty-ninth, but of course the Great Panathenea on which it was based was at least seven centuries earlier.[75] Olympia imitations in fact seem often to have been counted in this way,[76] to the sixty-second 'after the restoration', as at Tralles, more credibly back to historical founders, but there we are told again that this was a renewal after the Mithridatic war of a much older festival.[77] Perhaps. The imperial Pythia at Tralles was twice proclaimed as renewed, but never as having failed.[78] The sixty-fourth Artemisiad at Hypaipa sounds impressive, till we note that the victor has won it four times in a row as a boy;[79] clearly then it was an annual festival like the relatively unimportant Artemisia at Ephesus.[80] The *koinon Asias* festival at Smyrna calls itself misleadingly 'first' and was undoubtedly penteteric in the second century AD,[81] but how then can we have someone in AD 245 claiming to have been agonothete five times?[82] With luck, as with the ancient Ptoia of Akraiphia, a local benefactor will restore some of the missing funding of a failed festival, carefully however adding Kaisareia to the title, and in reality turning it into his own personal imperial cult festival.[83]

---

[73] Slater (1996) 200.   [74] *OMS* V 381 n. 5.   [75] Moretti (1953) 202.
[76] Festivals advertise themselves in Olympic style as in a numerical order, e.g. the ninth Nikephoria at Pergamum with Robert (1989) 23 n. 50, ninth Olympia at Kyzicus etc., but mostly in more secure imperial times.
[77] *I.Tralles* 133.   [78] *I.Tralles* 82; 143.   [79] *IGRR* IV 1609.
[80] Robert, *OMS* V 402 says that the Artemisia is well attested as sacred, but this is not so; Jones (2001) 46: 'probably of minor importance', even though at a time *eiselastic*. It is confused with the Epheseia.
[81] *I.Napoli* 50 Miranda = *IG* XIV 746.
[82] *EA* 36 (2003) 1 nos. 1 and 2.   [83] Oliver (1971).

Often a competition is called great (*megala*). We assume rightly that this means that a 'great' competition is a four-year competition while in the intervening years some minor competition, perhaps local or ephebic, was held at the same time, as with the Panathenaia of Athens or Ilion, the Haleia of Rhodes, the Klaria of Colophon, the Mouseia at Thespiae, even the Daidala of Thebes.[84] But this is not always true, and sometimes it just means 'great'; e.g. the *koinon* of Asia games were *megala* if held at Smyrna, Pergamum and Ephesus. The Didymeia were great when held in Miletus, not in Didyma. The Olympia is *megala* in Pisa to differentiate it from the thirty-six other known Olympia;[85] though *Olympionikes* does not always mean victor at Pisa. But often *megala* is omitted where it would be justified; and where we have no reference to *megala* we cannot assume that this is not the main four-yearly festival. As so often, use depends on the attitude of the writer. The Megala Epinikia at Ephesus is an oddity;[86] and such *ludi triumphales*—themselves in theory one-off celebrations—could economically and confusingly be attached to pre-existing festivals like the Hadriana Olympia Epinikia at Smyrna, and so repeatable.[87] In general, when a gymnasium contest of Leontopolis in Egypt in AD 220 is called the 'sacred *eiselastic* ephebic Antoninianos Heleios Leontios *isantinoios agon*', this is the result of uncontrolled title inflation, and also a sign that names no longer matter.[88]

Festivals change their management. The Dionysiac Artists—like the later athletic synod—start as a collegial selfhelp system, promoting jobs for their members, the μίσθωσις τῶν τεχνιτῶν

---

[84]	Robert (1966) 30 n. 4; Gauthier (1999) = *BE* 2000, 527; Knoepfler (1996) 162 with the troubling assumption of a penteteric festival which is only partly stephanitic; Paus. 9.2.7; when run by the Plataeans themselves, it was small, when with the Boeotians, it was great.

[85]	*IGRR* IV 1344 = *I.Mag.Sip.* 134, 6 = *TAM* V 1368; *SEG* 47, 2247.

[86]	*I.Ephesos* 3071, 20.

[87]	At Iasos Herakleia become the Herakleia Epinikia of Trajan to celebrate his victory: *EV* 218; Moretti (1955) 156. Robert (1966B) 104 n. 7 can be misunderstood; better *BE* 1959 no. 448; at *OMS* II 1140 he says that *epinikia* are *le plus souvent* not repeated, a view queried by Nollé (2003) and (1998) 331 n. 36. The issue deserves study.

[88]	*SEG* 40, 1568 with improvements *BE* 2002, 515.

('hiring of artists') to staff festivals;[89] then the further step was gradually taken, whereby the festival organisers contacted the association, and then the local association headquarters decided—more or less—who would go where; that is it would νέμειν τοὺς τεχνίτας, 'allocate the performers'.[90] At the Dionysia in Corcyra, set up by a testament about a century after the Chalkis decree, this hiring of the performers is what counts and entails explicit instructions;[91] the city is to send to the artists, and hire just enough for a competition with specific amounts of money, but as an extra the city must negotiate an unspecified sum for their maintenance costs, just as earlier the cities in Euboea had done; there is no provision for prizes or competition at all, even though the law invoked is that for the *agonothetes*, 'the competition organiser'; it would be a good guess that this person would have to provide the prizes, if any. Even from about 300 BC, this has become the normal way to get a festival going, which is why there is so much legalistic fuss about what happens when performers do not show up. At Iasos the artists' association voluntarily supply the staffing for the festival there, when the city cannot afford it.[92] Even so, often there would have been no competition in the absence of sufficient competitors and sufficient financing. But when some imperial euergete of Kaunos claims to have supplied the *hyperesia* (staffing) for the theatre, in fact he has just been employing the same procedure as cities had done for hundreds of years.[93] The euergetic wealthy had always subsidised festivals, either as *choregoi* or agonothetes or *philotimoi/munerarii*, and their contributions doubtless increased with time; of course they used agents to do the hiring. The guilds of the artists and athletes needed their festivals to be

[89] *IG* XI, 4, 1036, 10, detailing the foundation of the Demetrieia in early third-century BC Delos; after the provision of incense and contests follows the μίσθωσις τῶν τεχνιτῶν. The *technitae* were represented by their *ergolaboi*, contractors and agents and middlemen, at such times.

[90] As in Le Guen (2001a) no. 20, 35. First noted as a technical term by Wilhelm (1906), cited by W. Blümel on *I.Iasos* 152, 12.

[91] Laum (1914) II 3, no. 1; *IG* IX 1, 4, 798.

[92] *I. Iasos* I.152.

[93] The term *hyperesia* sometimes also means secondary dramatic staff, Aneziri (2003) 333–4; the Kaunos inscription (now *SEG* 50, 1109) is translated by Herrmann (1971) 36–9. For the well-documented changes from *choregoi* to *agonothetes* at Athens, see now the good summary of Summa (2003) 510–32.

regular and timely, and so they were naturally in the habit of pester-
ing the authorities even about matters that were strictly speaking
none of their business.[94] In drama, which had far lower prizes than
athletics (which could rely anyway on the local gymnasium), the
cities were not totally dependent on professionals, for there were
always local amateurs to provide a satyr chorus, or the relatives of the
agonothete to win in singing, as in Tanagra.[95] But drama and music
need experts, and at a certain point when the performers take greater
control, the competition can even be termed *nemetos*, 'allocated'.[96]
Only wealthy cities, or the great festivals of the—or rather, a—festival
cycle or *periodos*,[97] could, I think, safely assume that enough performing artists would show up of their own volition, and register
in the various categories several days in advance to be selected to
compete by a *krisis* or *kleros* (allotment).[98] Of all competition types,
save perhaps the later professional chorus, a drama performance
has especially high front-end costs; and so must seek to guarantee its
return on investment.

This industrial staffing mechanism does not correspond to the
spirit of open agonistic competition that is assumed and even
proclaimed by the ideology of inscriptions. Even Aristotle uses
'to compete' of performers who are not actually competing but
performing—on which see below—and it says a great deal for the
official refusal to acknowledge reality that *agonizesthai* can be used
epigraphically even of a solo performer, who is giving a display or a
free show, who is often not acceptable in any of the usual categories
of festival competition. Similarly the verb στεφανοῦν 'to crown'
means only 'to honour', especially when the 'crown' consists of a
statue.[99] Louis Robert, who pointed these facts out, insisted nonetheless on the 'radical distinction' between *epideixis*, 'display' and *agon*,

---

[94] *OGIS* 509, 7–8 = Roueché (1993) no. 50, 7–8; *OMS* II 1131.

[95] Calvet and Roesch (1966).

[96] Aneziri (2003) 283 n. 71.

[97] Wallner (2001) 92; Frisch (1991) 71–3; Caldelli (1995) 65 n. 13; Pleket on *SEG*
41, 1407 and 1750.

[98] *kleros*, 'tirage au sort', *Hellenica* VII 108; *krisis* has several meanings besides
'selection process'.

[99] Cf. Gauthier on *BE* 2002, 208.

'competition';[100] but, in reality, the term ἐπεδείξαντο ('displayed') is replaced by the completely equivalent ἠγωνίσαντο ('competed') in the formula of the Apollonia in Delos in the year 236 BC.[101] All of the competitors in the Artemisia of Eretria *c.* 340 BC are to 'compete' in the opening processional song, and we must understand this to mean merely 'participate'.[102]

What happens when contests are officially, and not just *de facto*, organised by the local or international association of the performers and/or their gymnic colleagues?[103] The issue is raised specifically by an inscription from Aphrodisias, which speaks of prizes in a musical competition of 'those from the association'.[104] It gives a list of these prizes, ending as often with the general dramatic-musical competition, the *dia panton*; then follows another section: 'for the gymnic contest of the boys (*paides*) of the city', which starts oddly with a list of competitions for men (*andres*), a technical designation[105] for gymnasium youth (*neoi*). The festival then appears to consist of a contest organised by and for musical professionals from the Dionysiac Artists and a gymnasium amateur athletic contest; both groups are competing in the same festival but separately, an interesting proof of what was, I think, a common expedient. Rouché says that the prizes there are provided by the guild, but what the guild brought was organisation and availability, while the local gymnasium provided the same for gymnic events, only of course much more cheaply, just as the overpaid imperial hymn singers of Ephesus were officially replaced with unpaid gymnasium students by thrifty Romans.[106]

---

[100] *OMS* VI 712; and see now van Liefferinge (2000). Of course the distinction between competition and demonstration does sometimes occur, as in *POsl.* 189 = Vandoni (1964) no. 13.

[101] Bruneau (1970) 74.

[102] *IG* XII 9, 189, 12–13 noted by Peter Wilson. Cf. the puzzlement of von Prott and Ziehen (1906) 255.

[103] I leave aside the well-known cases of Thespiae, Thebes, and Delphi, discussed by Aneziri (2003) 269ff.

[104] Rouché (1993) 178. For the official participation of the guilds in festivals, see the study of Aneziri (2003) 267ff. Forbes (1955) was misled into thinking here of the athletic guild.

[105] E.g. *IG* XII 9, 952 for the categories *pampaides, paides, epheboi, ageneioi, andres* who have a horse race.

[106] *I.Ephesos* 18d, 4ff.

One can obviously lose oneself in detail in such questions. To take only one example: in a list of victories of a pankratist at Ephesus we read:[107]

> ...Ζμύρναν
> κατὰ τὸ ἑξῆς Ὀλύμπια τὰ τῆς συνόδου
> Ἀδρίανα Ὀλύμπια ἀνδρῶν πυγμήν

> . . .Smyrna
> in succession: Olympia of the association
> the Adriana Olympia in the men's boxing

either with a comma after *synodou*, like Robert, or with commas after *synodou* and the first Olympia, as in *I.Ephesos*. Roueché and others speak therefore of the *Olympia apo sunodou*. Indeed a very fragmentary inscription from Delphi as read by Robert has a similar reference:[108]

> [Ἄλεια] ἐν Ῥόδωι· Γα [...]
> [...]συνόδου ΑΔ[.....]
> [...]ωι· Βαλβ[ίλληα ἐν Ἐφέσωι]
> [Haleia] in Rhodes; Ga[...]
> [...] of the association Ad[.....]
> [...]οἵ; Balb[illea in Ephesos]

which led Robert unwisely to restore exactly the same pair of contests as in Smyrna, so that we would then have two examples of this *Olympia apo synodou* or 'Olympia held by the association'. But what we need to read in the Ephesus inscription is '*ta tes synodou Adriana Olympia*' together, which can only be the same as the imperial Hadriana Olympia often mentioned in Smyrna; these are always different from another festival, the Olympia at Smyrna.[109] In this case the entire festival was apparently organised completely by the athletic guild.[110] The guilds independently therefore could operate closed—or at least partly closed—festival shops, either *apo*

---

[107] *I.Ephesos* 1615, 15ff.

[108] *FD* III 1, 549; *OMS* II 1158.

[109] The only exception is the list at *I.Ephesos* 1131, 29+30; if the illegible victories on the right side followed, as seems true, no distinction was made between Hadriana Olympia and Olympia.

[110] Whether the synodic Hadriana in the Delphic inscription is from Smyrna is another matter; the text is against it.

synodou, so that they could parade as agonothetes in procession
in their purple and gold finery along with the local élite, or via the
euergetic agonothetes who patronise them and whom they reward
with decrees and statues.

Status changes, and with it prizes, and these represent a confusing
picture. Crowns of vegetation are notoriously more prestigious than
cash. The best definition of a 'Panhellenic' festival upgrade is the
first, that of the islands of the Nesiotic league for the penteteric
isolympic Ptolemaia in Alexandria *c.* 280 BC:[111] specifically the honours
(*timai*) are to be in the various places the same as those established
by law in the individual islands for Olympic victors. We have the
evidence how Eumenes II put pressure on the Hellenes to get his pet
festival of Athena Nikephoros upgraded to stephanitic, 'crowned', in
182 BC, carefully defining its *isolympian* gymnic and hippic games
and *isopythian* musical ones.[112] Yet 'panhellenic' is not a technical
term of Hellenistic games.[113] The Asclepieia of Cos are not themselves given any specific upgrade of title, but its ambassadors ask in
242 BC to be treated with the same honours as those announcing
Olympia or Pythia or crowned games.[114] The best-known example
is when the Magnesians upgraded the festival of their own Artemis
called Leukophryene into a major international competition. The
first time, probably in 221 BC, other cities refused to sign on, but in
208 BC, the second time, the Magnesians did a better job by getting
the regal authorities on side, so that their festival was widely accepted

---

[111] *Syll.*[3] 390, 38 noted by Rigsby (1996a) 109.

[112] Welles (1934) nos. 49 and 50 with commentary; Rigsby (1996a) no. 178, 10ff.

[113] Rigsby (1996a) 64 on *Syll.*[3] 634; *LSCG* 73: 'the Greeks did not apply a word
"Panhellenic" to festivals. The games that all Greeks shared by sending theoroi, were
identified circumstantially: "crowned" "equal to the Olympia" "triumphal" etc. By
Roman times a favoured term had emerged, "sacred" games (the prize was dedicated
to the god). But that usage is a late development and all games were sacred to some
god. Hence ἀγὼν ἱερός is found early on as a poetic effusion, without implying a
contrast with ordinary games . . . with a cash prize. Of the technical usage the earliest
instance may be *ID* IV 1957 (*c.* 150–103 BC) cf. *SEG* 39, 1243, 7 (Claros late second
century BC); *AM* 33 (1908) 409 no. 40 (a statuette from Pergamum first century
BC?).' For Delphic and Clarian 'panhellenic' see now the careful remarks of Ferrary
(2001) 19–35; note esp. 35 n. 86 that those Hellenistic instances of the word Panhel-
lenes are usually in the context of the 'grandes fêtes panhelléniques, de concours ou
de spectacles réunissant des Grecs venus de toutes les cités'.

[114] Rigsby (1996a) 109.

as crowned, like other festivals of temples in the territory of Antiochus III: Klaros, Didyma, and others.[115] In the many letters, some apparently skillfully forged, which the hopeful Magnesians carved on their temple walls, there is no mention of the amount of the prizes.[116] On the other hand there is a repeated statement that the games are to be *isopythian*,[117] and it is specified that the *timai* (honours) or the *athla* (prizes) and *timai* and/or *philanthropa* and/or *siteresia* are to be *isopythian* (like the *isolympian timai* of the Ptolemaia);[118] but while it is clear that the standards of the Pythia—whatever they were—are to be applied, the prizes are to be the honours written in the laws for those victorious in Pythia (τὰς τιμὰς τὰς ἐν τοῖς νόμοις γεγραμμένας τοῖς νικῶσιν τὰ Πύθια).[119] This means of course, as with the Ptolemaia, not the laws of Magnesia, but the laws of the individual cities for their Pythian victors—save that parochially and inconsistently the Argives declare them *isonemean* and the Corinthians *isoisthmian*.[120] It follows that the Magnesians simply did not know what the rewards were to be for their own proposed games.

Prestige propaganda, especially in imperial inscriptions, may well lead us to assume that there were no financial rewards in stephanitic games.[121] The nice distinction of crown versus cash made by the

---

[115] Dignas (2002) 44; Rigsby (1996a) no. 66 with the necessary correction of line 16, though I have some doubts about the complete veracity of the Magnesians' account; cf. Rigsby (1996a) 188: 'I suspect that the Magnesians in 221 did not invite to the games all the Greek cities . . . but rather . . . the old Greek cities of Aeolis, Ionia and the Dorian south.' Flashar (1999) = *SEG* 49, 1501.

[116] Chaniotis (1999) 51–69. The dossier is now best read in Rigsby (1996a) 178–279.

[117] Cf. *IG* VII 1735b, where the Athenians—rightly Aneziri (2002) 274, with text—recognise that the Mouseia of Thespiae is to be *isopythic* and stephanitic, in that the ἆθλα are to be the same as the Pythian.

[118] *I.Magnesia* 34 = Rigsby (1996a) no. 84; *I.Magnesia* 111; *I.Magnesia* 85, 69 = *I.Tralles* 21, one of the latest of the archival inscriptions.

[119] *I.Magnesia* 50, 36–7 = Rigsby (1996a) no. 100; *I.Magnesia* 53, 37 = Rigsby (1996a) no. 102; and often.

[120] *I.Magnesia* 40, and 42.

[121] Poll. 3.153; for the prize system as money versus (symbolic) crowns see e.g. Frisch (1986) 38, citing Lucian *Anach.* 9; *Anthologia Graeca* IX 357; *Hellenica* VII 95–7; also Jones (1999) 164; Perpillou-Thomas (1993) 225; but Robert, *OMS* VI 710–19 is too emphatic; Caldelli (1997) 422 n. 41 justly notes the important objections of Pleket (1975) 49–89 to any simple system.

lexicographer Pollux conceals, as so often, much more complex conditions, certainly in earlier times, probably in later.[122] At the Dionysia in Athens the victorious poet got a crown of ivy leaves but also money in the form of a salary of some sort.[123] Common sense should tell us that an athlete or performer is not going to visit games where he is going to get no financial reward. Pleket has shown how fragile the notion of purist stephanitic games is.[124] Consider the regulations[125] for the sacred[126] Sebasta of Naples, which I understand like Robert to reflect the conditions of early imperial times.[127] There is a heading, *Concerning Prizes*, which contains three subsections: first, the prizes—*epathla*—followed by a gap of only a few words, perhaps, 'are according to the . . . law'; second, *opsonion* i.e. 'pay' or 'allowance' per diem, more usually called *siteresion*, set out at length; and third, *timai*, which are, despite the plural, specified as a crown of vegetation and nothing else. All of this has parallels. But in another later and unique section governing the daily calendar of the games, after the rules about sacrificing and the procession, we get a detailed list of those cash prizes—*epathla*—that were mentioned only as existing in the earlier chapter, but which are now listed according to the day on which they are disbursed, very useful information for a performer. They start with the thymelic, i.e. music and dramatic categories, but go on to the hippic,[128] before the stone breaks off, and we can assume they continued with the gymnic. It is not legitimate to assume that the thymelic portion was 'thematic', or cash only,

---

[122] Ebert (1982) 212 admits that his supplement of *I.Magnesia* 16, 28–9 with its award of a gold crown to the victor of an *isopythic* context is 'wohl ein Singularität' and that this represents a 'Missbrauch' of the term *stephanites*. Indeed; all the more reason to question his reading.

[123] Pickard-Cambridge (1968) 90, 98.

[124] Pleket (1975) 48–89.

[125] *I.Olympia* 56 with the supplements proposed by various scholars summarised in *SEG* 37, 356, mostly dealing with the three age categories.

[126] Already so called in Str. 5.6.7; Leppin (1992) 170 wants to dismiss this.

[127] See the long discussion referenced in Caldelli (1993) 30 n. 112. One must wait here for unpublished material.

[128] 'sebbene limitata all'agone musico', says Caldelli (1993) 34. At least seven lines at the end dealt with the *epathla* for horse racing, before the final break.

and the rest stephanitic, even in Augustan times.[129] This order is the actual order of the festival, and if thymelic and hippic get cash, then so does the gymnic.[130] Here is one of the very few examples where the prizes—or to be precise, 'extra-prizes'—for a sacred competition were announced;[131] but it is of a most unusual type, being found far from its place of origin, and destined for the information of competitors, not the general public.

We have seen the peculiar attitude to the word 'competition'; the same is true of crowns. As an example of the importance of the symbolism of crowns, we recall that the Delphians for some unknown but interesting reason shortly before 50 BC decided not only that they should not be awarding a crown (*sc.* of goldfoil) equivalent to a fixed sum of money to visiting artists, especially to *akroamata*—not, as far as we know, Pythic competitors, but we shall see how ambivalent even that term could be—but also that the numerical value of those that had been awarded should be chiselled off the relevant stones, the equivalent of incompetently shredding the evidence.[132] By a fortunate coincidence it is this shredding that has enabled epigraphists to deduce what they were up to, but not why; we are I suspect never going to find out, though Pomtow thought that such awards had 'disgusting overtones of illegality'.[133] Officially now, all that such artists were to get—or rather, were supposed ever to have got—were prestigious honours, including a crown, but not a crown worth a fixed sum of highly bankable goldfoil. Visiting artists were going to be paid somehow, and this had been an ingenious way to do so; but all that has happened is that it has been decided not to talk about their pay publicly. This we are glad

---

[129] Strasser (2002) 131; he seems to assume (n. 185) that choral kitharists are attested here for the first time; they exist much earlier in competitions in Teos and Athens.

[130] There is a section of the inscription which merely lists summarily the competitions in the three categories, with remarks apparently about which were open to non-citizens; of it only gymnic and hippic events are preserved, in that order. There is no 'second hippic' list as even Caldelli (1993) 30ff. seems prepared to admit; it is in the separate chapter listing money prizes. There is no justification for seeing two layers in the inscription at all.

[131] For *ep-athla* (extra prizes) cf. Nollé (2001) no. 120 compared to 121–8.

[132] *OMS* I 250–2; van Liefferinge (2000).

[133] Pomtow (1918) 85: 'einen odiösen ungesetzlichen Beigeschmack'.

to know, for the argument that 'we have no real evidence that ...'
does not work for documents designating prestige honours and
designed for public consumption. Yet these visitors to Delphi were
highly honoured artists, for the organ-player Antipatros had been
especially summoned along with his valuable instrument in 94/3 BC
from distant Eleutherna to display his skill for two days—the word
used is the usual misleading 'compete'—and he was officially
crowned in the *agon*—here the text is erased—perhaps at the Pythia,
but it was no *agon* in which he officially competed, unless we want
to contemplate a competition of hydraulic organ-players.[134] He was
also given a statue, perhaps suitably retrofitted. A non-competitive
but valuable crown was a normal solution for those on the fringes
but also for the more conventional artists. The comedian Nikophon
with his crew *c.* 200 BC apparently stopping off on his way home
to Ephesus, after doubtless some hard haggling on the quay, gets a
crown of 100 drachmas—not just 100 drachmas—and a string of
honours for two days' work, on tiny but prosperous Amorgos.[135] But
real victors in real contests, not just the odd visiting artist, were
awarded crowns of minutely weighed goldleaf, as at the Sarapieia of
Tanagra after 100 BC.[136] We find the award of gold crowns weighing
specific amounts and imitating vegetation attested for the victor
already in the musical contests (not the gymnic) of the Athenian
Panathenaia in the fourth century BC, though Aristotle carefully
does not mention them;[137] but cash is awarded even in addition to
this crown in some events. Such Hellenistic awards clearly fudge the
alleged division between panhellenic/sacred/crowned and 'thematic'
games. The city of Magnesia is said to have established its *isopythic*
competition giving a crown worth fifty *chrysoi*, but in all the other
inscriptions about this upgrade there is no mention of this valuable

---

[134] *Syll.*³ 737.   [135] *IG* XII 7, 226.   [136] Slater (1993).

[137] Arist. *Ath. Pol.* 60.3; the crown is specified as a gold crown of *thallos*, i.e. olive,
worth 1000 dr. with 500 silver dr. in addition. In other words the symbolism of the
victor's crown is all-important. The confusing testimonies of art and epigraphy are
assembled by Shapiro (1992), and note the important criticism of art evidence by
Hamilton (1996). Indispensable is the re-edited inscription by Shear (2003), though
some of the restorations are obviously debatable. The gymnic events were rewarded
with jars of oil, but also at some unknown point with a real olive crown: Shear
(2003b) n. 51. For further discussion of the complex organisation of these games see
Latini (2003) 311.

crown, and instead we have only the term *stephanites* applied to the Leukophryena.[138] While crowns of specific monetary value were a fashion taken over from the regular honours given by cities, a custom which lasted into the late Roman empire, it was obviously not something one advertised in festivals, certainly not after 50 BC. But there seems to be no fixed terminology for these Hellenistic upgraded festivals: the Asklepieia of Kos is not stephanitic or sacred but the Didymeia is stephanitic and the Klaria is sacred, but all are penteteric. Vial has pointed out these differences, and others connected with the armistices and truces required for festival organisation, and it is significant that only the Hellenistic kings, not the cities, attempted to create *isolympic* festivals.[139] We do find some other evidence for money being given as extra prizes even in sacred contests,[140] and in imperial times an agonothete of the penteteric Dionysia Kaisareia, the main festival of Teos, but apparently not sacred, can be specifically praised by the Dionysiac Artists for handing out *themata*, (extra?) money prizes, to the contestants;[141] why should this not happen at sacred imperial contests also? Robert showed that Pythia in later times had golden apples as prizes, and perhaps this piece of financial ingenuity too had its origins in Delphi.[142] A new inscription concerning possibly the last full year of independent Delos in 169 BC asserts that the two *choraulae*, choral pipeplayers, with their choruses actually 'competed' for prizes at the Apollonia, something previously hidden from us in the archon's listings.[143] They not only get the astonishing salary of 1,500 drachmas each, more than twice what the resident architect gets, but also a *siteresion*, that is living expenses, normal enough at the time for

---

[138] *I.Magnesia* 16, 29 = Rigsby (1996a) no. 66, 29 who accepts the reading of Ebert (1982), as does Vial (2003) 318.

[139] See the valuable analysis of Vial (2003) 316–23. Even the Panathenaia Eumeneia of Sardis had *isolympic* events added, *pace* Vial (2003) 323.

[140] Roueché (1993) 46 n. 26; Pleket (2001) nn. 52, 95, 96 rightly says that a victor could get a money prize from his home city, but that is a different matter, and belongs with such honours as *sitesis*; many examples in *OMS* V 356ff.

[141] *IGRR* IV 1568.

[142] See now the Delphic graffiti of apples inside a crown analysed by Queyrel (2001) from the first and second centuries AD.

[143] Prêtre (2000) = *SEG* 50, 725 where I should read [*auletes*] for [*nomon*] in l. 6; cf. Bruneau (1970) 72.

workmen generally, as well as a *niketerion*—a prize of only 40 drachmas and so presumably a sop to their egos, since they both get it;[144] but they also get a *choregema*, which could mean anything, and so we can translate it as 'business expenses' or 'managing fee' without having much of a clue what it was. Crowns are not mentioned, and *choraulae* are not yet found in formal victor-lists, though they will be. Yet they are obviously exceptionally wealthy and honoured performers, still apparently on the fringe; as pantomimes would be later.

But one item should be discussed, those important honours (*timai*) given to the victor by his own city when he returns home, i.e. especially *eiselasis*, the right to triumphal entry, and *sitesis*, free meals, apart from any other official monetary rewards and privileges in one's native land for registered *hieronikai*, 'sacred victors'. (Deciding who was a local *hieronikes* was already a critical task worth putting on one's resumé in the second century BC.[145]) It is often considered that these were the only real financial benefits to be gained from sacred competition, a doubtful proposition for travelling performers, who might seldom be at home anyway.[146] Later the victors would trade these privileges as cash among themselves.[147] But it follows that the real problem then in upgrading a festival was to get the victor's home city to spend on these honours, by agreeing[148] 'to accept the competition as stephanitic and confer the greatest honours on the victors'—honours for which the festive city did not have to pay. While we may be impressed with the cities that eventually signed on to the Magnesia *stephanites* upgrade,[149] we have to remember that many more did not, or if they did, were not prepared to grant everything asked, even though probably the invitation had

---

[144] Probably it was for an animal, a 'generous feast' for the chorus, Ceccarelli (2004) 94 n. 9.

[145] *SEG* 50, 1211 (Pergamum) with the comments and bibliography there.

[146] The basic early imperial texts on *sitesis* as the reward of sacred victory are: Cassius Dio 51.1.2.5 on the Actia; *I.Ephesos* 17, 46ff., the decree of Fabius Paullus, on the illegal payments to sacred victors from the Artemis temple funds.

[147] Perpillou-Thomas (1993) 232 n. 74 in an illuminating study; *P.Hal.* 1, 260–5 already gives tax relief for victors in Ptolemaic Egypt.

[148] *Syll.*³ 590, 40 in which the Koans are asked to support the Didymeia.

[149] These are listed in detail by Rigsby (1996a), who discusses (p. 182) the motives for the 'omission' by some cities of recognition of *asylia*.

gone out to 'all the Hellenes' as usual.[150] Blanket upgrades of Hellenistic *sitesis* in the *prytaneion* or expensive *eiselasis* under such circumstances were not really possible.[151] On the other hand one can see that the accumulation of citizenships and councillorships by performers was not quite the exercise in vanity that it might seem to be, if moveable feasts and other privileges came with them. When this haphazard system of recognition of festivals and sacred victors by other cities collapsed, an imperial recognition of 'sacred victors' appears; and since under the Romans a *hieronikes*, indeed even any hanger-on of the synod of the Artists, enjoyed tax advantages, it became essential to define which contests were sacred.[152]

Festivals had offerings for all comers. The philosophers and sophists and assorted cranks and charlatans who went to Olympia to perform were not in any programme; they went for the publicity.[153] However, sometimes these were fringe performers: mimes, jugglers, strong men, sideshow artists, story-tellers, animal shows, and all the other performances described under the general heading of *theamata* and *akroamata*—'things to hear and see'—most of whom will never appear in any festival programme or list, but who can, if found acceptable, eventually show up as offering free performances— *aparchai*, *epideixeis*, and *akroaseis*, and even just possibly may be included in regular competition. This is how re-performed tragedy entered the Athenian Dionysia. But consider, for instance, the early imperial young ladies from distant Tralles who won the Pythia in running at Delphi;[154] they had also won running competitions at the Asklepieia and Isthmia, and so show up in a *virginum certamen*

---

[150] Robert (1989) 53 emphasises the 'panhellenic' language.

[151] Perhaps considerations like this dictate who competes where; it can explain why victors from the Troad show up in the remoter games of Arcadia in late Hellenistic times.

[152] Good remarks in Nollé (2001) 447, noting that golden apples and also bulging moneybags were awarded in Side in a sacred contest. *Ateleia* for anyone at all admitted to the synod of Artists in AD 273: Frisch (1986) 44ff. Exemplary is *POxy.* 908: AD 199: 'Tiberius Claudius Didymus of the tax exempt *hieronikai* from the Dionyseum and the sacred guild.' Surely this is the meaning of *ateles* in Roueché (1993) 88, 6? Cf. *I.Ephesos* 3005, and the freedom from liturgies (*anenochlesia*) for a period victor in *Milet* VI 2, 939.

[153] Weiler (1997); for Olympia as a market and much else, see Zoumbaki (2001) esp. 59–60 on tourism; Farrington (1997).

[154] *FD* III 534 = *Syll.*³ 802; *Corinth* VIII.3.153; Kajava (2002).

(maiden's contest) in Corinth and a similar competition appears later in the Capetolia of Rome. Does all of this represent apparently a passing phase for pseudo-Spartan sexy stuff that disappeared as quickly as it came? Perhaps, but it is notably connected to the introduction of imperial cult by enthusiastic philo-Romans in these places. Where did this odd competition come from? Possibly the race of the *parthenoi* at the Heraia[155] at Olympia? The senate certainly wanted to suppress this resurgent feminism at Rome. But women runners appeared at the Capetolia, and we find local upper-class female runners as well as a female *choraula* in the Sebasta of Naples as late as AD 154, and there can be no real grounds to suppose they were not there from the beginning in 2 BC.[156] But the puzzle remains.

We should not insist then on too strict a dichotomy between familiar formal festival categories and the artists on the fringe.[157] This is I think particularly important in explaining the movement away from formal drama to mime and pantomime. One does not know quite what to make of the report of Polemon, writing in the second century BC, that a woman Aristomache of Erythrae was victorious as poetess at the Isthmia,[158] but at Priene soon after the Mithridatic war a generous donor, observing that the biennial Dionysia is not being held that year, hires a singer, a *choraules* and a kitharode for two days, an interesting example of what popular taste probably wanted, for this is one of the earliest specific mentions of the category *choraules*.[159] In the long list of choregic texts from Iasos from *c.* 195 to 126 BC, which list donations, probably under popular pressure, of performers at the annual Dionysia,[160] we should not be too surprised to find buried among the comedians, tragedians, and pipe players a lone female for a two-day stint, a *choropsaltria*, a female harp-player with chorus.[161] Someone obviously had the courage to try out a

---

[155] Dillon (2000).   [156] Caldelli (1993) 33 n. 134.

[157] Cf. Aneziri (2003) 222–3.

[158] Plu. *Moral.* 675B = Polemon fr. XXVII Preller.

[159] *I.Priene* 113,78; he had earlier hired the first known *pantomimos.*

[160] *SEG* 46, 1407 for the dating controversy. A useful chart can be found in Migeotte (1993) 270. See Crowther ch. 11 below.

[161] Athenaeus 538 reports that at Alexander's wedding tragedians and comedians and harp-players were the only artists with choruses.

new fashion, as happened in Delphi at the same time,[162] and she was popular enough to be asked for another day, but the experiment was not repeated. Did the guild object? Sadly, we shall never know if she brought her own chorus of singers or dancers or both with her, or if they were male or female, or if they sang a dithyramb, or if she just accompanied the Iasians at their festival. But she too found her place at the Dionysia, even without a proper prize. Of course this kind of thing was always going to happen, and we should expect it—let us not call it para-performance—as a permanent feature of all official competitions, whose conventions will be under attack in a mobile cultural world.[163] When the kitharode Athanadas of Rhegium arrived at the Delphic Soteria *c.* 150 BC, 'competed' for two days, then gave an *epidosis*—an extra gift—of a third day on popular demand, we cannot tell if he ever entered a real competition.[164] It is not easy to know what was going on. When we read that Menalkes of Athens, a kitharode, a hundred years earlier came to the Delphic Soteria, and

> τόν τε ἄλλον ἀγῶνα καλῶς καὶ φιλοτίμως ἠγωνίσατο καὶ
> προσεπέδωκε τῶι θεῶι καὶ τοῖς Ἀμφικτύοσι τὸν ἀγῶνα
>
> he performed well and generously and in particular donated the extra performance for Apollo and the Amphiktyons ...

I do not understand that the inscription 'explicitly stipulates' that he came to compete there, for there was no real competition, and he is not mentioned as one of the kitharodes in the relevant list, but as a (singing) member of a *choros* of five men; rather he probably performed twice, once as a singing member of a troupe (the first *agon*), where he could not win a prize anyway, and then as a

---

[162] A *choropsaltria* from Kyme is honoured at Delphi in 134 BC for donating a day free, and performing for two days, and 'being successful/popular at the contest of the Pythia': *Syll.*³ 689, with *OMS* I 253 for the formula. She is given a crown and a great deal of money, but the amount has been erased. Polygnota, a harpist from Thebes, is also honoured *c.* 86 BC: *FD* III 3, 249, though there is no likelihood at all that there was a contest of (female!) harpists, as affirmed in *Nouveau Choix* (1971) 69, or that she came 'pour participer aux Pythia', as van Liefferinge (2000) 157 writes. See also Bélis (1999) 54–5.

[163] Examples and bibliography are given by van Liefferinge (2002), and add Tedeschi (2003).

[164] Stefanis (1988) no. 55.

kitharode singing an extra solo outside of competition, both times for nothing.[165] Competition and performance are now ambivalent terms, and we still have the infinite variety of imperial times to come. Perhaps therefore it is not ritual stability, but gradual change and versatile adaptation, driven by internal dynamics from the fringe, that guarantee an enduring festival.

---

[165] My arguments against van Liefferinge (2002) 156, whom I quote, are: the Soteria at the time (Nachtergael 1977: 416 no. 8) were a demonstration by the Artists, and there seem to have been no prizes; φιλοτίμως usually indicates euergetism; finally the πρός in the verb suggests that this was *another* free gift to the Delphians. Menalkes is praised in the separate decree (Nachtergael 1977: no. 19) specifically as a kitharode, and must have performed as such the second time.

2

Theatre Rituals

Angelos Chaniotis

The shows in the ancient theatre did not only consist of theatrical and other artistic performances. A large variety of other activities, including ritual actions, took place both on the occasion of thymelic and musical competitions and in the context of other celebrations. After presenting an overview of the religious rituals performed in theatres, this paper focusses on non-religious rituals, such as the crowning of benefactors, the announcement of honours, ceremonial entrances of magistrates and honoured persons, acclamations, speech acts, and rituals of consecration. It is argued that stereotypical formulae in honorific decrees and other inscriptions reflect rituals of communication between mortals and immortals, between subject and ruler, between mass and élite, and between citizens and foreigners. Certain clauses in inscriptions should be interpreted as 'stage directions' for the successful performance of rituals. Theatre rituals were perhaps not meant to be spectacles; perhaps the theatre was chosen as their setting only because of the advantages it offered in a practical sense (acoustics, seats, large gatherings of people). But the choice of this particular setting, i.e. the space of *thea* (the watching of spectacles), sooner or later had consequences for the form of the rituals themselves.

MURPHY'S LAW OF RITUAL DISASTERS — OR, WHY RITUALS REQUIRE STAGING

In AD 365 Procopius, taking advantage of the absence of emperor Valens, attempted to conquer the throne with the help of a few soldiers. His attempt was successful—or at least so he thought. Ammianus Marcellinus describes the ceremony, hastily organised:[1]

Because a purple robe could nowhere be found, he was dressed in a gold-embroidered tunic, like an attendant at court, but from foot to waist he looked like a page in the service of the palace; he wore purple shoes on his feet, and bore a lance, and a small piece of purple cloth in his left hand . . . Then he appeared in public, surrounded by a number of armed men, and now advancing with more confidence and with upraised standards, attended with a fearful din of shields mournfully clashing together, which the soldiers from fear of his being pelted from housetops with stones or pieces of tile closely joined together over the very crests of their helmets . . . When the said Procopius had mounted the tribunal, and all were filled with amazement, fearing the gloomy silence, and believing (as indeed he had expected) that he had merely come to a steeper road to death, since a trembling which pervaded all his limbs hindered him speaking, he stood for a long time without a word. Finally he began with broken and dying utterance to say a little, justifying his action by his relationship with the imperial family. Then at first by the low whispers of a few, who had been hired for the purpose, later by the tumultuous acclamations of the people, he was hailed as emperor in disorderly fashion, and hastily went on to the Senate House. There finding none of the distinguished senators, but only a few persons of low rank, with rapid steps he hastened to the palace and entered it with ill-omened step.

(Ammianus Marcellinus 26.5.15–18)

If Procopius' *dies imperii* looks like the parody of a ceremony, it is because it was badly staged, hasty and disorderly. The new emperor could not find the appropriate costume, the right words and an enthusiastic audience that would hail him and not throw stones on him. This passage is an example of Murphy's law applied in ceremonies. Everything that could possibly go wrong, went wrong.

---

[1] I owe this reference to an unsuccessful ritual to Dr Thorsten Beigel.

Let us imagine for a moment how Murphy's law could work in a theatre, say in Priene. Dionysos' priest, who could not sleep all night because of diarrhoea, comes too late, only to find that his seat of honour has been occupied by a foreign envoy, who had not been told that he should enter the theatre when the herald announces his name. Because of the priest's weak voice nobody in the audience notices his prayer, and instead they all watch a fight in the fourth row; there, Aristodemos discovered himself seating next to Kallion whom he suspects as the person who had deprived his daughter of her virginity. After the libations and the prayer, both the *stephanephoros* (the chief magistrate) and the *agonothetes* (the organiser of the contest) stand up, hoping to have their short moment of glory and to be admired in their glamorous garments. They now look at one another because they do not know who is supposed to begin reading the announcements of crowns of honour; both of them start reading together, then both of them pause; both of them start again, until finally they agree, on stage, on the sequence of their speeches. While the *agonothetes* slowly reads the text of an honorific decree for a benefactor, he is interrupted by a man who enters the *orchestra* from the right *parodos*; it is Kriton, a benefactor, who has been waiting to hear the invitation to receive his seat of honour, alas, in vain; the secretary of the assembly had forgotten to put his name on the list that was read aloud by the herald; having lost his patience, he now enters uninvited and demands a seat in the front row. Now it is the spectators who lose their patience, for the announcements of honours decreed in the past years find no end. The tumult soon gets out of control, for the *agonothetes* incurred such high expenses on *kithara* singers that no money was left for the club-bearers needed to keep order in the theatre.

One does not really need a sudden rain, a strong wind, or an earthquake to ruin a day in the theatre, so eagerly anticipated by urban populations; bad organisation can sometimes be a much bigger disaster for a show.

People go to a cinema to enjoy a film, but this does not mean that they do not find the commercials entertaining and the previews informative. Similarly, the show in the ancient theatre did not consist only of theatrical and other artistic performances. A large variety of other activities, including ritual actions, took place both on the occasion of thymelic and musical competitions and in the context of other celebrations. Brigitte Le Guen (1995) has drawn attention to religious rites, such as the offering of sacrifices (e.g. at the Sarapieia in Tanagra), arguing for this reason—and correctly—that dramatic performances cannot be regarded as simply secular entertainment. A theatre often provided the ideal setting for all kinds of gatherings of people, from royal weddings (Chaniotis 1997) and meetings of the popular assembly, to courts and celebrations of emperor cult (see below). These gatherings were either aiming at the performance of rituals (weddings, emperor cult), or were accompanied by rituals (assembly).

An ancient theatre as public space is the locus of rituals. In some cases a theatre is even built so that the performance of a ritual can be watched by spectators, as in the case of the theatrical space added to the sanctuary of Artemis Orthia in Sparta so that spectators could watch the competition of Spartan youths in flogging themselves.

Unfortunately, rituals belong to the most elusive phenomena of ancient behaviour. As widely established, stereotypical activities, followed consistently and (at least in theory) invariably, they are rarely described and hardly ever explained by those who perform them; they are rather described by those who observe them and are astounded at the differences from the rituals of their own culture—or they are described by puzzled antiquarians (Chaniotis 2005). It is for this reason that our knowledge of theatre rituals is rather limited and usually based on indirect information. This article is dedicated to the information provided by the epigraphic sources.

RELIGIOUS RITUALS IN THEATRES

Among the rituals performed in theatres those of a religious nature are more often and more directly mentioned or described in inscriptions. A regulation (*diagraphe*) in the city of Priene which concerns the sale of the priesthood of Dionysos (*I.Priene* 174, second century BC) states: 'he will offer the sacrifices that are offered to Dionysos Melpomenos in the theatre and he will burn incense and will make the libation and the prayer on behalf of the city of Priene'.

Sacrifices are often followed by banquets, and, again, in Priene we do find an attestation of a banquet offered by the *agonothetai* 'in the theatre' for the citizens, the other population and the foreign sacred envoys (*I.Priene* 118, first century BC). The sacred law concerning the mysteries of Andania (*LSCG* 65) refers to purifications (*katharmoi*) to be performed in the theatre. And an inscription—possibly a pierre errante—found in Chalkis, describes the achievements of M. Ulpius Kallineikos, the Younger (*SEG* 29, 807, third century AD?). Kallineikos who had the function (or perhaps the nick-name?) 'the one who is carried' (*phoreimenos*), was carried on a phallus fifty-five times around the *orchestra* of the theatre (Veyne 1985; Csapo 1997). The expression *ep' agathoi* ('for a good outcome') in this text is not just a formula, but a reference to the fact that Kallineikos' acrobatic performance had taken place for the well-being of the community; it was an offering to the god.

Theatres were privileged ritual spaces also in connection with the cult of the emperor. When mortals communicate with the gods, by praying, sacrificing, or making a dedication, it is often expected, albeit not required, that others watch these expressions of piety. The necessity of spectators is far more important in the communication between polis communities and emperors as recipients of ritual actions. This is one of the reasons — certainly not the only reason — why theatres play an important role in the rituals of emperor cult: the citizens, the representatives of the imperial administration, the foreigners, sometimes the emperor himself, should watch how a civic community honoured the mortal divinity of an emperor. This is not the place to discuss the rituals of emperor cult that took place in theatres, especially since most of the material has already been collected and studied by Elizabeth Gebhard (1988 and 1996). I epigrammatically mention her discussion of processions that took place to and through theatres. Members of the procession assembled in a specified order at a shrine in the city or outside the walls and walked through the streets to the theatre carrying images which were finally set up in the theatre. At the end of the day or of the festival the images were returned to their place of origin.

The best-known procession of this type is the one at Gytheion (*SEG* 11, 923, AD 15). The *agoranomos* (the magistrate responsible for the market), the ephebes and the *neoi* (the age-class of young men aged from twenty to thirty), the other citizens, all dressed in white and wearing laurel crowns, the sacred virgins, and the women in their ritual garments proceeded from the sanctuary of Asklepios to the theatre. When they arrived there and before the performers entered, three painted *eikones* (images) representing Augustus, Tiberius, and Livia were set up, and a table with an incense-burner on it was placed in the middle of the theatre. The magistrates burned incense and prayed for the safety of the rulers.

The foundation of Salutaris at Ephesos involved the carrying of thirty-one figures of silver and gold from the sanctuary of Artemis, through the Magnesian Gates to the theatre, where they were set up in the cavea, creating thirty-one points of brilliant light as the sun struck the gold and the silver (*I.Ephesos* 27; Rogers 1991).

At Oinoanda the procession probably began at the temple of Apollo and moved through the theatre, where twenty *mastigophoroi* (bearers of whips) took care of order (Wörrle 1988; *SEG* 38, 1462 C, AD 125–6). The representatives of other cities were also escorted through the theatre (ll. 85–7): 'whatever sacrifices (i.e. sacrificial animals) are sent by other cities, these too should be escorted in procession (*pompeuesthai*) through the theatre and announced at the time they are sent'. I will return to the significance of the processions and the announcements for the understanding of inscriptions on theatre seats later.

I should also mention the performance of hymns for emperor Hadrian in the theatre of Ephesos on the occasion of his visit there (*I.Ephesos* 1145).

Some of the theatre rituals have left their traces both in its architecture, e.g. in the altar, in the *parodoi* (ceremonial entrances), and in the seats of honour, but also in its epigraphy. As I will argue, the number and complexity of ritual actions that took place in theatres made some kind of organisation and staging necessary, which again has left its traces in inscriptions both written in theatres and referring to theatres.

STEREOTYPICAL FORMULAE IN DECREES: STAGING DIRECTIONS FOR RITUALS?

A type of epigraphic evidence closely associated with rituals which took place in theatres is a stereotypical formula found in countless honorific decrees:[2] it provides for the crowning of local and foreign benefactors in the theatre and/or the announcement of this honour during a dramatic festival. The fact that we have a stereotypical formula should not be misinterpreted as evidence for a routine; the formula presupposes a stereotypical action, a ritual.

These 'crowning formulae' have the same structure. They provide information about the festival in which the crowning and/or announcement will take place, about the responsible magistrates, about the form and sometimes the value of the crown, in a few cases also about the exact text of the announcement, and occasionally about the repetition of this action year after year.

One of the most detailed instructions is given in the honorary decree of Kolophon for Ptolemaios (*c.* 130–110 BC):

He is to be crowned with a crown of gold and with a statue of gold for his virtue and his love of what is good for the people; the honours are to be announced at the Dionysia and the Klaria during the competitions; the *prytaneis* (presidents of the council) will be responsible for the announcement at the Dionysia, the *agonothetai* (those responsible for the competitions) at the Klaria; he is to be crowned, and an announcement of the honours by the herald should be made during the performance of the *pyrrhiche*-dance and during the gymnical competitions for ever; the announcement should be as follows: 'The *demos* crowns Ptolemaios, son of Pantagnotos, with a crown of gold and with a statue of gold, because he is a virtuous man and a lover of virtue, and generous towards the citizens, a man who never neglected the city's interests.'

(*SEG* 39, 1243 col. V 27–43)

The contemporary decree of the same city for Menippos (after 120/19 BC) is identical in the wording with regard to the honours, but not as regards the content of the announcement:

---

[2] On formulaic expressions in general see Rhodes and Lewis (1997) 18–23; cf. Chaniotis (1999). On the formulae concerning the announcement of honours see Henry (1983).

The *demos* crowns Menippos, son of Apollonides, natural son of Eumedes, with a crown of gold and with a statue of gold, because he is a benefactor, generous and a lover of virtue with regard to the citizens, a leader of the fatherland in difficult times.

(*SEG* 39, 1244 col. III 21–34)

In the text of the announcement one immediately notices an effort for an individual characterisation of the achievements of the two persons (cf. *I.Priene* 63).

Let us consider now the practical aspects of the announcement of the honours, looking again at the decrees for Ptolemaios and Menippos. In both cases the honours were to be announced at the Dionysia in the theatre for ever—as long as the honoured persons were alive, but possibly also after their death (cf. *SEG* 39, 759). Both decrees are roughly contemporary, so that it is most likely that for a period of time both announcements were made, one after the other, on the same occasion, in front of the same audience. If Ptolemaios and Menippos were present, one may assume that they stood up or even went to the stage to be hailed by the citizens. If such an honour was decreed for yet another benefactor every year, and taking into consideration life expectancy, one would have up to fifteen or twenty such announcements in a city of a medium size—and this in addition to other honours and ceremonies. Repetitions of similar texts and actions are as exciting as commencement ceremonies in American universities. They are tolerated only because all the persons involved as actors or spectators have a few seconds in which either they or a person they love stands in the centre of attention. What about an ancient audience that had come to the theatre for the performances and not for the 'commercials'? When would the point be reached at which the audience lost its patience?

As a matter of fact we have direct evidence showing that sometimes the announcement of honours took quite some time. The inventory of the treasurers of Athena and the Other Gods for the year 304/3 gives us an impression of the number of such announcements:

The following items were not delivered by the treasurers in office during the archonship of Pherekles to the treasurers in office during the archonship of Leostratos: the crowns that were announced at the Dionysia during the competition of the tragedians, announced[3] by Philippos, son of Nikias of Acharnai, the magistrate responsible for the administration (*epi tei dioikesei*), in accordance with the decree of the people that was proposed by Philippos, son of Nikias of Acharnai. The following crowns were announced: The people crown Antigonos with a crown with a value of 1,000 drachmas, etc.

(SEG 38, 143)

At least twelve crowns were announced on the same occasion: one for Antigonos the One-Eyed, four for Demetrios the Besieger, one for Antigonos and Demetrios, one for the council and the people by the Peparethians, one for the council and the people by the (new) *isoteleis* (privileged foreign residents), and four crowns for the councillors in office in four consecutive years, from 306 to 303. The repetition of the same text may have given this ceremony some solemnity, and most spectators some boredom, but among the audience we may expect some 2,000 men who were keen to experience this celebration: the 2,000 councillors of the past four years. Nonetheless some variation in the text would have been most welcome.

We find such variations not only with regard to the texts, but also with regard to the occasion and the event, during which the announcement or the crowning took place (see below). We usually find the instruction that the announcement has to take place during the festival of the Dionysia, i.e. on the occasion of the dramatic competitions. However, some decrees instruct the responsible officials to make the announcement at the 'first Dionysia' (Διονυσίοις τοῖς πρώτοις), i.e. during the next/coming Dionysia (*SEG* 35, 912: Kos, second century BC; *I.Priene* 4, 17, and 61: Priene, fourth and third century BC), some decrees do not. It was not self-evident that the honours were to be announced on the next occasion. The aforementioned inventory shows that some councillors had to wait for four years to see the crown that had been decreed for the council, in which they had served, announced in the theatre. A decree of the Aixoneis (*SEG* 36, 186, 313/12 BC) specifies the year of an honorific ceremony to be performed in the theatre during the competition of the comedies ('in the year after Theophrastos' archonship'), obviously in order to ensure a prompt announcement.

---

[3] Or, according to another restoration, 'brought back' (ἀνεκόμισεν).

The Dionysia usually lasted for several days and included a very diverse programme. For this reason some decrees specify exactly when the announcement was to be made, e.g. during the competition of the tragedians (*SEG* 34, 106: Eleusis; *SEG* 44, 699: Andros, third century BC; *SEG* 44, 949 I: Teos, third/second century BC; *I.Priene* 17: Priene, third century BC), during the new competition of the tragedians in Athens, both at the Great Dionysia (*SEG* 28, 60, third century BC) and at the City Dionysia (*SEG* 28, 75, *c.* 203 BC), or during the fair (*panegyris*) in an unknown city (*SEG* 29, 771, second century BC). A great honour was the repetition of the announcement in various festivals, e.g. in Kyme at the festival Dionysia and Attaleia in Kyme (*SEG* 29, 1216, second century). In some cases the instructions are very detailed. For instance, a decree in Kyme instructs the ceremony to take place 'on the next Dionysia during the competition of the boys' (*SEG* 33, 1035, second century BC); a decree in Priene is even more detailed: 'in the theatre, at the first (next) Dionysia, during the competition of the boys, when the *demos* performs the customary libations' (*I.Priene* 108, *c.* 129 BC). Similarly, another decree of Kyme specifies the appropriate moment for this honour during the festivals of the Great Soteria and the Rhomaia: 'when the *agonothetai* (the persons who preside over the competitions) perform the sacrifices in the theatre on the 13th day' (*SEG* 33, 1039, second century BC).[4] We may assume that at least in some years and in some cities the number of crownings and announcements could take such dimensions that provisions such as those presented here had to be taken in order to distribute these announcements among the festivals (dramatic or athletic), among the days of the celebration, and among the various events. Not every honoured person could expect an announcement in the coming festival.

---

[4] Cf. similar precisions in the following decrees: *I.Priene* 81: during the musical competition (Priene, *c.* 200 BC); *SEG* 29, 1072: 'during the musical competition when the people perform the choruses' (Halikarnassos, second century BC); *SEG* 29, 1089: in the theatre, 'when the people perform the musical competition' (Theangela, first century BC); *IG* XII 6.1, 150: 'the sacred herald should make announcement during the competition of the tragedians in the theatre naming each one of them separately, along with the father's name' (honorary decree for Koan judges, Samos, late fourth century BC).

Similar variations can be observed with regard to the persons responsible for the announcement. The announcement was often made by the persons who presided over the competition (*agonoth-etes*),[5] but in addition to the *agonothetai* we find references to many other magistrates and priests who undertook this task.[6] These differences are in part due to the duties of the officials, in part to their ambition to have their small share in glory when they stand up in the theatre, dressed in their best clothes, to be for a few minutes the centre of attention.

Even clearer are the differences in the type of the crown. They concern the value, the material, and the form (gold, ivy, myrtle, olive, decorated with the portrait of a god etc.).[7] The expression 'the greatest crown that the law provides for' (στέφανος ὁ μέγιστος ἐκ τοῦ νόμου: *SEG* 29, 752) suggests a hierarchy of crowns, not only in value, but probably also in form. Expressions such as 'a distinguished crown' (διαφέρων στέφανος: *SEG* 8, 529 ll. 44), 'a crown of merit' (στέφανος ἀριστεῖος: *I.Perge* 14 and 23; *I.Priene* 108), 'a crown of excellent behaviour as a citizen' (ἀριστοπολιτείας στέφανος: *I.Olympia* 465; *SEG* 46, 402), 'a crown of virtue' (ἀρετῆς στέφανος: *MAMA* VIII 408), or 'the crown of the god' (ὁ τοῦ θεοῦ στέφανος: *SEG* 43, 773; ὁ παρὰ τοῦ θεοῦ στέφανος: *SEG* 49, 1753) show that crown does not equal crown and that the rituals of the crowning and of the announcement of this honour were anything but uniform and monotonous, the more so when not only the announcement, but also the crowning itself took place in the theatre.

Unfortunately little is known about the procedure of crowning. It was usually less spectacular than the device that the Pergamenes attempted to apply in the case of king Mithridates VI in 88 BC. In the theatre, where they had assembled, they set up a machinery of some kind which would lower a statue of Nike holding a crown in her hand which would be placed on the king's head. However, when

---

[5] *SEG* 39, 1153 (Ephesos); *SEG* 29, 1216 and 33, 1039 (Kyme); *SEG* 35, 912 (Kos); *SEG* 39, 1243 col. V (Kolophon); *I.Priene* 4, 17, 61, 81 (Priene).

[6] E.g. *Basileis* : *SEG* 36, 1046 (Miletos). *Demarchos*: *SEG* 34, 106 (Eleusis). *Epi tei dioikesei*: *SEG* 28, 60, and 38, 143 (Athens). *Hieromnemon*: *I.Byzantion* 2. Priest of Dionysos and *prytaneis*: *SEG* 39, 1243 (Kolophon). *Strategoi*: *SEG* 28, 75.

[7] E.g. *SEG* 39, 1153 (Ephesos, third century).

the statue was being lowered towards Mithridates, it broke to pieces just as Nike was about to touch his head, and the crown went tumbling from her hand to the ground in the midst of the theatre (Plu. *Sulla* 11). Most honorees would probably satisfy themselves with a magistrate (rather than a beautiful virgin) who would place the crown on their head or hand it out, as the representations on documentary reliefs imply (Meyer 1989: 132–40). Of course it is difficult to find an answer to the question of how one crowns a foreign community or a council of 500 members.

I have discussed the ritual of crowning in some detail because it is so widespread and so well attested that it allows us to recognise not only the stereotypical formulations which one expects in inscriptions that concern rituals, but also individual features which are connected with staging instructions, without which the performance of a ritual can be either chaotic or monotonous and consequently inadequate for the audience in a theatre.

The last point makes all the difference in the world: we are dealing with a ritual that takes place before or during a performance for which hundreds or thousands of people have come to the theatre.

CEREMONIAL ENTRANCES

Theatre rituals have to compete with theatrical performances. Staging is more urgently needed than in other rituals that take place in a sanctuary, a private club, or at home. And the larger the gathering of people, the more difficult to stage the rituals in an orderly and aesthetically satisfying manner. An anonymous statesman in Chios, who served as an *agonothetes* of the first celebration of the festival for Dea Roma around 188 BC, was not only praised for his financial contributions and for a beautiful (καλός) musical *agon*, but he is also honoured because 'he took care of the proper conduct (εὐκοσμία) and good order (εὐταξία) with regard to/in the theatre (κατὰ θέατρον)' (*SEG* 30, 1073); he is praised for having succeeded where others had probably failed.

Proper conduct and good order do not primarily refer to the performers, although quarrels among them were not unusual—this is perhaps the context of the expression ἄμαχα (without μάχη, without combat, or 'unbeatable'?) in the backstage rooms in the theatre of Aphrodisias (Roueché 1993: 17–21). Proper conduct and good order primarily refer to the spectators, especially the less privileged spectators who did not have a seat of honour. In many theatres we have evidence for sectors or rows reserved for particular groups of the citizen-body. In the theatre of Herakleia Lynkestis in Macedonia (*SEG* 49, 720) seating inscriptions giving the names of tribes are written horizontally along the lowest row of seats. They name the tribes Asklepias, Artemisias, of the Sebastos,[8] Herakleios, and Dionysias. In Kaunos blocks with the names of the tribes Kranais and Rhadamanthis have been found (Ehrhardt 1997). The seat reservations may have played a role in the arrival of the citizens as spectators, but I have the impression that they were far more important for the occasions in which the citizens were themselves active participants. A Samian decree (*IG* XII 6, 172 A ll. 3–8) instructs the *prytaneis* to invite the members of the assembly, which convened in the theatre, to take their seats there according to the subdivisions of the citizen-body (*chilyastyes*); signs were to be set up in order to determine the place reserved for each *chilyastys*. The assembly was not the only occasion on which the citizens (or groups of citizens) were divided according to tribes. When citizens, ephebes, or young men attended processions, they did so divided into *phylai* (Chaniotis 1995: 156 n. 75). It follows that when these processions reached the theatre and entered it, the persons that attended the procession could take their seat in an orderly manner only if seats had been reserved for each tribe. Generalisations are very dangerous, but I would like to suggest that in some cases the tribal inscriptions written on the seats of theatres should be seen in the context of processions that ended in the theatre. White marble seats found near the theatre of Ephesos bear a long inscription which states that these seats were reserved for citizens—possibly for official representatives— of Keramos by the high priest Ulpius Aristokrates, who held his office on the second celebration of the Hadrianeia in AD 128 (*SEG* 34, 1168). The representatives of Keramos most likely entered the theatre

---

[8] I assume that the genitive Σεβαστοῦ does not refer to a priest of Augustus (ἱερεὺς Σεβαστοῦ), but to a tribe (φυλὴ Σεβαστοῦ).

all together, took their seats in a ceremonial way, and probably after the respective announcement. One may interpret the seats reserved for the *Apolloniatai* in the theatre of Antiocheia in Pisidia in the same manner (*SEG* 50, 1290, imperial period).

This brings me to another theatre ritual for which some staging was necessary: the invitation to take a seat of honour (*prohedria*). A ceremonial entrance in procession of the men and women for whom a *prohedria* was reserved is very probable. It is implied by the verbs καλεῖσθαι ('to be invited') and εἰσκηρύσσεσθαι ('to be invited by the herald to enter'), as in an honorary decree of Magnesia on the Maeander: Apollophanes was

to be invited by the herald to take a seat of honour together with the other benefactors in the competitions organised by the people, so that everyone knows that the people thankfully acknowledge the good and virtuous men and show the gratitude that benefactors deserve.

(*I.Magnesia* 92 a)

Everyone would have recognised the people's gratitude only if some kind of an announcement was made, and not if all these men entered the theatre together with the spectators. Their entrance was part of the show, exactly as the public appearances and the competition of the *choregoi* were part of the show in the Classical Athenian dramatic competitions (Wilson 2000: 95–102, 136–43).

Some decrees provide more details about the seat of honour, such as its exact location (e.g. next to the priest of Dionysos in *SEG* 36, 187) or its form (e.g. a throne as in the case of M. Ulpius Eubiotos Leuros in Athens in *IG* II² 82 = *SEG* 30, 82). An Athenian decree shows that the architect elected to be responsible for the sanctuaries had the burdensome task of accommodating the honoured persons (*SEG* 27, 60: κατανέμειν τὴν προεδρίαν : see Csapo, below).

The funerary epigram for the high priestess Romana in Side (late third century AD) mentions her office, which she owed to her husband Zosimos, in connection with her appearance in the theatre:

He did not only lead her to the wedding bed, the mother of his children, but he had her carried as a high priestess in the brilliant thymelic competitions, in purple dress, and placed on her head a crown of gold, a worthy present of her prudence.

(*I.Side* 226; Merkelbach and Stauber 2002: 158–9)

The interest of this text goes beyond the proof that high priestesses did not serve in their own right, but as wives of high priests (Herz 1992; Hayward 1998). It gives us an impression of the manner in which magistrates made their entrance to the theatre to receive their seats of honour, with impressive garments and crowns. This epigram makes sense only in the context of a ceremonial entrance—possibly in a procession—of all the persons who had a seat of honour, their names being announced as they entered. Such an entrance is reported about Agrippa I who arrived at a festival celebrated for the emperor in a theatre in AD 44. At daybreak on the second day of the festival, as Josephus narrates (*AJ* 29, 343), Agrippa, clad in robes of shimmering silver, made his way to the theatre to take advantage of the sunrise. The beams of light dancing off his robes as the sun came up made for a wondrous sight. A man in the crowd shouted out: 'You are more than mortal in your being.' Agrippa was punished for his arrogance and died within five days, but for many magistrates their entrance into the theatre was their moment of glory, for example for the priest of Dionysos in Priene (*I.Priene* 174). He was given the right 'to sit in the theatre in a seat of honour and to wear the garment which he chooses and an ivy-crown of gold'.

VERBAL RITUALS AND SPEECH ACTS

The announcement of honours and the invitation to members of the élite, benefactors, and guests of honour were alas not the only verbal rituals to which spectators were exposed, sitting in the hot sun and hungry, not only in a metaphorical sense. Other announcements, more or less important, were made. The Parian decree concerning the festival of Artemis Leukophryene in Magnesia on the Maeander provides, for example, for an announcement of the consecration of the city and the territory and of the new contest during the Dionysia in the theatre (*c.* 208 BC):

the magistrates should announce the *asylia* and the consecration of the city and the territory of the Magnetes in the theatre when we first celebrate the Great Dionysia in the competition of tragedies, and the envoys,

Molossos, Demetrios and Kallikrates should also announce the *agon* and
the *panegyris*.

(*I.Magnesia* 50)

In Philadelpheia, a letter of Caracalla concerning the *neokoreia* of the
city, that is its right to have a temple of the emperor, was read in the
theatre (*IGR* IV 1619 b, 18 November AD 213).

One of the largest groups of inscriptions concerning the Hellenistic theatre is the dossier of fifty-nine texts from Iasos that record
the contributions of citizens for the celebration of the Dionysia and
the construction of the theatre (*I.Iasos* 160–218; see Crowther,
below). Their chronology is a matter of controversy (Migeotte 1993;
Crowther 1995b), but there can be no doubt that we are dealing with
a long period of time. In these documents one finds three variants of
a stereotypical formula that express the fact that a person who had
promised to make a donation in the past fulfilled his promise. One
of the variants of this formula explicitly states that the promise
(ἐπίνευσις) was made during the celebration of the Dionysia
(τῶν ἐπινευσάντων πρότερον ἐν Διονυσίοις). The monotonous repetition of this formula suggests a ritual: during or at the end of the
competition of the Dionysia, the citizens were publicly asked to
make a contribution for the next year. The public performance of
such promises is suggested by Theophrastos (*Characters* 22) and
Athenaios (*Deipnosophistai* 4.168 f.; cf. Migeotte 1992: 23–4).

In this context one should also mention the manumission records
inscribed in or near theatres, for example in Bouthrotos and in
Delphi. Some of the Delphic manumission records (e.g. *SEG* 34, 403,
first century AD) refer to a law, according to which manumissions
were to be inscribed in the theatre in the sanctuary of Apollo
(ἐγχαράξας εἰς τὸ ἱερὸν τοῦ Πυθίου Ἀπόλλωνος εἰς τὸ θέατρον κατὰ
τὸν νόμον). The location may be related to the custom to announce
the manumissions in the theatre, either in meetings of the assembly
or in festivals. The invocations of the Muse Ourania in the theatre of
Aphrodisias (Roueché 1993: nos. 2, 4–5) also presuppose acclamations of the spectators at some point of the celebration. We have
direct evidence for such acclamations from Perge (*SEG* 50, 1342–3, *c.*
AD 275). Here, the quaestor pro praetore of the provinces of Lykia
and Pamphylia, Claudius Cornelianus Latro Apellianus impressed

the population with his building works; the people responded with acclamations inscribed on the balustrade of the theatre, the place where the acclamations probably took place—possibly after a speech of Cornelianus: 'Be fortunate, Cornelianus; you are constructing an Olympian work for the mother-city (of the province); take a seat of honour (or preside over)!' (εὐτύχη Κορνηλιανέ· Ὀλύμπιον ἔργον κτίζις τῆι μητροπόλι· προκάθηισε); 'be fortunate, Cornelianus; the entire building waits for you' ([εὐτύ]χη Κορνηλιανέ· ὅλον τὸ κτίσμα σὲ περιμένι).

Finally, we find numerous attestations of rituals of consecration that took place in the theatre, perhaps not every year, but quite often. I am referring to the dedication of the entire theatre, of separate sections, or of statues. The theatre of Gerasa was dedicated (ἀφιερώθη) to Domitian (*SEG* 27, 1009); the 'birthday' of the theatre of Aspendos was celebrated as an agonistic festival (*CIG* 4342 d, c. AD 150–175: ἀγὼν γυμνικὸς γενέθλιος τοῦ θεάτρου); in Ephesos a section of the theatre (σελίς) was dedicated to Artemis Ephesia and an anonymous emperor (*SEG* 48, 1383); and many dedicatory inscriptions from the theatre of Aphrodisias attest the dedications, possibly of parts of the theatre, as they were completed, to Aphrodite, the emperors, the *demos*, and the *patris* (Reynolds 1991). These acts of consecration were ritual acts, including sacrifices, and the same applies to the erection of statues. The honorary decrees for Apollophanes of Magnesia on the Maeander (*I.Magnesia* 92, early second century BC) mention the erection of his bronze statues in the most prominent place in the theatre; bronze statues of Aristomenes and Alexander the Great were dedicated in the theatre of Messene (*SEG* 48, 503–4). Denis Knoepfler (Knoepfler 1997) has suggested that Praxiteles' statue of Eros was removed from Thespiai by L. Mummius in 146 BC and given to Athens, where it was displayed under the *skene* of the theatre of Dionysos (Athenaios 13.591A; *Greek Anthology* 16.207), near Praxiteles' statue of Nike (*IG* II² 3089). In Ephesos, whenever the popular assembly took place in the theatre, statues representing the tribes, other personifications, deities, and local heroes were set up on bases (*I.Ephesos* 28–36).

CONCLUSIONS

I have argued that the stereotypical formulations used in inscriptions when referring to theatre are evidence for stereotypical actions, for rituals:

- rituals of communication between mortals and immortals,
- rituals of communication between subject and ruler/people and élite, and
- rituals of communication between citizens and foreigners.

These stereotypical actions were performed in front of the same audience that watched the theatrical and musical performances and on the same stage on which actors, musicians, mimes, and dancers impressed the audience with their skills and their costumes. This additional programme in the theatre, consisting of sacrifices and libations, the invitation to persons to take seats of honour, the cere- monial entrances of magistrates and benefactors, the announce- ments of honours and the crowning of benefactors, could not compete with the theatrical and musical performances, but it could certainly be assimilated into or influenced by them. I have suggested in the light of some evidence that there is an interest in the staging of these additional rituals, in the costumes, in the use of the space, the voice, the movement. Although there is no way to prove this, I suspect that this interest in staging originates in the influence of the theatrical performances (cf. Chaniotis 1997). If this is correct, it may have wider implications for the study of historical develop- ments in the Hellenistic and Roman imperial period. After a man had experienced a sacrifice offered in the *thymele*, in a magnificent setting, by a priest with impressive garments and a brilliant crown who has prayed in a room with excellent acoustics—after this ritual experience would a man be satisfied with the sacrifices in the sanctu- ary, in his club house, and his home? Theatre rituals were perhaps not meant to be spectacles; perhaps the theatre was chosen as their setting only because of the advantages it offers in a practical sense (acoustics, seats, large gatherings of people). But the choice of the space sooner or later had consequences for the form of the rituals.

The theatre is the place of *thea*, the place where people come to watch—usually artistic performances, but not only. This element of *thea*—an impressive show—is not absent in the other activities in this space, as my last example will hopefully show, precisely because it has nothing to do with either artistic performances or ritual actions, but with a trial. The honorary decree of Priene for Krates (*I.Priene* 111, early first century BC) is very fragmentary—especially in its most interesting passage (this is Murphy's law applied in epigraphy). This passage nonetheless makes clear that Krates successfully defended his city's interests together with other *ekdikoi* (public advocates) in Erythrai (l. 129: συνκατώρθωσεν μετὰ τῶν ἐκδίκων). Upon the announcement of this good outcome the city rejoiced and celebrated (ll. 129–30: συνησθέντες τοῖς γεγονῶσιν εὐημερήμασι ἑαυτοῖς ἐκ τῆς κρίσεως). Nothing is unusual in all this, and these phrases would suffice to demonstrate Krates' achievement. And yet the author of this decree found it necessary to mention the exact location in Erythrai where the trial had taken place (ll. 126–8): 'he presented the arguments on behalf of the city in the theatre of the Erythraians—in the presence also of a quite large number of other people, indeed of—.' For the author of the decree it was important to add that Krates had defended his city not only in front of judges, but in front of a large audience. The presence of an audience in the theatre made Krates' achievement more important, certainly for analogous reasons as an attack against a person in a theatre, that is in front of spectators, called for a more severe punishment.[9] People witnessed Krates' success, not in court, but in the theatre, the place of competition, but also the place of spectacles. Krates was not only praised for a successful diplomatic and legal mission, but also for a successful show.

---

[9] *Digesta* 47.10.9.1 (Ulp. 57 ad ed.): *sed et si in teatro vel in foro caedit et vulnerat, quamquam non atrociter, atrocem facit.*

3

The Organisation of Music Contests in the Hellenistic Period and Artists' Participation: An Attempt at Classification*

Sophia Aneziri

The basic issues addressed in this chapter are the role played by the associations of Dionysiac Artists in the organisation of Hellenistic music contests, and the participation of the Artists in them.[1] Music contests may be divided into three categories, on the basis of the nature of the involvement in them of the associations of Dionysiac Artists. These categories are: (1) contests organised by the associations; (2) contests in which the associations acted as co-organisers; and (3) contests in which the associations simply participated.

I. CONTESTS ORGANISED BY THE ASSOCIATIONS (MODEL 1)

Festivals were commonly organised by religious or other associations.[2] The Dionysiac Artists, being directly involved in contests,

---

* I would like to thank D. Hardy warmly for the translation of this text.

[1] The thoughts presented here form an elaborated version of the relevant chapter of Aneziri (2003). On the associations of the Dionysiac Artists (i.e. the guilds of the Artists—actors, poets, musicians etc.—who performed in festivals and competitions) see also Le Guen (2001a).

[2] Poland (1909) 246–69.

seem to have supplemented some of their own festivals with competitions. The only testimony at our disposal relates to the festival
held by the Athenian *Synodos* (i.e. guild) of Dionysiac Artists in
honour of the Cappadocian king Ariarathes V Eusebes Philopator.[3]
From it we learn that the guild determined the nature of the
contest and awarded the prizes to the victors.[4] There are grounds
for believing that similar contests accompanied the *panegyris* of the
Koinon (i.e. guild)[5] of Dionysiac Artists at Teos, for this *panegyris*
had an *agonothetes*.[6] The Artists proclaimed the festival, chose the
officials who presided over it[7] and further claimed their right to
exercise control over the whole *panegyris*.[8]

II. CONTESTS IN WHICH THE ASSOCIATIONS ACTED AS CO-ORGANISERS (MODEL 2)

The involvement of the Artists in the Mouseia at Thespiai, the
Dionysia at Thebes, and the Amphictyonic Soteria is particularly
clear.[9] With regard to the Mouseia at Thespiai and the Dionysia at

---

[3] *IG* II² 1330 (Le Guen 2001a: I. 67–74 no. 5; Aneziri 2003: 344–7 no. A3).

[4] *IG* II² 1330, ll. 42–6.

[5] For the terms *Synodos* and *Koinon*, which were used by different associations of Dionysiac Artists to refer to themselves, see Poland (1932) 1424–34 and Korneman (1924) 914–18; cf. Poland (1934) 2480–4 and Aneziri (2003) 23–5.

[6] *I.Magnesia* 54, ll. 32–3 (Le Guen 2001a: I. 210–12 no. 40; Aneziri 2003: 380–1 no. D8) and Daux 1935: 211–12, ll. 7–10, 26–7 (Le Guen 2001a: I. 231–9 no. 45; Aneziri 2003: 383–6 no. D10); cf. the contribution of J. Ma in this volume.

[7] *RC* 53 IC, ll. 5–8 (Le Guen 2001a: I. 243–50 no. 47; Aneziri 2003: 387–91 no. D12): [προεστῶσιν οἱ αἱρεθέντες] ὑφ ὑμῶμ (namely 'the tekhnitaî') πανηγυριάρχαι κατά τε τὴν ὑμ[ῶν αὐτῶν] τῆς πανηγύρεως ἐπαγγελίαγ καὶ κα[τὰ τὰ προστάγμα]τα τῶμ βασιλέων ('The panegyriarchs [chosen by you may preside over it] according to your proclamation of the festival and [the edicts] of the kings'; *RC* p. 225).

[8] *RC* 53 IIIB, ll. 1–5. For the demands of the *tekhnitai* and their clash with the Teians regarding the festival, see Aneziri (2003) 98–9, 186–8.

[9] For the Dionysia of Thebes and the Mouseia of Thespiai, see Schachter (1981–94) I. 189–91 and II. 163–79. For the Soteria, which was founded by the city of Delphi and the Amphictyony to celebrate the salvation of Delphi from the Gauls in 279/78 BC and was reorganised by the Aitolians around the middle of the third century (whence the distinction between Amphictyonic and Aitolian Soteria), see Nachtergael (1977).

Thebes (otherwise called *trieterides* and later Agrionia), decrees survive that yield significant information relating to their organisation: a decree dating from between 230 and 220 BC,[10] through which the Isthmian–Nemean *Koinon* of Dionysiac Artists recognises the reorganised Mouseia of Thespiai and decides to take part in it;[11] and amphictyonic decrees of the same decade through which the Delphic Amphictyony recognises the inviolability of the sanctuary of Dionysos Kadmeios at Thebes, together with the Dionysia celebrated there.[12] Eight catalogues of victors at the Mouseia, which cover the period from the late third to the early first century BC, are also preserved[13]—as well as the preamble of a similar catalogue for the Dionysia, which dates from the first century BC.[14] With regard to the Amphictyonic Soteria there are seven catalogues of participants in which the preambles are preserved; if we accept that the Amphictyonic Soteria were held annually, these catalogues date probably from 261/0 to 253/2 BC.[15]

II.1. Previous Research

These contests have given rise to most debate among scholars, since the evidence relating to them is apparently contradictory. The main questions that arise in connection with them are two: (1) How many associations were involved in their organisation? (2) Did the Artists who took part in them belong to one or more than one association?

---

[10] *Syll.*³ 457 (Le Guen 2001a: I. 141–6 no. 22; Aneziri 2003: 360–1 no. B4). For the date of the reorganisation see Knoepfler (1996) 156–67 (*BE* 1996, 272; *SEG* 46, 536).

[11] On the contrary, the inscription *IG* VII 1735b, which also relates to the recognition of the Mouseia, is not a decree of the Athenian Artists' guild (so Feyel 1942: 90–6 no. 2A; *BE* 1942, 69; Sifakis (1967) 144; Roesch (1982) 187–8 with n. 197; Knoepfler (1996) 154–5), but a decree of the Athenian state (for the argumentation see Aneziri 2003: 274–5; cf. Schachter 1981–94: II. 165 n. 1, 166 n. 2 and *SEG* 36, 466).

[12] *CID* IV 70–2 (Le Guen 2001a: I. 134–9 n. 20; Aneziri 2003: 358–60 no. B3).

[13] The preambles in Roesch (1982) 188–93 nos. 32–9 (*SEG* 32, 434–7). Full texts in Le Guen (2001a) I. 146–61 no. 23 and Aneziri (2003) 412–16 nos. Gb1–Gb8.

[14] *IG* VII 2447 (Le Guen 2001a: I. 140–1 no. 21; Aneziri 2003: 417 no. Gc).

[15] Nachtergael (1977) 407–24 nos. 3–5, 7–10; (Le Guen 2001a: I. 166–72 no. 24; Aneziri 2003: 403–12 nos. Ga1–Ga7). For the periodicity of the Amphictyonic Soteria cf. below n. 42.

Investigation to date has for the most part considered the two questions together and has linked the answers to them.[16] Pomtow and Poland rely on the priests ἐκ τῶν τεχνιτῶν ('from the Artists') who appear in the preambles to the catalogues of the Amphictyonic Soteria and the strong presence of Boeotians and Peloponnesians in the same catalogues, and recognise the *Koinon* of Isthmos and Nemea as the organiser of these contests.[17] Ferguson and Pickard-Cambridge support this view,[18] as, too, does Nachtergael.[19] Some of the representatives of this view (Pomtow and Poland) extend it to include the Mouseia at Thespiai and the Dionysia at Thebes, and unambiguously regard all Artists who participated in these games, and who therefore appear in the agonistic catalogues along with Athenians, and those who came from Asia Minor, as members of the *Koinon* of Isthmos and Nemea.

Another direction taken by scholars, the main representatives of which were Klaffenbach and Sifakis, argues that the three major associations (*Koinon* of Isthmos and Nemea, Athenian *Synodos*, *Koinon* of Asia Minor) were involved in the Soteria and the Mouseia. They interpret the many *ethnika* in the catalogues of these contests and also the variety of *ethnika* found in all agonistic catalogues as an indication that more than one association participated in these contests.[20]

Ghiron-Bistagne adopts a position intermediate between these two views, according to which the Mouseia and the Soteria were in the hands of the two associations of mainland Greece: the *Koinon* of Isthmos and Nemea and the Athenian *Synodos*.[21]

---

[16] Le Guen (2001a) II. 19 has recently expressed a very correct view on this point: 'It is not methodologically sound . . . to link the organisation of the festival with participation in the contests.'

[17] Pomtow (1897) 819–20; *id.* in *Syll.*³ 424 n. 1; Poland (1895) 15–16; Poland (1909) 134; no more so convinced Poland (1934) 2503.

[18] Ferguson (1934) 323–4 (cf. Flacelière 1937: 142–4); Pickard-Cambridge 1988: 283–4.

[19] Nachtergael (1977) 301–4, esp. 304 (cf. however pp. 337–8).

[20] Klaffenbach (1914) 20–1, esp. 21 n. 1 on the Mouseia: 'Mouseis Thespiis actis omnia tria sodalicia interfuisse titulos certe probare'. More generally Sifakis (1967) 145: 'all contests were frequented by Artists from all major guilds'.

[21] Ghiron-Bistagne (1976) 175.

II.2 Jointly Organised Contests

There is good evidence for the organisation of the Mouseia at Thespiai and the Dionysia at Thebes. We are informed that the competition at the Mouseia was considered to be a joint contest of the city of Thespiai (primarily also the Boeotian League) and the *Koinon* of Isthmos and Nemea and that the competition at the Dionysia was conducted jointly by the city of Thebes and the same *Koinon*.[22] It should be stressed, of course, that both Thespiai and Thebes were the main organisers of the contests: in the agonistic catalogues of the Mouseia and in the only surviving catalogue of the Dionysia the first magistrates cited (the archon, the priest of the Muses or Dionysos and the *agonothetes*) were officials of Thespiai (in the earliest catalogue there is also a federal archon);[23] it was Thespiai, moreover, that took the initiative of inviting the Artists to act as co-organisers of the Mouseia. In the case of the Dionysia, it is stated unequivocally that the festival was conducted according to the laws of the city of Thebes.[24] In other words, the joint organisation was a result of an initiative by the city involved, which continued to be the main organiser of the contests.

Let us now see what this joint organisation consisted of. First of all, the association of Artists was involved in the embassies dispatched by the people of Thespiai to announce the Mouseia, and by the Thebans to announce the Dionysia.[25] Practical proof of this is given by the embassy that approached the Delphic Amphictyony with requests relating to the Theban Dionysia, which was dispatched jointly by the Thebans and the Artists of the Isthmian and Nemean *Koinon*.[26] In the case of the Dionysia, we learn that this *Koinon* also participated, through its *epimeletai*, in the administration of the sanctuary of Dionysos Kadmeios at Thebes.[27] The officials of the *Koinon* involved in the conduct of these two festivals include not only the *theoroi* charged with the task of announcing the contests and—at least in some cases—the *epimeletai*, but also priests. The decree of the Artists

---

[22] *Syll.*[3] 457, ll. 11–13 (cf. n. 10); *CID* IV 70, ll. 1–3 (Le Guen 2001a: I. 134–9 no. 20; Aneziri 2003: 359 no. B3b).
[23] See n. 13, 14.   [24] *Syll.*[3] 457, ll. 8–27, 45–8; *CID* IV 71, l. 7.
[25] *Syll.*[3] 457, ll. 53–7; *CID* IV 70, ll. 13–14.
[26] *CID* IV 71, ll. 2–3.   [27] *CID* IV 70, ll. 14–15.

relating to the Mouseia leaves no doubt that the *Koinon* of Isthmos and Nemea appointed a special priest for the festival.[28] This is the priest of the Muses—in whose honour the festival was held—ἀπὸ τῶν τεχνιτῶν ('from the Artists'), who appears at the beginning of the same decree and in the records of victors at the Mouseia.[29] In some of these records other delegates of the association also appear: a priest of the Muses (in one case together with a priest of Dionysos) ἀπὸ τῶν τεχνιτῶν τῶν συντελούντων εἰς Ἑλικῶνα (that is, from the branch of the guild based in Helikon—the area of the specific festival) and torch-bearers from the whole guild (ἀπὸ τῶν τεχνιτῶν) or from the Helikon branch.[30] We need not analyse these references in detail here; what is significant is that the general expression ἀπὸ τῶν τεχνιτῶν without any further specification of the association or the like is used to qualify a special delegate, priest or torch-bearer, of a specific Artists' guild that is involved in the organisation of the contests. Furthermore there is a correspondence between the representatives of the Artists at the contests and the officials (priests, torch-bearers) of the city, with the former always following the latter in the record. A priest of Dionysos ἀπὸ τῶν τεχνιτῶν is also mentioned in the only surviving preamble of an agonistic catalogue of the Theban Dionysia.[31]

Using the presence of the priest ἀπὸ τῶν τεχνιτῶν as a criterion, the Amphictyonic Soteria may be added to the model of joint organisation. In seven catalogues of competitors from the amphictyonic phase of the festival a preamble is preserved.[32] These reveal the constant presence of a priest ἐκ τῶν τεχνιτῶν. Pythokles, son

---

[28] *Syll.*³ 457, l. 52.

[29] *Syll.*³ 457, ll. 3–4. The priests of the *tekhnitai* are recorded among the city magistrates in the preambles of these records: Roesch (1982) 188–93 nos. 32–9; cf. n. 10.

[30] Priests from the Helikon branch in Roesch (1982) 189–90 no. 33, ll. 8–11. Torch-bearers in Roesch (1982) 191 no. 36, ll. 6–7; no. 37, ll. 6–11; no. 38, ll. 10–12. On these officials cf. Aneziri (2003) 133–5, 137.

[31] *IG* VII 2447, ll. 4–6 (see n. 14). The inscription dates from the first century BC, while the decrees *CID* IV 70–2 in which the *Koinon* of Isthmos and Nemea appears as co-organiser of the Theban Dionysia dates, as we have seen, from about a century and a half earlier. It is however reasonable to link the delegate-priest with the earlier evidence that the *Koinon* of Isthmos and Nemea was involved in the organisation of the Theban Dionysia.

[32] For these catalogues see n. 15.

of Aristarchos, from Hermione appears in three catalogues and Philonides, son of Aristomachos, from Zakynthos in four.[33] These priests probably belonged to the *Koinon* of Isthmos and Nemea and were its delegates.[34] That the role of co-organiser of the Amphictyonic Soteria was played by only a single guild also emerges clearly from the phrase τὸ κοινὸν τῶν τεχνιτῶν ἐπέδωκε τῶι θεῶι καὶ τοῖς Ἀμφικτύοσιν εἰς τὰ Σωτήρια τὸν ἀγῶνα παντελῆ ('the *Koinon* of the Artists offered the whole contest of the Soteria to the god and the Amphictyons'), found in two preambles of the Amphictyonic Soteria.[35] The *Koinon* mentioned here can be only the one of Isthmos and Nemea that also sent the priest.[36]

What precisely can be meant by this phrase? According to the view held by many scholars, the phrase indicates that the *Koinon* of Isthmos and Nemea took part in the competition without payment, and guaranteed its entire conduct, which means that the competitors in these two catalogues came exclusively from the association of Isthmos and Nemea.[37] But the records of Artists in both catalogues, although fragmentary, appear to be no different in composition from these of the following Soteria in which the participating *tekhnitai* were not exclusively members of the *Koinon* of Isthmos and Nemea (see II.3). Furthermore, in the preamble of a catalogue of the Winter Soteria about a century later, the participation, gratis, of the Artists of the Isthmian and Nemean *Koinon* in the contest is indicated by an expression that has nothing to do with what we read in the two

---

[33] Stephanis (1988) nos. 2174, 2568.

[34] This emerges partly from their origins, and mainly from the fact that an honorary epigram for Pythokles (*IG* IV 682; also in Nachtergael 1977: 317–23, 429–30 no. 15*bis*) enumerates his victories, which were won exclusively in competitions in which the *Koinon* of Isthmos and Nemea played a decisive role: the Nemea, the Isthmia (the festivals whose names appear in the title of the guild), the Mouseia at Thespiai and the Dionysia at Thebes, to which reference has been made above. Cf. Nachtergael (1977) 321–2, who recognises a cryptic hint to this *Koinon* in ll. 3–4 of the epigram.

[35] Nachtergael (1977) 407–8 nos. 3, 4 (Aneziri (2003) 403–4 nos. Ga1–Ga2).

[36] Sifakis (1967) 146 takes the view that here the word κοινόν is not used in a technical sense, but means simply 'the *tekhnitai* in general acting as a unity', citing as examples the expressions τὸ κοινὸν τῶν ἀρχόντων, and τὸ κοινὸν τῆς κώμης. These examples are not apposite, in my view, since in these cases the word *koinon* is never used in a technical sense, whereas it is invariably so used in the world of the Artists.

[37] This view was advanced by Robert (1936b) 22; Ghiron-Bistagne (1976) 175; Nachtergael (1977) 300, 304; Le Guen (2001a) II. 19; cf. Ferguson (1934) 323–34.

preambles of the Amphictyonic Soteria. The preamble of the catalogue of the Winter Soteria lays emphasis on the fact that the *tekhni-*
tai sent by the *Koinon*, and listed in the catalogue that follows, will
compete free of charge ('and they sent these here who will compete
free of charge for the god').[38] On the contrary, in the phrase used in the
case of the Amphictyonic Soteria ('the *Koinon* of the Artists offered
the whole contest of the Soteria to the god and the Amphictyons'),
the emphasis is not on the sending of *tekhnitai*, but on the offering
of the entire competition by the *Koinon*.[39] Therefore in my view, the
phrase in question means that the *Koinon* of Isthmos and Nemea
undertook to meet all the expenses of the competition, that is, the
rewards for non-members as well. This offer is completely consistent
with the role of co-organiser, but does not seem to be a permanent
characteristic of the model of co-organisation. There is no such
reference in the preambles of the following five catalogues of the
Amphictyonic Soteria.

Although it cannot be ruled out that the same or a similar phrase
may have existed in one of the catalogues whose preamble has not
survived,[40] the questions arise in any case why the *Koinon* of Isthmos
and Nemea makes this offer in some and not all the occasions on
which it co-organises the Amphictyonic Soteria, and what benefit
it could have derived from a financial outlay of this kind. Bearing
in mind that the two catalogues in which the phrase in question
appears are the earliest of the total of seven catalogues in which the
preamble is preserved, it may perhaps be supposed that the *Koinon* of
Isthmos and Nemea undertook to offer the first celebrations after it

---

[38] *Syll.*³ 690, l. 4 (Le Guen 2001a: I. 173–4 no. 26; Aneziri 2003: 362–3 no. B7): καὶ
ἐξαπέστειλαν τοὺς ἀγωνιξομέ[νους τῶι θε]ῶι δωρεὰν τού[σδε].

[39] The verb ἐπιδίδωμι is frequently used in the context of music and dramatic
contests, when the Artist gives a performance outside the competition and without
payment (e.g. *Syll.*³ 689, ll. 5–6; *FD* III 3, 249, l. 6 = *Nouveau Choix* 10; *IG* XII Suppl.
p. 111, l. 7; cf. Robert 1929: 40; Liefferinge 2000). In my view, however, it is not a
technical term and consequently does not in every case mean 'give a free performance': it means more generally 'offer free of charge' (*LSJ*: 'give freely, bestow'),
and the precise significance is determined by the object of the verb on each occasion.
In the case of free performances by Artists, the usual object is ἡμέραν (i.e. a day of
performances or a performance).

[40] Nachtergael (1977) 404–6 nos. 2, 2*bis*, 412 no. 6 and 425 no. 11. The most likely
candidate is the catalogue Nachtergael (1977) 404–6 no. 2 (*FD* III 1, 478) which is
close in date with Nachtergael (1977) 407–8 nos. 3, 4.

became co-organiser of the contest. The assumption of the role of co-organiser by the *Koinon* of Isthmos and Nemea may well have had some connection with the withdrawal of the Athenian *Synodos* from the festivals at Delphi, which probably coincides with the Chremonidean war and its consequences for Athens.[41] It cannot be a coincidence that the earliest catalogues of the Amphictyonic Soteria, that is, those in which the *Koinon* of Isthmos and Nemea offer the contest, are dated roughly speaking to the time of the Chremonidean war or immediately afterwards.[42]

II.3 The Participation of the Artists

Having shed as much light as possible on the question of joint organisation, on the evidence of the relevant decrees and preambles, we turn now to the question of participation. The issue is whether Artists who were not members of the organising association had the right to take part in these contests.

In the lists of victors at the Mouseia and of those who competed at the Soteria, there is a surprising variety of *ethnika*. But the guilds, though consisting basically of Artists from the area of their influence, seem to be open to all Artists, irrespective of their geographical origins.[43] I therefore consider that, for methodological reasons, arguments based on the *ethnika* that appear in the catalogues of these two festivals should not primarily be taken into consideration in examining this particular issue.

There are, in my view, three arguments in support of the view that Artists participated in these competitions irrespective of the association to which they belonged.

A. There are some individuals who, while participating in the Amphictyonic Soteria, also appear in catalogues of victors at

---

[41] For the relevant arguments and the evidence for the links between Athens, Delphi, and the contests held there in the decades before the Chremonidean war, see Aneziri (2003) 39–41.

[42] The date of the catalogues depends on the periodicity of the Amphictyonic Soteria (annual or biennial system). On the basis of annual periodicity the two catalogues in question are dated to 265/4–263/2 or 261/60–259/8 (see Aneziri 2003: 338–41).

[43] Ghiron-Bistagne (1976) 174–6; Aneziri (2003) 230–43, esp. 236, 238. Cf. Le Guen (2001a) II. 41–6.

Athenian festivals (Dionysia, Lenaia), and in Athenian choregic inscriptions.[44] If, then, we assume that only Artists who were members of the organising association, the *Koinon* of Isthmos and Nemea, could participate in the Amphictyonic Soteria, we have to accept that while the Artists of the Athenian *Synodos* were not allowed access to the Soteria, of which the Isthmian–Nemean *Koinon* was co-organiser, the Athenian *Synodos* permitted Artists of the Isthmian–Nemean *Koinon* to participate in the Athenian contests, in which the *Synodos* certainly played a dominant role. A one-sided restriction of this kind is highly improbable. We are therefore led to the conclusion that Artists of the Athenian *Synodos* must have had free access to the competitions under the control of the *Koinon* of Isthmos and Nemea, and vice versa. Another related observation points to the same conclusion: in the second half of the second century BC, victories were won at the Mouseia by two Artists who may be regarded with certainty as members of the Athenian *Synodos*, since they also participated in the *Pythaides* sent by this *Synodos* to Delphi.[45] There are also

[44] Among twenty-five identifications about six are almost certain: (1) [D]einon from Aegina, cyclic aulete in *IG* II² 3080 and Deinon, son of Herakle[i]des, from Aegina, aulete in Nachtergael (1977) 413–16 no. 7, l. 28 (Aneziri 2003: 405–6 no. Ga4); (2) Herakleides, comic actor in *IG* II² 2325, l. 225 and He[r]aklei[des], comic synagonist (?) in Nachtergael (1977) 404–6 no. 2, l. 32 (see also Herakleides, son of Lykos, from Ambrakia, member of the comic chorus in Nachtergael 1977: 419–22 no. 9, l. 79; Aneziri 2003: 408–10 no. Ga6); (3) Hippokles from Boeotia, cyclic aulete in *IG* II² 3079, l. 3 and Hippokles, son of Smikron, from Boeotia, aulete in Nachtergael (1977) 422–4 no. 10, l. 16 (Aneziri 2003: 410–12 no. Ga7); (4) Lykis[kos], comic actor in *IG* II² 2325, l. 217 and Lykiskos, son of Lykos, from Kephallenia, comic actor in Nachtergael (1977) 416–19 no. 8, l. 61 and 422–4 no. 10, l. 68 (Aneziri 2003: 407–8 no. Ga5 and 410–12 no. Ga7); (5) Lysippos from Arkadia, *didaskalos* of a chorus in *IG* II² 3083B, l. 10 and Lysippos, son of Xenotimos, from Arkadia, *didaskalos* of auletes in Nachtergael (1977) 422–4 no. 10, ll. 17–18 (Aneziri 2003: 410–12 no. Ga7); (6) Pronomos from Thebes, *didaskalos* of a chorus in *IG* II² 3083A, l. 5 and Pronomos, son of Diogeiton, from Boeotia, *didaskalos* in Nachtergael (1977) 416–19 no. 8, l. 83 (Aneziri 2003: 407–8 no. Ga5). Cf. Stephanis (1988) nos. 590, 1075, 1282, 1561, 1587, 2148.

[45] First case: Theodotos, son of Pythion, paean singer, tragic synagonist in Tracy (1975) 60–7 n. 7h, ll. 39, 44, 50 (Le Guen 2001a: I. 117–23 no. 14; Aneziri 2003: 354–6 no. A11) and [Th]eodotos, son of Pythion, from Athens, rhapsode in Jamot (1895) 339–40 no. 13, ll. 17–18 (Aneziri 2003: 416 no. Gb8); Second case: Philotas, son of Theokles, paean singer in *FD* III 2, 47, l. 10 (Le Guen 2001a: I. 88–91 no. 10; Aneziri 2003: 350–1 no. A6) and Philotas, son of Theokles, from Athens, herald in Jamot (1895) 335–6 no. 10, ll. 11–12 (Aneziri 2003: 413–14 no. Gb4). Cf. Stephanis (1988) nos. 1146, 2573.

epigrams and honorific inscriptions for Artists who appear as participants or victors both at competitions jointly organised by the
Koinon of Isthmos and Nemea and at Athenian contests.[46]

B. The second argument relates to a decree by the *Koinon* of the
Artists of Asia Minor passed in the second quarter of the second
century BC.[47] It emerges clearly from this text that members of the Asia
Minor *Koinon* participated in competitions organised by the *Koinon*
of Isthmos and Nemea: the Soteria, Mouseia, and Dionysia, now
called Agrionia.[48] The presence of the Asia Minor association in
Boeotia, an area within the sphere of influence of the *Koinon* of
Isthmos and Nemea and the place where the Mouseia and Dionysia
were held, is also attested by the letter from Lucius Mummius to
the Asia Minor guild, which probably recognised the privileges of the
members of the association and was erected at Thebes.[49]

C. The third argument is of a more general nature. The view that
participation in competitions in which an association played the
role of co-organiser was restricted to Artists from this association
strongly conflicts with the efforts of the organisers of competitions
to secure as wide a participation in them as possible. This was the
precise objective of the numerous *theoriai* sent out by the organisers;
their aim was to ensure not only that official representatives were
sent to the festivals by cities and kings, but also the attendance
and participation of Artists, merchants, and general visitors from
every city and region. It would be difficult indeed to account for
the many *theoriai* sent by Argos and Delphi to Egypt, if members of

---

[46] I list only some cases: Stephanis (1988) no. 387 (winner in the Pythia, Nemeia,
Isthmia, in the Argive festivals and the Panathenaia); no. 1839 (winner in the Pythia,
Panathenaia, Lenaia, Isthmia and Basileia at Alexandreia); no. 3003 (winner in the
Great Dionysia at Athens, the Amphiktyonic Soteria, the Heraia at Argos and the Naia
at Dodona).

[47] Daux (1935) 210–30 (cf. n. 6).

[48] Daux (1935) 211–12, ll. 15–20. Klaffenbach (1914) 20 and Poland (1934) 2511
maintain that this passage refers to Artists in general and not specifically to the
members of the Asia Minor *Koinon* (cf. Daux 1935: 217–18). Obviously, the reference
here could be to Artists in general, but the effective answer has been given, I believe,
by Sifakis (1967) 141: 'It is unthinkable that the Ionians should speak on behalf of
other guilds if they were themselves banned from Greece or had no interest in her
festivals.'

[49] Roesch (1982) 198–202 no. 44 (Le Guen 2001a: I. 256–60 no. 51; Aneziri 2003:
361–2 no. D15).

the Egyptian guild were excluded a priori from the games in ques-tion.[50] The interest taken by Ptolemy IV and Arsinoe III in the Mouseia of Thespiai would also be strange if Artists from Egypt were excluded from them.[51]

Having reached the basic conclusion, that all Artists could partici-pate in the competitions regardless of the association to which they belonged, we may now venture further to assess the material pro-vided by the *ethnika*. Although, as we have seen, geographical origin does not by itself constitute secure evidence for the guild to which an individual Artist belonged, it may provide us with some information at a collective level. In other words, the fact that an individual Artist is a member of the *Koinon* of Isthmos and Nemea does not necessarily mean that he came from one of the headquarter cities, or even the sphere of influence of the *Koinon*, but there can be no doubt that the majority of the members of the *Koinon* came from these regions.[52] Consequently, the fact that the majority of the Artists in the catalogues of the Mouseia, Dionysia and Soteria came from Boeotia, the Peloponnese, and Central Greece[53] means that it was mainly the *Koinon* of Isthmos and Nemea that supplied members to these competitions, and precisely this fact seems to have been a major benefit to the association from its role of co-organiser.

Exactly how things were arranged is unknown, but a decisive factor seems to have been that the allocation (νέμησις) of those Artists who took part[54] lay in the hands of the *Koinon* jointly

[50] On the *theoroi* from Argos announcing Argive festivals (Nemea or Heraia) in Egypt see Bergmans (1979) 127–30; cf. Buraselis (1982) 165 with n. 189 and Buraselis (1993) 260. On the announcement of the Aitolian Soteria in Egypt see Nachtergael (1977) 228–35, 350, 354, 447–8 no. 28.

[51] Feyel (1942) 100–11 nos. 4, 5. Cf. Schachter (1981–94) II. 164–5, 166 with n. 1 and Barbantani (2000) 127–72. On a royal (Ptolemaic?) donation to the Thespian festival see Bringmann et al. (1995) no. 85[E] and Bringmann (2000) 103. The portrait of Arsinoe (III?)–Muse on a Thespian coin may have had some connection with the relations between Ptolemies and the Thespian Mouseia (*BMC* Central Greece, 92–3 nos. 14–26; cf. Schachter 1981–94: II. 166–7 with n. 4). On the relations between Egypt and Boeotia in the third century BC see Roesch (1989) 621–9.

[52] Aneziri (2003) 238.

[53] The *ethnika* recorded in the catalogues of the Amphictyonic Soteria are listed by Kahrstedt (1937) 380; Nachtergael (1977) 302; and Aneziri (2003) 453–4.

[54] In the context of music and dramatic contests νέμομαι and its participles mean the assignment or allocation of the *tekhnitai* to the contests. The term occurs with this meaning in Photius s.v. νεμήσεις ὑποκριτῶν ('the poets took three actors chosen

responsible for organising the contests[55] and this is apparently one more element of the model of joint organisation. Presumably, through the procedure of νέμησις the Artist-co-organisers determined the Artists-participants; they showed preference for their own members without excluding others. The involvement of representatives of the organising association in the *theoriai*/embassies that announced the competitions (see II.1) was perhaps designed to serve this very procedure.

It remains to examine the question whether the category of contests in which the guilds, more specifically the *Koinon* of Isthmos and Nemea, assumed the role of co-organiser had any general features in common. This category was certainly not restricted to competitions in which the prize was a wreath (ἱεροὶ στεφανῖται), since money prizes were awarded at the Amphictyonic Soteria and the role of the *Koinon* as co-organiser of the Mouseia at Thespiai goes back to an earlier period, presumably before the thymelic competition was upgraded to one in which a crown was awarded.[56] Similarly, it cannot be said that they were exclusively contests held at the headquarters of the *Koinon*. This is true, of course, of the Dionysia at Thebes and the Mouseia at Thespiai, but the Soteria took place in the panhellenic centre at Delphi, where no association seems to have been based. The role of co-organiser also seems, in my view, to have been played by the *Koinon* of Isthmos and Nemea in both the panhellenic festivals that appear in its title: the Isthmia and the Nemea. There can also

---

by lot—κλήρωι νεμηθέντας—to act in their plays'); Polybius 6. 47. 8 ('so that none of the *tekhnitai* or athletes who have not been allocated—τούς γε μὴ νενεμημένους—or who are not physically fit—ἢ σεσωμασκηκότας—can have access to the athletic contests'; cf. Laroche (1949) 49 and *BE* 1951, 55, p. 144) and in the inscription *IG* XII 1, 125, l. 4 (Ghiron-Bistagne 1976: 63–8 and *IG* II² 2323, l. 47).

[55] This emerges clearly from *CID* IV 71, ll. 5–9 (Le Guen 2001a: I. 134–9 no. 20; Aneziri 2003: 359 no. B3c): 'if one of the pipe-players or dancers or tragic or comic actors who have been allocated by the *tekhnitai*—νεμηθέντων ὑπὸ τῶν τεχνιτᾶν (i.e. the *tekhnitai* of the *Koinon* of Isthmos and Nemea)—to the *trieterides* (i.e. Dionysia) does not compete in the *trieterides* held in accordance with the law of the city of the Thebans, but, being healthy, is absent from the contest, neither he nor those co-operating with him shall have the privilege of security either in war or in peace'. That the collective term τεχνῖται in this case means the Artists of the Isthmian–Nemean *Koinon* is confirmed by the use of this term in another Amphictyonic decree (*CID* IV 70, ll. 13–15) which was also related to the Dionysia of Thebes, passed in the same year as *CID* IV 71, and was carved on the same stone.

[56] *Syll.*³ 457, ll. 23–7 (see n. 10). Cf. Schachter (1981–94) II. 163–4.

be no doubt that the *Synodos* of Athens played a decisive role in the conduct of Athenian competitions. The relationship of this role to the model of joint organisation examined earlier remains unknown.

III. CONTESTS IN WHICH THE ASSOCIATIONS MERELY PARTICIPATED

There is no concrete evidence for the role played by the associations in other competitions. Our safest tool is comparison with the situation at the Mouseia, Dionysia, and the Amphictyonic Soteria. For example, the amphictyonic decree relating to the Ptoia at Akraiphnia, which is akin to that relating to the Theban Dionysia in terms of both content and form, makes no reference to a guild or to joint organisation.[57] Moreover, lists of victors in numerous competitions fail to refer to a priest-delegate of the Artists.[58] It seems, then, that there were contests for which the associations provided Artists without being actively involved in their organisation and that these competitions were in the majority.

With the aid of a well-known inscription from Euboea (*IG* XII 9, 207), which dates from between 294 and 288 BC, we may perhaps form some picture of the manner in which the Artists participated in these competitions.[59] At the time of this inscription, there seems to have been no association of Dionysiac Artists in Euboea,[60] but only an informal gathering of *tekhnitai* at Chalkis, where the *Koinon* of Isthmos and Nemea later had a base.[61] According to the regulations, the Euboean cities are to send elected representatives to Chalkis

---

[57] Compare *CID* IV 76, ll. 12–16 with *CID* IV 70, ll. 14–16. On the Ptoia see Feyel (1942) 133–47; Schachter (1981–94) I. 70–2. Cf. Roesch (1982) 203–10, 225–55 (*SEG* 32, 439–49) and Rigsby (1987) 729–40 (*SEG* 37, 380; *BE* 1988, 393; Schachter 1981–94 III. 20–1).

[58] See e.g. Petrakos (1997) 520–1, 523–6, 528, 531; *IG* VII 541–3, 2727–8, 3195–7, 4147; *IG* XII 9, 91–2; Nachtergael (1977) 476–82 nos. 60–6; *IG* IX 2, 525, 528.

[59] *IG* XII 9, 207 is republished by Stephanis (1984) (*SEG* 34, 896).

[60] On the uncertain date of establishment of the Athenian *Synodos* and the Isthmian–Nemean *Koinon* see Aneziri (2003) 28–9, 52–6.

[61] *IG* XII 9, 910, second century BC (Le Guen 2001a; I. 183–5 no. 32; Aneziri 2003: 366 no. B10).

before the twentieth day of the month Apatourion in the Chalkidian calendar to assign work to the *tekhnitai*.[62] After this, the officials of Chalkis (*probouloi* and *strategoi*)—presumably acting in co-ordination—are to 'send a person to the *tekhnitai* to proclaim formally the job contracts'.[63] If we transfer this evidence to the world of the guilds, the following picture emerges: the emissaries of the particular organiser presented themselves to the association, asked for a specific number of Artists, and offered the corresponding number of contracts. This number depended on the money available to them and the nature of the competition—that is, whether it was local or panhellenic. The associations offered important services to these contests, although they were not involved in their organisation. For the organisers knew at any time to whom they should turn and where they would find what they needed to make their festival a success. This co-ordination was certainly not easy at a period when the number of competitions had increased significantly and when they occasionally coincided in time.[64]

IV. COMPARISON OF MODELS 2 AND 3— SIMILARITIES

The evidence available does not permit a detailed comparison between the two models of competitions. One similarity seems to be that Artists who did not fulfil their contract and failed to appear at the competition without reasonable cause were accountable not to the association, but to the organising city and its *agonothetes*, even in

---

[62] *IG* XII 9, 207, ll. 57–9: τὰς πόλεις ἑλομένας τοὺς ἄνδρας κατὰ τὴν διαγρα[φὴν πέμψαι] εἰς Χαλκίδα πρὸ τῆς εἰκάδος τοῦ Ἀπατουριῶνος μηνός, ὡς Χαλκιδεῖς ἄγουσιν, ὅπως ἂν ἐγδῶσιν τὰ ἔ[ργα τοῖς τεχ]νίταις. Cf. ll. 3–9: αἱρεῖσ[θαι ἄνδρας—οἵτινες παραγενήσοντες εἰ]ς Χαλκίδα διαδώσοντες τὰ ἔργα τοῖς τεχνίτα[ις].

[63] *IG* XII 9, 207, l. 59: τοὺς δὲ προβού[λου]ς καὶ στρατηγοὺς τοὺς Χαλκιδέων ἀποστεῖλαί τινα πρὸς τοὺς τεχνίτας, ἐπαγγε[λοῦν(τα) τὰς] ἐργολαβίας. Cf. *IG* IX 1, 4², 798, ll. 79–81 (Corfu, second century BC): ἀποστειλάντω οἱ ἄρχοντες ἐπὶ τὰν τῶν τεχνιτᾶν μίσθωσιν κατὰ τὸν ⟨τοῦ⟩ ἀγωνοθέτα νόμον.

[64] On the increase of festivals in the Hellenistic age see Robert (1984a) 36–7; Chaniotis (1995) 147–9, 151, 164–8, and Köhler (1996) 89–90.

cases where an association acted as co-organiser.[65] Stephanis reason-
ably concludes that in all cases Artists agreed their contracts directly
with the organisers of the contests, and not with the association.[66]
A clause that invariably accompanies the recognition of the privileges
of the Artists by the Delphic Amphictyony is, in my view, mainly
connected with these contracts: the Artists are 'secure' and 'inviolable', except in cases where they are bound by a private contract
(ἰδίου συμβολαίου ὑπόχρεως or χρέος ἔχων πόλει ὑπόχρεως
or πρὸς ἴδιον χρέος).[67] If, then, an Artist had broken his contract
and had not yet paid the penalty, he was not 'secure' and 'inviolable'
but 'liable to seizure everywhere'.[68] It is only when an association
sends its members to participate without payment in a competition,
as probably in the case in which the *Koinon* of Asia Minor sent Artists
to take part in the Dionysia at Iasos, that the members are accountable for any violations to the association itself.[69]

Another common characteristic is that, in addition to the competitors, the associations also sent *theoroi* to all music contests, those
in which the Artists acted as co-organisers and those in which they
merely participated. These are *theoroi* who represented the associations at the ceremonies of the various festivals and are not the same
as the *theoroi* who, as we have seen, undertook the task of announcing the festival, in cases where the association was involved in
its organisation.[70] Their role, like that of the *theoroi* sent by cities and
kings, was to take part in the sacrifices and processions held in
honour of the deity.[71] *Theoroi* of this kind are sent by the Isthmian–

[65] *CID* IV 71, ll. 9–10 (cf. n. 55).   [66] Stephanis (1984) 522.
[67] *IG* II² 1132, ll. 19–22, 82–5 (Le Guen 2001a: I. 62–4 no. 3; Aneziri 2003: 348–50
no. A5A). Cf. Gauthier (1972) 235; Bravo (1980) 947–53; and Lefèvre (1998) 245.
[68] *CID* IV 71, ll. 8–10 (cf. n. 55). See also *IG* XII 9, 207, ll. 44–5; cf. Stephanis (1984)
506, 539–40. On ἄγειν and ἀγώγιμος see Bravo (1980) 792 ff., esp. 799–808.
[69] *I.Iasos* 152, ll. 19–25 (Le Guen 2001a: I. 265–70 no. 53; Aneziri 2003: 392 no.
D13); cf. Robert (1937) 445–6 and Migeotte (1993) 285 with n. 56. In this case,
however, the violating Artists had not broken their contract, because, quite simply,
there was no contract. They could therefore only be disciplined as insubordinate
members, since they had violated an instruction from their association.
[70] On these two sorts of *tekhnitai–theoroi* see Aneziri (2003) 156–8.
[71] The participation of all the Artists, who competed in the musical contests of the
Artemisia at Eretria, in the *prosodion* (processional hymn), and the other religious
ceremonies of the festival (*IG* XII 9, 189, ll. 12–14, 37–9; *c.* 340 BC) may be a 'fore-
runner' of the more formalised role of the later Artists' *theoroi*, as Prof. P. Wilson

Nemean *Koinon* to the Thespian Mouseia.[72] They were also sent by the *Koinon* of Asia Minor to Samothrace and to the Leukophryena at Magnesia on the Maeander, a festival at which it is clear from the epigraphic evidence that the guild did not act as co-organiser.[73]

V. CONCLUSIONS

To sum up, it may be said that the picture of mutually conflicting evidence surrounding the role of the Artists in Hellenistic music competitions is clarified by two steps of a methodological character, which permit a better classification and evaluation of the material: (1) by distinguishing the various types of competitions, depending on the role played by the associations in them; and (2) by separating the organisation of the contests from participation in them.

On this basis, music contests may be divided into three categories: (1) contests organised only by the associations, which formed part of their own festivals; (2) those in which the associations acted as co-organisers, along with a city or a federal organisation like the Boeotian League or the Delphic Amphictyony; and (3) those for which the associations supplied Artists, without being involved in their organisation.

The evidence at our disposal relating to the Mouseia at Thespiai, the Dionysia at Thebes, and the Amphictyonic Soteria suggests that the participation of an association in the organisation of music contests in the second category entailed sending officials (priests, torch-bearers) of the Artists to them, the involvement of the association—in some cases, at least—in managing the finances of the festival, and above all, the announcement of the competition and the allocation of the participating Artists. Through this last procedure, the co-organising association met a large part of the needs

kindly remarked in a personal communication. This however is a question that requires further study.

[72] *Syll.*[3] 457, l. 53; cf. the *theoroi*-delegates who had to announce the same festival in *Syll.*[3] 457, ll. 55–7.

[73] *IG* XII 8, 163, ll. 35–9; *I.Magnesia* 54, ll. 34–40 (Le Guen 2001a: I. 288–9 no. 57, 210–12 no. 40; Aneziri 2003: 380–1 no. D8, 395 no. D19).

of the competition by supplying Artists who were its members, though without precluding the participation of members of other associations, or individual Artists. This secured the interests both of the association and of the basic organiser (city, Amphictyony, etc.) of the particular competition: the association primarily because it promoted the employment of its members (it remains unclear whether any other financial benefits accrued to the association from its participation as co-organiser) and the city, Amphictyony, etc. because it ensured the maximum success for its games through the wide participation of competitors.

There is less clear evidence at our disposal for the organisation of the third, largest category of games, but it does seem that the associations were not involved in it. Nevertheless, in this case, too, there seems to have been mutual support between the organisers and the Artists. On the one hand, the organisers had recourse to constant 'reservoirs' of Artists—the associations—thus ensuring that the games would take place. (The lack of competitors was by no means a negligible risk in the Hellenistic period.) On the other, the associations intervened and guaranteed work for their members in this case, too.

In conclusion, it should be emphasised that the attempt to classify music contests of the Hellenistic period on the basis of the degree and nature of the involvement of the associations in them, though based on a combined approach to the evidence, continues to have a hypothetical character. The evidence at our disposal, especially regarding the second category of games, relates only to the *Koinon* of Isthmos and Nemea, and cannot be used as a basis for generalisation.

Part II

Festivals of Athens and Attica

4

The Men Who Built the Theatres:
Theatropolai, Theatronai, and *Arkhitektones**

Eric Csapo

We depend mainly upon inscriptions for what little we know about the practicalities of the management and finance of the ancient Greek theatre. It is disappointing, therefore, to find no epigraphic attestation of the terms *theatrones* or *theatropoles*, figures absolutely central to theatre management and finance. These terms appear only in literary sources. Epigraphy, nonetheless, still has something to tell us of their function and their history, particularly in conjunction with another shadowy figure, the *arkhitekton*. In the past these figures have received little attention,[1] yet a close study of the evidence can shed some light on the organisation of the Classical and early Hellenistic theatre in and even beyond Attica. I will argue, moreover, that the history of these officials is relevant to a number of issues of current controversy: among them the shape of the early theatre, the date of the Lykurgan reconstruction of the theatre of Dionysos, and the background to the introduction of the Athenian festival fund (*theorikon*).

* For many helpful comments I thank audiences in Oxford, where this paper was delivered twice, in very different venues. Special thanks to Hans Goette, Scott Scullion, and William Slater for commenting on earlier drafts of this paper and helping me get my mind around several difficult questions.
[1] Caillemer (1877); Szanto (1896); Buchanan (1962) 86; Pickard-Cambridge (1968 [1988]) 266; Rhodes (1972) 125–6; Walton (1977) 82–6; Shear (1978) 56–8; Walton (1980) 69–73; Henry (1983) 293–4; Scullion (1994) 55–6; Wilson (1997b) 98; Moretti (2001) 221–2.

THEATRON-BUYERS AND *THEATRON*-SELLERS

Since late antiquity, *theatropolai, theatronai,* and particular figures referred to by the general term *arkhitektones,* have been lumped together as synonyms for theatre managers.[2] They *are* all theatre managers, but to stop there would be misleading. *Arkhitekton does* sometimes appear as a general term for a kind of theatre manager, but one with a very different function from the *theatrones* or *theatropoles.* Indeed I will argue that they have opposed and mutually exclusive functions.

Although the *arkhitekton* is different, at least *theatropolai* and *theatronai* really *are* just synonyms, so far as I can see. *Theatropoles,* '*theatron*-seller', is attested only once. It is cited by Pollux (7.199) from Aristophanes' *Phoenissai,* a play datable to the late fifth or early fourth century BC (*PCG* F 575):

ἐν ταῖς Φοινίσσαις θεατροπώλης ὁ θέαν ἀπομισθῶν.

In the *Phoenissai* a *theatropoles* is the man who rents out a place from which to view the spectacle.

Pollux records the term without any context. At a guess Aristophanes used the word in a metatheatrical reference to the greed or profits of the man who charged admission to the theatre of Dionysos at Athens. The *theatrones* '*theatron*-buyer', a word only twice attested, performs the same function. Theophrastos indicates that he is the man who charges and collects admission prices into the theatre (*Characters* 30.6):

καὶ ἐπὶ θέαν τηνικαῦτα πορεύεσθαι ἄγων τοὺς υἱεῖς, ἡνίκα προῖκ' ἀφιᾶσιν οἱ θεατρῶναι.

And he [the Niggardly Man] goes to the spectacle with his sons only as often as the *theatronai* offer free admission.

Money paid for admission into the theatre goes towards the *theatron*-buyer's profits. The greed of the '*theatron*-buyer' became

---

[2] Despite Shear (1978) 57 n. 162 who urged that 'a distinction should now be made between the elected *arkhitekton,* the custodian of sanctuaries, and the lessees who collected the price of admission', the distinction is only observed by Moretti (2001) 222.

something of a topos, thanks probably to Old Comedy. A recently published papyrus elegy by Nikarkhos suggests as much (*POxy.* 4502, 39–41 Parsons (first century AD?)):

πισ]τεύεις μυὶ τυρόν, ὄνῳ χόρτον, μέλι μην [ ].[
χησὶ σέριν, κυσὶν ὗν, παιδαρίοις ὑφίδα,
(ε)ἱμάτιον ῥιγοῦντι, θεατρώ{ι}νηι τὸ λόγευμα ...

(When you invite the seducer Damon to your house and introduce him to your wife, Alexis) you trust cheese to a mouse, hay to a donkey, honey to ?bees, chicory to geese, a boar to dogs, a wrap to slaves, a cloak to a freezing man, collected money to a *theatrones* ...

The *theatrones* 'theatron-buyer' and *theatropoles* 'theatron-seller' pretty clearly perform the same function. The two terms simply express different perspectives. 'Theatron-buyer' betrays the perspective of the state, which sells the franchise and this is doubtless the official term. The meaning of 'buyer' emerges clearly from an inscription which records the lease of a theatre in Peiraieus, which we will look at more closely in a moment. The Peiraieus lease refers three (?) times to the lessees of the theatre as 'buyers', twice as οἱ πριάμενοι and once as ὠνηταί. *Theatron*-buyers 'buy' or, more properly, 'lease' a theatre from the state. Attic comfortably uses 'buy' and 'sell', ὠνεῖσθαι and πωλεῖν, along with μισθοῦσθαι/μισθοῦν, to mean take out or let out on lease.[3] By contrast 'theatron-seller' betrays the perspective of the audience who buy admission from him, and this may simply be a comic or vernacular compound. But whatever the rationale behind the variation, the citations show both terms used indifferently, at least in non-official speech.

My translations deliberately avoid rendering *theatron* as 'theatre' because 'theatre-seller' and 'theatre-buyer' would be misleading at best. *Theatron* in Greek does not mean 'theatre' in the broadest sense including the rituals and entertainments which go on in a theatre building: the *theatropoles* is so far as we know not an impresario.[4]

---

[3] *Pace* Behrend (1970) 88, cf. 107. See And. *Myst.* 133–4, Lys. 7.2 with Gernet and Bizos (1924–6) ad loc., Arist. *Ath. Pol.* 47.2, 60.2 with Rhodes (1981) 552, 673, Aeschin. 1. 119.
[4] Notwithstanding the fact that the term can in Greek be flexed rhetorically (metonymically) to refer to performances: e.g. Plu. *Ant.* 9.3 (at night all he cared for were *komoi* and *theatra*).

Theatron normally refers only to the physical space in which theatrical entertainments take place, but the term is still ambiguous. '*Theatron*-seller' could imply selling the *theatron* in the broad sense of the entire theatre building, or simply in the narrow sense of the seating area or auditorium. The *theatron* in '*theatron*-seller' probably refers to this narrow sense of 'auditorium'. A literal translation of the Greek expressions for paying to get into the theatre is 'buy', 'rent', or otherwise put down money to 'get' a θέα. Θέα (like Latin *spectaculum*) is also ambiguous: it can mean both the place from which you watch and the spectacle you sit or stand to watch. But in this usage θέα generally refers unambiguously to the place and not the spectacle.[5] The idiom for paying theatre admission focuses on the venue rather than the entertainment, presumably, because this is what the *theatropoles* sells or rents out: not a *theatron* in the broad sense, but a place from which to watch the theatrical performances. But the other term '*theatron*-buyer' may be more ambiguous. The *theatron* that the *theatron*-buyer leases may be the whole theatre building. At any rate the Peiraieus lease shows that the terms extend to activities beyond the auditorium.

The Peiraieus lease shows pretty clearly how the operation worked:

Agora 19 (1991) L13 = *SEG* 33, 143 = *IG* II² 1176 + *Hesperia* 29 (1960) 1 no. 1 (*SEG* 19, 117) + *Hesperia* 32 (1963) 12 no. 10 (*SEG* 21, 521). Supplements following Stroud (1974) 290–8, and Walbank (1991), with some suggestions by myself and W. J. Slater (see apparatus). Non-stoich., 31 to 40 chars.

```
              lacuna
a+b      [τὴ ν?] σκηνὴν προ[. . . . . ]ασι [- - - - - - - - - - - -]
         [ἐ]άν τι βο[ύ]λωντ[αι πε]ρὶ τὴν οἰκοδομίαν·
         ἐξεῖναι δὲ αὐ[τοῖς χ]ρῆσθαι λίθοις καὶ
         γῆι ἐκ τοῦ τεμ[ένους] τοῦ Διονύσου· ὅταν δ'
    5    ἐξίωσιν παρα[διδόναι?] ἅπαντα ὀρθὰ καὶ ἑ-
```

---

[5] Thphr. *Char.* 9.5 (θέαν ἀγοράσας); *Agora* 19, L13 (below) l. 19; Philoch. *FGrH* F33 (δραχμὴ τῆς θέας); Lib. *Hypothesis to Dem. Olynthiac* 1 (ἔδει διδόναι δύο ὀβολοὺς καὶ καταβαλόντα θέαν ἔχειν); Phot. s.v. *theorikon kai theorike* Theodorides (μισθὸν τῆς θέας). Cf. Poll. 7.199 (θεατροπώλης ὁ θέαν ἀπομισθῶν); Σ Lucian *Tim.* 49 (τοὺς τόπους μισθοῦν). See also the honorary inscriptions granting *prohedria* and places in the theatre, below. Note, however, that Photius, possibly misunderstanding the use of the term in this context, uses θέα to refer to the spectacle (s.v. *theorika* 1 Theodorides μηκέτι προῖκα θεωρεῖν, ἐκμισθοῦν δὲ ταῖς θέαις τοὺς τόπους).

στηκότα. ἐὰ[ν . . . .]είψωσιν πρὸς τῆι σκη-
νεῖ, κέρα[μον καὶ ξ]ύλα ἀπίτω λαβὼν πα-

c   ΝΚ[- - - - -]ΔΔΙ· [ὁ δὲ χ]ρόνος ἄρχει τῆς μι-
σθώσεω[ς] Ἡγησίας ἄρχων· τοὺς δὲ δημό-
10 τας θεωρεῖν ἀργύριο[ν] διδόντας πλὴν ὅ-
σοις οἱ δημόται προ[εδρίαν δ]εδώκασι·
τούτους δ' ἀπογράψα[ι πρὸς τοὺς π]ρια[μέ]-
νους τὸ θέατρον· εἶν[αι δὲ τὴν προεδρίαν]
καὶ τῶι δημάρχωι κα[ὶ - - - - - - - καὶ τῶι κή]-
15 ρυκι καὶ εἴ τωι ἄλλωι [δεδώκασιν οἱ δημόται]
[τὴ]ν προεδρίαν· ὅσοι δ[ὲ - - - - - - - - - - - - - - - -]
[- - - - - - - - - - - - - -]Ν[- -]
    lacuna
    lacuna

d   [- - - - - - - - - - - τοὺς πριαμένους τὸ θέ]ατρ[ο]ν πα[ρέ]-
[χειν τοῖς δημότ]αις ἥδ[ω]λιασμένην τὴν θέαν [κα]-
20 [τὰ τ]ὰ πάτρια· ἐὰν δὲ μὴ ποήσωσιν κατὰ τὰς συνθ[ή]-
κας τὰς περὶ τὸ θέατρον, οἰκοδομῆσαι μὲν Πειραέας τὰ δεόμενα, τὰ δ' ἀναλώματα τοῖς πριαμένοις
εἶναι· ἐπιτιμητὰς δὲ αἱρεῖσθαι Πειραέας ὅταν πα-
ραδιδῶσι τὸ θέατρον τρεῖς ἄνδρας ἐκ Πειραέων·
25 ἀναγράψαι δὲ τὸν δήμαρχον καὶ τοὺς ταμίας ἀντί-
γραφα τῶν συνθηκῶν εἰς στήλην λιθίνην καὶ στῆσα-
ι ἐν τῆι ἀγορᾶι τῶν δημοτῶν· παραγράψαι δὲ καὶ τὸ
ὄνομα, παρ' ὧι ἂν κείωνται αἱ συνθῆκαι· ὠνηταὶ Ἀρι-
στοφάνης Σμικύθο: ΓΗ: Μελησίας Ἀριστοκράτο: ΧΗ
30 Ἀρεθούσιος Ἀριστόλεω Πήληξ: Γ: Οἰνοφῶν Εὐφι-
λήτου Πειραιεὺς: ΧΗ.   vacat
Καλλιάδης εἶπεν· ἐψηφίσθαι Πειραεῦσι· ἐπειδὴ Θεαῖος
φιλοτιμεῖται πρὸς τοὺς δημότας καὶ νῦν καὶ ἐν τῶι
ἔμπροσθε χρόνωι καὶ πεπόηκεν τριακοσίαις δρα-
35 χμαῖς πλέον εὑρεῖν τὸ θέατρον, στεφανῶσαι αὐτὸν θαλλὸ στεφάνωι ἀρετῆς ἕνεκα καὶ δικαιο-
σύνης τῆς εἰς τοὺς δημότας· στεφανῶσαι δὲ
καὶ τοὺς πριαμένους τὸ θέατρον Ἀριστοφάνην
Πειραέα, Μελησίαν Λαμπτρέα, Οἰνοφῶντα
40 Πειραέα, Ἀρεθούσιον Πήληκα.   vacat

1. e.g. εἰ περὶ τὴν σκηνὴν προστιθέασι   6. ἀλείψωσιν Meritt: ἐὰν δὲ παρα-
λείψωσιν Stroud: ἐάν τι ἐξαμείψωσιν / παραμείψωσιν Csapo: ἐὰν μὴ
Slater: 7–8. e.g. πᾶlν καὶ ὅτι ἄλλο

The deme of Peiraieus leased its theatre to a corporation of four men in 324/3 BC for 3,300 drachmas. The inscription preserves the terms of the lease and honours them for paying 10 percent, or 300 drachmas, beyond the expected price. It begins with a list of privileges and responsibilities with regard to construction in the theatre. The first line refers to alterations to the *skene* building. εἰ περὶ τὴν σκηνὴν προστιθέασι would fit: 'if they make any additions around the stage-building' something something 'if they should want anything with respect to the construction. But the lessees are permitted to use stones and earth from the sanctuary of Dionysos.[6] When the lease expires the lessees are to return everything in good repair: [Except where they change/alter] wood and tile on the stage-building,[7] he may depart taking all (i.e. wood and tile) away with him [and anything else they may have provided].'[8] The singular verb ἀπίτω seems to be a formula carelessly applied despite the plural verb in the conditional clause.[9] We continue with 'Let the lease take effect when Hegesias becomes archon. The demesmen are to pay cash to attend performances, all except those to whom the demesmen have granted *prohedria*. These are to be registered with the theatre lessees. The mayor,' the someone, 'and the herald are to have

[6] The stones and earth are likely to be of use in levelling the slope of the *theatron* and making foundations for the seating. Cf. the building inscriptions from Skepsis (fourth/third century BC) and Capua (second century BC): Wilhelm (1900) 54–7; Frederiksen (1959) 126, no. 6. I thank W. Slater for drawing my attention to these inscriptions.

[7] Meritt (1963) 12 and Stroud (1974) 297 supplement with forms of ἀλείφω, a common verb in building inscriptions, but 'if they do some plastering on the stage-building, let them take the tile and wood' is unfortunately a non-sequitur. So is καταλείψωσιν, 'leave behind'. I would suggest some compound of ἀμείβω to supplement the stone's ἐὰ[ν . . . .]είψωσιν. Satisfactory sense could be made from any of ἐὰ[ν τι παραμ]είψωσιν / ἐξαμ]είψωσιν / ἀνταμ]είψωσιν. William Slater suggests ἐὰν μή and takes κέρα[μον καὶ ξ]ύλα with the missing verb. My translation follows Slater's suggestion. For the form, cf. *IG* XII 5, 572. I assume the provision aims to keep the basic frame of the stage-building intact after expiry of the lease.

[8] My suggestion πᾶ|ν καὶ ὅτι ἄλλο may be a little too wide-open and generous for the language of contract. Cf. *SEG* 24, 203, 16–18 and *IG* II² 2499, 11–12 (ὅταν δὲ ὁ χρόνος ἐξίει... ἄπεισιν ἔχων τὰ ξύλα καὶ τὸν κέραμον καὶ τὰ θυρώ[μ]ατα. τῶν δ'ἄλλων κινήσει οὐθέν, 'when the term expires . . . He will leave taking the wood, the tile, and the door-fixtures, but he will displace nothing else.'

[9] Stroud (1974) 297.

prohedria as is anyone else to whom the demesmen have granted it. All those who ...' The stone breaks off, so there are at least one and two half-lines missing, before the non-joining fragment d, which reads:

the theatre lessees are to provide the demesmen with a θέα [i.e. a viewing area], fitted with wooden benchwork according to local custom. If they do not act according to the terms of the agreement concerning the theatre, then the people of Peiraieus will build what is required and the cost will fall to the lessees. When they hand over the theatre, the people of Peiraieus will choose three men from Peiraieus to act as inspectors. The mayor and the treasurers will have copies of the agreement inscribed on a stone stele and placed in the deme's agora. They will add the name of the person with whom the agreement is deposited. Lessees: Aristophanes, son of Smikythos—600 drachmas; Melesias, son of Aristokratos—1,100 drachmas; Arethousios, son of Aristoleos, of Pelekes—500 drachmas; Oinophon, son of Euphiletos, of Peiraieus—1,100 drachmas.

The rest is the honorary decree granting a crown to one Theaios for his civic zeal (*philotimia*) in inducing the lessees to pay 300 drachmas more than expected from the lease and also crowns to the lessees, doubtless as a return for being so induced. Unfortunately we know nothing of Theaios' role or function in these negotiations.

From the remains, as far as we can tell, the chief obligation on the part of the lessees (ll. 19–20) is the provision to the demesmen of a viewing place, a θέα, which is ἠδ[ω]λιασμένην according to local custom. The verb ἐδωλιάζειν is a rare but securely attested term meaning to fit with wooden benches.[10] In return the lessees are to

---

[10] Orlandos and Travlos (1986) 92. The ancient lexica treat the verb as an equivalent to ἰκριόω which refers to the building of wooden benches, usually stands or bleachers. The description, however, suggests a more casual construction. See esp. Bekker, *Anec. Gr.* 259.32 (cf. Suid., *EM*) ἐδωλιάσαι καὶ ἰκριῶσαι· ἔστι δὲ τὸ μὲν ἐδωλιάσαι οἱονεὶ συνθεῖναι ἔκ τινων ξύλων ἁπλῶς πρὸς τόπον τινὰ συντεθέντων. 'To build *hedolia* and to build *ikria*: to build *hedolia* is to put together as if from planks of wood put together in some place in a simple fashion.' The verb appears again in *IG* XI 2, 287 A 81 where it means, as here, to assemble wooden benches (see below). It apparently came also to mean 'seat on the wooden benches': Harpocration *s.v.* ἐδωλιάσαι cites Lykurgos (fr. 2) for the meaning συνκαθίζειν. Lykurgos may perhaps also be the ultimate source of Pollux' discussion of ἐδωλιάζειν (= συνκαθίζειν), though in Pollux it is cited as a theatrical term (4.121, 123).

get the entrance fees, which are to be paid by all demesmen except those to whom *prohedria* is granted. The lease also includes some stipulations regarding construction on or around the stage-building, though that part is all but lost. In the surviving document, the consideration, in the legal sense of *quid pro quo*, is the construction and resale of seating.

Similar arrangements may be attested by a couple of other inscriptions only two to three decades later than the Peiraieus decree. In these inscriptions another Attic deme and cities in Euboea dispose of money gained or expected from the leasing of their theatres. A decree of the deme of Akharnai *(IG II² 1206)* shows the deme at the end of the fourth century BC disposing of moneys 'collected' from the theatre.[11] Lines 4–12 read:

$$: \Delta \Delta : \delta\rho\alpha\chi\mu\grave{\alpha}s\ [\grave{\alpha}]\text{-}$$
5 $[\pi\grave{o}\ \tau o\hat{v}\ \grave{\alpha}\rho\gamma v]\rho\acute{\iota}ov\ \tau o\hat{v}\ \grave{\epsilon}\gamma\lambda\epsilon\gamma o\mu\acute{\epsilon}[v]\text{-}$
 $[ov\ \grave{\epsilon}\kappa\ \tau o\hat{v}\ \theta\epsilon]\acute{\alpha}\tau\rho ov\cdot\ \grave{\epsilon}\grave{\alpha}v\ \delta\grave{\epsilon}\ \tau\grave{o}\ \theta\acute{\epsilon}\alpha[\tau]\text{-}$
 $[\rho ov\dots\dots o]v\ \mathring{\eta}\iota,\ \delta\iota\delta\acute{o}v\alpha\iota\ \alpha\mathring{v}\tauo\hat{\iota}[s]$
 $[\tau\grave{o}v\ \delta\acute{\eta}\mu\alpha\rho\chi]ov\ \kappa\alpha\grave{\iota}\ \tau\grave{o}v\ \tau\alpha\mu\acute{\iota}\alpha v\ [o\mathring{\iota}]$
 $[\mathring{\alpha}v\ \grave{\alpha}\epsilon\grave{\iota}\ \mathring{\alpha}\rho\chi\omega]\sigma\iota v\ \tau\grave{o}\ \gamma\epsilon\gamma\rho\alpha\mu\mu\acute{\epsilon}v[ov]$
10 $[\grave{\alpha}\rho\gamma\acute{v}\rho\iota ov\ \epsilon]\mathring{\iota}s\ \tau\grave{\eta}v\ \theta v\sigma\acute{\iota}\alpha v\ \grave{\epsilon}\kappa\ \tau[\hat{\eta}s]$
 $[\kappa o\iota v\hat{\eta}s\ \delta\iota o]\iota\kappa\acute{\eta}\sigma\epsilon\omega s\ \tau\hat{\eta}s\ \tau\hat{\omega}v\ \delta\eta[\mu]\text{-}$
 $[o\tau\hat{\omega}v.$

Twenty drachmas from the money collected from the theatre. If the theatre is [missing word of seven letters] then the mayor and the treasurer in office at the time should give them the stipulated sum for the sacrifice from the deme's operating budget.

The term ἐκλέγειν here need not imply that the deme is collecting money directly; it is frequently used, for example, of collecting taxes that have in fact been farmed out to a tax-collector. One can perhaps compare the *theatrones'* λόγευμα in the Nikarkhos elegy. The revenues presumably come from leasing out the theatre. Much may depend on the five missing letters in line 7. Wilamowitz conjectured ἔλαττον, which would mean 'if the theatre is less',

---

[11] The connection (made by Köhler *apud IG* II 5, 587b) with Akharnai is based on the restored reference to Athena Hippia (cf. *IG* II² 1207, l. 4, *SEG* 43, 26 A, ll. 24–5, B, ll. 16–17, and Paus. 1.31.5).

which would then presumably have to be pressed very hard to mean 'if the revenues from the theatre fall short'. I suggest ἄπρατον, meaning 'but if the theatre is not leased'.[12]

We may note in passing that the *theatron* of Akharnai, like that of Peiraieus, was probably of wood. Its front row seating *(prohedria)* had not the separately articulated stone thrones we know from the Lykurgan theatre of Dionysos in Athens. A deme decree of 315/14 BC (*SEG* 43, 26 B 22) awards officials *prohedria* in perpetuity 'on the first bench' ἐπὶ τοῦ πρώτου βάθρου, using a word, *bathron*, which, when used of seating, normally seems to refer to a wooden bench. Indeed the expression is in Athens used interchangeably with πρῶτον ξύλον, literally 'first plank', used of the front row of the assembly and courts in Aristophanes' day, the former of which Lysias described as *bathra* and the latter of which the comic poet Pherekrates called *protobathron*.[13] If the *prohedria*, the seat of honour, was a wooden bench, then the rest of the *theatron* was also certainly of wood.

The custom of leasing the theatre was probably also standard in Euboea in the 290s BC. Wilhelm argued that the famous Euboean festivals decree assigns the cost of inscribing the decree and erecting the stele to expected income from leasing the theatres of Chalkis, Eretria, Karystos, and Oreos during the forthcoming Dionysia:[14]

τὰ δ[ὲ δό]-
[ξαντ]α ἀναγράψαι τοὺς ἄρχοντας ἐν ἑκάστ[ηι] τῶν πόλεων ἐν στ[ή]ληι λιθίνηι καὶ ἀν[α]θεῖναι εἰς τὴν πάρ[οδον]

---

[12] I am grateful to Robert Parker for bringing to my attention N. Papazarkadas' D.Phil. thesis (University of Oxford, 2004) which contains the same conjecture, arrived at independently. Papazarkadas gives full justification for the emendation.

[13] For *bathron* as 'wooden bench', see Hellmann (1992) 63, and the discussion below, pp. 103–7. Cf. πρῶτον βάθρον in Ar. *Ach.* 25, *V.* 90 (with *Σ*); Poll. 4.121, 8.133; Lys. 13.37; Pherecr. *PCG* F 260; cf. Steinhauer (1992) 182. *Bathron* can refer also to the base or foundation block upon which a seat is placed (as in Soph. *Ant.* 854). The stone foundations for the *prohedria* in the pre-Lykurgan theatre of Dionysus might have been referred to as *bathra*: upon them, I believe, wooden *klismoi* were placed.

[14] Wilhelm (1951) 79–83. Le Guen (2001a) I no. 1, ll. 54–7. Le Guen (2001a) I. 47 translates 'que la dépense pour la stèle soit imputée par chacune des cités, chez elle, sur les revenus de son théâtre, au moment où s'effectuera le paiement du loyer pour les prochaines Dionysies'.

[τοῦ] θεάτρου· τὸ δὲ ἀνάλωμα τὸ εἰς τὴν στήλην ὑποθεῖναι ἑκάστ[ου]ς
παρ᾽ ἑαυ[το]<ῖ>ς τῶι θεάτρωι, ὅταν ποή[σωνται τὴν]
[μίσθω]σιν κατὰ τὰ ἐπιόντα Διονύσια·

It is decreed that the archons in each of the cities have the decisions written up on a stone stele and erected in the entranceway of the theatre. Each is to apply the cost of the stele to their respective theatres when they lease them out for the upcoming Dionysia.[15]

If this is right the cost of publishing the decree is simply added to the cost of the lease, in much the same way that the cost of the sacrifice at Akharnai is simply added to or put against the anticipated income from the lease of the theatre.

THE THEATRE OF DIONYSOS AT ATHENS

We know, then, of *theatron*-buyers in deme theatres and probably foreign cities. Does this tell us anything about the practice in the theatre of Dionysos at Athens? Theophrastus' *theatronai*, being in the plural, are probably generalisations in reference to the normal arrangements at deme theatres. Aristophanes' *theatropoles*, being singular, could refer to the production context of *Phoenissai*, but we still cannot be sure that it was Athens. We have no direct

---

[15] μίσθω]σιν is a supplement by Wilhelm (1951); ἔγδο]σιν is a supplement by Wilamowitz, *addenda*, p. 176 to *IG* XII 9, 207. Both words are taken to refer to farming out the theatre on a lease. Cf. Stephanis (1984) 510. W. Slater, however, points out that the *misthosis* in question could refer to the hiring of Artists of Dionysus, which is also the subject of the next sentence: ὅπως ἂν γίνωνται ⟨αἱ ἐργολαβίαι suppl. Wilamowitz⟩, τὰς πόλεις ἑλομένας τοὺς ἄνδρας κατὰ τὴν διαγρα[φὴν] | [πέμψαι] εἰς Χαλκίδα πρὸ τῆς εἰκάδος τοῦ Ἀπατουριῶνος μηνός, ὡς Χαλκιδεῖς ἄγουσιν, ὅπως ἂν ἐγδῶσιν τὰ ἔ[ργα] | [τοῖς τεχ]νίταις. In this case we might obviate the necessity of Wilamowitz' supplement, reading 'let each city ascribe the cost of the stele to their theatre when they do the hiring for the upcoming Dionysia. And so that they (i.e. the hirings) take place, let the cities send men chosen according to the agreement to Chalkis before the twentieth of Apatourion in the Chalkidian calendar, so that they can assign the work to the Artists.' This may well be right, though it would require a difficult transition from singular μίσθω]σιν to plural γίνωνται and contradicts the strong discontinuity argued at this point in the text by Wilhelm (1951) 83 and Stephanis (1984) 513. Wilhelm's reading also makes better sense of the verb ὑποθεῖναι: Wilhelm (1951) 80.

evidence for *theatronai* in the theatre of Dionysos, but the circumstantial and comparative evidence makes their presence likely.

The Athenian theatre of Dionysos charged admission. We take admission charges for granted, but Alan Sommerstein (1997: 66–7) and Peter Wilson (1997: 97–8) have recently pointed out just how strange it was for Athens to have taken this step. The City Dionysia is the first Greek religious festival known to have exacted money for the right to participate. And at 2 obols the fee was something more than a nominal sum (presumably charged per entry into the theatre, so that full participation at the Dionysia would cost at least 1 drachma and 4 obols). Can we assume that Athens in the fifth century took the extraordinary measure of permitting entrance fees for the same reason that the deme of Peiraieus allowed such fees in the later fourth century? Can we assume, namely, that the *theatropoles* paid for the right to collect entrance fees in return for constructing and maintaining the *theatron*?

A difference in scale and construction might seem an obstacle to using procedures at Peiraieus as a model for explaining procedures at Athens. But new archaeological discoveries and better archaeological syntheses in the last forty years give good reason for questioning the belief that the scale and construction of the Athenian *theatron* differed greatly from that of theatres in the Attic hinterland.

There have, over the years, been many estimates of the seating capacity of the Athenian theatre in the fifth century. They vary widely. Limiting ourselves to estimates over the past ten years, we find the capacity of the fifth-century theatre of Dionysos pegged at: 3,700 (Dawson 1997), 5,500 (Korres 2002: 540), not more than 7,000 (Goette *per litteras*), 10,000 to 15,000 (Moretti 1999–2000: 395).

Moretti's figure of 10,000 to 15,000 is closer to the traditional view that the seating capacity of the fifth-century theatre was nearly the same as that of the later fourth-century Lykurgan theatre (influentially pegged by Pickard-Cambridge at 14,000 to 17,000 (1946: 141)). But for the capacity of the fifth-century *theatron* the evidence is very much in favour of the more modest estimates of Dawson, Korres, and Goette. We should probably think of audiences numbering somewhere between 4,000 and 7,000.

The reduced estimates are in line with archaeological evidence unavailable to the scholars, like Pickard-Cambridge (1946) and Dinsmoor (1951), who have shaped our traditional view of the architectural history of the theatre of Dionysos. They thought that the earliest stone theatre could be dated back to the time of Perikles. Many still adhere to this view, but the theory must be abandoned. In his Appendix to this chapter Hans Goette provides plans and a fuller description of the archaeological evidence for the *theatron* of the fifth-century theatre of Dionysos. The reader will find this a valuable supplement to the following summary.

Excavations during the 1960s in the sanctuary of Dionysos provided clear stratigraphical evidence that the foundations of the earliest stone theatre cannot be dated before the mid-fourth century.[16] The fifth-century *theatron* was therefore built almost entirely of wood. This inference is confirmed by Old Comedy where Aristophanes (*Thesmophoriazousai* 395, cf. scholiast ad loc.) and Cratinus (*PCG* F 360) both refer to the audience sitting upon *ikria*. This term is used only of wooden constructions. Moreover, Pollux (4.122) preserves, probably also from Old Comedy, the word *pternokopein*, 'heel-banging', which is one of the many means the Athenian audience employed to show displeasure at a performance. Heel-banging is doubtless what Cratinus refers to when he calls 'the noise of the wooden benches' the 'mother' of the audience (*PCG* F 360). No one with heels of flesh and bone will believe with Leyerle that *pternokopein* refers to an 'ominous noise made by heels drumming against the backs of the *stone* seats' (2001: 36, my emphasis).

Archaeological evidence also shows that the fifth-century *theatron* was much smaller than its Lykurgan successor. Doerpfeld's excavations uncovered an 'ancient road' (Appendix Fig. 1.9) running in a straight line on the south slope of the Athenian acropolis about ten metres to the south of the Lykurgan Peripatos (along the axis of the theatre). This is clearly the extension of the road that later curved

[16] Kalligas (1963); Travlos (1971). I am told that reports of recent excavations in the theatre, to be published soon in *Arkhaiologikon Deltion*, may provide confirmation of a mid-fourth-century date for the earliest stone *theatron* in Athens.

northward to form the Lykurgan Peripatos (running through the
Lykurgan theatre from Appendix Fig. 1.13). South of this ancient
road Doerpfeld uncovered wells and the walls of fifth-century BC
houses.[17] Still further south a rock cutting (Appendix Fig. 1.7) seems
to mark the northern boundary of the fifth-century *theatron* also in a
straight line. [18]

The only material remains of the fifth-century seating area are
some ten blocks which formed a platform for the fifth-century *prohedria*. The distinctive raised bands (anathyrosis) at the ends of these
blocks indicate that they are designed to abut one another to form a
straight line.[19] Thus, the Classical auditorium was constrained by
a straight face on the south and a straight back in the north. When
this evidence is combined with comparative evidence from other
fifth- and early fourth-century theatres, all of which are trapezoidal
or rectilinear, the case for a trapezoidal *theatron* for the fifth-century
theatre of Dionysos seems conclusive.[20] Thus the fifth-century
theatron had a much smaller seating capacity than its Lykurgan successor, not only because of its smaller extent, but also because of its
rectilinearity.

The extent and construction of the fifth-century theatre of
Dionysos allowed for audiences that were larger but not vastly larger
than some of the deme theatres. The Athenian *theatron* may have had
no more than about twice the capacity of the remote deme theatre of
Thorikos, for example, for which the latest capacity estimate is 3,200,

[17] See further Dörpfeld and Reisch (1896) 30–1, and fig. 7; Goette (1995a) 28–9.
The value of this evidence is limited, or obscured, by the judgement of Schneider that
the pottery associated with the walls dated no later than 450 BC. None of the pottery
fragments was published, and since knowledge of the chronology of Attic pottery was
slim and dating techniques were primitive in 1889, we can only wait for clarification
from further excavation in this area. Schneider's excavation notebooks are available in the archive of the Deutsches Archäologisches Institut in Athens. Recent
excavations in the area of the *theatron* and Peripatos should yield much more precise
and reliable stratigraphic information.
[18] The connection of this cutting with the Lykurgan *diazoma* has been disproved
by Korres (1980).
[19] See esp. Pöhlmann (1981).
[20] On Classical rectilinear theatres, see most recently: Goette (1995a); Moretti
(1999–2000); Junker (2004).

or Trakhones, where estimates run as high as 3,750.[21] Though still large by contemporary standards, the theatre of Dionysos very likely had less capacity than the *ekklesiasterion* of Pnyx I and II.[22] At 4,000 to 7,000 it could not have been much bigger than the theatre at Peiraieus which was sometimes used for assemblies of the Athenian *demos* (see further below).

If Athens invented admission charges, it was surely in order to deal with the extraordinary cost and bother of providing seats in the theatre. The theatre festivals, with an annual periodicity and a setting in the heart of a large urban centre, had more regular and much larger audiences than those which frequented most other musical or athletic festivals. It was just the kind of regular maintenance work which the Athenian democracy liked to farm out to private entrepreneurs. The demes and even cities outside Attica imitated the success of the City Dionysia, building theatres, appointing *choregoi*, and holding contests for dithyramb, tragedy, and comedy. Some at least would appear to have imitated the city in selling the work to entrepreneurs. The city stood only to gain by selling the franchise and lost no trouble or expense; the entrepreneurs profited by selling seats. Everyone was happy, excepting only Athenian theatre-goers, who blamed the greed of the *theatronai* for high admission costs or the scarcity of seats.

ENTRANCE FEES AND THE *THEORIKON*

If this seems plausible, it is not quite the way that ancient authors explained admission fees. Several late authors mention the introduction of admission fees in general accounts of the origin of the

---

[21] For the seating capacity at Thorikos: Palyvou (2001) 56. For Trakhones (Euonymon): Lohmann (1998) 195 (2,600–3,750); Tzachou-Alexandri (1999) 421 ('2,500 spectators at least').

[22] There is controversy too over the capacity of the Pnyx. Recent opinions include: Hansen (1991) 130–1, who estimates that Pnyx I held 6,000 participants, Pnyx II (after 403) held an estimated 6,500 to 8,000; Camp (2001) 46–7, who estimates that Pnyx I held 8,000 to 13,000.

festival dole, *theorikon,* in Athens.[23] They all agree that the root cause of the introduction of the *theorikon* was fierce competition for seats in the theatre of Dionysos. Two of the sources, Libanius and the scholiast to Lucian, add, apparently by way of explanation, that the theatre was not yet of stone. Unfortunately they make no effort to show how this could possibly exacerbate the competition for seats, and we may suspect that they have garbled their model. Four sources maintain that this competition led to physical violence in the *theatron* (Ulpian, *Σ* Lucian, Libanius, Photius s.v. *theorika);* the fifth *(Etymologicum Genuinum)* mentions the violence but without connecting it with the competition for seats. There is disagreement about whether the fighting was predominantly between rich and poor (*Σ* Lucian), citizen and foreigner (Photius s.v. *theorikon kai theorike , Etymologicum Genuinum),* or both (Ulpian). From here two authors move directly into an explanation of the *theorikon:* it was decided to provide money for all so that the rich (Ulpian), or the foreigners (Photius s.v. *theorikon kai theorike),* would not have the advantage in buying up the seats. But four sources have a more complex explanation: to stop the violence in the theatre the Athenians decided to charge admission (*Σ* Lucian, Libanius, Photius s.v. *theorika, Etymologicum Genuinum).*[24] The remedy then led to renewed conflict. The rich regularly bought up all the seats, so the *theorikon* was created to remedy the remedy (Harpocration, *Σ* Lucian, Libanius, Photius s.v. *theorika).* As a group, these sources offer nothing but confusion, non-sequiturs, and mutual contradiction. In particular, they do not explain how a theatre in wood is more conducive to violent confrontation than a stone theatre (was it because of its more restricted size?). And they do not explain how introducing entrance fees is any kind of solution to the competition for seats.

---

[23] Harp. s.v. Θεωρικά (includes Philoch. *FGrH* F33); Ulp. on Dem. *Olynthiac* 1.1 (Dilts); *Σ* Aeschin. 3.24; *Σ* Lucian *Tim.* 49; Lib. *Hypothesis to Dem. Olynthiac* 1; Phot. s.v. *theorikon kai theorike* (Theodoridis); Phot. s.v. *theorika* 1 (Theodoridis); *Et. Gen.* s.v. *theorikon argyrion* (Sylburg).

[24] It is not easy to see how charging admission stops violence. Only *Σ* Lucian offers further explanation by stating that the seats were then sold in advance and somehow reserved. But this might only remove the rioting from the *theatron* to the box office.

However Ulpian's version, probably the earliest of the group, shares none of this illogic. Unlike the other sources Ulpian does not make entrance fees the solution to civil strife, but its cause.[25] He assumes the existence of entrance fees to begin with, and he explains their existence by the fact that the theatre was constructed of wood (Ulpian on Dem. *Olynthiac* 1.1 (Dilts)):

ἐπειδήπερ χρήματα ἔχοντες στρατιωτικὰ οἱ Ἀθηναῖοι ἔναγχος αὐτὰ πεποιήκασι θεωρικά. ὥστε λαμβάνειν ἐν τῷ θεωρεῖν ἕκαστον τῶν ἐν τῇ πόλει δύο ὀβολούς, ἵνα τὸν μὲν ἕνα κατάσχῃ εἰς ἰδίαν τροφήν, τὸν δὲ ἄλλον παρέχειν ἔχωσι τῷ ἀρχιτέκτονι τοῦ θεάτρου (οὐδὲ γὰρ εἶχον τότε θέατρον διὰ λίθων κατεσκευασμένον) ... ἰστέον δὲ ὅτι τὰ χρήματα ταῦτα τὰ δημόσια θεωρικὰ ἐποίησεν ἐξ ἀρχῆς ὁ Περικλῆς δι᾽ αἰτίαν τοιαύτην· ἐπειδὴ πολλῶν θεωμένων καὶ στασιαζόντων διὰ τὸν τόπον καὶ ξένων καὶ πολιτῶν, καὶ λοιπὸν τῶν πλουσίων ἀγοραζόντων τοὺς τόπους, βουλόμενος ἀρέσαι τῷ δήμῳ καὶ τοῖς πένησιν, ἵνα ἔχωσι καὶ αὐτοὶ πόθεν ὠνεῖσθαι τόπους, ἔγραψε τὰ προσοδευόμενα χρήματα τῇ πόλει γενέσθαι πᾶσι θεωρικὰ τοῖς πολίταις.

When the Athenians got hold of military money they immediately turned it into festival money, so that each citizen received two obols for the festival, one to provide himself with food, the other to have something to give to the *arkhitekton* (they did this because they did not have a theatre built in stone in those days) ... It is important to know that Perikles originally made this public money festival money for the following reason. When there were many wishing to get into the theatre and there was fierce competition for places both among citizens and foreigners, and then when the rich bought up all the seats, Perikles wanted to please the people and the poor and decreed that the city's income be turned into festival money for all citizens so that they could have the means to buy seats.

Arguably Ulpian preserves the least garbled version of the account that lies behind this group. According to his source, from the time of Perikles, at latest, the admission fee went to pay the theatre manager, and this had something to do with the wooden construction of the theatre. The implication that the theatre manager was called the

---

[25] The same logic may lie behind Phot. s.v. *theorikon kai theorike*, but if so it is contradicted by Phot. s.v. *theorika* 1.

arkhitekton in the time of Perikles is an anachronism, as we will see, and most historians doubt the existence of a *theorikon* before the latter half of the fourth century. Plutarch also ascribes the *theorikon* to Perikles, and a common source, perhaps as early as the fourth century, is assumed for Plutarch and the later commentators: Theopompos and Philochorus have been named.[26]

I do not mean to imply that Ulpian's account of the *theorikon*, just because it is not illogical, or just because it does not completely garble a fourth-century BC author, is therefore somehow true. What interests me here, and what seems to me consistent with a late Classical/early Hellenistic source, is the logical association of entrance fees and wooden *theatra*.

WOODEN THEATRES

The emphasis placed in the Peiraieus lease upon the provision of wooden benches (rather than, say, a general provision for the maintenance of the theatre) suggests that something more than the mere maintenance of pre-existing structures is involved. Just how often was the *theatron* rebuilt?

It does not seem to have been the practice in antiquity to leave wooden seating in place very long before or after use. Epigraphy offers few references to the rebuilding of wooden *theatra*, but that is in itself interesting. The building accounts which might preserve such information refer only to expenditures from the public purse and the only theatres involved are those being built or rebuilt in stone. What the building accounts of various Greek cities do provide is a number of references to the erection of stands of wooden seats in stadia and lawcourts.

In Delos, for example, we have records of the payment of those who brought the wooden benches (*bathra*) into the stadium (and presumably installed them): this happened at least twice over a

---

[26] Meinhardt (1957) 38 (Philochorus); Wade-Gery (1958) 237 (Theopompos); Connor (1968) 111–16 (Theopompus). Cf. Stadter (1989) 116.

five-year period in the mid-third century BC.[27] The context makes it
clear that the installation was preparatory to the annual games (the
Apollonia). A few years later the Amphictyonic accounts for the
preparation of the Pythian games record a payment for the placing
of wooden stands for the spectators (*bathrosis*) in the stadium at
Delphi.[28] The same inscription may also refer to the *bathrosis* of the
theatre, although the line is heavily restored.[29]

It is perhaps easier to see why the seating at stadia should be
erected and dismantled on each occasion. Games are frequently
biennial, or quadrennial, and large tracts of land, especially in
remoter sanctuary locations, could be put to good use in the mean-
time: inscriptions show that the hippodrome in Delos, the stadium
in Libadia, and even the Panathenaic stadium in Athens were leased
for pasturage once the games were over.[30] The same logic would
govern the set up and removal of bleachers for viewing processions:
we have literary evidence from Athens for the erection of bleachers
for the Panathenaia from the second century BC, and architectural
evidence, in the form of postholes, for their regular periodic use as
early as the fifth century BC.[31] The stands were placed in the middle

---

[27] *IG* XI 2, 274 (Delos *c.* 255 BC) l. 24, with correction and supplement by Tréheux
(1984) 334 n. 33: τοῖς τὰ βάθ[ρα ἐνείγκασι - - '(paid) to those who carried in the
bathra'; *IG* XI 2, 287 A (Delos 250 BC) l. 81: καὶ ἐργάταις ἐδωλιάσασιν ⊢ 'and to
the workers who assembled the *hedolia* one drachma'; and l. 32: βάθρα ἐνέγκασι ‖
'to those who brought in the *bathra* two obols'. On *bathra* see above, p. 95 and
n. 13.

[28] *CID* II 139 (Delphi 247/6? BC), ll. 29–30: τὰν βάθρωσιν ἐν τ[ῶι] πυθικῶι
σταδίωι Νίκων, πόδας [: 1 |:], στατήρων : Π: 'for assembling the *bathra* in the Pythian
Stadium x feet by x feet, Nikon (received) six staters'.

[29] *CID* II 139 (Delphi 247/6? BC) l. 27: τὰν βάθρωσιν [τοῦ] θεά[τρου τοῦ
πυ]θικοῦ Μελισσ[ίων] : ΔΔΓΣΣΣ 'for assembling the *bathra* of the Pythian
Theatre (?), Melission (received) twenty-eight staters'. The *koilon* of the theatre seems
not to have been built in stone until the second century BC.

[30] **Delos**: *IG* XI 2, 104–11 A, 16–17; *IG* XI 2, 104–19 A, 11; *IG* XI 2, 104–26 A, 9; *IG*
XI 2, 149, 2; *IG* XI 2, 152 B, 6; *IG* XI 2, 158 A, 11; *IG* XI 2, 161 A, 11; *IG* XI 2, 162 A, 9;
IG XI 2, 199 A, 5–6; *IG* XI 2, 287 A, 32; *IG* XI 2, 352, 12; *IG* XI 2, 1417 B II, 114;
Homolle (1890) 390, 427; Hellmann (1992) 176. **Libadia**: Vollgraff (1901) 372.
Athens: *IG* II² 1035, 50.

[31] Ath. 4.167F (Hegesander): τοῖς δὲ Παναθηναίοις ἵππαρχος ὢν ἴκριον
ἔστησεν πρὸς τοῖς Ἑρμαῖς Ἀρισταγόραι μετεωρότερον τῶν Ἑρμῶν 'when
Hipparch he erected a bleacher for Aristagora by the herms which was higher
than the herms'. Cf. Poll. 7.125 s.v. *ikriopoioi*: ἰκριοποιοὶ δ' εἰσὶν οἱ πηγνύντες
τὰ περὶ τὴν ἀγορὰν ἴκρια 'bleacher-makers are those who emplace the bleachers

of the agora and would have to be removed immediately after the festival so as not to hinder normal activity.[32] More remarkable perhaps is to find the same ad hoc set-up and removal operation in the case of lawcourts, which met much more frequently. But we have evidence for this at Delos. One inscription uses the verb *hedoliazo* (the same verb used in the Peiraieus lease).[33] Another, if correctly restored, records payment for workers who bring in *and remove* 200 wooden benches from the lawcourts.[34] Roland Martin even argues that it was normal to construct and dismantle the benches for each meeting of the court of the Heliaia in Athens (1951: 325–7; 1957: 81).

The very terms employed for installing wooden seats seem to connote temporary structures. If the term *ikria* can be applied to such very different structures as the bleachers set up on the flat plane of the agora and the benches laid upon the rising ground of the theatre of Dionysos, it is probably because it connotes primarily any benchwork which is wooden and temporary. According to Martin (1957: 76): 'le terme designe toùt echafaudage, tribune, etc., de caractère temporaire élevé pour les assemblées, les fêtes, etc.'[35] The impermanence of the construction is also indicated by the vocabulary used in describing the way *ikria* or *hedolia* are put together: usually words like δέω, δεσμεύω, (συν)πήγνυμι, the seats, or often explicitly 'the planks', are 'affixed', 'emplaced' or 'assembled';

---

around the agora'. Postholes for the erection of bleachers have been found on the Panathenaic way: see Camp (1986) 45–6. These bleachers are not to be connected in any way with the alleged theatre in the agora: see the important discussion by Scullion (1994) 52–66.

[32] Cf. Plaut. *Curc.* 643–7: as a child Planesium was taken to see the Dionysia and lost in the confusion that followed when the stands (*spectacula*) collapsed. This does not refer to the Epidaurian theatre, since drama there formed part of the Asklepieia (and besides the sanctuary *theatron* was built into the hillside and of stone). The reference must be to stands built for spectators along the route followed by the *pompe* (cf. Plaut. *Cist.* 90).

[33] *IG* XI 2, 287 A, l. 81, cited above, n. 27.

[34] *IG* XI 2 no. 145 (Delos 302 BC) ll. 37–8 with *addenda*, cf. Tréheux (1984) 334 n. 33: [ἐργάταις βάθρα ὅ] | [τ'] ἦν τὰ δικαστήρια ταῖς ἱεραῖς γραφαῖς διακόσ[ια] κατενέγκασ[ι] ϙαὶ ἀπενέγκασι ⋅⊢⊢⋅ 'and two drachmas to the workers bringing in and taking out two hundred *bathra* when the courts met at the ?sacred sessions'.

[35] Cf. the *theatron* 'cobbled together' (ἰκριώσας) for a beast hunt by Caesar in Dio Cassius 43.22.2.

the ancient lexica describe *hedolia* as 'planks of wood put together in some place in a simple fashion'.[36] Moreover the building accounts often do not itemise the expense as a 'construction of benches', so much as a mere expenditure on the labour of 'bringing in' or 'carrying out' wood.

The evidence for the transitory nature of the Classical *theatron* sits well with the evidence for the rectilinear shape of the *orchestra* and *theatron* which we find in the older deme theatres of Attica.[37] The effort and expense of shaping a wooden *theatron* to fit a circular plan would hardly be worthwhile if the *theatron* were only being put up for a few days or a single festival season, especially when the decisions were being made by an entrepreneur who was mainly interested in maximising his profits. Not aesthetics, let alone Wiles' imputed rationalistic or antitheocentric values (1997: 23–62), but simple practical economics, *reine Zweckhaftigkeit* (Junker 2004: 28), dictated the rectilinear plan of all fifth- and early fourth-century theatres for which we have sufficient evidence. Aesthetic considerations take over once *theatra* are built of stone and with money directly dispensed from state coffers. We know of no circular theatres until the stone theatres of Lykurgos at Athens, Epidaurus, and Megalopolis.

The temporary character of the seating would also explain why the evidence shows the Athenian assembly meeting so rarely in the theatre of Dionysos. The fact is especially odd if one accepts the more

---

[36] δέω: Hsch. s.v. παρ' αἰγείρου θέα. δεσμεύω: *Suid.* s.v. ἴκρια: Σ Ar. *Th.*395. (συμ)πήγνυμι: Poll. 7.125; Lib. *Hypothesis to Dem. Olynthiac* 1; Hsch. s.v. αἰγείρου-θέα. The ancient lexica are cited above, n. 10. Cf. Martin (1957) 75–6.

[37] The theatres in question are Ikarion, Thorikos (see further below), Rhamnous, ?Peiraieus (Goette 1995a: 43 n. 32 finds the scant remains, mainly the drainage canal, reported by the nineteenth-century excavations, at least consistent with a rectangular *orchestra*), Trakhones, Oropos (Goette 1995a: 253–60 argues that it is mid-fourth century; Tzachou-Alexandri 1999: 421 would include it in the fifth century), Syracuse, Argos, Isthmia, Chaeroneia, Morgantina, ?Tegea, ?Phlious, ?Cyrene, Metapontum. The shape of most of these theatres is known from the *prohedria* which was of stone or had foundations in stone. Some early theatres, however, retained the rectangular form of the *theatron* and *orchestra*, despite the fact that the entire *theatron* was in stone, or substantially built of stone: Thorikos, for example, which has a *theatron* with nineteen stone seats dating to the early fifth century BC. In general, see most recently (with further literature) Moretti (2001) 121–36; Junker 2004. Calydon may also have had a rectilinear theatre: we await the publication of recent excavations.

traditional figures for seating capacity, by which the *ekklesiasterion* on the Pnyx had less space and probably no seating apart from the 'first benches'.[38] Yet, the only meetings of the assembly which were held in the theatre took place each year immediately after the Dionysia, and only, it appears, for the express purpose of reviewing the festival.[39] The infrequency of such gatherings is consistent with one or both of our earlier conclusions: namely that the capacity of the theatre of Dionysos was in fact smaller than or equal to the *ekklesiasterion* of the Pnyx and that seating was only available in the theatre during the festival season. Once the theatre was built in stone, it was regularly used in preference to the Pnyx.[40] The temporary convenience of available seating may also explain the pattern for assemblies in Peiraieus. Down to 188 BC all epigraphically attested assemblies held in the Peiraieus theatre in the third and second centuries BC took place during one of the three winter months, Poseideon, Gamelion, or Elaphebolion. Thereafter the assembly met frequently at any time of year. The building of the stone theatre at Zea is usually dated broadly to the mid-second century BC, but on this evidence, might be more narrowly dated to about 185 BC.[41]

---

[38] See e.g. Hansen and Fischer-Hansen (1994) 53.

[39] D. 21.8–10, 206; Aeschin. *Emb.* 61, *Ktes.* 52; *IG* II² 140.4 (353/2 BC), 223 (343/2 BC); Pickard-Cambridge (1968 (1988)) 68–70; Kourouniotis and Thompson (1932) 136–8; Kolb (1981) 93; Hansen and Fischer-Hansen (1994) 44–5. There was also a display of the ephebes in the theatre in Boedromion attested by Arist. *Ath. Pol.* 42.4, but this may refer to the time of the stone theatre; so also the assembly in late Anthesterion 331/0 BC reported by *IG* II² 350. The assembly of the deme of Myrrhinous after the rural Dionysia also met in the theatre to discuss the festival (χρηματίζειν περὶ Διονυσίων, *IG* II² 1183, 36).

[40] Moretti (2001) 118; Kolb (1981) 94–5, with some adjustments by Hansen and Fischer-Hansen (1994) 44 n. 82. The formula for meetings of the assembly which follow the Dionysia (ἐκκλησία ἐν Διονύσου) is consistently distinguished from the formula for other meetings (ἐκκλησία ἐν τῷ θεάτρῳ). Kolb claims that the latter appears in inscriptions first in 319/18 'als die vollständig aus Steinsitzen konstruierte Cavea des lykurgischen Dionysostheaters fertiggestellt war', and then regularly after the beginning of the third century (Kolb 1981: 95).

[41] Meetings in Peiraieus to 188/7 BC: *IG* II² 785 (Poseideon 239/8 BC); *IG* II² 849 (Gamelion *c.* 206/5 BC); *IG* II² 850 (Elaphebolion *c.* 200 BC); *Agora* 15.165 (?Poseideon *c.* 197/6 BC); *SEG* 25, 112 (Elaphebolion 196/5 BC); *IG* II² 890 (Poseideion 188/7 BC). After 184/3: *Hesperia* 40 (1971) no. 9 (Hekatombaion 184/3 BC); *SEG* 16, 89 (Metageitnion 175/4 BC); *SEG* 16, 91 (Metageitnion 173/2 BC); *SEG* 16, 94 (Maimakterion 173/2–168/7 BC, cf. *SEG* 21, 452); *IG* II² 910 (Gamelion 169/8 BC); *Hesperia* 5 (1936) no. 17 (Skirophorion 169–165 BC); *IG* II² 946 (Elaphebolion 166/5

Why *theatra* were reassembled for each festival or season of usage can only be a matter for speculation. The effect of spring rains and the summer sun on exposed and untreated wood may have been a primary concern. Anyone who has made the mistake of leaving furniture out on the balcony on a hot summer day in Athens will be able to estimate the potential for damage. Another possible reason is theft or vandalism. Long planks were a valuable resource. More pertinent, however, is the desire, especially on the part of entrepreneurs, to keep the wood in circulation. The texts just discussed may help form some impression of how frequently public seating needed to be transported and reassembled for festivals and public assemblies of all sorts. There seems little possibility that the planks were simply put into storage for safe-keeping until the next Dionysia.

THE *ARKHITEKTON*

It is time now to consider the third term in our trinity, the *arkhitekton*. The *arkhitektones* we meet in Greek inscriptions often seem to have little in common with what we would call 'architects'.[42] *Arkhitekton* might most often better be translated as 'general contractor'. But remoter still from what we consider architects are the official *arkhitektones*, who appear as salaried officials in various Greek states, beginning in the mid to late fourth centuries BC, and who work together with boards of *epistatai* or *epimeletai*. This figure more often functions as a combination of Chairman of the Public Works Dept. and Building Inspector. Not coincidentally, perhaps, the official *arkhitekton* is best attested in places like Athens, Delphi, and Delos during periods of major civic construction in the fourth and third centuries BC: at Athens from a little before the time of

BC); *SEG* 16, 96 (Gamelion 164/3 BC); *SEG* 16, 95 (Elaphebolion 164/3 BC); *SEG* 34, 95 (Boedromion 161/0 BC); *SEG* 16, 96 (?Gamelion *c.* 158 BC); *IG* II² 971 (Skirophorion 140/39 BC); *I.Delos* 1505 (Thargelion 150/49 BC); *IG* II² 974 (Gamelion 137/6 BC); *IG* II² 977 (month unknown, 131/0 BC); *IG* II² 978 (Anthesteria, *c.* 130 BC); *SEG* 21, 468 (month unknown, *c.* 130 BC). The exception is D. 19.60 which shows the assembly meeting in Peiraieus to discuss naval matters in summertime (27th Skirophorion, 347/6 BC).

[42] See most recently Svenson-Evers (1996) 505–9.

Lykurgos, at Delphi during the time of the reconstruction of the temple of Apollo, and at Delos during the great boom in public building in the period of independence from 314 to 240 BC.[43] The Delian inscriptions also seem to show that the official *arkhitekton* was, as we would expect, recruited from the ranks of professional builders, since some of them appear to have state contracts before and possibly even while they are in office.[44]

At Athens the first epigraphic attestation of *arkhitektones* salaried by the state is in an inscription of 337/6 BC.[45] The *Athenaion Politeia* indicates that the official *arkhitektones* were elected by the popular assembly, probably from the beginning, since elected *arkhitektones* are mentioned in inscriptions from as early as 333/2 BC.[46] An Athenian inscription mentions official *arkhitektones* in the plural *(IG* II² 244), and different offices are known. One of the *arkhitektones* specialised in the upkeep of sanctuaries and related buildings. We have direct evidence of the ἀρχιτέκτων ὁ ἐπὶ τὰ ἱερὰ χειροτονούμενος 'the *arkhitekton* elected to look after sanctuaries' from 270/69 BC.[47] His colleagues were the ἀρχιτέκτονες οἱ ἐπὶ τὰς ναῦς (χειροτονούμενοι) 'the *arkhitektones* elected to look after the ships' (*Ath. Pol.* 46.1). We see an *arkhitekton* elected possibly on an ad hoc basis to take charge of a large construction project at Eleusis in 333/2 BC: he is explicitly called ὁ κεχειροτονημένος ἐπὶ τὸν οἰκοδομίαν '(the *arkhitekton*) elected to look after the construction' *(IG* II² 1673 with Clinton 1971: 100–1).

The earliest full reference to the *arkhitekton* elected to look after sanctuaries is the Athenian decree honouring Kallias of Sphettos,

[43] Delphi: see esp. Burford (1969); Jacquemin (1990). Delos: see esp. Lacroix (1914). For literature on the Athenian *arkhitekton,* see below.

[44] Lacroix (1914) 304; Burford (1969) 139; sceptical, Svenson-Evers (1996) 510.

[45] *IG* II² 244 (337/6) where 'the *arkhitektones* salaried by the city', τοὺς ἀρχιτέκτονας τοὺς παρὰ τῆς πόλεως μισθοφοροῦντας, appears twice (with supplements).

[46] Arist. *Ath. Pol.* 46.1; *IG* II² 1673 + *SEG* 32, 167 + *SEG* 34, 122, ll. 59–60 (see below). cf. *IG* II²463 (307/6 BC) ἀρχιτέκτ]ονα τὸν κεχειρο[τ]ονημένο[ν] ὑπ[ὸ το]ῦ δ[ήμου] 'the *arkhitekton* elected by the people'; *SEG* 28, 60.98 (270/69 BC); *SEG* 37, 89 (third century BC?), *IG* II² 900.12 (185/4 BC); *SEG* 32, 129.9–10 (*c.* 185 BC). At Delphi the *arkhitektones* were appointed by the assembly or council, and by the *hieropes* at Delos: Jacquemin (1990) 85.

[47] *SEG* 28, 60.98, cf. *SEG* 27, 89 (third century BC?), and the second century inscriptions *IG* II² 839.29, *IG* II² 840.13, 21, *IG* II² 841.14, *IG* II² 842.2; *SEG* 34, 95.6.

dated 270/69 BC. Here the *arkhitekton* is instructed to provide Kallias
with *prohedria* in all the contests sponsored by the city (*SEG* 28, 60,
ll. 96–9):

> εἶναι δ-
> ὲ καὶ προεδρίαν αὐτῶν ἐν ἅπασιν τοῖς ἀγῶσιν οἷς ἡ πόλις τ[ί]-
> θησιν καὶ τὸν ἀρχιτέκτονα τὸν ἐπὶ τὰ ἱερὰ χειρο<το>νούμεν[ο]-
> ν κατ<α>νέμειν αὐτῶι τὴν προεδρίαν.

May he have *prohedria* in all of the contests which the city sponsors and may
the *arkhitekton* elected to look after sanctuaries assign him *prohedria*.

The formula for providing seats or *prohedria* for persons honoured
by the Athenians is a familiar one, though in other decrees it is
attached to 'the *arkhitekton*' *simpliciter*, without specifying 'elected to
look after sanctuaries'. I assume it is the same office. We have eleven
Athenian inscriptions, dating from 331–324 to 185/4 BC, which name
the *arkhitekton* in a formulaic clause granting perpetual *prohedria*
or one-off occasional theatre seats:[48] The formula normally reads
A+B or B+C as follows:

A εἶναι δὲ / ὑπάρχειν + dat. pronoun	+ καὶ προεδρίαν	ἐν ἅπασιν τοῖς ἀγῶσιν (οἷς ἡ πόλις τίθησιν/ ἂν τιθεῖ)
B τὸν ἀρχιτέκτονα	+ κατανέμειν + dat. pronoun	+ τὴν προεδρίαν / (τὴν) θέαν / τὸν τόπον
C εἰς τὰ Διονύσια *vel sim.*		

As Demosthenes (18.28.5) and Aeschines (2.55) use the same formula in relation to a decree of 346 BC, we can conclude that this is
our earliest evidence for the *arkhitekton* to look after sanctuaries. As

---

[48] *Hesperia* 43.322–3, ll. 27–30 (B+C, 331–324 BC); *IG* II² 456 fr. b, 31–2 (B+C,
307/6 BC); *IG* II² 466 fr. b, 52–3 (B+C, 307/6 BC); *IG* II² 567 fr. b, 22–3 (B+C, *fin s IV a*;
SEG 21, 343.3–5 (A+B, *ex s IV a*); *IG* II² 500, 23–4 (A+B, 302/1 BC); *IG* II² 512 (= *SEG*
31, 83), 6–8 (A+B, *c.* 300 BC); *SEG* 14, 65. 41–3 (A+B, 271/0 BC); *IG* II² 792, 7–9
(A+B, *c.* 230 BC); *SEG* 32, 129. 9–10 (A+B, *c.* 185 BC); *IG* II² 900, frs. 1–b, 11–13 (A+B,
185/4 BC). Note that the formula B+C is replaced by A+B sometime between 307/6
and 302/1. General discussion in Henry (1983) 291–4.

the name implies, this *arkhitekton* had duties in connection with all or most of the sanctuaries in the city, not just the theatre. Inscriptions show him taking care of the shrine of the Hero Doctor, probably the shrine of Kodros, Neleus, and Basile, and possibly the shrine of Aphrodite Hegemone or Aphrodite Ourania.[49] Despite a long-standing scholarly tradition, then, the *arkhitekton*, as an elected and salaried public official, with duties extending beyond the theatre, to the maintenance of all Athenian sanctuaries, is far from being just another name for a theatre lessee.

Nonetheless there are some similarities in function between the *arkhitekton* and the *theatrones*. The *arkhitektones* mentioned by these decrees have a special connection with the theatre and are clearly in charge of the distribution of seats. Just as the theatre lessees at Peiraieus are responsible for giving free admission and *prohedria* to those to whom it was granted by the demesmen of Peiraieus, so in the Athenian theatre by the mid-fourth century BC it is the *arkhitekton*. Perhaps the *arkhitekton* was now also required to see to the collection of the two obols which Demosthenes mentions as the cost of an ordinary seat in the theatre. If so, Ulpian's claim that the cost of theatre tickets went to the *arkhitekton* is correct but anachronistic, insofar as it is ascribed to the time of Perikles, and misleading (some of the other sources on the *theorikon* correctly state that the ticket money went 'to the polis'). The money is certainly no part of the *arkhitekton's* personal remuneration, as has sometimes been supposed.[50] Official *arkhitektones* have a relatively modest salary of one to two drachmas per day, as we know from inscriptions from Athens, Delphi, and Delos.[51] It would be absurd to think that, for this particular job, Athens threw in, as some sort of perk, an annual bonus of several talents.

So then what became of the *theatron*-seller of the theatre of Dionysos once the *theatron* was built in stone and no longer needed

---

[49] *IG* II² 839, 29–30 (221/0 BC); *IG* II² 840, 13, 22–3 (late third century BC); *SEG* 19, 78 (239/8 BC); *SEG* 34, 95.7 (161/0 BC); Cf. *IG* II² 841, 14–15 (early second century BC); *IG* II² 842, 2 (mid-second century BC). See also Shear (1978) 58; Rhodes (1972) 95–6, 126.

[50] E.g. Kahrstedt (1969 (1937)) 312. Cf. Buchanan (1962) 86–7.

[51] Lacroix 1914 (303–9); Burford (1969)140–1; Jacquemin (1990) 85; Svenson-Evers (1996) 503–4.

to be assembled and dismantled for each festival season? As mentioned earlier, the literary and architectural evidence both indicate
that the theatre of Dionysos—and for our purposes in particular
its *theatron*—was built of wood until the construction of the theatre
called 'Lykurgan'. But the Lykurgan theatre is in part earlier than this
name implies, since it had been under construction for some time
before Lykurgos. Of this the *theatron* was perhaps the first part to be
completed. A pre-Lykurgan drainage canal contains reused blocks
from the platform of the late fifth-century *prohedria*.[52] Also the base
of a statue of Astydamas was built into the west analemma of the
so-called Lykurgan *theatron*, and this fact perhaps suggests a date of
completion, at latest, around 340 BC.[53] We can therefore date the
beginning of the construction of the stone *theatron* in Athens to
several years before 340 BC, indeed about the time, 348 BC, that the
arkhitekton first appears distributing seats in the theatre.

I suggest that the need for leasing the theatre disappeared with the
building of a permanent *theatron*.[54] At this point the *arkhitekton* took
direct charge of the maintenance of the theatre. If we can compare
the situation at Delos and Epidauros we find plenty of epigraphic
evidence to show that the contracts for the construction and maintenance of the stone theatres, and in particular the stone *theatra*,
were tendered and paid directly by the *hieropoioi* or *epimeletai* upon
approval by the official *arkhitekton*.[55] There was no need for theatre
lessees or any other sort of middleman. Inscriptions are particularly
informative about work on the stone *theatron* in Delos, which was
underway by 305 BC.[56] Several of the accounts of the *hieropoioi*

---

[52] See Appendix 116–118; Goette (1995a) 25–6.

[53] Goette (1995a) 30. There are further indications that the *theatron* was completed around 330 BC before the beginning of building on the Panathenaic stadium.
See the inscription published by Heisserer and Moysey (1986) and also *IG* II² 351,
16–18 (*IG* II² 351 + 624 = *Syll.*³ 288 = Tod II, no. 198), date of *c.* 330/29, which
mentions provision of oxen for construction of the Panathenaic *theatron*. For the
connection between the building of the Panathenaic stadium and the work on the
theatre see Lauter and Lauter (1988) and, following them, Goette (1995a) 46 n. 81
and (1999) 25. On this inscription see most recently Dillery (2002).

[54] The reference to the *theatronai* in Theophrastos' *Characters* 30.6 is not evidence
for the survival of leasing arrangements in the main Athenian theatre. See above,
p. 96.

[55] See esp. Delos: *IG* II² XI 2, 150A, 10–13 (297 BC), with Vallois (1944) 231–2.

[56] Vallois (1944) 231–2.

record payments made, at the bidding of the *epimeletai* and the *arkhitekton*, to individuals who laboured on various parts of the *theatron*.[57] We have only one comparable account, from Epidauros. The accounts of the Epidaurian building commission for the theatre record payments for the laying of tiers of stone seats (*krepidia*), the construction of stone chairs (*thokoi*), probably intended for the *prohedria*, in addition to work done on the stagebuilding.[58] As at Delos, the work at Epidauros regularly requires the oversight and specific approval of the official *arkhitekton*.[59]

CONCLUSION

In sum, we know of leasing arrangements only for theatres built of wood. The main benefit of the lease is, for the state, income from the theatre without the regular expense and trouble of laying benches in the *theatron* for each festival season. The benefit for the lessees was the right to collect admission charges, thereby recovering the cost of the lease and chalking up what probably amounted to a handsome profit.[60] This arrangement fits well with the layout of the *theatron*

[57] *IG* XI 2, 142, 27 (305 BC); *IG* XI 2, 150 A, 10–13 (297 BC), with Vallois (1944) 231; *IG* XI 2, 163A, 24–6, (276 BC); *IG* XI 2, 203A, 82–8, 95–7 (269 BC); *IG* XI 2, 287A, 92–3, 94–6, 120 (250 BC). Cf. *ID* 291, b14.17, 30–1, c 16 + e15 (247 BC), with Vallois (1944) 233 n. 5; *I.Délos* 290, 176–92 (246 BC).

[58] Peek (1970–2) no. 19 (with Burford 1966: 296–300) A 8–9, 24–5, B 4–12, C 8–14 (Epidauros ?350 BC). For the meaning of *krepidia* and *thokoi* cf. *IG* XI 2, 203 A 95; Burford (1966) 299; Hellmann (1992) 149–50, 242–3.

[59] Burford (1966) 297; Burford (1969) 138–45; Svenson-Evers (1996) 415–28.

[60] In the case of the Peiraieus lease, the cost of the lease is 3,000 drachmas to which 300 were added out of civic zeal. Behrend (1970) 88 n. 178 reckons the income as follows. The theatre will not have had a larger capacity than the 'new theatre' at Zea, therefore no more than 5,000. At two obols a head, 9,900 paying customers, so at least two days of performances, are required to cover the initial outlay. He assumes that the costs for construction and upkeep amount to many times the cost of the lease, so that the lessees need at least ten days of capacity audiences to make a profit. But the costs of assembling wooden benches in the inscriptions from Delos and Delphi (two obols, two drachmas, six staters, or in the case of an entire theatre, twenty-eight staters) indicate that construction costs to the lessees were probably nowhere near as high as Behrend imagines. We do not know how many days the Dionysia at Peiraieus lasted. In 127/6 BC the ephebes who participated in the

which is rectilinear or trapezoidal in all early theatres. When theatres were built in stone, there was no need for such leasing arrangements and construction, maintenance, and repair now fell to the responsibility of the *arkhitekton,* or a commission advised by the *arkhitekton.*

It is hardly surprising, under these conditions, that the leasing arrangements came to an end. The need to construct the *theatron* was eliminated by the permanent theatre. The stone architecture reduced maintenance costs to a minimum. It also provided the state with vastly greater income from seat sales in a theatre with double the capacity of its predecessor. The state therefore had nothing to lose and everything to gain in discontinuing the former leasing arrangement. Perhaps the financial wizard Lykurgos was no less interested in the income the theatre brought to the state coffers than in the architectural glorification of his city. For although the maintenance of the theatres passed from private to public hands, admission fees certainly continued, despite the loss of their original justification.[61] This contradiction perhaps added some stimulus for the introduction of the *theorikon,* which is only directly attested after 343 BC. In any case, the appearance of the *arkhitekton* in Athens by 346 BC should be taken as evidence that the building of the stone *theatron* was well underway. Demes such as Peiraieus and Akharnai, and many foreign cities, like those of Euboea, continued to make use of leasing arrangements for their theatres until the end of the fourth

'Introduction' and sacrifice to Dionysos stayed for four days. There were at least three dithyrambic choruses ([Plu.] *Moral. (Ten Orators)* 842a) and tragedy and comedy (Law of Euegoros in D. 21.10). Assuming four days and admission paid upon each entry, one Dionysia would easily repay the lease (2 obols × 5,000 × 4 = 6,666 drachmas, twice the cost of the lease). The lease may have been longer than one year or one festival season. Aristotle *(Ath. Pol.* 47.4) gives ten years as the norm in Athens for the leasing of a *temenos.* Behrend (1970) 116, cf. Rhodes (1981) 556–7, also mentions a twenty-year lease of a *temenos* (though this is 418/17 BC and involves the planting of olive trees); 'exceptional' leases of thirty and forty years are also mentioned. The Euboean decree (above, pp. 95–6), however, implies that an annual lease was customary in the Euboean cities, and we must reckon with the possibility that other events in the theatre, closely following the Dionysia, might add to the lessee's income.

[61] D. 18.28.5. It is also clear from the Samian decree honouring Polos: (*SEG* 1, 362 = *MDAI(A)* 44, 16 no. 7, *c.* 306 BC) that Samos charged admission to its theatre and freely disposed of its revenue.

century and probably until they rebuilt their theatres in stone.⁶²
Through the influence of comedy, however, the reputation of the
theatre-lessees for greed survived as a literary topos even when
wooden theatres were a rarity, and on the evidence of Nikarkhos'
poem, even into the first century AD.

---

⁶² The earliest mention of the *arkhitekton* in relation to Peiraieus is in 307/6 BC.
This is a decree of the Athenian assembly granting honours to the people of
Kolophon. Among the many other honours, it includes in the last line a directive that
'the *arkhitekton* is to assign [the ambassadors of the Kolophonians] a seat at the
Dionysia in Peiraieus'. This is clearly the Athenian '*arkhitekton* elected to look after
sanctuaries' and the Athenians are exercising their usual central control over the
Peiraean Dionysia (Jones 2004: 134–5, 154). Contrast the wording of the Peiraean
decree granting *prohedria* in *IG* II² 1214, where there is no mention of the *arkhitekton*. The reason why the Athenians assign seats at the Peiraean Dionysia rather than
the City festivals has to do, presumably, with the date of the ambassadors' visit. The
decree is dated to Maimakterion, the month before the Peiraieus Dionysia. It is
interesting, however, that the Peiraieus lease makes no provision for seats assigned by
Athenian officials.

An Archaeological Appendix

Hans Rupprecht Goette

The Classical theatre of Dionysos was almost completely built over by the new, greatly enlarged building that was finished during the time of Lykurgos, perhaps in 329 BC. Little evidence remains with which to reconstruct the Classical theatre; thus, the reconstruction presented here must be hypothetical. Future excavation in the area of the *parodoi* and the *theatron* (i.e. *koilon*) may produce a more detailed picture of the theatre of Dionysos of *c.* 400 BC.

The following archaeological evidence provides the basis for the architectural reconstruction represented in Fig. 1:

(1) Three short walls made of Acropolis limestone ('SM 1, 2, and 4') were built north of the late Archaic temple of Dionysos on a higher level of the slope. One of these walls, which is curved ('SM 1'), prompted Doerpfeld to reconstruct a circular *orchestra* already for the late Archaic/early Classical period. But, in fact, much evidence (see the following) makes it clear that the *orchestra* was not circular. As we shall see, the three short walls ('SM 1, 2, 4') should be connected to one continuous terrace wall (Fig. 1 nos. 1–3), which divided the level of the temple from that of the theatre. It served the same purpose as the later 'wall H', which was erected almost at the same place.

(2) The *prohedria* was made of rectangular stone slabs with anathyrosis at their sides and can be dated to the late fifth century as indicated by the letter forms cut on their front. Thus the *prohedria* was a straight row of seats or adjacent supports for seats, yielding a straight line for the lowest step(s) of the *theatron*. Since most of the early theatres in the Attic demes (especially Trakhones-Euonymon) show the central part of the *theatron* flanked by wings, some stones of the Classical *prohedria* in Athens might have been situated at the sides of the *orchestra* as well, which therefore had an overall rectangular (or trapezoidal) form.

(3) Because open theatres collect much rain water, a drainage system had to be installed. There is a water channel, which leads from the east side of the *orchestra* in a southeastern oblique direction straight down the slope and out of the Dionysos *temenos* in the area of the later *propylon* to the sanctuary. Some lateral stones and some of the cover slabs of the northern portion of

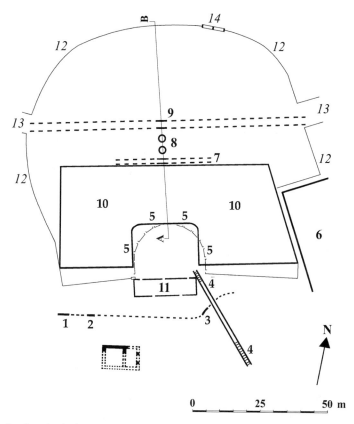

1–3: late Archaic terrace wall: 1: wall SM 4; 2: wall SM 2; 3: wall SM 1
4: water channel (drainage for the orchestra)
5: *prohedria*
6: Odeion of Perikles
7: rock cutting for theatre access (or foundation for back wall of theatre)
8: two wells belonging to a house
9: ancient road (later Peripatos)
10: reconstructed *theatron* of the Classical theatre
11: reconstructed *skene* of the Classical theatre
A–B: Doerpfeld's excavation trench through the *theatron*
12: outline of the 'Lykurgan' *theatron*
13: entry points of the Peripatos
14: choregic monument of Thrasyllos (320/19 BC) at the 'katatome'

Fig. 1 Reconstructed plan of the Classical Theatre of Dionysos with some 'Lykurgan' additions (bold: Classical; italics: 'Lykurgan').

this subterranean drainage channel once belonged to the Classical theatre's straight *prohedria*; thus at least this portion of the channel was built some time between the construction of the *prohedria* (*c.* 400 BC) and the inception of the new (rounded) theatre in the 360s B.C. Because one of these blocks was incorporated into the Lykurgan *theatron* wall at its south-western end, the construction of the channel most probably dates to the end of this four-decade period. The earlier channel starts on a lower level than the rounded channel of the Lykurgan theatre, to which it was connected when the new theatre was used. It is not clear, however, how far the earlier straight channel ran to the north. The pavement of the circular *orchestra* of Lykurgan times lies mostly on top of the levelled rock; according to Doerpfeld's excavation, few ancient cuttings were made into the rocky ground beneath the *orchestra*, and it is not clear if these were connected to the Classical drainage channel. The contemporary theatre in Trakhones might assist in the reconstruction: here the water drainage—a well, not a channel—was situated at the corner of the *theatron*, close to the *skene* and the east *parodos*. The same layout may have existed in the theatre of Dionysos in Athens.

(4) The east side of the Lykurgan theatre has an irregular shape, i.e. it runs parallel to the rectangular outline of the Odeion of Perikles. Since this Odeion was built later (mid-fifth century) than the theatre of Dionysos of *c.* 500 BC, and since it was connected to the theatre by the fact that the *proagon* was held in it, it is probable that its layout was designed with the old theatre in mind. Because the Odeion is parallel to the later Lykurgan theatre's *theatron* it is likely that the east side of the earlier theatre of the fifth century was parallel also. The reconstruction drawing (Fig. 1) shows the hypothetical east end in an oblique line, starting in the south at the point where the Lykurgan *theatron* terminates in an angle and ending in the north at the line of a rock cutting (Fig. 1 no. 7; Fig. 2).

(5) The excavation trench made by Doerpfeld through the *theatron* reveals a narrow, horizontal cutting in the bedrock about ten metres above the *orchestra* level (Fig. 2). This was thought to be the foundation of a *diazoma* of the Lykurgan theatre, but recent research by M. Korres indicates that this was not the case, so the cutting must have been for another purpose.

At about ten metres up the slope, Doerpfeld found two wells belonging to Classical houses, and cut into the bedrock above them an ancient road that again runs in a straight line. This 'antiker Weg'—hypothetically extended at the east and west—connects the access points of the later Lykurgan (curved) way through the theatre, and so the straight road of the Classical period was clearly already part of the Peripatos. Because there are wells indicating

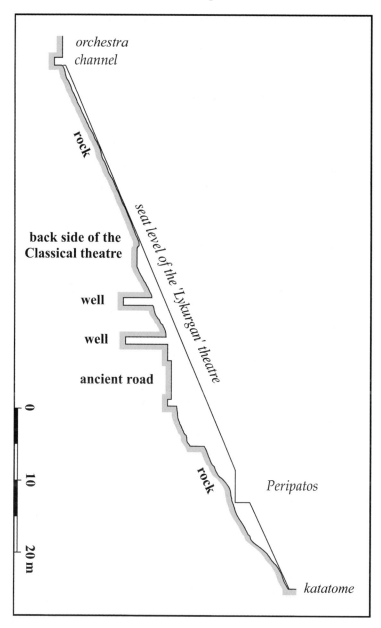

Fig. 2 Doerpfeld's excavation trench (A–B in Fig. 1) through the *theatron* (bold: Classical; italics: 'Lykurgan').

houses south of the road down the slope, the Classical theatre could not have reached to this higher level. It is probable that the narrower rock cutting (Fig. 1 no. 7) below the wells (nos. 8–9) marks the north boundary of the Classical *theatron*, either as the foundations for a back wall or, more probable, for another means of access to the theatre in addition to the *parodoi*. And because the 'antiker Weg' (no. 9) is laid out in a straight line and the cuttings for this road and the one (no. 7) below the wells are similar, one can conclude that the north side of the *theatron* also ran in a straight line and thus was parallel to the *prohedria* row at the centre of the Classical *orchestra*.

Unfortunately, no archaeological evidence exists for the layout of the *theatron* to the west. It may have joined the lower front of the *theatron* to the higher back with a 90° wall (as reconstructed in Fig. 1), in which case the *theatron* would have been similar to that in the theatre at Thorikos. But it is also possible that it mirrored the east side of the *theatron*, that is, that it was connected to the front and the back side of the *theatron* at an oblique angle.

The thickness and the exact inclination of the layer of earth on the rocky slope is also important for the reconstruction of the Classical theatre, but archaeological remains are of little help in this matter. In the area of the earlier theatre's *theatron*, the Lykurgan stone seats were set upon the bedrock (Fig. 2). But the wooden benches of the Classical theatre were surely placed on a layer of earth, which must have been levelled to create a stepped slope as is still preserved in several Attic deme theatres, for example, at Rhamnous or Trakhones. How thick this layer of earth once was; how much earth was removed for the construction of the Lykurgan stone *theatron*; and at which point between the end of the drainage channel and the Lykurgan *prohedria* the stepped slope began, cannot be determined with our present knowledge. Thus, it is not clear where the straight row of the Classical *prohedria* stones was once situated (in regard to the rounded *prohedria*). They may have been in line with the central throne of the later *prohedria* (as shown in Fig. 1), but it is also possible that they were placed a few metres further south of the position of the Lykurgan marble throne of the priest of Dionysos; then the *theatron* would have been broader (in a NS direction) and the Classical *orchestra* narrower than shown in Fig. 1, in which case there would have been more space for wooden benches as proposed by the reconstruction (Fig. 3). However it may have been, it is clear that the Classical theatre provided much less capacity for seats than its later incarnation, maybe just a little more than one-third of the *c.* 17,000 stone seats of the later rounded *theatron* belonging to the Lykurgan theatre.

Fig. 3 Model reconstruction of the Classical Theatre of Dionysos (photo courtesy of the Theatermuseum, Munich). The model shows the stone steps of the Classical *prohedria* and behind them the wooden benches on the slope in a straight line along three sides of the rectangular *orchestra*. The ninety-degree angle at which the left (east) side of this *theatron* is attached to the middle part is improbable, because this wing was parallel to the Odeion of Perikles and thus in an oblique line to the centre of the *theatron* (see Fig. 1).

5

Choregic Monuments and the Athenian Democracy*

Hans Rupprecht Goette

The Athenian democracy financed a substantial range of benefits for the citizens and the polis, including cultural events, by means of private sponsorship, that is, through the agency of wealthy citizens designated as *choregoi*.[1] Such sponsorship took many different forms—for example the trierarchs, the gymnasiarchs, and the *choregoi* for many festivals and competitions. This chapter is mostly concerned with the votive offerings erected by *choregoi* after victories in dithyrambic competitions in the Athenian theatre. A careful examination of the types of these choregic monuments, especially in their monumental architectural form,[2] indicates that they provided a forum not only for remarkable innovation, but also offered a means for leading citizens to proclaim their importance to the democratic community. As we will see, this role of the publicly endorsed victory monument, the result of private achievement, takes many forms and changes over time.

---

* I would like to thank the organiser of the conference, Peter Wilson, for the invitation to attend the interesting and stimulating symposium in Oxford and for his improvements of a draft of this article; and Judith M. Barringer for her helpful comments to this paper and her corrections of the English.
[1] For the bibliography, see Wilson (2000) 395–420.
[2] Goette (1989) 96–101.

I

Before examining the larger choregic dedications, the true architectural monuments, we might take a few moments to look quickly at four groups of minor choregic dedications or at least votive offerings that can be connected with the Athenian *choregia* of theatre productions, rather than those for the dithyrambic competitions.

The first group are votive reliefs. Within the huge number of such sculptures only a few examples can be securely identified as choregic dedications—some on the basis of their inscriptions, some by means of their images. One such example is a fragment of a Classical marble relief[3] found in the sanctuary of Dionysos in Ikarion where theatre productions are well attested;[4] there is a depiction of masks and a partly preserved inscription. Other reliefs of this kind with masks can be connected with the practice of dedicating images of theatre properties, although no votive inscriptions are preserved on any of these.[5]

In some rare cases a votive relief that is dedicated to Dionysos or Apollo presents a group of humans, a chorus, approaching the god— the leader of the chorus is very likely the *choregos*, who probably dedicated the relief.[6]

Closely connected to these votives is another kind of choregic monument, painted images. Unfortunately none of these so-called *pinakes* dedicated by *choregoi* have been preserved in the archaeological record,[7] but we learn of such offerings that were dedicated even by well-known *choregoi*, including important politicians, from ancient literary sources. The earliest known example is a dedication

---

[3] Athens, Nat. Mus. inv. 4531: *SEG* 32, 248; Wilson (2000) 241 fig. 24; Scholl (2002a) 553 no. 414 with fig.; Scholl (2002b) 32 n. 131 fig. 24.

[4] Biers and Boyd (1982) 1–18; Goette (2001) 262–4.

[5] Votive reliefs: (a) Athens, Nat. Mus. inv. 1750; (b) Cagliari, Museo Nazionale inv. 10918; (c) Munich, Glyptothek inv. 552: Scholl and Vierneisel (2002) 32 figs. 1, 5, 23, 25.

[6] See again the votive relief in Munich (n. 5 above) and others in Paris and elsewhere: Voutiras (1991–2) 29–55 and figs. 1–9; Scholl and Vierneisel (2002) 23 fig. 8.

[7] Reisch (1890) 116; Wilson (2000) 216, 242 summarises the bibliography since 1890; Scholl and Vierneisel (2002) 28 n. 111f.

from the year 476 BC when Themistokles, as a *choregos* for tragedy composed by Phrynichos, set up such a picture somewhere in Athens; although we do not know its location, it may have been in the sanctuary of Dionysos. Even centuries later such a *pinax* could be recognised as a dedication of Themistokles because of the choregic inscription and an epigram on it, as Plutarch tells us.[8] Further, Aristotle informs us that an Athenian named Thrasippos served as both *choregos* and *aulos*-player for the same production and was included in the depiction on such a *pinax*.[9] Thus, it seems likely that this was the norm: the *choregos* was included together with the participants of the theatrical production in the images on *pinakes*.[10]

Representations of this sort may have been predecessors to the practice of depicting actors or poets, identifiable by theatrical props, on Attic gravestones of the fourth century BC.[11] We will have occasion to refer to the relationship between choregic and funerary monuments again later in this paper; it is enough here to note that the production of Attic gravestones was brought to an end in 317 BC through a law against private luxury, while the choregic monuments, even the huge architectural ones, continued to be set up through Hellenistic times.

II

A second group of choregic dedications comprises herms, a type of monument closely connected with Dionysos Lenaios whose cult image was often depicted as a herm. Although no extant herm is identifiable as a choregic dedication, we possess bases on which

---

[8]   Plu. *Them.* 5.4–5.

[9]   Arist. *Pol.* 1341 a 35.

[10]   The *pinax* from the cave of Pitsa near Corinth in the National Museum of Athens (inv. 16464) may give some idea of such images, although a scene of a sacrifice is depicted: Kolonnas (2003) 227–8 no. 107 with colour fig.

[11]   Examples: a relief fragment in Lyme Park (Scholl 1995: 213–38 figs. 1–6) and another one from Salamis in the Peiraieus Museum (Scholl 1995: 230 n. 82 fig. 14; Steinhauer (2001) 301 fig. 447).

herms once stood, which are clearly dedications in honour of choregic victories: the marble bases in front of the Stoa Basileios (Royal Stoa), which were set up after victories at the Lenaia, are well known cases.[12] It is noteworthy that these herms were dedicated not by *choregoi* but by an Archon Basileus who was the state official in charge of the Lenaia;[13] he names the *choregos* in the inscription. These two herm bases are not the only examples of such dedications in connection with the Lenaian *choregia*: immediately next to them, in front of the Stoa Basileios, is a double throne dated to the fifth or, given that it is made of porous stone, perhaps even the late sixth century BC.[14] On the surfaces of both seats is a cutting for fixing a herm, so it is clear that the double throne served in a secondary capacity as a base for the two herm dedications. While we cannot be certain that this double throne with herms is a choregic dedication —an inscription does not exist—several factors do strongly suggest as much: the throne itself, which was a form used in the *prohedria* in Attic theatres;[15] its placement in front of the Stoa Basileios; and the use of herms, which serve as choregic dedications immediately adjacent to the throne. Like those, this double throne may have been a dedication by an Archon Basileus because it was placed close to his office.

III

As might be expected, inscriptions on bases attest that *choregoi* also dedicated large-scale statues, a third category of choregic dedications. Within this group is the well-known base of Sokrates,[16] who was

---

[12] *Agora* I.7168 and 7185: Camp (1986) 53 fig. 35.

[13] Wilson (2000) 30–1 fig. 1.

[14] Camp (1986) 53. This material was principally used during the sixth century BC. From about 500 BC on, Pentelic marble was the normal material as can be seen— mostly in the same form of a double throne—at various Attic theatres (see n. 15 below).

[15] Goette (1995a) 5, 14, 16 with plates 2.1, 3 for the double seats in Ikarion, Rhamnous, and Trakhones, all made of (different kinds of) marble.

[16] Mitsos (1965); *IG* I³ 969; Wilson (2000) 83 n. 140, 131–2 fig. 6.

a victor in a tragic competition at the deme Dionysia of Anagyrous in the late fifth century; the marble base with its much discussed inscription naming the poet and the chorus-members on the front side was found at Vari in Attica. On the top are two holes for affixing the feet of a bronze statue, one foot slightly in front of the other in contrapposto. Unfortunately there is not enough evidence to reconstruct anything more about the statue's appearance, but it seems probable that it was a short-clad or nude male figure since there is no trace, not even a weathered surface, of a long garment on the base.

Another inscribed base[17] from the same area, Vari, attests to another choregic statue, now lost. The inscription tells us that the statue was a joint dedication for two victories in tragedy and two victories in comedy in a Rural Dionysia of the deme of Halai Aixonides. The top of the marble base has a concave cutting to receive a circular tenon of a plinth, the usual support for a marble statue.

In addition to these more regular forms of base for choregic statue dedications, we find an example of an unusual kind of a base: a small inscribed pillar[18] dedicated around 350 BC by a father and his two sons in the sanctuary of Dionysos in Ikarion after they won a tragedy competition in that deme theatre. Because this narrow base, which was at least two metres high, has a top surface with anathyrosis there must have been a plinth of stone as the crowning member. And because of the large height of this base and its small rectangular plinth above, I propose a small bronze tripod as the votive of the three demesmen instead of a statuette, which would have been set too high in respect to its size.

A much larger, probably choregic dedication comprises three huge (160 cm × 80 cm) reliefs[19] found together in Athens (in Regillis Street), which seem to have been part of a single monument. A. Scholl[20] convincingly proposes that the reliefs decorated a base

---

[17] *IG* II² 3091; Wilson (2000) 248 n. 163.

[18] *IG* II² 3095; Goette (1995a) 10 n. 3; Wilson (2000) 249.

[19] Athens, Nat. Mus. inv. 3496–8: Kaltsas (2002) 288 no. 609 (illustration).

[20] Scholl (2002) 548 figs. 2, 3; no. 412 (illustration); Scholl and Vierneisel (2002) 24–7 nn. 87–9 figs. 10–12.

that once supported a (now lost) statue, probably of Dionysos, as all three depictions are thematically closely connected with this god: the panther frequently accompanies the god, and the production of wine by satyrs is a Dionysiac theme. Even the bull led by Nike may refer to a dithyrambic victory because Simonides and Pindar relate that the poet could receive a sacrificial bull for the team's festival meal; contemporary vases also show the bull together with the prize tripod, sometimes with Nike.[21]

Not every choregic dedication was made to commemorate a theatrical victory; such dedications were also made in other contexts and sometimes simply commemorated the performance of a liturgy (and not necessarily a victory). For example, a marble figure of Themis from a small treasury in the sanctuary of Nemesis in Rhamnous was dedicated by a *choregos*, as indicated by the inscribed base.[22] This work, impressive for its size, by the sculptor Chairestratos, dates to around 300 BC (as adduced from style and prosopography) and was dedicated by the Rhamnousian demesman Megakles who served in his community as gymnasiarch and *choregos* of a comedy.

IV

Another category of dedications made by *choregoi*, the fourth, leads us back to the god of the theatre, Dionysos: one group of votive sculptures are marble phalloi, ubiquitous throughout the ancient Greek world. The Hellenistic monument of Karystios in the sanctuary of Dionysos on the island of Delos[23] is a well-known and frequently mentioned impressive example of this kind of dedication.

---

[21] Pin. *O.* 13; Simon. *epigr.* 27 (P), 145 (B); Reisch (1890) 64; Wilson (2000); Scholl and Vierneisel (2002) 24 nn. 83–6. Not far from the Street of Tripods, a big relief with the depiction of a bull was found, which Miller (1970) thinks was part of a choregic monument; the relief is now stored in the Roman agora.

[22] Athens, Nat. Mus. inv. 231: *SEG* 40, 148; Kaltsas (2002) 272–3 no. 568 (illustration); Petrakos (1999) 99–100 no. 120 (illustration).

[23] *IG* XI 4, 1148; Bizard and Leroux (1907) 498–511, figs. 18–20, pl. xiii.

But there is one earlier example in Athens as well, possibly from the Classical period. From the area of the sanctuary of Dionysos[24] comes a marble sculpture, which combines a phallos with a feline, a sculpture that may have been erected on a base somewhere in or around the *temenos*.

V

Concluding this brief survey is a series of rectangular or three-sided bases for tripods, which served as victory monuments of dithyrambic competitions. As already mentioned, the victorious *choregos* of a dithyramb competition received a bronze tripod and an ivy wreath as prizes from the state of Athens. The *choregos* was then entitled to display the bronze trophy publicly on a marble base on which his name was inscribed even preceding that of the victorious poet or *aulos*-player. The chorus' tribe (*phyle*) was also inscribed on the base; so too was the name of the eponymous archon of Athens, which permits us to date these monuments to the exact year.[25]

The bronze tripods were fixed on the surfaces of marble bases with dowels and are the most frequent variety of choregic dedications that commemorate victories in dithyrambic competitions. Most of the bases are without any sculptural decoration, but some are decorated with reliefs; depictions of a winged Nike and Dionysos himself are well-attested images (Fig. 4).[26]

Other bases for bronze tripods stand to a remarkable height because they appear atop tall columns topped by three-sided capitals

---

[24] Dionysos theatre inv. NK 2253: Buschor (1928) figs. 29–30.

[25] *IG* II² 3027–62, 3073–89; Wilson (2000) 21–5, 199–235.

[26] E.g. the tripod base with two winged Nikai and a Dionysos, Athens, Nat. Mus. inv. 1463: Travlos (1971) 568 fig. 712; Kaltsas (2002) 244–5 no. 511 (illustration); Scholl and Vierneisel (2002) 27 figs. 13–14. There is a Roman imperial copy of this base in a private collection, once on loan to Basel, Antikenmuseum: Berger (1983). Another example of a marble tripod base decorated with reliefs, in this case a votive offering to Asklepios: Beschi (1969).

Fig. 4 Marble tripod base for supporting choregic tripod, with Dionysos and Nikai (Victories) in relief, found on the Street of Tripods.

(Fig. 5, nos. 3a–c).[27] These choregic dedications are already architectural in nature, even if they are merely isolated elements, and thus provide a transition to the main topic of this paper, architectural monuments erected by choregic victors.

[27] The following three tripod bases of this type are well known:

(a) at the southeast corner of the theatre of Dionysos' east koilon (fig. 5 no. 5e), set up by Drakontides in 175/4 BC: *IG* II² 3088; Amandry (1976) 28–32 figs. 12–13 (during the recent restoration of the site, a part of the unfluted column was erected and the capital was set on top of it); (b) above the *katatome* and the Thrasyllos monument (see below n. 32) in front of the Acropolis south wall (fig. 5 no. 3a): *IG* II² 3168; Amandry (1976) 79–87; Amandry (1997) 446–59; (c) next (east) to (b) (fig. 5 no. 3b): Amandry (1976) 79–87; Amandry (1997) 446–59; (d) west of (b) and (c) there was a third column which is lost; the only evidence for it is the cutting in the bedrock for its foundations (fig. 5 no. 3c): Amandry (1997) 455 fig. 8d. A few metres below, about eighty metres west of the Thrasyllos monument and on the same level with it, is a three-sided capital without an inscription; it lies in an ancient cutting for a choregic monument (see below n. 42 fig. 11) to which it does not belong. This capital, made of dark blueish-grey marble, may have crowned the now totally lost column, which was disassembled and reused, while the special form of capital was useless for the secondary purpose.

Other such tripod monuments were erected in sanctuaries with theatres outside of Athens as well, for example in the Amphiareion of Oropos: Amandry (1974) 231–2 figs. 43–5; Amandry and Ducat (1973) 35–6 fig. 19.

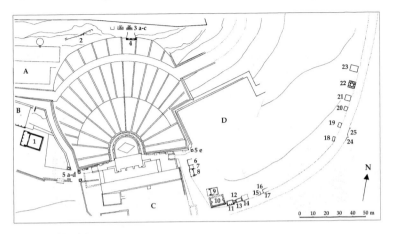

A   Asklepieion
B   Stoa of Eumenes
C   Sanctuary of Dionysos with temples and stoa
D   Odeion of Perikles
1   Choregic monument of Nikias
2   Rock cuttings for choregic monument
3   a–c Three columns belonging to tripod dedications
4   Choregic monument of Thrasyllos and his son Thrasykles
5   a–d Four foundations of columns for tripod dedications
     e   Column for the tripod dedication of Drakontides
6–25 Foundations of choregic monuments along the Street of Tripods
        11   Doric stoa
        22   Choregic monument of Lysikrates

Fig. 5 Plan of the sanctuary of Dionysos and adjacent areas.

VI

The victors' tripods were displayed in the precinct of Dionysos and
the immediate vicinity of the theatre of Dionysos (Figs. 5–6). But the
possibility existed, and was frequently exercised, to place the tripod
prominently along the festival road, which ran from the entrance of
the *temenos* of Dionysos to the Archaic agora and all around the
Acropolis before joining the Panathenaic way at the Eleusinion near

Fig. 6 Overview of the sanctuary of Dionysos from the southeast.

the Classical agora.[28] Because of the great number of tripods erected here, this street was called 'Tripod Street' by ancient authors, such as Pausanias (1.20.1). He described the road thus: 'A road leads away from the Prytaneion which is called Tripod Street. The area is named after the temples (*naoi megaloi*) which are, for this purpose, quite large, surmounted by bronze tripods and housing remarkable works of art. Among them is also a satyr of which Praxiteles is said to have been particularly proud.'

[28] *RE Suppl.* VIII (1956) 961–80 s.v. Tripodes (Riemann); Travlos (1971) 566–8 figs. 709–13; Choremi-Spetsieri (1994); Schnurr (1995); Knell (2000) 148–66; Hintzen-Bohlen (1977) 56–62; Greco (2001).

Fig. 7 Model of the sanctuary of Dionysos.

In this passage Pausanias describes a number of tripod bases that were not only simple marble blocks, but he also says—and this is particularly interesting for our discussion—that these bases were in the form of temples (*naoi*). This brings us to the architecture of a number of lavish choregic dedications.

Three such monuments are well known. In the year 335/4, the *choregos* Lysikrates erected a small round building on Tripod Street (Fig. 5 no. 22; Figs. 8, 15).[29] Except for the front, it was closed by large, rounded stone slabs. Corinthian capitals are used here for the first time in antiquity on the exterior of a building, and its almost completely closed drum with an extended open front in the inter-columniation high above the street level is an unusual design as well. Since it was later used as a monastery library, this monument, familiar to every visitor to Athens, has survived the centuries almost

---

[29] *IG* II² 3042; *RE Suppl.* VIII (1956) 266–347 s.v. Lysikrates-Monument (Riemann); Travlos (1971) 348–51 figs. 450–2; Bauer (1977); Amandry (1976) 71–9; Amandry (1997) 463–87; Wilson (2000) 219–26 figs. 12–14; Alemdar (2000); Knell (2000) 149–59; Scholl (2002) 551 no. 411 (illustration).

Fig. 8a The choregic monument of Lysikrates with open front in the intercolumniation facing the road.

Fig. 8b The choregic monument of Lysikrates reconstructed to show the bronze prize tripod secured above the akroterion on the roof.

intact, while another one[30]—still extant in medieval times and called the 'Lantern of Diogenes'—was later demolished. The Dilettanti Stuart and Revett still saw some marble fragments of its architecture in the late eighteenth century; one of these, today in the storerooms of the Acropolis Museum,[31] may be recognised in a slightly curved block decorated with a tripod in relief; it is therefore similar to the reliefs above the large stone slabs on the Lysikrates monument.

The second well-known example of a large choregic offering is that of Thrasyllos (Fig. 5 no. 4; Figs. 6–7, 9).[32] In front of a cave, in the

---

[30] *RE Suppl.* VIII (1956) 269.863–4; Wilson (2000) 234 n. 114.
[31] Inv. 7211 (2855): Walter (1923) 118 no. 260 (illustration).
[32] *IG* II² 3056 and 3083; Travlos (1971) 562–5 figs. 704–8; Townsend (1985); Amandry (1997) 459–60; Knell (2000) 159–61; Wilson (2000) 229–33 figs. 17–20.

Fig. 9 *Katatome* (vertical rock cutting) above the theatre of Dionysos with a reconstruction of the choregic monument of Thrasyllos (right) and an indication of the placement of another choregic monument set into a rock cutting (left).

vertically levelled surface of the Acropolis rock above the theatre of Dionysos, he built an impressive façade, consisting of three pillars bearing an inscribed architrave and frieze. The centre of the frieze shows the ivy wreath surrounded by a number of olive wreaths that Thrasyllos received for his victory. His prize tripod, together with a statue of Dionysos,[33] which was dedicated later by his equally victorious son, once surmounted the structure. Pausanias tells us that there was a depiction of the myth of Apollo and Artemis killing the

[33] London, British Museum 432: Smith (1892) 257–9 no. 432.

Fig. 10 Reconstruction of the façade of the choregic monument of Nikias.

Niobids decorating the narrow interior of the building; it must have been either a painting or a relief. The entire monument survived until 1827 and was recorded in several etchings before it was considerably damaged. But since almost all the architectural members of it survive in fragmentary form, it is now undergoing reconstruction.

In the same year as Thrasyllos, in 320/19 BC, the Athenian Nikias erected a small temple[34] with a six-columned front west of, and next to, the theatre of Dionysos to commemorate his victory in the boys' dithyramb competition (Fig. 5 no. 1; Figs. 6–7, 10). The entire superstructure above the foundations was dismantled in the third century AD and the blocks incorporated in the fortification wall of the Acropolis, in the so-called Beulé-gate. A careful examination of the building elements allows a complete reconstruction (Fig. 10).[35] Here we see for the first time that the term *naos* used by Pausanias is indeed justified because the monument looks exactly like a prostyle hexastyle temple.

---

[34] *IG* II² 3055; Travlos (1971) 357–60 figs. 459–63; Knell (2000) 161–4; Wilson (2000) 226–9 figs. 15–16; Korres (2000) 36 fig. 36.

[35] Choremi-Spetsieri (1994).

VII

While these are the best-known choregic monuments, in the last few years other foundations of choregic dedications along Tripod Street have been discovered and studied (Fig. 5 nos. 6–25).[36] Of these foundations, the substructure of sandstone blocks, sometimes of considerable height, is usually preserved. Occasionally only the lowest courses survive in situ; sometimes the limestone blocks of the foundations were reused in the immediate vicinity of their former location in the buildings of medieval churches (for example, in Ag. Nikolaos Rangavas on the northeast side of the Acropolis).

Foundations of several votive monuments have also been found east, and in front, of the propylon of the Dionysos sanctuary (Fig. 5 nos. 6–17; Fig. 7).[37] The first one of these foundations (Fig. 5 no. 10) was particularly large and is, in this regard, comparable to the Nikias monument.[38] But a reconstruction of its ground plan and the superstructure is nearly impossible as is the case for most of the votive monuments in that area because of its poor state of preservation.

In one instance, however, a number of better preserved foundation blocks are still extant (Fig. 5 no. 11). This enabled M. Korres[39] to determine that there had been a building open to the south with two columns between the lateral wall antae. Such a temple-like structure needed three architrave blocks to support a five-metre long frieze on its façade. Since the upper structure is completely missing, the possibility that the architecture was Ionic cannot be excluded. However, because of the column diameter, the axis width of the architrave, and a probable 2:3 proportion of metopes and triglyphs, a reconstruction of a Doric façade with three metopes over the intercolumniation is probable.

As part of this Doric frieze we might imagine a marble block

---

[36] Korres (1980) 16–18 fig. 1.
[37] Korres (1980) 14 fig. 1. The east side of the sanctuary, including the foundations of the propylon, has been excavated since this publication: Greco (2001) 31.
[38] Korres (1980) 16 fig. 1 no. 7. For the Nikias monument see above n. 34.
[39] Korres (1980) 16 fig. 1 no. 8 and fig. 4.

exhibited in the National Museum at Athens.[40] The measurements of the metope and the triglyphs, the dowel and clamp holes on the top surface, as well as the anathyrosis on both ends allow the reconstruction of a frieze five metres long with six metopes. Only one of these metopes together with two triglyphs at its sides survived. The relief on the metope depicts three women in mourning somewhere in a rocky landscape. The iconography of the scene is not, as is usually claimed, funerary, because such a scene does not exist among the *c.* 3,000 Attic grave stelai known; more likely, it is a mythological scene, maybe part of a Nekyia depiction, which continued on the other metopes.[41]

Korres does not offer dates for the various foundations at the beginning of Tripod Street. Nevertheless, these monuments cannot have been erected in the late fourth century because these are the best locations in front of the entrance to Dionysos' sanctuary and were surely already occupied at an early date; most probably, they should be connected to the new construction programme and layout of the *temenos* with its new propylon, which occurred around 370/360 BC.[42]

There is another case where the foundations allow a rough reconstruction of the superstructure of a choregic monument. Symmetrical to the central axis of the theatre of Dionysos (Fig. 5 no. 2), a counterpart to the Thrasyllos monument, approximately equal in size, stood high up on the Acropolis slope, where its base was cut directly into the limestone bedrock (Fig. 11).[43] At the back, the now completely lost architectural members were anchored to the rock by means of swallow-tail clamps, whose cuttings are still visible. The fact that the monument was aligned with the axis of the theatre of Dionysos demonstrates a deliberate placement, designed to create a visual pairing with the Thrasyllos monument, whose flat façade was probably reproduced in its counterpart (Fig. 9).

---

[40] Athens, Nat. Mus. inv. no. 1688: Kaltsas (2002) 188–9 no. 371; Goette (2004).

[41] Compare the scene on the krater by the Lykaon painter in Boston: Caskey and Beazley (1954) 86–93 pl. 16; for further comparisons see Goette (2004).

[42] Goette (1995a) and see the chapter by Csapo in this volume.

[43] Only mentioned by Travlos (1971) 526; publication under preparation by the author.

Fig. 11 Rock cuttings west of the *katatome* above the theatre of Dionysos in Athens.

VIII

Let us now turn to some isolated architraves identifiable by inscriptions as choregic dedications, which have survived without a known context. In addition to the poorly preserved foundations previously discussed, a number of marble blocks of superstructures are extant, most of which are housed today in the Epigraphical Museum of Athens.[44]

There is, for example, the architrave of a Doric building that the *choregos* Lysikles erected in 323 BC as indicated by the complete inscription (Fig. 12).[45] Despite later reworking we can still make out the remains of the mutulus slabs with their guttae, which allow us to imagine the remaining superstructure: the architrave ends at its narrow sides in anathyrosis. At the left end the joint is executed at the

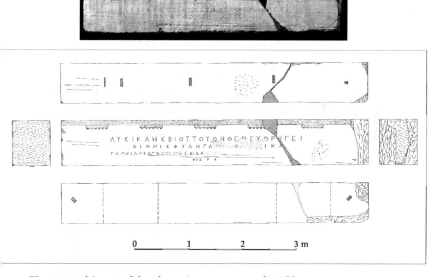

Fig. 12 Architrave of the choregic monument of Lysikles.

[44] *IG* II² 3040, 3052, 3054; Goette (1989) 96–9 listed under a, c, d; Goette (2004).

[45] *IG* II² 3054; Reisch (1890) 103–44; *RE Suppl.* VIII (1956) 877 listed under s; Goette (1989) 99 fig. 4; Goette (2004) 472 fig. 8.

right edge of the mutulus, which suggests that this mutulus was the last, the one at the corner so that the side architrave must have been attached there. The joint on the right side, however, was unusually situated within the mutulus slab, which means that the side architrave could not be attached here; thus an additional, equally large architrave block must be reconstructed to the right. And because we already have a complete inscription on the extant block, the restored architrave would be a symmetrical block with an additional inscription naming a second *choregos* of the same year. In that case, we might deduce a double *choregia*, possibly necessitated by a shortage of funds, for the year 323 BC or—less probably—we can posit a joint monument of two Athenians who wanted to commemorate two victories in two distinct full *choregiai*, which would have occurred within a short period of time (one year).

For the time being, the reconstruction of the Lysikles monument has to remain open, although it is certain that we are dealing here with a large-scale choregic monument in the Doric order. One other point is worthy of note: the metopes of this building were almost thirty centimetres wide—somewhat smaller than the mourning women metope[46]—and since the underside of the architrave shows dowel holes only at the ends, the structure possessed six metopes between the supports to judge from the extant remains. That means that the monument certainly had a most unusual form because the norm was two, or in some special cases even three, metopes above an intercolumniation.

IX

Between 317 and 307 BC, the old-style Athenian *choregia* was abolished by Demetrios of Phaleron and at the same time the erection of monumental grave stelai was also prohibited. From then on, the state took over the theatre competition and appointed an *agonothetes* in place of the *choregos*. He was perhaps still responsible for the costs, and he certainly was in charge of the entire management of the dithyrambic performance of his chorus. In spite of this change of

---

[46] See above n. 40.

management, the custom of awarding the *agonothetes*—should the chorus under his care win the competition—with a tripod displayed publicly on a more or less elaborate base still continued. Of the surviving agonothetic monuments, only two of several examples will be discussed here (the first one is a monument erected not for a victory in a dithyrambic competition, but in drama and comedy!); most of the others are known only by fragments of Ionic architraves.[47]

The first example[48] belongs to the well-known politician Xenokles of Sphettos or his brother,[49] erected in the year 307/6 BC, a monument that is especially remarkable in the history of western architecture. It is an Ionic marble architrave to which some years ago M. Korres was able to attribute parts of a lateral pillar (Fig. 13).[50] What results is a unique monument, specifically a gate, the front of which was inscribed with the name of the famous *agonothetes*. To my knowledge, this is the first example of an architectural form whose later examples are known as 'triumphal arches' or 'honorary gates'. It must have stood close to the eastern *parodos* of the theatre of Dionysos and spanned the entrance to the theatre, a prominent location chosen to advertise Xenokles' success in an extraordinary form.

The second example is that of Glaukon[51] from the year 280/79 BC. At the excavations in the Dionysos sanctuary in Athens, twelve[52] fragments of an agonothetic monument were found in 1862 that can be reconstructed to form a small, roughly square building. At the front, the restored architrave bears the choregic inscription, and the two sides showed, respectively, four and three wreath reliefs (Fig. 14).

---

[47] *IG* II[2] 3073, 3076, 3079, 3080; Goette (1989) 96–9 listed under g–j; Goette (2004).

[48] *IG* II[2] 3073; Goette (1989) 97 listed under g; Lambert (2003); Goette (2004).

[49] About the political career of Xenokles see Habicht (1988). Lambert (2003) discusses this inscription in detail and concludes that the *agonothetes* of *IG* II[2] 3073 might have been the brother of Xenokles, named Androkles, and that Xenokles himself erected another dedication as an *agonothetes* of a dithyrambic competition as known from *IG* II[2] 3077.

[50] Korres (1983).

[51] *IG* II[2] 3079; Goette (1989) 97 listed under i; Goette (2004).

[52] One of the fragments stored in the Epigraphical Museum (inv. 8707–11), no. VI in *IG* II[2] 3079, which shows the ivy wreath and the agonothetic inscription, was not to be found during my work in the museum.

Fig. 13 Architrave of the agonothetic monument of Xenokles and fragments of its lateral pillars, joined here in reconstruction to show the original form of the monument as a gate.

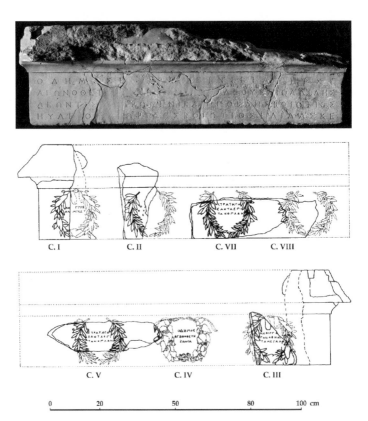

Fig. 14 Architrave and reconstruction of the sides of the agonothetic monument of Glaukon.

In the centre of the side with the three wreaths is an ivy wreath that encircles an inscription naming the *agonothetes* title which is flanked by olive wreaths; this combination of wreaths recalls the Thrasyllos monument. The two olive wreaths together with the four on the other side list the six liturgies or offices held by Glaukon. We should imagine the bronze tripod crowning the roof of this marble naiskos (approximately 1.5 m square).

X

In sum, this by no means complete survey of choregic architectural monuments reveals an amazing variety of form and size. I would even argue that in this type of monument we see the development of new architectural details and concepts that had not yet appeared in state building projects or anywhere else. In other words, this architectural genre may have provided the opportunity to experiment with architectural forms, and to judge from what remains, some of these efforts were completely innovative; the new wealth of overall architectural forms and details had never before occurred. Here we see them at the level of private initiative for public display.

Just to review this list, we might highlight the Lysikrates monument[53] with its Corinthian capitals on the exterior and its almost completely closed drum with an open front. Also remarkably new is the gate form of the Xenokles monument,[54] the real prototype of an honorary gate or—in Roman terms—a 'triumphal arch'. Extraordinary too is the Doric architecture of the Lysikles votive with its multiplied metopes over the intercolumniation.[55] By comparison, the already remarkable concept of the Nikias and Thrasyllos offerings seem rather tame although they copy parts of the Acropolis' fifth-century Propylaea;[56] in other words, here we find architectural quotations of an extraordinary Classical building being used simply as a support for the really important monument above, as bases for a prize tripod! These two last monuments appear to be parts of a wider

[53] See above n. 29.   [54] See above n. 49.   [55] See above n. 45.
[56] See above nn. 32 and 34; Felten (1997).

Fig. 15 Model of the Athenian Acropolis with choregic monuments on the Street of Tripods, viewed from the east.

architectural programme around the Athenian theatre, probably in the tradition of the policy of Lykurgos, who tried to canonise Classical achievements.[57] This programme also included a copy of the Nike temple used to record the lists of winners in the theatre competitions, a building attested by architectural remains[58] and inscriptions.[59]

Even in Pausanias' time, several centuries later, the Street of Tripods must have appeared amazingly sumptuous and made a tremendous impression on those who traversed it. We have to imagine the long row of relatively small but finely carved marble monuments on their high socles, surmounted by gleaming bronze tripods and abounding in a wealth of architectural forms, almost all taking advantage of the colossal, imposing backdrop of the Acropolis (Fig. 15).[60] Although in size and religious importance it could not measure up to the Panathenaic way, the relatively narrow Street of Tripods was most certainly one of the jewels of Athens and one of the

---

[57] Hintzen-Bohlen (1977) 135–40; Knell (2000) 167.

[58] Korres (1996) 132–3 under , 'Tempel D'.

[59] *IG* II² 2318.

[60] This impressive site was well described by Heliodoros in his monograph on the tripods on this street: see Athen. 6, 229c and 9, 406c.

heavily used urban veins connecting the Classical to the Archaic agora,[61] then proceeding to the important sanctuary of Dionysos. The fine choregic monuments were meant to impress the viewer and were absolutely inescapable for the citizens of and the visitors to Athens.

XI

At least in passing, it should be mentioned here that the large Athenian choregic monuments are not the only examples of this type of victory monument, which existed in other locations as well. Elsewhere in Attica, for example, we can note a Hellenistic building in the form of a covered exedra in the sanctuary of Dionysos in Ikarion[62] on the north slope of Mt Pentelikon.

Outside of Attica, on Thasos, we find a temple-like building[63] reminiscent of the Nikias monument with a group of large statues, including Dionysos, the Muses, and other personifications, placed on a base in a half circle.

In Boiotian Orchomenos, two other choregic buildings are attested by two surviving architectural members: a lintel with a choregic dedication[64] and an Ionic architrave, whose inscribed dedication permits its identification as a votive by a theatre producer.[65] Both monuments probably stood in the immediate vicinity of the theatre in Orchomenos in which many other tripod bases[66] have been excavated (some of them are exhibited in front of the *skene*, others are stored in the area of the Mycenean tholos tomb close to the theatre). These are, however, less impressive, since they are simple bases of a rectangular or triangular form.

---

[61] Schnurr (1995) with the older bibliography; Goette (2001) 54 n. 82; Goette and Hammerstaedt (2004) 87–98 fig. 18.

[62] See above n. 4; *IG* II² 3098.

[63] Daux (1967) 42–3 fig. 11; 130–3 nos. 29–32 figs. 69–71.

[64] Stored in the dromos of the Mycenean tholos tomb.

[65] Amandry and Spyropoulos (1974) 180–3 no. 3 figs. 7–9.

[66] Amandry and Spyropoulos (1974).

XII

After the mid-third century BC, choregic monuments diminished in size and are apparently fewer in number—at least we do not know of so many as in Classical times. No other architectural dedication by an *agonothetes* is known to us although theatre competitions continued.

To close this survey, we might leap ahead a few centuries to see how the choregic monument evolved in Athens under the peaceful conditions of the Roman imperial period, when, from the reign of Augustus to Hadrian and the Antonines, Athens flourished economically and as a cultural centre. Victorious *choregoi* of theatre competitions continued to set up prize-tripods;[67] in some cases their marble bases were quite large and even decorated with reliefs,[68] such as the bases with Nikai and Dionysos (Fig. 4).[69] Another is the large three-sided monument crowned by an anthemion frieze found in the Athenian agora;[70] it bears a long inscription naming Loukios Flavios Flammas as the *agonothetes* who served in his office for all the tribes in around 100 AD.

XIII

Remarkably, one of the most generous *choregoi* in Roman Athens elected *not* to erect a choregic monument to celebrate his victory but instead memorialised himself in a different way. A quick glance at this case enables us to grasp the profound changes that occurred in the ideal of the civic benefactor and his relationship to the city between the Classical Athenian democracy and the early second century AD.

[67] *IG* II² 3112–20; Follet and Peppas-Delmousou (2001).

[68] See, for example, the impressive so-called Sarapion monument: *IG* II² 3704; *SEG* 28, 225; Follet and Peppas-Delmousou (2001) 100–2 no. 5. A smaller tripod base with a relief depiction is the one on the Roman agora (once in the Tower of the Winds): *IG* II² 3120; Follet and Peppas-Delmousou (2001) 113–14 no. 13.

[69] See above n. 26: Berger (1983); see n. 68 above.

[70] *IG* II² 3114; Travlos (1971) 568 figs. 711, 713; Amandry (1976) 42–3; Follet and Peppas-Delmousou (2001) 99–100 no. 4.

Around that time C. Iulius Antiochos Philopappos,[71] who lived until AD 112/14, was *choregos* for all the choruses of *all* the tribes in a single year, an extraordinary service to the Athenian state since a *choregos* usually financed only *one* chorus of *one* tribe in a given year. But he did not proclaim this financial support for the city state with a choregic monument in the usual fashion, that is, a tripod base, which we would expect because of his wealth and his civic position—at least such a monument is not attested. But we know of an honorary statue of Philopappos erected by the tribe Oineis in the theatre of Dionysos, which commemorates his efforts as an *agonothetes*;[72] the existence of this portrait at that place supports the hypothesis that he himself did not dedicate a lavish choregic monument. It seems that, instead, he perpetuated his glory by constructing a huge mausoleum for himself at the most prominent point in Athens, opposite the Acropolis on top of the Mouseion hill,[73] and surprisingly, neither the inscriptions nor the sculptural decoration make any mention whatsoever of his generosity to Athens during his lifetime.

In the upper storey Philopappos is depicted in a free-standing statue as a Hellenistic king[74]—he was, in fact, a descendant of the Kommagene monarchy, and in the main frieze beneath the statue, Philopappos, who had been a *consul suffectus*, presents himself in relief as a consul in Rome during the ceremony of the *processus consularis* or the *pompa circensis*, although he never actually took part in such a ceremony in Rome.[75] He stands in a quadriga accompanied by the twelve lictors of the city of Rome. Such images suggest that Philopappos wished to portray himself, and be perceived as, a Hellenistic king and simultaneously as a member of the Roman aristocracy, which now ruled the world. Such self-presentation in a monument for a prominent individual, an important *choregos*, differs dramatically from its predecessors, both funerary and choregic monuments, in the Greek world; for a glance back at the fourth

---

[71] Byrne (2003) 308–10 no. 37 with bibliography.

[72] *IG* II² 3112; Follet and Peppas-Delmousou (2001) 97–8 no. 1.

[73] *IG* II² 3451; Travlos (1971) 462–5 figs. 585–7; Kleiner (1983).

[74] The type of the statue is 'heroic', i.e. almost naked with only a mantle around the hips; the ends of the diadem on the shoulders as well as the inscription below the statue naming him *basileus* point to the depiction of a Hellenistic king.

[75] Schäfer (1989) 380–1 no. B 13.

century BC reveals a situation that is almost the contrary to that of Philopappos' mausoleum.

XIV

Although the Athenian *choregoi* commemorated their victories in monumental form, they always portrayed themselves as part of a larger civic entity.[76] They surely celebrated their own civic-mindedness and generosity, but the individual was presented within the context of the city's cultural programme. Even when commemorating the dead, which, we might remember, always occurred outside the city, the individual Athenian citizen was honoured within a family tomb plot even though such monuments were sometimes large and prominently placed along main roads to draw attention to notable families or individuals.[77] Yet it is noteworthy that the funerary monuments of Athenian citizens—stelai and the sometimes large grave precincts of the very wealthy—never were as huge and elaborate as contemporary choregic architectural dedications.[78]

While the lavish grave monuments were prohibited by the sumptuary legislation of 317 BC and the old-style *choregia* changed under the same laws, it is important to note that monuments to civic liturgies and theatrical victories, now erected by *agonothetai*, persisted. In other words, one type of display that celebrated the wealth and power of individual families was discontinued but another kind, the liturgy monument that celebrated civic-mindedness and the contribution to the community and its well-being, and whose

---

[76] Wilson (2000) esp. 172–97.

[77] Bergemann (1997) 15–17, 131–42, 227–30. The negative characterisation of the Athenian *choregia* as an 'empty grave (*kenotaphion*) of the vanished estates' of a wealthy *choregos* may go back to Demetrios (Plu. *Moral.* 349a; see Wilson 2000: 95, 125, 169, 380 n. 20). It appears to be a general criticism of the lavish expenditure of financial resources; the description is not a comparison between funeral and choregic monuments of Demetrios' (or Plutarch's) time, because the prize awarded to the victorious *choregos*, the tripod (not the lavish choregic monument), was—according to Plutarch (or his source)—ridiculous, much too small in regard to the financial outlay.

[78] It seems as if the largest funeral monuments were erected by people who were not Athenian citizens; see Scholl (1994).

architectural innovation was so markedly different from the past and so extraordinary, continued to thrive. As the votive inscriptions explicitly tell us, the *demos* was now said to serve as the overall *choregos*, and occupied first place, while the individual *agonothetes* served the *demos*. The tripod dedication of a *choregos* or *agonothetes* was the manifestation of the well-functioning city and its democratic institutions, where the agonistic character of all the citizenry and its festivals was engaged to benefit the community—and conversely, the community permitted its civic benefactors to erect choregic monuments.

By contrast, the self-representation of Philopappos highlights a break with that Athenian civic tradition: although Philopappos had been one of the most generous *choregoi* and even an archon of Athens, he did not choose to represent himself as a benefactor of the city; rather, he erected a prominent monument that glorified only himself and his ancestors, not the city. Yet in the case of Philopappos, the family took an even more extravagant form in that he pronounced his descent from a Hellenistic monarchy and portrayed himself as a high-ranking official of the city of Rome. Here Philopappos uses a new visual language, influenced by both Hellenistic rulers and Roman officials and emperors, a language far removed from the traditional self-representation of Athenian democratic benefactors, whose choregic monuments, while remarkably innovative, even daring, always represented a careful and strategic balance between the individual and the larger democratic community.

6

Performance in the *Pythion*: The Athenian Thargelia*

Peter Wilson

Athens' principal urban festival for Apollo, the Thargelia, has been aptly described as 'a festival of the arts . . . second only to the *City Dionysia*'.[1] Although much about the festival remains a mystery, it has received none of the sort of integrated historical and socio-political analysis that has been so productive for our understanding of the urban festivals of the Dionysia and Panathenaia. This chapter will initiate such analysis, with an emphasis on the performance practice of the festival as evidenced principally through epigraphy.[2]

* Thanks to Barbara Kowalzig, Simon Hornblower, Eric Csapo, Ian Rutherford, Paola Ceccarelli, Julia Kindt; and above all to Stephen Lambert, whose generosity and learning were invaluable in the final stages of writing this chapter.

[1] Parker (1996) 95. Celebration of the Thargelia in the demes (its existence doubted by Parker 2005: 74 and n. 99) will not be considered here. The main evidence is *IG* I³ 256*bis* = *SEG* 33, 147 (Thorikos); *IG* I³ 255A15 = *LSS* 18B (Erkhia): see Humphries (2004) 161, 179, 187.

[2] For full literary testimonia relating to the Thargelia (though much of it referring to places other than Athens and of doubtful reliability) see Nilsson (1906) 105–15; Deubner (1932) 179–98. For an indispensable treatment of the Athenian material see now Parker (2005) 481–3.

INTRODUCTION

The Thargelia was not a week-long event like the Dionysia or Panathenaia, but held over just two days, the sixth and seventh of the month Thargelion (late May). The first day saw the ritual cleansing of the city and expulsion of *pharmakoi*, the second, the procession through the newly cleansed city to the *Pythion* outside the old city walls that conveyed the stew of first fruits in a vessel known as the *thargelos*—a procession in which the Sun and Seasons were also honoured. On this day, at least in the Classical period, choral contests between five choruses of men and five of boys took place. Robert Parker makes the telling point that it was these contests that probably dominated most Athenians' thoughts of the festival, as they do our sources.[3] And yet there has been little attempt to integrate them into a broader understanding of the festival.

In fact, the Thargelia has an awkwardly split identity in current scholarship. On the one hand, the presence of the scapegoat ritual long tended to dominate interest, fed by the possibility of human sacrifice, or at least penis-flagellation.[4] This led to an anthropological vision of the festival with many of the characteristics of a Lévi-Straussian 'cold' society, primitive and achronic, outside the exigencies of the political, even of history. The effect has been to retard exploration of the potential social and political dynamism of the cult. On the other hand, the Thargelia is seen as an 'arts' festival of the living Classical city. Yet even in this guise it has attracted little more than the passing interest of the literary historian for having hosted another set of (generically embarrassing) dithyrambic contests—a neglect also fostered by the lack of surviving 'texts' from these contests, and by the absence of drama from it in any period.[5]

---

[3] Parker (1996) 95.

[4] Human sacrifice: Harrison (1903) 78–108; cf. Frazer (1913) 253–8. Penis-flagellation: Tz. *Chil.* 5.726–30 = Bergk *PLG*³ frs. 4–9: ἑπτάκις γὰρ ῥαπίσαντες ἐκεῖνον εἰς τὸ πέος, σκίλλαις σύκαις ἀγρίαις τε καὶ ἄλλοις τῶν ἀγρίων.

[5] Deubner (1932) represents the interpretative imbalance in striking fashion: after twenty pages devoted to the first day and its rituals, his final paragraph is devoted to the choruses of the second, thus: 'Der frohe Charakter des zweiten Tages äußerte sich auch in agonistischen Darbietungen, Männer- und Knabenchören, deren Choregen der Archon Eponymos zu besorgen hatte.'

I suggest we try to bridge this divide.[6] It is not present in many ancient traditions relating to the festival, which frequently link the ritual *pompe* closely to the choral *agones*.[7]

Robert Parker has neatly elucidated the festival's basic ritual logic: 'on Thargelion 6, bad things are driven out, while on Thargelion 7, good things are carried in, in a pattern whose appeal on an expressive level is self-evident'.[8] Consideration of the 'good things' brought in on the second day has been limited to the first-fruits of the agricultural year symbolised in the seeds boiled in the *thargelos* and carried in procession. But given that this day was dominated by choral performances, an attempt should be made to fit them into this same ritual logic. Nor is that hard to do. These groups of the city's finest boys and men, trained in the order-and beauty-creating activity of *khoreia*, represent at the civic and collective level the 'fairest and finest' (καλοὶ κἀγαθοί) to set against the 'most ugly and base' individuals ejected as *pharmakoi* on the preceding day, who are described with terms like ἀγεννεῖς, ἄχρηστοι, φαῦλοι, εὐτελέστατοι, ἀηδέστατοι.[9] This looks like a clear instance of choral performance as an affirmation or symbolic creation of a hierarchical civic order, as an antidote to impurity. The 'goods' of which Apollo Pythios was described as the *exegetes* should include these choruses.[10]

---

[6] Calame (1990) 321–2 has led the way in this; cf. also Parker (2005) esp. 203.

[7] As in the law of Euegoros: D. 21.10 (with MacDowell 1990: 234): Θαργηλίων τῆι πομπῆι καὶ τῶι ἀγῶνι; or in the third-century stele discussed below 169–71; cf. also Michael Apostolius *Corpus Paroemiographorum Graecorum* 3.31.19: ἐν ἧι [sc. ἑορτῆι] ἦψουν ἀπαρχὰς τῶι θεῶι τῶν πεφηνότων καρπῶν, ἵσταντο δὲ ἐν αὐτῆι καὶ χοροὶ καὶ ἀγὼν Θαργήλια; Suid. θ49; Phot. θ p. 80.3.

[8] Parker (1983) 25.

[9] Deubner (1932) 184 n. 5 for sources. On the likely contents of the *thargelos* see Parker (2005) 185 (cf. 417). The prominence of a very wide range of 'good things' carried in procession fits well with the prominence of the boys in the festival contests. (Parker 2005: 204 hypothesises an important place for children in the procession.)

[10] Apollo Pythios as ἐξηγητὴς τῶν ἀγαθῶν: *SEG* 21, 469.9 (second-century), drawing on a much older formula: cf. *IG* I³ 137.4–5 (422–16 BC): ἐχσεγετέ[ν τον ἀl]γαθον Oliver; Pl. *R.* 4.427c; Suid. θ49: καὶ ἀγαθῶν Θαργήλια.

DIACHRONY

Athenian domestic participation in the cult of Apollo Pythios has been plausibly hypothesised as early as the eighth century,[11] but the attentions of the Peisistratids represent the first clearly attested activity, part of more extensive development of the whole region around the *Pythion* in the southeast part of the city.[12] And the evidence is more solid than for the much-discussed sixth-century Dionysia. Peisistratos the elder constructed a temple in the *Pythion*.[13] The sanctuary may have even then been the site of choral contest and the dedication of tripods.[14] The younger Peisistratos dedicated in this sanctuary the altar that Thoukydides describes and that still survives. The date was almost certainly 522/1.[15] An important part of the context of this Peisistratid interest in Pythian Apollo at home is the unhealthy relations they entertained with him at Delphi.[16]

---

[11] Parker (1996) 27–8. Karouzou (1954: pls. 10–11) interprets a Geometric Attic vase with dancers (male and female) and tripods as a representation of the Thargelia.

[12] Camp (2001) 36–7.

[13] Zen. *Epitome* ed. Miller 1868, 367: τὸν ναὸν τοῦ Πυθίου ᾠκοδόμησεν ὁ Πεισίστρατος; *Corpus Paroemiographorum Graecorum* 1.406–7 L.-S., no. 66: Πεισίστρατος ᾠκοδόμει τὸν ἐν Πυθίωι ναόν; related sources from the paroemiographic tradition discussed by Lynch (1984). Suid. π3130 and Phot. s.v. Πύθιον record that Peisistratos founded a sanctuary, rather than specifying construction of a temple. The elder rather than the younger: Parker (1996) 72. If it had been the younger, Th. 6.54.6 would surely have indicated as much.

[14] Implied perhaps by the expression used in Suid. and Phot.: 'a sanctuary that came into existence under Peisistratos, in which the victors in the *kyklios khoros* at the Thargelia erected their tripods' (ἱερὸν Ἀπόλλωνος Ἀθήνησιν, ὑπὸ Πεισιστράτου γεγονός, εἰς ὃ τοὺς τρίποδας ἐτίθεσαν οἱ τῶι κυκλίωι χορῶι νικήσαντες τὰ Θαργήλια). Late sources are however perhaps unlikely to have had much more than Thoukydides on which to base their remarks. See also n. 2 above.

[15] Th. 6.54.6; *IG* I³ 948. Arnush (1995) attempts to down-date the altar to *c.* 495 and sees it as Peisistratos junior's attempt to remind the Athenians of his service as arkhon some twenty-five years earlier. Aloni (2000: 84–7) gives a full refutation; cf. Angiolillo (1997) 23.

[16] Philoch. *FGrH* 328 F115 for the tradition that the Peisistratids were responsible for the arson of the Delphian temple. As Jacoby notes ad loc. this can only have been a story spread by their enemies in Athens, but is suggestive of bad relations. The observation of lightning over Harma to initiate a theoric mission to Delphi (Str. 9.2.11) took place from the altar of Zeus Astrapaios, which was probably in or near the *Pythion*, and may have been timed to coincide with the Thargelia: Colin (1905) 11–12. For evidence unknown to Colin see now Lambert (2002) F1A, 26–30 and F6 (now *SEG* 52, 48); *SEG* 21, 541 (Erkhia calendar); cf. also Lambert (2005) no. 13.

The precise boundaries of the *Pythion* have not been identified, but it lay southeast of the Acropolis, outside the ancient city walls (by virtue of its purificatory function[17]), along the western bank of the Ilissos. Its general location is well known, largely because of the find-spots of the altar dedicated by Peisistratos, and of various dedications set up by victorious Classical Thargelian *khoregoi* (which apparently sat quite happily alongside the Peisistratid altar).[18]

Epigraphic evidence for the competing choruses starts some seventy years later, with the (lost) fragment of a khoregic dedication, dated to just before 450.[19] The scrap of another inscription found on

Among the intriguing items carried by Athenians for Apollo on the Pythais of *c.* 403/ 2–400/399 are a tripod and ἐπιτοξίδας (F1A, 28) which, following Phot. s.v.—ἀγκυρ- ίδες σιδῆραι δίβολοι—Stephen Lambert (2002: 371) suggests may be 'little anchors as symbols of Athens' status as colonial metropolis'. See below, p. 164.

[17] Simon (1983) 74.

[18] Travlos (1971) 100–3. The promised study of the site by Matthaiou (cf. Matthaiou 2003a: 91 n. 35) is eagerly awaited. Smaller sanctuaries of Pythian Apollo are attested or claimed for: the northern slope of the Acropolis; Daphne; Oinoe (Philoch. *FGrH* 328 F75); Thorikos (see n. 1 above): Lupu (2005) 143–4. His promin- ence in the Marathonian Tetrapolis is ancient, and includes the *Pythion* at Oinoe and a Delion at Marathon: Colin (1905) 62–70. The continued presence of the Peisistratid altar in the *Pythion* alongside khoregic memorials is particularly interesting given the deletion by the *demos* of the inscription on the Altar of the Twelve Gods in the Agora (Th. 6.54.7), and the fact that Peisistratid activity in the *Pythion* may have become a focus of anti-tyrannical sentiment, as formulated in the expression 'to shit in the *Pythion*': Hsch. s.v. ἐν Πυθίωι χέσαι.

[19] *IG* I[3] 963, '*ante a.* 450?' This stone was found near the Ilissos: Pittakis (1835) 184; Makres (1994) 326. In addition to those mentioned subsequently in the text, the following are the major inscriptions relating to the Thargelian *agones*:

- Khoregic dedications: *IG* I[3] 964 (*c.* 435), 965 (430–405), 966 (425–404 boys), *IG* II[2] 3072 (late fifth—early fourth century), *IG* II[2] 3029 (early fourth century: Amandry 1976: 44–6), *IG* II[2] 3071 (400–375), *IG* II[2] 3064 + *SEG* 18, 69 (384/3 men), *SEG* 41, 141 (380/79 men), *Hesperia* 4 (1935) 54 no. 16 (before 365), *IG* II[2] 3065 (365/4 boys), *IG* II[2] 3066 (364/3 boys), *IG* II[2] 3070 (perhaps 358/7 or 356/5, or before 365: Amandry 1977: 179 boys), *SEG* 27, 12 (363/2 boys), *SEG* 27, 13 (362/1 boys), *SEG* 27, 14 (361/0 boys), *SEG* 27, 15 (360/59 boys), *SEG* 27, 16 (359/8), *IG* II[2] 3067 (358/7 or 356/5 boys), *SEG* 27, 17 (355/4 boys), *SEG* 26, 220 (354/3 boys), *SEG* 27, 18 (352/1 boys), *SEG* 27, 19 (349/8 boys), *ADELT* 25, p. 60, cf. *SEG* 30, 127 (mid- or late fourth century), *IG* II[2] 3068 (344/3 boys), (?) *IG* II[2] 3069 (344/3 festival uncertain), *SEG* 21, 694 (fourth century: Amandry 1976: 42).

IG II[2] 3022 records past victories in the *gymnasiarkhia* and *euandria* at the Panathen- aia plus a boys' chorus at the Thargelia (mid-fourth century, boys).

- Other: *IG* II[2] 1629.196–9, 325/4: trierarchic *agon* prizes announced at Thargelian *agon*.

the south side of the Acropolis from around this time may be part of a decree regulating the cult.[20] There is at any rate a suggestion of heightened activity mid-century—though as a matter of method we should not assume a simple correspondence between epigraphical developments and developments in cult practice.[21] The evidence becomes more abundant throughout the fifth and into the fourth century, when the cult of Apollo Pythios seems to have been identified more closely with that of Apollo Patroos.[22] This is the period for which we are best informed about the festival and its *agones* from a variety of sources, but there is at least one testimony to the continued dancing of men and boys at the Thargelia during the period when so much goes quiet, the third century (see below p. 169).[23]

The cult—with a choral contest still (or again) operative—also received the full attention of the civic authorities in the 'époque de renaissance des cultes nationaux'[24] of the later second century, as evidenced by an extensive decree of 129/8 BC. This may represent a revival from near or total inactivity. What has often been overlooked in discussion of this important document is the decision to inscribe it on a reused khoregic dedication of the festival's hey-day, the fourth century. The curved surface of a triangular base had been reworked so as to form a stele—a neat physical instantiation of the decree's proud 'renovation' of the Classical cult.[25]

---

[20] *IG* I³ 143, perhaps dating to *c.* 450: too fragmentary for sure conclusions, but line 5 suggests a regulation. The connection to the Thargelia could be more secure:

```
_ _ _ _ν ἐαμ μὲ α-   5
[_ _ Θαρ]γελίοι τ-
_ _ _ _ν τοι θεοι
_ _ _ _ν
```

[21] Cf. Shapiro (1996) 102: 'precisely *because* of the physical removal of the League headquarters from Delos, the Athenians felt it necessary to embrace more enthusiastically than ever the cult of Apollo'. Cf. Hornblower (1992) and below pp. 175–82.

[22] De Schutter (1987) and below p. 182.

[23] Mitsos (1970) 393–5. Cf. Parker (1996) 273.

[24] Sokolowski (1962) 39.

[25] *LSCG* 14 = *SEG* 21, 469 and 694. Amandry (1976) 40–2 correctly dates the remains of the reused khoregic dedication. Sutton (1989) 101 is wrong on the date and festival; Ieranò (1997) 361 gets the festival right but the date wrong. Cf. Mikalson (1998) 272–4.

PRACTICALITIES OF PERFORMANCE

The performances of the Classical Thargelia consisted of two choral contests, a category of men and one of boys. There were five choruses in each category, and fifty members in each chorus.[26] The design seems to be modelled on, and so in this form probably post-dates, that for the Great Dionysia, with its tribally patterned two-times-ten choruses of fifty; except that at the Thargelia there were half the number of competing choruses. The Kleisthenic tribes (which had, after all, been selected by Apollo Pythios) were paired off—randomly, by lot, until some time in or near the 370s[27] and thereafter, as Amandry has shown,[28] operating in fixed pairs, so as to produce the unique phenomenon of competing tribal choral 'teams'. Economy may not be the only, or even the most plausible, reason for this arrangement. The desire to 'mix' constituencies of tribes further may be another.[29] If participation in choral contests was in any sense a means of reducing internal social tensions through 'safe' group cultural contest,[30] this further pairing of tribes will have taken the original Kleisthenic 'mix' a step further. A desire for distinction from the Dionysian pattern may also have played a part. The pool of available singing talent will have been twice that for Dionysian choruses.

It is easy to see why the tribal pairs were fixed once and for all. The provision of *khoregoi* and the need to alternate the duty (and honour) between randomly paired tribes over successive years will have been a source of potential confusion and dispute. The normal operational arrangement seems to have seen the task of providing a *khoregos* for the (in total) ten choral groups assigned to one each of the tribes. Each tribe thus provided one *khoregos* each year, in one of the two performance categories. In the next year each tribe will presumably have had the obligation to provide a *khoregos* for the other category. Every tribe thus had choral representation (and, we

---

[26] For the number of choreuts: Wilson (2000) 119.

[27] After 380 (*SEG* 41, 141) and by 365 (*IG* II² 3065–70).

[28] Amandry (1977) 166–9. Bodensteiner (1891) 71 first noted that the inscription formula for Thargelian dedications was modelled on that for the Dionysia.

[29] Wilson (2000) 304.   [30] Cf. Wilson (2003).

assume, actual participation) in both categories every year; but only in every second year will the men or boys of Aiantis have had an Aiantid *khoregos* organising and 'leading' their performance.[31]

It has been plausibly argued that, until some date in the latter part of the fifth or early fourth century, there was in fact only one category of chorus—the boys.[32] Whether or not the men were a later addition, the overwhelming majority of evidence relates to the boys' choruses,[33] and this surely reflects a real prominence, fitting to a cult of Apollo. For instance, we have a fascinating set of more than a dozen khoregic dedications, all from the boys' category, covering a period from c. 365 to the late 340s. These are on cylindrical marble bases of a standard type, whose uniformity encouraged Amandry to describe them as having 'une sorte de caractère administratif'.[34] Most of them were found together on the southern bank of the Ilissos and so may have come from an area of the *Pythion* especially devoted to the presentation of victors in the boys' event. Such apparent systematisation of boys' *khoreia* in these decades may reflect a role accorded to choral training and dancing for Apollo as a precursor to the marked

[31] Thus Amandry (1977) 166 n. 4, the best discussion of the topic. The most important (though cryptic) text is Arist. *Ath. Pol.* 56.3. The subject is the arkhon's reception of *khoregoi* appointed by the tribes: ἔπειτα παραλαβὼν τοὺς χορηγοὺς τοὺς ἐνηνεγμένους ὑπὸ τῶν φυλῶν εἰς Διονύσια ἀνδράσιν καὶ παισίν καὶ κωμωιδοῖς, καὶ εἰς Θαργήλια ἀνδράσιν καὶ παισίν (εἰσὶ δ' οἱ μὲν εἰς Διονύσια κατὰ φυλάς, εἰς Θαργήλια ⟨δὲ⟩ δυοῖν φυλαῖν εἷς· παρέχει δ' ἐν μέρει ἑκατέρα τῶν φυλῶν). Cf. Rhodes (1981) 624.

[32] Evidence for men's choruses: *IG* II[2] 1138 (the Thargelian *khoregiai* referred to probably date from the early fourth century to c. 360); *IG* II[2] 3064 + *SEG* 18, 69, 384/3; *SEG* 41, 141, 380/79. This is the idea of Ieranò (1997) 242. But I do not understand how he can write on the previous page that Antiph. 6.11 attests 'la compresenza agli agoni delle Targelie dei cori di uomini e di ragazzi'. In fact the latter part of §11 may imply the existence only of boys' choruses. Having said he commenced recruiting his chorus, the *khoregos* goes on to describe a series of actions that he did not need to undertake (imposition of fines, application of compulsion, etc.) which make better sense in the context of a boys' chorus, when a *khoregos* must deal with parents. And the initial description of his appointment—Ἐπειδὴ χορηγὸς κατεστάθην εἰς Θαργήλια—in not mentioning a category, may suggest that his audience knew there was only one (and that, notwithstanding the fact that they presumably knew this was a trial concerning the death of a boy choreut).

[33] We have in addition the testimony that young well-born Athenian males danced for Apollo in another configuration probably related to the Thargelia (see below p. 166 on the *Orkhestai*).

[34] Amandry (1977) 177; at 167 he reports the existence of three further such bases that are 'anépigraphiques': M 925, M 926, M 1145.

concern for *paideia* in the Lykourgan period that led, among other things, to the formalisation of the *ephebeia c.* 335. Prominence of the boys' category would make ritual sense, too, in that it would fit nicely with the idea that these choruses restated, in a different, musical and human medium, the promise of the first-fruits in the *thargelos*.[35]

The prize awarded at the Thargelia was a large bronze tripod. Although it has proved more difficult to deduce much about the size and shape of these tripods compared with their Dionysian counterparts (because no good examples of the crowning block of stone that surmounted the cylindrical bases and onto which the tripod was affixed have survived), Amandry has shown that those awarded in the boys' category stood somewhere in the region of a formidable 2.1 to 2.8 metres in height.[36] They were dedicated by their victorious *khoregoi* on an inscribed base and—like their Dionysian counterparts—Thargelian *khoregoi*, or their friends, could later allude to their presence in the *Pythion* when speaking in court to demonstrate their civic virtue.[37]

The epigraphic practice followed in these victory-dedications is distinctive for the prominence it gives to the *khoregos*. He is normally listed first, with patronymic and demotic, often as the victor (χορηγῶν ἐνίκα; cf. *IG* I³ 964.2 of *c.* 440–430: ἀνέθηκ[ε]ν νικήσα[ς]), though sometimes that is simply implicit (ἐχορήγει), with the two tribes following in the dative as the instruments of his victory (e.g. *IG* II² 3065: Ἀκαμαντίδι Πανδιονίδι). When included, the competition category (παίδων) is next, followed by the *didaskalos*, the *aulos*-player and finally, arkhon. The *aulos*-player only starts to be named at all in the fourth century. He is first securely attested in 384/3, after the *didaskalos*; and over the course of the relatively well-documented

---

[35] *Paides* may also have played a role in the procession: *Σ* Ar. *Eq.* 729.

[36] Amandry (1977) esp. 202.

[37] Is. 5.41, 7.40; cf. Pl. *Grg.* 472a. Wilson (2000) 201–5. Further on khoregic dedications see the chapter by Goette above. Voutiras (1991–2) argues that a relief in the Louvre (Ma 756) is a Thargelian dedication that, uniquely, bears no sign of having housed a tripod. The relief—dated on stylistic grounds to *c.* 320–300—shows two adult males approaching Apollo as dedicators of a sacrifice, followed by seven (?) boys. Voutiras explains the absence of a tripod prize on a Thargelian monument by reference to the *agonothesia*. It is however likely that tripods continued to be awarded under the *agonothesia*, and the association of the relief with the Thargelia in particular (as opposed to Apollo) is far from proven.

period of 360–340, gradually wrests epigraphic priority from the *didaskalos*—and, definitively so, from 354 (*SEG* 26, 220).[38]

In a very small percentage of cases the tribes are named as the victors (*IG* II² 3072, late fifth to early fourth-century, *SEG* 27, 14 of 361/0), which shows that this was a generic possibility but presumably not the way the contest was normally conceived. That the prominence of the *khoregos* counted for much in the conception and memorialisation of Thargelian choral contest is also shown by the fact that the order in which the two tribes are listed is not neutral. When we are able to identify it, the *khoregos'* own tribe always comes first. It is likely that such favouritism, however mild, translated into the more practical realm of recruitment, training, and care of *khoreutai*.[39] Such partiality is further illuminated by a fragmentary decree of the tribe Hippothontis (*IG* II² 1153, mid-fourth century). In this, one Polynikos moves to honour a Metagenes, also of Hippothontis, for having voted for the victory of their tribe at the Thargelia: ἔκρινε τὴν [φ]υλ[ὴν] νικᾶν Θαργήλια. Metagenes is said to have 'judged in a fine and just manner, and without taking bribes'. Given the parallels, the decree doubtless went on to praise Metagenes further and award him a crown (of olive or gold.)[40] This document opens a fascinating window onto tribal back-patting, but also onto the attempt by one tribe to appropriate a shared victory as its own (note τὴν φυλὴν νικᾶν, in the singular)— even if that is only in the relatively secluded context of the tribe's own meeting-place. If the tribal pairing was intended to be a mechanism to nuance tribal allegiances, it has not succeeded here. We should assume that the *khoregos* of this chorus was also a Hippothontid. It would not be surprising if it were Polynikos himself, or a close associate of his.

This fragmentary document raises, but tells us very little about, the issue of the mechanics of judgment at the Thargelia. It may imply that Thargelian *kritai* (judges) were appointed on some form of

---

[38] Amandry (1977) 178.

[39] As much is implied rather than contradicted by the manner in which the Thargelian *khoregos* on trial in Antiphon 6 claims (§13) to have taken such pains to ensure that he had appointed to assist in his *khoregia* 'another man of Kekropis [the tribe with which his own had been paired] who regularly convened his tribe'.

[40] Jones (1999) 185.

tribal representation (as at the Dionysia), and at least hints at the existence of a similar system of regulation to that at the great dramatic and choral festival.[41] Moreover, the virtuous terms in which Metagenes' service as judge is described (excellence, justice, and freedom from favour) suggests the common presence of their opposite vices in the process.

POETS AND PIPERS

We know the names (but little more) of about a dozen *didaskaloi* who performed at the Thargelia, and those of about ten *aulos*-players. *Didaskaloi* came to Athens for Apollo's festival from a wide range of places, some of them well-known centres of musical and poetic excellence—Megara, Thebes, east Lokrian Opous (two), Sikyon, and Phleious. The Sikyonian was working with an *aulos*-player from his home city, the Phleian with one from nearby Sikyon (the dates are 344/3 and 359/8 respectively).[42] This is probably not a coincidence. It seems likely that *aulos*-players at the Thargelia were chosen (and paid?) by *khoregoi* once the *khoregoi* had been allotted their *didaskalos*, in which case collaboration between professionals (poets and pipers) with pre-existing relationships could work to the benefit of the production.[43] As the importance of the musical element increased, however, it is possible that the allocation of *aulos*-players

---

[41] Wilson (2000) 98–102; Marshall and van Willigenburg (2004) 103–5.

[42] [E]pikouros of Sikyon, *didaskalos* at Thargelia 344/3, with Satyros, *aulos*-player from Sikyon (*IG* II² 3068); Hegemon of Phleious, *didaskalos* at Thargelia 359/8, with Alkathous, *aulos*-player from Sikyon (*SEG* 27, 16). For other known Thargelian musicians and *didaskaloi* see Stephanis (1988) and Sutton (1989) 125.

[43] In the later fifth century *didaskaloi* were assigned by lot to *khoregoi* at the Thargelia (Antiphon 6.11), but this probably represents the allotment of order of choice (Wilson 2000: 68). We have no direct evidence as to how *aulos*-players were involved in the production, and practice is very likely to have changed over time. At the Dionysia in the mid-fourth century (D. 21.13) the arkhon used the lot to assign an order of choice of *aulos*-players. It seems that the role and hence the formal treatment of *aulos*-players came closer to that of poets: they ceased to be hired by poets and came to be allocated by the polis in a separate operation: [Plu.] *Moral.* (*de Mus.*) 1141d; Ath. 617b–c; Wilson (2000) 69, 336–7 nn. 85–6.

was also controlled by the polis separately with the use of the lot, as it was at the Dionysia by some time in the fourth century.[44]

The 'struggle' for epigraphic priority between these two is one index of a shift in the relative importance of poet and piper. I have hesitated to translate the term *didaskalos* because there is some doubt whether those who 'trained' such choruses were always poets composing and teaching the words and music of new compositions.[45] Pantakles (of unknown origins) is one of the few *didaskaloi* we know to have performed repeatedly and successfully in Athens and at the Thargelia and about whom we know something more than a name.[46] His career spanned the second half of the fifth century.[47] Aristotle (fr. 624R) indicated in his *Didaskaliai* that he was a poet (ποιητής): the use of this term, and his inclusion in that work, may imply he was a 'creative artist' rather than simply a trainer. But the fact that Aristotle made the point at all (or that his *Didaskaliai* was later used to make the point) may suggest that it was in fact an issue.[48]

[44] See previous note and cf. Amphis fr. 14 K–A, with Wilson (2000) 69–70. On the first day the *pharmakoi* were ejected to the sound of a special tune, the 'tune of the fig-branch' played on the *aulos* (Hsch. s.v. κραδίης νόμος). We can only guess as to whether this was played by one of the competing pipers.

[45] The term διδασκαλία could be used purely of choral training, with no necessary implication of poetic composition: Xen. *Mem.* 3.4.4; cf. Pl. *Grg.* 501e, where ἡ τῶν χορῶν διδασκαλία καὶ ἡ τῶν διθυράμβων ποίησις seems to be a way of describing dithyrambic performance as a whole. But if Thargelian performances used pre-existing compositions and were in effect re-performances, we might expect the sort of epigraphic variation we find used to signal the re-performance of Timotheos' *Elpenor* nearly a century after it was composed. The relevant phrase of the inscription (*IG* II² 3055, of 320/19) reads: 'Pantaleon of Sikyon played the *aulos*. The song (ἆισμα): the *Elpenor* of Timotheos.' On the issue see Amandry (1977) 177 n. 21; Robert (1938) 31–5.

[46] Stephanis (1988) 352; Makres (1994) 288–9.

[47] The evidence for Athenian victories: *c.* 450–444, with Akamantis (*SEG* 10, 322 = *IG* I³ 958; *c.* 430–20, with (?)Aigeis (*SEG* 26, 44 = *IG* I³ 959: Amandry (1977: 183–5) argues this is a Thargelian victory); another with unknown tribe (*IG* I³ 967); another with Antiokhis is likely (St. Byz. 142, 10, Ἀτήνη). He was also *didaskalos* for Erekhtheis and Kekropis in the unhappy *khoregia* of Antiphon 6, *c.* 419: Wilson (2000) 116–20, cf. 68.

[48] Harpokration preserves the fragment of Aristotle's *Didaskaliai*: I 96.6: ὅτι γὰρ ὁ Παντακλῆς ποιητής, δεδήλωκεν Ἀριστοτέλης ἐν ταῖς Διδασκαλίαις. Though we know so little about the *Didaskaliai*, if it was little more than an (annotated?) compilation of epigraphic evidence, a reader may have had not much more to judge

In this period the line between choral poet and musician was blurring, as musical composition *per se* took on far greater prominence, and pipers like Pronomos of Thebes were known for musical *and* poetic composition, as well as execution and technical innovation;[49] when song, and perhaps dance, had become increasingly virtuosic and a pipeplayer could take over the training of a Dionysian chorus when its 'corrupt' *didaskalos* absconded.[50]

The case of Oiniades throws a little more light on this issue. In the entire Athenian epigraphic corpus, he is the only *aulos*-player to be recorded on a victory-monument with the addition of his patronymic.[51] The reason for this special honour is clear enough. This was the son of the most famous *aulos*-player of antiquity, the great Pronomos of Thebes. Oiniades was (at least) twice victor at the Thargelia: once in 384/3, the second time a full thirty years later, in 354/3.[52] And he too is known to have been a poetic and musical composer in his own right. The *Kyklops* of Oiniades was performed, by the famous *aulos*-player Timotheos of Thebes, also in 354.[53]

One other name stands out among known Thargelian *didaskaloi*: a Eukles, who was victorious at the Thargelia at least *seven* times in a ten-year period around the middle of the fourth century.[54] In all the cases where the category is known, these were boys' choruses, so Eukles may have been a specialist. His career coincides with what looks like an administrative 'rationalisation ' of the Thargelia— perhaps, as I have suggested, motivated in part by increased polis attention to the choral training of the young.

---

by than 'ἐδίδασκε'. It is impossible to decide whether the Pantakles mocked by Aristophanes (and Eupolis ?: fr. 318 K–A) is the same man. Storey (2003: 275–6) is inclined to think he is.

[49] Paus. 9.11.5–6.

[50] D. 21.17.

[51] A possible second case: Lamprias on *IG* II² 3029 (Stephanis 1988: no. 1528), partly restored. That he was probably an Athenian (thus *LGPN* vol. 2) may be relevant to this choice.

[52] *SEG* 18, 66; *SEG* 26, 220.

[53] Duris *FGrH* 76 F36 = Didymos Σ D. 11.22, col. 12.43ff. Some (Raubitschek in *Hesperia* 1960: 86, and Foucart before him) emend the text to make this a reference to Timotheos of Miletos' *Kyklops*.

[54] Wilson (2000) 304. Eukles was probably an Athenian, since no ethnic is given on any of the extant monuments.

IN THE GARDENS BY THE ILISSOS

The question of where Thargelian choruses danced has only very recently been posed.[55] Epigraphic and other evidence speaks of 'gardens' (κῆποι) in connection with the *Pythion*.[56] Did these provide a suitably open space within the sanctuary, or on the banks of the Ilissos nearby, in which choruses of fifty men and boys could dance, sing, and be viewed by a large audience?[57] That is possible, and an important lesson of Csapo in this volume is his reminder of the impermanence of the seating structures of the theatre itself before *c*. 335, and of the availability and ready use of mobile, temporary seating. Perhaps such seating was also used in the *Pythion*.

The alternative would be to imagine that the performances were held in the theatre of Dionysos, at least from a date when that had become 'the' place for large-scale choral contest in Athens. But apart from pure 'theatrocentric' prejudice, the only possible indication of this in our sources is the fact that a meeting of the assembly may have been held in the theatre of Dionysos after the Thargelia, as it was after the Great Dionysia, to discuss the conduct of the festival, especially allegations of misconduct actionable under the *probole* procedure.[58] If the *agones* did take place in the theatre, the consequent disjunction between the localities of *thysia* (sacrifice) and *agon* makes it is easier to see why the sense that these choruses were somehow οὐδὲν πρὸς τὸν Ἀπόλλωνα ('nothing to do with

---

[55] Leduc (2001) 24.

[56] *SEG* 21, 469.26–7: sacrifices and processions held ἐν τῆι Θαργηλίων ἑορ[τῆι] ἐν Κήποις. At 34ff. the *agon* is described as taking place [πρ]ὸς τοῦ Πυθίου. Mikalson (1998) 273 translates 'near the *Pythion*', but I suspect this may mean 'for the Pythian'. See also Paus. 1.19.2.

[57] Leduc (2001) 25 thinks the *Pythion* itself was too small to accommodate many spectators.

[58] D. 21.10, the law of Euegoros. MacDowell (1990) 14 infers the existence of a law relating to the Thargelia like that for the Dionysia in D. 21.8. See Scafuro (2004) esp. 132–3. She very convincingly revives Drerup's reading of the MSS at 21.10 of ΚΑΘΑ ΘΑΡΓΗΛΙΩΝ, 'just as at the Thargelia'. This would restrict the law mentioned at 21.10 to festivals of Dionysos but also imply that another law already existed about the seizure of property at the Thargelia when it was framed.

Apollo'), and more about spectacle than piety, might have taken further root.

Wherever they sat, just prior to the *agon*, a Thargelian audience heard the herald of the council announce the gold crowns awarded to victors in another important civic *agon*—the annual contest between trierarchs in preparing their ships for service.[59] That such honouring of the city's economic élite was at home as a prelude to the performances of the Thargelia is interesting, though most will be content with the pragmatic explanation that this festival coincided best with the demands of the military calendar. But if Apollo's Pythian cult at some time looked in some way to the Athenians' mastery of the sea, this honouring of trierarchs will have been all the more appropriate.

THE PROBLEM OF GENRE

This 'problem' is well known and easily stated: at Athens' most important city festival for Apollo, we apparently find him honoured by the performance of *dithyrambs* for the observable course of the Classical period, while we look in vain for performances of paeans or kitharodic *nomoi* in his honour in Athens.[60]

The solution has taken three avenues: the first is, in effect, to embrace Platonic despair and to concur with the vision of a decline into generic and religious chaos, propelled by growing democratic political self-confidence, conjured by *Laws* 700. But this is to treat the atopic fantasy of the *Laws* as an eye-witness, objective account of Athenian cultural history, which lays the blame for this generic confusion at the door of those 'leaders of unmusical illegality, poets who though by nature poetical, were ignorant of what was just and lawful in music . . . [and who] in a Bacchic frenzy and unduly possessed by pleasure, mixed dirges with hymns and paeans with

---

[59] At least in the fourth century: *IG* II² 1629a, 196ff.; cf. [D.] 51.1, 6. See below 182.
[60] Pickard-Cambridge (1962) 4, 32; MacDowell (1990) 230, 234: 'dithyrambs'; Simon (1983) 78: 'contests of dithyrambic choruses of boys and men'; Ieranò (1997) 248: 'agoni ditirambici'; Matthaiou (2003a) 90: ἀγῶνες διθυράμβου. Others are more cautious: e.g. Parke (1977) 148: 'hymns at the Thargelia'.

dithyrambs.'[61] The hedonistic Athenians long ago lost the ability to distinguish a paean from a dithyramb, and so the 'problem' of dithyrambs for Apollo at the Thargelia is merely one symptom of the broader problem of Athenian religious, performative, and political chaos.[62]

The second solution is denial: these were in fact paeans, though no ancient document comes close to describing them as such.[63] Or else they were 'Apollo's other genre', the kitharodic *nomos*.[64] This last is one theory at least that can be proven wrong, since epigraphy makes it abundantly clear that these were *choral* events, and that their musician was an *aulos*-player, not a kitharode.

The third avenue is a more honest variant on denial and despair— the attempt to save the phenomena, and to argue that dithyrambs were (or became) a suitable form of song-dance with which to worship Apollo.[65] Proponents of this view offer a variety of arguments. They point to Apollo's familiarity with the dithyramb—or at least, of its beginning and end—from his Delphic sanctuary, on departure and arrival in the winter months;[66] and to Aiskhylos' description of 'Apollo in ivy, the bacchic prophet' ὁ κισσεὺς Ἀπόλλων, ὁ βακχειόμαντις (fr. 341).[67] Then there is the broader sharing of cult at Delphi and elsewhere between the brothers,

---

[61] Pl. *Lg.* 700a–701a; cf. *Grg.* 501e.

[62] Modern scholarship has shown itself unusually willing to accept this Platonic vision of generic and more broadly cultural decline uncritically, and to judge the practitioners of music and poetry in the late fifth and early fourth century accordingly: see Csapo (2004), Csapo and Wilson (forthcoming). One of the paradoxes of over-reliance on this passage is that the relation between paean and dithyramb has come to be seen as more polarised than it was in practice. Contrast our earliest text that presents a relation between these two 'genres', Pindar *Threnos* 3 = fr. 128c: here paeans and dithyrambs are complementary, and contrasted rather with varieties of *threnoi*. Calame (forthcoming).

[63] Bodensteiner (1891: 48): hyporchemes for the boys, paeans for the men. Colin (1905: 13) is even more imaginative, introducing contests of rhapsodes and kitharodes held in an 'old' Odeion on the banks of the Ilissos.

[64] Rutherford (1995).

[65] E.g. Ieranò (1997) 170–1. The most straightforward testimony is a *scholion* to Dionysios Thrax *Grammatici Graeci* I, 3, p. 451 Hilgard: Διθύραμβός ἐστι ποίημα πρὸς Διόνυσον αἰδόμενον ἢ πρὸς Ἀπόλλωνα, παραπλοκὰς ἱστοριῶν οἰκείων ⟨περιέχων⟩; cf. *An. Ox.* IV, 314 Cramer (= Ieranò 1997: 25, test. 33).

[66] Pickard-Cambridge (1962) 4; with greater subtlety, Calame (1990) 364–9.

[67] West (1983: 70) distributes this phrase between Orpheus and the chorus so that the two were distinguished rather than assimilated; cf. Eur. fr. 477 (*Likymnios*).

including the tradition that Dionysos had a tomb there;[68] the fact that we have Philodamos' paean, unmistakably composed for Bromios,[69] as well as the evidence discussed here by Ceccarelli and Milanezi that Apollo in Cyrene apparently received dithyrambs that were very explicitly described as such; that the tripod awarded as prize for dithyramb at the Athenian Dionysia, as at the Thargelia (and also dedicated to Dionysos at Orkhomenos in Boiotia), is a markedly Apollonian object;[70] and that at various points in the Classical period, and certainly later, the iconography of the two gods shows some remarkable swapping and merging of attributes.[71] We could add to this list some other features of the Thargelia that hint at the meaningful co-presence of Dionysos. There is the strange, faintly Dionysiac name of σύβακχοι given to the scapegoats; and the possibility that the guild of young Athenian noble dancers who performed around Apollo's temple in the context of the Thargelia were kitted out as Silens (unless they were in fact wearing Theran cloaks, which would be easier to accommodate to Apollonian principles).[72]

All the same, a distinct unease persists, particularly on the part of historians of religion.[73] We need to pull away from the restrictive arguments of later generic criticism, which throws a long shadow that obscures its very object of study,[74] and start instead by asking how the Athenians who participated in these performances in the *Pythion*

---

[68] Plu. *Mor.* (*de E*) 389c. Cf. the sacrifice to be performed for Dionysos *and no other* in Apollo's month of Apellaios at Delphi by the Labyads: Homolle (1895) esp. 12; Rougemont (1977) no. 9.

[69] See esp. Käppel (1992) 222–84.

[70] Tripods at Athenian Dionysia: Amandry (1976); for Dionysos in Orkhomenos: Amandry and Spyropoulos (1974). Note also the eight marble thrones in the theatre of Dionysos for priests of Apollo: Maass (1972) 103–4, 107–8, 123–4, 128, 135–6, 138, 140.

[71] Moret (1982); Stewart (1982).

[72] σύβακχοι: Hellad. *ap.* Phot. *Bibl.* p. 534b; Calame (1990) 308. The young Athenian dancers are the *Orkhestai* mentioned by Theophrastos (fr. 119) in his *On Drunkenness*, and said to have worn ἱμάτια τῶν Θηραικῶν. LSJ translate Θηραικόν as 'a dress worn in the satyric drama at Athens, invented in the island, Thera'. I assume this is based on Poll. *On.* 4.118: καὶ τὸ θήραιον τὸ Διονυσιακὸν, καὶ χλανὶς ἀνθίνη, καὶ φοινικῶν ἱμάτιον, καὶ χορταῖος, χιτὼν δασύς, ὃν οἱ Σειληνοὶ φοροῦσιν.

[73] Confronted by Parker (1996) 95. Deubner (1932: 198) referred only to 'Männer- und Knabenchören.'

[74] Some recent work on lyric poetry has tended to undermine a tenet of generic

themselves in the first instance described them; and then, more broadly, how they conceived of them.

The answer to the first question is relatively easy, and revealing. They called them two things: the 'men' and the 'boys,' or 'the men's chorus', and sometimes in the genitive plural (ἀνδρῶν, παίδων) with the ellipse of the word 'chorus' (or perhaps 'contest') common in the terminology of festivals.[75] And they called them κύκλιοι χοροί or 'circular choruses'.[76] These two formulations are always used of the performances at the Thargelia, from epigraphic records to public oratory to the descriptive systematisation of the *Ath. Pol.* The word διθυραμβός is *never* used of them.[77] That is not to say that the scholarly presumption that the Athenians thought of them as dithyrambs has no basis whatever. Its principal basis is a *scholion* to Aiskhines' *Against Timarkhos* that states bluntly that in the Athenian context 'dithyrambs are called circular choruses'.[78] And it is supported more generally by the way in which, in comedy, the term διθυραμβοποιός is used of poets who produce κύκλιοι χοροί.[79] But very few people have gone to the trouble of asking just why the expression *kyklios khoros* in particular took on such prominence at

criticism that stresses a tight correlation between type of song and (divine) recipient: cf. e.g. Rutherford (2001) esp. 36–58, 86–9 on the paean; Calame (forthcoming); d'Alessio (forthcoming) is an important contribution.

[75] ἄνδρες, παῖδες e.g. Arist. *Ath. Pol.* 56.3; Wilhelm (1909) 148–9. *IG* II² 1138 shows the use of the dative (ἀνδράσι, παισί) to describe the events; cf. ἀνδρικὸς χορός at Lys. 21.1, 6; Krates fr. 27 K.-A.; D. 39.23–4. Dedicatory inscriptions with the event-markers ἀνδρῶν and παίδων: the '*Fasti*' of the Dionysia: *IG* II² 2318; many khoregic dedications, e.g. *IG* II² 3038–3040, and now proposed for the Atarbos base (*IG* II² 3025) by Shear (2003a) 166–8. As the inscription published in this volume by Ma shows, the use of the genitive plural διθυράμβων as the header for an agonistic event is possible (in second-century Teos), but there it is further qualified by the term ἄισμα—'With the song *The Horse*'—already used in the last quarter of the fourth century in Athens: see above n. 4–5.

[76] κύκλιος χορός of the Thargelia: *Suid.* s.v. Πύθιον (π3130); Phot. π472.25.

[77] Cf. d'Alessio (forthcoming): 'apart from the book of Bakkhylides' *Dithyrambs*, there is no literary or epigraphic text mentioning "dithyrambs" performed outside of a Dionysiac context'. Ceccarelli (forthcoming) is an important discussion of the evidence of the Hellenistic period. See also Käppel (2000).

[78] Σ Aiskhin. *against Timarkhos* 10, discussing Athenian practice: λέγονται δὲ οἱ διθύραμβοι χοροὶ κύκλιοι καὶ χορὸς κύκλιος.

[79] Ar. *Av.* 1377–1409, with Σ 1403a, on Kinesias: κυκλιοδιδάσκαλον· ἤγουν τὸν διθυραμβοποιόν. Cf. Ar. *Nu.* 333; *Ra.* 366.

all in the language of festivals in Athens and beyond, and just what its relation to the term διθυραμβός is.[80] I would suggest that the reason lies in its blandly modal form of expression, stressing the *shape* of the dancing chorus and so avoiding any more explicit generic, or cultic, markers. To that extent it is not a generic term at all, as commonly understood in the study of Greek lyric poetry.

Apollo was worshipped with contests of circular choruses, just as Dionysos was. In Athens, the songs for Dionysos were the privileged form that such circular choruses took, and their predominance may have caused features of the Dionysian *kyklios khoros* to migrate to their Apollonian counterparts, in the way that sharing and mixing of forms had always been characteristic of Greek religious and poetic expression. But *kyklios khoros* was never an exact synonym for 'dithyramb'. It was in the first instance a description of a format of performance that represented a larger category than 'dithyramb', but which was closely associated with it in Athens.[81] There were evidently reasons why even in the case of the Great Dionysia the two major choral events for Dionysos tended to be known as 'circular choruses' rather than simply 'dithyrambs'. The use of the somewhat blander term in that context may register the fact that an issue of performative and generic change is at stake.[82] There is surely a core of

---

[80] Fearn (2003) is an important exception; also d'Alessio (forthcoming) and Ceccarelli (forthcoming). Cf. Pickard-Cambridge (1962) 32: 'The name "circular chorus", which always means dithyramb'.

[81] And, perhaps, in Thebes: in Pindar's dithyramb for the Thebans (fr. 70B.1–5, with d'Angour 1997), the 'song of dithyrambs' is described as taking on a *new* form in which 'the young men are stretched out in well-centred circles' (διαπέπ[τ]α[νται δὲ νῦν εὐο]μφάλ[οις κύ/]κλοισι νεανίαι).

[82] Athen. 4.181c describes the distinctive culture of *mousike* at Athens as follows: τῶν μὲν Ἀθηναίων τοὺς Διονυσιακοὺς χοροὺς καὶ τοὺς κυκλίους προτιμώντων—'while the Athenians preferred Dionysiac choruses and cyclic ones'. It would be possible, as Fearn (2003: 130) argues, to see a disjunction here between Dionysiac and 'cyclic' choruses, if only in Athenaios' mind. The modal nature of κύκλιος as a competition category is also suggested by the evidence of third-century victor-lists from the Koan Dionysia, where the genitive plural κυκλίων, used as an event marker (see n. 75 above), is qualified (we might say, given generic character) by the addition of τᾶι πυρρίχαι (e.g. *ED* 234, A.9–11, 21–3); cf. Ceccarelli (1995). For signs of the early debate about the 'genre' dithyramb see the reference to the quarrel between Kallimakhos and Aristarkhos in *POxy.* 2368 col. I.8–20; and the remains of the learned discussion preserved in the context of an analysis of Pindar's Theban dithyramb in *PBerol.* 9571v: Ieranò (1997) test. 219; d'Alessio (forthcoming).

abused truth in the Platonic image of Athenian culture: the massed, spectacular dithyrambs of the Dionysia, and—perhaps to a lesser extent—the *kyklioi khoroi* of the Thargelia became 'theatricalised' choruses under the impact of developments in music that grew principally out of the increasingly competitive, professional—and lucrative—sphere of the Dionysia. Just what impact these developments had on the choruses of the Thargelia in particular is very hard to say: they might have been similarly 'theatricalised'; or they might have become something of an enclave for a less 'modern' form of performance.

I have already begun to broach the second, more difficult question—Athenian *attitudes* to these performances. I have suggested that we should stop viewing these contests as an embarrassing accretion to a first-fruits festival of civic cleansing and, more broadly, break down the presumed disjunction between choral *agon* and the rest of the festival, a disjunction driven by *interpretatio Platonica*, but not present in other Athenian sources. I add to this discussion a document that appears never to have been properly integrated into the literature on the festival. It is a fragmentary inscribed stele, published in 1970 by Mitsos (Athens, E.M. 6117; Fig. 16):

]οσινος	_ _ _
]τερως	Δ[
]σιμος	Ζω[
]ομας	
]γαθος	Επι[
]δοκας	Ροδ[
]νος	Φ[
]ων	Σε[
]ος	Φο[
]νδρος	Επ[

[ὁ] δῆμ[ος]

Θαργη-

λίων

The upper part of the stone, which is broken at the top and right-hand side, has a catalogue of fragmentary names in two columns. The lower part has a carving of a vessel, possibly intended to suggest

Fig. 16 A third-century stele from Attica with two columns of fragmentary names and a vesssel with the word Thargelion inscribed on it.

bronze, with the word Θαργηλίων inscribed across its body. This must be a depiction of the very *thargelos* full of the stew of seeds that was the central ritual object at the Thargelia.[83] And the two columns of names are very likely to be those of the men and the boys who were in the winning choruses of a particular year. Underneath the names and above the vessel are what appear to be the remains of the words 'The *Demos*', in slightly larger letters. This implies it was erected by the polis, and suggests the existence of an *agonothesia* in connection with the festival by this time.[84]

Apart from presenting a neglected item of evidence for the conduct of the Thargelia in the third century and the persistence at it of choral performance, this document illustrates very nicely that the Athenians may have been predisposed to see quite a close relationship between the central ritual event of the festival and its choral *agones*.

A better knowledge of the mythology relating to the festival would doubtless give us further insight into the role the choral *agones* played in it. What we do know suggests that the ritual patterning continued at the level of myth. It is likely that the—or a—mythical *aition* of the purification rite was the story of the Athenian murder of Minos' son Androgeos, and the need to cure the city of the disease that resulted from it.[85] If so, we might propose that the model for

---

[83] Hsch. and Suid. s.v. Θαργήλια. This is more likely than, as Mitsos (1970: 394) suggests, that the vessel is a prize given to the choruses. The word must be the genitive plural of the festival name (Θαργηλίων) rather than the month-name (Θαργηλιών).

[84] The prominence of 'The *Demos*' in this document recalls agonothetic inscriptions of the period, with the preface ὁ δῆμος ἐχορήγει: see Xenokles' monument of 307/6, *IG* II² 3073 with Wilson (2000: 273) and Goette in this volume; and Lambert (2003) for the convincing suggestion that the dedicator of this monument was in fact Xenokles' brother, Androkles. In the second century there appear to be *agonothetai* (plural) of the Thargelia (might these be past officers processing?), and *khoregoi* are involved: *SEG* 21, 469.34ff. However Stephen Lambert cautions (*per litteras*) that the restoration [ὁ] δῆμ[ος] is far from certain (a name ending in -*demos* is also possible), and that the deduction of an *agonothesia* at this time is correspondingly insecure (a prize or honorific reward granted by the *demos* could also be imagined).

[85] Thus Hellad. *ap.* Phot. *Bibl.* 279, p. 534, after a description of the *pharmakos*-ritual at Athens: τὸ δὲ καθάρσιον τοῦτο λοιμικῶν νόσων ἀποτροπιασμὸς ἦν, λαβὸν τὴν ἀρχὴν ἀπὸ Ἀνδρόγεω τοῦ Κρητός, οὗ τεθνηκότος ἐν ταῖς Ἀθήναις παρανόμως τὴν λοιμικὴν ἐνόσησαν οἱ Ἀθηναῖοι νόσον, καὶ ἐκράτει τὸ ἔθος ἀεὶ καθαίρειν τὴν πόλιν τοῖς φαρμακοῖς.

the dancing *paides* of the Thargelia was in some sense the group of youths taken to Krete by Theseus as tribute for the murder—and brought back again, via Delos (and this mythic thread between Pythian Apollo and Delos is noteworthy).[86]

The mythology of that great role-model to Athenian youth, Theseus, is further associated with the *Pythion*. He had a dominating presence in the region.[87] Pausanias (1.19.1) associates the Delphinion closely with the *Pythion*, and this was the site of Aigeus' royal palace (Plutarch, *Theseus* 12.3). It was also the site of a renowned deed of early youthful power by Theseus. Newly arrived in the city, dressed in a long robe and with well-coiffed hair, he shocked the workman building the temple who mistook him for an unmarried girl by hurling the oxen from his waggon higher than its roof. The story is obviously one appropriate to the rituals of transition from boyhood to early manhood, and might make us ask whether the boys' *agon* of the Thargelia that took place in this region represents a cognate expression, at the broad level of cyclical civic festival, of the same concerns. At any rate, the mythology of the great Athenian synoecist and 'purifier' *par excellence* is entirely fitting for the Thargelia, and is likely to have found expression in its *kyklioi khoroi*.

In this context I would add further weight to arguments put

---

[86] At some time the ills of the first day were associated with a religious transgression. Harpokration, citing Istros' *Epiphanies of Apollo* (*FGrH* 334 F50, third century), indicates that the *pharmakos*-ritual was a mimesis of the punishment by Akhilleus and his men of the theft of sacred *phialai* of Apollo by one Pharmakos (who may have been the priest of Apollo). The fact that this is preserved as a gloss on a speech of Lysias (*Against Andokides, for impiety* 6.53) gives us reason to believe that it describes the *pharmakos* ritual as it existed in Athens. Might those *Orkhestai* from the 'first' families of Athens who danced about the temple (Thphr. fr. 119) have been imitating the actions of Akhilleus and his men? Harp. *Lexicon in decem oratores Atticos* (Φ5) Φαρμακός· Λυσίας ἐν τῶι Κατ' Ἀνδοκίδου ἀσεβείας, εἰ γνήσιος. δύο ἄνδρας Ἀθήνησιν ἐξῆγον καθάρσια ἐσομένους τῆς πόλεως ἐν τοῖς Θαργηλίοις, ἕνα μὲν ὑπὲρ τῶν ἀνδρῶν, ἕνα δ' ὑπὲρ τῶν γυναικῶν. ὅτι δὲ ὄνομα κύριόν ἐστιν ὁ Φαρμακός, ἱερὰς δὲ φιάλας τοῦ Ἀπόλλωνος κλέψας ἁλοὺς ὑπὸ τῶν περὶ τὸν Ἀχιλλέα κατελεύσθη, καὶ τὰ τοῖς Θαργηλίοις ἀγόμενα τούτων ἀπομιμήματά ἐστιν, Ἴστρος ἐν α' τῶν Ἀπόλλωνος ἐπιφανειῶν εἴρηκεν. The variant reading ἱερεὺς for ἱερὰς makes Pharmakos the name of a priest of Apollo who stole the *phialai*. The fall of Troy was at some stage associated with the 'good' of the second day: Damastes *FGrH* 5 F7; cf. Hellanikos *FGrH* 4 F152a.

[87] Plu. *Thes.* 14.1, 18.1, 22.4, 27.4; cf. Wycherley (1963) 78. Musti and Beschi (1982) 328–9.

forward by others that Bakkhylides' poem, the *Theseus* (18), was probably composed for a boys' chorus at the Thargelia.[88] The comparatively simple style and structure of the song point in the direction of boys, with its clear role for a leader in the 'Aigeus' figure which might well be undertaken by an older singer, or perhaps simply by the most accomplished *pais*, perhaps even by their *khoregos*. The intense focus on the sheer physical power and military potential of the unknown 'boy at the threshold of manhood' ($\pi\alpha\hat{\iota}\delta\alpha$ ... $\pi\rho\acute{\omega}\theta\eta\beta o\nu$ 56–7) making his way to Athens from Troizen, also fits such a context very well. And when the chorus attempts to calm their fears in lines 12–15, they may hint—extra-diegetically—at their own identity as *neoi*, as they sing to Aigeus: 'you, if any mortal, have the aid of valiant youth ($\dot{\alpha}\lambda\kappa\acute{\iota}\mu\omega\nu$ $\dot{\epsilon}\pi\iota\kappa o\nu\rho\acute{\iota}\alpha\nu$ ... $\nu\acute{\epsilon}\omega\nu$) at hand, O son of Pandion and Kreousa!' In this, they are surely proffering themselves as *neoi* ready to come to the aid of the Athenian king. Only here is Kreousa made the wife of Pandion and mother of Aigeus.[89] Has the lineage been made to fit performance by a combined chorus of Pandionids and Aigeids?

The narrative and dramatic tension that drives this short choral song derives its force from a productive irony. Its participants and internal audience—both Aigeus and the Athenians—are ignorant of the identity of the awesome youth announced as making his way to 'brilliant Athens', while the external audience ought to know what is going on at least by line twenty, with the mention of Sinis. In addition to the various exploits narrated in this poem, the external audience very probably knew too that Theseus had already been required to recover the sandals and sword left under a rock by his father on the road from Troizen to Hermione that were the tokens of his birth, and that he was bearing these to Athens with him.[90] Quite apart from the immense dramatic force with which this endows the song, this dynamic of carefully

---

[88] Jebb (1905) 235. Maehler (1997: 212) suggests a possible link with the Thargelia as a festival of purification, given the role of Theseus as 'purifier' here. As he notes, there is no evidence to suggest that the Theseia ever hosted choral performance (Merkelbach 1973 argued for performance by an unattested ephebic chorus there). Zimmermann (1992) 100 for a boys' chorus.

[89] Jebb (1905) 392–3.

[90] Jebb (1905) 230.

constructed ignorance and uncertainty would also be especially fitting if, as many believe, it was within the context of the Thargelia that some phratries met to perform their function of admitting new members by recognising naturally legitimate and adopted children presented by their fathers.[91] In this performance the paradigmatic Athenian recognition of son by father is anticipated with all the anxiety and fear appropriate to the preliminary phase of so significant a ritual transition, an anxiety exemplified in the mythic variant which saw Medea try to murder the young Theseus on his return to Athens—and the spot where the poisoned cup fell was enclosed in an area of the Delphinion, adjacent to the *Pythion*.[92]

Bakkhylides' *Theseus* is the most likely candidate for a choral song designed for the Thargelia, but in truth we have no single text that we can confidently declare to have been performed there. There is no sign that the Athenian polis kept records of the choral poets (or pipers) who performed at any of their festivals, or of their works, as they may have for tragedy and comedy (nor, for that matter, that individual tribes did so). In the so-called *Fasti* of the Great Dionysia only the names of victorious tribes and of their *khoregoi* are recorded for dithyramb.[93] Neither the traditions of transmission, nor such texts as survived, supplied the information to permit the inclusion by Hellenistic scholars of editorial details of the kind Οἰνηΐδαις καὶ Αἰαντίδαις εἰς Θαργήλια παίδων or the like. At some point it became one possible editorial practice to collect some choral songs by reference to their thematic titles, as with Bakkhylides, whose 'dithyrambs' are collected in alphabetical order.[94] Many of these are in all probability what (at least in the Athenian context) would be termed *kyklioi khoroi*, for they demonstrate characteristics which

---

[91] Lambert (1993) 216–17; cf. Parker (1996) 104–9.

[92] Plu. *Thes.* 12.3.

[93] Though the fact that Aristotle in his *Didaskaliai* mentioned Pantakles (see above p. 161) may point to the existence of more extensive production records that covered non-dramatic performances; or it may indicate that this is another Pantakles, or that the choral poet also composed drama. Cf. Milanezi (2004).

[94] The earliest clear example of this is the inclusion of the title of a dithyramb by Timotheos, the *Elpenor*, on the architrave of the monument of Nikias that dates to 320 (above n. 45).

prompted the employment of the broader and less explicit category of *kyklios khoros*, in particular the inclusion of extensive heroic narrative which might have little or nothing to do with Dionysos.[95]

THARGELIA AND DELIA

The remainder of this chapter turns to a more speculative argument: my suggestion is that the Athenians exported choral practices they had developed in their domestic festival of the Thargelia to the great festival for Apollo 'abroad'—on the island of Delos that was, for much of the Classical period, effectively offshore Athenian territory. The effect (and probably the aim) was to make the extremely malleable circular chorus available at the heart of the league and empire to forge and validate in performed myth the city's hegemonic cultural and political identity—and, moreover, to involve the allied states themselves in the performance.

The Delia under Athenian management certainly had a contest of choruses. The Athenians manufactured tripods to be awarded as victory-prizes (νικητήρια) in this *agon*, and saw to their transportation from Athens. The same ship also carried a number of Athenian choruses and bulls that were doubtless to be sacrificed as part of the same festival.[96] As part of the process of purifying the island and developing the festival in 426, the Athenians rejuvenated a contest that had fallen into decline.[97] It may be from this date that the model of the Thargelian *agones* became particularly influential. But poor relations with the Delphian cult for much of the fifth century, combined with the Athenian drive to forge an identity as the leader of a maritime alliance centred on Delos, will have been reason enough to

[95] For further argument along these lines see Fearn (2003). Cf. now Negri (2004) on the Alexandrian editorial treatment of Pindar.

[96] *IG* II² 1635aA, esp. 33–9 = *I.Délos* 98; Rhodes–Osborne no. 28: accounts of the Athenian administration of Delos, 377–3. See Rutherford (2004), especially on the relation between the Athenian theoric chorus and the competitive choruses on Delos. I suggest that any chorus sent could have been both 'theoric' and competitive.

[97] Th. 3.104.2, 6. Cf. the *Pythian* oracle recorded in D. 21.52 that ordains the setting-up of choruses after a plague. Hornblower (1991) 519.

promote a link between the domestic Pythian and the Delian cults from a date much earlier in the century.[98]

The reason for positing a direct connection with the Thargelia rests on a very material basis. The tripods taken to Delos by the Athenians were the same in size and design as those awarded as prizes at the Thargelia.[99] How much else came with these 'Pythian' tripods—and precisely when—we cannot say. The Delian tripod bases have no surviving inscriptions, and can be dated only very generally to the fifth or fourth centuries. But prizes are highly symbolic items and the distinctive badges of their particular festivals, so we should not underestimate the import of this connection. There can be little doubt what it signifies: this was worshipping Apollo in the Athenian way.

Thargelian influence on the Delian festival would also help explain the fact that, in Athens, Apollo *Delios* could be identified with Apollo *Pythios* of the Thargelia. In describing a group of young Athenian dancers called the *Orkhestai*, for whom as a youth Euripides served as cup-bearer, Theophrastos locates their activity 'about the temple of Delian Apollo' and goes on immediately to add: 'this is the Apollo for whom they conduct the Thargelia'.[100] On my hypothesis, such an association between Delian Apollo and the Thargelia is perfectly intelligible: the 'temple of Delian Apollo' was that in the *Pythion* itself, which through its links to the cult on Delos could be referred to as a sanctuary of both Delian and Pythian Apollo.[101] A distinguished

[98] The activity in 426 may have mirrored an operation undertaken by Peisistratos during the first purification (Ieranò 1989; 1997: 281)—and he had promoted the cult of Pythian Apollo at home. The expulsion of Thargelian *pharmakoi* was said to purge plague from the city, so the festival and its choruses may have taken on special prominence in the wake of the cleansing of the city of Athens itself from plague in 430; and likewise, in cleansing Delos a few years later, Thargelian choruses will have presented themselves as a suitable ritual model. Tz. *Chil.* 5.726–30; Hedrick (1988) 209.

[99] Amandry and Ducat (1973) esp. 40–1.

[100] Fr. 119: ὠρχοῦντο δὲ οὗτοι περὶ τὸν τοῦ Ἀπόλλωνος νεὼν τοῦ Δηλίου τῶν πρώτων ὄντες Ἀθηναίων καὶ ἐνεδεύοντο ἱμάτια τῶν Θηραικῶν. ὁ δὲ Ἀπόλλων οὗτός ἐστιν ὧι τὰ Θαργήλια ἄγουσι.

[101] Leduc (2001) 19 draws attention to the lack of evidence for a sanctuary of Apollo Delios in Athens, and suggested that the city's principal veneration of Delian Apollo took place on Delos. She does not mention the modest temple built for him at Phaleron in the 430s. Lewis (1960) argued that the Athenian state had taken

parallel for such a co-joining at the level of festival celebration had long existed in the Pythia and Delia (*Πύθια καὶ Δήλια*) of Polykrates.[102] Closer to home, Peisistratid attentions to Delos went hand-in-hand with renovation of the Pythian cult in Athens at another time when relations with Delphi were poor. In the period of their Aigean hegemony, the Athenians will have had similar reasons to forge ties between their domestic, polis worship of Apollo and their leading role in his cult on Delos: the chorus was a principal mechanism of that process.[103]

The major difference between the Delian and the Thargelian choral contests from the point of view of performance lay in the fact that, rather than Attic tribes, the choruses on Delos represented visiting members of the Delian League and Athenian empire, modelled on the *panegyris* of Ionians that had long since gathered to meet and dance on Apollo's sacred island.

The songs performed competitively on Delos would, I suggest, have been called 'circular choruses'.[104] They might also, from time to time, have been classified for other purposes as paeans, dithyrambs, or *prosodia*, but the broader term was probably that in common use for Athenian choral contest abroad, as at home. Surviving examples

---

over a private cult of Apollo Delios at Phaleron, but recent analysis of the relevant inscription (Matthaiou 2003) has undermined the connection with Apollo Delios. In the final stages of completing this chapter I had access to the important study of Matthaiou (2003a), in which he argues that the *Pythion* in Athens was also the temple of Apollo Delios. He adduces the fact that inscriptions relating to the cult of Apollo Delios—in particular, what appears to be the first account of the Amphiktyons after the founding of the second Athenian confederacy in 378/7: *IG* II² 1635)—were found in close proximity to the region beside the Ilissos where Thargelian dedications were found. Cf. Aloni (2000) 88. The temple of Apollo at Prasiai on the east coast of Attica, possibly associated with a tomb of the hero Erisykhthon (and the *genos* Erisykhthonidai), was the final staging-post for the gifts of the Hyperboreans on their way to Delos: Parker (2005) 82.

[102] Burkert (1987).

[103] See Hornblower (1991: 521) also stressing the reaffirmation of the 'Ionianism' of the Delian League as part of the same process. In 420 Delphi reversed the Athenian decision to expel the islanders: Th. 5.32.1. Santucci (2002) 161–2.

[104] Kall. *Hymn* 4.310–15 gives what looks like an *aition* for the Athenian mission of choruses to Delos that depicts the original dance, under Theseus' leadership, as a circular dance about the altar (with the implicit suggestion that it mimicked their movements in the Kretan labyrinth.) Cf. esp. 313: κύκλιον ὠρχήσαντο, χοροῦ δ' ἡγήσατο Θησεύς.

of songs possibly performed under these conditions on Delos include Bakkhylides' seventeenth dithyramb (*Youths*) and Pindar's fifth paean.[105]

Only two short stanzas of the original eight that made up this paean survive,[106] but that is enough to show that the song—performed, very probably, by Athenians on Delos—told a story of the progressive Athenian–Ionian colonisation of the islands.[107] As our fragment begins, with the closing phrase of the sixth strophe, we hear that 'they took Euboia and dwelt there' (36). The seventh strophe then opens with the refrain to Apollo—'*Ieie* Dalian Apollo!'—and goes on to recount the colonisation (ἔκτισαν 39) of the Kyklades, culminating in the 'gift' from Apollo of the body of Asteria—that is, Delos itself (40–2): a legitimation of possession of the crucial sacred island (and all that its ownership implied) as a gift of Apollo (δῶκεν 41).

Some date Bakkhylides' *Youths* as early as 480 or even 500, but a period after the formal foundation of the league seems most likely.[108] Classed among the poet's dithyrambs in antiquity, the song has invited classification as a paean because of the way, at the end of its narrative, with the epiphanic return of Theseus from the waves, the Athenian youths raise a paean (124–9).[109] At that point the narrative frame immediately closes and the concluding address, in the here and now of performance by the Kean chorus, is a request to Dalian Apollo to promote 'god-sent fortune of good things ... taking pleasure in his heart in choruses of Keans' (130–2).

Claude Calame has made the attractive suggestion that the myth of Theseus' heroic leap in this song, and his protection of the Athenian youths against the predations of Minos, can be read as an *aition* for the regular performance on Delos by choruses of Athenian youths and maidens *as well as* for the righteous assumption of

---

[105] Simonides composed dithyrambs for Delos: Str. 15.3.2. There was an important Dionysia on the island, but this usage may intend 'dithyrambs' in the looser sense applied to Bakkhylides' songs: Rutherford (1990) 203–6; Ieranò (1989).

[106] Rutherford (2001) 293–8, esp. 296, for the intriguing suggestion that a scholiast interpreted the song as a re-enactment of the original colonisation. Rutherford (2004) 82–9.

[107] A *scholion* to l. 35, ἀπ' Ἀθηναίων, suggests that the colonists were Athenians.

[108] Maehler (1997) 167–70.

[109] For the debate as to whether Bakkh. 17. is a paean or dithyramb, see Maehler (1997) 167–8, with earlier bibliography.

Athenian thalassocracy over the Aigean.[110] What is most striking, however, is the fact that such a freighted ideological message is danced and sung by means of Kean ventriloquism. This certainly represents an extraordinary deviation from the standard expectation of the relationship between poet, commissioning city, and festival. We look in vain in this poem for anything about distinctively *Kean* myth and traditions. Such ventriloquism is of course particularly beneficial when performed by a friend rather than oneself. Keans happily sing and dance 'the song of the Athenian empire', as Ian Rutherford has dubbed it.[111] But perhaps this chorus was in fact packed with Athenian-Keans, for the place was an Athenian foundation and doubtless had many Athenian citizens dwelling there.[112] Many of the choruses competing on Delos will have hailed from states that had a significant population of Athenians, whether or not as a formal kleroukhy. It may be that many of the performers on Delos in Naxian, Andrian, Kean, or Samian choruses, were in fact resident Athenians who had trained as boys in domestic *kyklioi khoroi*. And we might suppose that the impact of those Athenians abroad, in terms of the commissioning and performance of these songs, was great.

Whatever the make-up of the choruses who came to compete on Delos, Athenian pre-eminence in the event was assured. It is to the 420s that we ought to attach the discussion that Xenophon puts in Sokrates' mouth regarding Athenian choral hegemony. He explains this pre-eminence by Athens' collective devotion to *philotimia*, which in this context might best be understood as the driving psychological force of empire: 'Did you never reflect that when one chorus is set up from this city, like the one that is sent to Delos, no chorus from anywhere else can ever come into the running with it . . .?'[113]

We may catch a further echo of the tightening of the Athenian choral and ideological grip on the Delian festival in a fascinating fragment of Eupolis' comedy the *Poleis*, a work generally dated to the

---

[110] Calame (forthcoming).

[111] Rutherford (2004) 82.

[112] Hdt. 8.46 and Th. 7.57.4 both describe Keos as an Athenian foundation, though we have no indication of a kleroukhy. See esp. Parker (1994).

[113] Xen. *Mem.* 3.3.12. Rutherford (2004).

420s and much concerned with the condition of the empire.[114] This hints suggestively at the intersection of imperial politics and choral organisation: fr. 239 K.-A. ἄνδρες λογισταὶ τῶν ὑπευθύνων χορῶν. 'Gentlemen auditors of the choruses under scrutiny ...' This looks like a variant on the familiar topos of appeal—or threat— to the judges of the comic contest to secure favour for one's cause. It seems the judges at the current Dionysia are being assimilated to the accountants of empire, scrutinising the accounts rendered of themselves by the choruses as though they were subject-states having their tribute payments audited. The effect is to turn the choruses of the comic *agon* into subject-states of empire, tribute-bearers under scrutiny. This is especially resonant in a comedy whose chorus was itself made up of subject-states of the Athenian empire, the *poleis* of its title. And it may imply a wider perception of the time that the Athenians were fully in charge not only of all economic judgments to be made in the empire, but of choral judgments too. Such a trope may also point to Delos and recent Athenian impact on the organisa- tion of its choral contest. The possibilities for comparison will have been extensive between the 'contributions' brought by the allies in the form of choruses to the Delia and their contribution in coin to the coffers of the Athenian empire, brought at the time of the Dionysia.

Whatever the nature of their formal relation, the choruses of the Thargelia and Delia were very probably both sites for the develop- ment of an Ionian cultural and political identity centred on leader- ship of a maritime empire. Central to the mythology of both festivals, Theseus played the lead role in this development.[115] The Thargelia is emphatically identified by ancient sources as a festival characteristic of Ionian communities.[116] And Ionianism features prominently in Bakkhylides' *Theseus*, which I argued was performed by boys at the Thargelia. The opening phrase of the song, in which Aigeus is addressed as 'King of holy Athens, lord of the soft-living Ionians', strikes a strong note of apparently positive valuation of soft-living Ionianism. This may be a further item of evidence to

---

[114] Storey (2003) 216–30.   [115] Mills (1997); Calame (1990).
[116] Nilsson (1957) 109. Gebhard (1934) lists fifteen Ionian cities in which Θαργη- λιών (or an equivalent) occurs as a month-name; to which now add Hermonassa on the north shore of the Black Sea: *SEG* 44, 659.

add to that of Thoukydides (1.6.3), that in Athens of the (?) 470s this version of Ionian culture that was to take on associations of eastern softness and élitism later in the century was still available for positive civic identification. Unless of course the whole point of stressing the soft-living ways of the Athenian–Ionians at the start of this performance, and markedly before the arrival of the young warrior Theseus, is to contrast a 'pre-Thesean' softness with a change to come with the arrival of this tough, physically powerful militaristic hero and future king—'this man so vigorous, valiant and bold' (38–9), 'intent on the past-times of Ares, on warfare and the clangour of battle' (57–9: Jebb's translation).[117] This young Theseus is wearing a Lakonian cap, purple tunic, and woolly Thessalian mantle (50–4)—nothing very Ionian about that get-up, though as Barron pointed out, the unique use of the adjective οὔλιος to describe the mantle as 'woolly' (ostensibly used as a synonym of οὖλος, rather than its usual sense of 'destructive'), points suggestively to Apollo, for it must allude to the vow Theseus made to Apollo Oulios for his safe return before he embarked.[118] The representation of Theseus in this song implies that Ionian identity was not a culturally fixed quality. If the choruses of the Thargelia were an important site for the formulation of Athenian Ionianism as it became enmeshed with Delian and Athenian imperial ideology over the course of the century, this would help explain the remarks of Plato (echoed by Plutarch and others) to the effect that Minos received such terrible press in Athenian poetry. Tragedy comes to mind first, and others have suggested epic, but that may only be because we have none of the dozens of choral songs that might have expressed similar views of Minos as the tyrannical thalassocrat from whom Theseus liberated the flower of Athenian—and Ionian— youth forever.[119] This would serve as a perfect mythological decoy

---

[117] I owe this suggestion to Frances Muecke.

[118] Barron (1980) 1, citing Pherek. *FGrH* 3 F149. In a similarly prominent opening phrase of the song for the Keans on Delos, the young Athenians are described as ἀγλαοὺς . . . κούρους Ἰαόνων (2–3).

[119] [Pl.] *Min.* 318d–320e; 321a; Philokh. *FGrH* 328 F17; Pl. *Thes.* 16.1; D.S. 4.60.4; Paus. 1.27.10; Apollod. 3.15.7–8. Giesekam (1976: 241) stresses that poetry other than tragedy is probably meant, but thinks only of epic. As I noted, the story of Androgeos' murder and the subsequent need for the city's purification after Minos sent plague seems to have been the—or a—mythic *aition* of the Thargelia.

for the youth of a city that was itself fast becoming a tyrannical thalassocracy.[120] In short, the representation of Athens' role as metropolis of the Ionians could thus have been developed in the choruses of the 'Ionian' Thargelia for subsequent dissemination on Delos, whose major festival was evidently moulded by the Athenians into a *panegyris* promulgating their own special vision of Athenian–Ionian mastery of the Aigean.[121]

The cult of yet another Apollo that was apparently unique to Athens,[122] that of Apollo Patroos, also became associated with that of Apollo Pythios at least by the fourth century, and perhaps earlier.[123] Whenever this happened, it suggests that the Apollo of the Thargelia had by then become identified as 'ancestor' of all Athenians through his son, *Ion*, and that this identification played an important part in Athens' claim to being the mother-city of all Ionians.[124] This looks very much like the formulation on the banks of the Ilissos of a new idea about being Ionian whose elaboration we first know of from a work produced on the southern slopes of the Acropolis, in the sanctuary of Dionysos.

---

[120] If the Thargelia and its choruses did look to Delos and play some part in helping mould the ideology of Athenian maritime power, the fact that its *agon* was preceded by the announcement of the winner in the trierarchic contest (see above p. 164) seems less incidental.

[121] Shapiro (1996) argues, principally from the iconographical evidence, for a special Athenian concern with Apollo as ancestor of the Ionian Greeks in the last three decades of the fifth century. See also Connor (1993).

[122] Hedrick (1988) 206; Colin (1905) 8–9.

[123] Cf. D. *de Corona* 141. Hedrick (1988: 205) argues that the cult of Apollo Patroos was associated with Pythios in Athens from its inception. See also de Schutter (1987).

[124] Hedrick (1988) 200–2; *SEG* 21, 469.9ff.

Part III

Beyond Athens

7

Dithyramb, Tragedy—and Cyrene

Paola Ceccarelli and Silvia Milanezi

The traditional emphasis on Athens in the study of dramatic and musical performances is to some extent justified by the abundance of the documentation and the importance of theatrical activities for the cultural life of the city. Yet increasingly other localities of the ancient Greek world are receiving the attention they deserve.[1] Still, the problems facing those intent on broadening the Atheno-centric horizon are enormous. And so, any attempt to extend the geographical scope turns almost inevitably into a study in the empirical and methodological difficulties involved in writing anything like a history of dramatic culture outside Athens. Nevertheless, the fact that such interpretive efforts will often have to remain hypothetical or speculative should not be considered sufficient excuse for forgetting that much was going on elsewhere in the Greek world.

Cyrene, the focus of this chapter, is a case in point: despite its numerous theatres and some important documentary evidence, the Libyan city is still frequently forgotten in surveys of ancient drama. The hazards of archaeological discovery have had a hand in making it the Cinderella of theatrical studies: of the two documents around which the whole issue of theatrical and dithyrambic performances at Cyrene revolves, one—*SEG* 9, 13—was published in 1933, too late for

---

[1] Cf. e.g. Sifakis (1967), with its focus on Delos and Delphi; for the rest of the Greek world, the recent survey in Wilson (2000) 279–302 (including a reference to the Cyrenaean tragic choruses, 290).

inclusion in Pickard-Cambridge's authoritative survey (1927); and the other—*SEG* 48, 2052—has been published only very recently. These two documents will be at the centre of our discussion: if they raise more questions than it is possible to answer, they also give us tantalising glimpses of the cultural life of a Greek city in the fourth century BC.

TWO INSCRIPTIONS FROM CYRENE

Among the inscriptions brought to light in the excavations of the agora of Cyrene are the so-called accounts of the *damiergoi*. Thirty-eight of these accounts, ranging from the very end of the fifth to the second half of the second century BC, have survived, in a more or less fragmentary state. Their format is relatively standardised. The heading mentions the eponymous priest of Apollo and the names of the three *damiergoi* in charge; this is followed by the evaluation (τίμασις) of various kinds of agricultural produce, and by the total of the revenues for that specific year (τὸ πᾶν ἐσιὸν τῶ ἐνιαυτῶ). The *damiergoi* then note the expenses of the year (ἐξιόν), and the difference between the two (λοιπόν); the sum to be paid to the *damiergoi* as (symbolic) compensation (παρόρεγμα) closes each account. Since their publication in 1933, these texts have been scrutinised more than once, mostly for what they can tell us about the economy, agriculture, and prosopography of Cyrene.[2]

As a rule these accounts are very detailed on the evaluation of the agricultural produce, but give only a lump sum for the expenses;[3] two however, the afore-mentioned *SEG* 9, 13 and *SEG* 48, 2052, both

---

[2] The most important discussions are Oliverio (1933); Laronde (1987) 241–5 and 325–36; and Chamoux (1988). For the agricultural, religious, and civic vocabulary see Dobias-Lalou (2000) 195–246. For a general, updated account of the topography and history of Cyrene, see Bonacasa and Ensoli (2000).

[3] Three of them (*SEG* 9, 11 and 16: ἐξιὸν βουθυσιᾶν ἤσσᾶν, and *SEG* 9, 17: βο-]λυθυσίας ἔ[σσας - -) specify that the total of the expenses is inclusive of the sacrifices.

dated *c.* 335 BC, are in this respect exceptional, because they detail the expenses as well.[4] These two accounts are the only known documents that mention tragic and dithyrambic choruses in Cyrene; moreover, they share a very specific vocabulary that sets them apart from the rest of Cyrenaean inscriptions. Why the *damiergoi* of the year in which Eukleidas was priest of Apollo (just as the unknown *damiergoi* of the other, fragmentary, inscription) decided to go into details about their expenses, which are not greater than those incurred in the immediately preceding or following years, is not known: we can only make guesses. At any rate, this is what they chose to register:

Θ[εοί]. | .Ἰαρεὺς τῶ Ἀπόλ[λων]ος Εὐκλείδας Παραιβάτα, | δαμιεργοὶ Λῦσι[s] Ἀνδροκλεῦς, Τιμῶναξ Πρώρω, | Ἀντίμαχος Δαιλέ[ο]ντος. Καρπῶ τίμασις· κριθαὶ ||5 ἂν Z >, σπυροὶ ἂν Z [>] > > >, ὄσπρια ἂν Z > >, κάρφη ἤμερα | ἂν ⋛ ⋛ ⋛, ἄγρια ἂν ⋛ ⋛, ἄχυρα ἂν ⋛ ⋛, σπυραμινὰ ἂν ⋛ ⊏, | σταφυλὰ ψυθία ἔνδος τᾶς προκλησίας ἂν ⋛ Z, ἔξος | ἂν ⋛, μέλαινα ἔνδος τᾶς προκλησίας ἂν ⋛, ἔξος | ἂν ⊏ Z > > –, σταφὶς ἂν Z >, σῦκα ἂν > > > >, ἐλαῖαι ἂν Z, || 10 ἔλαιον ἂν ⋛ ⋛, κύμινον ἂν ⋛ >. Τὸ πᾶν ἐσιὸν τῶ | ἐνιαυτῶ M ⋛ ⊏ Γ = – X X X ⋛ ⋛ ⋛ ⊏ Z > Δ Δ, ἐξιὸν ἱαροθυσίας, | ἄρκωι τροφᾶς, Ἀρτάμιτι Καταγωγίδι ἐς τά ἰαρ[ά, ἱ]αρέαι | Ἀ⟨θ⟩αναίας τροφά, περιακτριαι ἐ[ς τὸ]ν κόσμον, χοροῖς | τραγικοῖς τρισὶ ἑκάστωι βοῦς, διθυραμ[βικ]ῶι χορῶι ||15 βοῦς, ἐξάρχοις, κάρυξι τρισὶ ἐς ἡμάτ[ια κ]αὶ ἐς τρο-|φάν, αὐλητᾶι, γροφεῖ, ταμίαι, μαγίρω[ι, π]ρωροῖς, λυ-|χνοκαιία Ἰατρῶι ποθ᾽ ἑσπέραν· ἐπισκ[ευᾶ]s τῶν μη-|ρῶν τῶν βοέων, εὑρόντων ἂν τρισκ[αίδε]κα στατῆρας | ἑκάστω βοὸς τῶν μηρῶν· τὸ πᾶν ἐξ[ι]ὸν τῶ ἐνιαυτῶ || 20 σὺν ἱαροθυσίαις M ⋛ Γ – X X X ⋛ ⋛ Z > > – Δ Δ, λοιπὸν | M ⊏ = ⋛ Z > > > Δ Δ Δ Δ. Παρόρεγμα δαμιεργοῖς : M = –

12: Oliverio; ἄρκωι τροφᾶς Ἀρτάμιτι Καταγωγίδι ἐς τά ἰαρ[ά] Dobias-Lalou || 16–17: Dobias-Lalou; π]ρωροῖς λυ|χνοκαιία, ν ἰατρῶι ποθ᾽ ἑσπέραν, ἐπισκ[όποι]s Oliverio; πρωροῖς, λυ|χνοκαιίαι, ἰατρῶι, ποθ᾽ ἑσπέραν ἐπισκ-|[όποι]s Chamoux 1988.

Gods. Priest of Apollo Eukleidas son of Paraibatas, *damiergoi* Lysis son of Androkles, Timonax son of Proros, Antimachos son of Daïleon. Estimate

---

[4] They correspond to Oliverio (1933) no. 12 (cf. also *SEG* 38, 1875, and *SEG* 43, 1186) and Marengo and Paci (1998). We give here only a very selective apparatus. *SEG* 9, 13 is one of a group of five texts (*SEG* 9, 11, 12, 13, 14, and 15) all inscribed on a single stone and all dating to the second half of the fourth century BC: 11 and 12 were inscribed on the left side, 13 on the front, 14 and 15 on the right side; the fourth side was not prepared for inscription and must have been put against a wall. These five are the only accounts of which beginning and end are preserved.

Fig. 17 An inscription from the agora of Cyrene, with accounts of the *damiergoi*, civic officials with responsibility for administering sacred properties and mentioning tragic and dithyrambic choruses (*SEG* 9, 13: *c.* 335 BC).

of the agricultural produce: barley [5] 1 drachma and 1 obol, wheat 1 drachma and 4 obols, pulse 1 drachma and 2 obols, cultivated hay 12 drachmas, wild hay 8 drachmas, straw 8 drachmas, wheat flour 6 drachmas, early grapes among the choice ones 5 drachmas, outside the choice ones 4 drachmas, black grapes among the choice ones 4 drachmas, outside the choice ones 3 drachmas, two obols and a dichalcous, raisins 1 drachma and 1 obol, figs 4 obols, olives 1 drachma, [10] olive oil 8 drachmas, cumin 4 drachmas and 1 obol. Total revenue for the year: 308 minae (= 30,800 drachmas) and 75 drachmas, 1 obol and 2/10. Expenditure: for the sacrifice, to the Bear for maintenance, to Artemis *Katagogis* for the ceremonies, to the priestess of Athena maintenance, ?(to the) *periaktriai*? for the adornment, to each of the three tragic choruses an ox, to the dithyrambic chorus [15] an ox, to the *exarchoi*, to the three heralds for dress and maintenance, to the *aulos* player, the secretary, the treasurer, the sacrificer, the guards, illumination for Iatros towards the evening; for the preparation of the thighs of the oxen, having been evaluated at 13 staters for the thighs of each ox. Total expenditure for the year, [20] sacrifices included, 20,669 drachmas, two obols and 7/10. The difference, 10,205 drachmas, 3 obols and 4/10. Contribution to the *damiergoi*: 300 drachmas.

The text of the inscription is well established; there is however disagreement concerning the division into clauses and the interpretation of single words.

The first problem occurs in ll. 11–13: Oliverio (1933: 117–18 and 133) understood them as listing four different items of expenditure (sacrifice; maintenance of the bear; ceremonies of Artemis *Katagogis*; and maintenance of the priestess of Athena). Dobias-Lalou (1993: 27–8) however, on the basis of her study of the sacred regulation *SEG* 9, 72, links the bear to Artemis *Katagogis* and suggests that only three items are meant (sacrifice; maintenance to the bear for the ceremonies of Artemis *Katagogis*; and maintenance of the priestess of Athena).[5]

---

[5] A priestess of Athena at Cyrene is also mentioned in *SEG* 9, 21, 3 and in *SEG* 48, 2052, 15–16. As for the 'bear', Chamoux (1953) 319 had already suggested that she might be the priestess of Artemis *Katagogis* (cf. Hsch. α 7280 ἄρκος· καὶ ἱέρεια τῆς Ἀρτέμιδος); a bear is attested at Cyrene also in the *lex sacra SEG* 9, 72 (revised text in Dobias-Lalou 2000: 307–9) and in *SEG* 48, 2052 (discussed below).

This is as yet an unresolved problem;[6] but whatever the choice, it does not greatly affect our understanding of the document. It is however very interesting to find that a bear, Artemis *Katagogis*, and Athena are mentioned in the same context.

The second difficulty concerns the term περιακτριαι in the clause of l. 13: both its case and its meaning are in dispute. The term is a *hapax*. Oliverio, who did not translate it, considered it a dative and thought of a priestess in charge of adorning a divine statue.[7] Another possibility is to take the term as referring to revolving machines used to change the scene on stage.[8] Such an interpretation would imply that the Cyrenaean theatrical performances had a relatively high degree of sophistication. The possibility of theatrical machines has however been recently dismissed by Dobias-Lalou (1993: 29) in favour of a third hypothesis, namely, that the term (the derivation of which from περιάγω she accepts) should be understood as referring to a female leader of processions, who would have needed to dress up expensively for the occasion.[9] This is a possibility to be considered; on the other hand, her objections to theatrical machines are not altogether convincing. The first objection is based

---

[6] Cf. Callot (1999) 254 and n. 343; Dobias-Lalou (2000) 208. The meaning of the unique epithet *Katagogis* is not certain: it might refer to a dress, to the celebration of returns called *katagogia* (usually however these are linked to Dionysos), or to a term deriving from κατάγω, 'to bring one down', in some relation to the topography of Artemis' cult in Cyrene. Cf. Gentile (1999) and Dobias-Lalou (2000) 218 and n. 61.

[7] Oliverio (1933) 119, with reference to money spent in Delos in 250 BC εἰς κόσμησιν τῆς Ἥρας καὶ ταῖς κοσμούσαις, IG XI 2.287A68; and to the ἱέρεια ἡ περιρ[ά]πτρια (who took care of the dress?) of IG II² 2361 = Syll.³ 1111 (*orgeones* of the goddess Belela in Athens, beginning of the third century AD).

[8] Thus the 1940 *addenda* to LSJ, with reference to the Cyrenaean inscription. περίακτος is found in Plutarch (*Mor.* 2.348e: μηχανὰς ἀπὸ σκηνῆς περιάκτους), and as a noun in Vitr. 5.6.8 and Poll. 4.126. For Bieber (1961) 75–7 this kind of device may go back to the fifth century BC; Sifakis (1967) 134–5 links them to the introduction of the high stage and the separation between chorus and actors typical of the Hellenistic period, and advances the hypothesis that the τόρνισκος constructed at Delos in 279 BC (*IG* XI 161A65, 162 A53) may have been a support for the *periaktoi* (ibid., 51–2). At Cyrene such a structure might have existed already in the second phase (fifth century BC) of the theatre on the terrace of the Myrtousa in the sanctuary of Apollo, which definitely had a central rectangular cavity for staging apparitions from underground: cf. Stucchi (1975) 3, who however prefers to refer the expenses for the choruses of the account SEG 9, 13 to the third phase (mid-fourth century) of the theatre of the Myrtousa: ibid. 69 and n. 4.

[9] See now also Dobias-Lalou (2000) 238–9.

on the inappropriateness of the use of a dative for an inanimate object. But περιάκτριαι could be taken as nominative plural. It comes after the clause on the maintenance (τροφά) and before that concerning the prize (βοῦς), which are both in the nominative;[10] and as both Pollux and Vitruvius make clear, there were always two of these *mechanai*, on the two sides of the stage. The rationale of her second objection—namely, the fact that the term occurs before and not after the prizes for the choruses—is unclear: the important point in favour of machines is surely their closeness to theatrical performances. Her third argument, the difficulty of seeing a relation between theatrical machines and the κόσμος, can also be disputed: in the same paragraph on the organisation of the *scaena* in which he mentions the *periaktoi*, Vitruvius uses *ornatus* twice, and twice *speciem ornationis*.[11] In the present state of the evidence, it may be better to leave open whether we are here dealing with expenses for theatrical machines, for a female leader of processions, or for a priestess in charge of adorning the statue of a god.

The third problematic point in the understanding of the text concerns the meaning of *exarchoi*. Are they officials, as proposed by Oliverio,[12] who connected them to the heralds, the *aulos*-player, the secretary, the *mageiros* and the guards, as people concerned with the organisation of the festival(s), or should they be distinguished from the following personnel and considered, as in a famous passage of Aristotle, leaders of the dithyrambic choruses?[13] Oliverio assumed the

---

[10] In giving the items of expenditure, the list oscillates in seemingly random fashion between datives, objective genitives, and nominatives.

[11] Vitr. 5. 6.8: *Ipsae autem scaenae suas habent rationes explicitas ita uti mediae valvae ornatus habent aulae regiae, destra ac sinistra hospitalia, secundum autem spatia ad ornatus comparata, quae loca Graeci* περιάκτους *dicunt ab eo quod machinae sunt in his locis versatiles trigonos habentes in singula tres species ornationis, quae cum aut fabularum mutationes sunt futurae seu deorum adventus cum tonitribus repentinis ea versentur mutentque speciem ornationis in fronte.*

[12] Oliverio (1933) 119, with reference to Heliod. *Aeth.* 6. 3, 26. *Exarchoi* are also mentioned in the extremely fragmentary account *SEG* 9, 21, 2, which may also refer to an *agon*; cf. below.

[13] Thus Chamoux (1988) 152–3 and Dobias-Lalou (1993) 30. For ἔξαρχος with the sense of 'head of the chorus', besides Arist. *Po.* 1449a11 (οἱ ἐξάρχοντες τὸν διθύραμβον) cf. Dem. 18 (*De Corona*) 260. ἐξάρχειν appears already in Archil. fr. 120 and 121W, respectively for a dithyramb in honour of Dionysos, and for a paean; ample discussion in Ieranò (1997) 175–85.

existence of a *vacat* after the choruses, signalling a change in the kind
of expenses. But a look at the photograph (Fig. 17) shows that this
space cannot have been intended to mean anything (or we would
also have to assume a *vacat* at l. 10, after *elaion*, and that would be
absurd). In fact, the layout does not give any indications that might
help in deciding how the different rubrics relate (or do not relate) to
each other.

The fourth problem concerns ll. 16–17 λυχνοκαιία ἰατρῶι ποθ'
ἑσπέραν. Oliverio (1933: 120) thought that we had two items of
expenditure: for the illumination, and for calls on a doctor in the
evening.[14] This clause may however also be understood as referring
to an evening ceremony for the healing god Iatros.[15] In this case, the
expenses of the *damiergoi* from the revenues of the terrains of Apollo
would have concerned personnel explicitly linked to the following
gods: Artemis, Athena, and Iatros. To these we should add Apollo, to
be regarded as an implicit presence in the list, and possibly Dionysos,
because of the choruses.[16]

---

[14] He could refer to similar cases: the Delian accounts for the year 270 BC report
expenses under λαμπάς, λαμπάδες; in 279, the term was δᾶιδες, as well as ἔλαιον
καὶ ἐλλύχνια (*IG* XI 2, 161A112: χορῶι τῶι γενομένωι τοῖς Ῥοδίων θεωροῖς
δᾶιδες; cf. *I.Délos* 316, 76–80, 88, 89). And *Syll.*³ 596, 18 offers a case of a doctor
offering special service during a festival. Moreover, *SEG* 9, 1, 44 (the *diagramma* of
king Ptolemy I) testifies to the existence of public doctors in Cyrene (ὅστις ἐκ τοῦ
πολιτεύματος δημοσίαι ἰατρεύηι) besides public *kerukes* and teachers.
[15] Dobias-Lalou (1993) 33–5; Dobias-Lalou (2000) 225–6. Iatros is however
attested at Cyrene only from the second century BC onwards (*SECir* 158, 18; the other
attestations are all of Roman times), and usually with his *paredros* Iaso. Iatros and
Iaso are the epichoric version of the couple Asklepios–Hygieia: Callot (1999) 255–6
(cf. *SEG* 9, 46 for a fourth-century BC dedication to Asklepios). Dobias-Lalou (1993)
34–5 stresses the independence from Apollo (and Asklepios) of both Iatros and
Paian; but surely, if the expenses for this god were part of the accounts of the
damiergoi, his cult must have been part of the general organisation of the sanctuary
of Apollo. In one of his Cyrenaean odes Pindar stresses both the healing and
the musical capacities of Apollo (*P.* 5.63–5); cf. Krummen (1990) 145. Might not
Opheles, who also had from the very beginning an *oikos* and a cult on the agora
(Krummen 1990: 107 and n. 21), be hiding behind the *Iatros* of the inscription?
[16] For Dionysos cf. Dobias-Lalou (1993) 30 and 38; for the closeness of Apollo and
Artemis, Chamoux (1953) 138–40; Callot (1999) 254 and n. 340, who underlines the
proximity, both cultic and topographical, of the *Apollonion* and the *Artemision*:
the rituals and the administration were conducted jointly. The same situation (a close
relation between Apollo and Artemis) is attested at Brauron, where there were also, as
in Cyrene, bears: Peppas-Delmousou (1988).

This list of expenditures raises numerous questions. In particular, it would be important to know in which context the choral performances took place. Until a few years ago, this text was almost unique (with the extremely fragmentary *SEG* 9, 18 and 21 for company). Now, a fragment found in the same region where the other accounts were found, near the Apollo temple of the *agora*, and joining with *SEG* 9, 18, offers some terms of comparison.[17] Here is the text:

----| [ἀχύρ]ων ῥῖπο[ς price σταφυλά] | [ψυθί]α ἔνδος τᾶ[ς προκλησίας] |
[price] :μέλαινα ἔ[νδος τᾶς πρ]-|[οκλ]ησίας [Z > > -[ψυθία ἔξος]||5 [τᾶς]
προκλησία[ς price μέλαινα] | [ἔξ]ος τᾶς προκλ[ησίας price] | [ἔλ]αιον ⊰ ⊰ Z:
ἐλ[αῖαι price] | τὸ πᾶν ἐσιόν :Μ:⊰[--- ἐξιόν?] | τάδε ἔξος ἰαρο[θυσίας : τραγ-
] | |10 οἰδικῶν χορῶν [----] | Μ: - ⊰ ⊰ [: ἐπιθεν[--- :Μ: ?] | X X X X ⊰ ⊰ [:
διθυ[ραμβικῶν] | χορῶν τῶι : νικ [--:Μ: ---| τᾶι ἄρκωι τροφ[ά ---] ||15 θρα :
Μ = X X : τᾶι [ἰαρέαι τᾶς Ἀθ]- |αναίας :Μ: = : τ[οῖς ἐξάρχοι]-|ς:Μ = X:
κάρυξ[ι τρισὶ ἐς τροφά]-|ν καὶ ἡμάτια[:Μ: ---?] | πρωροῖς τρι[σί? :Μ: ---τα]-
||20 μίαι :Μ:Γ= = ⊰ [---αὐλ]-|ητᾶι :Μ: = = X[---] | τὸ πᾶν :Μ: > [---] | τὸ
πᾶν ἰαρ[οθυσίας ---] | ἰ τὸ τιμαχ[εῖον ---? :Μ : ---]|| 25 = X X⊰ ⊰ [[---τὸ
πᾶν ἐξιόν] | τῶ ἐνι[αυτῶ --- ? :Μ: ---] | Γ = - X X [---] | λοιπ[όν :Μ: ---] | [Z]
> > [---? ||30----

4: [ψυθία ἔνδος] edd. pr. || 10: [τῶι νικάθρωι?] edd. pr. || 13: νικ [άθρωι edd.
pr. || 17–30 = Oliverio no. 17, *SEG* 9, 18.

... hurdle of straw [price; early grapes] among the choice ones [price],
black [among the choice ones] 3 drachmas, 2 obols and a half; [early grapes
outside] [5] the choice ones [price; black] outside the choice ones [price];
olive oil 9 drachmas; olives [price]; total of the revenue 200 minae (20,000
drachmas) and [--]. [Expenditure?] without the [sacrifice:] [prize?] [10]
for the tragic choruses 110 drachmas, on top, [minae ?---] 90 drachmas,
prize? [--] for the dithyrambic choruses [sum]; maintenance for the Bear
[- -], [15] ?-*thra* 2 minae and 40 drachmas, to the priestess of Athena,
2 minae, to the *exarchoi* 2 minae and 20 drachmas, to the [three?] heralds
for maintenance and dress [sum, something else ?] to the three (?) guardians [sum..., to the] treasurer [20] 9 minae and 4 drachmas; [---to the]
auletes 4 minae and 20 drachmas; [something else]; total, minae [10+];
total of the sacrifice [- - -] and the *timach*[*eion* ?---], [25] 2 minae and
50 drachmas [--. Total expenditure] for the year [? minae]; difference,
[minae --] [30]

---

[17] *SEG* 48, 2052, published by Marengo in Marengo and Paci (1998).

Fig. 18 An inscription from the agora of Cyrene, with accounts of the *damiergoi*, civic officials with responsibility for administering sacred properties and mentioning tragic and dithyrambic choruses (*SEG* 48, 2052 upper part comprising ll.1–17: *c.* 335 BC).

First a few technical points. The stone is broken on all sides except the right; the editors established the approximate line-length on the basis of ll. 3–4, whose restorations are almost certain, because they feature standard formulas for the evaluation of the produce. At l. 4 however [ψυθία ἔξος] must have been meant, because the category [ψυθί]α ἔνδος τᾶ[ς προκλησίας] is already mentioned at l. 2.[18] This gives a line-length of twenty-two letters; but it is necessary to make allowances for the possibility of longer or shorter lines, because the lettering is not very regular, and because, as the comparison with the left margin of *SEG* 9, 13 shows, we should not expect a regular end of line.

These two inscriptions present marked similarities which distinguish them from all other Cyrenaean inscriptions, but some differences as well, which may help in the overall interpretation. The principal difference between *SEG* 48, 2052 and *SEG* 9, 13 seems to be, apart from the absence of Artemis *Katagogis*, a structural one. In the new text the expenditure is divided into subsections: a first long one concerning choruses and excluding the *hiarothusia* (sacrifice); another one on the *hiarothusia*; and then the total sum. In keeping with its care about the different rubrics, the new text carefully records the sum spent on each item of expenditure, allowing us to evaluate their relative importance.

TRAGIC AND DITHYRAMBIC CHORUSES: FOR WHOM?

Our texts do not give explicit indications as to the god to whom the choruses were dedicated, nor as to the festival in which the dances were performed. It is however quite extraordinary to find dithyrambic choruses epigraphically attested in Cyrene, for the term διθύραμβος and its related forms are rarely found in inscriptions: the rest of the Greek world seems to have preferred such denominations as

---

[18] For the meaning here attributed to the phrase ἔνδος / ἔξος τῆς προκλησίας cf. Oliverio (1933) 111; Marengo and Paci (1998) 389 n. 31. Chamoux (1988) 150 and Dobias-Lalou (2000) 199–200 prefer to think of a specified amount whose price was fixed beforehand, and of the surplus.

κύκλιος χορός, χορὸς παίδων, χορὸς ἀνδρῶν, *et similia* (see Wilson, above, p. 167). How interesting, then, but also how puzzling, since just in the one place where we encounter the markedly Dionysiac term 'dithyramb', there are no attestations of the cult of Dionysos prior to the first century BC![19]

It is not easy to decide which god was honoured by the performances of tragic and dithyrambic choruses at Cyrene. *SEG* 9, 13 explicitly mentions only two goddesses, Artemis and Athena; *SEG* 48, 2052 is from this point of view even less helpful. To these two, one may want to add Iatros and, as an implicit presence, Apollo, if we accept that the *damiergoi* administered the revenues of his terrains.[20]

As Dionysos is the god of the dithyramb and of theatre *par excellence*, most scholars have suggested that these choruses were associated with his cult. However, even if the archaeological findings show that he was not unknown in Cyrene, there are no direct literary or epigraphic references to his cult before the first century BC.[21] It

---

[19] Cf. Dobias-Lalou (2000) 221. The first epigraphical attestations consist in the dedication of a statue by a priest of Apollo to a Dionysos Charidotas (an epiclesis better attested, and at an earlier date, for Hermes), and in an honorific inscription for a priest of Dionysos in the *kome* of Mgernes (respectively, *SEG* 9, 103, from the sanctuary of Apollo, dated to the first century BC, and *SEG* 9, 354, which Laronde (1987) 335 would date in the Augustan period); in the first century AD a statue and a temple are consecrated to the god in the extramural sanctuary of Demeter and Persephone (*CIG* 5139). Cf. Callot (1999) 94, 142, and 258–9: Dionysos in Cyrenaica had privileged relations with Delphic Apollo and with the Eleusinian goddesses, and his popularity may have increased due to his role as protector of the Lagids. The theophoric anthroponym Dionysios is also very rare before the second century BC.

[20] Marengo and Paci (1998) 387–8 doubt this; it is true that nowhere in the accounts is Apollo mentioned. But that the *damiergoi* administered his properties still seems to be the most reasonable explanation of their activities; cf. Chamoux (1988) 147–8. *Damiergoi* are not mentioned in the *diagramma* of Ptolemy on the constitution of Cyrene (*SEG* 9, 1); the only document, apart from the accounts, in which they are mentioned is *SEG* 9, 5, a decree of the Cyrenaeans on cultic regulations dated *c.*110 BC, specifying that the various magistrates must decorate their official buildings with crowns, while the *damiergoi* and the *hiarothytai* must decorate the *prytaneion* and the porticoes on the agora and sacrifice for the kings. This sets them apart from the other magistrates and qualifies them as religious functionaries, associated with a *hiarothysia* still in the second century BC.

[21] For the possibility of identifying with a temple for Dionysos the anonymous *naiskos* situated near the theatre, outside the sanctuary of Apollo, cf. Callot (1999) 152, 258–9. Epigraphical attestations: above, n. 19. Archaeological data: below, n. 30. In Sparta too the cult of Dionysos was of minor significance: cf. Parker (1988) 99–103; for Dionysos in Lakonian pottery, see Pipili (1987) 52–4.

thus seems difficult to maintain with Chamoux that in Cyrene 'the cult of Dionysos must have been flourishing':[22] the *komos* of men mentioned by Pindar in his ode for Arkesilas of Cyrene, on which Chamoux's argument rests, need not have been Dionysiac—*komos* could be used for any chorus, and anyway, this one is explicitly said to be a delight for Apollo.[23] It is also dangerous to assume that all of the theatres that were built in Cyrene were dedicated to Dionysos:[24] Dionysos is associated with the theatre in a great number of Greek cities, but neither the building nor dramatic or circular choruses are exclusively linked to this god. Even before Hellenistic times, dramatic performances were associated in various cities with divinities other than Dionysos: at the end of the fifth century, Archelaos instituted the festival of the Olympia in Dion, which comprised dramatic representations; there were tragic performances for Athena at Coronea. Dramatic performances were also on the programme of the Soteria at Delphi, of the Heraia of Argos, and of the Naia at Dodona, as is shown by the list of victories of a third-century tragic actor from Tegea in Arcadia.[25] The theatres of Cyrene and Delos were built in the

---

[22] Chamoux (1953) 271; cf. Laronde (1987) 335 and n. 136.

[23] Pi. *P.* 5.22: δέδεξαι τόνδε κῶμον ἀνέρων, Ἀπολλώνιον ἄθυρμα; at 5.103 Phoibos of the golden sword/lyre (χρυσάορα, an epithet particularly apt for the double character, musical and military, of the Karneia: cf. Giannini, in Gentili (1995) 538) must be invoked ἐν ἀοιδᾶι νέων. Krummen (1990) 98–151 shows that this epinician was performed by a chorus of young men on the occasion of the Karneia (esp. 114–16; cf. also Gentili 1995: 160): a festival of Apollo would have been appropriate, since the king's victory was obtained in an Apollinean contest. For the synonymity of *komòs* and *choros* cf. Ieranò (1997) 268–70.

[24] For these theatres, cf. Chamoux (1953) 271; Bonacasa and Ensoli (2000) 103, 123. The one on the Myrtousa, just west of the *Apollonion*, seems to have existed already at the time of the Battiadai; Stucchi (1975) 34–6 has published foundations which might have supported a wooden *skene* at the end of the sixth century, with a second phase in the first half of the fifth century; this would have been substituted by a stone *skene* in the second half of the fourth century, ibid. 69–70. The three other theatres are all late (after the second century AD): Stucchi (1975) 289, 291, and 262. A fifth theatre, of pre-Roman date (see Luni 2006a and b), has recently been found by the Italian archaeologists in the vicinity of the sanctuary of Demeter.

[25] Archelaos: D.S. 17.16.3; Coronea: *TrGF* I DID B 12; victory list from Tegea: *Syll.*³ 1080. Cf. Sifakis (1967) 1–2; Scullion (2002) 112–14. The latter's case for dramatic performances for Apollo in Amorgos, based on *IG* XII 7.226, seems less clear-cut: the fact that the decree honouring Nikophon of Miletos for having produced three dramas 'for the god' was inscribed on the wall of the temple of Delian Apollo does

sanctuary of Apollo; such may have been the case already in Syracuse.[26]

The case of the dithyramb is different, however: this song carries specifically dionysiac connotations. In view of the evidence, the most likely solution is to think that theatrical performances, including the specifically Dionysiac dithyrambs, might have been included in the celebrations of another divinity. Apollo would then seem the best candidate, all the more so if we recall that in Classical times the most important non-Dionysiac festivals of which circular choruses (principally the dithyramb) formed part were those of Apollo.[27]

But there might be other possibilities: if in his *Fifth Pythian* Pindar insists on the brilliance of the festival of Apollo *Karneios*, he elsewhere mentions games (*teletai*) organised in honour of Zeus Olympios, Athena, and Ge Bathykolpos.[28] Athena was very important in Cyrene, especially in the Archaic and Classical periods—and she is mentioned in our accounts. The same applies to Artemis: besides the extremely fragmentary account *SEG* 9, 21 (discussed below), an inscription of the Hellenistic period mentions the sacrifice of 120 oxen for the Artamitia; the latter was an important festival, attested in three more inscriptions.[29]

Thus, both Athena and Artemis might be candidates for the festival to which our inscriptions refer. Demeter might have a claim too: besides the fact that some of the pottery dedicated in her sanctuary presents Dionysiac themes, Demeter and Kore are perhaps

---

not necessarily imply that the plays were produced for Apollo—all the more so since the honours given by the same Minoans in Amorgos to unknown judges (*IG* XII 7.225) are to be announced by the *strategoi* at the Dionysia and the Heraia (l.11), but are to be inscribed on the temple of Apollo (l.12).

[26] Again, Scullion (2002) 114 (mentioning also the theatres of Poseidon at Isthmia, of the hero Amphiaraus at Oropos in Boeotia, and of Hera at Samos).

[27] At Athens, for example, at the Thargelia: on these see Wilson above. There were however circular choruses for Athena at the Panathenaia, for Prometheus at the Prometheia and for Hephaistos at the Hephaisteia: cf. Ieranò (1997) 255–8; Pickard-Cambridge (1962) 8–10.

[28] Pi. *P.* 9. 97–103.

[29] *SECir* 161 and 162 (two copies of the same epigram) commemorating the sacrifice offered by Hermesandros son of Philon; *SEG* 9, 66, 3; *SEG* 9, 72, 92; *SECir* 145, 2.

associated with Dionysos in a relief dated to *c.* 300 BC and found in the sanctuary of Apollo; moreover, a theatre has recently been identified in their sanctuary.[30]

Still, the case for the Karneia seems overwhelming: that choruses performed in this festival is suggested by Callimachus in his *Hymn to Apollo* (85–7), and a sacrifice of bulls is also mentioned in that context (77–9). Dithyrambs for Dionysos could have been part of a festival for Apollo: in this connection, a well-known volute-krater from Taranto (a Spartan colony) is particularly important, for it represents on one side (Fig. 19a) Dionysos sitting on a rock, while on the other (Fig. 19b) it has on the upper register Perseus showing the Gorgon's head to scared satyrs (a typical subject for dithyrambs), and, on the lower register, girls and youths with wide leafy crowns (*kalathiskoi*) dancing besides a pillar inscribed *Karneios.*[31]

If Denoyelle (2002: 606) is right in thinking that its composition may be understood as the Italiote answer to an Attic masterpiece such as the Pronomos-vase from Ruvo—and the two kraters indeed show the same kind of thematic balance, having on the one side, Dionysos and his *thiasos*, on the other, a theatrical/satyric representation—then the Italiote Karneia were considered by the locals as comparable to the Attic Dionysia, both at the level of the type of performances and at the religious/cultural level.

---

[30] For Attic ceramic with Dionysiac imagery from the sanctuary of Demeter and Kore cf. Elrashedy (1985); Moore (1987); and McPhee (1997) 74; cf. also the Laconian cup with Dionysos dated to *c.* 520–480 in Schaus (1985) 43 n. 225, pl. 14. No significant pattern seems however to emerge from the range of mythological scenes reproduced on the vases found in this sanctuary. The relief, whose interpretation is uncertain, is now in Edinburgh, Nat. Mus. Scotland inv. 1956. 364, cf. *LIMC* IV 870 n. 308 and *LIMC Suppl.* VIII 964 n. 139. The comparison with the Akrokorinth, where a theatrical area was part of the sanctuary of Demeter and Kore, suggests itself; in addition to theatrical masks and terracotta figurines possibly representing Dionysos, four inscribed *pinakes* were found there, bearing the inscriptions Διονύσου, Παιᾶνος, Ὁλολυνγοῦς, Ἀλφιαίας: cf. Stroud (1968) 323–6 and 328–30; Bookidis and Stroud (1997) 247; Lavecchia (2000) 223–5; other instances of Dionysos and Demeter linked in dithyrambic contexts in Lavecchia (2000) 114, 116.

[31] Krater: Taranto, Nat. Mus. IG 8263, found in 1898 at Ceglie del Campo; *LCS* p. 55 no. 280; *LCS Suppl.* III, p. 19; Malkin (1994) 157 and n. 58; bibliography in Denoyelle (2002), who sees the vase as the result of the collaboration of a 'Karneia painter A' and of the painter of Brooklyn–Budapest.

Fig. 19a Red-figured krater from Ceglie del Campo, now in Taranto, side A: Dionysos sitting on a rock.

Fig. 19b Side B of the same: Perseus showing the Gorgon's head to satyrs; girls and youths dancing near a pillar inscribed *Karneios*.

AN ATHENIAN INFLUENCE AT WORK?

In her study of the accounts of the *damiergoi,* Dobias-Lalou (1993: 35) had suggested that the number of the tragic choruses—three— that we find in *SEG* 9, 13 could be a reflection of the programme of the Athenian Dionysia. The new text shows that the tragic choruses need not always have been three; nonetheless, the hypothesis of an Athenian influence deserves consideration, as Athens was in Classical times the centre of dramatic culture.[32]

The iconography of two funerary reliefs from Cyrene of the last quarter of the fifth century BC might lend weight to this hypothesis if, as Laronde (1987: 140) has suggested, the artist was influenced by the *Alkestis* of Euripides: the play, produced at Athens in 438 BC, might have been reperformed not much later in the theatre of the sanctuary of Apollo at Cyrene.[33]

On the other hand, we do not necessarily need a Cyrenaean repre- sentation of Euripides' *Alkestis* to explain these reliefs: the play itself alludes to songs in honour of Alkestis during the Karneia. Just after the death of the queen, the chorus sings for her (ll. 445–51), adding that the servants of the Muses will often celebrate her, both on the seven-toned mountain tortoise and with lyreless hymns, in Sparta when the season of the Karneia comes around, as well as in Athens.[34] These verses involve two distinct oppositions: the first one between song and spoken verse, or, as seems more likely, between songs to the

---

[32] The important finds of Panathenaic amphorae in Libya and more specifically in Cyrene show that there were close relations between the two *poleis*: cf. Laronde (1987) 142–5 (and 140–2 for a list of imported Attic vases); Maffre (2001a) 25–32 and pls. 8–12; Maffre (2001b) 1066–79; and Luni (2002).

[33] The reliefs, kept in the Archaeological Museum of Cyrene, are reproduced in Laronde (1987: 138–9 pls. 36–7); cf. also Bonacasa and Ensoli (2000) 211–12 and Quattrocelli (2006).

[34] Eur. *Alc.* 445–54: πολλά σε μουσοπόλοι | μέλψουσι κατ᾽ ἑπτάτονόν τ᾽ ὀρείαν | χέλυν ἔν τ᾽ ἀλύροις κλέοντες ὕμνοις, | Σπάρται κυκλὰς ἁνίκα Καρνεί-|ου περινίσεται ὥρα | μηνός, ἀειρομένας | παννύχου σελάνας, | λιπαραῖσί τ᾽ ἐν ὀλβίαις Ἀθάναις. | τοίαν ἔλιπες θανοῦσα μολ-|πὰν μελέων ἀοιδοῖς. This is Diggle's text; at l. 448 κυκλὰς is a correction of Scaliger almost universally accepted, but the codices have κύκλος (maintained by Nilsson 1906: 118). Full discussion of the possibilities (including 'round dance') in Dale (1954) 90; cf. also Susanetti (2001) 215–17.

lyre and songs to other instruments;[35] the second one between Sparta
and Athens, conveying the idea that Alkestis' fame will spread
throughout the Greek world. We know that Phrynichos had composed an *Alkestis*, and that her story had also formed the subject of
a lost play by Sophocles, the *Admetos*: when mentioning Athens,
Euripides may have been alluding to these dramatic performances.
Similarly the mention of the Karneia opens the possibility of a more
specific understanding (by the Spartans and the Cyrenaeans): the
Karneia was the most important festival of both Sparta and Cyrene,
dedicated to Apollo—and in view of the important role of the god in
the *Alkestis* it has been suggested that the story of Alkestis might have
been elaborated (or at least sung) precisely in that context.[36] But then,
the funerary reliefs can be explained independently of a performance
of Euripides' *Alkestis* in Cyrene: Alkestis' story might have been
known through performances at the Karneia, at Sparta but also in
Thera and Cyrene.[37] Alkestis is, already in Hesiod (fr. 37.16–22 M–W),
the daughter of Pelias, and thus closely related to the Argonautic
story, in its turn related to the foundation of Cyrene. According
to Pausanias' description of the Chest of Cypselos (5.17.9–11),
Admetos, Iason, and Euphemos participated in the funeral games for

---

[35] Thus Dale (1954) 90, who remarks that the terms μέλψουσι and μολπὰν
μελέων ἀοιδοῖς would be more appropriate with the second alternative. For song to
the αὐλός as ἄλυρον μέλος cf. Arist. *Rh.* 3.6.7, 1408a.

[36] Weber (1930) 12–20. The song of the chorus in the second stasimon is defined
by Dale (1954) 88 'a study in prosodiac-enoplian', something which may suggest that
Euripides is here 'picking up' an older tradition; similarly, it might just be possible
that the term κύκλος, which has caused difficulties to the commentators (who—as
now Diggle, n. 34 above—generally correct to κυκλάς), may refer allusively to cyclic
choruses.

[37] The name Admetos is particularly frequent in Thera among the priests of
Apollo Karneios. The name is attested twice in Cyrenaica, in two inscriptions of the
second century BC; once in Delos and twice in Thasos, also in the second and first
century BC; and eight times in Thera, in inscriptions dating from the second century
BC to the second century AD (cf. *LGPN* I s.v.; Malkin's reference (1994: 158 n. 64) to
an Admetos master-dancer at the Karneia is wrong: the text has Eumelos). Six of
these are priests of Apollo Karneios; particularly interesting are *IG* XII 3.868 and 869
(imperial period), because Admetos son of Theokleidas, priest of Apollo Karneios
διὰ γένους, claims to descend from Lakedaimonian kings and from the Thessalian
ones Peleus and Pheres. This recalls the genealogy of the Aigeidai: cf. Krummen
(1990) 140–1. The comparison with Athens, where the name is attested only four
times (cf. *LGPN* II s.v.), is instructive. In Sparta, Admetos is attested twice (father and
son), and given the scarcity of information on Sparta this is not little.

Pelias; Alkestis was portrayed (the only woman to be named) on the other side of the chest.[38] Alkestis might thus have been at home in Libya, and her story might have been sung in the Cyrenaean Karneia. This does not necessarily exclude Athenian influences: but it rather points towards local traditions.

The same applies to the presence of a bear. Brauron comes to mind. But this parallel need not be explained as a direct Attic influence: bears appear, in a more or less marked way, in many regions of the Greek world.[39]

One further bit of information may lie in the number three: three *damiergoi*, three *karukes* (heralds), three *phrouroi* (guards). As a Dorian colony, Cyrene had three *phylai* (which were kept in place

---

[38] On the links between the three sons of Tyro Pelias, Pheres, and Aison and their offspring Alcestis, Admetos, and Iason cf. Gantz (1993) 189–95; a Euphemos, very likely the Argonaut central to Pindar's *Pythian* 4, appears among the contestants in the funeral games for Pelias, together with Kastor, Admetos, Alastor, Amphiaraos, and Hippasos, on a late Corinthian krater from Berlin (now lost: F1655). In that same *Pythian* 4.126, Pheres and Admetos come on hearing of Iason's arrival. Later Callimachus attests to this same connexion by numbering Cyrene, the daughter of the Lapith king Ipseus, among the participants in the funeral games at Iolcos (*Hymn to Artemis*, 3.206–8); cf. also Malkin (1994) 158. The name Admetos is attested twice at Cyrene: cf. Marengo (1991).

[39] Having examined some sixty sanctuaries (including the temple of Artemis in the sanctuary of Apollo at Cyrene) in which, according to archaeological reports, images of animals were a fairly common form of votive, Bevan (1987) found bears in six: the Acropolis of Athens; the Argive *Heraion*; the *Artemision* of Thasos; the sanctuaries of Artemis Orthia in Sparta (terracotta and ivory figurine of the Archaic period, possibly a rough relief on a limestone plaque) and of Athena Alea in Tegea; and the sanctuary of Artemis Hemerasia in Lousoi, where the bear is represented by the teeth which some worshippers chose to dedicate there. To this evidence should be added the Cyrenaean inscriptions (not mentioned by Bevan); the temple-legends of the *arkteia* at Brauron and Mounichia (on which see Guarisco (2001)), and the Arcadian legends of Kallisto and Atalanta, which are related to motherhood and the upbringing of infants: the bear was for the ancients a symbol of motherhood (cf. Plu. *Mor.* 494). Moreover, an inscription of the early second century BC from Arcadian Stymphalos (*SEG* 25, 445; cf. Moretti *ISE* 55) mentions a Brauronian Artemis at Stymphalos (Paus. 8.22.7 saw a temple of Artemis there). A sanctuary of Athena has also been excavated on the acropolis of Stymphalos; intriguingly, a late Archaic Attic *kore*, more than a century older than the temple, has been found in the vicinity of the latter. It is not clear how the statue got there; Williams and Schaus (2001) 85 suggest that it either belonged to an earlier phase of the sanctuary, or it was brought later from Athens, possibly when Artemis Brauronia was given a sanctuary in Stymphalos. Bevan (1987) supposes on the other hand that the bear in the cult may have come to Attica from the Peloponnese at some time before the fifth century.

by the reformer Demonax of Mantinea: Herodotus 4.161) and it organised its Karneia just as the Spartans did. Athenaeus (4.441 e–f), quoting Demetrios of Skepsis, affirms that during that festival at Sparta nine men were installed in nine *skiades* (tents), where they took their meals and responded to the command of a herald. In each *skias* members of three *phratriai* were united, and the festival lasted nine days. Musical contests were organised for the occasion; according to Callimachus (*Hymn to Apollo* 85–7) the Cyrenaean Karneia featured dances by young armed men and Libyan women.[40] If the Cyrenaeans had maintained the Karneia in their city, as the Aigeidai of Sparta had originally established them at Thera and then in the new colony,[41] the number three appearing repeatedly in *SEG* 9, 13 and 48, 2052 could be a hint of the phyletic organisation of the festival.[42]

THE PRIZES FOR THE DITHYRAMBIC
AND TRAGIC CHORUSES

Let us now focus on the dithyrambic and tragic choruses. As we have seen, *SEG* 9, 13 mentions four choruses, three tragic and a dithyrambic one; all receive an ox.

[40] Cf. Hellanikos (*FGrH* 4 F85–6), quoted by Athen. 14, 635c-f. The latter, citing Sosibios Περὶ χρόνων (*FGrH* 595 F 3), affirms that the musical contest was established in the twenty-sixth Olympiad (676–672 BC). On the Cyrenaean Karneia as presented in Callimachus' *Hymn to Apollo* see Nicolai (1992); Krummen (1990) 108–10.

[41] For the links between Sparta, Thera, and Cyrene cf. Hölkeskamp (1993) 416–18; Malkin (1994), *passim* (specifically on the Karneia, 143–58); Karneia were also celebrated at Argos, Cos, and Thera, and more generally in the Dorian world: cf. Nilsson (1906) 118–29. On the relationship between Battiadai and Aigeidai, cf. Nafissi (1985). But Arcadia is also (not surprisingly: cf. the reforms of Demonax of Mantinea, Hdt. 4.161.2–3) very present: *damiorgoi* are attested in an Archaic inscription from Thera, *IG* XII 3.450 1–2 and 5–6, but in Arcadia as well, cf. Th. 5.47; *Syll.*³ 183; and *Syll.*³ 314B 4–5, where we have a γροφεὺς δαμιοργῶν.

[42] On the organisation of Cyrene cf. Hölkeskamp (1993), esp. 409–19. In the fourth century there were still three *phylai*. Φυλαί, πάτραι, and ἐννῆα ἑταιρήας are mentioned in the famous stele of the founders of Cyrene (fourth century BC): *SEG* 9, 3, 15–16. On the other hand if the number of the tragic choruses was two in *SEG* 48, 2052, the choral performances can hardly have been organised on a phyletic basis.

The oxen are prizes to be sacrificed and eaten together, as is clear from l. 19, where thighs, that is portions, are mentioned. This could mean that both the tragic choruses and the dithyrambic one consisted of locals, and that the *mageiros* (butcher) mentioned at l. 16 as having been in charge of preparing the thighs might also be connected with this festival. Such a prize brings to mind Pindar's verses on the 'ox-driving dithyramb': there were cultic associations between Dionysos and the bull, and the ox or bull is attested as a prize for dithyrambic *agones*, even if mostly in sweeping statements.[43] At Athens, the winners in the lesser *agones* of the Panathenaia (those which were reserved to citizens: *pyrrhiche, euandria, lampas,* and *neon hamilla*) also received an ox as a prize.[44] As for Cyrene, there all choruses, tragic and dithyrambic, received an ox; it is difficult to tell how usual this was.

It is possible to form an idea of how much the prizes for the tragic and dithyrambic choruses weighed on the general expenditure of the year: the thighs of an ox cost thirteen staters (a sum corresponding to the price of the animal); in the Cyrenaean monetary system, thirteen staters are the equivalent of fifty-two drachmas.[45] The expenditure for the four oxen amounted thus to 208 drachmas—which is not much if compared with the total expenditure of about 20,000 drachmas! The reason for registering these specific expenses cannot then have been the wish to account for an important sum.

The fact that an ox was given as a prize to each of the choruses, irrespective of whether they were dithyrambic or tragic, allows some inferences about their relative size and importance. If the prize

[43] Cf. Pi. *O.* 13.17–19 S.–M.; 'Simonides' epigr. 27 Page (*AP* 6.213, 1–2); *schol. vet.* Pl. *Rep.* 394c; *Σ* Pi. *O.* 13.26a; Suid s.v. *Ταυροφάγον· τὸν Διόνυσον. Σοφοκλῆς ἐν Τυροῖ ἀντὶ τοῦ ὅτι τοῖς τὸν διθύραμβον νικήσασι βοῦς ἐδίδοτο,* a comment which is also found, attributed to the grammarian Apollonios, in *Σ* Ar. *Ra.* 357, and attributed to Aristarchos in Tzetz. *Comm.* in Ar. *Ra.* 357 (with an interesting additional remark: *Τζέτζης δὲ διθυραμβικοῖς καὶ λυρικοῖς φησιν ἔπαθλον δίδοσθαι ταῦρον, οὐ μέντοι γε τραγικοῖς ἢ κωμῳδιῶν διδασκάλοις*). Cf. Ieranò (1997) 57, 70–1, 172–4, 247, and 271–2; Pickard-Cambridge (1988) 78; Pickard-Cambridge (1962) 6–7, 52 and n. 3. Apart from the prize, at Athens a bull was sacrificed before the contest: cf. *IG* II² 1006, 12; and Ieranò (1997) 243–4.

[44] *IG* II² 2311, 71–81 (first half of the fourth century).

[45] And are equivalent to thirty-nine Attic drachmas: Laronde (1987) 331 and n. 86; 324 and n. 10.

allotted was the same, they must have been formed of roughly the same number of participants. The difference from what we know of the situation at Athens is notable here. Moreover, at least in the case of the tragic choruses it seems difficult to speak of 'contest' and 'winners': if all three choruses received the same prize, they should be considered participants in a celebration rather than a competition. The oxen could be simply a compensation for their performance in honour of the gods.

This is however one of the points in which the two inscriptions part company. In ll. 10 and 13 *SEG* 48, 2052 mentions tragic and dithyrambic choruses, in the same order as in *SEG* 9, 13, but in the genitive;[46] the mention of the dithyrambic chorus at l. 13 is followed by the article in the dative (τῶι), a sign of interpunctuation, and a tantalising νικ[, after which the stone breaks.[47] Some word from the semantic field of 'victory' is almost inevitable. Marengo and Paci (1998: 383–4) suggest restoring νικ[άθρωι], a term otherwise unattested at Cyrene, which they then also restore in l. 10 (there, the word fills the lacuna, adding up to twenty-three letters, which is about the assumed line-length of the inscription).[48] Besides Hesychius (ν 564 νίκαθρον· ἔπαθλον, ἐπινίκιον), *nikathron* is found only once, in a Spartan inscription of the Augustan period (*IG* V 1.267,10: νίκαθρον B[ορθέαι]), where it denotes not the prize received by the victor, but the offer to Orthia of the stele and the victory (hence *LSJ* 'thank-offering for victory'). Sparta is a very convenient location, even if the period is not the same, because of its close relationship with Cyrene; but the meaning in the Spartan stele seems to be quite

---

[46] No particular significance can be attributed to the use of τραγωιδικός instead of τραγικός.

[47] The presence of the interpunctuation here is problematic. Elsewhere in this account the interpunctuation is used sensibly; this would be the one disruptive case. It is however difficult to imagine a sentence ending with an article in the dative, and then a new entry; moreover while usually in the inscription the interpunctuation occupies a space of its own, here it seems to have been squeezed—possibly at a second stage—between the two letters; we may then have to assume an error of the stonecutter.

[48] Dobias-Lalou (2000) 22 may have had doubts as to the correctness of the restoration, because she does not mention the rare use of νίκαθρον in her study of the dialect of the Cyrenaean inscriptions, even though she does cite as an example of shortening of the ω before a vowel the [τραγ]-λοιδικῶν of *SEG* 48, 2052, 10. An alternative would be τῶι νικ[ῶντι.

different from what we should assume in Cyrene. The same oscillation in meaning appears however in the corresponding Attic Greek νικητήριον, a prize dedicated to a god as a thank-offering for victory, but also a special kind of prize to be shared collegially in a feast among the winners.[49] The prize in Cyrene may have been oxen for the sacrifice and the ensuing banquet, and a clue may come from the sum allotted to the tragic choruses: 110 drachmas is roughly double the 52 drachmas which were paid, in *SEG* 9, 13, for an ox. Two tragic choruses might then have participated, and each might have received an ox.[50] In this case the (probable) use of νίκαθρον need not have implied a contest.

Another difference in respect to *SEG* 9, 13 is however that there seems to be an additional something (the fragmentary ἐπιθεν- at l. 11 has to be connected with ἐπιτίθημι, something added on top). This might have been an additional prize, for example for a second position, or also an expense related to the activities of the tragic choruses, such as the hire of the costumes.[51]

---

[49] For the first meaning cf. the accounts of the Athenian treasurers of Athena and the Other Gods, where, as of 402/1 BC, a crown dedicated by the polis as *niketeria* of the citharode is mentioned (*IG* II² 1372, B3, restored on the basis of *IG* II² 1388, A37; the formula is consequently restored in the entire series). On the other hand, the prizes of the lesser *agones* at the Panathenaia figure under the heading νικητήρια— and they are oxen. A *niketerion* need not be very valuable: at Delos in 189 BC the *niketerion* for the *hamilla* (naval competition) at the Posidonia cost only 12 drachmas, while the ox sacrificed at the same festival cost 120 drachmas (*I.Délos* 401, 21); around 190 BC, the ox cost 72 drachmas, and the *niketerion* was worth 10 drachmas (*I.Délos* 406, B74). In 179 BC the payment to the two *auletai* for the Delian Apollonia was 3,000 drachmas, to which were added 470 drachmas for the *siteresion*, the *choregemata* and the *niketerion*—it is unclear whether the latter was given to both or only to the first one (*I.Délos* 442, A86 and 128). At the Apollonia of the year 192 BC the pay for the *auletes* Telemachos was 1,500 drachmas, the *siteresion* 130, the *niketerion* 60, to which were added 50 drachmas for the *choregemata* and as much as a *xenion*, for a total of 1,790 drachmas (*I.Délos* 399, A56–7); cf. Sifakis (1967) 31 n. 1. On the other hand, still in Delos but during the period of Athenian domination, in 377 BC the *niketeria* for the choruses were tripods worth at least 1,000 drachmas (*IG* II² 1653, 33 = *I.Délos* 98A33—the rest of the sum is in a lacuna). Even this was not so much, when compared with what was spent in the same year on the oxen for the festival: one talent and 2,419 drachmas.

[50] So Marengo and Paci (1998) 384 n. 23. Our hypothesis concerning the number of the *exarchoi* (below) falls in neatly with this.

[51] A Delian account, *IG* XI 110, 17–18, mentions (using the expression οὐ κατεθέμην) the fact that the archon did not put the expense for the hire of the costumes on the account, having paid for it personally: Sifakis (1967) 40–1.

As for the dithyrambic choruses, it is impossible to advance guesses as to their number or the prize, since the sum allotted is lost. The festivities in Cyrene may have been organised so as always to add up to four choruses—but on the scanty evidence, it might be better to refrain from even this inference.

We do not know why the changes in the type of performances occurred (from one to more dithyrambic choruses), nor how they were financed. Clearly these choruses performed in a civic cult, and the city was responsible for the prizes offered.[52] But where did the *choreutai* come from, who chose them, and who paid for their training?[53] These questions are not answered by the inscriptions. The most plausible guess seems to be that the tragic and dithyrambic choruses were composed of locals (whether organised along phyletic lines or not, is difficult to tell). And what exactly is meant by χοροῖς

---

[52] The presence of tragic choruses and in general of dramatic performances at Cyrene finds a striking complement in the paintings covering the walls of a second-century AD tomb, the Tomba dei ludi funerari. According to Bacchielli (1993) 86–95 on the far side of the tomb are represented a scene from comedy, two dithyrambic choruses (for Strasser 2002: 98 and n. 9, however the scene represents a *pythaules* and a *chorokitharistes*, both with seven choreuts, while a *choraules* figures on another painting of the same tomb), and a scene from tragedy; for the latter, Bacchielli thinks of the *Orestes* or of the *Heraclidae*. One of the figures is clearly Heracles: one might be tempted to suggest a scene from the *Alcestis*. As the inscriptions which were painted besides (and sometimes over) the characters have not yet been published, interpretation must wait.

[53] An inscription from Mgernes of the end of the first century BC (*SEG* 9, 354: discussion in Laronde 1987: 334–5), shows that under precise circumstances a citizen could be liberated from liturgy, while being entered among the priests of Dionysos (l. 10–14: [ἐγ]γράψα[ι δὲ] αὐ-Ιτὸν καὶ ἐς τὸς ἱαρεῖς τῶ Διονύσ[ω] | ἱαρατευκότα, ἦμεν δὲ αὐτὸν κα[ὶ] | ἀλειτούργητον); the priests of Dionysos in Mgernes seem to function as those of Apollo in Cyrene (on the latter, see Robert 1940: 3–15). Can we assume that in the fourth century the Cyrenaeans were submitted to a *khoregia* as the Athenians were? Wilson (2000) 290, while thinking that the choruses were organised along phyletic lines, leaves the question open. For *leitourgia* and *leitourgein* in Cyrenaica cf. also *SEG* 9, 8, 57 (an *edictum* of Augustus stating that citizens from Cyrenaica who receive honours will have to be leitourgists nonetheless; cf. also ll. 104, 114–15, and 136); the honorary decree from Arsinoe (end of the second–first half of the first century BC) *SEG* 26, 1817, 48 and 53 (respectively ἐχοράγησε and λειτουργεῖν, in a matter concerning the acquisition of wheat); and Reynolds (1977) no. 18, 15 (decree of the Jewish *politeuma* of Berenice exempting from any *leitourgia* and honouring a citizen who has undertaken at his own expense the plastering of the floor and the painting of the walls in the amphitheatre, first century BC to first century AD).

τραγικοῖς τρισί (or by τραγοιδικοῖς χοροῖς): tragic choruses, as in the narrative referring to the changes introduced in Sicyon by the tyrant Kleisthenes (Herodotus 5.67), or the tragic choruses of three tragedies? A straight answer to the question of the kind of spectacle performed by the tragic choruses mentioned in our inscriptions is impossible: the only clue to the solution may lie in the use of the term *periaktriai*. If the *periaktriai* were revolving stage machines, then we must admit that we are dealing with tragic choruses of tragedies. On the other hand if the *periaktria* was a priestess, then the tragic choruses may have pertained to tragedies, but may also have performed particular bravura pieces simply *qua* choruses.[54] At any rate, it is extremely interesting to be able to add one more reference, and a relatively early one at that, to the meagre dossier concerning tragic performances by choruses in the Hellenistic period.

As for the possibility of imported artists, there are as yet in Cyrene no traces of tragic actors. One case of a foreign performer might be the *aulodos* Apollodoros, mentioned in a much-discussed inscription, the so-called 'stele of the σῦλα'. This document shows that around 335 BC a group of Cyrenaean ambassadors was sent to Megalopolis in order to pay 4,000 minae (an enormous sum) to a not otherwise known *aulodos*, Apollodoros, as right of reprisal.[55] It is however by no means certain that the Cyrenaeans had incurred this debt because of any musical performances on the part of Apollodoros. By the third century, on the other hand, a Cyrenaean *komoidos* had entered the international artistic circuit: around 260–252 BC, a Polyaratos, son of Eudoxos, from Cyrene performed at

---

[54] For the various possibilities (persistence of a tragic chorus; performances of tragedies without choruses; bravura pieces in solo-song by *tragodoi*; amoebean song between an actor and a chorus), which may often have depended on the composition of a specific theatrical troupe, see Sifakis (1967) 113–20 (persistence of tragic choruses); Gentili (1979) 16–31 (no tragic choruses); Wilson (2000) 308–9 (diversity, among which a possibility is the combination of a small professional chorus with local *choreutai*).

[55] *SECir* 103 and pl. 81; *SEG* 20, 716. New fragment: *SEG* 27, 1194; *SEG* 30, 1783. Photograph, text, and discussion (with suggested date of *c.* 335) in Laronde (1987) 149–61 (*SEG* 38, 1879). At ll. 20–2, it is specified that the group led by Karnedas, son of Spondarchos, has to go to Megalopolis in order to reimburse Ἀπολλόδωρον τὸν αὐλῳδὸν (no patronymic, but in the inscription the creditors are all simply characterised by their activity, their origin, or a physical particularity). It is unlikely that this Apollodoros was a Cyrenaean, as supposed by Stephanis (1988) no. 250.

the Soteria in Delphi. He was also granted proxeny, *enktesis, isotelia,* and *asphaleia* by the people of Oropos around the middle of the third century BC: these distinctions may have underlined the excellence of this individual.[56]

THE *EXARCHOI* AND THE REST OF THE PERSONNEL

SEG 9, 13 lists at ll. 16–17 expenses for different kinds of experts (*exarchoi* and *karukes,* an *auletes,* a secretary, a treasurer, a butcher, and guards), who are possibly connected to the performances of the tragic and dithyrambic choruses. The entire issue revolves around the *exarchoi.* While Oliverio saw in them simple guides, Chamoux, on the basis of Demosthenes *De Corona* 260, suggested that the *exarchos* was the chief of the chorus. Similarly, Dobias-Lalou considers that the *exarchoi* are the equivalent of the phrase οἱ ἐξάρχοντες τὸν διθύραμβον used by Aristotle in a famous passage of the *Poetics* in order to describe those that became the protagonists of tragedy.[57]

How does the evidence of *SEG* 48, 2052 fit into the picture? As has been mentioned above, the vocabulary and the syntactical arrangements of this inscription are not the same as in *SEG* 9, 13. There, the officials followed directly after the choruses; here the mention of the choruses is followed by two lines concerning expenses for the bear (and thus probably for the cult of Artemis); then come a –*thra* which is difficult to understand and a mention of expenses for the priestess of Athena; the list of the officials begins only at this point.

All of this is however 'bracketed', as it were, by the indications of l. 9 (τάδε ἔξος ἱαροθυσίας, 'without including the sacrifice') and 22–3 (τὸ πᾶν 'total'; and τὸ πᾶν ἱαροθυσίας 'total including the sacrifice').

---

[56] Delphi: *Syll.*³ 424, col. I, 67 = *GDI* 2563, 260–252 BC; cf. Ghiron-Bistagne (1976) 352–3; Sifakis (1967) 159; Stephanis (1988) no. 2090. Proxeny decree for Πολυάρα-τος Εὐδόξου Κυρηναῖος and his descendants: *SEG* 15, 265 = *Arch. Eph.* 1952, 171/2 no. 3 (cf. also *SEG* 16, 298); he does not seem to have been affiliated to an Artists' association.

[57] Oliverio (1933) 119; Chamoux (1988) 152–3; Dobias-Lalou (1993) 30, cf. Dobias-Lalou (2000) 239, and above n. 13.

We might then want to consider all the expenses listed within these lines as pertaining to some specific festival. While for the *exarchoi* and the *aulos*-player we may be in doubt as to whether they participated in the festival as performers or only as officials, the rest of the personnel named had to do with the organisation and the functioning of that same festival. This makes sense of the presence of three guards (the πρωροί): three are not enough in case of serious trouble, but they may form some kind of official escort to a procession. The same applies even more clearly to the rest of them, secretary, treasurer, and *mageiros*: they cannot have been performers, but they may have been directly connected with a specific festival. Thus, in light of the scanty evidence available, the best solution may be to link the *exarchoi* with the choruses (both tragic and dithyrambic), and to think of all the others as personnel of the festival.[58]

Something of the duties of an *exarchos* can be gathered from a passage of Eratosthenes. In it the Cyrenaean defines the role of the *exarchos* in respect to the chorus, the *auletes* and the *kitharistes*, saying that, in the absence of musical accompaniment, the leader of the chorus would take up and speak the *tenella* outside the song, and the chorus of the komasts would contribute the *kallinike*.[59] For Eratosthenes, then, the *exarchoi* had to do with choral performances: they may have had a role similar to that of the ἡγεμόνες τοῦ χοροῦ

---

[58] An interesting fact, even though it cannot be pressed too hard, is that κήρυκες, αὐληταί and μάγειροι appear in the same order of *SEG* 9, 13 in a passage of Herodotus (6.60) attesting that at Sparta these functions were transmitted from father to son. If we admit that the same or a similar structure may have obtained in Cyrene as well, then this is another reason to separate the *exarchoi* from this group. There is space to restore a *mageiros* (as well as a *gropheus*) in *SEG* 48, 2052, 17–21; their order is however not the same as in *SEG* 9, 13. We probably should recognise these officials in the unique ὑπη[ρεσίαις] of the account *SEG* 9, 33, 9.

[59] Σ Pi. *O.* 9.1k = *FGrH* 241 F44: περὶ δὲ τοῦ τήνελλα Ἐρατοσθένης φησὶν ὅτι ὅτε ὁ αὐλητὴς ἢ ὁ κιθαριστὴς μὴ παρῆν, ὁ ἔξαρχος αὐτὸ μεταλαβὼν ἔλεγεν ἔξω τοῦ μέλους, ὁ δὲ τῶν κωμαστῶν χορὸς ἐπέβαλλε τὸ καλλίνικε, καὶ οὕτω συνειρόμενον γέγονε τὸ τήνελλα καλλίνικε. Geus (2002) 291–301, in particular 294 n. 36, thinks that in the passage cited Eratosthenes did not want to discuss Pindar's verses, but rather Ar. *Av.* 1764, and considers his explanation of the *tenella* as a vocal replacement for the missing musical accompaniment (an explanation which coincides with that offered by Σ Ar. *Av.* 1764) a likely one (*contra* Dunbar 1995: 769–70). It may be worthwhile to point out the careful wording of the fragment: συνειρόμενον is a technical term, cf. Pl. *Lg.* 654a: ᾠδαῖς τε καὶ ὀρχήσεσιν ἀλλήλοις ξυνείροντας.

recently discussed by Slater, both leaders of the chorus and first singers.[60] It is interesting to note that Eratosthenes does not connect the *exarchoi* with a specifically Dionysiac performance, but with choruses *tout court* (and in fact, the scholiast who is quoting him adduces his opinion in the context of the *tenella kallinike*, a victory song). This ties in well with the fact that in *SEG* 9, 13, where only one dithyrambic chorus is mentioned, the *exarchoi* are a group: if indeed they are to be linked to the choruses, they took care of the dithyrambic and of the tragic choruses as well. Our last bit of evidence for ἔξαρχοι in Cyrene, an extremely fragmentary account, also dated to the fourth century BC, confirms our hypothesis. The stone is broken on all sides, so that we cannot know how much is missing from either the beginning or the end. What is preserved is a word *kallisteia*, followed by the final part of the sum allotted to it and by a mention of *exarchoi*, and, on the following line, of the priestess of Athena.[61] Here, the *exarchoi* would seem to be located in a position where there is no room for choruses—unless the *Kallisteia* (a competition in beauty among women, possibly, in view of the presence of a bear in Cyrene, linked to the Arkadian nymph Kallisto?) themselves imply the presence of choruses.[62] The latter seems the better option: for if choruses are not explicitly mentioned near the *exarchoi*, neither is there room for any of the other officials.

---

[60] Cf. Slater (1997) 97–106; Wilson (2000) 166 and 358 n. 50. The word *hegemones* appears at Cyrene only in *SEG* 9, 61, 2 (ἡγεμόνες ἐπὶ τῆς θεραπείας), after 128 BC, in a very different context (military officers honouring Kleopatra III).

[61] *SEG* 9, 21: ⸗]καλλιστηιαις--|⸗ ⧘: ἐξάρχοις [--|--Ἀ]θαναίας ἱαρέα[ι--⸌⸗ = = X ⧘ ⧘ ⧘..||5--]X X[. According to Dobias-Lalou (2000) 82 n. 4 and 271, the reading of Oliverio (1933) 92, followed in the *SEG*, is wrong: the stone has – ΚΑΛΛΙΣΤΗΙΑΤ–, to be understood as a nominative plural (either a 'beauty contest', or a special prize—an *aristeion*—for the best chorus, comparable to the *epithen-* of *SEG* 48, 2052, or also the best offering for a sacrifice) followed probably by the article in the dative for the recipient of the expense (Oliverio's photograph, t. XIII fig. 9, 22, seems to corroborate this).

[62] Σ Hom. *Il.* 9.129 mentions καλλιστεία in Lesbos, in connection with the cult of Hera, and also a competition in beauty in Tenedos. There was also an Arcadian ἀγὼν κάλλους which took place among women in honour of Demeter Eleusinia at Basilis (Athen. 13.609e); the participants were called χρυσοφόροι. Interestingly, the term recurs for male priests in a fragmentary inscription of the first century BC from Cyrene, *SECir* 120 (οἱ ἱερατευκότες καὶ χρυσοφορέ[ντες). Finally, the Hesychian lemma πυλαιΐδες· αἱ ἐν κάλλει κρινόμεναι τῶν γυναικῶν καὶ νικῶσαι may be connected to Demeter Pylaia. Cf. Nilsson (1906) 57 and 336; Guarisco (2001) 77–8.

The amounts paid to the priestesses and to the various officials may give us some further indications. The bear receives food and possibly something else for a total value of 240 drachmas, while the priestess of Athena is given 200 drachmas.[63] The *exarchoi* receive 220 drachmas, and if this is the total of the expenses for the *exarchoi*, then there were either two or four of them, receiving 110 or 55 drachmas each;[64] the *auletes*, who had the most important role, receives 420 drachmas—a far cry less than what the *auletai* received, a century later it is true, at Delos, but still not a small sum; the treasurer is the best paid, with 508 drachmas. As for the sums paid to the rest of the personnel, they have disappeared in the lacunae.

CONCLUSION

It is difficult to draw any clear-cut conclusions from the evidence surveyed. The inscriptions mention important expenses on some religious festival—very likely the Dorian Karneia—that included in its programme dithyrambic and tragic choruses, and that presented a high degree of organisation. It is not possible to say in detail how

[63] After the word *tropha* the text breaks off; the following line has a –*thra* and then a sum. As observed by Marengo and Paci (1998) 384–5, the options are to think of a clause referring to the bear, who would receive food and something else, for a total value of 240 drachmas; or to imagine a sum after *tropha* (two minae, as for the priestess of Athena) and then a new clause. The word to be restored should be linked to the cult; among the possibilities (for which see Buck and Petersen (1948) 325–6) are the Hesychian glosses γεῖθρον· ἔνδυμα (dress, which gives a line of twenty-three letters: τᾶι ἄρκωι τροφ[ά καὶ ἐς τὰ γεῖ]-lθρα); νίκαθρον, attested for Artemis Orthia in Sparta (see above); or κύριθρα (wooden-masks, giving: τᾶι ἄρκωι τροφ[ά καὶ ἐς κύρι-[-lθρα). The latter gloss is connected with the Hesychian gloss κυριττοί· οἱ ἔχοντες τὰ ξύλινα πρόσωπα κατὰ Ἰταλίαν, καὶ ἑορτάζοντες τῆι Κορυθαλίαι γελοιασταί, and thus with Artemis Korythalia; Athen. 4.139b speaks of an Artemis called Korythalia in the neighbourhood of Sparta, for whom dances were performed. Apollo was also connected to Artemis Korythalia: cf. Nilsson (1906) 183–7.

[64] The sum cannot be divided neatly among three; five, at forty-four drachmas each, would be a possibility. Two or four *exarchoi* would tie in well with the hypothesis advanced by Marengo and Paci (1998) 384 n. 23 as to the number of tragic choruses: see above n. 50. In theory, the 220 drachmas might also be what each *exarchos* receives, but the wording speaks against this hypothesis; so does the comparison with the indemnity allocated to the three *damiergoi*, three minae, one mina each.

things worked, but it is at any rate clear that many influences and models were at play in Cyrene: the Libyan polis was by no means cut off from the rest of the Greek world. The complexity of the situation is due to the fact that we have to take into account cultural interactions between the Spartan (and more generically Dorian) traditions (to be expected in Cyrene because of the origin of the polis); the Arkadian strand, attested since the reform of Demonax, and still strong in the fourth century, as is shown by the stele of the *sula*; the Athenian influence, which exerted itself, culturally and economically, throughout the Aegean; the relationship with Delphi, particularly important already at the moment of the foundation, and still very much alive in the fourth century;[65] and the continuing existence of strong local traditions. All of this goes some way towards explaining the presence of unique cultic associations, as well as the use of a terminology which is unique in respect to the rest of the Greek world.

---

[65] Cf. Bousquet (1952) 71–5 for the relations between Cyrene and Delphi; in particular, the construction of the treasury of Cyrene at Delphi dates to the second half of the fourth century (*c.* 335–330 BC) and is contemporary with the architectural reorganisation of the sanctuary of Apollo at Cyrene, and with the reconstruction of its temple. For the contacts between the philosopher Plato and important Cyrenaean families cf. Laronde (1987) 110–16 and 129–31; the theories of the famous mathematician Theodoros, who appears in Plato's *Theaetetus*, might explain the structural relationships of the different elements of the treasury of the Cyrenaeans at Delphi: Bousquet (1952) 77–98.

8

A *Horse* from Teos: Epigraphical Notes
on the Ionian–Hellespontine Association
of Dionysiac Artists*

John Ma

Peter Herrmann zum Gedächtniss

I. TEOS: EPIGRAPHY, TERRITORY, HISTORY

The ancient Ionian city of Teos is important and interesting, especially in the context of a volume on the 'epigraphy of the Greek theatre'; it deserves to be presented briefly. Teian epigraphy is abundant, and rich in famous texts:[1] the wealth of epigraphy reflects the twofold articulation of Teian history, which it shares with many other *poleis*: as a smaller entity caught in the high politics of war and conquest; as a stable actor in its own history, living its life as a political unit and pursuing its own aims at a regional scale.

* Many thanks to the following colleagues: Peter Wilson for his invitation to publish this paper; Hasan Malay for assistance with the stone in Sığacık; Angelos Chaniotis and Christian Habicht for reading an early version of this chapter and much improving it with comments; Charles Crowther, David Fearn, Peter Thonemann, William Slater, for helpful suggestions when this paper was first read out; Glen Bowersock and Christian Habicht for permission to work on the squeezes of LB–W 91 and 93; Bob Kaster for checking measurements on these squeezes; Panayiotis Hatzidakis and Jean-Charles Moretti with help on Delos; Jim Coulson for pointers on architecture. Responsibility for mistakes remains my own.
[1] Inscriptions from Teos are compiled by McCabe and Plunkett (1985), an unpublished fascicle in the 'Princeton Epigraphy Project'; also Ruge (1934) 539–43. Unpublished texts mentioned by L. Robert: *OMS IV* 149 (there announcing the near-completion of an epigraphical corpus for Teos); *BE* 69, 496.

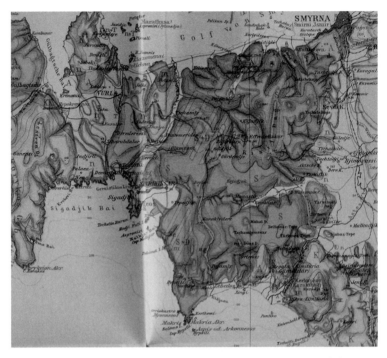

Fig. 20 Smyrna and the region of Teos: extract from A. Philippson, *Geologische Karte des westlichen Kleinasien, Blatt 3* (in Philippson 1911).

The wealth of Teian epigraphy is also the reflection of a long history of travellers to the site, easily accessible from Smyrna (Fig. 20). The ancient town itself, however, is not well known, apart from the temple of Dionysos; alluviation has covered the remains which were visible in the nineteenth century, and which some French test work in 1924 showed to be extremely interesting.[2] What can still be seen now is disappointing (or perhaps 'evocative'), except for the temple.[3] The site lies to the south of a peninsula, near the modern resort of Akkum and its rapidly spreading holiday real estate; in the

[2] Bécquignon and Laumonier (1925).
[3] Ruge (1934) 569–70; Bean (1966) 136–46, mostly for a summary description of the site; Mitchell (2000) 97–8, 148, mentions recent work, with reference to Turkish publications.

nineteenth century, this site was known as Bodrum (recorded with all the variant spellings of the old travellers: Boudroum, Budrun, etc), the castle. To the north of the ancient site, on the other side of a still surprisingly rural headland, lies the rapidly mushrooming village of Sığacık, with its Genoese castle, and the second of Teos' harbours. From there, a dusty hour's walk will take you, past Teos' marble quarries,[4] to Seferhisar, a small provincial Turkish town: this is where the bus from Izmir/Üçkuyular stops, on a junction on the big coastal road; the town serves as a nodal point and administrative centre for the area. Along the northern road towards Urla, there are several villages where ancient inscriptions were found, notably Ulamış (modern spelling; the old spelling 'Olamiş' is prevalent in scholarly literature; a famous inscription concerning synoikism still sits in a cemetery wall, opposite an olive oil-press[5]) and Hereke (now Düzce, with its disused hammam and its mosque and disused medrese built on an ancient temple). The name Hereke indicates that this was once a fortified site (Charax), probably a polis in earlier times, before absorption by Teos.[6] Near Hereke, there once existed a village named 'Güzellir' (Boeckh), or 'Ghésusler' as printed in *LB–W*, explicitly identifying it with Güzellir; pencil notes on Le Bas's squeezes call the place 'Goesusler' (Fig. 21). This place seems to have disappeared as a village, and no traveller mentions it after Le Bas; inscribed stones from the cemetery of 'Ghésusler' were later seen by R. Démangel and A. Laumonier in Seferhisar.[7]

---

[4] Fant (1989).

[5] Most recently, Chandezon (2003) 205–12 no. 53.

[6] On Hereke, see L. Robert, in Devambez (1962) 5–6; *SEG* 41, 1007 is an imperial-era dedication, from a gymnasium, in the disused hammam in Düzce (Hereke); it might come from Teos.

[7] On Güzellir (Turkish Güzeller, the fair ones?), *LB–W* 79 and *CIG* 3046, 3052 (assigned to 'Güzellir'), 3116 ('sesquilapide à Severhisar'); Boeckh, in *CIG* II 627, discussing Chandler, *Inscr. Syll.*, p. iii, which should be expanded to R. Chandler, *Inscriptiones antiquae, pleraeque nondum editae: in Asia Minori et Graecia, praesertim Athenis, collectae. Cum appendice* (London, 1747), introductory section entitled '*Syllabus et notae*': '*fortasse, paucis annis, nec supererit memoria loci Guzellir, quippe in quo tuguriolum nunc tantum unum et Moschea ruinosa. Distat semihora a Severhissar, Boream atque occidentalem coeli partes versus.* Anglice, the NW'. Güzellir is not in the list of provenances for Teian inscriptions in McCabe (1985). It appears as a 'Ru[d] Mosque' atop a rise, on the British Admiralty Charts 'Asia Minor. Sighajik Bay' and 'Asia Minor. Island of Khios and Gulf of Smyrna' based on a survey of 1836; it no

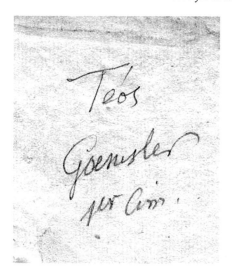

Fig. 21 'Téos, Goesusler, 1er cim(etière)'. Pencil note by Philippe Le Bas on a squeeze of *LB–W* 93, now kept in the Institute for Advanced Study, Princeton.

From Seferhisar, roads lead into the hills then the mountains, a world of small villages, still badly known from the archaeological point of view; one such village is Benler, where Petzl and Baran found a cave dedicated to the Nymphs (and, oddly enough, a graffito purporting to be that of a king Antiochos; but that is another story); somewhere in these highlands existed a small community, Oroanna.[8] The high ground stretches from the Bay of Smyrna and the 'Two Brothers' range south towards the point of Cape Myonessos (where the old Greek village of Ispili is now Doğanbey; in 1999, I saw *SEG* 2, 644 still in place in the big village well).[9] The high ground dominates a coastal strip; R. Chandler describes the 'low mountain on our left hand, with an opening in it', as he journeyed south from Teos towards Lebedos;[10] the opening is doubtless the saddle of the pass

longer figures in Kiepert (1908), Philippson (1911), Tanoğlu et al. (1961). The site has doubtless been swallowed by the northwards building sprawl. Inscriptions shifted from 'Ghésusler' to Seferhisar: Demangel and Laumonier (1922) 355, re *LB–W* 121 (note also 103 (*CIG* 3084), 105 (*CIG* 3085), transported from Sığacık to Seferhisar).

[8] Benler: Baran and Petzl (1977–8); Oroanna: Robert and Robert (1976) 172–4 (*OMS* 7, 316–18); the localisation of Oroanna proposed by R. Meriç must remain a hypothesis (noted in Mitchell 1990: 98).

[9] Demangel and Laumonier (1922) 353 no. 68; earlier, less complete text in *LB–W* 133.

[10] Chandler (1817) 114.

towards the valley leading into the plain south of Smyrna. The coastal strip is now solidly taken over, down to the island of Myonessos (Üçgen Adası), by *front de mer* apartment and vacation houses, and the great road that serves them. Across the Bay of Teos, along the southern side of ancient Mt Korykos, lie further villages, one of which, Yeni Demircili, is near the ancient site of Airai.[11] Some of the landscape is olive and fruit trees; much of the hills, once devoted to vines, are now pasture since the turn of the twentieth century devastation of *phylloxera* and the departure of wine-drinking Greeks. The network of communications between sea, harbour village, resort spot, provincial town (ilçe), and hill villages reflects a complex geography of micro-regions, which in ancient times added up to form the sizeable and diverse *chora* of the Teian polis (Fig. 20).

In April 1997, and again in September 1999, I spent some time in the area on a bicycle, with P. Herrmann's warm, if bemused, encouragement. I approached from the east, cycling from Adnan Menderes airport to Seferhisar, via the Karakoç valley: this easy road through the woods and the hills, with its villages low and high, old bridges, rivers, wells, fountains, orchards, fields, farms, stables, collapsed terraces, gardens, old abandoned cemeteries, roadside cafes and fruit stalls (drably deserted in winter, welcoming in summer) is obviously an important *lieu de passage* (it allows quick access to the coastal strip from the airport and the great plain south of Smyrna, now urbanising as part of the Izmir megalopolis). This was probably a route in ancient times—yet another of the micro-regions of Teian geography. The corridor leads from Cumaovası/Menderes, on the edge of the plain south of Smyrna, to the hamlet of Kavakdere, at which point lies a crossroads. From this point, the road leads left, to Lebedos,[12] or right, to Teos. The Teos branch leads past a disused cemetery, then up a not inconsiderable saddle; from there, a long, exhilarating glide down the bare hills takes the cyclist into the coastal plain—this is the 'opening in the hills' which Chandler saw, but from

[11] Robert and Robert (1976) 165–7 (*OMS* 7, 309–11); Mitchell (1990) 98 noting survey work by R. Meriç at Airai.

[12] French (1988) nos. 482, 496 (Diocletianic milestones; they indicate that in the third century AD at least, a road ran from Teos into the hills, past the modern hamlet of Kavakdere and the west–east corridor from the plain south of Smyrna, and onwards to Lebedos (the modern highway hugs the coast).

the Teos side. In Seferhisar, in Sığacık, in Ulamiş, in Düzce, I was surprised to see inscriptions preserved in modern contexts, most published, some unpublished.

Several of these Teian sites play a role in the present chapter, which is why I have spent a little time presenting the geography; Teian inscriptions were found scattered across this area, and this holds true for documents of a particular class: those relating to a particular Association of Dionysiac Artists, τὸ κοινὸν τῶν περὶ τὸν Διόνυσον τεχνιτῶν τῶν ἐπ' Ἰωνίας καὶ Ἑλλησπόντου, the Association which was installed in Teos, from the late third century to the mid-second century BC. The material has recently been gathered, republished, and analysed in two analytical studies, by B. Le Guen (2001a) and S. Aneziri (2003).

II. VICTOR-LISTS FROM TEOS

Among the Teian documents concerning the Artists, three documents seem very similar in formulation and nature: they are victor-lists for thymelic contests. They have recently been reproduced by Le Guen, more or less as follows.

1. *LB–W* 91 (Le Guen 2001a: TE 46 A). This text comes from Sığacık, or more precisely the actual ancient site, 'Boudroum', near the theatre.

[		ἱ]ερέως β[	
		Σατύρων	Ἀμυ– –
[	]πος	Ἀναξίων Θρασυκλείδου	
[	]ηι	Μυτιληναῖος	ὑπε[κρίνετο
[	]ς Βακχίου	Δράματι Πέρσαις	Ἀριστ– –
		ὑπεκρίνετο Ἀσκληπιάδης	
		Ἡρακλείδου Χαλκιδεύς	

Le Bas' facsimile shows ὑπεκρίνατο (followed by Le Guen), the text in *LB–W*, correctly, ὑπεκρίνετο.

2. Pottier and Hauvette-Besnault (1880) 176–8 no. 37 (Le Guen 2001a: TE 46 C). This text comes from Seferhisar ('maison de Hassan

Effendi', as the editors, E. Pottier and A. M. Hauvette-Besnault write).

[ἐπὶ ἱερέως Ἀπελ]λικῶντος καὶ ἀγωνοθ[έτου   ]
[Διθ]υράμβων
[Δημήτριος Μ]ενίππου Φωκαιεὺς
[Ἀ]νδρομέδαι
[ἐκιθαρώιδει δ' ὁ] αὐτός

3. *LB–W* 93 (Le Guen 2001a: TE 46 D). This text comes from the 'first cemetery of Ghesusler', or, to spell it as Le Bas did on his squeezes, 'Goesusler'; from 'Goesusler' also comes *LB–W* 92 (TE 46 B), an inscription recording the dedication of masks and crowns by a victor at the Dionysia, a text which I will not treat here.

[ἐπ]ὶ ἱερέως Δημητρίου, ἀγωνοθέτου δὲ καὶ ἱε[ρέως - - - - - -
                                                        τοῦ δεῖνος, οἵδε]
[ἐνίκησαν ἐν τῶι ἀγῶνι] τῶι τεθέντι Ἀττάλ[ωι]
        Διθυράμβων   Σατύρων
Νίκαρχος Ἑρμόνακτος Περγαμηνός   [Ζηνό]δ[οτος]
Φερσεφόνει   [---]
ἐκιθαρώιδει Δημήτριος [Μ]ε[νίππου]   ὑπεκ[ρί]νετο [ὁ δεῖνα]
Φωκαιεύς   Καλ . . . . Μ

The dispersion of stones is not surprising: one needs think only of the dispersion of the texts relating to the *asylia* of the shrine of Dionysos and the city of Teos; two texts, of exactly the same type, relating to the fortifications of Teos, were found, the first in Seferhisar, the second in Hereke (*SEG* 2, 582–3). The provenance of the first list from the ancient site proper guarantees, if need be, that all these texts originally came from Teos.

From Le Bas's squeezes, now kept in the Institute for Advanced Study in Princeton, the similarity in script appears clearly; a second-century date is suggested by the wide, broken bar alphas, the big, round omicron and theta, with central dot; the pi with equal verticals, and the parallel horizontals on sigma; omega is smaller, and raised above the line. These appear on *LB–W* 91, the clearest of the squeezes; the same features can be seen on *LB–W* 93 (Figs. 22–5). In both texts, the letters measure between 2.3 and 2.5 cm; the omega is 1.5–1.7 cm, raised 0.7 cm off the base of the line. On *LB–W* 91, some of the alphas are extremely wide, 3.2 to 4 cm; in *LB–W* 93 the

Fig. 22 Squeeze of *LB–W* 91, now kept in the Institute for Advanced Study, Princeton.

Fig. 23 Squeeze of *LB–W* 91 (detail), now kept in the Institute for Advanced Study, Princeton.

alphas are *c.* 2.5 cm. In spite of the difference in size, these letters are very similar to those on the stele bearing several documents concerning Kraton of Khalchedon, Michel 1016 (from *CIG* 3068),[13] now in the Fitzwilliam (this stone, not a stele but a pilaster, groups documents issued over a period of time, but the date of inscription is that of the heading, which is not the heading of the first decree but of the whole dossier: some time before 158 BC). They do not look like

---

[13] The old text in Michel, taken from a squeeze, is more accurate than either Aneziri's or Le Guen's. I will present this stone more fully elsewhere. On Kraton see the chapter by Le Guen below.

Fig. 24 Squeeze of *LB–W* 93, now kept in the Institute for Advanced Study, Princeton.

Fig. 25 Squeeze of *LB–W* 93 (detail), now kept in the Institute for Advanced Study, Princeton.

the lettering on the decree concerning the foundation of Polythrous, which dates to the earlier second century BC (Fig. 26).

There is a similarity in layout in all three texts: a preamble with dating formula, then the victors by category of contest: in the first text, satyr-play, flanked by two other categories; in the second text, dithyramb; in the third, dithyramb and satyr-play. From the similarity in nature, formulation, order of contests, and general layout, I believe we should reconstruct a single model for these lists: a long heading, with dating formula, unfolding over at least three columns for at least three thymelic categories (dithyramb, satyr-play, and one or two more categories: tragedy and/or comedy).

The documents are all dated in the same way: by reference to an eponymous priest and to an *agonothetes* who is also a priest of an Attalid king. This can be seen most clearly in the second and third

Fig. 26 Foundation of Polythrous (*Syll.* 578).

texts, and can probably be restored in the first text. The officials involved are not Teian officials, as Le Guen tentatively writes (2001a: I 239) but, a possibility Le Guen also canvases, officials of the Association of Artists. The reason is that this dating formula is that used by the Artists, as Le Guen notes (priest—of Dionysos), followed by *agonothetes*–priest of king Eumenes). The two relevant documents are Michel 1016 A (*CIG* 3068 A, the printed text of which is reproduced as Le Guen 2001a: TE 48 and Aneziri 2003: D11), a decree of the Artists, where the *agonothetes*–priest of Eumenes is also mentioned as an official at line 10,[14] and *OGIS* 325 (also in Le Guen 2001a: TE 49), a letter of Kraton to the Attalistai, where the eponymous priest is followed by an *agonothetes* who is also priest of the god Eumenes).[15]

---

[14] ἐπὶ ἱερέως Σατύρου, καὶ ἀγωνοθέτου κ[αὶ] ἱερέως βασιλέως Εὐμένου vac. Νικοτέλου[ς].

[15] [Βασιλε]ύοντος Ἀττάλου Φιλαδέλφου, ἔτους ἑβδό[μου, μηνὸς Δ]ύστρου, ἐπὶ δὲ ἱερέως τῶν τεχνιτῶν Κρατίν[ου, καὶ ἀγνω]οθέτου καὶ ἱερέως θεοῦ Εὐμένου Ἀρισταίου.

Le Guen argues against the view that the officials on the three victor-lists, as reproduced above, are officials of the Artists rather than of Teos: her argument is the absence of patronymic and *ethnikon* for both the priest and the *agonothetes*, whereas the victors are named with patronymic and *ethnikon*. This argument cannot hold. The patronymic and *ethnikon* are not required in dating formulae: these elements are lacking in the other documents, mentioned above, where the priest and the *agonothetes* are named as eponyms. In contrast, the name with patronymic and ethnic is necessary in lists of victors in contests between international competitors (the polis identity of the victor is part of the point).[16] Most decisively, in the polis of Teos, the eponymous official is not a priest, but a prytanis (at least on decrees of civic subdivisions; I see no reason for the prytanis not to have been the eponymous magistrate generally).[17] If the officials are not Teians, but Artists, the contests were not the Teian Dionysia, but contests celebrated by the Artists. The dating formula in the three documents should therefore read ἐπὶ ἱερέως τοῦ δεῖνος, καὶ ἀγωνοθέτου / ἀγωνοθέτου δὲ καὶ ἱερέως βασιλέως Εὐμένου *vel* θεοῦ Εὐμένου τοῦ δεῖνος, 'When So-and-so was priest, and So-and-so was *agonothetes* and priest of King Euemenes *or* of Eumenes the god.'

The contests involved are probably not the Dionysia of the polis of Teos, but rather one of the contests which the *agonothetes* of the Artists organised in his year of office (Michel 1016 B, reproduced in Le Guen 2001a: TE 44, at l. 10), perhaps the '*panegyris* of the *koinon*' (*I.Magnesia* 54 and 89, same documents Le Guen 2001a: TE 40 and 45; *RC* 53, same document Le Guen 2001a: TE 47). Does the joint office as *agonothetes* and priest of Eumenes II hint at a festival for that king? I see no reason to assume that this is necessarily the contest involved in the first and second lists. In the case of the third list, the contest was set up for 'Attal[os]'. Which Attalos? He has usually been identified as Attalos II; but the answer needs elaboration. If the contest was set up for a living king (Attalos II or III during their reigns), we would expect βασιλεῖ Ἀττάλωι, 'to King Attalos'; if for a deceased

---

[16] Robert (1967) 18–26 = *OMS* V, 358–66.
[17] Sherk (1991) 250 no. 180, with examples, to which add *GIBM* 1032 / *SEG* 4, 598 (McCabe 1985: no. 36).

king, we would expect θεῶι Ἀττάλωι, 'to Attalos the god', just as in the cases where there is a priest of Eumenes the god. The solution, suggested during the 'Epigraphy of the Greek theatre' conference by P. Thonemann, is a mention of Attalos the brother of the king (the future Attalos II) or Attalos the son of the king (the future Attalos III).

The joint office as *agonothetes* and priest of the king appears on these documents, and also in the decree of the Artists and the letter of Kraton, both quoted above, but this office is absent from other documents involving the Artists: in a decree of the *synagonistai*, Kraton is mentioned first as priest, then as *agonothetes* (also *CIG* 3068 B, also Michel 1016 B, whence Le Guen 2001a: TE 44); in a decree of the Artists inscribed on Delos, Kraton appears as priest of Dionysos and *agonothetes tout court*, twice (*IG* XI.4, 1061, same document Dürrbach *Choix* no. 75; Le Guen 2001a: TE 45; Aneziri 2003: D10).[18] As Le Guen has shown, the decree of the *synagonistai* should be dated not too long after 188, say in the 180s or 170s; the decree of the Artists found on Delos should be dated *c.* 171. Therefore, the introduction of a priesthood of Eumenes held in association with the *agonothesia* comes later: our three victor-lists date to the 160s at the earliest.

In consequence, the three victor-lists from Teos can be dated to the second quarter of the second century BC, in the Attalid period, and should be reconstructed as follows.

1. *LB–W* 91 (Le Guen 2001a: TE 46 A)

[ἐπὶ ἱερέως τοῦ δεῖνος, καὶ ἀγωνοθέτου / ἀγωνοθέτου δὲ καὶ ἱ]ερέως
β[ασιλέως Εὐμένου τοῦ δεῖνος, οἵδε ἐνίκων...]

		[Τραγωιδιῶν ?]
[Διθυράμβων]	Σατύρων	Ἀμυ–
[ ]πος	Ἀναξίων Θρασυκλείδου	
[ ]ηι	Μυτιληναῖος	ὑπε[κρίνετο
[ἐκιθαρώιδει . . .]ς	Δράματι Πέρσαις	Ἀριστ[
Βακχίου		
[ethnikon]	ὑπεκρίνετο Ἀσκληπιάδης	
	Ἡρακλείδου Χαλκιδεύς	

---

[18] Aneziri (2003) 128–32, on the office of priest and *agonothetes*.

[When (*name*) was priest and (*name*) was *agonothetes* and priest, the following were victors.]

(Of the) dithyrambs: ....pos, [son of (*name*), of (*polis*)], with [(*title of dithyramb*)].... [(*name*)] son of Bakchios, of (*polis*) ..., [was kitharode].

(Of the) satyr-plays: Anaxion, son of Thrasykleides, of Mytilene, with a drama, the *Persians*. Asklepiades son of Herakleides, of Chalkis, was actor.

[Of the tragedies ?] Amy––, [son of (*name*), of (*polis*), with a drama, (*title*). (*name*)], son of Arist– , [of (*polis*)], was actor.

At line 1 I could make out a few more letters in [ἱ]ερέως than there appear in the printed text of *LB–W*. Since the heading mentions a priest of king Eumenes, and not Eumenes the god, the document dates before the death of Eumenes II in 158 BC. This cannot be dated by the priest of king [Attalos], since under Attalos II, Kraton's letter is dated by a priest of Eumenes the god (*OGIS* 325, also in Le Guen 2001a: TE 49). The restoration seems to be sure, because the place where these letters appear in the line fits in a long heading, such as the third list allows us to see at the beginning. I have added the formula οἵδε ἐνίκων, though the name of the contest cannot be restored.

The column on the left must be for the victor in the dithyrambs, though this reading cannot be confirmed on the squeeze. The following line contains the name of the victor, ending in [-ip]pos, for instance, [Kallip]pos; at any rate, the squeeze makes clear that the line is aligned with Anaxion, the victor of the satyr-play contest. *HI* must be the ending of the victorious work, in the dative, as in the two other victor-lists, though in the third list (see below), the ending is the Attic style *EI*; I do not think this a definite obstacle; see Michel 1016A, for the Attic dative used in a contemporary decree of the Artists). For instance, from attested titles of dithyrambs, we might hypothesise *Niobe, Danae, Europe, Pasiphae, Semele*;[19] or *Ariadne, Andromache, Hekabe*, or another feminine name drawn from myth; or a masculine name such as Philoktetes. The lettering is slightly more worn in this column, but is the same as in the other two columns (a slightly tilted chi appears in this column and the middle one).

---

[19] Sutton (1989).

The third line must be the name of the kitharode, –s son of Bakchios.[20] The actor in the satyr-play, like the document, should be dated roughly to the second half of the second century. The third column might be tragedies, the author of the play would be one Amy—, as Waddington correctly read on the squeeze, and Le Guen carefully notes (Fig. 22). Then there would come his *ethnikon*; then follows the name of his actor, Arist—. There is a slight problem in that the letters *AMY* are aligned, on the squeeze as on *LB–W*'s facsimile, with the title Σατύρων; presumably the word Τραγωιδιῶν 'Tragedies' (?) was a line higher, to accommodate the very long lines necessary for the names of the author and actor of the satyr-play.

2. Pottier and Hauvette-Besnault (1880) 176–8, no. 37 (Le Guen 2001a: TE 46 C)

[ἐπὶ ἱερέως Ἀπελ]λικῶντος καὶ ἀγωνοθ[έτου καὶ (?) ἱερέως βασιλέως *vel* θεοῦ
Εὐμένου τοῦ δεῖνος, οἵδε ἐνίκων...]
[Διθ]υράμβων   [Σατύρων ?]
[Δημήτριος Μ]ενίππου Φωκαιεὺς
[Ἀ]νδρομέδαι
[ἐκιθαρώιδει δ ὁ] αὐτός

When Apellikon [was priest] and . . . was *agonothetes* [and priest of king Eumenes/the god Eumenes ?, the following were victors].
    (Of the) dithyrambs: [Demetrios son of M]enippos, of Phokaia, with *Andromeda*. The same [was kitharode].
    [(Of the) satyr-plays: ?]

The priesthood of Eumenes could be of king or god; or it could not be there at all, if the *agonothetes* was not yet priest of Eumenes: in which case, this text would date before 171 BC.
    The surviving column is the beginning of the at least three columns of the victor-list. Demetrios Menippou is the restoration of Pottier and Hauvette-Besnault, based on the following list (see below, and section 3). Strikingly, he performed his own composition, as kitharode.

---

[20] I note Stephanis (1989) no. 512, Bakchios son of Bakchios of Athens, a lyric poet in the early first century BC.

The name Apellikon is one with strong associations at Teos, since
the most famous bearer of the name was Teian. But this does not
necessarily mean that the priest is Teian, since the name is widespread in Ionia; furthermore, even if this were a Teian, it would not
necessarily imply that this priesthood is a Teian office, since it is
conceivable that a Teian could hold office within the *Koinon* of the
Artists.[21] The name is therefore not a decisive objection against my
argument that the eponymous officials in this list are not officials of
the *polis* of Teos, but those of the Artists.

3. *LB–W* 93 (Le Guen TE 46 D).

[ἐπ]ὶ ἱερέως Δημητρίου, ἀγωνοθέτου δὲ καὶ ἱε[ρέως βασιλέως vel θεοῦ
Εὐμένου τοῦ δεῖνος, οἵδε ἐνίκων ἐν τῶι ἀγῶνι]
τῶι τεθέντι Ἀττάλ[ωι   ]

                                                                  E

Διθυράμβων   Σατύρων
Νίκαρχος Ἑρμόνακτος Περγαμηνός   Ζ[ηνό]δο[τος]
Φερσεφόνει   δ[ρ]άματι[- - -]
ἐκιθαρώιδει Δημήτριος [Μ]ε[νίππου]   ὑπεκ[ρί]νετο [ὁ δεῖνα]
Φωκαιεύς   Καλλιπ[που] Μ- - -

When Demetrios was priest, and . . . was *agonothetes* and priest of [king / the
god Eumenes . . . these were victors in the contest] celebrated for Attalos
[the brother / son of the king].

(Of the) dithyrambs: Nikarchos son of Hermonax, of Pergamon, with
Persephone. Demetrios, son of [M]e[nippos], of Phokaia, was kitharode.

(Of the) satyr-plays: Z[eno]do[tos, son of (*name*), of (*polis*)], with a
drama, [(*title*)] , [(*name*)] son of Kallip[pos], of M..., was actor.

This is a very long squeeze, made of several sheets; the stone was over
90 cm long. This text, at least, was carved on an architectural block
rather than a stele. As the squeeze shows, there is nothing to the
left of the words τῶι τεθέντι Ἀττάλ[ωι] (Figs. 24–5). The first two
lines were a centred heading above a number of columns of victors;
the dithyrambic victor came in the first column on the left. A mention of a priesthood held by the *agonothetes* is certain. Demetrios, the

[21] Very few (three) Teians are attested as Artists: Aneziri (2003) 90, 239–40.

eponymous priest, might be identical to the kitharode in this document and in the first list. As mentioned above, the date is made certain by the rest of the heading, with a mention of either the brother or the son of Eumenes II: between 167 and 158. We should read οἵδε ἐνίκων for LB–W, οἵδε ἐνίκησαν. The phrase, ἐν τῶι ἀγῶνι, 'in the contest' is unusual. Normally, victor-lists would start with an expression such as οἵδε ἐνίκων τὸν ἀγῶνα τῶν Θησείων or οἵδε Νέμεια ἐνίκων (*Syll.* 667, 1057, cf. 1058, 1079). For parallels, in victor-lists, to the expression found here, see *I. Magnesia* 88 c; *SEG* 28, 1246, ll. 5–7, which might offer a model for any restoration: οἵδε ἐνίκων ἐν τῶι ἀγῶνι τῶν ǀ Ῥωμαίων τῶι τεθέντι ὑπο τοῦ κοινοῦ τῶν Λυκίων. The name of the festival is lost: Attaleia, specifying which Attalos—brother or son of Eumenes II—was honoured?

If this was the brother, the future Attalos II, the text might have read Ἀττάλ[ωι βασιλέως Ἀττάλου],[22] or Ἀττάλ[ωι τῶι ἀδελφῶι τοῦ βασιλέως].[23] If this was the future Attalos III, if the list dates to Eumenes II, the text might have read Ἀττάλ[ωι τῶι υἱῶι τοῦ βασιλέως];[24] under Eumenes' successor, Attalos II, the text might have read Ἀττάλ[ωι (τοῦ) βασιλέως Εὐμένου].[25] I cannot see any way of determining which restoration is the correct one.

In the first column, the restoration of the name of the kitharode is due to Pottier and Hauvette-Besnault (see below, section 3). The second column is very worn and difficult to read on the squeeze. For the satyr-play, the list names the author, Z[eno]do[tos] (I could not make out the delta on the squeeze or on photographs; I read Z . . . . . O. The following line must have mentioned the play, in the form δράματι + title of the play in the dative, as in the first

---

[22] The same expression in *I.Pergamon* 64, 65, 168, 174; similar is the expression Ἀθήναιος βασιλέως Ἀττάλου in *I.Asklepieion* 3 (Athenaios, brother of Eumenes II).

[23] The same expression in *MAMA* 6.173, ll. 10–11 and *SEG* 49, 1540, l. 3, with Thonemann (2003) 104 (proposing to date these two documents, and the title 'brother of the king', after the birth of Attalos (the future Attalos III) *c.* 168).

[24] The expression is similar in *I.Didyma* 488, ll. 39–40, where the male relatives of Eumenes II are named as οἱ ἀδελφοὶ αὐτοῦ . . . καὶ ὁ υἱὸς Ἄτταλος.

[25] This expression occurs in *OGIS* 319, ll. 16–18, same document *I.Magnesia* 87 (with article τοῦ), and in the heading of the ephebic list published at Schröder, et al. (1904) 170–3 no. 14, l. 9.

list. The facsimile in *LB–W* bears . . . *A*; the present reading comes from the squeeze. Then comes the actor, whose name I suppose followed immediately after ὑπεκρίνετο and is lost; Kal[....] should be understood as the beginning of his patronymic, followed by *M*—, his *ethnikon* (rather than the Kal—m of Stephanis, Le Guen). The present reading comes from the squeeze, 'son of Kallippos'.

I do not know what to make of the letter *E* on the facsimile in *LB–W*. I could not make out this letter on the squeeze. It must lie under the long heading in lines 1–2, and hence belong to the third column of victors (Κ[ωμωιδιῶν] ?)

The *Koinon* of the Artists of Ionia and the Hellespont, based at Teos in the second century BC, enjoyed a rich agonistic life, even though the exact details are obscure. It is unclear whether all of the performers and poets involved were necessarily members of the *Koinon*: does the formula 'Ionia and the Hellespont' designate the primary area of activity of the Association, or the area of origin of its members? Perhaps both; I consider membership of the Association almost certain in the case of the kitharode from Phokaia, and for the poets from Pergamon and Mytilene, problematic in the case of the actor from Chalkis in Euboia.[26] The genres attested— dithyramb, satyr-play—are certainly Dionysiac and appropriate for the festivals of the Dionysiac Artists.

From these lists, three titles emerge, contributing to the roster of titles of Hellenistic works known by epigraphy.[27] First, a satyr-play called the *Persians*: we can only wonder about the sources for this (Aischylos? Timotheos?), and any contemporary relevance in Attalid, post-Seleukid Asia Minor (it is tempting to posit a relation with the concern shown by Eumenes II to cast himself in an 'Athenian' light in the visual arts). Second, two dithyrambs: *Phersephone* and *Andromeda*; the form is now sung by a kitharode. Traditionally dithyramb involved a chorus, a *chorodidaskalos*, and an *auletes*. Were these elements compatible with the kitharode? That they are not

---

[26] In fact, the only Artists whose origin is securely known come from Kalchedon, Samos, and 'Laodikeia' (presumably Laodikeia on Lykos): Aneziri (2003) 238.

[27] See *I.Magnesia* 88 for titles of 'new dramas' from the Rhomaia at Magnesia on Maiandos.

mentioned on the lists is no argument against their presence; but the presence of a kitharode, rather than a kitharist, might imply a solo performance. The change might be explained, because the chorus is a civic form, organized by civic subdivisions, unsuited for the Dionysiac Artists.[28] In all three lists, the dithyrambic contest is mentioned first: the prominence of dithyramb mirrors, and perhaps competes with, the increased importance of choral forms in the Hellenistic cities.[29]

III. FINDING A TEIAN *HORSE*

In the courtyard of the primary school at Sığacık are kept two inscribed stones. The first is a stele, bearing a Teian *symmoria* decree (*SEG* 35, 1152). The second is a marble block, long upside down and half-buried, now proudly presented unearthed, cleaned, and right side up (Fig. 27). I studied this stone with H. Malay, to whom I owe excellent photographs. It is 87 cm wide, 37 cm high, 53 cm thick. At the front, a large zone of moulding was knocked back, and the first line of the text substantially erased. In spite of damage, it is clear that the top and bottom surfaces were originally dressed, to receive a block on top, and to rest on other blocks below. The back is smoothed, with a small moulding (Fig. 28). This is not an *anta*, nor

[28] On Hellenistic and post-Hellenistic dithyramb (mostly choral with *auletes*, in the old style), the meagre evidence is gathered by Pickard-Cambridge (1962) 75–80; see now P. Ceccarelli's forthcoming paper in the proceedings of a conference on dithyramb held in Oxford, summer 2004 edited by B. Kowalzig and P. Wilson. Bélis (1995) 1054–5, presents some evidence for 'kitharodic dithyramb', but apart from the victor-lists at Teos, it is scarce. Paus. 8.50.3, Plu. *Phil.* 11, show the famous kitharode Pylades performing Timotheos' *Persians* at the Nemeia in 205; however, this is not a dithyramb (as Bélis seems to believe), but a kitharodic *nome* (albeit one which presumably illustrates Timotheos' importation of 'dithyrambic style' into the *nome*). There is a problematic dithyrambic victory at the Lenaia in Athens attested for the mid-third-century kitharode (?) Nikokles, son of Aristokles (Stephanis 1988: no. 1839); the identity is based on a combination of *IG* II² 3779 (list of victories by Nikokles Aristokleous) with Paus. 1.37.2; see Wilson (2000) 391 n. 155.

[29] The importance of choral performance for local identity in the Hellenistic period is argued for in Wilson (2003) 166.

Fig. 27 New victor list from Teos.

Fig. 28 Back of the block with the new victor list.

an architrave, but part of the wall of a monumental building—in some way connected to the Associations of Dionysiac artists. I have no information on the provenance of the block.

	ΠΟ. . . . Α	
	Διθυράμβων	*Σα[τύρων]*
	Κάλλιππος Παντοκρατίδου	*Δημόφιλ[ος τοῦ δεῖνος]*
Σ	*Μαρωνίτης ἄισματι* Ἵππωι	*Περγ[αμηνός]* 4
	ἐκιθαρώιδει Δημήτριος	*Δρ[άματι . . .]*
	Μενίππου Φωκαιεύς	*[ὑπεκρίνετο ὁ δεῖνα]*
	(traces of a heading)	

(Of the) dithyrambs: Kallippos, son of Pantokratides, of Maroneia, with a song, *the Horse*. Demetrios, son of Menippos, of Phokaia, was kitharode.

(of the) satyr-plays: Demophilos, son of [(*name*)], of Pergamon, with a drama, [(*title*). (*Name*) was actor].

(Looking at my notebook, I am embarrassed to admit that I first restored *Σα[λπινκτῶν]*, 'trumpeters').

The *sigma* at the left of the text is not exactly aligned with the two columns, and may come from another victor-list.

This inscription is a new, fourth, victors' list from Teos. It is the only surviving example of this category of document, unless the others turn up, say in Seferhisar (highly unlikely). Its provenance, Sığacık, is another illustration of the wide scatter of Teian material: none of the four victor-lists was found in the same spot—Teos, Sığacık, Seferhisar, Güzellir, the names map the dispersion of Teian inscriptions. The first line contains the traces of a heading, and perhaps a dating formula (though there does not seem to be a formula in *ἐπί* followed by an eponymous official); nothing is secure or usable. Dating will depend on palaeography.

The letters measure *c.* 2 cm. The contrast in style with the second-century victor-lists is immediately apparent. Here, alpha has a straight cross bar, with a very slight hint of a curve; round letters are slightly smaller than the other letters, and slightly off the line. Pi has uneven verticals, the right one being shorter than the left one, if not considerably so. There are slight apices; the letters are neat, except for a rather wobbly sigma; all straight lines show no trace of the bendiness (side legs of mu, top and bottom horizontals of epsilon) that characterises documents of *c.* 200 (first *asylia* requests,

Fig. 29 Decree concerning a gift of land to the Dionysiac Artists (*Tekhnitai*) (*SEG* 2, 580).

decrees relating to Antiochos III: Fig. 29[30]). The palaeography of Teian inscriptions is known thanks to dated examples: in the late fourth century, the Ulamış *sympoliteia* document;[31] in the third

[30] Herrmann (1965) 48–50.
[31] Robert and Robert (1976) 176–9 = *OMS* VII 320–3.

Fig. 30 Extract from a Teian decree for Antiochos III (*SEG* 41, 1003 II).

century, the Teian decree for the Dionysiac Artists (Fig. 30),[32] the
isopoliteia treaty between Temnos and Teos;[33] the decree concerning
sympoliteia with Kyrbissos;[34] the recently found decree about pirates
occupying the Teian harbour;[35] the dossier relating to the Seleukid
takeover and presence (Fig. 29);[36] in the second century, the documents mentioned earlier; and in the later part of the century, the
Teian decree concerning Tyre, which probably dates after 142 BC.[37]
In addition, there are two bodies of documents relating to the *asylia*
of Teos, one in the late third century, and one in the second quarter
of the second century.[38]

The closest parallel is the Teian decree in favour of the Dionysiac
Artists, *SEG* 2, 580 (Fig. 29). The straight bar alphas and small round
letters, especially the theta with its central dot, are similar. Le Guen
has recently argued convincingly for dating this document to the late

---

[32] *SEG* 2, 580; the present photograph courtesy of the French Archaeological
School in Athens.
[33] Herrmann (1979) 242 and pl. 67.2 on the palaeography of this document,
dating to the late third or early second century BC.
[34] Robert and Robert (1976) 156–9 = *OMS* VII: 300–2.
[35] Şahin (1994), whence *SEG* 49, 949; pp. 12–14 on palaeography.
[36] Herrmann (1965), whence *SEG* 41, 1003.
[37] Bécquignon and Laumonier (1925) 305–8, whence *SEG* 4, 601, with Rigsby
(1996a) 481–5. On the palaeography of Teian documents, Herrmann (1965) 49–50;
Herrmann (1979) 242; Şahin (1994) 12–13.
[38] Rigsby (1996a) 289–90; I owe thanks to C. V. Crowther for photographs of
documents from the 'second series' of *asylia* decrees.

third century, 218–203. Should our new victor-list go as early as this, into the third century BC? Another parallel is the large lettering on 'Block F' among the Seleukid documents published by P. Herrmann: straight lines, slightly smaller round letters, slight apices, no curved bar on the alpha; this letter must date between 203 and 190.[39] It is true that the letters on the new list are of a monumental size, which is always difficult to date: it is less straightforward than it might seem to compare these letters to the letters of *SEG* 2, 580 (1.1 cm) or to the letters of the decrees concerning Antiochos III (1.2 cm), let alone the lettering on the Kyrbissos *sympoliteia* document (5–7 mm) or the 'pirate decree' (5–7 mm). On the other hand, the two victor-lists securely dated to the second quarter of the second century, and documented in Le Bas's squeezes, are also carved in monumental lettering, and hence can be legitimately compared with the lettering on the new list. The comparison makes it clear that the new list is earlier, and hence should be dated to the late third or early second century. It is more the pity that we cannot read the dating formula on the stone: if there had been a priest of the ruler-cult, Attalos I, Antiochos III, or Eumenes II would settle the matter of dating. In spite of the absence of dating formula, I still think it most likely that this list is the same in nature as the three other lists from the second century: a list of victors at a festival celebrated by the Artists rather than at the Dionysia or Leukathea of Teos.

The political context is hence either the last years of the Attalid presence at Teos, or in the early 190s, in the period of Seleukid dominance, or the years immediately following the Seleukid defeat. Noteworthy is the Pergamene victor in the contest for satyr-plays. If the contestants, and victors, at the contests organised by the Artists were members of the Association of Artists, some consequences follow for the date of this victor-list. An attractive hypothesis of K. Rigsby, accepted and refined by S. Aneziri,[40] is that the Association at Pergamon was founded during the period of Seleukid domination of Teos (probably 204–188). If this hypothesis is right, the presence of the Pergamene victor would date the list either to before 204 or to after 190, since in between these years, there was a separate

[39] See Herrmann (1965) 157–9 and pl. V on the lettering of 'Block F'.
[40] Aneziri (2003) 73–4.

Association in Pergamon, distinct from the Ionian Association, and our Pergamene victor would presumably have belonged to this Pergamene Association.

The kitharode's name survives in full. Demetrios, son of Menippos, of Phokaia (Stephanis 1989: no. 636). Earlier, we only had separate attestations of his name: in the first list, *LB–W* 93 (Le Guen 2001a: TE 46 D), Δημήτριος . ε. . . . Φωκαιεύς; in the second list, Pottier and Hauvette-Besnault 1880: 176–8 no. 37 (Le Guen 2001a: TE 46 C), the name is [- - - M]ενίππου Φωκαιεύς. Pottier and Hauvette-Besnault put the two texts together, to produce the full name, and their restoration is fully vindicated. If the new list dates to the late third century, or even if it dates to the early second century, Demetrios of Phokaia had a long period of activity as kitharode, since the other two victor-lists where he appears can be dated to the 160s, forty-odd or thirty-odd years; we should date these two victor-lists early in the 160s. This is a long time for a successful opera-singer-cum-virtuoso instrumentalist to be performing at his peak. (Another possibility is that the Demetrios Menippou in the new, third-century document is the grandfather of the Demetrios Menippou of the long-known, second-century documents.)

The poet of the dithyramb is one Kallippos, son of Pantokratides, of Maroneia. Our list is the first attestation of this man. However, Stephanis 1989: no. 1995, lists a Pan[ta]kratides, son of Kallippos, of MA– in *IG* XI.4 no. 705, honoured in the very late third century BC.[41] (Thanks to A. Chaniotis for spotting this, and discussing the whole issue).

ἔδοξεν τῆι βουλῆι καὶ τῶι δ[ήμωι· Ἀρισ]-
τείδης [Τηλεμ]νήστου εἶπε[ν· ἐπειδὴ Παν]-
[τα]κρατίδης Καλλίππου Μα[　　　ἀ]-

---

[41] On the *rogator*, Aristeides Telemnestou, Vial (1984) 98–9: our Aristeides (II) belonged to 'the greatest family which Delos had in the purely political sphere'; he proposed the decrees *IG* XI 4, 704, 705, 1031. He appears as a public debtor, 209–200, and is mentioned in *I.Délos* 406 B 30 (the reference must be as part of the 'address' of a house offered as security for a loan from the Delian moneys; the text is to be dated after 188: Kent 1948: 301). In addition, Aristeides Telemnestou is the proposer of a decree accepting the Leukophryeneia of Magnesia on Maeander as *isopythios* in 208 (Rigsby 1996a: no. 99; earlier version of document in *I.Magnesia* 49). Many thanks to Chr. Habicht for these indications.

[νὴ]ρ ἀγαθὸς ὢν διατελεῖ π[ερί τε τὸ ἱε]-
[ρ]ὸν καὶ [τὸν] δῆμον τὸν Δηλ[ίων καὶ χρείας]
[πα]ρέχεται καὶ κοινῆι τῆι [πόλει καὶ ἰδίαι]
[τοῖς ἐντ]υγ[χά]νο[υσιν αὐτῶι Δηλίων
κτλ.

It was resolved by the council and the p[eople. Aris]teides, son of [Telem]nestos proposed: [since Panta]kratides son of Kallipos, of Ma[...], is continuously a good man towards the shrine and the people of the Delians, and provides services both publicly to [the city and individually to those of the Delians who meet him], etc.

The name should be corrected, in line with the new text from Teos, as K. Hallof confirms from examining a squeeze of this inscription in Berlin: in line 3, an omicron can be read in [Παντ]οκρατίδης.[42] The name Pantokratides is not hitherto attested in the Greek onomastic material (that in itself is no cause for surprise); in any case, similar names are attested (Pankrates, Panukrates, Pasikrates).[43] This Pantokratides Kallippou might well be the brother of [St]ratippos Kallippou, the *thearodokos* of Delphi at Maroneia, mentioned on the great list from Delphi, specifically in those parts to be dated to the late third century.[44]

The Delian stele is further illustrated with a document relief or emblem (Fig. 31): not a lyre, as Roussel writes in *IG* (repeated in Stephanis), but a *kithara*. This emblem is not an illustration of the honorand's polis,[45] but a reference to his identity as *mousikos*: either a

---

[42] I checked on the stone in the Delos Museum, by kind permission of P. Hatzidakis, *epimeletes* of Delos; my warmest thanks to Jean-Charles Moretti for brokering this. I could make out the omicron.

[43] Bechtel (1917) 357, 359, 361. The root Panto- appears at nearby Samos, in the name Pantonaktides: *CIG* 3091, l. 14, with Preuner (1924) 35; *SEG* 1, 366, l. 2; *OMS* II 1091. My thanks to Chr. Habicht for these references. See now *LGPN* 4.

[44] Plassart (1921) col. III 93; on the date, 230–220, Hatzopoulos (1991). However, J. Oulhen will apparently assign this part of the *thearodokoi* list to Ainos rather than Maroneia (I owe this information to E. Matthews at the *LGPN*, but am not clear as to the reasons; my thanks also to L. Loukoupoulou for checking her Maroneian prosopographical notes).

[45] Maroneia does not use Apollo's *kithara* as an emblem on its coinage; the traditional motifs are horse + vine, and from 188 (?) onwards images of Dionysos (head, cult statue): Schönert-Geiss (1987). On *parasemata* see Knoepfler (2001) 30, with earlier bibliography, notably Ritti (1970).

Fig. 31 Delian decree (late third century BC) honouring the musician of the *kithara* Pantokratides Kallipou, from Maroneia (*IG* 11.4, 705).

kitharode, or a writer of poetry for the *kithara*. There are several similar Delphian examples: a carved *kithara* accompanying a proxeny decree for Nikodromos, son of Theodoros, of Chalkis (third century BC) must indicate the honorand's activity as a *kithara*-player or poet for the *kithara*; a carved lyre accompanying a proxeny decree for two poets from Aigira, Thrason and Sokrates, the sons of Patron, reflects the honorands' performance of λυρικὰ συστήματα extracted from ancient poets (second century BC); an incised *kithara*-player, next to a decree granting citizenship to Theseus, son of Heroxenos, of

Athens, presumably informs the viewer of the honorand's activity.[46]
The Delian decree perhaps went on to describe his literary and
artistic activity in the missing lines: for instance, he may have given
performances of (kitharodic? dithyrambic?) poetry concerning
Delos, and gained good repute (εὐδοκιμεῖν) in the process. At any
rate, it is clear that we are dealing with two generations of men
who were involved in some way with the *kithara* and with poetry.
The new Teos document, and *IG* 11.4.705 are both to be dated in the
late third century or very early second century, which means that
the activity of Pantokratides, the father, and Kallippos, the son, over-
lapped. It is likely that both poet, from Maroneia, and performer,
from Phokaia, belonged to the Association of Artists. In addition,
it is possible that the actor in the third victor-list from the years
between 167 and 158, *LB–W* 93 (*name*), son of Kallippos, of the
polis M—, is from Maroneia and in fact a son of the Kallippos
Pantokratidou Maronites in the new Teian list. These Maroneian
artists are members of the Ionic–Hellespontine Association. The
city was free, indeed an ally of Rome,[47] but was close to the Attalid
dominion in the Chersonese; in addition, it was close to the
Hellespont. The Association recruited from Maroneia, as well as
from Kalchedon; if its title reflects geographical origin of members,
'Hellespont' was taken broadly.

The poet who wrote the victorious satyr-play is from Pergamon,

---

[46] Nikodromos: *FD* III 2, no. 207 (the emblem is carved in the pediment of a
stele-shaped panel in the polygonal wall next to the treasury of the Athenians); it
is clearly not a lyre, as the editor, G. Colin, writes (also in *Syll.* 432; Ritti 1970: 279–
80), but a *kithara* (thick wooden arms and integral sound-box). Nikodromos might
be identified with the kitharode mentioned in D. L. 6.89 (Stephanis 1989: no. 1829).
Thrason and Sokrates: *FD* III 1, no. 49 (clearly a lyre—curved, horn-shaped arms,
small oval sound-box), carved on the base of a statue of Philopoimen. The incised
kitharode next to a decree granting citizenship to Theseus, son of Heroxenos, of
Athens (second-century AD) is probably an image of Apollo: Ritti (1970) 283, on *FD*
III 2 no. 104. The proxeny decree from Lousoi for one Olympichos, son of Polykles,
of Charadra, is carved on a bronze plaque decorated with a lyre (according to the
editor, A. Wilhelm), perhaps a reference to his activity as *mousikos*: *IG* V 2, 389 with
Ritti (1970) 294–5; Stephanis (1989) no. 1939. From Wilhelm's photograph, *JÖAI* 4
(1901) 64, I could not tell if the *parasema* represented a lyre (Wilhelm), or a *kithara*
(Ritti).

[47] *SEG* 35, 823 gives the text of the alliance between Rome and Maroneia (after
167).

like the dithyrambic poet of the third Teian list (*LB–W* 93); he bears a common name, Demophilos, which turns up twice in Pergamon, once in *I.Pergamon* 332 and once in *I.Asklepieion* 123. I do not think we can identify him.

The new text gives us a complete text for the dithyrambic victors, whereas those known earlier were not so well preserved. Noteworthy is the expression ἆισμα, song, to describe the dithyrambic piece. On a textual level, we might restore ἆισματι + title in dative in the first victor-list (*LB–W* 91, Le Guen 2001a: TE 46 A) and in the second (Hauvette-Besnault and Pottier 1880: 176–8 no. 37; Le Guen 2001a: TE 46 C), but certainly not in the third (*LB–W* 93; Le Guen 2001a: TE 46 D), as can clearly be seen from the squeeze (Fig. 25): there are no letters to the left of the title Φερσεφόνει, which is centred.

More generally, the new text makes clear the contrast between *drama*, the word used for satyr-play, and *asma*, song, used for dithyramb. The word in itself does not imply any difference between 'choral' and 'solo' song, and so does not necessarily confirm my suggestion that the Artists performed dithyramb as solo pieces.[48]

The title of the victorious dithyramb was *The Horse*. I notice, without much comment, that the name of the author was itself a horse compound; after all, the fact that you're named after a horse isn't enough reason for going on about them. This title presumably refers to the Trojan Horse, the *doureios hippos*; the new text from Teos gives us a reference to treatment of the theme in Hellenistic times. The Horse is mentioned in a dedicatory epigram by Alkaios of Messene, as one of the themes (Ἵππου ἔργματα, the 'deeds of the Horse') in a song performed by a chorus and accompanied by an *auletes*, Dorotheos, son of Sosikles, of Thebes (*Anth. Planud.* 7, Gow–Page Alcaeus 10; Stephanis 1989: no. 812): this must be a traditional dithyramb.

Σύμφωνον μαλακοῖσι κερασσάμενος θρόον αὐλοῖς
Δωρόθεος γοερὸυς ἔπνεε Δαρδανίδας

---

[48] On the meanings and context of *asma* see Wilson (2000) 227–9.

καὶ Σεμέλας ὠδῖνα κεραύνιον, ἔπνεε δ' Ἵππου
ἔργματ', ἀειζώων ἁψάμενος Χαρίτων·
μοῦνος δ' εἰν ἱεροῖσι Διωνύσοιο προφήταις
Μώμου λαιψηρὰς ἐξέφυγε πτέρυγας,
Θηβαῖος γενεήν, Σωσικλέους· ἐν δὲ Λυαίου
νηῶι φορβειὰν θήκατο καὶ καλάμους.

Mixing the song of many accorded voices with soft pipes, Dorotheos piped the mournful Trojans, and the labour of Semele, struck by lightning, and he piped the deeds of the Horse, having reached the eternal Graces; alone among the sacred prophets of Dionysos, he escaped the swift wings of Blame. By birth, he was a Theban, son of Sosikles; in the temple of Dionysos, he dedicated his mouth-strap and his reeds.

Another epigram, by Dioskorides, describes a woman, Athenion, 'singing the Horse', presumably in a private performance or a festival *epideixis* (*AP* 5.138, also Gow–Page, Dioskorides no. 2; Stephanis 1989: no. 72).

Ἵππον Ἀθήνιον ᾖσεν ἐμοὶ κακόν· ἐν πυρὶ πᾶσα
Ἴλιος ἦν, κἀγὼ κείνῃ ἅμ'ἐφλεγόμαν,
†ουδεισας Δαναῶν δεκέτη πόνον· ἐν δ' ἑνὶ φέγγει
τῶι τότε καὶ Τρῶες κἀγὼ ἀπωλόμεθα

Line 3: On grounds of meaning, Gow and Page dislike the MS οὐ δείσας, 'having endured without fear' (Fr. Dübner), 'I had braved the ten years' effort of the Greeks' (W. Paton). They propose συστείλας, 'contracting, shortening', which seems equally unsatisfactory. Perhaps simply σὺ δ'ᾖσες/σὺ δ'ᾆσας ('you sang') ? The repetition of δέ is awkward.

Athenion sang the Horse, an evil for me; all Troy was on fire, and I burned with it . . . the ten years' toil of the Greeks; but on that same day, the Trojans and I perished.

Both epigrammatists date to the late third century, and hence provide evidence for performance of songs on the theme of the Trojan Horse contemporary to the dithyramb written by Kallippos and performed by Demetrios.

Sources for Kallippos' *Trojan Horse* would have included the *Odyssey*, Cyclical epic (the *Little Iliad* being much read in the Hellenistic period), tragedy (Sophokles' *Laokoon* ? *Sinon* ?), and various passages in lyric poetry.[49] A special role might have been played by Stesichoros' poem on the Trojan war, whose title survives on a papyrus as

$$\Sigma TH[\Sigma IXOPOY]$$
$$I\Pi\Pi[$$

'Stesichoros' *Horse*'. The fragments are published at *POxy*. 2803; West (1971) combines this text with the Stesichorean fragments *POxy*. 2619. The *Horse* seems to have covered elements of the sack of Troy, so that we may be dealing with an 'alternative or informal designation' (West) for Stesichoros' *Iliou Persis—Sack of Troy* (a known title).

In conclusion, the new list from Teos is the earliest document of its nature; it belongs to the dossier of the rich festival activity of the Dionysiac Artists, which ran in its own time, parallel with the festivals and activities of the Teian polis, even though the two activities shared the same physical space. It left its own traces, inscribed in the monumental structures of Teos town; the dispersion of this material mirrors the dispersion of the civic inscriptions of the Teians. The new inscription can be read in a precise context, modern and scholarly, but also ancient and institutional as well as monumental.

The new document provides us with information on the nature of Hellenistic dithyramb—a song, *asma*, at least in the hands of the performers at the festivals of the Artists. One such performer was Dionysios of Phokaia, appearing as a very young man, *c.* 200, at one of these festivals, singing—alone, without a chorus—a freshly minted dithyramb, *The Horse*, specially composed for the competition by a poet, himself the son of a poet or artist. We can only try to imagine this song—its prelude, its invocation, its hymnic elements, the praise of god and polis and the all-important sensitivity to place; the sense of solidarity and identity of the Dionysiac

---

[49] Bakchylides *Dithyrambs*, fr. 9, from Servius, *ad* Verg. *Aen.* 2.201 *sane Bacchylides de Laocoonte et uxore eius vel de serpentibus a Calydnis insulis venientibus atque in homines conversis dicit*, 'Bacchylides certainly speaks of Laokoon and his wife, and of snakes coming from the islands of Kalydnai and turning into people', seems to concern Laokoon, and perhaps in some way the conclusion of the Trojan legend. Many thanks to David Fearn for this reference.

Artists; the combination of kitharodic virtuosity and quotations of choral song; the sensitive intertextual weavings; the metre, the dialect; the overall hearable structure of the poem; a lot of alliteration, the piling up of composite epithets for the deadly artifact and its craftedness; the variation in rhythm between extended elaborate purple ekphrastic passages and swift narrative: Sinon, Kassandra, perhaps Laokoon, portents, gods, the debate about the Horse, foreshadowing of the sack of Troy; meaningful, allusive, tactful, reworkings of panhellenic myth to fit the politics, especially to construct relations between Troy, Pergamon, Asia Minor, and perhaps already Rome;[50] the abrupt beginning and end.

My hypothesis is that the Hellenistic professionals offered 'pseudo-choral' poetry, put on by virtuoso solo artists but, perhaps, evoking the still-ongoing group performances of old dithyramb. Nothing of this is more than speculation, and none of this exists any more; but I am trying to raise the possibility that such artistic forms were comparable in form, nature, and quality to Archaic Greek poetry, 'lyric' and 'choral', produced by professionals at frequent occasions, in well-attended festivals. The epigraphy of the Dionysiac Artists at Teos belongs to the lost world of Hellenistic literatures, as well as to that of the Greek festival and generally of Greek theatre.

---

[50] On the politically useful myth work performed by the Trojan legend see Gruen (1990) 5–33; Erskine (2001).

9

Kraton, Son of Zotichos: Artists' Associations and Monarchic Power in the Hellenistic Period*

Brigitte Le Guen

Kraton, son of Zotichos, from Calchedon, is undoubtedly the *aulos*-player from the ancient world about whom we are best informed.[1] A musician active in the second century BC and an eminent member of the Association of Dionysian *Technitai* in Asia Minor (a group of stage performers under the protection of the god of the theatre), he is known to us through around ten items of epigraphic evidence.

This corpus has been the subject of excellent analysis by Daux, whose main objective was to provide a chronological order for the various items.[2] Even so, it is still impossible to date some of them as precisely as we would like. In a book dealing with the Associations of *Technitai* in the Hellenistic period (Le Guen 2001a), I translated and provided commentary on all the inscriptions relating to Kraton, though without providing a continuous analysis.[3] A second book on

---

* Mes plus chaleureux remerciements vont à Peter Wilson, qui non seulement a accepté de publier mon texte dans son ouvrage, mais en a en outre effectué la traduction.

[1] Stephanis (1988) no. 1501; Bélis (1999) 215, 226.

[2] Daux (1935) 210–30.

[3] Le Guen (2001a). This work, the product of a habilitation thesis of 1999, consists of two volumes: a documentary corpus (vol. I), in which the reference TE designates an epigraphic text; and a synthesis (vol. II). For reasons of convenience, epigraphic references will on the whole be cited according to my own corpus, where previous bibliography may be found. The dossier on Kraton is currently made up of nine

the same subject appeared in 2003 (Aneziri 2003), but neither does it have a chapter specifically devoted to Kraton.[4]

In addition, two recent articles have returned to several points of controversy in the dossier: one forms part of an analysis of the royal cult in Hellenistic Pergamon;[5] the other responds to the discovery in the hinterland of Pergamon of an unpublished inscription that documented a new Association from the time of Eumenes II.[6]

It therefore seems a particularly appropriate moment to present a synthesis of all the information available about this famous musician. To this end I shall begin by looking at his personality and career, going back to the chronology provided by the inscriptions that relate to it. I shall then examine the nature and the status of the various Associations which, at the same time or in succession, had close relations with Kraton: the *Koinon* of synagonists; the *Koinon* of the *Technitai* of Ionia and the Hellespont, and those gathered under Dionysos Kathegemon; the *Koinon* of the Attalists; and lastly, the *Koinon* of the *Technitai* of the Isthmos and Nemea. Finally, I shall show what the example of this well-connected *aulos-player* tells us about the links formed between the artists and political power in the Hellenistic period.

I. KRATON: THE MAN, THE ARTIST AND THE WEALTHY PROPERTY OWNER

I.1. The man

Although a number of significant facts about his life are known, the dates of his birth and death remain obscure, and they can only be approximated from our available sources. The period in which

---

documents, as follows: a list inscribed in the theatre of Iasos (*IGSK* 28, 1, 163, l. 9 = *LB–W* 255); five decrees, issued by various authorities (TE 33, TE 44, TE 45, TE 48, TE 52); two letters, by different authors (TE 49, TE 51); a funerary inscription (TE 50).

[4] Aneziri (2003). See my review, Le Guen (2004b) 279–99.

[5] Schwarzer (1999) 249–300. The essentials of this article are recapitulated in Schwarzer (2002) 221–46, with figs. 1 and 2 on 227–8.

[6] Müller and Wörrle (2002) 191–235. When I refer to Wörrle (2002), I mean the first part of this article, which he produced, though the work is the fruit of collaboration.

he was born can be estimated on the basis of the first reference to him in the epigraphic evidence (*IGSK* 28, 1, 163, l. 9). There he is engaged to take part in the Dionysia of Iasos at a date which the specialists place no earlier than 193/2 BC.[7] He died at Pergamon (TE 52, l. 15) in the years 146–138, or 146–133: the appearance of his name in a letter dated to 146/5 or 145/4 leads one to believe that he was still alive at that time (TE 51).[8] As for the *terminus ante quem* of 138 or 133, this derives from the fact that a monarch by the name of Attalos was to present Kraton's heirs with the will of which he was trustee (TE 52, ll. 17–18). It is impossible today to decide between these two dates, although the first is undoubtedly the more plausible.[9] Supposing that the *aulos*-player was born towards the end of the third century (based on the hypothesis that he began his career in the 190s around the age of twenty), he would have been between seventy-two and sixty-four years old if he died under Attalos II, between 146 and 138 BC;[10] if under Attalos III, between seventy-two and seventy-seven.

What little we know of his identity does not add up to much: a name, a patronymic and two successive *ethnika*. Son of a man named Zotichos[11] and originally from Calchedon in Bithynia, during his lifetime Kraton acquired Pergamene citizenship, as shown by a decree of the Association of the *Technitai* of the Isthmos and Nemea (TE 33, ll. 1–2). Although it contains nothing that might date it, this document can nonetheless be given a context thanks to another inscription which is very precisely dated to February 152. This is a letter written by the musician to the Association of Attalists (TE 49).[12]

The twin reference at the beginning of the letter—to the seventh year of the reign of the sovereign Attalos II Philadelphos and to the

---

[7] Crowther (1990) 145 and (1995b) 228; Migeotte (1993).

[8] See Le Guen (2001a) I.262 and Aneziri (2003) 82. For the reference to Kraton in this letter, see below section II.1.

[9] See below II.1.

[10] If he founded the Attalists at the very end of the reign of Eumenes II, he would have been at most fifty.

[11] According to *LGPN*, this name is widely attested in the Greek world.

[12] Schwarzer wrongly imagined that this was the *aulos*-player's will (or the letter accompanying the will). As I have already indicated (Le Guen 2001a: I.262), and as Wörrle (2002: 201–2 n. 34) has also remarked, the document is formally dated to 152 BC, while Kraton very probably died after 146, if we may trust the inscription TE 51.

eponymous magistracies of *Technitai* of Asia Minor—only makes sense in relation to the author of the letter.[13] The reference to the priesthood of Dionysos, in close association with the priesthood and *agonothesia* of king Eumenes, is explained by Kraton's position in the Anatolian Association. On the other hand, the decision to date the letter by reference to the year of the reign of the Attalid monarch can, it seems to me, be explained solely by the fact that the *aulos*-player was by then in possession of his new status as a citizen of Pergamon (*Περγαμῆνος*).[14] In addition, the month referred to—*Dystros*—belonged to the Macedonian calendar used in the capital of the Attalid kingdom.[15] The year 152 thus constitutes a *terminus ante quem* for the granting of Pergamene citizenship to the musician.

As far as other chronological indicators for the life of Kraton the following is a summary of what we can say:[16]

---

[13] It goes without saying that this provides no indication as to the place where the recipients of the letter resided. Nor does it throw any doubt on the fact that the magistrates mentioned are those of the Anatolian *Koinon*: the detail *τῶν τεχνιτῶν* which follows the name of the eponymous priest is the result of the author's wish to differentiate clearly between the Association of Asia Minor and the group of Attalists. For a similar interpretation see Wörrle (2002) 201 n. 28 and Aneziri (2003) 130–1. On the other hand, I do not share the opinion of Aneziri when she asserts that the fact that it was dated by reference to the eponymous magistrates of the Anatolian college rather than by reference to the year of the reign of Attalos II had nothing to do with the *Technitai*. In a letter, the method of dating bears no relation to the person or persons receiving it, as the Egyptian papyri teach us for private correspondence, or numerous inscriptions for royal correspondence. Kraton dated his letter not by reference to the position of the Attalists, but as a consequence of his double status as a member of the Anatolian Association and a citizen of Pergamon, which is where he was when he drafted it.

[14] Note that Kraton has no *ethnikon* in this document. The significance of this observation is however considerably limited by the fact that most often only his name and patronymic are indicated on the stones (cf. TE 45, ll. 3, 6, 22, 34; TE 48, ll. 3, 7; TE 49, ll. 3–4; TE 52, l. 2).

[15] Had he written it from Teos, Kraton would only have made reference to the magistracies effective in the Associations to which he belonged and which constituted an entirely separate state within the city where it was based (cf. Le Guen 2001a: II.77–82). Further confirmation of this special status is provided by the recent publication of a tetradrachm with a reference to '[money] of the Dionysiac *Technitai*'. This is the first numismatic evidence to date for the Dionysiac Artists (cf. Lorber and Hoover 2003: 59–63).

[16] The chronology proposed by Daux still seems to me to be beyond debate (cf. Le Guen 2001a: I.228). This is also the view of Wörrle (2002: 196 n. 12) and Aneziri (2003: 107f., 123, 385).

TE 44 (under Eumenes II, *c.* 180–170): a reference to the irreproachable conduct of the *aulos-player* towards 'the gods and the kings' enables us to assign this text to the third period of Attalid rule over Teos. As with the next inscription, which contains an almost identical expression (TE 45, ll. 12–13), it can be placed, at the earliest, around the time of the peace of Apamea, as Daux has shown. At this date, Attalos I is dead, Eumenes II has succeeded him and Kraton—referred to as Καλχηδόνιος (ll. 2, 19, 29–30)—is honoured by an Association called the '*Koinon* of the synagonists'.[17]

TE 45 (*c.* 171–167): later than the previous document, this decree (ll. 6–7) shows that, having held in succession the priesthood and *agonothesia* which are also referred to in TE 44 (ll. 5, 10), Kraton goes on to hold them both again at the same time, by special concession (TE 45, l. 9). The reference to the festival of the Mouseia—the chronology of which has recently been analysed by Knoepfler (1996: 165)—might even suggest a date after 171 BC.[18] The reference to the Delian people (l. 38) ensures that it is in any case earlier than 167 BC, when the renewed Athenian control of the island began.

TE 48: this decree follows the inscriptions TE 44 and TE 45 since it refers to 'honours already awarded in the past' to the musician (ταῖς προυπαρ-χούσαις τιμαῖς, l. 9). In any case, it dates to before 158: the reference to a priest of king Eumenes in the first line of the title implies that it was issued during the lifetime of the ruler;[19]

TE 49: a letter written by Kraton himself in February 152 BC;

TE 50: this inscription, engraved on a funerary monument from Teos, featuring both Kraton and the Attalists, certainly follows the creation of the *koinon*—whose prior existence is attested in the previous text;

TE 51: this letter is dated to 146/5 or 145/4 as it comes from a Roman general, identified by the specialists as L. Mummius;

TE 33: this new decree in honour of Kraton—now in possession of Pergamene citizenship—is to be attributed to the *Technitai* of the Isthmos and Nemea. Its abbreviated header contains no part of a dating formula. Only certain indications, to which I shall return, suggest that it might come shortly after TE 51.

Finally, it is possible that the musician may have been rewarded during his lifetime with three crowns, represented in a relief-carving found at Teos. These were dedicated, at an unspecified date, by,

---

[17] On this see below, II.1.   [18] See Le Guen (2001a) I.235.
[19] On the date of the death of Eumenes see Petzl (1978) 264f.

respectively, the ephebes, the *strategoi* and the people of the city (*LB–W* 1558). However the stone has only the name 'Kraton', without patronymic or *ethnikon*: his fame could explain such a lack of further specification, unless it is another person of the same name.[20]

If it were in fact the son of Zotichos, this would be further evidence of the extent of his connections and of his popularity. It would suggest that he did not merely associate with the narrow circle of his fellow-artists, but had ties with the magistrates and citizens of the polis where the *Technitai* were based.[21]

I.2. The artist

Kraton's professional career was as a musician—more specifically, as an *aulos*-player, a reed instrument that Bélis[22] and many others[23] have often reminded us should not be identified with a flute—just like its Latin equivalent the *tibia*—nor should it be translated as such.

He makes his first appearance in our sources as an αὐλητής, responsible for providing two days of performances at the theatre of Iasos (*IGSK* 28, 1, 163, ll. 9–10). Subsequently he is always designated with this term without any further qualification (TE 44, l. 2; TE 45, l. 6, 22–3; TE 48, l. 3, 7), with only one exception. In TE 33, l. 2 he appears as a 'cyclic' *aulos*-player—that is, an instrumentalist who did not play as a soloist as a 'Pythic' player did, but accompanied by a dithyrambic chorus.[24]

---

[20] Kraton is a fairly widespread name in the Greek world. See s.v. in the various volumes of *LGPN*.

[21] We know that a statue in his honour had been erected in the theatre of Teos, among other places where he did not reside. This was to be crowned during the festivals celebrated by the civic community itself, both the Dionysia and all other contests (TE 45, ll. 28–9).

[22] Among a large bibliography, I would mention e.g. Bélis (1999: 16), who defines the *aulos* as a 'wind instrument with two pipes, played through two double reeds' and Landels (1999: 1–2), for whom 'The *aulos* was a pair of pipes, with vibrating reeds in their mouthpieces, held out in front of the player.' See also his chapter 2a—'The Aulos'—which has a number of illustrations.

[23] Landels (1999) 24.

[24] Whence his other title, '*aulos*-player of dithyrambic choruses'—of *andres* or *paides*—(Bélis 1988: 230–1).

According to Bélis (1988: 227–50; 1999: 72–3), while 'the position of the *aulos*-player was at the bottom of the social scale', this was nonetheless not true of all players of the *aulos*, as 'the social status held by musicians was not inherent in the instruments they played but in the activities they pursued'.[25] She cites, among the least respected activities, those of the *aulos*-player on warships or at funeral ceremonies.

There is thus no reason to be surprised by the respect enjoyed by Kraton during his lifetime.[26] To take the example of two of his colleagues: Dionysodoros[27] and his contemporary, the famous Ismenias,[28] were able, through their art, 'to amass genuine fortunes and to carve out a prominent place in society' (Bélis 1999: 73).[29]

With regard to Kraton, however, the evidence says nothing about the size of his fees nor about the way he pursued his profession, and his name does not feature in any victor- or competition-list in our possession. We do not know which genre of music he excelled in, nor which type of *aulos* he used among the various models known to have existed.[30] We do not know if he was able to perform outside the context of the Associations,[31] nor if he had any career as a soloist rather than an accompanist of choruses (dithyrambic, comic, or

---

[25] On the place of the *aulos* in the musical life of the Greeks and on the status of the *aulos*-player after the death of Alexander the Great, see Scheithauer (1997) 107–27.

[26] I have some doubts about the hypothesis of Aneziri (2003: 216 and n. 74) to the effect that *aulos*-players would have enjoyed a privileged position in the Anatolian *Koinon*—assuming the prosopographical identifications of Stephanis (1988) are correct, since we find those named Satyros (TE 48, l. 1 = Stephanis 1988: nos. 2232, 2240) and Kratinos (TE 49, l. 2 = Stephanis 1988: nos. 1493, 1495) exercising the high office of priest of the Association. It is perhaps not so much their status as professional *aulos*-players as their social position (in relation to the powerful?) that secures them such an honour.

[27] Cf. Stephanis (1988) no. 753.

[28] See Stephanis (1988) no. 1295. The basic documents relevant to the *aulos*-players of antiquity are assembled in this prosopographical work.

[29] See likewise, in the previous bibliography, and for an enlightening comparison with the Greek world, Baudot (1973) ch. 4, 79–89: 'Profanes et professionnels: préjugés et passions'.

[30] See Landels (1999: 40), who cites different types of *auloi*—the *parthenikos*, *paidikos*, *kitharisterios*, *teleios*, and *hyperteleios*.

[31] See Le Guen (2004a) 77–106, esp. 94ff. The reasoning applied there to actors is equally valid for the musicians affiliated to the Associations of *Technitai*.

tragic); and whether this was due to his own preference or because he was obliged by the contracts to which he was bound as an artist affiliated to an Association.

But Kraton's is far from being an isolated case: the sources that deal with the Dionysiac corporations generally make no mention of the artistic talents of their members. They seem concerned only to stress their exceptional piety. Their purpose was to underline the sacred character of the activities of the *Technitai*,[32] and they were not intended to provide information on their professional merits. As paradoxical as it may appear, Kraton the musician remains an enigma for us.

I.3. The wealthy property owner

Although the available evidence establishes no explicit connection between Kraton's remarkable social standing and his status as an artist, in a position to be handsomely remunerated, the image provided of him unanimously by the sources is one of a wealthy man. While we have no precise indications as to the origin of his fortune,[33] we know indirectly what it was made up of (in part or in total), thanks to the list of goods that he left to the Association of Attalists which he founded. This is the inventory:

- a capital of 10,500 silver Alexandrian drachmas: he directed the members of the *koinon* to invest this, as the interest was to be used to finance their meetings and sacrifices (TE 52, ll. 24–7);[34]

---

[32] We should recall that one of the principal activities of the *Technitai* was participation in contests of all kinds, indissociably connected to divine cult (Le Guen 2001a: II.84).

[33] It could have come from his family, be the result of a brilliant international career, or a combination of these two hypotheses. The fact that the sum of money bequeathed by Kraton to the Attalists is expressed in a coinage widely diffused throughout the Greek world—and well after the death of the Macedonian conqueror—and not in cistophoric drachmas, which were the official currency of the kingdom of Pergamon, seems to me to be the sign of a fortune acquired, at least in part, thanks to the profession which made him criss-cross the Greek world (TE 52, ll. 24–7).

- slaves: all the necessary details concerning them were given in the will itself (TE 52, ll. 27–30);
- a sanctuary (TE 52, l. 30: τεμένει) or *Attaleion*, located close to the theatre (TE 52, l. 20: τό τε Ἀττάλειον τὸ πρὸς τῶι θεάτρωι); and objects to be used for its upkeep (TE 52, l. 30);[35]
- a house adjoining the royal palace whose previous owner was called Mik[ka]ros (TE 52, ll. 21–3: τὴν συνοικίαν τὴν πρὸς τῶι βασιλείωι, τὴν πρότερον οὖσαν Μικ[κά]ρου).[36]

The question of the location of the sanctuary and the house has been endlessly disputed. Scholars sometimes opt for Pergamon, sometimes for Teos, depending on whether they see the Attalists as an Association based in the one or the other of these *poleis*. I would like to take up this debate[37] that Aneziri prefers to leave an open question,[38] while Wörrle for his part basically accepts the argument of Schwarzer in favour of Teos.[39]

Although the fact of the donation by Kraton to the Attalists of a sanctuary (or *Attaleion*) and of a house (*synoikia*) is not in dispute, the main question to be examined, it seems to me, is the issue of the name of the city in which the musician owned his property.

For as long as Kraton bears the *ethnikon* Καλχηδόνιος in the documents, we may assume that it is in Calchedon—and nowhere else—that he holds the privilege of the right to own land and property (ἔγκτησις γῆς καὶ οἰκίας) attached to the status of citizen. But from the day he obtained Pergamene citizenship (cf. TE 33, ll. 2–3), he became free to enjoy full legal property rights at Pergamon.

And so, if we rely solely on the information provided by the epigraphic corpus, the only place where Kraton was able to acquire land and property was not Teos but Pergamon. This is, logically,

---

[34] This practice operates in religious foundations; cf. Poland (1909) III.490–1 and Laum (1964²) *passim*.

[35] The list of these objects is found partially preserved on the back of the present inscription. See *CIG* 3071 with the corrections of Rigsby (1996b) 137–9.

[36] The name appears to be a *hapax*. Perhaps it should be replaced by 'Mikkalos', attested in the Aegean islands (Chios, Crete, Delos, Rhodes, Samos) as well as Doris, according to *LGPN*.

[37] See Le Guen (2001a) I.254–4, 262–5.

[38] Aneziri (2003) 108 n. 489.   [39] See Wörrle (2002) 200 n. 24.

where we should look for the sanctuary and the house that formed part of his patrimony. To resist this conclusion requires us to assume that Kraton was *also* honoured with citizenship of Teos, because while based in this city, the *Technitai* were nonetheless not citizens of it. The only alternative is to suppose that the Teans granted him the extraordinary favour of the right to acquire a meeting house[40] in their territory, as well as a sanctuary as a base for the cultural Association he had created. There is no evidence whatever for such a supposition, even though we may imagine that Kraton had relations with the citizens and magistrates of Teos.[41] It is on the other hand one item in the dossier of Kraton that irrefutably attests his status as a citizen of Pergamon.

We should now compare these conclusions with the recent analysis of Schwarzer, recalling first the interpretations given by the specialists of the relevant archaeological data, which are diametrically opposed.

Those who maintain the Pergamene hypothesis[42] believe that the royal palace that serves to locate the house owned by Kraton (τὴν συνοικίαν τὴν πρὸς τῶι βασιλείωι) is simply one of the structures built on the acropolis where the dynasty dwelt. Similarly, the theatre that helps place the *Attaleion* (τὸ Ἀτταλεῖον τὸ πρὸς τῶι θεάτρωι) is none other than the famous monument built on the side of the hill that overlooks the valley of Caicus. Some maintain that the *Attaleion* is the Ionic temple built at the northern end of the terrace of the theatre—sometimes attributed to Dionysos Kathegemon, sometimes to the dynastic cult—while others believe it is the

---

[40] Wörrle (2002: 202 n. 35, with reference to Hellmann 1992: 397) has shown that it is not a question of a 'house', as in the translation I have given of *synoikia*, but of a 'technical term for a boarding house'. This is not incompatible with my translation/ interpretation. Owner of a *synoikia*, previously the property of the Mik[k]aros mentioned, Kraton could very well have occupied one part, while renting out the others if, in the use of this term, it is the notion of cohabitation that is primary. As Boeckh (1828: I.111) commented, the Attic language certainly makes 'a distinction between domestic houses (*oikiai*) and houses for rent (*synoikiai*)', but 'in truth, it can happen that a domestic house be rented out or that a house for rent be dwelt in by the owner. One designates this a shared house, even if one of them does not pay rent'.

[41] See *LB–W* 1558, TE 44, TE 50.

[42] Allen (1983) 153; Cardinali (1906) 151 and n. 1; Fraenkel (1890) 138; Hansen (1971) 419; Lüders (1873) 22; Ohlemutz (1940) 100–3; von Prott (1902) 168 ff., 178–82; Rostovtzeff (1930) 600.

building cut into an alcove excavated on the southern slope of the theatre.[43]

For their part, supporters of the Tean hypothesis[44] stress the fact that the majority of the inscriptions relating to Kraton were found in the territory of ancient Teos and not at Pergamon.[45] They believe that the *Attaleion* is a sanctuary to be found in the vicinity of the theatre whose ruins are still visible today on the site of Teos. As for the royal palace, they are compelled to propose that the Ionian city possessed one comparable to that which is attested for Tralles.[46]

Following a close re-examination of the remains of the Attalid capital, Schwarzer has recently joined their ranks. He found no building that might correspond with the *Attaleion*.[47]

The building cut into an alcove: this complex set of structures, made up of several terraces and long since in a very poor state of preservation, would have housed the meeting place of the branch of artists of Pergamon known as the *Technitai* of Dionysos *Kathegemon*. As proof Schwarzer cites two elements of its architecture: the presence of an area on the rocky surface with no traces of covering;

---

[43] Wensler (1989) 33–42; Radt (1999) 222.

[44] *OGIS* I. 500 n. 13; Kern *RE* II s.v. '*Attaleion*', col. 2516; Klaffenbach (1914) 27; Poland (1909) I.140; Rigsby (1996b) 137–9; Ruge (1934) col. 567; Virgilio (1993) 55.

[45] According to the first editors, the inscriptions TE 44, TE 48, and TE 33 were found in the village of Sığacık, inscribed on the same stone, and in an order that does not respect chronological order. Given that in TE 44, l. 26 it is stipulated that the decree should be erected next to the *Dionyseion*, the provenance of the three inscriptions might correspond to the place where the Anatolian Association posted its major decisions. Unfortunately we do not know whether the stone was found in situ: see the discussion in Ma's chapter of the dispersal of Tean epigraphy. The letter addressed by Kraton to the Attalists (TE 49) comes from a Turkish cemetery in the vicinity of Sevrihissar, a locality whose Turkish name designates an elevated fortress. We should definitely recognise in this the fortified enclosure mentioned in connection with the find-spot of the inscription TE 50. The same is true of the decree of the Attalists (TE 52), on the back of which Kraton's will was inscribed. As for the crown engraved on the funerary monument (TE 50), according to Pottier and Hauvette (1880: 164) it was discovered 'in an ancient Turkish cemetery, to the north-east of the village and several metres from the fortified enclosure'. Perhaps this is the same cemetery as that mentioned in reference to TE 49 and TE 52.

[46] Vitr. 2, 8, 9; Plin. *HN* 35, 172.

[47] Schwarzer (1999: 265–72) also attaches great importance to the find-spot of the inscriptions relating to Kraton, especially to the funerary crown discovered on the site of ancient Teos and dedicated by 'the Attalists and Kraton' (TE 50).

and its position next to another cultic space, equipped with a niche capable of accommodating statues of greater than normal height. According to Schwarzer (who shares the view of Radt), such an arrangement would have been particularly well suited to the celebration of Dionysiac mysteries, and we know from other sources that these formed part of the state cult of Dionysos Kathegemon.[48] It follows that one must look elsewhere for the site of the *Attaleion*. And given that there is no suitable structure in close proximity to the theatre of Pergamon, the Tean hypothesis necessarily follows.[49]

The hypothetical temple devoted to the cult of the sovereign: the location of this building, to the south of the gate of the citadel, had in the past been deduced from its ground-plan, which recalls that of Hellenistic *heroa*.[50] But now Schwarzer has recognised that the very configuration of the place and the profane structures nearby prevent us from identifying in it a sanctuary sponsored by a monarch.[51] He concludes from this that the *temenos* was built by a private person. This could not, however, be the college of Attalists, as Radt would like.[52] Our sources clearly locate the *Attaleion* in close proximity to the theatre, which is not the case with the sanctuary in question. Schwarzer has thus identified a further argument for locating the *Attaleion* bequeathed by Kraton at Teos, and not at Pergamon.

Let me say straightaway that I do not find the case based on the archaeology of the area convincing: incontestable proof that would bring an end to the debate has never, to my mind, been adduced. In reality, the only reliable conclusions may be summarised thus:

The building cut into an alcove is closely connected with premises belonging to a society and suggests Dionysiac practices;

---

[48] In this he follows the opinion of Radt (1999: 223). One can compare this place with the two grottoes excavated in the sanctuary of Poseidon at the Isthmos (the northeast grotto and the grotto said to be part of the theatre), which hosted Dionysiac Associations until the fourth century, and then again in the second century AD (cf. Broneer 1973: 33–46; Gebhard 1973: 4).

[49] See more recently Schwarzer (2002) 223–5.

[50] Excavated in 1927 by Wiegand, it was published ten years later by Boehringer and Krauss in *Altertümer von Pergamon*, Band IX. Wensler (1989: 33–42) has shown that it could only have been built in the early years of the reign of Eumenes II.

[51] See the plan of the entire *temenos* given by Schwarzer (2002: 2).

[52] Radt (1999) 247.

The *temenos* located to the south of the gate of the citadel is the concern of a private cultic association and not of some state institution.

The archaeology can certainly identify two sites of religious activity, as well as defining their particular status (public, private, or even royal). But by itself it does not allow us to say whether the Attalists or the *Technitai* of Dionysos Kathegemon conducted their activities in one of them. The reason is simple, and the textual evidence confirms it: the practices of these two Associations, both devoted to the cult of the Attalids, were far too similar.[53] And so there is no major obstacle to continuing to see in the building cut into an alcove in the theatre the seat of the Attalists, while reserving for the *Technitai* of Dionysos Kathegemon the sanctuary formerly called 'Temenos für den Herrscherkult' ('*Temenos* for the Rulercult').[54]

Interpretations based on the find-spots of inscriptions are no more effective. Already in 1902 Prott, followed by Ohlemutz, had objected that the texts unearthed at Teos were very probably simply copies of originals erected at Pergamon.[55]

---

[53] This is beyond doubt. See also Wörrle (2002) 200–1.

[54] The analysis of Wensler (1989: 33–42) remains valid: the repetition of the article (τό τε Ἀττάλειον τὸ πρὸς τῶι θεάτρωι) requires us to draw a distinction between the famous official building devoted to the dynastic cult and the *temenos* of the artists. I believe we must therefore distinguish between the *Attaleion*/alcove-building that was the seat of the *Koinon* and the *Attaleion* that was a private sanctuary of the royal family where the cult of the monarch was conducted, which Schwarzer situates by the site of the great altar of the capital. I do not find the position of Schwarzer (2002: 227) particularly compelling. He argues that the *Technitai* of Dionysos Kathegemon cannot be associated with the supposed 'Temenos für den Herrscherkult': on the one hand because, under Roman domination, they no longer had any influence at Pergamon and on the other because, in the Hellenistic period, only one Association could practise the royal cult (and likewise for the imperial cult in the Roman period). In the first place the Anatolian Association is still attested in TE 56, under Sulla (*c.* 84 and 81 BC) and I have tried to show (Le Guen 1997: 73–96; 2001b: 273–82) that its Pergamene branch had certainly not conducted its affairs at Elaia, as is usually stated, on a mistaken interpretation of the inscription TE 54: thus Wörrle (2002) 197–8 n. 14; second, there is no reason why, after the disappearance of the *Technitai* of Dionysos Kathegemon, the local meeting-place should not have been reused by another cultic association.

[55] Prott (1902) 166. This hypothesis is vigorously rejected by Wörrle (2002) 200 n. 24, with reference to Dittenberger (*OGIS* 326 n. 1) and Klaffenbach (1914: 27). In fact Klaffenbach simply refers to Poland (1909: I.140), who without any discussion, evokes the foundation at Teos of an Association of Attalists.

In fact there is nothing surprising about the discovery at Teos of documents that in all probability formed part of the archive of the Association of Asia Minor, of which Kraton was an eminent dignitary.[56] Some of them—and here I pick up the argument of Prott—could certainly have been inscribed in multiple copies and erected in a number of places, such as the decree of the *Technitai* of the Isthmos and Nemea (TE 33). This was found at Teos, but one can easily imagine that it was also present in one of the bases, or even the headquarters, of this other *Koinon*. An example is the honorific decree passed before 167 by the *Technitai* of Anatolia, which is known to us through a single copy from Delos (TE 45) but which we know to have accompanied statues of the musician erected in two other places; another, the letter found at Thebes in Boeotia (TE 51), that a Roman magistrate addressed to the Anatolian *Technitai*, and which includes the name of Kraton.

The situation is different with the funerary monument, which contains the following reference, inscribed within a crown:[57] 'The president Kraton, son of Zotichos, and the Attalists.'[58] The anonymous deceased person (the first editors of the text thought of a *para-prytanis*) is honoured here by a number of other groups, political as well as religious.[59] And given that he was the leader of an association of a similar nature, Kraton may have been concerned to join in

---

[56] The place where documents relating to the Anatolian Association were posted should be situated at Teos πρὸς τῶι Διονυσίωι, according to TE 44, l. 26. It is without doubt the same place as the archive of the Association of Asia Minor. By way of comparison, we know that the Association of the *Technitai* of the Isthmos and Nemea kept the archives of both its constituent elements at its headquarters in Thebes (TE 12A, l. 41). It is possible that a duplicate of part of these archives was kept at Pergamon, as in the local headquarters of the Association of the Isthmos and Nemea.

[57] This monument carried a total of fourteen crowns, of which five no longer have any trace of letters.

[58] This translation seems to me to be preferable to the one I gave in TE 50 (Le Guen 2001a: I.255), namely 'The Attalists under Kraton's presidency', which incorrectly stresses the former over the latter.

[59] They are: the *synarchontes* presided over by Metrodoros, son of Metrodoros; the *thiasos* of [Si]malion; the *orgeones* presided over by Athenodotos, son of Metrodoros; the *paraprytaneis* presided over by Metrodoros, son of Onesimos and grandson of Anaxibios; the *Samothrakistai* presided over by Athenodotos, son of Metrodoros; the *mystai* presided over by Athenodotos, son of Metrodoros.

paying his respects to this leading figure of Teos. He might have had a relationship with the magistrate during his stays in the city, just like the Attalists (or at least some among them). There is no reason to believe that they both dwelt in one and the same place—as it happens Teos, where the document was found.[60]

II. KRATON IN THE CONTEXT OF THE ASSOCIATIONS: A LIFE OF SERVICE

Many aspects of Kraton as a private individual, an artist and a wealthy property owner remain unknowable. But thanks to the nature of the available evidence, we are better informed about him as a character entirely devoted to the life of the Associations and abundantly generous to groups of diverse status and lustre. I shall survey them briefly before examining the specific ties that Kraton formed with each of them.

II.1. Local and international Associations

The first Association with which we find Kraton connected, according to the chronology established earlier,[61] is that of the synagonists, for which we possess a single epigraphic attestation (TE 44).

In 1997 Sophia Aneziri showed that this *Koinon* existed on the margins of the Association of Asia Minor,[62] to which it was always closely tied, but independent in its organisation. It brought together

---

[60] To form the *Koinon* of Attalists, Kraton could have chosen men of any profession and origin whom he knew in Teos and who had had some connection with the deceased citizen (magistrate?). While conceding that the Attalists (or at least some of them) had been artists (see the discussion of their identity below), they—like Kraton himself—could certainly have continued to exercise their profession at Pergamon, as at Teos, and kept company there with the individual honoured on the funerary monument TE 50 before he died.

[61] Cf. Section I.1 above.

[62] Aneziri (1997) 62. Aneziri (2003: 317–35) returns to a general discussion of the synagonists, with a number of modifications that do not affect my argument here. See also Le Guen (2001a) I.229–30.

in its ranks all manner of stage artists, with no discrimination as to specialism, who participated in spectacles during musical and/or dramatic *agones*, but were not permitted to compete for any reward.

From reading the decree issued by the synagonists, it is not clear whether, when they honour Kraton, it is as a real member of their Association, or if they grant him these rewards as a former colleague. The ambiguity of the expression used in the formula encouraging the synagonists 'to honour their own (τοὺς ἐξ ἑαυτῶν) at every opportunity' in effect allows for both interpretations.[63] All the same, the second seems to me to be preferable: when he was just embarking on his career, not (yet) playing as a soloist but basically occupied as the accompanist of dramatic choruses (which are still attested in the Hellenistic period), the *aulos*-player would have won over the sub-group of synagonists to concerns that were closest to his own. Then, as he advanced in his career, and became a figure of note in the Anatolian *Koinon*, he would have continued to demonstrate the greatest concern for those with whom he used to associate not long ago and who, in the shadow of the more famous, remained specialists essential to the artistic life of the period.

The second Association with which our sources link Kraton—in this instance certainly as a member—brings together the 'Dionysian *Technitai* of Ionia and the Hellespont and those gathered under the patronage of Dionysos Kathegemon'. This is an Association whose title is only attested, in this double form, after 188 BC. We must assume that in the aftermath of the peace of Apamea, the *Technitai* of Ionia and the Hellespont, based at Teos in the course of the third century, united (or were strongly encouraged to unite) with the *Technitai* of Dionysos Kathegemon, established at Pergamon and close to the Attalid monarchy.[64]

Then we have the *Koinon* of Attalists,[65] the first reference to which appears in the letter that Kraton addressed to its members in February 152 (TE 49, ll. 1–2). According to Wörrle, it is not possible to assign its creation to the year 158 BC, when the reign of Attalos II begins, in which case it would follow by a little the correspondence of

---

[63] See Le Guen (2001a) I.229 and Aneziri (2003) 325.
[64] Cf. Le Guen (2001a) I.236–7, II.29–30; Aneziri (2003) 105–6.
[65] Cf. Le Guen (2001a) II.30 and n. 132.

the *aulos*-player. The decree published by the Attalists after the death of Kraton in fact speaks of 'the *philanthropa* (acts of generosity), many and fine, directed at the Association on behalf of the kings' (TE 49, ll. 9–11). Wörrle believes that such a plural can only be explained because the Association, with its ties to the royal family and household, already existed in the time of Eumenes II.[66]

In light of the available evidence it is by no means certain that he is correct. His analysis requires that Attalos II was at the same time the sovereign entrusted with conveying to the Attalists the will of Kraton (TE 52, l. 18).[67] The identification is not proven.[68] It could just as easily be Attalos III: if so, the *Koinon* of Attalists would have come into being under Attalos II, and the authors of these royal benefactions would have been Attalos II as well as his successor, Attalos III.[69]

Arguments from plausibility are all that we have to try to settle the question—based on the accepted average longevity of the period and taking into consideration a number of elements from the dossier. While Kraton could have died around the age of seventy—the figure required by the hypothesis of Attalos III—it is surely more reasonable to place his death under his predecessor, king Attalos II. In this hypothesis, the foundation of the *Koinon* of Attalists—which would date back to the reign of Eumenes II—could be a consequence of the king's arbitration in the dispute between the Tean branch of the Anatolian *Technitai* and the city of Teos (TE 47). Kraton would have made use of his influence with the sovereign to support the case of the organisation; and with the *Koinon* itself, to ensure that Eumenes II was thanked, in a manner fitting the services rendered, by a vote of cultic honours.[70] In return for his incomparable devotion

[66] Ll. 12–13 of the document (TE 52) also attest it: τῆς ἑαυτῶν ἐπωνυμίας.

[67] Wörrle (2002: 202) asserts that Attalos himself would have sent to the *Koinon* of Attalists at Teos the will representing his *hieros nomos*. In fact Wörrle is simply repeating the erroneous assertions of Schwarzer (1999: 266ff.), who follows the study of Klimov (1986: 102). Klimov places the foundation of the college of Attalists under Eumenes II, and the death of Kraton under Attalos II.

[68] In this debate Aneziri (2003: 107–8) shows all due caution.

[69] There would thus be no difficulty in explaining the plural βασιλέων (TE 52, ll. 9–11), picked up by the pronoun ἑαυτῶν (ll. 12–13).

[70] This is attested indirectly by the existence, at the heart of the Anatolian Association, of a priesthood of the king, combined with the task of *agonothetes* (TE 48, l. 1).

and effectiveness, the *aulos*-player for his part would have obtained a range of privileges from the Association of Asia Minor (cf. TE 48), and Pergamene citizenship from the king.[71] But every gift requires a return gift, and Kraton would have founded a *Koinon* exclusively devoted to the cult of his beloved sovereign comparable to that of the *Eupatoristai* of Delos, established in honour of Mithridates VI Eupator,[72] or to that of the *Basilistai* of Upper Egypt.[73] And he would have given it a name that evoked the ancient founder of the dynasty.[74]

This act of naming in no way resolves the difficult matter of the identity of the Attalists,[75] which earlier scholarship has often regarded as an evident truth.[76] It is far from being so. The letter which Kraton wrote to the Attalists (TE 49), as well as the decree drafted by the *Koinon* after the death of the *aulos*-player (TE 52), contain—in almost identical form—very limited information. We read only that the musician personally undertook to bring the members of the new Association together (τοῖς ὑφ᾽ ἑαυτοῦ συνηγμένοις in TE 49, l. 4, τῶν ὑφ᾽ ἑαυτοῦ συνηγμένων in TE 52, l. 6); he had also chosen them, if we may trust the further detail provided by the decree of the Attalists, with Dittenberger's restoration (TE 52, ll. 6–7: καὶ κε[κρι]μένων).[77]

---

[71] In TE 33, Kraton has the ethnic of Pergamene, but no text tells us when or how he obtained this privilege, which in my opinion only the king—and not the city of Pergamon—could have granted him.

[72] *OGIS* 367.   [73] *OGIS* 130, l. 6.

[74] The decree drafted by the Attalists evokes an Association worthy of the eponymy of the Attalists (TE 52, ll. 12–13). For the divergent interpretations suggested by the name of the Attalists see Le Guen (2001a) I.254 n. 738 and I.262 n. 761. I entirely share the view of Aneziri (2003: 108): even if the foundation date of the *Koinon* is to be placed under Eumenes II, the origin of its name must be understood in relation to the divinisation of Attalos I; and after that of Attalos II, if that was later than the death of Eumenes II.

[75] See Le Guen (2001a) I.255, 258–9, 265; II.30–1. Aneziri (2003: 108) thinks that the Attalists were mostly *Technitai*, especially in light of the letter addressed to them by Mummius (TE 51) which, according to her, may be a reply to a petition drafted jointly by the Anatolian *Koinon* and that of the Attalists. But why would the latter have turned to the Roman magistrate? As Attalists, devoted to the cult of the Attalids, they could expect nothing from him for the practice of their activities. These were of no concern to L. Mummius.

[76] Préaux (1987) I.264; Rostovtzeff (1989) 1137 n. 76.

[77] Boeckh and Lüders for their part restore κε[ι]μένων. Since Chishull did not specify the length of the lacuna, it is difficult to decide between the two proposed participles.

However that may be, according to Wörrle, the Attalists should not be identified with either the *Technitai* of Ionia and the Hellespont, nor with the branch of Pergamene Artists who were connected with them, even though the Anatolian *Koinon* (understood in its two constituent elements) and that of the Attalists constituted two groups that were very close to one another.[78] As indicators of their shared characteristics Wörrle cited not only the figure of Kraton himself, an incontestable feature of the link between the two *Koina*, but also their shared place of operations—Teos;[79] the system of dating used by the *aulos*-player in his correspondence;[80] and finally, the reference to the musician and the Attalists together in the letter attributed to L. Mummius (TE 51).[81]

I shall confine myself to this last point, since the others have been fully discussed already:[82] I would stress that this can only be considered a matter of debate if we accept the restoration that has been adopted thus far, [καὶ τοῖς] σὺν Κράτω[νι Ζωτίχου Ἀτταλισταῖς. . .].[83]

---

[78] Wörrle (2002) 200–1 and n. 31. *Pace* Wörrle, I do not believe that a discussion of the validity of the restoration of the inscription TE 51 reveals 'unnecessary complications'; nor that partial citation of certain of my remarks out of context (e.g. p. 200, n. 27) is sound method.

[79] If, as I believe, the Attalists were based in Pergamon, it is necessary to replace Teos with Pergamon. For his part, Kraton was present at Teos, but also at Pergamon, not only as president of the *Koinon* of Attalists but equally as a member of the *Koinon* of which the *Technitai* of Dionysos Kathegemon, based at Pergamon, were a constituent element.

[80] For Wörrle (2002: 200) the reference to the eponymous magistrates of the Association of Asia Minor shows at which point the Attalists were close to the *Technitai*. But the dating of the letter does not necessarily have to be set in relation to its recipients (see I.1 above).

[81] It began thus: 'To good fortune! / [. . . . .] Rom[an] consul [to the Association of the] Dionysiac *Technitai* [of Ionia and the Hellespo]nt and of those grouped around [Dionysos Kathegemon and the Attalists] presided over by Kraton, [son of Zotichos, greetings]'.

[82] See I.3 above for the place where the *Koinon* of Attalists was based and I.1 for the double dating.

[83] It is necessary to correct in my book (Le Guen 2001a: I.256 and 258 n. 752) the placement of the square bracket that follows (and should not precede) the final sigma of the article τοῖς.

However, there is no reason to do so.[84] I fear that the justification by reference to the inscriptions in which Kraton and the Attalists are in effect mentioned together (TE 49, TE 50) is in reality faulty,[85] and that it has led in turn to a completely circular argument: the Attalists were *Technitai* because L. Mummius addressed himself jointly to them and to the two corporations, of Asia Minor and of the Isthmos and Nemea: L. Mummius addressed himself to the Attalists because they were *Technitai*.

On reflection, it seems to me more and more surprising that a representative of the authority of Rome should have concerned himself with an Association whose principal activity was—as its very name indicated—to display unshakable loyalty to the sovereigns of Pergamon, and to serve their cult. It is easy to understand that in 146/5 or 145/4 L. Mummius was concerned to reassure (by the renewal of privileges essential to the conduct of their artistic activities), the two corporations of Anatolia and the Peloponnese,[86] who were anxious over the new political situation in those regions—Boeotia, Phokis, not to mention Macedon itself—where they had for a long time practised their craft and taken part in numerous dramatic and musical competitions of panhelenic status; but it is more difficult to envisage that the Roman magistrate should have any concern for a *Koinon* of a fundamentally local character and whose interests were very far removed from the high concerns of inter-state politics.

There is in fact no indication that L. Mummius had *also* written to the Association of Attalists, which would make sense of the

---

[84] This position led me to draw the following conclusion in my book: since L. Mummius could only have been addressing himself to artists, along with the Association of Anatolian *Technitai*, it was necessary either to accept the restoration of the name of the Attalists and, in that case, to reckon that it was a matter of the members of an 'Association coming from an artistic milieu'; or to reject the restoration and complete the lacuna differently, e.g. with a reference to the synagonists attested in TE 44 (cf. Le Guen 2001a: 259).

[85] If the union of Kraton and the Attalists is intelligible and legitimate at the local level, whether that be Teos or Pergamon, or at the very most, across the entire region (of western Anatolia), the same is not true outside such a context. Wörrle (2002: 201 and n. 29) also underlines the change in context implied by the letter of Mummius, but from a different perspective, since he does not utilise the traditionally accepted restoration; and he naturally draws conclusions different from mine.

[86] Inscribed on the same stone, another letter of L. Mummius would in effect have been directed to the appeal of the *Technitai* of the Isthmos and Nemea (TE 34).

appearance of Kraton's name. Even though the exact length of the lacuna is not known, one can imagine some such restoration as this: immediately after the full naming formula of the Anatolian Association there appeared the greeting formula, *chairein*; after this a new phrase began, making reference (for example) to the ambassadors who, under the leadership of Kraton, had come to air their grievances on behalf of the *Technitai* (οἱ σὺν Κράτωνι πρεσβευταί, or better οἱ σὺν Κράτωνι ἀποσταλέντες παρ' ὑμῶν πρεσβευταί, *vel simile*), in keeping with the formulae frequently used in correspondence between cities and Roman magistrates.[87]

This is why it seems preferable to me not to have recourse to the letter attributed to L. Mummius in discussion of the identity of the members of the *Koinon* of Attalists. That does not prevent us from supposing that Kraton was able to choose his own people (all or in part), from among the *Technitai*, for the simple reason that this was the environment most familiar to him.[88] But he could as readily have drawn them from among the citizens of Teos,[89] or among the acquaintances he had made in the course of his career as a travelling musician.[90]

The final example to date of an Association connected to the figure of Kraton is provided by a decree that the Association of the Isthmia and Nemea passed in his honour. Unfortunately the only part that remains of this is the header, which is, moreover, drafted in an abbreviated form (TE 33).

As a result we do not know when or how Kraton came into contact with his members. One thing is certain: he met them on more than one occasion. The text declares, in accordance with the usual structure and phraseology of honorific decrees, that the *aulos*-player, currently being rewarded, had earlier already (l. 2 πρότερον) given clear proof of his good-will towards the *Technitai* of the Isthmos and Nemea, in both his private and public capacity (l. 3).

The first hypothesis that comes to mind is that they got to know

---

[87] See for example the texts collected by Sherk (1967).

[88] Here I return to the interpretation of Wörrle, but by a different route.

[89] See I.3 n. 60 above.

[90] This is why I find it difficult to write, following Wörrle (2002: 201), that the two *koina* (*Technitai* of Anatolia and Attalists) were devoted to serve the interests of the *Technitai*.

one another when they took part in the same sacred contests, the celebration of such *agones* that were the principal concern of the Associations of Dionysiac artists. It remains to determine the place in which they practised their shared profession.

If Asia Minor or Aegean islands such as those of the Dodecannese are not to be excluded a priori,[91] one might prefer a site in mainland Greece, in particular Boeotia and Phokis, which were the cradle of the great panhellenic competitions. In fact in another decree (TE 45, ll. 18–20), we find it recorded that the privileges granted to the *Technitai* (with no distinction among the various Associations) allowed them to participate above all 'in the contests in honour of Apollo Pythios, the Heliconian Muses and Dionysos at Delphi during the Pythia and Soteria; at Thespiai during the Mouseia; and at Thebes during the Agrionia'. Various agonistic lists confirm the presence at such performances of specialists drawn from the entire Greek world.[92]

In addition, the letter written by L. Mummius to the *Technitai* of Asia Minor that mentions Kraton (TE 51) was found at Thebes in Boeotia, engraved on the same stone as another letter which was very probably drafted for the attention of the *Technitai* of the Isthmos and Nemea (TE 34). This report authorises the following proposition: on the occasion of a contest held in the city or region,[93] Kraton was

[91] For the list of contests attested in the Hellenistic period see most recently, with reference to earlier bibliography, Vial (2003) 311–28. The only certainty is that Kraton went to Delos, where a statue was erected in his honour, to be crowned—as the text puts it (TE 45, l. 30)—'there too by the *Technitai*', although the identity of this last group cannot be specified.

[92] It is true that while the lists of competitors which we have for these contests record artists from the Peloponnese and mainland Greece, as well as artists of Anatolian origins, they never mention that these same artists belonged to such an Association of *Technitai*, and as a consequence we do not know whether they competed or not in their capacity as *Technitai* dispatched by their organisation. Cf. Sifakis (1967) 148–71; Mette (1977) 44–71; Le Guen (2001a) I.31–2, I.166–7, I.173, II.42–6; Le Guen (2004) 77–106.

[93] It is perhaps not necessary to assume the existence of a contest at which L. Mummius made known his intentions to the *Technitai* of mainland Greece and Asia Minor. The place where the stone was found might have been the central site of publication or archive of the confederation of the Isthmos and Nemea. The fact that the letter addressed to the Anatolian *Technitai* had been engraved on the same stone shows that Thebes was at the centre of the common concerns of the *Technitai* of the Isthmos and Nemea and those of Anatolia, since the city was at the heart of an intense artistic life.

to speak, before the Roman general, for the cause not only of the *Technitai* of the Anatolian Association (which had mandated him to do so, if the restoration I have proposed for TE 51 is correct), but also that of his colleagues, members of other Associations,[94] gathered during the great contests of mainland Greece. He would have claimed for all the Artists the right to come to compete in the same places and with the same advantages as in the past. It is for an intervention of this kind that he could have been thanked by the Association of the Isthmos and Nemea.

II.2. Kraton: a *Technites* with multiple responsibilities and a benefactor handsomely rewarded

Let us now try to specify the position and the role held by Kraton in the various Associations which have been mentioned in turn.

Among the achievements of the musician, he evidently at first assumed a certain number of responsibilities in the Anatolian Associations that may be summarised thus: he held the highest magistracies attested in the religious associations;[95] then he was priest—twice—in the Association that united the *Technitai* of Teos and Pergamon (TE 44, ll. 6–7; TE 45, ll. 14, 32); and he also discharged, until his death, the priesthood of the *Koinon* of the Attalists which he had founded (TE 52, ll. 1–2). He was also agonothete on two occasions in the Association of the *Technitai* of Asia Minor (TE 44, l. 10; TE 45, ll. 7, 9). This was an office distinct from but close to that of *hiereus*, the two magistracies being both concerned with the religious activities of the Association. It is also possible that Kraton led an embassy to L. Mummius in the second half of the second century (TE 51, l. 13; see above).

In addition to his exercise of these functions—testimony to his sense of his responsibilities,[96] to his profound commitment to the life

---

[94] It is not impossible that L. Mummius had addressed a third letter to the *Koinon* of the *Technitai* of Athens, also very much concerned by the contests of Boeotia and Phokis.

[95] See Poland (1909) 337–43; Le Guen (2001a) II.65–6; Aneziri (2003) 127–33.

[96] His *kalokagathia* is referred to in TE 45, l. 14.

of the Associations, and further (as the texts vie with one another in detailing) to his great piety (TE 44, ll. 6–7; TE 45, ll. 14, 32)—Kraton was a benefactor of the first rank;[97] so much so that the label of '*euergetes*' becomes his habitual epithet, at first accompanying and eventually replacing that of *auletes*.[98]

It was principally in the exercise of his duties—to which he owed the most distinguished titles of the day, those of priest and agonothete[99]—but equally outside the context of the Associations,[100] that he never ceased to render service,[101] to demonstrate a generosity[102] that was, on several occasions, modestly evoked under the ordinary term of benevolence (*eunoia*),[103] and sometimes more explicitly stated,[104] and to respond assiduously to requests put to him by individuals or groups.[105]

Kraton's exemplary behaviour in relation to the Associations of which he was (with the exception of the *Koinon* of *Technitai* of the Isthmos and Nemea) an essential member, if not the guiding force, secured him every kind of reward. They were moreover the markers of his unrivalled status.

Celebrated, like so many other benefactors, by commemorative inscriptions and decrees inscribed on *stelai* erected in the most

---

[97] Kraton is designated *euergetes* in TE 45, ll. 3, 23, 34; TE 48, ll. 3, 7.

[98] In the decree drafted by the Attalists in (posthumous) honour of Kraton (TE 52), they do not mention his profession. Even if it might be claimed that such precision is not absolutely required by the purpose of the document, its absence is surprising all the same, especially if the Attalists were (all or in part) *Technitai*.

[99] TE 44, l. 11: αἰείμνηστο. See also TE 45, ll. 9–10.

[100] Deduced from the funerary crown (TE 50) and the other links between Kraton and the city of Teos revealed by the homage rendered to his statue in the theatre during festivals of the civic community (TE 45, ll. 28–9).

[101] See TE 44, ll. 3–4: λέγων καὶ πράττων αἰεὶ τὰ συμφέροντα; TE 48, l. 4: τῶν κοινῆι συμφερόντων; TE 48, l. 6: πράττων τὰ συμφέροντα; in TE 33, ll. 2–3, Kraton is also a benefactor on an international scale, as he gives the *Koinon* of the Isthmos and Nemea πολλὰς καὶ μεγάλας (. . .) χρείας κατ᾽ ἰδίαν . . . καὶ κοινῆι.

[102] TE 44, l. 9: οὔτε δαπάνας οὔτε φιλοτιμίας οὐθὲν ἐλλείπων. See also TE 45, ll. 14–15; TE 48, l. 5; TE 52, l. 8 (the *philotimia* of Kraton). In TE 52, ll. 13–14 we read: τῶν ἰδίων ἐπιδιδοὺς καὶ χορηγῶν διατέλει.

[103] TE 44, l. 2: εὔνους ὢν διατέλει. For the *eunoia* of Kraton, see TE 44, ll. 20, 30; TE 45, ll. 3, 24–5; TE 48, l. 5; TE 52, ll. 5, 11, 19–20. For his *arete* see TE 44, ll. 19, 30; TE 45, ll. 3, 24.

[104] TE 44, ll. 9, 12; TE 45, ll. 9–10; TE 48, l. 5; TE 52, ll. 7–8, 13–15.

[105] TE 45, l. 15; TE 48, ll. 4, 6, 8; TE 52, ll. 5–6.

visible sites (TE 33, TE 44, ll. 25–7, 27–9; TE 45, ll.35–6; TE 48, TE 52), he also obtained numerous crowns that were drafted with a remarkable inventiveness.[106] The crown that the *Koinon* of synagonists awarded him for life (TE 44, ll. 15–17) must have in effect been proclaimed by the archons successively in charge in two different places, indicative of his double religious and professional status: on the one hand, the banquet at which the members of the college gathered; and on the other, the theatre.[107] The crowns further conferred on Kraton for life by the Anatolian Association must have been proclaimed in the same places, and at highly symbolic dates. One of these award ceremonies was planned for the day of the general gathering of the Association, after the award, in the theatre, of crowns thanking benefactor cities;[108] the other, the 'day of King Eumenes', on two successive occasions: after the passage of the procession, during the crownings and during the *potos* (drinking) of the banquet, once the libations had been offered.[109]

Among the other awards conferred upon the *aulos*-player should be mentioned that of a painted portrait on the part of the *Koinon* of synagonists (TE 44, ll. 27–8); and a public eulogy (TE 48, l. 7) and several honorific statues (TE 45, ll. 26–31) from the Anatolian Association. One of these was to be erected in a location chosen by Kraton himself, the other on Delos, so that those *Technitai* present might crown it (this in no way implies the existence of an Association on the island).[110] As for the third, it was to be placed in the theatre of Teos and crowned by the agonothete of the Association on

---

[106] This same inventiveness is found in the honours conferred by civic communities. See Le Guen (2001a) I.252 n. 730.

[107] Likewise, it was the archons who, in the Anatolian Association, performed this task on the 'day of king Eumenes' during the banquet of the Association (TE 48, l. 12); at this date the proclamation made in the theatre fell to the agonothete and priest of king Euemenes (TE 48, ll. 9–10), while later this was the responsibility of the agonothete of the *Koinon*, on the occasion of the *panegyris* it organised (TE 45, ll. 25–6). *Pace* Wörrle (2002: 199 n. 21), when I wrote of 'a banquet bringing the archons together' (Le Guen 2001a: I.253), this was in the context of a broader discussion which he does not cite. I was simply establishing a parallel with civic practice, without implying that I believed that only the archons were present at this communal meal.

[108] TE 45, ll. 23–4.   [109] TE 48, ll. 9–12.

[110] Le Guen (2001a) I.260 and n. 756; Le Guen (2001b) 288–96; Aneziri (2003) 86–7.

the occasion of its annual general gathering, and during the celebration by the Teans of the Dionysia, or any other contest. It was beside this same statue that the *Technitai* later decided, as an addition to the pre-existing honours (TE 48, l. 9: ταῖς προυπαρχούσαις τιμαῖς), to have a tripod and *thymiasterion* (censer) installed, with instructions to the agonothete and priest of king Eumenes officiating in the Association (TE 48, ll. 13–15) to burn incense during the festivities given for Eumenes II.[111]

This ritual is fairly well attested in the context of the practices of families and associations: the *Technitai* of Athens had likewise decreed, shortly before 130 BC, that the censer be used for the cult statue (*agalma*) of the sovereign Ariarathes V of Cappadocia (TE 5, l. 37). Similarly, in the regulation of Diomedon, which stipulates the crowning of statues of his ancestors, we find a reference to three gilded bronze censers.[112] And according to Cicero (*Verr.* 4.46–7), every family in Sicily needed to possess, for the purposes of its cult practices, a *phiale*, a plate, and a censer—items that are moreover found on the inventories of cult sites and in the excavations of numerous sanctuaries.

Even though in the case of Kraton the statue for which the censer is to be used is described as an *andrias* (as is usual for honorific statues) and not an *agalma* (used only of cult statues),[113] the similarities that develop between their practices show the extent to which the boundary between honorific privileges and cult honours became blurred. While he was still alive, Kraton's contemporaries saw him as an exceptional man, of a status close to that of the gods, heroes, or the dead, for whom large quantities of incense and other perfumes were burnt.

It is only with his death, however, that we see him receive the supreme honour of a cult—an honour also conferred on a number of great benefactors (*euergetai*) of the late Hellenistic period.[114] The formal evidence for this is the inauguration by the *Koinon* of Attalists

---

[111] The text refers to processions (πομπαῖς) and to θέαις, on which see Le Guen (2001a) I.253 and Aneziri (2003) 107 n. 480.

[112] *LSCG* 177A, ll. 118, 153.

[113] On the distinction *andrias/agalma* see most recently Briant (1998) 216–20, citing earlier bibliography.

[114] See Gauthier (1985) 53–66.

of festival days named after him, in keeping with a practice current in religious corporations (TE 52, ll. 35–6).[115]

III. KRATON AND ATTALID POWER

If he had simply been a benefactor, Kraton would be a figure of real interest for the historian for the way he enriches our already plentiful dossier of evidence about the great family of benefactors. But his value is much greater than that. For he illuminates not only the role played by the Associations of *Technitai* in the practice and diffusion of royal cults,[116] but also the manner in which sovereigns conducted themselves in the face of the artists and their own realms.

III.1. Kraton, the Associations of *Technitai*, and the royal cult of the Attalids

From the very first references to the *aulos*-player in our sources we see him, in his capacity as a priest of the Association of Asia Minor, demonstrating great piety towards the protective divinities of the arts.[117] That devotion is only matched by the fervour he displays towards the reigning monarch, Eumenes II, his family, and the entire dynasty of the Attalids (TE 44, ll. 6–7; TE 45, ll. 12–13).[118] It emerges clearly from the decree awarding him the opportunity to choose the site of one of the statues that had been voted to him. The text in fact

---

[115] See Poland (1909) 250–1, 523.

[116] See Le Guen (2001a) II.29–31, 88–90; Le Guen (2003) 353–5. Wörrle (2002: 198) concurs with my own analysis when he speaks of the 'protectorate of Eumenes II' over the Anatolian Association.

[117] In TE 45, ll. 11–12, Dionysos, the Muses, and Pythian Apollo are explicitly mentioned.

[118] The text names the queens, namely Apollonis, widow of Attalos I, and Stratonike, wife of Eumenes, as well as the brothers of king Eumenes, i.e. Attalos II, Philetairos, and Athenaios. The adverb ὁσίως, which was suitable for gods and kings (whose cult is no longer attested) is replaced respectively by the substantives *eusebeia* (for gods), *philotimia* (for kings) and *eunoia* (for members of the royal family as well as those of the Association).

specifies the reason: it was necessary that there 'be a permanent record of his *philodoxia* in his dealings with kings and queens, and of his good will (*eunoia*) toward the brothers of king Eumenes and the Association of Dionysiac Artists' (TE 45, ll. 31–4).

But the best evidence for the excellent relationship between the Artists and the Attalids is the cult set up by the Anatolian *Koinon* while king Eumenes was alive, and that continued after his death,[119]— though we cannot always assess their degree of spontaneity.[120] A special priest (not the priest of Dionysos) had responsibility for it and at the same time held office as agonothete. It follows that the celebration of the Attalid sovereign brought with it the management of one (or more) competitions.[121]

Among the other elements of the cult was a 'day of the king',[122] with a procession, proclamation of honorific crowns, and various spectacles: it has been observed that on this very day, each year, the priest and agonothete of the sovereign had to announce one of the crowns awarded to Kraton in the theatre and go on to honour the statue with incense. The close relationship between the musician and the representative of the Attalid dynasty could not be more neatly expressed, nor in a more official manner.

In the history of the (increasingly strong) ties which bound the *Technitai*, and Kraton in particular, with Pergamene power, the creation of the *Koinon* of Attalists appears as the final culmination. A study of the single decree that we possess from this Association

[119] In TE 49, l. 3 it is a question of a priest of the god Eumenes, no longer a priest of the king, as in TE 48, l. 1.

[120] The expressions habitually used in the documents (which are our only sources) do not allow us to decide. We are equally ignorant of the degree of religious fervour in the founding of the civic cults in honour of Hellenistic monarchs.

[121] We have a fragment of a catalogue that documents a contest organised in honour of a sovereign by the name of Attalos (*LB–W* 93). Perhaps it formed part of a cult created by the Dionysiac Artists on the model of that established in honour of Eumenes II. The header of this text is similar to that in TE 48 and TE 49.

[122] Wörrle (2002: 199 and n. 20) says that 'the day of the king' Eumenes has nothing to do with the birthday of the sovereign, as I claimed. Once again he does not cite my argument in its entirety, nor with its various qualifications. Cf. Le Guen (2001a) I.252 n. 731, where the assimilation of the day of the king with his birthday in fact rests on the analysis of Robert (1937: 31 and n. 1; 1926: 499), and where the reference to Habicht (1970: 148, nn. 41–2), then to Gauthier (1989: 65–7) serves to document birthday festivals.

informs us that its president and life-long priest—Kraton—had been charged by the monarchy with the duty of conveying to him the gifts that were owed to him. It also tells us of the significant choice that the musician had made to entrust his will to a sovereign of Pergamon (TE 52).

Unlike the *Technitai* who were grouped in Associations under the aegis of Dionysos, and who worshipped—in addition to their favoured god—the traditional divinities of the Greek world, along with the most recent creations of the Hellenistic period, such as the kings, the Attalists—under the leadership of an especially valued musician and the artistic colleagues of his age and of the ruling dynasty—formed an Association entirely devoted to the glorification of the Pergamene monarchy.

Even though the precise nature of the cult practised by this *Koinon* escapes us, it nevertheless appears to have had a Dionysiac character. Included on the inventory of goods bequeathed by Kraton to the Attalists are two tripods, alongside couches, blankets, cushions, and other items essential for the gatherings and banquets of any religious association.[123] These are, of course, emblematic items of the cult of Dionysos. And they would take on a special significance if they had been taken to the site of the building cut into an alcove at Pergamon (or, in my opinion, the *temenos* of the Attalists), whose rocky walls have, it seems, revealed the existence of Dionysiac practices—and even of mysteries, according to Radt's hypothesis.[124]

Thus the *Koinon* of Attalists may be seen as one of those numerous religious associations of the Hellenistic period known for having

---

[123] *CIG* 3071, with the new readings of Rigsby (1996b) 137–9.

[124] See Radt (1999) 223. However, such practices did not *ipso facto* make *Technitai* of the Attalists. It should be remembered that this arrangement (of a piece with the rocky walls) led Schwarzer (2002: 224–5) to make of the place the headquarters of the *Technitai* of Dionysos Kathegemon, in whose civic (or state) cult mysteries are indeed attested. However there is no cause to believe that the Pergamene branch of the *Technitai* of Asia Minor worshipped the god of the great theatre in the capital under a mystic form. As Robert (1984b: 495ff. n. 41; 1937: 25ff.) explained long ago, under the epithet of Kathegemon (referring to his role as leader or guide of the 'Bacchic troupe'), Dionysos is above all 'the god of the theatre and of literature, the god of festivals, favoured by the monarchy'. However that may be, we can see how dangerous it is to differentiate on the basis of archaeological evidence alone the *Technitai* of Ionia and the Hellespont, *Technitai* of Dionysos Kathegemon, and Attalists, whose activities had certain elements in common but differences also.

venerated the Attalids, at Pergamon and throughout the kingdom, through rituals borrowed from the cult of Dionysos and his *teletai*.[125] In their own way the Attalists would have played their part in highlighting the Dionysiac element in the ideology of the monarchy, such as we find revealed with some skill in an epigram dated to the very end of the third century BC. Engraved—at the behest of Dionysodoros, son of Deinokrates, from Sikyon—on the base of a statue of a satyr, it associates in the same praise the sovereign Attalos I and the god Dionysos, qualified in this case as the son of Thyone.[126]

III.2. The *Technitai,* the Attalists, and royal 'Dionysism': Kraton in the title-role

While the 'Dionysism' of the Hellenistic monarchies has been much studied, the role of the theatre—understood as the site where the political, religious, and artistic practices of the era converge—has not been sufficiently emphasised.[127] And yet that role was significant in a context in which theatrical buildings continued to be built and the number of new Dionysia and other festivals with both theatrical and musical events on their programmes multiplied.

In order to appear as 'new Dionysoses'—whether overtly or not[128]— it was not enough for sovereigns, of whichever kingdom, to secure for their populations safety, peace, and above all prosperity, nor to secure the basis of their power through victory, in the image of the civilising god par excellence, Dionysos. In keeping with mythological tradition, he should have returned victorious from campaigning in

---

[125] See Musti (1986) 122; Burkert (1993) 261, 264–8; and Müller (1989) 547, for whom the Bacchants 'of the euastic god' (τοῦ εὐάστου θεοῦ) who, around the middle of the second century, honour the dead king Eumenes II, should be worshippers not of some mystic Dionysos, but of Dionysos Kathegemon, who we know was closely tied to the Attalid monarchy.

[126] Müller (1989) 547.

[127] This has been emphasised as far as the Lagids is concerned, especially by Dunand (1986: 85–103), but less in relation to the Attalids, where the principal interest has been in the cult of Dionysos Kathegemon: e.g. Musti (1986) 111–28. See Le Guen (2001a) II.90–3 and Le Guen (2003) 353–5.

[128] In this respect the Lagids and Attalids behaved somewhat differently, though their common imitation of Dionysos was based on the rivalry between the contemporary monarchies.

India, and dispensed great promises of happiness both in this world and beyond the grave.[129]

It was not enough either for sovereigns to venerate an Alexander who had, very early on, been assimilated to the god Dionysos (to a large extent as a result of Lagid propaganda) and then to have themselves represented with Dionysiac traits in both sculpture and on the coins that circulated in their kingdoms and sometimes much further beyond their frontiers. Nor was it enough to encourage—in some cases while fully controlling—the development of the cult of Dionysos: thus the Lagids in Egypt and the Attalid kings at Pergamon, who from the closing years of the third century promoted the god under the specific epithet of Kathegemon;[130] nor to support the formation of Associations of a Dionysiac or mystic character, intended to honour themselves at the same time—as I believe was the case with the *Koinon* of Attalists.[131]

They also needed to reinforce the position of the theatre in their territories. Mithridates made the theatre—at Pergamon itself, and certainly in the tradition of Attalids—the site of his crowning by a Victory.[132] To this end rulers allied themselves with the leaders in the field of the activities that took place on the stages of the Greek and Hellenised worlds—that is to say, the Dionysiac *Technitai*. In the course of his conquests, Alexander had already organised numerous festivals and contests for which he arranged the appearance of artists from the entire *oikoumene*, with the double purpose of celebrating his great military deeds and exalting his conception of power, in showing that, like Dionysos, he provided unrivalled wealth and victory.[133]

---

[129] His numerous epithets testify to the many spheres of his influence: for instance, he is successively or at the same time the god of wine, god of new vegetal growth, god of the theatre, god of mysteries (Lévêque and Séchan 1990: 401).

[130] On the meaning of the cult of Dionysos Kathegemon at Pergamon and under the Attalids, see e.g. Ohlemutz (1940: 90–122); and Müller (1989: 539–53), who, following Robert, notes that the god, as he was venerated at Pergamon through the intermediary of a priest appointed for life by the sovereigns, did not serve in the role of 'progenitor' ('Stammvater') of the Attalids, as von Prott had proposed.

[131] Müller (1999) 540–50; Schwarzer (2002) 235; Müller and Wörrle (2002) 191–233.

[132] Plu. *Sull.* 11.1–2. See Chaniotis in this volume.

[133] See e.g. Plu. *Alex.* 4, 11; 29.1–3; Ath. 12.538c; Arr. *An.* 2.1, 4.

The successors of the Macedonian conqueror followed the path that he had opened up for them: by supporting cultural life and providing artists with the financial means necessary to the exercise of their profession, they offered them their 'benevolent protection', when they did not put them formally under their control.

In Egypt the official names of the Associations of Ptolemais and of Cyprus[134] show that the Lagids patronised the *Technitai* and, on the island, the loyalty of the people of the royal court was indicated by the reference in the list of their court titles to their membership in the branch of the Association that was based there.[135]

As for the Seleucids, even if their relations with the *Technitai* are hardly documented (which is curious, given the extent of their kingdom), we do know that at the end of the third century, one of their number, Antiochos III, took steps at Teos 'to be pleasing to the people *and to the Association of Dionysiac Technitai*' established in the city (TE 42, B, ll. 16–17). In return for this the Teans set up a civic cult of the king and queen, in which the *Technitai* specifically took part.

As far as the Attalids are concerned, I have already drawn attention to just how close their relations with the *Technitai* were and shown the particular involvement of Kraton in this respect. Let us also remember that the union of the two branches of *Technitai* attested in Anatolia (those of Ionia and the Hellespont, based at Teos, and those placed under the patronage of Dionysos Kathegemon at Pergamon) should in all likelihood be ascribed to their actions—that is to say, to their powers of persuasion or of intimidation (expressed under the rubric of *eunoia*). As much is shown by the official name used in the epigraphic dossier from the 180s.

The Attalid kings at Teos and Pergamon thus made use of artists who were ready, as members of Associations under the aegis of Dionysos, to serve and to propagate the ideal of a *tryphe* (luxurious-ness) embodied by the god and dear to the monarchy. In Kraton they had the perfect man to accomplish this task, for he was the most

---

[134] The documents refer to the Associations of *Technitai* under the patronage of Dionysos and the Brother Gods (TE 60, ll. 1–2; TE 61, ll. 1–2); and then Epiphanes (TE 62, ll. 3–4; TE 69, ll. 4–5; TE 70, ll. 2–3).

[135] See e.g. TE 67, TE 68, TE 69.

Dionysiac of the artists. Not only, as an *aulos*-player, did he of all musicians embody one of those closest to Dionysos,[136] but he was in addition the representative of all the god's skills that the Attalids were concerned to be seen to recognise in equal measure.

In his capacity as a member of the Association of the *Technitai* of Asia Minor, he exercised the high offices of priest and agonothete and competed in the theatre for victory. As founder of the *Koinon* of Attalists, whose Dionysiac practices perhaps also had a mystic dimension, he played his part in validating and diffusing the images of saviours which the sovereigns wanted to project of themselves: the epithet of *Soteres* associated with their names is clear evidence of this, as is the specific form that they had given to the cult of Dionysos Kathegemon. We know that it included mysteries at Pergamon, and that the priest in charge of them was elected for life by the sovereigns and chosen from the entourage of those closest to the royal family.[137]

In addition to glory, wealth, and victories, it was pleasure and happiness that Dionysos offered in the theatre; while in his mysteries he brought an answer to the soteriological concerns of his followers. In this his course was no different from that followed by the Hellenistic kings and, more especially, by the monarchs of the Attalid dynasty.

Through the intervention of the Dionysiac *Technitai*, and with the exemplary participation of the *aulos*-player Kraton, son of Zotichos—also president–founder of the *Koinon* of Attalists—the sovereigns of Pergamon had no need to appropriate the actual title, in order to impose themselves, with the greatest subtlety, as 'New Dionysoses'.

Translated by Peter Wilson

---

[136] While the *kithara* was associated with Apollo, the *aulos* was very closely linked to the god Dionysos, even if its use was not restricted to his cult.
[137] *RC* 65, 66, 67.

10

Theoria and Theatre at Samothrace: The *Dardanos* by Dymas of Iasos*

Ian Rutherford

I. THE DATA

Around 200 BC, the island state of Samothrace, at this time a popular sanctuary for cities in the North and East Aegean,[1] passed two decrees in honour of a certain Dymas, son of Antipatros, a poet of tragedies whose home was Iasos in Karia.[2] In the first decree, passed when Sosiphanes was *basileus* ('king' or chief magistrate), Dymas is granted a golden crown, and citizenship of Samothrace. The second, passed when Theoteles was *basileus,* awards Dymas, now a citizen, another golden crown, and goes into detail about the nature of his accomplishments:

. . . (he) has always proved his own nature and composed an account (*pragmateia*) of the doings of Dardanos in the form of a drama—the greatest memorials . . .[3]

---

* Thanks to Angelos Chaniotis, John Ma and Lucia Prauscello.

[1] Cole (1984).

[2] *I.Iasos* 153; see appendix. The name Dymas has only one parallel in the region: the father of an envoy in a third-century inscription from Karian Theagela: Robert (1936) n. 54, 29. In mythical–poetical tradition one Dymas was the eponym of the Dorian tribe of the Dumaines (cf. the tradition of the foundation of Iasos from Argos), and another was the father of Hekabe.

[3] Lines 19–20. The Greek here is tricky. I take it that the 'memorials' are (a) the proving of his nature and (b) composing the account of the doings of Dardanos, these being distinct.

Both decrees conclude with instructions that a proclamation is to be made at the Samothracian Dionysia and the text put up in the temple of Athene. The second contains in addition the instruction that copies of both decrees are to be given to the next *theoroi* (sacred ambassadors) who arrive from Iasos for proclamation at the Dionysia there; matching Dionysias, mediated by interstate *theoria*.

About the content of the drama we have to guess. Dardanos was an important hero, founder of the royal family of Troy. Recent excavations at the West Sanctuary of Ilion have revealed a series of clay plaques depicting a rider from the Hellenistic and Roman period, which may be evidence for a hero cult of Dardanos, possibly connected with a hypothetical mystery cult there.[4] But he had been born on Samothrace, son of Zeus and the Pleiad Elektra. He had two siblings: a brother, Aetion or Iasion, who stayed in Samothrace, and founded the local mysteries, and became the lover of Demeter, and a sister Harmonia, at least in some versions, who of course married Kadmos (providing a link to the Theban Kabeirion?). The *praxeis* of Dardanos will presumably have included how he left Samothrace and brought certain sacred items to the Troad, where he founded Troy. He also founded the city of Dardanos in the northern Troad, so we would expect that to have been included as well.

Dymas was not the only poet that Samothrace honoured.[5] A decree from Priene, dated around 100 BC, reproduces a Samothracian decree honouring Herodes, son of Poseidonios from Priene who wrote an epic poem for the sanctuary, concerned with Dardanos, Aetion (i.e. Iasion), Kadmos, and Harmonia.[6] The chances are that Dymas' poem covered much the same ground.

Dymas' hometown of Iasos had an ancient and turbulent history, stretching back at least to the late Myceneaen period, archaeological

---

[4] Lawall (2003) 97–9, referring to Rose (1998) 88.

[5] Another possible case: Hegemon from Alexandra Troas (third century BC?) composed a poetic work called *Ta Dardanika*: Ael. *NA* 8.11 (*SH* 462). Cameron (1995) 66 and 212 claims that Kallimachos of Cyrene may have performed the poem from which comes fr. 115 (*Aet.* 3) on Samothrace as well, but the reconstruction of Massimilla (1993) calls into question a direct connection between this fragment and Samothrace.

[6] *I.Priene* 68; 69 is the reply of the Prienians; 70 is another decree relating to Samothrace. For the text, see Merkelbach (1995).

remains from which period seem at least roughly consistent with the tradition that it was founded from Argos.[7] By the period our records become informative, Hellenisation, both on the level of religion and that of language, is almost complete.[8] In the Hellenistic period it changed hands several times. It was under Ptolemaic control early in the third century BC, passing (perhaps after a period of independence) to the Macedonians in 227 BC, before being handed over to the Seleukids in 197 BC, and then finally liberated, thanks to Roman intervention a few years later.[9]

Iasos had been a home to Greek poetry since at least the fourth century BC when Khoirilos of Iasos wrote an epic about the exploits of Alexander the Great. While he could not claim that he lacked material, he seems to have lacked skill, at least according to the judgment of posterity: Horace said of him that he was bad in the special way that his one or two good lines caused laughter and surprise.[10] An even later source tells us that Alexander himself is supposed to have said: 'I'd rather be a Thersites in a poem of Homer than an Achilles in a poem of Khoirilos.'[11] By the early second century BC, if not before, a system of *khoregia* had become established at Iasos to bankroll performances of tragedy and comedy.[12] In a khoregic list from the early 190s, Dymas is one of three people who funded a performance by a *komoidos* (comic actor). So in the literary economy of Hellenistic Iasos he occupies a double role, both a poet and a financier.[13] If Dymas was a poet of tragedies, it seems possible, at least, that they were performed in Iasos. The khoregic lists are evidence that there were performances there, and they occasionally mention *tragoidoi*.[14] All things being equal, Dymas need not have

---

[7] See Biraschi (1999).

[8] Religion: Laumonier (1958) 591–9; language: Blümel (1994).

[9] On the history see Ma (1999); Mastrocinque (1979).

[10] Hor. *Ars P.* 357.

[11] Porph. on Hor. *Epist.* 2.1.232.

[12] *I.Iasos* 160 = Csapo and Slater (1995) 171, 205–6. On the khoregic lists see Migeotte (1993); Crowther (1995b); Delrieux (1996) and Crowther in this volume.

[13] *I.Iasos* 160 = Csapo and Slater (1995) 171.

[14] A Herakleides in *I.Iasos* 166; and Lykophron in *I.Iasos* 167. We also know that the *Tekhnitai* sent artists to Iasos. See *I.Iasos* 151 = Le Guen (2001a) TE 53.

been the only Iasian tragic poet; there could have been a whole Iasian school.

II. *THEORIA* FROM IASOS TO SAMOTHRACE

The Samothracian decree talks about *theoroi* from Iasos to Samothrace who are to take the decree back. There is other evidence for Iasian *theoria* to Samothrace as well: another decree honours two Iasian *theoroi,* Gryllos and Euktos, probably dating from about 240 BC.[15] And among the large number of *theoroi* visiting from various places whom Samothrace designated as *proxenoi* as a reward for the service we find two Iasians, Antileon and Billaros.[16] That is probably just the tip of the iceberg, and *theoroi* most likely went from Iasos to Samothrace more or less every year, probably to attend the festival there, though we are not told when that was. In fact, there is more evidence for Iasian *theoria* to Samothrace than for Iasian *theoria* anywhere else.[17]

This was not just a religious enterprise, and it must have had political significance as well. These were turbulent times in southeast Asia Minor. In 197 BC, or soon afterwards, Iasos passes from the control of the Macedonians under Philip V to the Seleukids under Antiokhos III and Laodike, and then it seems to have been liberated by Rome in 190 BC. There were similar changes at Samothrace.[18] But as Susan Cole says, the significance of Samothrace was probably communal:[19]

Samothrace, as neutral territory where *theoroi* of the Aegean area met to worship together, may have enjoyed special recognition by all of the three major Hellenistic dynasties because of their common Macedonian past.

And I would add that this common Macedonian heritage may have implicitly or explicitly been perceived as different from, or even in

---

[15] Habicht (1994), a re-edition of *I.Iasos* 160.

[16] *IG* XII 8, 170e.70–1. The name Billaros also in *I.Iasos* 265, 4.

[17] Other Iasian *theoriai*: in 182 BC they recognised a decree reorganising the Nikephoria at Pergamon: *I.Iasos* 6 (Robert 1930: 338–40); and they made dedications at Didyma: *I.Didyma* 32.6 etc.

[18] Ma (2000) 247, 335.

[19] Cole (1984) 24.

opposition to, the heritage of mainland Greece. That point comes out from the *theoriai* lists, which show that *theoriai* to Samothrace come more or less exclusively from Thrace and Asia Minor, rarely from the mainland.[20]

A further possibility is that the increasing influence of Rome was beginning to change the significance of Samothrace in this period. For diplomatic purposes Romans had probably allowed themselves to be represented as the heirs of the Trojans since the late fourth century BC, and this tendency became even more marked when Rome became involved in the Aegean around 200 BC.[21] Roman contact with Samothrace may have started as early as dedications there by Marcellus in 212 BC, and later on Samothrace came to be important in Roman ideology because of the notional origin there of the *Penates*, believed to have been the very sacred objects that Dardanos brought from Samothrace to Troy. A relation of *syngeneia* between the cities of the Troad and Rome is already explicit in the appeal of Lampsakos to Rome in 197–196 BC, and it would not be surprising if the idea of Samothracian origins was part of this. It is conceivable, then, though impossible to prove, that *theoria* to Samothrace in this period could have been a gesture of loyalty to Roman traditions, especially after the liberation of Iasos in 190 BC.[22]

One particular aspect of poetry composed in the context of *theoria* deserves to be mentioned: a tendency to try to establish links, mythological or ritual, between the sanctuary and the home-city of the poet or the performers.[23] We see this tendency already in the choral lyric of the fifth century, and there may be signs of it here as well. Herodes' poem may also, conceivably, have developed mythological links between Samothrace and Priene, since, as Louis Robert pointed

---

[20] One exception is a document relating to a *theoria* to Samothrace from the Thessalian Federation recently published by Pounder and Dimitrova (2003).

[21] See the elegant presentation of the evidence in Jones (1999) 83–8.

[22] Appeal of Lampsakos: Curty (1995) no. 39; Jones (1999) 95–6. Lampsakos in fact invokes two different *syngeneia*-relations at the same time: with Rome itself, in virtue of common connection with Ilion, and with Massilia, which, like Lampsakos, was supposed to be a colony of Phokaia. For the role of Rome in general see Cole (1989).

[23] This rhetoric of *syngeneia* is best attested in prose decrees; see Jones (1999); Curty (1995).

out, there were ancient traditions linking Priene and Kadmos. One tradition asserts that the original name of Priene was 'Kadmos'.[24] If, as seems reasonable, we would expect a poet celebrating a sanctuary to include traditions that link it to his own city, and if Dymas of Iasos had wanted to make a connection between Samothrace and Iasos, I would suggest that he might have started from the name Iasion, brother of Dardanos and founder of the Samothracian Mysteries; Iasion sounds awfully like Iasos.[25]

III. THE *POETI VAGANTI*

The inscriptions relating to Dymas and Herodes are two examples of a common type of honorific decree issued by sanctuaries and cities in honour of foreign poets, musicians, and intellectuals. They date mostly from the third and second centuries BC, and were collected into a corpus by the great Italian epigrapher Magherita Guarducci in 1930.[26] Most of the poets are pretty obscure, with one probable exception: Delphi honoured a Nikander of Kolophon, describing him as the 'epic poet', and this is probably the earlier of the two Hellenistic poets of that name.[27]

These decrees do not mention contests, but rather commemorate a presence, an *epidemia,* to use the Greek term, and the poet's behaviour—his/her *anastrophe*—in the sanctuary. Some of them are fascinating in their detail. The Delphic decree in honour of Kleokhares of Athens from 230 BC honoured him for writing a

---

[24] *I.Priene* test. 405 = Hsch. s.v. Καδμεῖοι. οἱ Πριηνεῖς, ὡς Ἑλλάνικος (*FGrH* 4, 101); cf. Str. 14.636: λέγεται δ' ὑπό τίνων ἡ Πριήνη Κάδμη, ἐπειδὴ Φιλωτᾶς ὁ ἐπικτίσας αὐτὴν Βοιώτιος ὑπῆρχεν· One may contrast this with claims for *syngeneia* between Priene and Athens made in Prienian theoric decrees from about the same time. Iasos and Priene: see also *I.Iasos* 74 = *I.Priene* 54, 35–6.

[25] It would be complementary to the origin-story for Iasos known from other sources, according to which its founders came from Argos: cf. Biraschi (1999).

[26] Guarducci (1929); Chaniotis (1988) includes a selection of the decrees, including some that Guarducci omitted. A few decrees are known from the Roman period also, and are discussed e.g. by Cameron (1965), Weiss (1990). For the *poeti vaganti,* see also Hunter and Rutherford (forthcoming).

[27] Cameron (1995).

prosodion, paean and hymn: the *paides* are to sing, and the *khorodidaskalos* is instructed to train them in his songs. Amphikles of Rheneia in 165/4 BC put on *akroaseis* at Delos, wrote a *prosodion,* and taught *paides* to sing the *melos* to the *lyra.* Dioskourides of Tarsus was honoured by Knossos for writing a Homeric *enkomion,* which he sent his pupil Murinos to Crete to perform. From Delphi comes a decree, around 160 BC, honouring the brothers Thrason and Sokrates from Aigira who put on performances 'through the lyric compositions of the ancient poets which were appropriate for the god and our city'. Another Delphian decree honours Kleodoros and Thrasyboulos of Phenea who made *epideixeis* through the musical arts, expressing rhythms of ancient poets. In a Delian decree, Demoteles of Andros is rewarded with a laurel crown for writing local *mythoi* for the Delians. Women-poets are honoured as well: Alkinoe, a poetess from Thronion in Lokris, was honoured by Tenos for writing a hymn to Poseidon and Amphitrite. And Aristodama of Smyrna is honoured by both Lamia in Thessaly, and by Khaleion in Western Lokris; Khaleion honours her for writing a poem which narrated the traditions of their ancestors, and awards her a share from the sacrifice of Apollo, which is to be sent all the way to Smyrna.[28]

Sometimes poetry becomes a diplomatic technique. The Cretan cities of Knossos and Priansos passed a decree in honour of Herodotos and Menekles of Teos, two ambassadors sent out by Teos to obtain recognition for the status of 'inviolability' (*asylia*) for their home-city. Menekles was honoured for performing with the *kithara* songs of Timotheus and Poluidos and 'our ancient poets' (i.e. Cretan ones?), and putting on 'a cycle narrating stories about Crete, gods and heroes in Crete, making a selection from many poets and historians'. At Teos, at this period the headquarters of the Asiatic

---

[28] Kleokhares of Athens: Guarducci (1929) = G 7 = *FD* III 2.78; Amphikles of Rheneia in 165/4 BC: G11 = *I.Délos* 1497 = *Syll.*[3] 3.66; Dioskourides of Tarsus: G16 = *IC* I 8, 12 = *I.Délos* 1512; Thrason and Sokrates from Aigira: G31 = *FD* III 1, 49; Kleodoros and Thrasyboulos of Phenea: G32 = *Syll.*[3] 703; Demoteles of Andros: G8 = *IG* XI 4, 544 = *SIG* 382; Alkinoe: G18 = *IG* XII 5, 812; Aristodama of Smyrna: G17 = *IG* IX 2, 62; G17* = *FD* III 3, 145.

branch of the Artists of Dionysos, music and politics were so closely interwoven that even its ambassadors could sing.[29]

The decrees date from the third and second centuries BC, which is when the epigraphic habit gets established. Hence the absence of such decrees from earlier centuries does not mean that this was not a very old mode of poetic practice. One might therefore ask to what extent the behaviour of poets like Simonides, Pindar, and Bakkhylides might be thought of as resembling the Hellenistic data. The possibility of fifth-century poets acting as diplomats, carrying out negotiations between cities, suggests itself. And one gets a real sense of the surprising intricacy of the Greek poetic network, with dozens, even hundreds of centres competing for the attention of poets.

Another question we can ask about the *poeti vaganti* inscriptions is: to what extent does the role of the poet who visits the sanctuary resemble that of *theoroi*? *Theoroi* are delegates sent out by their cities to sanctuaries to represent the cities, and *theoria* to sanctuaries was often accompanied by song-dance performance of various sorts. In so far as *poeti vaganti* at sanctuaries represent their own cities, the correlation between being a *poeta vagante* and being a *theoros* is not obviously very great, as in the case of the delegates representing Teos. On the other hand, *poeti vaganti* are not always regarded as representing their cities, but sometimes seem to be thought of as general panhellenic experts. And in these cases, it may be sensible to think of a tripartite model, comprising the sanctuary itself; the *theoros* who visits the sanctuary, representing his city-state; and the poet or musician, who visits the sanctuary, and is commended not because he represents well the city that sent him, but because of artistic skill which stands outside the system of panhellenic *theoria*, or transcends it.

---

[29] G36 = *IC* I 8.11; I 24.1; see Chaniotis (1988), who compares epigraphic testimony from Mylasa (*I.Mylasa* 652 and 653) that poems of Thaletas were performed by Cretan ambassadors. For poets as diplomats cf. also the role of the Athenian comedian Philippides, discussed in Sonnabend (1996). For further connections between music and politics in the region of Teos see the chapter by Le Guen above.

IV. PERFORMANCES AT SAMOTHRACE

To return to Dymas' poem, it is pretty clear that it fits into the general type of *poeti vaganti* inscriptions mentioned here. It happens to be one of only two examples of a foreign poet thanked for composing a drama. The only other example is Zotion of Ephesos, τραγαϜυδία[ς ποειτὰς κὴ σατ]ύρων ('poet of tragedy and satyr-dramas'), honoured by Koroneia in the middle of the second century BC for memorialising events that had taken place there through poetry.[30] Epic poetry (like that of Herodas) is by contrast much more common, particularly in Delphian decrees. At Delos and Delphi we also find a few visiting poets honoured for composing hymns and other forms of choral lyric. Perhaps if we had more such decrees from Samothrace we would find examples of lyric as well.

The question arises of whether or not and under what circumstances Dymas' tragedies were actually performed. The first thing to say is that the decrees do not mention performance, whereas many of the other *poeti vaganti* decrees do.[31] Might the drama then have been a purely writerly affair, neither performed nor intended for performance? It is not out of the question that the Samothracians honoured Dymas simply because he had immortalised the island in a work of literature, but the hypothesis of performance must surely be likelier.

Like many Greek sanctuaries, the sanctuary of the Great Gods at Samothrace had a small theatre, lacking a stone *skene*, probably built in the second century BC.[32] Even if this exact structure was not

---

[30] Chaniotis (1988) E69. Dramatic performances certainly went on. The Athenian Artists of Dionysus who accompanied the Athenian *theoriai* to Delphi at the end of the second century BC and the beginning of the first seem to have staged dramatic performances. And a Delphic decree from 165 BC (*FD* I 48, 1) praises a certain Nikon of Megalopolis who was a τραγωιδός.

[31] Chaniotis (1988) 346 suggested that Dymas composed the drama quickly to fill a gap in dramatic performances in Samothrace, pointing to the phrase κατὰ τά[χ]ος in l. 4 of the second decree, but this was corrected by Louis Robert to the more formulaic διὰ [παν]-τος. See Blümel (1985) ad loc., in *I.Iasos*, with bibliography.

[32] Chapouthier et al. (1956); Nielsen (2002) 134–6. And there is some evidence that the *Tekhnitai* of the Hellespont visited Samothrace: Le Guen (2001a) TE 57 = *IG* XII 8, 163C, 35–8, date uncertain.

around when Dymas composed his work, there is likely to have been some place in the sanctuary where simple performances could be put on. In fact, we could perhaps see both Dymas' play and the new theatre as reflecting a desire on the part of the Samothracians for a serious engagement with theatrical performance.

On the other hand, Inge Nielsen has recently argued forcefully that many 'cultic theatres' were not designed, at least primarily, for literary dramas, but rather for the enactment of dramatic rituals.[33] We know virtually nothing about the ritual side of the Samothracian cult, but song must have played a role in it.[34] One detail we do know of comes from the historian Ephorus who attests that in his day people looked for Harmonia at Samothracian festivals.[35] This sounds like a crude ritual drama, re-enacting an episode from the myth of Kadmos and on another level perhaps symbolising the political 'harmony' and *communitas* generated in interstate festivals.[36] One could easily imagine this happening in the Samothracian theatre, which was very much in the ritual heart of the sanctuary, directly opposite the altar. And if the Samothracians had one ritual drama, they could easily have had more; hence there is a chance at least that the drama of Dymas was used for this purpose.

One objection to this might be that Dymas' work is likely to have had literary pretensions, whereas 'cultic dramas' would have been cruder in their aesthetic quality. But whatever Dymas' work was like, an absolute distinction between the crude and cultic on the one hand and the refined and literary on the other does not really work for ancient Greece. One has to think only of the choral poetry of Pindar, which was aesthetically complex and ritually useful at the same time. There is, however, another objection to the hypothesis that Dymas'

---

[33] Nielsen (2002). The distinction between 'ritual drama' and 'literary drama' is laid out in the introduction of her book (9–10), though later on in her conclusion (276) she flirts with the possibility that it is unimportant.

[34] There is no evidence of *theoriai* from surrounding towns ferrying choruses of singers, as at Delos, or as at Klaros in the second millennium BC. There is, however, a famous frieze of dancing women from the sanctuary, and Karadima-Matsa and Clinton (2002), who published an inscription with the female name Korranme, have suggested that she might have been a singer.

[35] *FGrH* 70 F120: καὶ νῦν ἔτι ἐν τῆι Σαμοθράκηι ζητοῦσιν αὐτὴν ἐν ταῖς ἑορταῖς ('even now in Samothrace they are looking for her at the festivals').

[36] See Kowalzig (2005) 41–72.

drama had a cultic function. The story of Dardanos was not a central concern of the Samothracian cult, as far as we know. Dardanos was best known for having founded Troy, and this myth would have had most significance to cities in the Troad, including Ilion itself, which had close relations with Samothrace, and the eponymous town of Dardanos on the northern shore, which is attested as having sent the most *theoroi* to Samothrace of any city.[37] Dymas' play could have provided a literary account of the foundation of these cities, and a ritual aetiology for their links to Samothrace.

Another factor behind the genesis of Dymas' drama might have been the coming of Rome. The very same sacred items that Dardanos brought to Ilion were supposed ultimately to have been taken by Aeneas to Rome, where they became known as the *Penates*. Rome became interested in Samothrace in the late Hellenistic period, and it seems likely that the myth of the origin of the *Penates* was part of that; it is perhaps not entirely clear whether Rome's strategic interest in the area or the myth of origins came first. Now, we know that at almost exactly this period Rome was operating in the Aegean coast of Asia Minor, and in fact liberated Iasos from Seleucid control around 190 BC. It thus becomes very tempting to link Dymas' poem with Roman interests. Could Dymas' *pragmateia* perhaps have traced the *Penates'* future transportation to Rome?[38]

V. THE ECONOMICS OF FAME

More generally, it seems likely that Samothrace was not overly represented in the Greek literary record before Dymas and Herodas. So what we perhaps find here is that Samothrace is particularly anxious to be written about, because commemoration in literature means achieving the status of a panhellenic centre. And it seems more than likely that Samothrace actually encouraged, or even commissioned, such compositions. It may be that a particular need was felt for this in the early second century BC, which was perhaps the period when

---

[37] Cole (1984).   [38] On Rome and Samothrace: Kowalzig (2005) 69.

interest in the cult was at its height, a period which coincided with the Romans becoming interested in the cult.

Samothracians might have written this sort of material themselves, but foreign poets had a special value in the system. The foreign poet brings an external, transcendent perspective, and his stamp of approval elevates the sanctuary to a transregional status. This is what is going on in all the *poeti vaganti* decrees. We might particularly single out those in which the foreign poet is praised for having repackaged a myth that belongs to the local cycle of the sanctuary, like Demoteles of Andros in Delos, or Menalkes and Herodotos in Crete. And this had been going on for centuries. We think of the traditions about the Lydian Alkman and Sparta, or the Cretan Thaletas. Similar comments could be made about Pindar, or about the last years of Euripides' life. Relevant here also is Richard Martin's analysis of the poet Hesiod as a 'metanastic poet', who is able to claim transcendent, panhellenic status precisely because his hometown has been destroyed. His very statelessness gives him a broader perspective. So the transcendent *kleos* offered by the poet of foreign origins is at the heart of this phenomenon.[39]

But there is another side to this as well. As at earlier periods of Greek literature, the poets are not just bestowers of fame, but they seek it for themselves, partly precisely so that they are in a position to bestow it, as we see from the end of Pindar's *First Olympian*. And one of the reasons that Dymas of Iasos was attracted by the idea of writing a tragedy for Samothrace was, no doubt, that the prospect of becoming a sort of poet laureate for the Samothracian sanctuary was something that would enhance his own reputation as a poet. And so it may well have done, at least for a while. This reciprocal economy of fame is a good way of summing up *I.Iasos* 153. Dymas has celebrated Samothracian myth, so Samothrace honours and memorialises Dymas.

---

[39] Euripides: Revermann (1999–2000); Taplin (1999); Hesiod: Martin (1992). For the role of 'experts from a distance' in traditional cultures, see Helms (1988).

Appendix. Text of the Decrees, *I.Iasos* 153

First decree

[ἔδο]ξεν τῆι βουλῆι· βασιλεὺς Σωσιφάνης Σωφάνους εἶπε[ν·]
[ἐπ]ειδὴ Δύμας ποητὴς τραγωιδιῶν ἀεί τι λέγων καὶ γράφων
[κ]αὶ πράττων ἀγαθὸν διατελεῖ ὑπὲρ τοῦ ἱεροῦ καὶ τῆς πόλε[ως]
[κ]αὶ τῶν πολιτῶν, ἡ δὲ βουλὴ προβεβούλευκεν αὐτῶι περὶ ἐ[παίνου]
5   καὶ στεφάνου καὶ πολιτείας· ἀγαθῆι τύχηι· δεδόχθα[ι τῶι]
δήμωι· ἐπαινέσαι Δύμαντα ἐπὶ τῆι πρὸς τὴν πόλιν εὐνοίαι καὶ στεφα[νῶ]-
σαι χρυσῶι στεφ[ά]νωι Διονυσίων τῶι ἀγῶνι τὴν ἀνάρρησιν ποιουμένου[ς·]
ὁ δῆμος στεφανοῖ Δύμαντα Ἀντιπάτρου Ἰασέα χρυσῶι στεφάνωι εὐσ[ε]-
βείας ἕνεκεν τῆς εἰς τοὺς θεοὺς καὶ εὐνοίας τῆς εἰς τὸν δῆ[μον·]
0   τῆς δὲ ἀναρρήσεως ἐπιμεληθῆναι τοὺς προέδρους καὶ τὸν ἀγω-
[νο]θέτην· εἶναι δὲ αὐτὸν καὶ πολίτην μετέχοντα πάντων ὧν καὶ [οἱ]
[ἄ]λλοι πολῖται μετέχουσιν· ἀναγράψαι δὲ τὸ ψήφισμα εἰς τὸ ἱερὸ[ν]
[τ]ῆς Ἀθηνᾶς.

Decree of the council; Sosiphanes son of Sosiphanes, *basileus*, said:

Since Dymas, poet of tragedies, has continuously spoken, written and performed something good on behalf of the sanctuary, the city and the people, and the council has previously made a decision in his favour concerning praise, crown and citizenship:

in good fortune: the people have decided to praise Dymas for his goodwill to the city and to garland him with a gold crown at the Dionysia making the proclamation:

'the people crowns Dymas, son of Antipatros of Iasos with a gold crown on account of his piety to the gods, and his good will to the people'.

The *proedroi* and the *agonothetes* should deal with the proclamation. He should be a citizen, sharing all the rights that citizens are entitled to. The decree should be inscribed in the temple of Athene.

Second decree

[ἔ]δοξεν τῆι βουλῆι· βασιλεὺς Θεοτέλης Ἀριφάντου εἶπεν· ἐπε[ιδὴ]
5   Δύμας ποητὴς τραγωιδιῶν τά τε πρὸς θεοὺς εὐσεβῶς δια[γό]-
μενος καὶ τὰ πρὸς [τ]ὴμ πόλιν οἰκείως καὶ φιλανθρώπως ἀεί τι λ[έγων]
καὶ γράφων καὶ πράττων ἀγαθὸν διατελεῖ περὶ τῆς νήσου, διὰ [παν]-

[τ]ός τε ἀπόδειξιν ἐποιήσατο τῆς αὐτοῦ φύσεως καὶ πραγματείαν σ[υνέ]-
ταξεν ἐν δράματι τῶν Δαρδάνου πράξεων τὰς μεγίστας μνημοσ[ύνας,]
20 ἡ δὲ βουλὴ προβεβ[ο]ύλευκεν αὐτῶι περὶ ἐπαίνου καὶ στεφάνου· [ὅπως]
οὖν καὶ ὁ δῆμος φαίνηται τοὺς εὐεργετοῦντας αὐτὸν τιμῶν ἀξίω[s]
διὰ παντός· ἀγαθῆι τύχηι· ἐψηφίσθαι τῶι δήμωι· ἐπαινέσαι Δύμα[ντα]
ἐπὶ τῆι πρὸς τὴμ πόλιν εὐνοίαι καὶ στεφανῶσαι αὐτὸν χρυσῶι στε[φάνωι]
Διονυσίων τῶι ἀγῶνι τὴν ἀνάρρησιν ποιουμένους· ὁ δῆμος στεφα[νοῖ]
25 Δύμαντα Ἀντιπάτ[ρ]ου χρυσῶι στεφάνωι ἀρετῆς ἕνεκεγ καὶ εὐν[οίας]
τῆς εἰς αὐτόν· τῆ[ς] δὲ ἀναρρήσεως ἐπιμεληθῆναι τοὺς προέδ[ρους]
[κ]αὶ τὸν ἀγωνοθέτην· εἶναι δὲ αὐτῶι καὶ ἄλλο ἀγαθὸν εὑρέσθαι ὅτ[ι ἂν]
[β]ούληται παρὰ τοῦ δήμου· ἀναγράψαι δὲ τὸ ψήφισμα τὸμ βασιλέα [εἰς τὸ]
[ἱε]ρὸν τῆς Ἀθηνᾶς· ἵν[α δ]ὲ φανερὸν ἦι καὶ Ἰασεῦσιν ὅτι ὁ δῆμος τιμᾶ[ι τοὺς]
30 [κα]λοὺς καὶ ἀγαθοὺς ἄνδρας ἀξίως τῆς αὐτῶν ἀρετῆς, δοῦν[αι τόδε]
[τὸ] ψήφισμα τὸμ βασιλέα τοῖς πρώτοις παραγενομένοις θεωροῖς ἐ[ξ Ἰασοῦ]
[καὶ] τὸ γραφὲν ἐπὶ Σωσιφάνους ἀνενεγκεῖν τῆι βουλῆι καὶ τῶι δήμ[ωι τῶι]
[Ἰα]σέων, καὶ παρακε[κ]λῆσθαι Ἰασε[ῖ]ς ἐπιμεληθῆναι φιλοτίμως ἵνα [τὰ]
[ψ]ηφίσματα ἔν τινι τῶν ἱερῶν ἀναγ[ρ]αφῆι καὶ οἱ στέφανοι ἀν[ακη]-
35 [ρυχ]θῶσιν ἐν Διο[νυ]σίοις εἰδότας δι[ό]τι ποιήσαντες τὰ ἠξι[ωμένα]
[χα]ριοῦνται τῶι δ[ήμ]ωι.

Decree of the council; Theoteles son of Ariphantos, *basileus*, said:
Since Dymas, poet of tragedies, has continued to behave in a pious
manner towards the gods and in an appropriate and kind manner
towards the city, always saying, writing and doing something good with
respect to the island, and has always proved his own nature and composed an account of the doings of Dardanos in the form of a drama—
the greatest memorials—and the council has previously passed a decree
in his favour concerning the award of praise and a crown; so that the
people too should be seen to honour its benefactors in a worthy manner
always:
in good fortune: the people have voted: to praise Dymas for his good-will
to the city and to crown him with a gold crown at the Dionysia, making this
proclamation.
'the people crowns Dymas, son of Antipatros with a golden crown on
account of his virtue and good-will towards it.'
The *proedroi* and the *agonothetes* should deal with the announcement. It
should be possible for him to obtain any favour he wishes from the people.
The *basileus* should inscribe the decree in the temple of Athene.
So that it is clear to the Iasians as well that the people honours good and
virtuous men in the way their virtue deserves, the *basileus* should give this
decree to the first *theoroi* who arrive from Iasos and take the one written in
the kingship of Sosiphanes to the council and the people of Iasos, and the
Iasians are asked to deal with them in an honourable manner, so that

the decrees are inscribed in one of the temples and crowns are proclaimed at the Dionysia, knowing that by doing what is worthy they will please the people.

11

The Dionysia at Iasos:
Its Artists, Patrons, and Audience

Charles Crowther

I. INTRODUCTION

Strabo illustrates his discussion of the dependence of the coastal Carian city of Iasos on its fishing grounds with a carefully constructed story of how a recital from a *kitharoidos* was disturbed by the bell of the fish-market which abruptly drew away the audience, except for the one man who could hear neither the performance nor the signal.[1] The impression of an uncultured, indifferent community that could easily be deduced from Strabo's anecdote would, however, be a misleading one. The performance interrupted by the bell was also in its way typical of the ancient city. The epigraphical corpus of Iasos has preserved a continuous record of the dramatic life of the city over the course of the second century BC and offers the contrasting picture of a community that attended tenaciously to its civic and cultural life and amenities even through adversity.

Although the epigraphical evidence for performances at the Iasian Dionysia has attracted attention in recent years from a variety of perspectives,[2] there remain a number of issues, of transmission,

---

[1] Str. 14.2.21.

[2] Crowther (1990); Migeotte (1992) 197–8; (1993); Crowther (1995b); Delrieux (1996); Wilson (2000) 296; Maurizi (2000). When I tried to resolve some chronological problems in the Iasian inscriptions in 1990, I hoped to provide a framework for dating any new second-century inscriptions that might emerge from the

reading, and context, that are still fully to be explored. In this chapter I attempt to offer a general perspective across the evidence and at the same time to address some of these specific questions in the light both of new discoveries at Iasos and of renewed study of older and incomplete texts.[3]

II. IASOS IN THE HELLENISTIC PERIOD

Iasos was an ancient community.[4] In spite of the indifferent fertility of its hinterland, its coastal situation, fine harbour, and command of the sheltered Gulf of Bargylia are reflected in the extensive evidence that has emerged from the excavations carried out by the Italian Archaeological Mission since the early 1960s of its settlement history from the middle Bronze Age onwards. Although Iasos was not an important or vital city, its epigraphy is relatively rich, and above all inter-connected. In a series of inscriptions dating from the second quarter of the second century BC onwards, Iasos has left one of the fullest records of the ephebic, gymnasial, and agonistic life of a small Greek community.[5] This material—worthy of study in its own right—complements, although it only partially overlaps,[6] the evidence for dramatic performances.

The public epigraphy of Iasos is also rich in formal records of decisions by the assembly and of interactions with external powers,[7]

continuing Italian excavations at Iasos. On the last count (Maddoli 2000: 15) there are in the region of 130 inscriptions still to be published (120 in Maddoli 1995), many of them no more than fragments.

[3] New discoveries: Maddoli (2000) B1–3, with the discussion of Maurizi (2000). For new readings, see section V below.

[4] The Iasians seem to have been conscious of this: at the beginning of the second century we can see the Iasians asserting an implicit claim about the antiquity of their origins in two decrees honouring travelling judges from Priene (*I.Priene* 53–4, with Crowther 2007).

[5] *I.Iasos* 23, 84, 93, 98–102, 107–12, 114–15, 120–4, 245–8, 269–369.

[6] The most notable contributor to the theatre and Dionysia in the first half of the second century, Sopatros the son of Epikrates (Appendix 1, no. **177**), was also a major benefactor of the gymnasium (*I.Iasos* 250).

[7] *I.Iasos* 1 (Mausolus); 2–3 (Ptolemy I, Polemaios, Aristoboulos); 4–5 (Antiochos III and Laodike); 30 (Alexander); 32 (Eupolemos); 35, 150 (Olympichos, Philip V and Rhodes).

which offer both an intermittent narrative and an institutional back-drop for the city's cultural life. A late fourth-century decree reveals that Iasos had a developed democratic system and that limited public payment was available for attendance at the assembly.[8] A series of early second-century proxeny decrees indicate the extent of this par-ticipation, preserving voting figures both for the Iasian council[9] and for the assembly.[10]

In the fifth century Iasos appears in the Athenian Tribute Lists, with a contribution rising from one to three talents.[11] Contacts between the Iasians and Athens during the Peloponnesian war have recently been brought into focus by the discovery of an Iasian copy of an Athenian honorific decree from the late fifth century, which seems to have been kept in the archives at Iasos for 200 years until it was published at the turn of the third and second centuries BC—exactly the moment at which the evidence for the dramatic life of the city begins to be recorded in the theatre in the form of lists of contribu-tors to performances at the Dionysia.[12] The awakening of epigraphical memory in this form also coincided with the beginning of an embattled period in the city's history.

In the later third century Iasos faced damaging incursions into its territory by an agent of the local Carian dynast Olympichos, and an appeal for Rhodian support was required to lift the threat.[13] An interval of freedom and autonomy under Rhodian patronage was ended by the imposition of a garrison during Philip V's Carian expedition in 201. The four years of Macedonian occupation that followed proved particularly difficult for Iasos, not only because of

---

[8] *I.Iasos* 20 with Gauthier (1990) (resumed in *SEG* 40, 959).

[9] Voting figures for the Council of 68 (*SEG* 41, 932, 10–12) and 83 (*SEG* 41, 929, 34–5) suggest a membership of up to 100; *SEG* 41, 930–1 and *I.Iasos* 25 from the same stephanephorate year have different lists of *prytaneis*, indicating that the latter rotated.

[10] Voting figures of 841 (*SEG* 41, 932, 13–14) and 858 (*SEG* 41, 929, 35). The monthly sum allocated for assembly pay in *I.Iasos* 20, 180 drachmas, is compatible with a similar level of attendance; see the discussion of Gauthier (1990) 441–3.

[11] *IG* I³ 263 V 21 (1 T: 450/49); 270 IV 29 (1 T: 442/1); 279 I 69 (1 T: 433/2); 280 I 63 (1 T: 432/1); 285 I 91 (3 T: 421/0).

[12] Maddoli (2000) 15–22, A, with Habicht (2001).

[13] We learn of this episode from a series of Rhodian documents published at Iasos (*I.Iasos* 150), discussed by Meadows (1996).

the initial exigencies of the expeditionary force after it became blockaded in the Gulf of Bargylia, but also because of the severe earthquake that struck southwest Asia Minor in 199/8 BC.[14] A letter from Laodike III, dating probably to 196 or 195 BC, after the departure of the garrison that Philip had left behind, when Iasos had recovered its notional autonomy under the tutelage of Antiochos III,[15] acknowledges the troubles experienced by the Iasians.[16] Antiochos and Laodike provided limited assistance to the city; oracular advice was solicited as well as the counsel of the king and the Iasians appear to have called on neutral judges from friendly cities to resolve subsisting internal disputes within the citizen body (*OGIS* 237).[17] Nevertheless, the city was hosting a Seleucid garrison at the beginning of the Syrian war and a group of exiles accompanied the Roman army under L. Aemilius Regillus which blockaded the city in 190 BC (Livy 37.17.3–8). The exiles appealed successfully to the Rhodians to avert a direct Roman assault upon the city itself, but not before its territory had been devastated. The renewed turmoil within the city that ensued in the aftermath of Macedonian and Seleucid control and occupation, the expulsion and return of exiles, and the interruptions to economic activity caused by warfare and earthquake is reflected in a further series of decrees for foreign judges.[18] Recovery may have been a slow process, and other troubles seem to have supervened. A decree of the Dionysian *Technitai* dating to the middle of the second century alludes to the Iasians' difficult circumstances (*I.Iasos* 152, 26–8),[19] while another, less closely dated, text establishes

---

[14] For the history of Iasos during this period see Crowther (1995a).

[15] *I.Iasos* 4, 47–8: τὴν δὲ ἡμετέραν πόλιν πρότερό[ν | τε] ἐγ δουλείας ῥυσάμενος ἐποίησεν ἐλευθέρα[ν] ('having previously rescued our city from enslavement he made it free').

[16] *I.Iasos* 4, 6–9: 'when he (Antiochos) recovered your city which had been afflicted by unexpected natural disasters (συμπτώμασιν περιπεσοῦσαν ἀπροσδοκή|τοις), he restored to you your freedom and your laws'.

[17] Republished as *I.Iasos* 4, 51–62, but see Crowther (1989), with Ma (2000) 336–7 no. 28. Foreign judges at Iasos in the 190s: Crowther (1995a).

[18] Crowther (1995a).

[19] ἵνα δὲ καὶ Ἰασεῖς ἐπιγειν<ώ>σκωσιν τὴν τοῦ πλήθους ἡμῶν σπουδὴν | καὶ ἣν ἔχομεν πρὸς τοὺς φίλους ἐκτένειαν ἐν τοῖς ἀναγκαιοτά|τοις καιροῖς ('in order that the Iasians may recognise the zeal of our company and the devotion which we have towards our friends in circumstances of the greatest necessity').

a subscription for a grain distribution (*sitometria*)—'to strengthen the democracy'.[20]

The epigraphical documentation for choregic and other contributions to support performances at the Iasian Dionysia during the second century BC unfolds against this persistent background of external pressure and internal tensions.[21] The evidence consists of a series of lists, each dated by the eponymous magistrate of Iasos, the *stephanephoros*,[22] of individual contributors. Fifty-six lists, together with four notices of contributions towards building work on the theatre,[23] have survived, in whole or as fragments, spanning the course of the second century to the early years of the Roman province.[24]

III. TRANSMISSION AND CONTEXT

The inscriptions recording the lists of contributors have a history of discovery of their own which is worth reviewing briefly because it sheds light on their original location—and so the context in which they were placed and seen and, perhaps, sometimes read.

The site of Iasos was a frequent destination for European travellers visiting the western coast of Turkey in the eighteenth and nineteenth centuries, in part because of the excellence of its harbour, which, as L. Robert noted, also contributed to the dispersal of its epigraphy.[25] The first oblique notice of the theatre lists comes from Richard Chandler, who visited Iasos in 1765:[26]

---

[20] *I.Iasos* 244 dated by Hicks (1887: 100–1) to the middle of the second century BC. The phrase quoted is partially restored (by A. Wilhelm); see, in general, Migeotte (1992) 232–6 no. 74: [οἵδε ἑκόντ]ες βουλόμενο[ι ἐπὶ πλεῖ]ον αὔξειν (?) τὴ]ν δημοκρατί-[αν ἐκ τῶν ἰδίων ἐπέδωκ]αν ἀργύριον [εἰς σιτωνίαν] ('[the following individuals willingly] wishing [to strengthen to a greater degree] the democracy contributed money [from their own resources towards a grain fund]').

[21] Migeotte (1993) 277–8.

[22] Sherk (1991) 256–7 no. 20.

[23] LB–W 275–6 (*I.Iasos* 179, 180, 182, 183).

[24] LB–W 252–68, 270–80, 282–99; *I.Iasos* 160–7, 170–218; supplemented now by Maddoli (2000) B1–3.

[25] Robert (1936) 73–4. [26] Chandler (1775) 181–2; cf. Ross (1850) 122.

In the side of the rock is the theatre, fronting 60 m east of north, with many rows of seats remaining, but covered with soil or enveloped in bushes. On the left wing is an inscription in very large and well-formed characters ranging in a long line, and recording certain donations to Bacchus and the people.[27] Beneath, near the bottom, are several stones inscribed but not legible.

Chandler's left wing of the theatre is the north *parodos* wall, where fragments of the dedicatory inscription, recording the contributions made by Sopatros, the son of Epikrates, to the reconstruction of the theatre were rediscovered and reinstated during the initial campaign of the Italian Archaeological Mission.[28] The identity of the other inscriptions mentioned by Chandler is clarified by Ph. Le Bas, who visited Iasos in 1843 and made the fullest record of the lists of contributors before they were lost in the middle of the nineteenth century. His squeezes, notes, and transcriptions formed the basis for W. H. Waddington's edition (*LB–W* 252–99) on which the texts in W. Blümel's Iasian Corpus, in turn, are largely based.

As well as recording the dedicatory inscription noticed by Chandler, Le Bas copied a series of other texts inscribed partly 'sur le bandeau du théâtre' and partly lower down on the theatre wall. The drawing published in *LB–W* indicates that these texts were inscribed on the supporting wall of the cavea running along the north *parodos*.[29] The south *parodos*, in contrast, remained uninscribed. Le Bas's 'bandeau' is the inset course of dressed blocks *c.* 0.35 m high running the length of the *parodos* wall *c.* 2.15 m above ground level,[30] in the middle of which the dedication by Sopatros was inscribed.[31] The

---

[27] *LB–W* 269 (*I.Iasos* 249, partially extant): ⟨Σ⟩ώπατρος Ἐπικράτου χορηγήσας καὶ ἀγωνοθετήσας καὶ στεφανηφορ[ή]σας τὸ ἀνάλημμα καὶ τὴν ἐπ᾿ αὐτοῦ κερκίδα καὶ τὸ βῆμα Διονύσωι καὶ τῶι δήμωι ('Sopatros the son of Epikrates having served as *choregos* and *agonothetes* and *stephanephoros* (dedicated) the supporting wall and the seating segment (resting) on it and the podium to Dionysos and the People').

[28] Levi (1963) 541–2 with fig. 60.

[29] Le Bas's drawing shows the arrangement of the texts and offers a profile of the wall.

[30] The latter measurement is taken from Texier's elevation drawing of the theatre: Texier (1849) pl. 144.

[31] Levi (1963) 543 n. 1: 'l'iscrizione termina a m. 7,45 dallo spigolo del muro; se esse era collocata nel centro della parete, che misura m. 21,98, la sua lunghezza totale doveva essere di m. 7,08'.

right extension of this course to the edge of the *parodos* has been
preserved and is blank; so that the texts recorded by Le Bas must
have been cut to the left of the dedication by Sopatros, between it
and the entrance to the theatre. The wall blocks of the *parodos* below
this level have either been lost or are buried under accumulated soil.
Chandler's 'several inscribed stones' near the bottom of the wall
should correspond to the texts recorded by Le Bas below the
'bandeau', which consist of a series of eighteen lists (*LB–W* 282–99)
disposed around a decree of the *Koinon* of *Technitai* of Dionysos,
itself cut in two columns (*LB–W* 281; *I.Iasos* 152). Le Bas's copies and
squeezes are the sole source for these texts, which have not been seen
since his visit.[32]

Le Bas was also the first to record systematically a further group of
theatre texts which had been glimpsed only briefly by a previous
visitor. Ch. Texier, who stopped at Iasos in 1835 and carried out an
important survey of the theatre, noted a long inscription in the area
of the *orchestra* on a marble pilaster, divided into five sections.
Although he had the stone cleared of overlying soil and bracken, he
had no time to record the inscription himself,[33] and it was left to Le
Bas to copy and squeeze the inscription in full, including additional
series of texts continuing on its laterals.

The inscribed pilaster remained at Iasos for a further sixteen years
until it drew the attention of an Anglo-Irish visitor who had become
enthused by epigraphy in the course of a voyage along the Aegean
coast of Turkey, from Rhodes to Smyrna.[34] When Lord Dufferin
stopped at Iasos on 15 June 1859, he found the pilaster lying at the
foot of the theatre and had it taken on board his steam-yacht
Erminia,[35] and transported back to his family home at Clandeboye,

---

[32] Unless by Ludwig Ross who visited Iasos in June 1844 and noted their impending publication by Le Bas (Ross 1850: 122).

[33] Texier (1849) 139: 'Dans le voisinage de l'orchestre, j'ai aperçu une longue inscription composée de cinq tableaux. Elle est tracée sur un pilastre de marbre, écrite en caractères très-menus. Je la fis dégager des terres et des broussailles qui la couvraient, mais le temps me manqua pour la copier.'

[34] For Lord Dufferin's voyage from Rhodes to Constantinople in June 1859, which became in part an inscription hunt see Crowther (1994).

[35] We have his own account of how he found the inscriptions. The entry for 17 June, 1859 in Lord Dufferin's journal reads as follows:

County Down.[36] There it remained, removed from professional scholarly attention, until its presence was reported by J. P. Mahaffy in a notice in the *Athenaeum* review in 1897.[37]

The pilaster seems originally to have formed part of the gateway in the *parodos* through which the audience and performers would have passed on their way to the *orchestra* from the agora.[38] The twenty texts inscribed on it mark the beginning of the published series of lists of contributors to the Dionysia and cover a period of thirty years, from the beginning of the second century through to the early 160s.[39] The interval between the two series is unlikely to have been an extended one,[40] and the lists seem to have been continued directly on to the *parodos* wall rather than on to the other side of the gateway.[41] It is possible that the opposite pilaster may already have been partially occupied by other texts,[42] but there is also a stronger reason for the discontinuity. The inscriptions on the *parodos* wall necessarily post-date the dedicatory inscription of Sopatros, whose own eponymous year is recorded on the third list on the right lateral of the pilaster, since the dedication marks the construction of the supporting wall of the cavea at this point. When the *parodos* supporting wall had been reconstructed, it was natural that the continuation of the lists of

Went out (from Myndos) under steam. Arrived at Jassus about 12 o'clock. Landed went round the whole place looking for inscriptions. Found a large marble mass in two pieces at the foot of the theatre on the left hand side. Then went down the right towards the Aqueduct. Surveyed the Venetian fort at the top, and so in and out of every nook and corner. A beautiful little harbour with a mole and a tower guarding it. In the evening all hands on shore, dragging down the marble inscriptions.

[36] Crowther (1994).

[37] Mahaffy (1897).

[38] So *LB–W* 80: 'cette inscription (252), ainsi que les six suivantes, se trouve sur la face latérale du montant de la porte du théâtre'.

[39] The date of the beginning of the series is discussed in the following section and chronological questions in Appendix 2.

[40] Crowther (1990) 148.

[41] So Migeotte (1993) 284.

[42] The front face of another pilaster from the theatre found reused in the Roman *proskenion*, on the left lateral of which three lists of contributors were later inscribed (*I.Iasos* 167, 201, and 215), had already been used in the late third or early second century to record a decree of Euromos in honour of Pantainos (*I.Iasos* 151), perhaps, but not certainly, the eponymous *stephanephoros* of *LB–W* 253 (*I.Iasos* 161). The dimensions of this block (width: 0.425 m; depth: 0.45 m) are different from those of the Clandeboye pilaster (width: 0.51 m, measurable depth: 0.31 m).

contributors should have flanked and underlined the notice of Sopatros' great work.

The additional lists of contributors discovered during the Italian excavations in the 1960s also derive from the theatre, as does a further block found in 1973.[43] There are few parallels for the concentration of this documentation.[44] Spectators of performances at the Dionysia would have passed along a wall and through a gateway thickly inscribed with the names of those who had made the performances possible and under the name of Sopatros who had sponsored a substantial section of the cavea in which they sat.

I turn next to the lists themselves and what they can tell us about performances at the Dionysia.[45]

IV. THE THEATRE LISTS

The theatre inscriptions fall into two distinct series. The first consists of seven lists (*I.Iasos* 160–6; *LB–W* 252–8), which show a number of variations as well as common features in their formulation. *LB–W* 252 (*I.Iasos* 160), the earliest of the lists, is typical of this group of texts:[46]

ἐπὶ στεφανηφόρου Ἀπόλλωνος τοῦ μετὰ Νημέρτεα·
οἷδε ἐπέδωκαν· ἀγωνοθέτης Ἀπολλόδωρος
Χάρμου Σωσύλον τὸν κωμωιδὸν ἡμέρας δύο,
καὶ ἡ [πάρ]οδος εὗρεν δραχμήν, ἡ δὲ θέα ἐγένετο
5   δωρε[άν·] ᵛᵛ Δύμας Ἀντιπάτρου τῆς ἐπιδόσεως ἧ[ς ἐπ]ένευσεν χορηγῶν ἐν τῶι ἐπάνωι ἐνιαυτῶ[ι]
Σωσύλον τὸν κωμωιδόν, καὶ ἡ πάροδος εὗρεν
δραχμήν, ἡ δὲ θέα ἐγένετο δωρεάν· ᵛᵛ Βλόσων
Πυθίωνος τῆς ἐπιδόσεως ἧς ἐπένευσεν χορηγῶν

---

[43] Maddoli (2000) B1–3.

[44] The *parodoi* walls of the theatre at Sparta, which in the first and second centuries AD were thickly inscribed with career inscriptions, provide a remarkable, if distant parallel: Woodward (1924–5).

[45] In this section I draw on the important study of Migeotte (1993).

[46] I have made small corrections to the text in *I.Iasos* at the ends of ll. 6, 13, 15, 20, where letters have been lost or damaged on the edge of the stone, and also signalled blank punctuation spaces dividing individual contributions.

10 ἐν τῶι ἐπάνωι ἐνιαυτῶι Σωσύλον τὸν κωμωιδόν,
    καὶ ἡ πάροδος εὗρεν δραχμήν, ἡ δὲ θέα ἐγένετο
    δωρεάν· ᵛ Νημέρτης Θεοτίμου τῆς ἐπιδόσεως ἧς
    ἐπένευσεν στεφανηφορῶν Εὐάλκην τὸν κιθαριστήν,
    καὶ ἡ πάροδος εὗρεν δραχμήν, ἡ δὲ θέα ἐγένετο
15 δωρεάν· ᵛᵛᵛ Μένων Ἀρτέμωνος χορηγῶν Εὐάλκην
    τὸν κιθαριστήν, καὶ ἡ πάροδος εὗρεν δραχμήν, ἡ δὲ
    θέα ἐγένετο δωρεάν· ᵛ Μενέδημος Ἀρτέμωνος
    χορηγῶν Εὐάλκην τὸν κιθαριστήν, καὶ ἡ πάροδος εὗρεν
    δραχμήν, ἡ δὲ θέα ἐγένετο δωρεάν· ᵛ Ἑρμόδωρος
20 Δρακοντίδου τῆς ἐπιδόσεως ἧς <ἐ>πένευσεν ἀγωνοθετῶ[ν]
    ἐν τ[ῶι ἐπά]νωι ἐνιαυτῶι δραχμὰς τριακοσίας.

In the stephanephorate of Apollo after Nemertes, the following made contributions: as *agonothetes* Apollodoros, the son of Charmos, (paid for) the comic poet Sosylos for two days, and his appearance brought in a drachma and viewing was free; Dymas, the son of Antipatros,[47] from the contribution which he assented to make in the previous year when he was *choregos* (paid for) the comic poet Sosylos, and his appearance brought in a drachma and viewing was free; Bloson, the son of Pythion, from the contribution which he assented to make in the previous year when he was *choregos* (paid for) the comic poet Sosylos, and his appearance brought in a drachma and viewing was free; Nemertes, the son of Theotimos, from the contribution which he assented to make when he was *stephanephoros* (paid for) the *kitharistes* Eualkes, and his appearance brought in a drachma and viewing was free; Menon, the son of Artemon, as *choregos* (paid for) the *kitharistes* Eualkes, and his appearance brought in a drachma and viewing was free; Menedemos, the son of Artemon, as *choregos* (paid for) the *kitharistes* Eualkes, and his appearance brought in a drachma and viewing was free; Hermodoros, the son of Drakontides, from the contribution which he assented to make in the previous year when he was *agonothetes* (paid) 300 drachmas.

Although other forms of contributions are also recorded in some of the texts in this group,[48] most of the entries are for payments made by individuals identified as current or former *stephanephoroi*, *choregoi*, or *agonothetai*, covering the costs of designated artists for one or more days of the festival. A standard formula (καὶ ἡ πάροδος

---

[47] Dymas' other career as a tragic poet, attested in an inscription whose lettering seems to be contemporary with the record of his contribution to the Dionysia (*I.Iasos* 153), is discussed by Ian Rutherford elsewhere in this volume.

[48] Appendix 1 nos. **84, 87, 104, 106.**

εὗρεν δραχμήν, ἡ δὲ θέα ἐγένετο δωρεάν: 'the appearance brought in a drachma and viewing was free') indicates that the contribution enabled the performance to be viewed by the audience without charge, although a token sum of one drachma was paid to the city for the performer's right to appear.[49]

The date of the beginning of the series deserves attention. A *terminus ante quem* is provided by the third list, LB–W 254 (*I.Iasos* 162), which shares the same *stephanephoros*, Kydias, the son of Hierokles, with *I.Iasos* 4, the letter of Laodike cited earlier, which seems likely to belong in 196 or 195.[50] On this basis LB–W 252, dated to the year of Apollo after Nemertes, would have fallen at least two years before, and the stephanephorate of Nemertes himself, during which Dymas, Bloson, and Menedemos served as *choregoi* at the Dionysia and Hermodoros as *agonothetes*, a year earlier still.[51] The contributions pledged in Nemertes' year should, accordingly, belong no later than 198, and possibly to 199 BC, the year of the earthquake, and, at any rate, during the period of the Iasians' avowed 'enslavement' to Philip V.[52]

The continuation of celebrations of the Dionysia even through critical times is noteworthy, but the decision to inscribe publicly and permanently the names of the individuals who supported the festival performances is equally significant. The moment at which this decision was made cannot be fixed precisely, but it seems possible that it preceded the departure of the Macedonian garrison.[53]

---

[49] For this explanation of ἡ πάροδος εὗρεν δραχμήν, see Wilhelm (1923) 435–9 (438 on the meaning of ἡ πάροδος), with Migeotte (1993) 271; for the sense of εὑρίσκω more generally see now also Jones (2004) 476–7.

[50] Crowther (1990) 143–4; Migeotte (1993) 276–7 with Crowther (1995b).

[51] The close sequence in which LB–W 252–4 (*I.Iasos* 160–2) are inscribed on the stone suggests, although it cannot prove, that they belong to successive years: the cutter of 253 initially began inscribing immediately below the last line of 252, but stopped at the second nu of Πανταίνου, erased the letters already cut, and began again after inserting a dividing marker. 254 also follows 253 closely. Between 254 and 255, in contrast, there is an interval of 0.17 m. LB–W 255–8 (*I.Iasos* 163–6), which belong to consecutive years, are also inscribed in sequence, separated only by dividing markers.

[52] Enslavement (δουλεία): *I.Iasos* 4, 41–50.

[53] Ma (2000) 85, following J. and L. Robert (1983) 178, suggests that Antiochos' viceroy Zeuxis had already secured Iasos in the summer of 197, before the king's own arrival.

The seven lists in the first series inscribed on the front face of the Clandeboye pilaster cover the period to the early 180s.[54] Subsequent texts record uniform payments of 200 drachmas by Iasian citizens and 100 by *metoikoi*.[55] The first list of this form (*LB–W* 259; *I.Iasos* 170) appears at the head of the left lateral of the pilaster; thereafter the pattern is constant.[56] *LB–W* 263 (*I.Iasos* 174) provides a full example of these second series lists:[57]

ἐπὶ στεφανηφόρου Ἀ-
πόλλωνος τοῦ ἔκτου
μετὰ Κλεάνακτα Θε-
οκλείους, ἀγωνοθέ-
5 του δὲ Ὀμφαλίωνος
τοῦ Εὐβουλίδου· οἵ-
δε τῶν πρότερον ἐ-
πινευσάντων ἐν Διο-
νυσίοις ἀπέδωκαν·
10 Ἀπολλώνιος Παιω-
νίου δραχμὰς διακο-
σίας, Ἰάσων Ἀρεταίου
φύσει δὲ Μενίππου δρα-
χμὰς διακοσίας, Μητρό-
15 φαντος Δημοφῶντος
δραχμὰς διακοσίας,
Μέλας Πόλλιος δρα⟦χμ⟧-

---

[54] I have argued elsewhere (Crowther 1990: 145) that the first series of lists formed a relatively tight sequence and probably ended in 190/89 or not long after. Migeotte (1993) 277 favours a slightly more extended dating range.

[55] Three texts (*I.Iasos* 167, 199 (*LB–W* 284), 217) revert in part of their formulation to the pattern of the first series to record additional contributions to support specific performances; for these see the discussion of Migeotte (1993) 269–70, 280.

[56] Prosopographical connections and their immediate collocation on adjoining faces of the pilaster suggest that the second group of texts was not separated from the first by an extended interval: Crowther (1990) 145–6.

[57] I have corrected the reading in *I.Iasos* for the end of l. 17, where the stone-cutter inscribed *ΔΡΑΧΜ* before deciding that there was insufficient space to complete δραχμάς and erasing the last two letters to obtain a linebreak after *ΔΡΑ*. There are similar cutting revisions in *LB–W* 264 (*I.Iasos* 175), l. 2 (Ἀπόλλωνος ⟦νος⟧ τοῦ); and *LB–W* 265 (*I.Iasos* 176), where the initial inscription of the first line ended at *ΑΠΟΛΛΩ*, with the last three letters, *ΝΟΣ*, cut on the line above; the line was then recut from eta of στεφανηφόρου onwards so that the whole of Ἀπόλλωνος could be fitted in before the linebreak.

χμὰς διακοσίας, Διό-
δωρος Σατύρου δρα-
20   χμὰς διακοσίας, Δρο-
μέας Θεοδώρου Νε-
αιτῖνος δραχμὰς ἑκατόν,
Λίβανος Ἀμφικλείους
Μύνδιος δραχμὰς ἑκα-
25   τόν.

In the stephanephorate of Apollo for the sixth time after Kleanax the son of
Theokles, and when Omphalion the son of Euboulides was *agonothetes*:
from those who had previously assented (to make contributions)[58] at the
Dionysia the following made payments: Apollonios, the son of Paionios,
200 drachmas; Iason, the (adopted) son of Aretaios, and natural son of
Menippos, 200 drachmas; Metrophantos, the son of Demophon, 200
drachmas; Melas, the son of Pollis, 200 drachmas; Diodoros, the son of
Satyros, 200 drachmas; Dromeas, the son of Theodoros, from Neaiton, 100
drachmas; Libanos, the son of Amphikles, from Myndos, 100 drachmas.

The contributors in this text and a number of the other lists are not
identified by function,[59] but the arrangement of their names follows
an unvarying pattern in which the first named contributor is the
agonothetes of the preceding year. The pattern can be verified in
sequences of lists, even where the title is not explicitly recorded,
from the *agonothetes* recorded in the antecedent list; so Apollonios,
the son of Paionios, the first contributor in LB–W 263 (sixth
stephanephorate of Apollo after Kleanax, the son of Theokles)
appears as *agonothetes* in LB–W 262 (*I.Iasos* 173), which is dated to
the immediately preceding year (fifth stephanephorate of Apollo
after Kleanax). In the first twelve lists from the second period neither
the preceding *agonothetes* nor the other contributors are identified
explicitly,[60] but since in subsequent lists the latter are qualified as
choregoi, the same identification can also be assumed for the cases

---

[58] The use of ἐπινεύειν, 'to nod assent', implies, as Migeotte notes (Migeotte 1993:
274–5) a public procedure. This formula seems specific to Iasos.

[59] LB–W 259–68, 270–1, 285; in LB–W 291, LB–W's E[ἰ]ρη[ναῖος] was corrected
by Brinck (1886) to ⟨χ⟩[ο]ρη[γοί].

[60] LB–W 259–68, 270–1 (*I.Iasos* 170–7, 204, 206–7).

where the title is not specified.[61] In most, but perhaps not all, cases the *choregoi* will have been those of the preceding year, although this is again left unstated.[62]

The distinction between the groups of lists points to a reform or institutionalisation of the way in which contributions were made during the 180s, well analysed by Migeotte.[63] Both the *agonothetes* and the *choregoi* seem to have been expected *ex officio* to commit to making contributions of 200 drachmas to the funding of subsequent Dionysia. In a number of cases the *agonothetes* had also himself served as *choregos* and made a separate pledge and contribution for each office.[64] Although the sum of the contribution seems to have been fixed, the language of assent employed in the lists implies that the obligation was at least formally voluntary.[65] At the same time, one of the offsets of voluntarism was the commemoration of the necessary gesture—publicly and permanently on stone.

The contributions, of 200 drachmas (100 for metic *choregoi*), were neither trivial nor exigent,[66] and the burden of payment was shared. Although certain individuals reappear,[67] the great majority of those listed contributed (and served as *agonothetes* or *choregos*) only once.[68] Nevertheless, the group was a select one. It is instructive to set the names of the contributors against the names of *prytaneis* (rotating members of a steering committee of the council, which seems likely to have been representative) attested in the headings of a number of

---

[61] So also Migeotte (1993) 280–1.

[62] Migeotte (1993) 281, noticing the variations in numbers of named *choregoi*, argues plausibly that the numbers of *choregoi* listed are in many cases too high to represent only the *choregoi* of a single year.

[63] Migeotte (1993) 277–8.

[64] LB–W 272, Appendix 1 no. **176**; 287, no. **17**, 295 no. **187**; 296 no. **134** (*I.Iasos* 208, 186, 194–5).

[65] Migeotte (1993) 290.

[66] Immediate Iasian comparisons are offered by the 300 drachmas maximum size of dowries funded by Laodike's gifts of grain to the city in the 190s (*I.Iasos* 4, 11–25) and the two surviving contributions towards a grain fund in *I.Iasos* 244 (Migeotte 1992: no. 74) of 600 and 200 drachmas. Migeotte (1992) 316–19 discusses the size of contributions in public subscriptions, the majority of which are somewhat lower (the modal value in large subscriptions, for example, for the Samian Corn law (*IG* XII 6, 172) and for a Smyrnaian building project (*I.Smyrna* 688–90) is 100 drachmas).

[67] See, e.g., Appendix 1, nos. **10**, **42**, **70**, **87**, **93**, **131**, **157**, **177**.

[68] Of 206 individual citizen contributors (listed in Appendix 1 below), 170 make a single appearance.

early second-century Iasian decrees (*I.Iasos* 4, 25, 76, 77; *SEG* 41, 930, 932). There is an element of circularity in the comparison, but of thirty-three identifiable *prytaneis* only one, Menoitios son of Hierokles (Appendix 1 no. **137**), is separately attested as a contributor in the lists. Responsibility for supporting performances at the Dionysia appears to have fallen on a relatively limited class of citizens—but to have been shared evenly among this group. *Grands évergètes citoyens* were in short supply at Iasos.[69] The one individual who perhaps belongs in this category is Sopatros, the son of Epikrates, former *choregos*, *agonothetes*, *stephanephoros*, and gymnasiarch, whose contributions to the refurbishment of the theatre are matched by the construction of a portico for the gymnasium commemorated, as in the theatre, by a dedicatory inscription cut in beautiful and prominent lettering across the architrave of the stoa (*I.Iasos* 250).[70]

The regular succession of pledges and contributions established during the 180s BC seems to have formed an effective system which ensured the continuity of dramatic and musical performances at the Dionysia for more than fifty years. The few gaps in the sequence of lists are likely to reflect incompletenesses of epigraphical survival as much as interruptions in performance. One interval can be securely associated with a moment of difficulty, but its duration seems to have been brief. *I.Iasos* 152 (*LB–W* 281) records a decree of the *Koinon* of *Technitai* of Dionysos at Teos offering assistance to the Iasians for their celebration of the Dionysia.[71] The considerations section of the decree is poorly preserved, but an emphatic declaration of the Iasians' zealous commitment to the performance of dramatic contests in previous times[72] is countered by a reference in the resolutions to current pressing circumstances and an undertaking by the *Koinon* to send three representatives and a group of performers with

---

[69] For *grands évergètes citoyens*, see Gauthier (1985) 53–75.

[70] Theatre: *LB–W* 269 (*I.Iasos* 249), quoted in n. 26 above. Gymnasium: *I.Iasos* 250: Σώπατρο[ς Ἐπικ]ράτου γυμνασια[ρχήσας] τῶν τε νέ[ων καὶ τῶν π]ρεσβυτέρων τὴν στοὰν τῶι δήμωι καὶ τοῖ[ς νέοις καὶ τοῖς πρεσβυτέροις ἀνέθηκεν] ('Sopatros, the son of Epikrates, having been gymnasiarch of the *neoi* and the *presbyteroi* [dedicated] the stoa to the People and the [*neoi* and the *presbyteroi*]').

[71] English translation in Csapo and Slater (1994) 252–3 no. 45.

[72] *I.Iasos* 152, 7–8 (with the good supplement of Aneziri 2003: 392 D13 for l. 8): ἔν τε τοῖς πρότερον χρόνοις [πᾶσ]αν σπουδὴν καὶ φιλοτιμίαν [δείξαν|τες] περὶ τῆς τῶν ἀγώνων ἐρ[γολαβείας].

supporting teams to Iasos to ensure choral performances in accordance with the Iasians' established regulations.[73] The implication seems clear:[74] that the Iasians had been unable to sustain performances at the Dionysia and had petitioned the *Technitai* for assistance. The inscribed text is notarised with an Iasian date ('in the third stephanephorate of Apollo after Menes, the son of Tyrtaios, sixth day of Apatourion') which allows the event to be set against the sequence of inscribed lists of contributors. One of the new lists found in the course of the Italian excavations, *I.Iasos* 217, is dated to the stephanephorate of Menes Tyrtaiou and records, three years before the Iasians' appeal to the *Technitai*, a full set of four citizen choregic contributors (Appendix 1 nos. **4, 22, 56, 116**), one of whom contributed additionally as *agonothetes* of the previous year (**22**: Aretaios, son of Aischines, natural son of Phanias), and two metics (**244, 256**). The lists for the following two years, when the stephanephorate was assumed by Apollo, in default of citizens able to meet the costs of the office,[75] are missing, but it seems to have been during this interval that the Iasians' difficulties arose. In an earlier article on the chronology of the lists I suggested a *terminus post quem* for the decree of the *Technitai* of 157/6, but new publications of inscriptions have now pushed this limit down at least five years and the decree is likely to have been somewhat later still.[76] Unfortunately, the precise circumstances to which the *Technitai* allude cannot be recovered.

The decree offers other insights into the Iasian Dionysia. In order to ensure continuity of performance according to the Iasians'

---

[73] *I.Iasos* 152, 12–17: [νέμειν τ]ῶι Διονύσωι καὶ Ἰασεῦσιν εἰς τοὺς [συντελουμ-έν]ο⟨υ⟩ς | παρ' α⟨ὐ⟩τοῖς τῶι Διονύσωι ἀγῶν[ας ἐκ] τῶν ἐνγεγραμμένων τεχνιτῶν καὶ με[τεχόντων τῆς [ἡ]⟨με⟩[τ]έρ[ας συνόδ]⟨ου⟩ (?) φιλίας ὑπαρχούσης ἡμῖν ἐκ παλαιῶν χρόνων, ‖ αὐλητὰς δύο, τραγωιδοὺς δύο, κωμωιδοὺς δύο, κιθαρωδόν, κιθαριστήν, ὅπως | ἄγωσιν τῶι θεῶι τοὺς [χ]ορούς κατὰ τὰς πατρίους αὐτῶν διαγραφάς, προσ⟨ν⟩εί⟨μ⟩αι δὲ τού[των καὶ τὰς ὑπηρεσίας --- ('[to designate] for Dionysos and the Iasians, from the number of those who are registered as Artists and those who participate in our [company], in view of the friendship which we have from ancient times, two *aulos*-players, two tragedians, two comedians, a singer to the *kithara*, and a *kithara*-player for the contests [conducted] at Iasos in honour of Dionysos, so that they may perform the choruses in accordance with their ancestral regulations').

[74] Good discussions by Migeotte (1993) 285–6; Le Guen (2001a) 268–9.

[75] Migeotte (1993) 269 n. 7, with the references cited there.

[76] See the chronological notes in Appendix 2.

established prescriptions, the *Technitai* undertook to assign two *auletai* (pipers), two tragedians, two comedians, a *kitharoidos*, and a *kitharistes* to the Iasians. This assignment can be compared with the recorded lists of performers in the first series of Iasian lists: four days of one comedian, three days of one *kitharistes* (*LB–W* 252); two days of one *auletes* and two days of one *kitharistes* (*LB–W* 253); one day of one *kitharistes*, two days of one *auletes*, two days of one singer to the *aulos* (*LB–W* 254); two days of one Boiotian *auletes*, two days of the *auletes* Kraton Zotichou, five days of one comedian (*LB–W* 255); one day of one tragedian, two days of one comedian, two days of a second comedian, one day of one *kitharoidos* (*LB–W* 256); five days of one comedian, three days of one *choropsaltria* (*LB–W* 257); two days of one *auletes*, four days of one tragedian (*LB–W* 258). The performances subsidised by contributors in *LB–W* 256 come closest to this pattern, but the divergence of the early lists from the roster followed by the *Technitai* suggests that in the difficult conditions of the early second century BC, only a limited range of performances could be supported. The regular pattern of contributions instituted thereafter, four sets of choregic donations of 200 drachmas together with 200 from the preceding *agonothetes* and two payments of 100 drachmas by metic *choregoi*, a total of 1,200 drachmas, would perhaps have met the costs of the full list of performers (with their supporting teams).

V. TEXTUAL NOTES

In this section I turn to the texts themselves. The theatre lists on the laterals of the Clandeboye pilaster have been re-edited with minor corrections in W. Blümel's valuable Corpus-Repertorium, but have not been systematically collated since Le Bas recorded them in situ.[77] The lists inscribed on the left lateral of the pilaster, from top to bottom, form a sequence of years dated from the stephanephorate of Kleanax Theokleous (*LB–W* 259–265). The first text on the right

---

[77] Dimensions of the pilaster (in m): 2.95 high, 0.51 wide, 0.23–0.31 deep; 0.265 for the lower right lateral.

lateral, *LB–W* 266 (*I.Iasos* 177), dated to the ninth stephanephorate of Apollo after Kleanax, the son of Theokles, follows immediately the last text inscribed at the base of the left lateral, *LB–W* 265 (*I.Iasos* 176: eighth stephanephorate of Apollo), but was inscribed *c.* 0.6 m below the top of the pilaster. *LB–W* 267 (*I.Iasos* 204), which belongs to the year after *LB–W* 266, since the list of contributors in 267 begins with the *agonothetes* of the previous year Hermonax Poseidippou, who is also named as *agonothetes* in 266, follows after an interval of 0.075 m. There follows a short gap to the next list, which belongs to the stephanephorate of Sopatros; and a further interval of 0.27 m to the final three texts on the lateral (*LB–W* 270–2; *I.Iasos* 205, 207, 208), which extend to its foot and form a sequence of three years.

The final three lists are only partially transcribed in current editions.[78] A visit to Clandeboye house in 2000 provided an opportunity to review these and the other texts on the pilaster and to take new squeezes and photographs.[79] In the case of *LB–W* 270 and 272 the texts recorded by Le Bas (and inherited in *I.Iasos*) can be corrected or supplemented in important details; the readings for the second text offered in *LB–W* and *I.Iasos*, in contrast, are so incomplete that the edition offered here effectively becomes a new inscription.

LB–W 270 (*I.Iasos* 205; Brinck 1886: 234 no. 125)

The text occupies a vertical space of 0.33 m, with a preserved width varying between 0.265–0.26 m Letter height 0.012–0.015, line interval 0.005 m Letter forms: alpha with straight crossbar, pi with overhanging top bar, finished with serifs, and a shorter right hasta; sigma and mu have parallel outer strokes with deeply inset internal bars; theta is oval; rho has a large, rounded loop.

---

[78] Cf. *I.Iasos* I, pp. 2–3: 'die Buchstaben auf der vorderen und auf der linken Seite sind im wesentlichen gut lesbar; auf der rechten Seite ist der Stein so stark abgenutzt, daß nur noch die drei oberen Inschriften zu entziffern, von der übrigen nur noch schwache Reste erkennbar sind'.

[79] I am very grateful to the Marchioness of Dufferin and Ava for allowing me to revisit the stones and to the Clandeboye archivist, Lola Armstrong, for her assistance.

ἐπὶ στεφανηφόρου Εὐθιά-
δου τοῦ Μελανθίου τοῦ
δεύτερον στεφανηφοροῦν-
τος, ἀγωνοθέτου δὲ Δρα-
5 κοντίδου τοῦ Ἑρμοδώρου·
οἵδε τῶν πρότερον ἐπινευσά[ν]-
των ἐν Διονυσίοις ἀπέδωκαν·
Μόσχος Μόσχου δραχμὰς διακοσίας, ᵛ Στησίοχος Δημέου καθ᾽ υ[ἱ]ο-
10 θεσίαν δὲ Φερετίμου δραχμὰς διακοσίας, Φίλων Ὀλυμπιοδώρου
δραχμὰς διακοσίας, ᵛ Ὄβριμος
Κτησιφῶντος δραχμὰς διακοσία[ς,]
Ἑκαταῖος Διος[κουρίδου]
15 δραχμὰς διακοσίας· ᵛᵃᶜ
Ἑκαταῖος Οὐλιάδου ᵛᵃᶜ
[δρ]α̣[χ]μ̣ὰ̣ς διακοσίας, . . ⁴⁻⁵ . .
. ο̣ς Ν̣ικοτ[έ]λ[ο]υ̣ς? (i)-- ᶜ· ¹⁰ --
δρα̣χμὰς ἐκ[α]τ[ό]ν̣.

Critical notes

4–5: ἀγωνοθέτου δὲ Δρ[α]|κ[ο]ντίδου τοῦ Ἑρμοδότ[ου] LB–W, corrected by
Blümel in *I.Iasos*, following Brinck: Δρ[α]|κοντίδου τοῦ Ἑρμοδώρ[ο]υ. The
reading can now be completed from stone and squeeze.

6–7: οἵδε τῶν πρότερον ἐπινευ[σάν]|των ἐν Διονυσί[οις ἀπ]έδωκ[αν], LB–W,
followed by *I.Iasos*.

12–14: δραχμὰς δια[κοσίας -----] | Κτησιφῶντος [δραχμὰς δια]|κοσία-
[ς -----], LB–W, followed by *I.Iasos*. Omicron and sigma are compressed
together at the end of line 12 and the loop of rho is incomplete, but the
reading Ὄβριμος at the end of l. 12 otherwise seems secure; Obrimos
appears, apparently as a patronymic, in LB–W 273 (*I.Iasos* 209), and is the
name of the *stephanephoros* of LB–W 299 (*I.Iasos* 214). The transmitted
reading of LB–W for the beginning of l. 14 (ΚΟΣΙΑ) is seriously astray;
διακοσία[ς] can be read almost in full at the end of l. 13, and a name is
required here: the vertical of epsilon is incomplete, but otherwise Ἑκαταῖος
is clear. The following patronymic, beginning Διος-, is more marginal, but
seems likely to belong to Διος[κουρίδου]. A Διοσκορίδης Ἑκαταίο is named
among the Iasian *tamiai* ('treasurers') in the decree concerning the sale of
property belonging to conspirators against Mausolus (*I.Iasos* 1, 8–9), but a

familial relationship cannot be assumed for a homonym over the course of almost three centuries.

15: [δραχ]μὰς δια[κοσίας], *LB–W*, followed by *I.Iasos*; but the squeeze offers a fuller reading.

16–17: Ἑκαταῖος Οὐλιάδου [δρα]χμὰς] διακοσία[ς, -----], *LB–W*, followed by *I.Iasos*. The first half of l. 17 is eroded, but traces on the squeeze and the position of διακοσίας indicate that the line began with [δρ]α̣[χ]μάς and that there was a short vacat after the patronymic Οὐλιάδου at the end of the preceding line. The name of the last contributor, who seems to have been a metic, begins at the end of l. 17 and carries over with a nominative termination in -ος at the beginning of 18. The patronymic seems to have begun Νικ-. Traces on the squeeze suggest that the following letters may have been a small omicron and an overhanging tau: perhaps Νικοτ̣[έ]λ[ους]. The ethnic cannot be distinguished among the remaining letter traces to the end of the line.

18–19: [----- δρα]χμὰς ἑκ]ατόν, *LB–W*, followed by *I.Iasos*. After δραχμάς, which was missed by *LB–W* at the beginning of 19, traces of ἑκ[α]τ[ό]ν after initial epsilon and kappa are tightly compressed and hard to separate, although *LB–W*'s reading of *ATON* is not qualified as problematic.

Translation

In the stephanephorate of Euthiades the son of Melanthios, who was *stephanephoros* for the second time, and when Drakontides, [5] the son of Hermodoros, was *agonothetes*, the following of those who previously indicated their assent at the Dionysia paid (contributions[): Moschos, the son of Moschos, 200 drachmas; Stesiochos, the son of Demeas, by adoption [10] the son of Pheretimos, 200 drachmas; Philon, the son of Olympiodoros, 200 drachmas; Obrimos the son of Ktesiphon, 200 drachmas; Hekataios, the son of Dios[kourides], 200 [15] drachmas; Hekataios, the son of Ouliades, 200 drachmas; -- the son of Nikot[eles (?) from --] 100 drachmas.

LB–W 271 (*I.Iasos* 207; Brinck 1886: 234 no. 126)

Inscribed immediately below *LB–W* 270; the text occupies a vertical space of 0.315 m, its preserved width varying between 0.26 and 0.23 m. Letter height 0.011–0.012 m, line interval 0.005–0.006 m.

The lettering, so far as it can be judged from the eroded surface, is broadly similar to that of *LB–W* 270.

ἐπὶ στεφα[ν]ηφόρου Ὀμ[φα]-
λίωνος τ[οῦ Ε]ὐ[βου]λίδ[ου,]
ἀγωνοθέτο[υ] δὲ Σ[ι]μάλ[ου]
το[ῦ] Ἀμυν[αίου·] οἵδ[ε] τῶ[ν]
5   πρότερον ἐπινευσά[ν]-
των ἐ[ν] Διονυσίοι[ς]
ἀπέδωκαν· Δρακοντίδ[η]ς
Ἑρμοδ[ώρ]ο[υ δραχμὰς]
διακοσίας, ῎Α[ν]τιγέ[νη]ς
10   Μενεκλείους δραχ[μὰς δι]-
ακοσ{ισ}ίας, Διονυσικ[λῆς]
Πανταίν[ο]υ δ[ραχμὰ]ς [δι]-
ακοσίας, Κλεα[ίν]ετος Κ[λε]ά-
νακτος δραχμὰς δια[κ]οσί-
15   ας, Σωστρατίδης Σωσ[τρά]-
του δραχμὰς διακοσίας,
Μενεκράτης Ἑρμίου Μυλα-
σεὺς δραχμὰς ἑκατόν.

Critical notes

LB–W 271 records the eponymous dating in lines 1–2 (ἐπὶ στεφα[ν]η[φόρ]ου Ὀ[μφα]λ[ίων]ος [τοῦ Ε]ὐ[βουλίδου,]), but otherwise has only sporadic letter traces for the remaining lines, for some of which Blümel in *I.Iasos* 207 offers possible interpretations, but no more than the shell of a text. Sufficient traces are discernible on the squeeze, however, for the whole list to be reconstructed.

1–2: ἐπὶ στεφα[ν]η[φόρ]ου Ὀ[μφα]λ[ίων]ος [τοῦ Ε]ὐ[βουλίδου], *LB–W*, followed by *I.Iasos*, on the basis of *LB–W* 272 (*I.Iasos* 208) 10–12.

3–5: [ἀγ]ω[ν]οθ[έτου δὲ ---- | ----- οἵδε | τῶν πρ]ότε[ρον ἐπινευσάντων ἐν Διονυσίοις], *I.Iasos*, from the letters recorded by *LB–W*. *LB–W*, followed by *I.Iasos*, offers [Δ]ίνυλλο[ς | Εἰρη]ναίου as the name of the former *agonothetes* and first contributor in *LB–W* 272 (*I.Iasos* 208, 7–9), but the two lists are consecutive and the name of the *agonothetes* can be completed and confirmed from one to the next.

6: . Ω . Ε . . . . N, *LB–W* ad init.; [ἀγ]ω[νοθ]έ[της (?)], Migeotte 1993: 280 n. 33.

7: *AΘ .. IΩ, LB–W* ad init.

7–8: the first contributor, Drakontides the son of Hermodoros, is *agonothetes* in *LB–W* 270 (*I.Iasos* 205); the two lists are accordingly consecutive.

8: . . *OΔ* . . *O, LB–W* ad init. Letter traces after Ἑρμοδ[ώρ]ο[υ] should belong to δραχμάς, but are hard to reconcile with individual letters. There seems to have been a short vacat at the end of the line.

9: *Δ, LB–W* ad init.

9–10: Antigenes the son of Menekles is *agonothetes* in *I.Iasos* 180, 4–5 (*LB–W* 276).

10–11: [----- δραχμὰς δι]ακοσί[ας -----], *I.Iasos* from the traces recorded by *LB–W*.

11: *ΑΚΟΣΙΣΙΑΣ, lapis.*

11–12: Dionysikles, the son of Pantainos, is *agonothetes* in *I.Iasos* 183–4.

12: . *A* . . . . . . *Ω, LB–W* ad init.

12–13: [δραχμὰς δι]ακοσίας, Πολέ[μ]α[ρχος], *I.Iasos* (*ΠΟΛΕ . . A, LB–W*).

13–14: Kleainetos, the son of Kleanax, should be the son of Kleanax, the son of Kleainetos, in *I.Iasos* 163, 13 (*LB–W* 255).

15: . . *ΣΟ, LB–W* ad init.

16: . . . . . *O, LB–W* ad init.

17: *E, LB–W* ad init.

18: *EK, LB–W* ad init.

Translation

In the stephanephorate of Omphalion, the son of Euboulides, and when Simalos, the son of Limnaios, was *agonothetes*, the following of those [5] who had indicated their assent previously at the Dionysia paid (contributions): Drakontides, the son of Hermodoros, 200 drachmas; Antigenes, the [10] son of Menekles, 200 drachmas; Dionysikles, the son of Pantainos, 200 drachmas; Kleainetos, the son of Kleanax, 200 drachmas; [15] Sostratides, the son of Sostratos, 200 drachmas; Menekrates, the son of Hermias, from Mylasa, 100 drachmas.

LB–W 272 (*I.Iasos* 208; Brinck 1886: 235 no. 127)

Separated from *LB–W* 271 by an interval of 0.05 m. The text occupies
a vertical space of 0.43 m, with an uninscribed space below of
c. 0.25 m to the foot of the pilaster; the preserved width is 0.255 m.
Letter height 0.013, line interval 0.005 m. There is a left margin
of 0.015 m. The outlines of the lettering have been eroded somewhat by exposure to time and rain, but seem to diverge from those
of the preceding two inscriptions. The right hasta of pi descends
closer to the base-line, phi is compressed to fit within the regular
height of other letters; the right hasta of nu is raised above the
base-line.

```
   ἐπὶ στεφανηφόρου
   Ἀρχελάου τοῦ Δράκ[ον]-
   τος, ἀγωνοθέτου δ[ὲ]
   Μενίππου τοῦ Μεν[ίπ]-
5  που· οἵδε τῶν πρότερ[ον]
   ἐπινευσάντων ἐν Διο-
   νυσίοις ἀπέδωκαν· ἀγω-
   νοθέτης Σίμαλος
   Λιμναίου δραχμὰς
10 διακοσίας, στεφανή-
   φορος Ὀμφαλίων Εὐ-
   βουλίδου δραχμὰς δ[ι]-
   ακοσίας· ᵛᵛ χορηγοί· Σίμ[α]-
   [λο]ς [Λ]ιμναίου δραχμὰ[ς]
15 διακοσ[ίας, - - -]
   . ΕΙ[- - - δραχμὰς]
   διακοσίας, [ᵛᵛ Π]υθ[ί]ων
   [Πα]ρμενίσκου καθ᾽ υ[ἱοποί]-
   [αν δ]ὲ Ἑρμαΐ[σ]κου [δραχμὰς]
20 [διακο]σίας, ᵛᵛ Σώ[π]α[τρος (?)]
   . . . σέου δραχμὰς [δια]-
   [κο]σίας, ᵛᵛ Νίκων . . . .
   . . . . ου Ἀχαῖος δραχμ[ὰς]
   [ἑκα]τόν.
```

Critical notes

4–5: Μενίππου τοῦ [Κράτη]|τος, LB–W, questioned by Brinck; ΠΟΥ is clear on the stone at the beginning of 5 for LB–W's ΤΟΣ, and the first three letters of the patronymic at the end of the previous line seem to be mu (damaged on the right), epsilon (lower bar missing), nu.

5: οἵδε τῶν πρ[ότερον], LB–W, followed by *I.Iasos*.

7–9: [ἀγω]|νοθέτης [Δ]ίυλλο[ς | Εἰρη]ναίου, LB–W, followed by *I.Iasos*; but the reading on the stone is clear.

10–11: στεφα[νη]|φορῶ[ν Ὀμ]φαλίων Εὐβουλίδου δραχ[μὰς δι]|ακοσί[ας], LB–W, followed by *I.Iasos*. The present participle was questioned by Maddoli (2000) 30, who suggested στεφα[νη]φόρο[ς], which can now be confirmed from the stone.

13–14: . Χ . . . . . Ι . ΟΣ, LB–W, followed by *I.Iasos*; the omicron in the second letter space in l. 14 is now lost, but the reading of 13–14 seems otherwise assured. It is interesting to see Simalos, the son of Limnaios, who contributed in fulfilment of a pledge as *agonothetes* in the preceding year, also having made a similar commitment as *choregos*.

15–24: the stone is now fractured across ll. 15–17 and has lost 2–3 letters and the margin on its left edge; the gap in 15–17 has been filled with cement and plaster, so that no traces of the original surface remain. Readings transmitted by *LB–W* are underlined.

17: ad fin. [Λά]σο[ς], LB–W. The first half of l. 17, where LB–W read διακοσίας, is now lost; letter traces in the second half of the line are likely to correspond to the name of a contributor (whose patronymic and adopted name follow in ll. 18–19), separated from διακοσίας by a short vacat. Where LB–W read sigma, the stone seems to show the branches of upsilon; the following round letter could be theta as well as omicron and is separated by a short letter space from omega and nu, suggesting [Π]υθ[ί]ων.

18–20: Παρμενίδου δ[ραχμὰς | δ]ιακο[σίας . .]ΟΥ[. . .], *I.Iasos*, following LB–W. In l. 18 the stone seems to show sigma followed by a compressed kappa after ΠΑΡΜΕΝΙ. Instead of the delta read after the patronymic by LB–W the traces visible now on the stone suggest kappa followed by the lower half of an alpha, the central dot and eroded outline of theta and the branches of upsilon. The letters recorded by LB–W at the beginning of l. 19 are incompatible with letter traces on the stone which seem to belong to epsilon followed by the patronymic Ἑρμαί[σ]κου. The reading inherited by *I.Iasos* from LB–W would require an unusually short name–patronymic combination to allow an additional contributor to be inserted into ll. 19–20. The new readings indicate instead that the name of the contributor in ll. 17ff. was an extended one, including a notice of adoption in 19–20, where καθ᾽ υ[ἰοποί]αν] (cf. *I.Iasos* 215, 2; 230, 2) fits the lacuna better than the more common formula καθ᾽ υἱοθεσίαν, with the sum of the contribution recorded at the beginning of l. 20, where the letter traces suggest [διακο]σίας.

20–22: ------------- | [----]έου δραχ[μὰς --], *I.Iasos* following *LB–W*, but more can now be read on the stone. After [διακο]σίας a vacat of two letter spaces is followed by the upper bar and internal angle of sigma, a clear omega, an indistinguishable trace, alpha, and room for a further 4–5 lost letters, indicating Σώ[π]α[τρος]. Traces of a possible sigma before [--]έου in l. 21 suggest that the contributor's patronymic may have been Thraseas ([Θρα]σέου) rather than Aristeas, Demeas, Menneas, Proteas, or Hybreas.

22–4: ------------ | [------]αιου[-- δραχμὰς] | ἑκατόν, *I.Iasos*, following *LB–W*. The name and ethnic of the metic contributor are new, but little otherwise can be added to *LB–W*'s readings.

Translation

In the stephanephorate of Archelaos, the son of Drakon, and when Menippos, the son of Menippos, was *agonothetes*,[5] the following of those who had indicated their assent previously at the Dionysia paid (contributions): as *agonothetes* Simalos, the son of Limnaios, 200[10] drachmas; as *stephanephoros* Omphalion, the son of Euboulidou, 200 drachmas; as *choregoi*: Simalos, the son of Limnaios, 200[15] drachmas;—the son of—200 drachmas; Pythion, the son of Parmeniskos, adopted son of Hermaïskos, 200[20] [drachmas]; Sopatros, the son of -seas, 200 drachmas; Nikon, the son of -os, from Achaia, 100 drachmas.

Appendix 1: Contributors to the Iasian Dionysia

(n.n. indicates a lost name)

1. Admetos, son of Hekataios: as *choregos* paid for the *auletes* Nikokles (*LB–W* 254; *I.Iasos* 162).
2. Aerion, son of Hierokles, son of Aristogenes: 200 dr. (*LB–W* 285; *I.Iasos* 200).
3. Aischines, son of Apollonios: 200 dr. (*LB–W* 260; *I.Iasos* 171).
4. Aischines, son of Phanias: 200 dr. as *choregos* of previous year (*I.Iasos* 217).
5. Aischines, son of Theodoros: 200 dr. as *choregos* of previous year (Maddoli 2000: B3).
6. Aison, son of Stephanios: 200 dr. as *agonothetes* of previous year (*I.Iasos* 201).
7. Anaximenes, son of Apollodoros: 200 dr. as *choregos* of previous year (*I.Iasos* 184).
8. Androkles, son of n.n.: 200 dr. as *choregos* of previous year (*I.Iasos* 203).
9. Antheas, son of Meniskos: [200 dr.] as *choregos* of previous year (*LB–W* 293; *I.Iasos* 192).
10. Antigenes, son of Menekles: 200 dr. (*LB–W* 271; *I.Iasos* 207); separately attested as *agonothetes* in *LB–W* 276 (*I.Iasos* 180).
11. Antikrates, son of n.n. (Maddoli 2000: B1).
12. Antipatros, son of Menekles: 200 dr. as *choregos* of previous year (*LB–W* 287; *I.Iasos* 186); probably father of Menekles, son of Antipatros (no. 126).
13. Apollodoros, son of Charmos: as *agonothetes* paid for the *komoidos* Sosylos for two days (*LB–W* 252; *I.Iasos* 160).
14. Apollonides, son of Aristippos: 200 dr. as *agonothetes* of previous year (*LB–W* 265; *I.Iasos* 176).
15. Apollonides, son of Hekataios: 200 dr. as *choregos* of previous year (*LB–W* 296; *I.Iasos* 195).
16. Apollonios, son of Dionytas: 200 dr. (*LB–W* 268; *I.Iasos* 206).
17. Apollonios, son of Iatrokles: 200 dr. as *agonothetes* of previous year (*LB–W* 287; *I.Iasos* 186); a second contribution of 200 dr. as *choregos* of previous year (*LB–W* 287; *I.Iasos* 186).
18. Apollonios, son of Menipos: 200 dr. as *choregos* of previous year (*I.Iasos* 201).

19. Apollonios, son of Menodoros: 200 dr. as *choregos* of previous year (*LB–W* 293; *I.Iasos* 192).
20. Apollonios, son of Paionios: 200 dr. as *agonothetes* of previous year (*LB–W* 263; *I.Iasos* 174).
21. Archytas, son of n.n.: 200 dr. as *choregos* of previous year (*LB–W* 289; *I.Iasos* 188).
22. Aretaios, son of Aischines, natural son of Phanias: 200 dr. as *agonothetes* of previous year; also contributed 200 dr. as *choregos* of previous year (*I.Iasos* 217).
23. Aristeas, son of Aristeas, natural son of Thaumasios: 200 dr. as *choregos* of previous year (*LB–W* 292; *I.Iasos* 191).
24. Aristeas, son of Aristeas: 200 dr. as *choregos* of previous year (Maddoli 2000: B3); possibly to be identified with no. 23, but the names are common and the papponymic in 23 may be used to avoid ambiguity.
25. Aristeas, son of Melanion: 200 dr. as *choregos* of previous year (*LB–W* 297; *I.Iasos* 196).
26. Aristeas, son of Philokles: 200 dr. (*LB–W* 268; *I.Iasos* 206).
27. Aristeides, son of Antimenes: 200 dr. (*LB–W* 265; *I.Iasos* 176).
28. Aristides, son of Menekrates, adopted son of [-]menes: 200 dr. as *agonothetes* (*LB–W* 274; *I.Iasos* 178).
29. Aristion, son of Sophron: 200 dr. as *choregos* of previous year (*LB–W* 284; *I.Iasos* 199).
30. Aristippos, son of Dorotheos: 200 dr. (*LB–W* 264; *I.Iasos* 175).
31. Aristokritos, son of Aristokritos: 506 dr. contribution to construction of theatre (*LB–W* 276; *I.Iasos* 180),
32. Aristokritos, son of Glaukos, adopted son of Diodoros: as former *choregos* paid for the *auletes* Kraton Zotichou of Kalchedon for two days (*LB–W* 255; *I.Iasos* 163).
33. Aristokritos, son of Menestheus: 200 dr. as *choregos* of previous year (*I.Iasos* 215); brother of Isidoros (no. 97) and Menestheus (no. 130).
34. Aristomachos, son of Eirenaios: 200 dr. as *choregos* of previous year (*LB–W* 297; *I.Iasos* 196).
35. Ari[-], son of n.n.: 200 dr. as *choregos* of previous year (*I.Iasos* 202).
36. Artemidoros, son of Diotimos: 200 dr. as *choregos* of previous year (*I.Iasos* 201).
37. Astiades, son of Pindaros: 200 dr. as *agonothetes* of previous year (*LB–W* 286; *I.Iasos* 185); separately attested as *stephanephoros* in *I.Iasos* 202.
38. Bloson, son of Pythion: as *choregos* of previous year paid for the *komoidos* Sosylos for one day (*LB–W* 252; *I.Iasos* 160).
39. Bloson, son of Pythion: probably grandson of Bloson (no. 38); 200 dr. as *agonothetes* of previous year (*LB–W* 291; *I.Iasos* 190).

40. Boethos, son of Dionysodoros: 200 dr. as *choregos* of previous year (Maddoli 2000: B2).

41. Bryon, son of Aristoneikos: 200 dr. (*LB–W* 260; *I.Iasos* 171).[80]

42. Chares, son of Chares: 200 dr. as *choregos* of previous year (*LB–W* 292; *I.Iasos* 191); a second contribution of 200 dr. as *agonothetes* of previous year (*LB–W* 297; *I.Iasos* 196).

43. Charidemos, son of Theophilos: as former *choregos* paid for the *komoidos* Athenodoros (*LB–W* 255; *I.Iasos* 163).

44. Chrysippos, son of Apollonios: 200 dr. as *choregos* of previous year (*LB–W* 288; *I.Iasos* 187); subsequently attested as gymnasiarchos of the *presbyteroi* in *I.Iasos* 23, 8–9.

45. Deinon, son of Diouches: as *choregos* of previous year paid for the *auletes* Nikon for one day (*LB–W* 258; *I.Iasos* 166); probably the father of Diouches, son of Deinon (no. 59).

46. Demetrios, son of Alexis: 200 dr. as *choregos* of previous year (*LB–W* 293; *I.Iasos* 192).

47. Demetrios, son of Apollodoros: as former *choregos* paid for the *komoidos* Athenodoros Herakleidou for one day (*LB–W* 257; *I.Iasos* 165).

48. Demetrios, son of Automates: 200 dr. as *choregos* of previous year (*LB–W* 298; *I.Iasos* 197).

49. Demetrios, son of Demetrios, adopted son of Menekles: 200 dr. as *agonothetes* of previous year (*LB–W* 284; *I.Iasos* 199).

50. Diodoros, son of Satyros: 200 dr. (*LB–W* 263; *I.Iasos* 174).

51. Diogenes, son of Melanthos: 200 dr. as *choregos* of previous year (*LB–W* 283; *I.Iasos* 198).

52. Diognetos, son of Diophantos: 200 dr. as *choregos* of previous year (*LB–W* 288; *I.Iasos* 187).

53. Dionysikles, son of Pantainos: 200 dr. (*LB–W* 271; *I.Iasos* 207); separately attested as *agonothetes* in *I.Iasos* 183–4.

54. Dionysios, son of Menippos: 200 dr. as *choregos* of previous year (*LB–W* 294; *I.Iasos* 193).

55. Dionysios, son of Pamphilos: 200 dr. (*LB–W* 264; *I.Iasos* 175).

56. Dionysios, son of [-]nos: 200 dr. as *choregos* of previous year (*I.Iasos* 217).

---

[80] Bryon's name is restored as Βρ⟨ί⟩κων at *I.Iasos* 171, 15–16 (these lines are omitted in *LB–W*), but the letters have been painted in misleadingly on the Clandeboye pilaster and Maddoli (2000) B3, 2–3 (ἀγωνοθέ|[τ]ου Ἀριστονείκου τοῦ Βρύωνος: 'when Aristoneikos, the son of Bryon, was *agonothetes*') now offers the correct form; Aristoneikos, the son of Bryon, may be the son of Bryon, the son of Aristoneikos, although an interval of more than half-a-century separates them.

57. Dionytas, son of Dionysodoros: 200 dr. as *choregos* of previous year (Maddoli 2000: B2).

58. Diotimos, son of Diotimos: 200 dr. as *choregos* of previous year (*LB–W* 287; *I.Iasos* 186).

59. Diouches, son of Deinon: 200 dr. (*LB–W* 262; *I.Iasos* 173).

60. Dorotheos, son of Minnion: 200 dr. [as *agonothetes* of previous year] (*LB–W* 285; *I.Iasos* 200).

61. Drakon, son of Nebrides: 200 dr. as *choregos* of previous year (*LB–W* 286; *I.Iasos* 185).

62. Drakontides, son of Diokles: 200 dr. as *choregos* of previous year (*LB–W* 295; *I.Iasos* 194).

63. Drakontides, son of Hermodoros: 200 dr. as *agonothetes* of previous year (*LB–W* 271; *I.Iasos* 207).

64. Dymas, son of Antipatros: as *choregos* of previous year paid for the *komoidos* Sosylos for one day (*LB–W* 252; *I.Iasos* 160); separately attested as tragic poet honoured twice by the Samothracians (*I.Iasos* 153).

65. Eirenaios, son of Hermias: 200 dr. as *choregos* of previous year (*I.Iasos* 184).

66. Eirenion, son of Sostratos: 200 dr. as *choregos* of previous year (Maddoli 2000: B2).

67. [Eu]damos, son of Kydikles: 200 dr. as *agonothetes* of previous year (*LB–W* 299; *I.Iasos* 214).

68. Euthiades, son of Melanthios: 200 dr. as *agonothetes* of previous year (*LB–W* 262; *I.Iasos* 173); separately attested twice as *stephanephoros* in *LB–W* 267 (*I.Iasos* 204) and 270 (*I.Iasos* 205).

69. Glaukos, son of Aristeas: 200 dr. (*LB–W* 285; *I.Iasos* 200).

70. Glaukos, son of Hybreas: 200 dr. jointly with his brother Menippos (no. 133) and Lysis the son of Phaidros (no. 118) (*LB–W* 261; *I.Iasos* 172); another contribution of 200 dr. (*LB–W* 265; *I.Iasos* 176).

71. Hegemon, son of Po[seidip]pos: 200 dr. as *choregos* of previous year (*LB–W* 297; *I.Iasos* 196).

72. Hekataios, son of Dios[kourides]: 200 dr. (*LB–W* 270; *I.Iasos* 205).

73. Hekataios, son of Menekles: 200 dr. as *choregos* of previous year (Maddoli 2000: B2).

74. Hekataios, son of Ouliades: 200 dr. (*LB–W* 270; *I.Iasos* 205).

75. Helenos, son of Theodotos: 200 dr. probably as *choregos* of previous year; separately attested as current *agonothetes* in same text (*LB–W* 267; *I.Iasos* 204).

76. Heliodotos, son of Aristokritos: 200 dr. as *choregos* of previous year (*LB–W* 295; *I.Iasos* 194).

77. Heraios, son of n.n.: 200 dr. as *choregos* of previous year (*LB–W* 286; *I.Iasos* 185).
78. Herakleitos, son of Phormion: as former *choregos* paid for the *komoidos* Athenodoros (*LB–W* 255; *I.Iasos* 163).
79. Hermaiskos, son of Epigonos: 200 dr. (*LB–W* 262; *I.Iasos* 173).
80. Hermias, son of Leodamas: 200 dr. (*LB–W* 264; *I.Iasos* 175).
81. Hermias, son of Melas: 200 dr. as *choregos* of previous year (*I.Iasos* 184); Hermias, son of Melas, epistates in *I.Iasos* 39, 2–5, may belong to an earlier generation of the same family.
82. Hermias, son of Meno[dot]os: 200 dr. as *choregos* of previous year (*LB–W* 289; *I.Iasos* 188); possibly to be identified, as in *I.Iasos*, with Hermias, son of Menophilos (no. 83).
83. Hermias, son of Menophilos: 200 dr. as *choregos* of previous year (*LB–W* 297; *I.Iasos* 196).
84. Hermodoros, son of Drakontides: 300 dr. pledged as *agonothetes* of previous year (*LB–W* 252; *I.Iasos* 160); probably the father of Drakontides, son of Hermodoros (no. 63).
85. Hermogenes, son of Apollodoros: 200 dr. as *choregos* of previous year (*LB–W* 283; *I.Iasos* 198).
86. Hermogenes, son of Minnion, son of Hermogenes: 200 dr. as *choregos* of previous year (*LB–W* 287; *I.Iasos* 186); separately attested as *strategos* in *I.Iasos* 264, 2.
87. Hermonax, son of Poseidippos: as former *choregos* paid for one stone bench (*LB–W* 256; *I.Iasos* 164); a second contribution of 200 dr. as *agonothetes* of previous year (*LB–W* 267; *I.Iasos* 204).
88. Hierokles, son of n.n.: 200 dr. as *choregos* of previous year (*I.Iasos* 203).
89. Hierokles, son of Phi[lon]: as *choregos* of previous year paid for the *tragoidos* Herakleides for one day (*LB–W* 258; *I.Iasos* 166).
90. Hippokleides, son of Herakleides: 200 dr. pledged perhaps as *agonothetes* of previous year; the payment was made by his children through their *epitropoi* Minnion, son of Menippos, and Pausanias, son of Herakleides, presumably because Hippokleides had died in the interval (*I.Iasos* 184).
91. Hippokrates, son of Dionysi[-]: 200 dr. as *choregos* of previous year (*I.Iasos* 216).
92. Hippokrates, son of Leontiskos: 200 dr. as *choregos* of previous year (*LB–W* 292; *I.Iasos* 191).
93. Hippokrates, son of Metrodoros: as former *choregos* paid for the *komoidos* Athenodoros Herakleidou for one day (*LB–W* 257; *I.Iasos* 165); a second contribution of 200 dr. as *agonothetes* of previous year (*LB–W* 261; *I.Iasos* 172).

94. Hysaldomos, son of Antigonos: 200 dr. as *agonothetes* of previous year (*I.Iasos* 215).

95. Iason, son of Aretaios, natural son of Menippos: 200 dr. (*LB–W* 263; *I.Iasos* 174).

96. Iason, son of Proteas: 200 dr. as *choregos* of previous year (*I.Iasos* 201).

97. Isidoros, son of Menestheus: 200 dr. as *choregos* of previous year (*I.Iasos* 215); brother of Menestheus (no. 130) and Aristokritos (no. 33).

98. Kallimedes, son of Plousion: 200 dr. as *agonothetes* of previous year (*LB–W* 283; *I.Iasos* 198).

99. Kleainetos, son of Kleanax: 200 dr. (*LB–W* 271; *I.Iasos* 207).

100. Kleanax, son of Kleainetos: as former *agonothetes* paid for the *komoidos* Athenodoros (*LB–W* 255; *I.Iasos* 163); probably father of Kleainetos, son of Kleanax (no. 99).

101. Kleanax, son of Theokles: as former *choregos* paid for the *tragoidos* Lykophron (*LB–W* 256; *I.Iasos* 164); separately attested as *stephanephoros* (*LB–W* 259–66; *I.Iasos* 170–7).

102. Kleon, son of Antinikos: 200 dr. (*LB–W* 264; *I.Iasos* 175).

103. Ktesias, son of Metrodoros: as former *choregos* paid for the *komoidos* Athenodoros (*LB–W* 255; *I.Iasos* 163).

104. Kydias, son of Hierokles: as *agonothetes* paid for the Boiotian *auletes* Mnasias Pyrrilou; also met the costs of the procession, sacrifices and perquisites of Dionysos (*LB–W* 253; *I.Iasos* 161); as *stephanephoros* paid for the *kitharistes* Pythion and *auletes* Nikokles (*LB–W* 254; *I.Iasos* 162).

105. Kydias, son of Menexenos: as *agonothetes* jointly paid for the *komoidos* Eukles, son of Iambos, for two days (*LB–W* 284; *I.Iasos* 199); separately attested as *stephanephoros* in *LB–W* 286 (*I.Iasos* 185); possibly the son of the Iasian ambassador Menexenos, son of Kydias, in *I.Priene* 53, 37 (190s BC).

106. Kydias, son of Poseidippos: former *choregos*, paid for one stone bench (*LB–W* 256; *I.Iasos* 164).

107. Kydikles, son of Kydikles: contributed 500 dr. to the construction of the theatre (*I.Iasos* 183).

108. Kydikles, son of Lysen: 200 dr. as *agonothetes* of previous year (*LB–W* 266; *I.Iasos* 177).

109. Lachares, son of Athenodoros: 200 dr. (*LB–W* 261; *I.Iasos* 172).

110. Leon, son of Demetrios: as *choregos* paid for the *kitharistes* Apollonios Theogenou from Myndos (*LB–W* 253; *I.Iasos* 161).

111. Leon, son of Iason: as former *choregos* paid for the *komoidos* Athenodoros (*LB–W* 256; *I.Iasos* 164).

112. Leon, son of Menon (patronymic given as Menoitas in *LB–W* 297; *I.Iasos* 196): 200 dr. as *agonothetes* of previous year (*LB–W* 298; *I.Iasos* 197).

113. Leon, son of n.n.: 200 dr. as *choregos* of previous year (*I.Iasos* 216).

114. Leontiades, son of Herakleides, natural son of Demeas: 200 dr. (*LB–W* 267; *I.Iasos* 204); a second contribution of 200 dr. as *stephanephoros* of previous year (Maddoli 2000: B2). Leontiades seems to have been *stephanephoros* twice (see Appendix 2 below).

115. Leontiades, son of Hermias: 200 dr. as *choregos* of previous year (*LB–W* 286; *I.Iasos* 185).

116. Leontiskos, son of Hippokrates: 200 dr. as *choregos* of previous year (*I.Iasos* 217); probably father of Hippokrates, son of Leontiskos (no. 92).

117. Limnaios, son of Eudoros: 200 dr. as *agonothetes* of previous year (*LB–W* 292; *I.Iasos* 191).

118. Lysis, son of Phaidros (grandson of Hybreas, the son of Menippos): 200 dr. jointly with Glaukos, the son of Hybreas (no. 70) and the latter's brother Menippos (no. 133) (*LB–W* 261; *I.Iasos* 172).

119. Mandron, son of Phanokritos: as former *choregos* paid for the *komoidos* Athenodoros Herakleidou for one day (*LB–W* 257; *I.Iasos* 165).

120. Melanippos, son of Ephesios: 200 dr. (*LB–W* 259; *I.Iasos* 170).

121. Melanthios, son of Melanippos: 200 dr. as *choregos* of previous year (*LB–W* 298; *I.Iasos* 197).

122. Melas, son of Pollis: 200 dr. (*LB–W* 263; *I.Iasos* 174).

123. Menedemos, son of Artemon: as *choregos* paid for the *kitharistes* Eualkes (*LB–W* 252; *I.Iasos* 160); probably brother of Menon (no. 139).

124. Menedemos, son of Menedemos, son of Damokrates: 200 dr. as *agonothetes* of previous year (*LB–W* 289; *I.Iasos* 188).

125. Menedemos, son of Menekrates: 200 dr. as *choregos* of previous year (*LB–W* 294; *I.Iasos* 193).

126. Menekles, son of Antipatros: 200 dr. as *choregos* of previous year (*LB–W* 292; *I.Iasos* 191).

127. Menekles, son of Hekataios: 200 dr. (*LB–W* 266; *I.Iasos* 177).

128. Menekles, son of Hierokles: as *choregos* paid for the *auloidos* Metaneiros for two days (*LB–W* 254; *I.Iasos* 162).

129. Menestheus, son of Isidoros: 200 dr. as *agonothetes* of previous year (*I.Iasos* 216); probably the father rather than the son of Isidoros, son of Menestheus (no. 97).

130. Menestheus, son of Menestheus: 200 dr. as *choregos* of previous year (*I.Iasos* 215); brother of Aristokritos (no. 33) and Isidoros (no. 97).

131. Menexenos, son of Poseidippos: 200 dr. (*LB–W* 260; *I.Iasos* 171); a second contribution of 200 dr. [as *agonothetes* of previous year] (*LB–W* 268; *I.Iasos* 206).

132. Menippos, son of Aristeus: 200 dr. as *choregos* of previous year (*LB–W* 284; *I.Iasos* 199).

133. Menippos, son of Hybreas: 200 dr. jointly with Glaukos, son of Hybreas (no. 70) and Lysis, son of Phaidros (no. 118) (*LB–W* 261; *I.Iasos* 172).

134. Meniskos, son of Drakon, son of Meniskos: 200 dr. as *agonothetes* of previous year, with a second contribution of 200 dr. as *choregos* of previous year (*LB–W* 296; *I.Iasos* 195).

135. Menitas, son of Maiandrios: as former *choregos* paid for the *komoidos* Athenodoros (*LB–W* 255; *I.Iasos* 163).

136. Menodotos, son of Apollonios: 200 dr. as *choregos* of previous year (*LB–W* 286; *I.Iasos* 185).

137. Menoitios, son of Hierokles: as *choregos* paid for the *kitharistes* Apollonios Theogenou from Myndos (*LB–W* 253; *I.Iasos* 161); separately attested as *epistates* of the *prytaneis* in *I.Iasos* 4, 36–9.

138. Menoitios, son of Satyrion: 200 dr. as *choregos* of previous year (*LB–W* 298; *I.Iasos* 197).

139. Menon, son of Artemon: as *choregos* paid for the *kitharistes* Eualkes (*LB–W* 252; *I.Iasos* 160); probably brother of Menedemos (no. 123).

140. Menotimos, son of Podon: 200 dr. as *choregos* of previous year (*LB–W* 294; *I.Iasos* 193).

141. Metris, son of Metris: 200 dr. as *choregos* of previous year (*LB–W* 283; *I.Iasos* 198).

142. Metrodoros, son of Menophilos: 200 dr. as *agonothetes* of previous year (*LB–W* 288; *I.Iasos* 187).

143. Metrophantos, son of Demophon: 200 dr. (*LB–W* 263; *I.Iasos* 174).

144. Metrophantos, son of Eudamis: 200 dr. as *choregos* of previous year (*LB–W* 286; *I.Iasos* 185).

145. Mnesitheos, son of Athenodoros, natural son of Menedemos: 200 dr. as *agonothetes* of previous year (*LB–W* 294; *I.Iasos* 193).

146. Moschion, son of Antiphon: as *agonothetes* of previous year paid for the *auletes* Nikon for one day (*LB–W* 258; *I.Iasos* 166).

147. Moschos, son of Aglaophon, natural son of Menedemos: 200 dr. as *choregos* of previous year (*LB–W* 284; *I.Iasos* 199).

148. Moschos, son of Moschos: 200 dr. [as *agonothetes* of previous year] (*LB–W* 270; *I.Iasos* 205).

149. Nemertes, son of Theotimos: paid for the *kitharistes* Eualkes in fulfilment of pledge made as *stephanephoros* of previous year (*LB–W* 252; *I.Iasos* 160).

150. Noumenios, son of Noumenios, son of Sosibios: 200 dr. (*LB–W* 285; *I.Iasos* 200).

151. Nysios, son of Ktesikles: 200 dr. as *choregos* of previous year (*LB–W* 283; *I.Iasos* 198); a second contribution of 200 dr. as *agonothetes* of previous year (Maddoli 2000: B3).

152. Obrimos, son of Ktesiphon: 200 dr. (*LB–W* 270; *I.Iasos* 205).

153. Olympiodoros, son of Phi[lon]: as *agonothetes* paid for the *tragoidos* Herakleides for one day (*LB–W* 258; *I.Iasos* 166); Olym[piodoros Philonos] is also partially restored as a former *choregos* paying for a second day's performance by Herakleides (*LB–W* 258; *I.Iasos* 166); probably the father of Philon, son of Olympiodoros (no. **159**).

154. Omphalion, son of Euboulides: 200 dr. as *agonothetes* of previous year (*LB–W* 264; *I.Iasos* 175); a second contribution of 200 dr. as *stephanephoros* of previous year (*LB–W* 272; *I.Iasos* 208).

155. Onatas, son of Menophilos: 200 dr. (*LB–W* 285; *I.Iasos* 200).

156. Ouliades, son of Athenagoras: 200 dr. as *choregos* of previous year (*LB–W* 298; *I.Iasos* 197).

157. Pantainos, son of Hierokles: as *stephanephoros* paid for the Boiotian *auletes* Mnasias Pyrrilou (*LB–W* 253; *I.Iasos* 161); subsequently as *agonothetes* paid for the Boiotian *auletes* Satyros Aristokleious for two days (*LB–W* 255; *I.Iasos* 163).

158. Philokles, son of Aristeas: 200 dr. (*LB–W* 259; *I.Iasos* 170); a second contribution of 200 dr. as *agonothetes* of previous year (*LB–W* 260; *I.Iasos* 171); probably the father of Aristeas, son of Philokles (no. **26**).

159. Philon, son of Olympiodoros: 200 dr. (*LB–W* 270; *I.Iasos* 205).

160. Phrixos, son of Satyros: 200 dr. (*LB–W* 285; *I.Iasos* 200).

161. Pixodaros, son of Pixodaros: 200 dr. (*LB–W* 268; *I.Iasos* 206).

162. Polemarchos, son of Artemon: 200 dr. (*LB–W* 259; *I.Iasos* 170); a second contribution of 200 dr. as *agonothetes* of previous year (Maddoli 2000: B2).

163. Polyainos, son of Dorotheos: 200 dr. (*LB–W* 260; *I.Iasos* 171).

164. Polygnotos, son of Demophon: 200 dr. (*LB–W* 266; *I.Iasos* 177).

165. Porphyros, son of Porphyros: 200 dr. (*LB–W* 268; *I.Iasos* 206).

166. Poseidippos, son of Symmachos: 200 dr. (*LB–W* 262; *I.Iasos* 173).

167. Posittas, son of Aristokrates: contributed 500 dr. to the construction of the theatre (*I.Iasos* 183),

168. Pyrgion, son of Pyrgion: 200 dr. as *choregos* of previous year (*I.Iasos* 201).

169. Pyron, son of Lasios: 200 dr. (*LB–W* 259; *I.Iasos* 170).

170. Pythion, son of Parmeniskos, adopted son of Hermaiskos: 200 dr. as *choregos* of previous year (*LB–W* 272; *I.Iasos* 208).

171. Python, son of Skylax: as former *choregos* paid for the *choropsaltria* Kleino Euandrou for two days (*LB–W* 257; *I.Iasos* 165).

172. P[...]tes, son of Theudotos: contributed 1500 dr. to the construction of the theatre (*I.Iasos* 182).

173. Samios, son of Eupolemos: 200 dr. as *choregos* of previous year (Maddoli 2000: B3).

174. Simalos, son of Kydias: 200 dr. as *agonothetes* of previous year (*LB–W* 293; *I.Iasos* 192).

175. Simalos, son of Laios, possibly the same man as Simalos, son of Limnaios (no. **176**): 200 dr. as *choregos* of previous year (*LB–W* 286; *I.Iasos* 185).

176. Simalos, son of Limnaios: 200 dr. as *agonothetes* of previous year (*LB–W* 272; *I.Iasos* 208); a second contribution of 200 dr. as *choregos* of previous year (*LB–W* 272; *I.Iasos* 208).

177. Sopatros, son of Epikrates: 200 dr. [as *agonothetes* of previous year], (*LB–W* 259; *I.Iasos* 170). Additionally made major contribution to the repair of the supporting wall of the theatre, a segment of seating and the *bema* (*LB–W* 269; *I.Iasos* 249). Separately attested as *stephanephoros* (*LB–W* 268; *I.Iasos* 206), as well as former *choregos* (*LB–W* 269; *I.Iasos* 249), and gymnasiarchos and dedicator of a stoa (*I.Iasos* 250).

178. Sopatros, son of [-]seas: 200 dr. as *choregos* of previous year (*LB–W* 272; *I.Iasos* 208).

179. Sostratides, son of Sostratos: 200 dr. (*LB–W* 271; *I.Iasos* 207).

180. Sotadas, son of Nikaristos: 200 dr. as *choregos* of previous year (*LB–W* 288; *I.Iasos* 187).

181. Stesiochos, son of Demeas, adopted son of Pheretimos: 200 dr. (*LB–W* 270; *I.Iasos* 205); possibly, son of the *stephanephoros* Demeas, son of Stesiochos (*I.Iasos* 150, mid-210s BC).

182. Taurion, son of Hekataios: as former *choregos* paid for the *komoidos* Athenodoros (*LB–W* 256; *I.Iasos* 164).

183. Telesias, son of Te[lesias]: 200 dr. as *choregos* of previous year (*LB–W* 289; *I.Iasos* 188).

184. Thalieuktos, son of Antiphon: 200 dr. (*LB–W* 265; *I.Iasos* 176).

185. Theaitetos, son of Melanion: as *agonothetes* of previous year paid for the *komoidos* Athenodoros Herakleidou for one day (*LB–W* 257; *I.Iasos* 165); also paid for [the same] *komoidos* for one day as former *choregos* (*LB–W* 257; *I.Iasos* 165).

186. Theodoros, son of Laios: 200 dr. as *choregos* of previous year (*LB–W* 293; *I.Iasos* 192).

187. Theodoros, son of Melanion: 200 dr. as *agonothetes* of previous year (*LB–W* 295; *I.Iasos* 194); a second contribution of 200 dr. as *choregos* of previous year (*LB–W* 295; *I.Iasos* 194); separately attested as secretary of the *strategoi* in *I.Iasos* 264, 7–8.

188. Theodotos, son of Theodotos, son of Timarchos: 200 dr. as *choregos* of previous year (*LB–W* 284; *I.Iasos* 199).

189. Theodotos, son of Theodotos: 200 dr. as *choregos* of previous year (*LB–W* 295; *I.Iasos* 194).

190. Theophilos, son of Anaxippos: 200 dr. as *choregos* of previous year (*LB–W* 294; *I.Iasos* 193).

191. The[-], son of [-]teros (?): 200 dr. as *choregos* of previous year (*I.Iasos* 184).

192. Thraseas, son of Asandros: 200 dr. (*LB–W* 266; *I.Iasos* 177).

193. Xenokrates, son of Apatourios: 200 dr. as *choregos* of previous year (*LB–W* 288; *I.Iasos* 187).

194. Zoilos, son of Mneseas: 200 dr. as *agonothetes* of previous year (*LB–W* 290; *I.Iasos* 189).

195. [-]anos, son of Hermokrates: 200 dr. (*LB–W* 280; *I.Iasos* 212).

196. [-]demos, son of n.n.: [200 dr.] (*LB–W* 280; *I.Iasos* 212).

197. [-]enes, son of Apollas: 200 dr. as *choregos* of previous year (*I.Iasos* 202).

198. [-]tios, son of Eikadion: 200 dr. as *choregos* of previous year (Maddoli 2000: B3).

199. n.n., son of Androklos: [200 dr.] as *choregos* of previous year (*I.Iasos* 203).

200. n.n., son of Apollodoros: 200 dr. as *agonothetes* of previous year (*I.Iasos* 202).

201. n.n., son of Aristokrates: 200 dr. as *choregos* of previous year (*I.Iasos* 216).

202. n.n., son of Demetrios: 200 dr. as *choregos* of previous year (*LB–W* 291; *I.Iasos* 190).

203. n.n., son of Hierokles (Maddoli 2000: B1).

204. n.n., son of n.n., son of Diokles: 200 dr. as *choregos* of previous year (*LB–W* 291; *I.Iasos* 190).

205. n.n., son of Obrimos: 200 dr. (?) (*LB–W* 273; *I.Iasos* 209).

206. n.n., son of [-]onos: 200 dr. as *choregos* of previous year (*I.Iasos* 202).

Metic contributors:

207. Agathinos, son of Leon (Apameia): 100 dr. (*LB–W* 294; *I.Iasos* 193).

208. Agathoboulos, son of Dionysios (Alinda): 100 dr. (*LB–W* 262; *I.Iasos* 173).
209. Agathokles, son of Hierokles (metic): as former *choregos* paid for the *komoidos* Athenodorus Herakleidou for one day (*LB–W* 257; *I.Iasos* 165).
210. Apollonios, son of Bion (metic): former *choregos*, paid for the *choropsaltria* Kleino Euandrou for two days (*LB–W* 257; *I.Iasos* 165).
211. Apollonios, son of Phanokritos (metic): former *choregos*, paid for the *komoidos* Theodoros (*LB–W* 256; *I.Iasos* 164).
212. Asklepiades, son of Hipponikos (Phaselis): 100 dr. (*LB–W* 264; *I.Iasos* 175).
213. Damotheos, son of Alexandrides (Myrina): 100 dr. (*LB–W* 293; *I.Iasos* 192).
214. Demetrios, son of Zotikos: 100 dr. (*I.Iasos* 216).
215. [Demo]phon?, son of Polytimos (Antiocheia): 100 dr. (*LB–W* 295; *I.Iasos* 194).
216. Diogenes, son of Menandros (Berytos): 100 dr. (Maddoli 2000: B3).
217. Diogenes, son of [T]anybotos (?) (Kallatis): 100 dr. (*LB–W* 298; *I.Iasos* 197).
218. Dionysios, son of Antigonos (Alabanda): 100 dr. (*LB–W* 264; *I.Iasos* 175).
219. Dionysios, son of Nikanor (Hierapolis): 100 dr. (*LB–W* 286; *I.Iasos* 185).
220. Dioskourides, son of Apollonios (Sinope): 100 dr. (*LB–W* 288; *I.Iasos* 187).
221. Dromeas, son of Theodoros (Neaiton): 100 dr. (*LB–W* 263; *I.Iasos* 174).
222. Eirenaios, son of Mandrogenes (Magnesia): 100 dr. (*LB–W* 265; *I.Iasos* 176).
223. Epinikos, son of Aristeas (Lysimacheia): 100 dr. (*I.Iasos* 184).
224. Euchares, son of Chares (Apameia): 100 dr. (*LB–W* 297; *I.Iasos* 196).
225. Euenemos, son of Apollonios (Marathos): 100 dr. (*LB–W* 285; *I.Iasos* 200).
226. Hekataios, son of Athenodoros (Stratonikeia): former *choregos*, paid for the *komoidos* Theodoros (*LB–W* 256; *I.Iasos* 164).
227. Hekataios, son of Menogenes (Laodikeia): 100 dr. (*LB–W* 297; *I.Iasos* 196).
228. Hekataios, son of Zonios (Thrace): 100 dr. (*LB–W* 292; *I.Iasos* 191).
229. Herakleitos, son of Kallisthenes (Magnesia-on-the-Maeander): 100 dr. (*LB–W* 285; *I.Iasos* 200).

230. Hermias, son of n.n. (incomplete ethnic: [-]nos): 100 dr. (*LB–W* 280; *I.Iasos* 212).

231. Hermon, son of Agathokles (Antiocheia by Daphne): 100 dr. (*LB–W* 261; *I.Iasos* 172).

232. Hierokles, son of Hierokles (Myndos): [100 dr.] (*I.Iasos* 215).

233. Iason, son of Drakon (Euromos): 100 dr. (Maddoli 2000: B3).

234. Iason, son of Hekatonymos (metic): former *choregos*, paid for the *auloidos* Metaneiros (*LB–W* 256; *I.Iasos* 164)

235. Kasios, son of Ariston (Seleukeia): 100 dr. (*LB–W* 265; *I.Iasos* 176).

236. Kineas, son of Protoarchos (Tralles beyond the Tauros): 100 dr. (*LB–W* 287; *I.Iasos* 186).

237. Libanos, son of Amphikles (Myndos): 100 dr. (*LB–W* 263; *I.Iasos* 174).

238. Lysimachos, son of Iason (Antiocheia): 100 dr. (*I.Iasos* 201).

239. Melas, son of Demetriou (Euromos): 100 dr. (*LB–W* 283; *I.Iasos* 198).

240. Menekrates, son of Demetrios (Laodikeia) (*LB–W* 284; *I.Iasos* 199).

241. Menekrates, son of Hermias (Mylasa): 100 dr. (*LB–W* 271; *I.Iasos* 207).

242. Menes, son of Papiades (Alinda): 100 dr. (*LB–W* 293; *I.Iasos* 192).

243. Menoitas, son of Proteus (Alinda): 100 dr. (*LB–W* 288; *I.Iasos* 187).

244. Menoitios, son of Demetrios (incomplete ethnic: [-]seus): 100 dr. (*I.Iasos* 217).

245. Menophilos, son of Dionysios (Mallos): 100 dr. (*LB–W* 283; *I.Iasos* 198).

246. Neon, son of Pythagoras (Phokaia): 100 dr. (*LB–W* 266; *I.Iasos* 177).

247. Nikanor, son of Diophantos (Antiocheia): (*LB–W* 284; *I.Iasos* 199).

248. Niketas, son of Iason (Jerusalem): 100 dr. (*LB–W* 294; *I.Iasos* 193).

249. Nikon, son of n.n. (Achaia): 100 dr. (*LB–W* 272; *I.Iasos* 208).

250. Nous, son of Demetrios (Antiocheia by Daphne): 100 dr. (*I.Iasos* 184).

251. Nymphon, son of Archagathos (Syracuse): 100 dr. (*LB–W* 266; *I.Iasos* 177).

252. Pileos, son of Philistides (Kyme): 100 dr. (*LB–W* 292; *I.Iasos* 191).

253. Poseidonios, son of Bennetos (Herakleia Pontica): 100 dr. (*LB–W* 287; *I.Iasos* 186).

254. Protos, son of Dionysios (Antiocheia): 100 dr. (*LB–W* 268; *I.Iasos* 206).

255. Pythes, son of Aristeides (Bithynia): 100 dr. (*LB–W* 298; *I.Iasos* 197).

256. Sosibios, son of Apolloniou (Seleukeia): 100 dr. (*I.Iasos* 217).

257. Sosilos, son of Protoarchos (Tralles): 100 dr. (*LB–W* 295; *I.Iasos* 194).

258. Symmachos, son of Demarchos (Antiocheia): 100 dr. (*LB–W* 289; *I.Iasos* 188).

259. Thal[-], son of n.n. (metic): 100 dr. (*I.Iasos* 202).

260. Theodoros, son of Theodoros (Alinda): 100 dr. (*LB–W* 289; *I.Iasos* 188).

261. Theodotos, son of [-]mos (incomplete ethnic: M[-]) (*LB–W* 284; *I.Iasos* 199).
262. [-]imos, son of Sannos (Amyzon): 100 dr. (Maddoli 2000: B2).
263. n.n., son of Amphikles (metic): 100 dr. (*LB–W* 274; *I.Iasos* 178).
264. n.n., son of Demetrios (Mylasa): 100 dr. (*I.Iasos* 202).
265. n.n., son of Nikoteles (metic): 100 dr. (*LB–W* 270; *I.Iasos* 205).
266. n.n., son of Philon (Selge): 100 dr. (*LB–W* 278; *I.Iasos* 210).

Appendix 2: The Chronology of the Theatre Lists

The recent publication of three new lists of contributors (Maddoli 2000) requires some modifications to the chronology of second-century Iasian *stephanephoroi* proposed in Crowther 1990.[81] The suggestion there that the name of the *agonothetes* of *LB–W* 275 (*I.Iasos* 179), Poseidippos, the son of An[-], may have been misread by Le Bas and that this text should belong to the same second stephanephorate of Apollo after Leontiades, the son of Herakleides, as *I.Iasos* 182, although the *agonothetes* in the latter is Panatainos Hestiaou, now seems unlikely to be correct since one of the new texts published by Maddoli records a different *agonothetes* for the year in which Leontiades was *stephanephoros* (Maddoli 2000: B2, 4–5: Polemarchos, son of Artemon, Appendix 1 no. **162**) from that in *LB–W* 274 (*I.Iasos* 178), which has Aristides, the son of Menekrates (Appendix 1 no. **28**).[82] It seems to follow that Leontiades, the adopted son of Herakleides (Appendix 1 no. **114**) was *stephanephoros* twice and that on both occasions his tenure was followed by a sequence of years in which Apollo was eponym. The relative sequence of the two series of years dated from Leontiades' separate stephanephorates cannot be determined with certainty, but it seems very likely that the five lists inscribed on the dressed course of the *parodos* wall (*LB–W* 273–7; *I.Iasos* 209, 178–81) preceded Maddoli 2000: B2 and *I.Iasos* 182. *I.Iasos* 182 was inscribed below two texts belonging to the year of Hermias, the son of Aristeas (*I.Iasos* 184, 183) and closely followed by a list of contributors dated to the year of Astiades, son of Pindaros, which itself is the first of a sequence of at least seven years,[83] closely followed by a further series of seventeen years, beginning with the stephanephorate of Kleanax, the son of Kleanax.[84]

---

[81] Restated with qualifications in Crowther (1995b).

[82] A full discussion in Maurizi (2000) 49–63.

[83] Astiades, son of Pindaros (*I.Iasos* 202), Apollo after Astiades, Apollo for [the second time] after Astiades (*I.Iasos* 203), Menes, son of Tyrtaios (*I.Iasos* 217), Apollo after Menes, Apollo for the second time after Menes, Apollo for the third time after Menes (*LB–W* 281; *I.Iasos* 152).

[84] In my 1990 article I followed *LB–W* in restoring the date of *LB–W* 284 (*I.Iasos* 199) as the third(?) year of Apollo after Kleanax. Whatever may have been inscribed on the stone, however, it is clear from the *agonothetes* contributor named in *LB–W* 284 (Demetrios, the son of Demetrios, Appendix 1 no. **49**) that it belongs to the second year of Apollo after Kleanax and that the list for the third year of Apollo is

The confirmation that there was a second stephanephorate of Leontiades, the son of Herakleides, introduces an additional series of at least three consecutive years and requires a number of other rearrangements to the table of second-century Iasian *stephanephoroi* in Crowther (1990). On the assumption that *LB–W* 273–7 (*I.Iasos* 209, 178–81) preceded Maddoli 2000: B2 and *I.Iasos* 182, they should also precede *I.Iasos* 183–4 (stephanephorate of Hermias, the son of Aristeas). *LB–W* 278–80 (*I.Iasos* 210–12), which were inscribed alongside them on the dressed course of blocks on the *parodos* wall, should also precede *I.Iasos* 183–4.

Earlier in the sequence of *stephanephoroi*, two additional years (of Hierokles, the son of Iason, already known from *I.Iasos* 25, and Basilides, the son of L[-]) attested in *SEG* 41, 930–2 are likely to belong between the eponymous years attested on the front and left faces of the Clandeboye pilaster.[85] To them I would also add the *stephanephoros* of *I.Iasos* 76 ([-] the son of Apollonios), which now seems to me on palaeographical grounds to belong after the peace of Apameia rather than in the aftermath of the Iasians' engagement with Olympichos.[86]

A further eponymous year, for the second year of Apollo after Theaitetos, is added towards the end of the list of second-century *stephanephoroi* by the last of the new theatre texts published by G. Maddoli (Maddoli 2000: B3). This list can be added to a sequence of texts from the *parodos* wall recording contributions in the years of Hekataios, the son of Antigenes, Theaitetos, the son of Theaitetos, for the second time, and Apollo, after Theaitetos (*LB–W* 296–8; *I.Iasos* 195–7).[87]

missing or was omitted. The continuous sequence of *stephanephoros* years from Kleanax, son of Kleanax (*LB–W* 282; *I.Iasos* 213) to the second year of Apollo after Antigonos, the son of Antigonos (*LB–W* 295; *I.Iasos* 194), accordingly, extends to seventeen years, rather than sixteen as argued in Crowther (1990).

[85] So Crowther (1995b) 233–4.

[86] So Crowther (1995a) 109–12, but I have since been able to examine the squeeze of the inscription in the epigraphical collection of the Institute for Advanced Studies at Princeton, and its lettering is so different from the proxeny decree for Olympichos inscribed immediately above it on the same stone (*I.Iasos* 35) that a later date seems more appropriate. I am grateful to Christian Habicht and Glen Bowersock for the opportunity to examine the squeeze.

[87] The context and interpretation of Maddoli (2000) B1 remain unclear, in spite of the detailed and careful study by Maurizi (2000) 45–9. The edition of B1 in Maddoli (2000) omits a line of text between ll. 4–5.

12

An Opisthographic Lead Tablet from
Sicily with a Financial Document
and a Curse Concerning *choregoi**

David Jordan

For Anne Miller Zartarian, its pioneer editor

Here I present a reading, from autopsy, of an unusually interesting
lead tablet of the earlier fifth century from southeast Sicily, which
is now in the Rare Book Room of the Library of the University of
North Carolina at Chapel Hill. It is opisthographic, both sides
inscribed in West Greek, one bearing a record, in the 'blue' alphabet
(+ = *chi*), of a financial transaction that took place in the presence
evidently of a *proxenos*, the guarantor being one Apellis. This Apellis
later writes, or causes to be written, on the other side and in the
earlier 'red' alphabet (↓ = *chi*), a magical curse to ensure ἐπὶ τᾶι
φιλότατι τᾶι Εὐνίϟο, 'because of his love/friendship for Eunikos',
that this Eunikos, a *choregos*, shall defeat other *choregoi* in a
competition.

If it is like other early lead curse tablets, this tablet, with its curse,
would have been deposited in a grave or a chthonic shrine and therefore presumably not reused. The financial document, despite its
later alphabet, is therefore no doubt the earlier of the two texts;
this side I call *A*. Its later 'blue' alphabet was no doubt the official

* I am grateful to Dr Zartarian for encouraging my study of this tablet. All dates
are BC.

chancery style, adopted evidently fairly recently. For the curse, on what I call Side *B*, its writer used the older alphabet with which he was more familiar, learned before the official introduction of the 'blue' alphabet. Because most southeast Sicilian cities that made the change from the 'red' to the 'blue' alphabet did so around the 470s, this is the earliest period to which the financial document can be assigned.

Anne P. Miller (now Zartarian), with only a hand-held magnifying glass at her disposal, first edited the tablet as her doctoral dissertation (1973). Her texts of both sides have been reproduced, with a few different interpretations, by Laurent Dubois (*IGDS* 134) and, unchanged, that of Side *A* by R. Arena[1] and H. Van Effenterre and F. Ruzé,[2] that of Side *B* by M. del Amor López-Jimeno.[3] With a binocular stereoscopic microscope I was able to derive fuller readings, especially of Side *B*. A significant advance for the understanding of *A* has been William West's study of *A* 7, his report of which (1997: see note on *A* 2 below) includes my transcription of both sides, with his own punctuation and supplements, including Miller's Ἀνθ]εμόκριτος in *A* 2. G. Manganaro,[4] using that transcription, has recently printed the text of *A* again, restoring and punctuating differently. Here I give my transcriptions once more, this time with my own comments.

The dealer from whom the tablet was bought stated that it came from a grave in southeast Sicily. For the letter forms, see Miller and West; for matters of dialect, Miller and Dubois. On the basis of its letter forms and dialect Miller concluded that certainly Side *B* and possibly *A* were inscribed in Gela, around the middle of the fifth century. West maintains Miller's date but, arguing also from letter forms, proposes Kamarina as the provenance of at least Side *A*.

Rare Book Room	height 0.062, width 0.171 m	Side *A*, *c*. 470 BC or slightly later
University of North Carolina at Chapel Hill		Side *B*, not long afterwards?

---

[1] Arena (1992) 36 no. 80.   [2] Van Effenterre and Ruzé (1995) 36 no. 50.
[3] López-Jimeno (1991) 110–31 no. 17.   [4] Manganaro (2004) 65f.

SIDE A

The tablet is complete at its top, bottom, and right-hand edges. The right-hand edge of the textblock is rather ragged. There is certainly one division within a word at line-end, 3/4 ξέ/[-], and 4/5 Σ/[-] may show a division within a numerical expression.

1 (Hand II) [Μ]ύσκον Δάμιος τοῦ Κοβέτου. *vacat c. 7*
2 (Hand I) [Δ]εμόκριτος ἐφίετο Ἀπέλιλν ἐνγυάσασθαι. *vacat c. 4*
3 [há]μα δὲ ἔφα εἴμειν. κατελάζετο τὸν Λεοντίνον ξέ-
4 [νον] Μύσκονα ἐν τᾶι πλατεία<ι> θοκέοντα. Σ- *vacat c. 4*
5 [ΣΣ?] ἀργυρίον ἔχον hῖκε βοὸν τιμάν. οὐκ ἐπρίατο
6 [δὲ·] ποτ' Ἐνπεδοκλêν Μνασιμάχου ποτεν<ε>θετο. *vacat c. 2*
7 (Hand II) γενέσθο ἐν[γ]υάσασθαι. *vacat c. 20*
        vacat

1 :του, vertical at left of υ   Κοβέτου, left-hand descender of υ doubled   2 Ἀπέλιλν: horizontal, apparently inadvertent, in centre of first Λ: Ἀπέλλιν   4/5 Σ/[ΣΣ]? Σ/[ΣΣΣ]?   6 Μνασιμαχου: left-hand descender of 2nd A doubled

1 Κορέτου for Κοβ- Manganaro 2 Ἀνθ]εμόκριτος Miller, Dubois Ἀπέλ⟨λ⟩·⟦ν⟧ Miller, Ἀπέλ(λ){ε}⟨ι⟩ν Dubois 3 μαδε ἔφα Miller, [há]μαδε Jeffery *apud* Miller, .A..IOA Dubois, [σô]μα Manganaro 3/4 Λεοντίνον ξε/[ ] Miller, Λεοντῖνον/[ ] Dubois, Λεοντῖνον Ξε/[?νιν] Manganaro 4/5 θοκέοντας/[ ] Miller, Dubois; θοκέοντας· /[οὐκ]Manganaro 5 hῖκε, βοὸν τιμᾶν Manganaro 6 .αι ποτ' Miller, [ ] ποτ' Dubois, α̣ὶ ποτ' Manganaro   ποτένθετο 'went' Miller, ποτένθε το Dubois, ποτενθέτο West, ποτένθει Manganaro

(Hand II) Myskon (son) of Damis the (son) of Kobetos.
(Hand I) Demokritos asked Apellis to be guarantor. And at the same time he (*sc.* Apellis) said he was. He (Apellis?) found the *proxenos* of the (people of) Leontinoi, Myskon, sitting in the *plateia*. He came having three (?) staters of silver, (as) cattle price. He did not buy, however: with Empedokles son of Mnasimachos he made a deposit.
(Hand II) Let this be the guarantee.

1. The first line is in larger letters than the rest of the text. Here we evidently have a label, for the filing of the document. Myskon, identified with patronym and presumably papponym, has, in his capacity as *proxenos* (3–4) for visitors/metics from Leontinoi, over-seen their financial transactions, whose minutes need to be filed in the public archives. Such minutes form the text of *A* 2–6, evidently in the hand of a court recorder or such, the label in *A* 1, evidently in the hand of the archivist, showing where in the archives the tablet is to be kept—in the files of Myskon—and *A* 7, evidently again in the same archivist's hand, certifying that the minutes are acceptable for the official record and are now on file. Side *A* of the tablet is presumably an official copy given to the guarantor of the transaction, Apellis. This interpretation is based on a number of assumptions, and other interpretations may of course be envisaged. (Miller assumed a lawsuit between [Anth]emokritos and Myskon, Van Effenterre and Ruzé an 'imprécation contre un parténaire malhonnête' and translate *A* 7 '… que [le malheur?] arrive [à qui?] se porterait garant!'; but this was before the lengths of the left-hand lacunae could be estimated. West: 'I reconstruct as follows: Myskon is one of the litigants. He deposes to the facts of the case. Anthemokritos (the judge?) bade Apelles provide surety. He (the defendant?) came upon the host of the Leontines, Myskon, sitting along the avenue. He came with money, the price of the cattle, but he did not buy (i.e. the cattle). [Direct Discourse] "Let him go to Empedokles son of Mnasimachos. Let him provide surety." The dispute involves an agreement in which a contract of sale was aborted. The litigant seeks to enforce it.' Manganaro: 'Myskon figlio di Damis, figlio di Koretos. / Anthemocrito [?] ha indotto Apellis a prestare garanzia, / ma (Apellis) uno schiavo disse di essere, egli (Anthemocrito?) convinse il leontineo Xenis (?) (come garante) / per Myskon, nella via maestra sedendo (ambedue). / (Non) avendo denaro [Myskon?] è venuto, per il prezzo (alto) dei buoi non ha comprato. / Ma se (Myskon?) si recasse presso Empedocle figlio di Mnasimachos, / sia possibile dare garanzia.' Against Manganaro's assumption that Apellis was a slave—his 3 [σῶ]μα δὲ ἔφα εἴμειν—is the consideration that if the record of the transaction was intended for an archive, there would be no point in even mentioning Apellis if he, as a slave, played no role in the transaction.

From Sicily there is evidence for such archives in the form of lead tablets, above all a register of propertied citizens at Kamarina;[5] very probably three later sales contracts there (*IGDS* 124–6, 300 BC or slightly earlier) bespeak other such archives in Sicily, as do a record of indebtedness (*IGDS* 177, area of Gela, 450–400 BC), and several contracts from Kamarina and Morgantina (Manganaro 1989: 300–100 BC).

We find the name Myskon at Syracuse (Th. 8.85.3[6]) and at Kamarina (*SEG* 27, 650 = *IGDS* 126, second century BC) and the forms $Μύσϙος$ at Selinous (a prominent citizen in whose grave plot state sacrifices were made: *LSSel* A 9, earlier fifth century BC), $Μύσκελος$ at Kroton (her founder[7]) and in a graffito from Monte di Marzo (ancient Erbessos?) near Gela (*IGDS* 168; fifth century), and not only a $Μύσσκελος$ among the targets of Side *B* of the present tablet but a $Μύσκελος$ among those of a fifth-century lead curse tablet that I am in the course of editing, now at Oslo in the Schøyen Collection and said to come from Gela.

2. Miller considered $Δ]εμόκριτος$ and $Ἀνθ]εμόκριτος$, the two quotable names ending in $]εμόκριτος$. The former would have to be Ionic ($Δ]ε̄μ$-) and therefore initially suspect in a text otherwise in West Greek, which would have the spelling $Δ]αμ$-. She therefore, and Dubois after her, restored $Ἀνθ]εμόκριτος$. This implied that the lacuna had a minimum of three letters and that, if the left-hand edge of the text-block was originally fairly even, *A* 7 could not be intact at its left. (*A* 7 corresponds to *B* 1–3, the left-hand edge of whose text is in fact preserved; the conclusion was that at some point before the reuse of the tablet for the curse, the entire left-hand edge of the financial document had been lost.) West later observed (1997), from autopsy, that the edge of the tablet at the left of *A* 7 had never been broken away. Because the first $ε$ of its $γενέσθο$ stands directly below the $]ε$ of *A* 2, the Ionic $Δ]εμόκριτος$, being shorter by two letters is inevitable. Dubois had already noted that an Ionic name here might be related to the mention of the Ionic-speaking town of Leontinoi.[8] As, thanks to West, the now secure lengths of the left-hand lacunae

---

[5] Cordano (1992), *c.* 450 BC .   [6] Cf. Lenschau (1933).
[7] Zwicker (1933); see Masson (1989) for the name.
[8] Drögenmuller (1969).

show, this relation proves to be the key to the understanding of the document as a whole: Demokritos and his guarantor Apellis in lines 3–4 find Myskon, the ξε/[—] of the people of Leontinoi, the home of Demokritos, who is therefore not a citizen of the town where the transaction takes place and therefore needs a guarantor, asking Apellis to act as such (ἐγγυάσασθαι).[9]

3. The simple λάζομαι is found in epic poetry, in Ionic, and in Megarian (*LSJ* s.v.), but the compound καταλάζομαι (= Attic καταλαμβάνω) occurs only here and is to be added to the lexica. From the verb I see no reason to conclude, with Dubois, that the encounter was necessarily violent: 'il s'emparait (brutalement) de l'hôte léontin'.

If, as we assume, Apellis as citizen acts as representative of the non-citizen Demokritos, Apellis is no doubt the subject of the remaining finite verbs. It is he, presumably, who makes contact with Myskon. As for this last, we may with some confidence restore the accusative ξέ/[νον], with ξένος in the sense of *proxenos* now also to be added to the lexica. It is uncertain what the πλατεία was in which he was found seated. A wide place in the road (sc. ὁδῶι), almost as in today's usage (cf. *OGI* 491.9, fourth century, the first such attestation in this sense)? The proper name of a 'broad' public building—ἐν τᾶι πλατεία<ι> (sc. e.g. Στόαι)—where Myskon as civic official sat?

4–5. Before the size of the lacuna could be confidently estimated, one could entertain the possibility of the plural θοκέοντας, i.e. that Myskon was not sitting alone. Now that only two or three letters are available for restoration in 5, it seems likely that we have a quantity of silver staters, Σ/[ΣΣ] or Σ/[ΣΣΣ], the price of the cattle, even if there would have been room to write out the number at the end of 4.

5–6. The transaction was not a purchase, however. Once he had brought the money (Demokritos), Apellis apparently deposited (?) it with Empedokles, son of Mnasimachos. The verb is not completely sure: before West's discovery that 7 is complete at the left, Miller

---

[9] For the concept of this last see Berneker (1967a) and (1967b) with the bibliography cited there.

envisaged three possibilities: (1) an 'unaugmented aorist middle of προσεντίθημι, (2) the aorist active of ποτέρχομαι and the neuter article, or (3) the aorist middle of the same verb'. Because we can no longer assume a lacuna after ποτεν-θε, the possibility that Dubois chose, this now has to be ruled out. (Manganaro has inadvertently omitted the final το.) A middle second aorist of the verb ἔρχομαι (3), evidenced only at *Batrachomyomachia* 179, seems equally unlikely. We are left with (1), even though the verb occurs only here. There is no need, however, to assume an intentionally unaugmented aorist: I should print ποτεν<έ>θετο and assume an oversight. The verb would mean 'deposit' or such. On such surety deposits Miller quotes J. W. Jones:

Early law everywhere turns to the use of sureties as a means of giving some measure of collateral backing and indirect legal sanction to the credit or uncompleted agreements for which no place has been found in the legal scheme of things, but which social and commercial requirements make indispensable. Where the concept of contractual obligation has not yet been accepted, the purchaser who has not the available cash at hand must provide a pledge or surety.[10]

Apellis, to be sure, has agreed to act as the ἐγγυητής of Demokritos, but it is not clear whether Jones' general description of pledges and surety fits this particular case: the silver for the cattle is spoken of as their τιμάν, not as a down-payment or pledge. Nor is it clear what role Empedokles played: was he the owner of the cattle? May it be that Demokritos' non-citizen status left him unable to buy the cattle themselves, having to lease them and to deposit their price as security for the period while they were to be in his care (and he presumably claiming such products as calves, or milk)? I see nothing to suggest wrong-doing or criminal charges. In any case, the record as we have it is to us so elliptical as to elude interpretation today. This, though, is why it is so important as evidence for official legal transactions in fifth-century Sicily: the record would not have seemed at all elliptical to the ancient reader who chose to consult it in the town archives. This means that the transaction was so generic as not to need

---

[10] Jones (1956) 225f.

explanation. For this reason the document, as a new attestation of the ordinary working of ancient legal machinery, deserves more attention from the legal historian.

7. Those readers who remember both the excitement in the popular press when a few years ago it was announced that the statement γενέσθω at the end of a papyrus document concerning lands belonging to Cleopatra was in the queen's own hand and the deflation that ensued when papyrologists pointed out that the imperative was no more than a chancellery convention meaning that the document was validated as part of the public record may welcome an early example, perhaps the first, of the word in this sense. The writer of line 1—himself, if my assumption is correct, an official in charge of public archives—here notes that he affirms that this tablet is an acceptable record of Apellis' assurance of Demokritos' transaction. This note of approval may belong to a much older tradition. It has long been recognized that ἀρ(ρ)αβών, an expression used by Greeks for such surety (first attested in another such financial document, *SEG* 38, 1030.7, a lead tablet from Pech Maho, fifth century), has a Semitic background (cf. Hebrew *ērābōn*). E. Masson has speculated that the Greeks got it from Phoenician traders.[11] Roy Kotansky (1994) has noted that the vocable Θωβαρραβαυ, frequent in much later Greek magical texts, is in fact the Greek transliteration of a Semitic expression meaning 'the surety/deposit is good' or 'let the surety/deposit be valid', curiously similar to the last two words of our Greek document. He cites Biblical parallels for the Hebrew expression in pledges.

SIDE *B*

1   (I) *Τύχα*. (II) Ἀπέλλις ἐπὶ φιλότατι τᾶι ΕὐνίϘο <—> μεδέν’
    [*E*]ὐνίϘο σπευ-

2   δ[αι]ότερον ἔμεν μεδὲ φιντίονα, ἀλλ’ ἐπαινê<ν> καὶ ἐϘόντα
    κἀεϘ-

[11] Masson (1967) 30f.

3 ὄντα καὶ φιλετᾶν. (III) ἐπὶ φιλότατι τᾶι Εὐνί℘ο ἀπογαράφο τὸ-
4 ς χοραγὸς πάντας ἐπ 'ἀτελεία<ι> κέπέον καὶ ἔργον καὶ τ-
5 ὸς παῖδ{ι}ας {ἀπὸ} τένον καὶ τὸς πατέρας κἀπρακτίαι κέν ἀγô-
6 νι κέχθὸς ἀγόνον οἵτινες μὲ παρ 'ἐμ'ἀπολείποιεν. (IV) Καλεδίαν
7 [ἀπογ]αράφο ἀπ 'Ἀπέλλιος καὶ τὸςς τενêι πάντας ἐπὶ μεσοτέρ-
8 [ο _____ᶜ·³] ἐντάδα. (V) Σοσίαν ἀπογράφο ἀπὸ τô καπελείο Ἀλκιαδᾶν ἐπὶ τâ-
9 [ι Μελ?]ανθίο φιλότατι. (VI) Πυρία<μ>, Μύσσκελον, Δαμόφαντον καὶ τὸν
10 [____ᶜ·⁴]ον ἀπογράφο ἀπὸ τôμ παιδôν καὶ τôμ πατέρον καὶ τὸς ἄλλ-
11 [ος πά]ντας οἵτινες ἐντάδε ἀφικνοίατο, μεδέν 'Εὐνίκο σπευδαιó-
12 [τερο]ν γενέσθαι μέτ 'ἄνδρεσι μέτε γυναίκεσσι. (VII) ὃς οὗτος ⟨ὁ⟩ βόλιμος, τὸς ΤΕ-
13 [____ᶜ·⁵]ΟΔΙΑΙΤΙΜΑΝ ἐρύσαιντο Εὐνίκοι ἀὲ νικᾶν παντê. (VIII) ἐμ βολύμοι ἐπ-
14 [ὶ φιλ]ότατι τâι Εὐνίκο γάρφο.

1 Τύχα or Εὐχά 3 ἀπογράφο 7 ἀπογράφο 13 ἀεί 14 γράφο

1 Ἀπελλâς Miller, Ἀπέλλι⟨ο⟩ς Dubois 1/2 σπευ/δότερον Miller 2 Φίντονα Miller, Dubois ἐπαινê⟨ν καὶ⟩ Miller, Dubois 3 Φιλέταν Miller, Dubois 6 παρεμ Miller 7/8 μεσοτέρ/[....] εντάδα (π)εντάδα? Dubois) Σοσίαν Miller, Dubois 8 καπελείο· Ἀλκιάδαν Miller, Dubois 9 Μελ?]ανθίο Miller, Μελ]ανθίο Dubois 10 παῖδον Dubois, but see Greg. Cor. 317S. for West Greek perispomenon παιδôν 11 ἀφικνοίατο. Μεδέν' Miller, Dubois 12 τοσοῦτος Miller, τοσούτος Dubois 12/13 βολιμος τος τε/[....]ο Διοτίμαν Miller, βολίμος τὸς τε/[νεῖ, β]ο-λίμο τιμάν 13 ἐμ βολύμοι: εμοαυνσον Miller, PMOAY... Dubois

This side is much harder to interpret than Side A. The earliest extant Greek curse tablets are Sicilian (*SGD* 84–122; *NGCT* 54–80; Curbera 1999), largely from Selinous (*SGD* 94–108, *LSSel.* pp. 125–31; *NGCT* 64–77; Curbera 1999: nos. 17–30), and date from the end of the sixth century or the beginning of the fifth. Because of their repeated local formulae and their grammatical simplicity, the Selinuntine texts are relatively easy to understand. Repetitions in the present curse suggest that it too was constructed from traditional formulae, even if their syntax and sense as they appear on the tablet are obscure. Formulae imply that Apellis, the *defigens*, probably turned to a practising magician for the curse. If this is right, there are mistakes and possibly omissions, however, that suggest either that the magician was unaccustomed to expressing himself very lucidly or that he produced a (papyrus?) model for another (the proverbially erring 'sorcerer's apprentice'? perhaps even Apellis himself?) to inscribe on the tablet. (As I interpret it, the Schøyen curse shows— see note on VI—a misunderstanding of a written model, and some of its formulaic phrases are in fact similar to those of the present tablet.)

Here my modest intention is to present, based on my autopsy at Chapel Hill, a fuller transcription, which leads to a new interpretation of parts of this curse, one of the purposes of which was to affect the outcome of a choregic competition. Readers of this volume will surely have more to say than I about the *choregoi* of the text, and much of what I write is necessarily speculative. If Miller's suggested Geloan provenance is correct, we must remember that Aischylos was in the town in the 470s;[12] neither he nor Pindar is likely to have been attracted to Gela if the city had no structure of poetic competitions; indeed, no one should be blamed for musing on the possibility that illustrious poets such as these wrote the words for the performances mentioned here. Nor should the reader of Apellis' curse on behalf of his friend the competitor Eunikos be blamed for remembering that the subject of Pindar's *First Olympian* was also that of supernatural assistance given by an older male to a young competitor of whom he was fond.

It will be convenient to consider the text according to the sections that I have defined above.

I. Τύχα

A heading, the traces of its first letter compatible equally with ε and τ. I have not found either word heading the text of a curse tablet. Which of the two would be likelier here I cannot say: my Τύχα has no better grounds than that the curse is meant to affect a competition. Miller and Dubois, assuming Εὐχά, further assumed

---

[12] See Vogt (1964) and Wilson's chapter below.

that the name following it must be a misspelled genitive (Miller: Ἀπελλᾶς; Dubois: Ἀπέλλι<ο>ς) and that the title must extend to ταῖ Εὐνίϙο. The letters ΑΠΕΛΛΙΣ are clear, though, and even after Εὐχά need not be emended, for the name in the nominative could easily be the subject of a verb that is implied or to be restored after ἐπὶ ταῖ φιλότατι ταῖ Εὐνίϙο: cf. the prepositional phrase before the main verbs of III and IV.

II. Ἀπέλλις ἐπὶ φιλότατι ταῖ Εὐνίϙο <—> μεδέν᾽[E]ὐνίϙο σπευ[2]δ[αι]ότερον ἔμεν μεδὲ φιντίονα, ἀλλ᾽ἐπαινέ<ν> καὶ ἐϙόντα κἀεϙ[3]όντα καὶ φιλετᾶν.

It is not clear what the verb should be. A similar phrase in VIII has γράφω. ἀπογράφω, the meaning of which is not perfectly clear in this text, may also be suitable, for in VI it governs the phrase μεδέν᾽ Εὐνίκο σπευδαιό[12][τερο]ν γενέσθαι, which is much like what would follow it here. There, however, and in III–VI it evidently requires an object, against which it connotes a hostile action. The possibly local form σπευδαιότερον, which we meet with again in 11/12, occurs only in this text; σπουδ- is the form elsewhere. Dubois suggests 'appliqué' or 'accompli'.

The name Φίντονα (acc.) as read by Miller and kept by Dubois ('pourrait être un concurrent d'Eunikos') is easily paralleled. Inspection with a microscope shows an unmistakable ι after τ, however, which leads me to assume, although a proper name Φιλτίων is attested, that here we have a correlative of σπευδαιότερον, the comparative of an adjective *φιλτ- (cf. the irregular comparative and superlative φίλτερος, φίλτατος of φίλος), of which the non-Attic form would be *φιντ- (cf. Epicharmos fr. 56 φίντατος). For both *φιλτ- and *φιντ- the evidence is mainly onomastic.[13] We read later that Eunikos is to compete against *choregoi* and that the purpose of the text is to assure his victory. The Greek of these opening lines seems to have a slightly different nuance, however: 'Apellis <requests (?)> that no

---

[13] See Bechtel (1917) 454f. and *LGPN* I, III.

one be more enthusiastic (?) or more friendly than Eunikos but may he (Eunikos) praise (me) both willingly and unwillingly and be affectionate.'

This last word Miller and Dubois took to be a proper name, Φιλέταν,[14] but it seems easier to think of a correlative of ἐπαινεῖν: φιλεῖταν, from *φιλητάω, an unexceptionable if unattested denominative of φιλητής and its family.

III. ἐπὶ φιλότατι τᾶι ΕὐνίϘο ἀπογαράϕο τὸ[4]ς χοραγὸς πάντας ἐπ' ἀτελεία<ι> κέπέον καὶ ἔργον καὶ τ[5]ὸς παῖδ{ι}ας {ἀπὸ} τένον καὶ τὸς πατέρας κἀπρακτίαι κὲν ἀγô[6]νι κέχθὸς ἀγόνον οἵτινες μὲ παρ᾽ ἐμ᾽ ἀπολείποιεν.

χοραγός: cf. Athenaeus 14.633b: ἐκάλουν δὲ καὶ χορηγούς, ὥς ϕασιν ὁ Βυζάντιος Δημήτριος ἐν τετάρτωι Περὶ Ποιημάτων, οὐκ ὥσπερ νῦν τοὺς μισθουμένους τοὺς χορούς, ἀλλὰ τοὺς καθηγουμένους τοῦ χοροῦ, καθάπερ αὐτὸ τοὔνομα σημαίνει.

The condition of ἀτέλεια κέπέον καὶ ἔργον is wished on victims of curse tablets from Selinous, *IGSD* 29, 32, 37 (= *SGD* 94, 97, 99f. = Curbera 1999: 17, 20, 22f.). See Jordan (1997) for a general discussion of the use of ἀτέλεια and its congeners in Selinuntine curses. We also read in the Schøyen curse that each of its victims is to be ἀτέλεστος, as well as his ἔπεα καὶ ἔργα.

In τ[5]ὸς παῖδ{ι}ας the writer has obviously made a mistake: evidently he thought of the neuter παιδία before he realized that his article τός required the masculine, and then in adding -ς he did not cancel his -ι-.

Whatever the precise meaning of ἀπογράϕω, it is constructed with ἀπό + genitive in IV–VI; ἀπὸ τένον here is awkward, however. I assume that influenced by this construction the writer inadvertently added ἀπό and then, whether or not he noticed his mistake, he failed, as in παῖδ{ι}ας, to cancel it. Questions to be asked are whether the *choregoi* are to be expected to be of an age to have children and

---

[14] Dubois (1989) 'pas très courant', citing Bechtel (1917) 453; *SEG* 1, 398 (Samos); Masson and Mitford (1986) 40.

whether their fathers played a role (in supporting them?) in the contest.

Το κἀπρακτίαι (*hapax*) we may compare ἐπὶ δυσπραγί[αι τὸν] κερδὸν on a mid-fifth-century curse tablet from Kamarina (*SGD* 88 = Curbera 1999: 5).

The relative clause at the end puzzles. Its phrase παρ' ἐμ(έ) is acceptable West Greek for παρ' ἐμοί (Buck 1955: §136.2): '*chez moi*, "in my hands"'. Dubois (reading οἵτινές με): 'Tous ceux qui dans mon entourage pourraient me laisser tomber'; such placement of the pronoun με, if this is the intended meaning, is unexpected. One may think, instead, of 'those who leave me isolated (παρ'ἐμέ = Attic παρ' ἐμοί)' or, perhaps better, of οἵτινες μέ, with Καλεδίαν (here assigned to IV) the object of the verb: 'those who would not leave Kaledias in my hands'. But then who, we may ask, is this Kaledias? Another of Apellis' ἐρώμενοι? But why, then, does the curse announce itself as being written in friendship specifically of Eunikos?

IV. Καλεδίαν[7] [ἀπογ]αράφο ἀπ 'Ἀπέλλιος καὶ τὸςς τενêι πάντας ἐπὶ μεσοτέρ[8][ο——c. 3——] ἐντάδα.

Another awkwardness in taking Καλεδίαν to be part of the previous sentence is that ἀπογράφω elsewhere consistently follows its object; therefore I put it here. We may, in any case, ask why Apellis 'writes' anyone 'away' (if this is what ἀπογράφω means) from himself. Miller translated 'along with Apellis', but this is difficult. Dubois's assumption that 'le rédacteur maudit Καλεδια ou Καλεδιας (masc.) pour la/e séparer d'un autre Apellis' seems too elaborate: surely Apellis here is the *defigens*, even if we cannot explain the sentence. Do we have a renunciation by Apellis, now (?) favouring Eunikos, of this Kaledias? The ἐπὶ μεσοτέρ[8][ο——c. 3——] ἐντάδα is difficult; presumably it means something like the ἐντάδε ἀφικνοίατο of VI.

V. Σοσίαν ἀπογράφο ἀπὸ τὸ καπελείο Ἀλκιαδᾶν ἐπὶ
τᾶ[9][ι Μελ?]ανθίο φιλότατι.

Miller: 'Sosias I curse, along with his shop'; Dubois: 'Sôsias, je
l'inscris pour l'arracher à sa boutique'. It is not immediately clear, in
any case, why a καπελεῖον 'shop', 'tavern' should figure in a curse
concerning *choregoi*. This is worth thinking about, however, and
readers should ask whether supporters of a particular *choregos* or
his team in fifth-century Sicily could include owners/customers
of *kapeleia*. Miller and Dubois print the singular Ἀλκιάδαν;
the resultant syntax is awkward, however. I assume the name of the
kapeleion or of its family of owners; indeed Miller herself mooted
the possibility that ἀλκιαδαν might modify καπελείο; at least two
Athenian taverns are thought to have had their own proper name:
DTWü 70.1–3 καταδήσω . . . τὸ καπηληῖον Ὀλυμπον· [κ]αταδήσω . . .
τὸ καπηληῖον Ἀγάθωνα (fourth century).

As a supplement, Melanthios, unnamed elsewhere in the text, must
be considered *exempli gratia*. It seems incongruous, in any case, for a
curse with the phrase ἐπὶ φιλότατι τᾶι Εὐνίϙο (II, III) to include
also ἐπὶ τᾶ[9][ι Μελ?]ανθίο φιλότατι here, as a second interest of
Apellis', but it is probably better to assign this last phrase to V than to
VI, which includes the wish μεδέν' Εὐνίκο σπευδαιό[12][τερο]ν
γενέσθαι.

VI. Πυρία<μ>, Μύσσκελον, Δαμόφαντον καὶ τὸν[10][——c. 4——]ον
ἀπογράφο ἀπὸ τὸμ παιδὸν καὶ τὸμ πατέρον καὶ τὸς ἄλλ[11][ος
πά]ντας οἵτινες ἐντάδε ἀφικνοίατο, μεδέν' Εὐνίκο
σπευδαιό[12][τερο]ν γενέσθαι μέτ ᾽ἄνδρεσι μέτε γυναίκεσσι.

Here four persons are cursed in a formula very much like that of III.
It is not to be ruled out that Mysskelos is related to the Myskon of *A*.
For the lacuna, which Miller and Dubois printed as [....], D. C. Young
apud Miller suggested [υἱὸν]όν, a homonymous grandson of
Damophantos. The idea has its attractions, but if the supplement is
right the phrase τὸμ παιδὸν καὶ τὸμ πατέρον later in the line
means that this section curses as many as five generations, and we

may ask whether the Damophantos actually named here, if he is a rival of the *choregos* Eunikos, is likely to be a grandfather. Probably a better approach is to consider the writer's letter-spacing: letters become gradually smaller and closer together as the text progresses. 7]α is directly below the χ of 6 -νι κἐχθός, of which the letters νικε occupy 0.02 m; this is the length, then, of the lacunae of 8–14. Now if we turn to the right-hand ends of lines 7–13, we see that 0.02 m can accommodate more than 4 letters there:

Line	Letters	Line	Letters
7	5–6	11	6
8	4–5	12	6
9	5	13	*c.* 6
10	5		

This means that we may consider for 10 [—] a slightly longer word than Miller envisaged; [χοραγ]όν comes to mind, with Pyrrias, Mysskelos, and Damophantos, all known to Apellis by name as members of a competing chorus, the fourth target their unnamed *choregos*.

VII. ός (= Attic ὡς) οὗτος ⟨ὁ⟩ βόλιμος (= Attic μόλυβδος) ⟨–––⟩, τὸς (= Attic οὕτως) *TE*[13][_c. 5_]*OΔIAITIMAN* ἐρύσαιντο Εὐνίκοι ἀὲ νικᾶν παντ̂ε.

Here we have an example of sympathetic magic, a technique used in the contemporary Schøyen curse:

θ̂ος (= Attic ὡς)ἀτέλεστος Ὀλτὶς ἀπόλετο *EΣTENOΣIAΣA*, θὸς (= Attic οὕτως; *EOΣ* tab.) Μύσκελος ἀτέλεστος καὶ {καὶ} Ϝέπεα (θ*EΠEA* tab.) καὶ ἔργα ἐν τᾶι δίκαι. (Here Ὀλτίς, with an elsewhere unattested proper name, and as *EΣTENOΣIAΣA*, evidently a participle, shows, a woman, is no doubt the deceased into whose grave the tablet was deposited.) A fourth-century Attic example in which the condition of the lead itself figures in the sympathetic magic: *DTWü.* 106 *b* καὶ ὡς ο⟦τως ὁ μόλυβδος ἄχρηστος, ὡς ἄχρηστα εἶναι τῶν ἐνταῦθα γεγραμμένων καὶ ἔπη καὶ ἔργα.

VIII. ἐμ βολύμοι ἐπ̣[14][ὶ φιλ]ότατι τᾶι Εὐνίκο γάρφο.

A recapitulation, with the verb γράφω, which is possibly to be understood in II.

13

Sicilian Choruses*

Peter Wilson

The document David Jordan has presented here in Chapter 12 is a unique and quite extraordinary glimmer within a great darkness. As John Herington wrote of the cultural and social history of western Greece from the time of Hieron's succession in 478 to Aiskhylos' death in 456: 'most of the details in the picture that are not missing . . . are obscure'.[1] This lead tablet opens a (small, dirty and broken) window onto the festival culture of a Greek community in mid-fifth-century Sicily, almost certainly that of the flourishing city-state of Gela at its height.[2] It gives evidence of a festival there that had choral contests, perhaps of some scale, and hints at the mechanics of their operation. In metropolitan Greece, our usual access to such precious information is by deduction (our own or that of ancient scholars) from the self-referential suggestions of ritual and choral action that can be gleaned from the surviving texts of Archaic melic poetry;[3] or, in the case of Classical Athens, through epigraphy and the comment of contemporaries (the orators, Aristotle, and others[4]). Virtually

* Thanks for invaluable suggestions to friends and colleagues in Sydney who participated in a discussion of this text, and to Eric Csapo, Archibald McKenzie, and Lindsay Watson in particular. Likewise, thanks to Paola Ceccarelli, Pat Easterling, Simon Hornblower, Barbara Kowalzig, Leslie Kurke, and Robert Parker for advice and criticism. None of these should be held responsible for the faults that remain.
[1] Herington (1967) 74.
[2] *BTCG* 8.19: all the evidence points to the very middle of the fifth century as the peak of Gela's prosperity. It was razed to the ground in 405 by the Carthaginians.
[3] See e.g. Calame (1977); Krummen (1990); Stehle (1997); Kurke (2006).
[4] See e.g. Wilson (2000).

nothing comparable survives for all the rest of the great western Greek city-states.[5]

I offer here a (tentative) translation of and some further comments on this intriguing item of evidence, with a two-fold aim: the first, to try to say something more about the broader contexts—cultural, historical, and political—from which it emerges; the second, to offer a few specific remarks on points of detail that arise in its interpretation.

A TRANSLATION OF SIDE *B* OF JORDAN'S NEW TEXT

(I) Prayer.[6] (II) Apellis, for love of Eunikos ⟨prays⟩ that no one be taken more seriously or be more popular than Eunikos but that all praise and admire him both willingly and unwillingly. (III) For love of Eunikos I mark down[7] all the *khoragoi* so that they be ineffectual both in word and deed, along with their sons and fathers; and so that they fail both in the contest and outside the contests—whoever does not leave him (*sc.* Eunikos) with me.[8] (IV) I mark down Kaledias to

---

[5] An inscribed mid-fifth-century tablet found with, but not one of, a collection of lead tablets identifying membership of civic units from the temple of Athena in Kamarina (Cordano 1992: no. 6; cf. *SEG* 42, *s.* no. 846, p. 245) was, when first published, thought to reveal the existence of an intriguing singing contest in this nearby Sicilian city, that included a member of the ruling family of Akragas and some sort of military club: 'Thrasys, an Emmenid, is supreme at singing among all the Doristomphoi.' However Cassio (1994) has shown that for the crucial word ἀείδων ('singing') should in fact be read ἀκίδων ('arrows'), producing: 'Thrasys, an Emmenid, is supreme with his spear over the arrows of all the boasters.' See the full discussion of Cassio, who suggests (1994: 16) that these may have been iambic lines.

[6] Preferring εὐχά to τύχα.

[7] Cf. the hostile intent of ἀπογράφω in the Attic legal sense of 'enter a person's name for the purpose of accusing him', 'denounce', *LSJ* III.1.

[8] My suggested translation for the phrase οἵτινες με παρ' ἐμ' ἀπολείποιεν. This clause should express an action, actual or feared, on the part of the rival *khoragoi* that has given rise to Apellis' curse. If we understand the object of the verb ἀπολείποιεν to be Eunikos (easy enough given the sentence's—indeed the whole document's—focus on him), we might construe: 'whoever does not leave him (= Eunikos) with me'. Apellis' fear is that rivals—in choruses, and perhaps also in love—will take Eunikos from him. See Jordan, Chapter 12 above.

keep him apart from Apellis,[9] and all those (??) in between there and here.[10] (??) (V) Sosias I mark down, the one from the shop of the Alkiadai, because of his love of [Mel]anthios.[11] (VI) Pyria⟨s⟩ Mysskelos, Damophantos and the[ir *khorag*]os I mark down, along with[12] their sons and fathers, and all the others who arrive here. May no one be taken more seriously than Eunikos either among men or women. (VII) As this lead, so [. . .[13]] may they support Eunikos to be victorious always everywhere. (VIII) On the lead for love of Eunikos I write.

---

[9] Assuming that the Apellis mentioned here is the author of the curse, I (tentatively) understand the difficult phrase Καλεδίαν [ἀπογ]αράφο ἀπ' Ἀπέλλιος to mean 'I mark down Kaledias [as failures] apart/in a separate category from Apellis. . .'

[10] καὶ τὸςς τενεῖ πάντας ἐπὶ μεσοτέρ-[ο - c. 3 -] ἐντάδα. Archibald McKenzie suggests to me that this phrase may mean something like 'and all there [for instance, in Syracuse or some other important centre from which Kaledias may have come to compete in Gela] for more middling [placings ?] here'. Cf. Pl. *Prt.* 346d for the meaning 'mediocre' for μέσος. Another possibility would be to place a stop after πάντας, remove that after ἐντάδα, and understand: 'and all those there [either "in the house of Kaledias" or with reference to a specific centre such as Syracuse]. Here in the middle [of the text] I mark down Sosias . . .'.

[11] This translation eradicates the incongruity (remarked upon by Jordan) of understanding 'for love of [Mel]anthios' as a second interest of Apellis. On the interpretation offered here, Sosias is targeted because of *his* love of [Mel]anthios: Sosias thus looks like a rival supporter of another competitor.

[12] This is perhaps the most difficult phrase for which to maintain consistency in our construal of ἀπό after the verb ἀπογράφο as implying separation from. In (V) I have already construed it not as indicating separation, but specification—'the Sosias from the shop. . .'. If such consistency were desired here, it might mean 'I mark down Pyria⟨s⟩, Mysskelos, Damophantos and the[ir *khorag*]os so that they do not have the benefit of their sons and fathers.' Archibald McKenzie suggests that 'the sons' and 'the fathers' here—and in (III)—might refer to choral competition categories (comparable to παῖδες and ἄνδρες in that function in Athens and elsewhere, though a fathers' event would to my knowledge be entirely unparalleled). He suggests as a translation for the usage in (III): 'and (I list) the sons and the fathers (as choral categories) (to be separated) from them (the *khoragoi*)', retaining as not an error the ἀπό bracketed by Jordan before τένον. Here he would translate: 'I list Pyria⟨s⟩, Mysskelos, Damophantos and the[ir *khorag*]os (to be separated) from the sons and from the fathers (as choral categories).'

[13] For a suggested restoration see below.

KHORAGOI AND CHORAL CONTESTS
IN GREEK SICILY

Although there is nothing in the text of the document to tie the anticipated agonistic activity to any particular festival or cult, in the Classical period formal contests (*agones*) are unknown outside such a context, and we should assume the existence of one here. What that cult might be can be little more than a guess. Possible candidates known from Gela are that city's cults of Athena Lindia (on the acropolis), the founder-hero Antiphamos, Apollo, Gelas (the river-deity), and—most prominent of all—the chthonic goddesses.[14] It is a striking fact that many theatrical structures in Sicily are found in close proximity to sanctuaries associated with chthonic cults.[15] The political importance of the cult of Demeter and Kore in Gela was enormous, and of long standing. The Deinomenid tyrants apparently claimed the hierophancy of the cult by hereditary title; a claim that was used to legitimate the maintenance of their power.[16] One other, even more tantalising possibility for the context of performance is a cult for the heroised tragic poet Aiskhylos that included the competitive re-performance of his dramas.

The only other explicit evidence known to me for the mechanics of theatrical, choral, or more broadly musical contests in all of Classical Sicily is confined to two items from the literary tradition that concern the business of judging such contests:[17] a fragment of

[14] *BTCG* 8.8, 10–28. For the archaeological evidence for the cult in Gela see esp. Hinz (1998) 55–69.

[15] Todisco (2002) 29. To these we may add the *Thesmophorion* by the recently excavated theatre in Cyrene.

[16] Hdt. 7.153.2–4; *Σ* Pi. *P.* 2.27b; Pi. *Pyth.* 2.15–16 with Gentili et al. (1995) 370–1; Dunbabin (1948) 64–6; Luraghi (1994) 120, 122–3. Cf. also Pi. *O.* 6.94–6 for Hieron's promotion of the cult of Demeter and Kore in a Syracusan context.

[17] We must wait for the late second or first century for the (limited) epigraphic evidence for the existence of Associations of *Tekhnitai* at Syracuse. One of these is in relation to a cult of Apollo, Dionysos, and the Muses, whose activities were likely to have been based in the *Mouseion* identified by archaeologists in close proximity to the Syracusan theatre; the other, in honour of Aphrodite Hilaria, and probably experts in the form of comic parody of tragic themes of a sort originally associated with Rhinthon of Syracuse or Taras (third-century): *IG* XIV 12–13; Moretti (1963); Le Guen (2001a) I.319–26 [TE 73–5], II.77; Aneziri (2001–2), (2003) 400–2 [F1–4]. On the *Tekhnitai* of Aphrodite see also Fountoulakis (2000).

Sicilian Epikharmos (fr. 237 K.–A.) '[the verdict] rests on the knees of the five judges': ἐν πέντε κριτᾶν γούνασι κεῖται;[18] and the more general (and seemingly incompatible) observation made nearly a century later in Plato's *Laws* (659b–c) that in Sicily and Italy (as in Greece in the past), theatrical judgments are 'nowadays' assigned to the entire body of spectators who acclaim the winner by show of hands (ἐξῆν γὰρ δὴ τῶι παλαιῶι τε καὶ Ἑλληνικῷ νόμῳ, καθάπερ ὁ Σικελικός τε καὶ Ἰταλικὸς νόμος νῦν, τῶι πλήθει τῶν θεατῶν ἐπιτρέπων καὶ τὸν νικῶντα διακρίνων χειροτονίαις . . .) These are slim pickings. But as Luigi Todisco has pertinently remarked, they do imply that, broadly speaking, the organisational parameters of the performance traditions in 'western' Greece were in some ways modelled on or parallel to those in metropolitan Greece (a related gloss of Hesychius on the phrase 'five judges' explicitly comments that 'that was how many judged the comic competitors not only in Athens but also in Sicily').[19]

We thus see for the first time something of the mechanics of a cultural festival in a city whose ruling powers have always been known as poetic patrons on a grand scale. The Deinomenid tyrants Gelon (who seized power in the city *c.* 491) and Hieron were it seems the first in the West to recognise the enormous political potential of agonistic victories in the great panhellenic centres and—crucially— of their subsequent publicity in choral performance.[20] During his

---

[18] cf. K.–A. ad loc.

[19] Hsch. π 1408 πέντε κριταί· τοσοῦτοι τοὺς κωμικοὺς ἔκρινον, οὐ μόνον Ἀθήνῃσιν, ἀλλὰ καὶ ἐν Σικελίαι. Cf. Todisco (2002) 18. Todisco's work offers a good synthetic discussion of the current state of evidence for theatrical and other performance culture in *Megale Hellas*. Cf. also Todisco (2003). He places the remarks of Aristoxenos of Taras on the 'barbarisation' of musical and theatrical activity in Poseidonia and Taras (Athen. 14.632a = fr. 124 W) in the same context. On this see Meriani (2003) ch. 1 and Csapo (2004a) 234–5, making the convincing case that the degener- ation of south Italian Greek culture lamented in this work—with its talk of the 'barbarisation' of theatres by 'utterly populist music'—refers to the late Classical phenomenon of the 'New Music' well known from Athens and Plato's criticisms, but here at work in the West. If that case can stand, this is another element of continuity of musical tradition (including at the level of criticism) between western and metro- politan Greece.

[20] Cf. esp. Luraghi (1994) 354–68; Harrell (2002). On Gela see also Privitera (1980); Dunbabin (1948) 410–34.

regency at Gela (485–478), Hieron clearly entertained and realised great ambitions to assert and express his power—in part spurred by rivalry with his more glamorous brother Gelon, who had won at Olympia in 484[21]—through a cultural politics to which musical and poetic performance were central.

Gela was, as Jordan reminds us, also sufficiently attractive to lure Aiskhylos thither. The Athenian poet's stay is reported with some security as having spanned the last three years of his life, 457–455. By that date the major Sicilian city-states, Gela included, may have become democracies,[22] although the sources imply that the stay in Gela, like the trip some years earlier for the founding of Aitna (476), came at the instigation of Hieron.[23] We cannot therefore be quite sure whether Aiskhylos spent his final years in a democratic Gela or one still ruled by the Deinomenids. Nor can we date our document with sufficient precision to determine whether the agonistic events to which it refers were held in a tyranny or a fledgling democracy.

It is worth taking a closer look at the principal source for this final journey of the Athenian tragedian. The anonymous *Life* reports (10) that he spent his last three years in Gela, greatly honoured by tyrant and people alike (11). The Geloans gave him a lavish burial in the public burial-grounds, and there was inscribed the famous epitaph (*TrGF* 3 T162).[24] Most intriguing is the following reference to the way the tomb thereafter became a site of pilgrimage—formal hero-worship is clearly meant—and performance for those in the

---

[21] *Olympionikai* 158; *I.Olympia* 143; Paus. 6.9.4.

[22] D. S. 11.68, 72–3, 76, 86; Berger (1989) 304 makes the point that our single most important source for the introduction of these 'democracies', Diodorus (writing in the first century) conceived of democracy in a fairly simplistic way, as the antithesis to tyranny. Cf. Herington (1976).

[23] Anonymous *Life of Aiskhylos* 10: καὶ σφόδρα τῶι δὲ τυράννωι Ἱέρωνι καὶ τοῖς Γελωίοις τιμηθεὶς ἐπιζήσας τρίτον ἔτος γηραιὸς ἐτελεύτα κτλ. In §11, it is perhaps important that only the Γελῶιοι are mentioned in relation to Aiskhylos' death and burial (see above), and Hieron's death is normally dated to 466/5: D. S. 11.66.4. Dougherty (1993) ch. 5 is an excellent study of Hieron's use of choral poetry and Aiskhylean tragedy within his colonial ambitions.

[24] Cf. also the *Marm. Par.* ep. 59: ἐτελεύτησεν ἐγ [Γέλ]ᾳ τῆς Σικελίας (465/5), 'he died in [Gel]a, in Sicily'; *TrGF* 3 T K; Herington (1976) esp. 76 on the authority of the sources for Aiskhlyos' death in Sicily; Griffith (1978).

tragic trade: 'those who made their livelihood in tragedy made frequent trips to the memorial, where they made offerings[25] and staged
dramas', or—perhaps more precisely—'and staged *his* dramas',
taking the article τὰ in a defining rather than a generic sense.[26] (εἰς τὸ
μνῆμα δὲ φοιτῶντες ὅσοις ἐν τραγῳδίαις ἦν ὁ βίος ἐνήγιζόν τε καὶ τὰ
δράματα ὑπεκρίνοντο.) The *Life* does not indicate how long after his
death this practice arose, but the way the author moves immediately
from the death and burial to the worship may be felt to imply no
long gap of time. It is, therefore, a possibility that our tablet relates to
competitive tragic performance staged as part of a hero cult for
Aiskhylos in Gela. The contest envisaged in the tablet seems to
anticipate the arrival of outside competitors (see below): this would
fit well with the idea of a 'pilgrimage' hero cult observed by tragic
professionals from across Greece. In this case the *khoragoi* are perhaps more likely to have been producers, close to the Athenian leitourgical sense (see below).[27] That, sadly, is as far as one can go in
such attractive speculation.

This tablet is thus our first (and only good) evidence for choral
contest in that city which may have seen both choral *epinikia*, and
tragedy, in the very period in which it was incised and buried.[28] Gela
probably had its own theatre (or a space that could be used as a
theatre) in the fifth century. The presence of Aiskhylos in the city
implies the existence of such a space, and some relevant remains may
have been seen in the nineteenth century on the coastal side, though
the identification may have been in part the result of wishful local

[25] Note the use of the verb ἐναγίζω, properly of offerings to the dead brought by
families to non-family. It is often used of cult worship of heroes.

[26] Thus also Clay (2004) 127.

[27] On hero cults of poets see now Clay (2004), with brief remarks at 81 and 127 on
Aiskhylos in Gela.

[28] Gela is also one of the first Greek cities in Sicily to show the importation of
Archaic Korinthian *aryballoi* and *alabatsra* (c. 600) with 'padded dancers' on them:
Todisco (2002) 47. Its interest in dramatic subjects on ceramic is also very well
represented in the record: see Catucci (2003) esp. 7, 28; at 42–3 she suggests a link
between the wealth of Gela in the early fifth century and the city's importation of
Attic ceramic in quantity. That trade is itself further evidence of the direction in
which the cultural aspirations of the élite were oriented.

pride.[29] The indications are that the events referred to in this tablet were of some scale and more than local importance. They were for instance apparently attractive to outside contestants. Note the emphasis in lines 10–11 on 'all the others who arrive here'—these very probably being other *khoragoi*.[30] And if we take the plural ἀγόνον—'contests'—in line 6 to be a deliberate and specific reference rather than a generalising 'cover-all' phrase of magic ritual, we can say that the festival in question had more than one choral contest.[31] If there were outside competitors, we have an intriguing example of a choral (and/or theatrical) contest that perhaps drew on a regional or wider catchment. Jordan identifies what may be at least five 'local' competitors (in ll. 9–10); presumably the outsiders are in addition to their numbers.[32]

We know of one other mobile chorus in Greek Sicily, this time moving across the straits from Messana to Rhegion. Pausanias describes a dedication at Olympia commissioned by 'the Messenians on the straits' in response to a choral disaster. The Messenians, 'according to an ancient custom',[33] sent a chorus of thirty-five *paides* (children, probably boys or a mixed chorus), along with a *didaskalos*

---

[29] For the nineteenth-century report see Todisco (2002) 175, 222; *BTCG* 8.5–65 (Canzanella and Buongiovanni). This was a curvilinear stone structure near the so-called Torre dell' Insegna. However Battaglia (1957) cast serious doubt on the identification, adding (p. 172) that in the fifth century one should not expect an elaborate stone theatre but the use of wood, the shaping of a natural slope, and a flattened open space for an *orchestra*. More recently, Fischer-Hansen et al. (2004: 194) are more optimistic: 'The stay of Aeschylos at Gela surely implies that the city had a theatre in C5m.'

[30] As Jordan notes, the difficult expression of ll. 7–8 may refer to something similar: 'all those (??) in between there and here (??)'. The specificity of this phrase suggests a particular centre from which (some) competitors come to Gela, and at any time in this general period, Syracuse is the most likely candidate: n. 10 above.

[31] However, the fact that it is coupled with the singular—'and (I mark down to failure) both in the contest and outside the contests'—perhaps speaks in favour of the 'generalising' plural.

[32] The locals would be Eunikos, Pyrias, Mysskelos, Damophantos, and τὸν [- *c.* 4 -]-ον of ll. 9–10 (in (VI)). However, Jordan's very attractive supplement of καὶ τὸν [χοραγ]ὸν for that gap would, as he notes, imply members of or those associated with a particular competing chorus and its leader, and so reduce that to a single team of local competitors. The various persons named in (IV) and (V) may also be local rivals. See further below p. 365.

[33] Reading ἔθος rather than ἔτος at Paus. 5.25.2. Both are in the MSS: see Cordano (1980) 436.

and an *aulos*-player, to a local festival of the Rhegines (ἐς ἑορτήν
τινα ἐπιχώριον Ῥηγίνων 5.25.2). In one year the treacherous
passage took the entire ship, and the Messenians honoured the
memory of those lost by dedicating at Olympia what must have been
a major monument, consisting of the entire group, sculpted in
bronze by Kallon of Elis. (The impulse to dedicate so costly a
memorial in Olympia can be seen as another illustration of western
Greek desire to assert cultural connectedness with and pre-eminence
in the prestige arenas of metropolitan Greece.[34]) Pausanias gives us
the fascinating detail, from autopsy, that this offering bore two
inscriptions. The original one probably indicated little more than the
identity of the dedicators and sculptor (5.25.4); while a later one (by
perhaps just one or two decades) was in elegiac couplets, composed
by Hippias of Elis. The reasons behind this intriguing further commission are left unexplained. The Elean's intellectual fame and his
associations with both the region of dedication and with Greek Sicily
are obviously relevant.

It has been plausibly suggested that the members of the young
chorus were descendants of the families, originally from Rhegion,
who had passed over the straits to the Sicilian shore when Messana
was founded on the site of Zankle by the tyrant Anaxilas.[35] It is perhaps likely that the occasion at which they had been intending
to perform was a more cultic than theatrical event, to use an unsatisfactory but useful opposition.[36] There is in any case no indication
from Pausanias' account that they were in competition with other
choruses.

What more can be said about the possible nature of the choral
events in the southwest of the island? Much depends on our interpretation of the word *khoragos* (χοραγός). As Jordan argues, it is
likely that these *khoragoi* are themselves performers, presumably
the participating leaders of choruses. Most scholars who have

[34] On this see further Shepherd (1995) 74–6, making the important point at p. 75:
'It is no accident that we have virtually no evidence of colonial activity in mother-
cities and a great deal of it in the pan-Hellenic sanctuaries: the colonial dedications
were the result of self-assertion, not of nostalgia.'
[35] Cordano (1980) 437; Maddoli and Saladino (1995) 337.
[36] Likely divine honorands are Apollo and/or Artemis: Schneidewin (1832) 20;
Mosino (1977); Cordano (1980) 438.

commented on this document consider that they are unlikely to be leitourgical financiers, the meaning with which we are most familiar with the term in its Attic-Ionic form (χορηγός, *khoregos*) from the Athenian environment.[37] Rather, they appear to be what is sometimes called (in ancient and modern terminology) *koryphaioi*, the 'leaders of the chorus' in a more participatory, performance-oriented sense.[38] Unless, that is, they are trainers and/or poets, and/or producers of choruses. (The two—or three, or four—roles could, of course, be undertaken by the same person.)[39] However many or few of these tasks were undertaken by these Sicilian *khoragoi*, their active, participatory role in the contest is virtually guaranteed by the language of the tablet itself: little reason otherwise to curse them 'to ineffectuality both in word and *deed*'.

A number of parallels not cited by Jordan for *khoragoi* (and related terms) in the western Greek context might usefully be brought into the picture. The lexicon of Pollux reports (9.41–2) that Dorian Greeks in particular (and Gela is a thoroughly Dorian foundation[40]) used the word *khoregeion* where others used *didaskaleion*; they used *khoregos* for *didaskalos*, and the verb *khoregein* where others

---

[37] Thus e.g. Dubois (1989) 156: 'Il n'est pas ici question de liturgie.' Faraone (1991) 12 was undecided between 'liturgists . . . or actual performers'.

[38] Jordan cites the passage of Demetrios of Byzantium's *On Poems* book 4 *apud* Athen. 14.633b that traces this semantic and historical shift—from 'those who lead the chorus' to 'those who hire the choruses'—on which see further Calame (1977) I.93.

[39] Gilula (1995), (1996) has argued that a *Khoragos* in a western Greek context was a commercial provider of costumes and props to dramatic productions. The argument is based on (1) the evidence of (second-century) Plautine comedy, with its roots in western Greek tradition; and (2) interpretation of the intriguing *Khoregoi* vase from Apulia (*c.* 430–380), on which see Taplin (1993) esp. 55–66 with further bibliography. The case for this usage in the second century is strong; but the *Khoregoi* vase is too weak a basis to project that usage back to the late fifth or early fourth century. There is also a danger of homogenising all the very limited evidence of western Greek practice so as to produce a coherent, single image. But that tradition represents more than half a millennium and hundreds of different centres that doubtless had their own distinctive practices. I would in any case resist the implicit assumption of this argument that the chorus was effectively absent from western Greek dramatic traditions. The sense of 'provider of costumes and props' seems implausible for the mid-fifth-century Geloan context—Gilula does not claim it—(though some may be tempted to explain 'the shop of the Alkiadai' (l. 8) in this connection).

[40] Cf. esp. Th. 6.4.3; Luraghi (1994) 120.

used *didaskein*.[41] Although Pollux' language is highly compressed, it seems fairly clear (especially from Attic–Ionic usage) that the meanings of these various terms are 'training-room' (especially for the training of choruses), 'trainer' or 'trainer/poet' and 'to train' (a chorus). In other words, this is evidence for the meaning of 'trainer' or 'trainer/poet' or '(trainer/poet)/producer'[42] for the Dorian χοραγός.

Pollux in fact cites the work of an early western Greek poet to make his point—Epikharmos, who very probably came from Syracuse and lived and produced there under Hieron. Syracuse succeeded Gela as the epicentre of Deinomenid power by at least 485, and with the transfer thither of Gelon.[43] It certainly possessed a theatre by the early fifth century (at a conservative estimate), and rebuilt a state-of-the-art version around 460. This, as Dearden comments, 'must have been of considerable dramatic influence to Sicily as a whole'.[44] Epikharmos is the most famous practitioner of Sicilian comedy in the early fifth century (at his peak around 480), and he was certainly not the only one.[45] In fact, the western Greek dramatic

---

[41] Poll. 9.41–2 (a list of the various physical components of a city):

πόλεως δ' αὖ μέρη καὶ στοαὶ καὶ δρόμοι καὶ στρατήγια καὶ ἀρχεῖα καὶ γραμματεῖα καὶ διδασκαλεῖα, ἃ καὶ παιδαγώγια καὶ φωλεοὺς ὠνόμαζον. ἐκάλουν δὲ τὸ διδασκαλεῖον καὶ χορόν, ὁπότε καὶ τὸν διδάσκαλον χορηγὸν καὶ τὸ διδάσκειν χορηγεῖν, καὶ μάλιστα οἱ Δωριεῖς,(42) ὡς Ἐπίχαρμος ἐν Ὀδυσσεῖ αὐτομόλωι, ἐν δ' Ἁρπαγαῖς χορηγεῖον τὸ διδασκαλεῖον ὠνόμασεν.

Pollux does not cite the Dorian forms of these terms (χοραγός etc.), but his point is not a dialectal one in that sense.

[42] For διδάσκειν to mean 'produce' (with or without the implication of poetic composition) compare its common usage in Attic khoregic and 'didaskalic' inscriptions; and note, for what it is worth, that Suid. ε2766 uses the expression διδάσκων ἐν Συρακούσαις of Epikharmos' production of comedy in Syracuse. Cf. Wilson above p. 161.

[43] Hdt. 7.156.2. Luraghi (1994) 273–88.

[44] Dearden (1990) 232; Polacco and Anti (1990) esp. 155–9 for a late sixth-century date for the first phase of the large theatre at Syracuse. The post-*c.* 460 theatre had a trapezoidal *orchestra*.

[45] Others include Phormos of Syracuse (early fifth century, said to have been the tutor of the tyrant Gelon's sons: Suid. φ609; *PCG* 1), Dinolokhos of Syracuse or Akragas (fifth century, among whose titles may be a *Komoidotragoidia*: *PCG* 1). In the fourth century there is Apollodoros, from Gela itself (Suid. s.v.); and Philemon may have been Syracusan by birth (Suid. s.v.) Two titles of works ascribed to Phormos are the *Sack of Ilion* and the *Horse* (Suid. φ609), which as Kaibel originally pointed out are very probably alternatives for the same work (see *PCG* 1.174). This is

tradition must have been very vigorous, and far from dependent on infrequent visits of luminaries like Aiskhylos.[46] At least as far as comedy is concerned, it has a much better claim to the title of 'inventor' than Athens. We should also remember that in later years talent moved east as well as west; and that there was a home-grown tradition of tragic poetry in the region around Gela. The fifth-century tragic poet Karkinos (I) was said by some to have been Akragantine, but was in fact probably an Athenian from Thorikos.[47] However, his grandson of the same name—Karkinos (II)[48]—also a tragic poet, is closely associated with Sicily and was probably born in Akragas, a city itself founded (in part or whole) by Gela (*c.* 580).[49] Another Akragantine tragic poet is the Empedokles who moved to Syracuse when the Athenian expedition arrived and whose tragedies Aristotle described as 'political' (Aristotle fr. 70; *TrGF* 1, 50). The tradition continued vigorously in the fourth century, with the tyrants Dionysos of Syracuse and Mamerkos of Katane (*TrGF* 1, 87) prominent at home and abroad; while Akhaios of Syracuse, author of at least ten tragedies, won at the Attic Lenaia around 330.[50]

To return to the discussion of choral terminology in the West: Pollux writes that in his comedy the *Seizures* (Ἁρπαγαί, fr. 13 K.–A.) Epikharmos used the term χορηγεῖον instead of διδασκαλεῖον,[51] while his *Odysseus the Deserter* (Ὀδυσσεὺς αὐτόμολος, fr. 103 K.–A.) is referred to without quotation for the more general phenomenon (of *khoreg-* for *didask-* roots to refer to choral/theatrical training). This Doric and west Greek tendency

---

thus another example, to add to that of Stesikhoros, of *Horse* being an alternative name for a *Sack of Ilion*—and so further supporting Ma's case above (Chapter 8) that the Teian *Horse* was on the Trojan subject.

[46] The presence of Attic vases with images probably related to Attic tragedy is another indication of the wider interest in (Attic) tragedy in Sicily, and in Aiskhylos in particular. Many significant finds come from Gela: Todisco (2002) 53; and see now the compendium of material in Todisco (2003); for greater detail, see Kossatz-Deissmann (1978); cf. Allan (2001).

[47] *TrGF* 1, 21.

[48] *TrGF* 1, 70.

[49] Th. 6.4.4; Σ. Pi. *O.* 2.15a. See Luraghi (1994) esp. 28, 125.

[50] *IG* II² 2325.242; *TrGF* 1, 79.

[51] Epikharmos would in fact probably have used the form χοραγείων: K.–A. *ad* fr. 13.

to use 'choral' words for 'training' or 'production' terms should not be taken to imply that the chorus itself had ceased to be a meaningful institution—on the contrary, if anything it points to a choral pre-ponderance. And there is good reason to believe that the works of Epikharmos themselves had a chorus, and interacted with a wider choral culture. There are for instance the many 'collective' titles of his works implying choruses—and among them, a *'Choreuts'* (*Χορευταί* or *Χορεύοντες*, cf. *Bakkhai*, *Thearoi*, *Komasts*, *Months*, *Islands*, *Persians*, *Citizens*, *Sirens*, *Trojans*; and cf. Sophron fr. 136); as well as the presence of a trapezoidal orchestra in the theatre at Syracuse.[52]

Photius and the Suda record another example of an early western Dorian *khoragos*, and though it is not made explicit, he too—on the evidence of Pollux—is very probably a trainer/poet (*didaskalos*). This is a fragment of the contemporary (fifth-century) Syracusan composer of mimes, Sophron. It is simply the phrase 'the *khoragos* scratches himself' or 'the *khoragos* is scratched'—ὁ χοραγὸς ξύεται (fr. 147 K.–A.). This is cited without any further illuminating context apart from proximity to another phrase—αἴ τις τὸν ξύοντα ἀντιξύει—that may draw on a proverb along the lines of 'you scratch my back, I'll scratch yours'. The proverb however is in evidence only much later, and Hordern (2004: 174) wonders whether Sophron himself may not be the origin of it. There is in any case little reason to believe that the two phrases were continuous in the original mime.[53] Pure speculation aside, we can say little else about this other than that it conjures an image of a choral trainer (*didaskalos*) being literally or metaphorically scratched by himself or another.[54]

All this implies that in the broadly Dorian, and specifically Sicilian, Greek performance traditions, from which our tablet certainly emerges, a *khoragos* is perhaps likely to be a trainer and/or poet—of a

---

[52] Cf. Kerkhof (2001) 151–3. One could also cite the story of the Athenian soldiers in the aftermath of the defeat in Sicily who supposedly won their freedom from Syracusans by performing Euripidean songs in particular, among them presumably many choral songs (more likely to be known by ex-chorus-members among the soldiers): Satyr. *Vit. Eur.* fr. 39 XIX; Plu. *Nic.* 29.

[53] See Hordern (2004) 174.

[54] Hordern (2004: 174) speculates about a chorus comically beset with an attack of itching.

production that involved choruses, to be sure. We should probably think of Eunikos and the other *khoragoi* in our tablet in this light. It is also likely that such trainer/poets were themselves active participants in the contest; that the differentiation we find elsewhere between poet and chorus-leader, or trainer and chorus-leader, did not apply.

It is an intriguing coincidence that the targets of attack in the only good parallels for this 'choral' curse-tablet (and they come from a non-Dorian context) are described as διδάσκαλοι (*didaskaloi*) and ὑποδιδάσκαλοι (*hypodidaskaloi*). These are two fourth- or third-century *defixiones* from Attica.[55] In one, the intended victims are described, with the repetition characteristic of such obsessive ritual, as 'all the trainers/poets and assistant trainers with Theagenes, both the trainers/poets and assistant trainers'.[56] Faraone is surely right to identify Theagenes as an Attic (leitourgical) *khoregos*, one with a formidable support-team at his disposal.[57] There are parallels in the way Apellis has taken such care to list a variety of opponents ranged against his Eunikos, including their sons and fathers (ll. 4–12). And the other Attic example, though less complete, evidently included 'all the children (*paides*)' in its attack, along with 'all the *didaskaloi* with Si-[ ]'—the last probably the partial name of another *khoregos*; while the children are probably the boys in his chorus.[58]

The case for a leitourgical *khoragia* in Gela revealed by this document certainly cannot be ruled out, however. The case against it, on the basis of Pollux, would be more compelling if he had not qualified his point with the word 'especially' (μάλιστα). The subject of the sentence about the use of these choral terms is 'the Greeks' in general. Among the Greeks, the Dorians 'especially' used *khorag*– terms for *didask* – words: that means that at least some other Greeks did so too; and it does not mean that Dorian practice was completely uniform.

---

[55] *CIA App.* 33 and 34. See Gager (1992) 49.

[56] *CIA App.* 34: το[ὺ]ς παρὰ Θε[α]γένει πάντας [δι]/δασκά(λους καὶ ὑποδιδα-(σκάλους)/καὶ διδασκάλο(υς)/καὶ ὑποδιδασκ(άλους).

[57] Faraone (1991) 12; Wilson (2000) 357 n. 34.

[58] *CIA App.* 33: [τ]ῶν / Μαντία / τοὺς παρὰ ΣιΛΟΚΣΑΛΗΙ / [δι]δασ[κ]άλους / πάντας / πάντας παῖδας.

What little we know of the political and cultural conditions of mid-fifth-century Sicily and Gela in particular is entirely consistent with the presence of rich and powerful élites keen to assert their position through cultural expenditure. A single individual example would be Psaumis of Kamarina, Olympic victor and poetic commissioner (Pindar *Olympian* 4 and 5), a man who also personally helped rebuild his city after its destruction by Gelon in the 480s. Whether the tyrants would have countenanced contest among such men in their cities' festivals is an open question. As we have seen, our document may in any case derive from the period after their fall in Gela, which is likely to have been a period that saw a broadening of possibilities for élite participation in public life.[59] But it is important to note that the leitourgical institution of the *khore/agia* was by no means exclusive to democratic polities. Nor should we take refuge in the hypothesis that its presence in Gela should be ascribed to its introduction there by visiting Athenians like Aiskhylos.

A leitourgical interpretation of our tablet could in fact iron out some of its apparent eccentricities. I would suggest, on this working hypothesis, that its author, Apellis, was himself a competing *khoragos*, and that Eunikos was in his 'team', a star performer of some kind, actor or singer. The prayer is, after all, a request for his success, and Apellis' 'love' for Eunikos is far from being inconsistent with his having a personal interest in his agonistic victory.

Most of the others named are also competing *khoragoi*. Following the inclusive 'all *khoragoi*' of (III), we move to specific, named rivals: Kaledias; Sosias—whose own star performer, [Mel]anthios, is also mentioned, perhaps too along with a reference to the source of his financial support (the shop or bar); Pyria⟨s⟩, Mysskelos, Damophantos and the[ir *khorag*]os (adopting the reading suggested by Jordan) become members or supporters of another team.[60]

It is a striking fact that the manner in which Apellis has expressed his wish for Eunikos' success makes it quite likely that he expected

---

[59] For the possibility of leitourgies under the Peisistratids see Wilson (2000) 14–17.

[60] Alternatively we could continue to regard Apellis as having no direct involvement in the contest, and see Eunikos as a *khoragos* among these others. The pair of Sosias and [Mel]anthios, however, may incline us towards seeing a two-tier competitive pattern of 'backers' and performers.

there to be women in the audience of the choral contest in which his friend was competing. Having 'marked down' the group of competitors and their male relatives in (VI), Apellis goes on to pray that no one be more σπουδαῖος than Eunikos 'with men or with women'. I have translated the adjective here as '(worthy to be) taken more seriously', but perhaps closer to the mark is something like 'arousing enthusiasm or admiration'. The expression captures the charismatic power of the successful contender, beautiful, skilled, and victorious. The idea and language are evocative of Alkibiades, and in particular of the response he was said to have generated habitually in the spotlight of a huge theatrical audience: 'whenever he was *khoregos*' he wore a gorgeous purple robe in the procession and 'was the object of the adoring gaze (ἐθαυμάζετο) not only of men, but of women too' (Athenaios 12.534c). The last phrase offers a striking parallel to that in line 12 of our document. In wishing for this sort of charismatic adulation for Eunikos (which would in turn doubtless reflect back on himself as his lover), Apellis inadvertently alerts us to the likely presence of women in the Geloan festival audience.

EROS AND THE CHORUS

Apellis' prayer is, so it seems, first and foremost an attempt to win the affection of Eunikos. It fits into a well-known category of curses or prayers that has a fundamentally erotic orientation and objective— the securing of the affections and charms of a particular target within a context of fierce rivalry.[61] In that respect, it may be best termed a *charitesion*. It also takes its place alongside the only two other known examples, both from fourth- or third-century Attica, of curses from the choral, agonistic sphere (mentioned above). The Sicilian tablet is, however, the only one in which these two spheres of 'competition'—the choral and the erotic—explicitly intersect. That intersection is, however, paralleled in other sources.[62] Apellis' core wish—that 'all praise and admire (Eunikos) both willingly and

[61] See Gager (1992) 78–115; Faraone (1999).

[62] Wilson (2000) 254–6 for the Athenian khoregic context; Calame (1977) I for Alkman and the wider phenomenon.

unwillingly' (ll. 2–4)—recalls some of the language and sentiments expressed in the seventh century by Spartan girls in choruses for their leader-figures—including a *Hagesikhora* ('Leader-of-chorus'). I think in particular of the point at which the girls who sing Alkman's first *Partheneion* declare their awestruck affection for their leader (probably the Agido they have just described as brilliantly glowing as the sun): 'But our glorious *khoragos* does not allow me either to praise or blame her' (ἐμὲ δ' οὔτ' ἐπαινῆν οὔτε [μ]ωμήσασθαι νιν ἁ κλεννὰ χοραγός οὐδ' ἁμῶς ἐῆι, fr. 3 Calame ll. 43–5).[63]

The further self-description of the interaction between (as it appears) members of this chorus and the leader-figures of Agido and Hagesikhora is similarly charged with erotic overtones (see esp. ll. 74–7); as is that from another maiden's chorus by Alkman who sing of 'limb-loosening desire', seemingly directed towards a choral leader called Astymeloisa ('Darling of the town') whose swiftly moving long legs and beautiful hair are fleetingly evoked (fr. 26 Calame ll. 61, 70–2).[64] While the Spartan girls seem to have a limit placed on the (in any case somewhat stylised) expression of their erotic emotions for their leaders, as part of the rite of passage in which they are engaged, in Gela it seems we catch a glimpse of the rawer expression of a desired affection sought of a choral performer by another male (whether older or younger we cannot say, though Jordan's assumption that Apellis is the *erastes* is most plausible). It does seem quite likely that Apellis himself is directly involved in the choral contest in some way: he is certainly extremely well informed about it.[65]

---

[63] Calame (1983) 326–7.

[64] Calame (1983) 403–13. See also Stehle (1997).

[65] Another relevant *comparandum* is the erotic graffiti found in or near sanctuaries or gymnasia which praises the balletic skills of love objects or compares skill in dance with skill in sex. The best-attested examples come from Thera, where rock-cut inscriptions praising the erotic charms of males, along with their dance-skills, were probably associated with the cult of Apollo Karneios and competitive dance in that cult. See Powell (1991) 171–80 with earlier bibliography. Two examples: *IG* XII 3, 543: 'Barbax dances well and has given [me] pleasure'; *IG* XII 3, 536—a set of agonistic, 'capping', graffiti: 'Pheidippides got fucked here. / Timagoras and Empheres and I—we got fucked too. / Emp(h)ylos [did] this [got fucked too? carved these words?]. . . / Empedokles wrote this. And he danced, by Apollo!' Translation of Powell (1991: 180), who adds, 'This youthful pederastic boaster not only writes—he dances too!' For similar inscriptions on Thasos see Garlan and Masson (1982).

COMPARATIVE CHORAL PRACTICE

Further comparison with the choral culture of Archaic Sparta may throw some light on the inclusion of Sosias and the shop (or bar) of the Alkiadai in Apellis' curse ((V), ll. 8–9). I think of the passage in Alkman's first *Partheneion* (fr. 3 Calame) in which the girls air the possibility of 'going to the house of Ainesimbrota' to secure some sort of aid in their struggles, choral and erotic. Opinion divides as to whether this Ainesimbrota is more probably a (rival?) expert in choral leadership or a *pharmakeutria* who might dispense love-magic.[66] A shop or bar ($\kappa\alpha\pi\epsilon\lambda\epsilon\acute{\iota}o$ l. 8) is perhaps not intrinsically a very likely term to use to describe a place of choral training; but a shop may all the same have been put to that purpose in Gela, a city whose Rhodian and Cretan roots may have made its élite less precious than that of Athens about matters mercantile.[67] As Jordan suggests, we may see here a form of collegial choral organisation—and perhaps, of sponsorship—based around a commercial business.

In the first and principal verbal act of this document (III), Apellis 'marks down' all the *khoragoi* to ineffectuality in word and deed. By deed we are perhaps encouraged to think especially of their dance-movements or, if leitourgical *khoragoi*, of their practical support of their teams.[68] They are also marked down for failure both in and outside the *agones*—*along with* their (male) children and their fathers. This generational smiting may be part of the formulaic sort of 'root and branch' rhetoric of curse, but Jordan asks pertinently whether there may not be a more pragmatic aspect to their inclusion: does this imply that these *khoragoi* were of an age to have sons; and did fathers (– and sons? –) play some role, perhaps in supporting *khoragoi* in the contests?

---

[66] Calame (1983) 337.

[67] On *IGDS* 130 (dated *c.* 500), one of the few funerary inscriptions from Gela, the trade of the deceased in life—a cord-maker ($[\kappa]\alpha\lambda o\pi o\iota\acute{o}s$)—is explicitly marked. This is unusual for any region at this date: Dubois (1989) 148.

[68] Cf. the use of expressions such as $\chi\rho\acute{\eta}\mu\alpha\sigma\iota$ $\kappa\alpha\grave{\iota}$ $\sigma\acute{\omega}\mu\alpha\tau\iota$, 'with money and in person' (e.g. Lys. 19.58) of leitourgical contributors in Athens: Wilson (2000) 135–6.

As for the idea of paternal support for their son's choral endeavours, this is entirely plausible, and parallels could be drawn from the Theban ritual of the Daphnephoria. Here, in Pindar's day, son and father of a noble house—as well, it seems, as mother and daughter—are all involved with different roles in a choral event that expresses and asserts the position of the house within wider Boiotian social and political networks.[69] There is also the clearly observable phenomenon in the context of the Athenian theatre that saw theatrical and other musical crafts being transmitted through generations of the same family. We might note in particular the claim preserved in the Suda regarding the practice of the tragic poet Karkinos (who, as I have noted, has Sicilian connections): in forming his choruses, he 'introduced [his sons as khoreuts] to dance in his own dramas'.[70] The sons of tragic poets and actors evidently often entered the trade.[71] Also relevant from the Athenian context is the practice of fathers and sons sharing the same monuments recording their agonistic victories with choruses.[72]

Sosias may, I think, be one of the Alkiadai mentioned as shop-owners in (V) himself: 'Sosias I mark down, the one from the shop of the Alkiadai, because of his love of [Mel]anthios.' It is an intriguing coincidence that one of the very few epigraphic finds from the Archaic Geloan necropolis (on Capo Soprano), consists of the remains of a substantial funerary monument in the shape of a Doric *naiskos*, dated to around 500 BC, with a list of some ten or more names on it—and among them, a Sosias and an Alkias (Fig. 32).[73] The presence of a Sosias and an Alkias on the same funerary monument certainly suggests they were related; the monument itself implies social elevation of the family; and the find-spot and relative rarity of the names speak for a possible relation to the Sosias and the

---

[69] Pi. fr. 94b S.-M.; Kurke (2006); Stehle (1997) 93; Wilson (2000) 280–1.

[70] Suid. κ 396.

[71] Sutton (1987).

[72] Wilson (2000) 228–9, 232.

[73] Dubois (1989) 148–50 no. 131, Museum of Syracuse no. 20087; Jeffrey (1990) no. 56. Dubois (1989) 149 reads ten names, including as a separate name rather than an ethnic one Geloios. There appear to have been at least two other names, now illegible, on the monument. See Gentili (1946) 11–13.

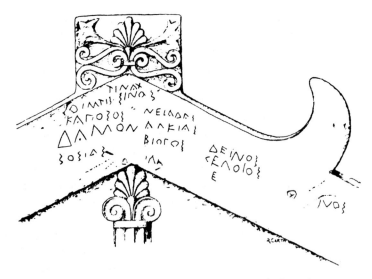

Fig. 32 Line-drawing of the inscription, consisting of a list of some ten or more names, on a monument from the Archaic necropolis of Gela (Capo Soprano), in the shape of a Doric *naiskos*, dated around 500 BC.

'offspring of Alkias' in our document.[74] It is therefore quite likely that the Sosias of our tablet (perhaps the grandson of that on the funerary monument?) was one of the Alkiadai who owned the shop. Perhaps they, as a family group (recalling our document's reference to fathers and sons), formed a competing chorus.

I must defer to the experts on the matter, but I am not convinced that this was necessarily a funerary monument, and I would like to air the possibility that it may rather have been a dedication, quite

[74] Sosias is recorded 26 times in *LGPN* 1 (including 6 times in Kyrenaica), 52 in *LGPN* III, 25 times in *LGPN* IIIa (which includes western Greece and Sicily—with 13 Sicilian attestations), 36 times in *LGPN* IIIb and 26 times in *LGPN* IV; the corresponding figures for Alkias are: 5, 9, 20 (this figure again includes *Megale Hellas*: just 2 in Sicily, this one and another in Hellenistic Syracuse), 11; the name Alkiadas is recorded only in *LGPN* IIIa, 4 times (the single Sicilian occurrence is on our lead tablet, understanding Ἀλκιαδαν in line 8 as a proper name), and once in *LGPN* IIIb. Alkiadas is clearly confined to Doric and in particular western Greek contexts, while Alkias is slightly more broadly spread and Sosias much more widely diffused, though far from common.

possibly marking the victory or performance of a chorus. The form of the monument—a *naiskos* – and, more strikingly, the nature of its inscription, are equally if not more compatible with a dedicatory monument. The names are merely listed, with no indication of the relationship of their owners to one another,[75] no patronymics and nothing whatever by way of the traditional diction of epitaph. We might contrast the use of the explicit τὸ σᾶμα—'the funerary marker'—on two of the very small number of other Geloan monuments (*IGDS* 128 and 129); while a third (*IGDS* 130) furnishes the patronymic, as well as indicating the trade, of the deceased. The list on the *naiskos* seems too numerous and too imprecise in its formulation to be that of the dead within a tomb. Some other reason for their being collected in this way is needed.[76] There is, however, admittedly little that explicitly points to an agonistic group. The most suggestive element in that direction is the quite extraordinary name that heads the list, in prominent position—Τιναξσίνοος (Tinaxinoos). Guarducci drew attention to the 'lyric' and possibly erotic associations of this name, drawing for comparison on Sappho fr. 47 L-P: Ἔρος ἐτίναξέ μοι φρένας—'Eros has shaken my mind'.[77] This is entirely without parallel, and perhaps too outlandish for an ordinary name. It would however serve very well as a 'stage-name' for a star—'Mind-shaker'; or should that be 'Heartthrob'?

In fact, the few archaeologists who have discussed this intriguing monument seem to agree that the names were in fact probably added to it at a later date, but not long after it was erected—either 'through piety or for amusement' ('per pietà o per ozio', as Guarducci 1949–51: 110 put it). Thus they have been classified as *graffiti* names, and probably not in fact those of the deceased within.[78] By 'pietà' I suppose Guarducci envisages some friend or relative adding names that were omitted from the original design,

---

[75] At least one of the names—Kaposos—is indigenous (Dubois 1989: 149).

[76] Cf. e.g. the choral monument of Sokrates and Euripides from Anagyrous in Attica: *IG* I³ 969, *c*. 435. The names of the fourteen *tragoidoi* here have no patronymics or demotics. On this see Wilson (2000) 131–3.

[77] Guarducci (1949–51) 111 n. 1. The erotic associations of this name, if a performer, are apt.

[78] Gentili (1946) 11; Jeffrey (1990) 273. Cf. Dubois (1989) 148: 'très négligement gravés'.

or perhaps the names of family members who died after it had been erected.[79] That would not explain the negligence of the inscription, but few inscriptions of this date in this region are made with especial care.[80] Much could come under the rubric of 'ozio'. But, although the names are rather roughly formed and ill-organised, they are not the scrawls of an idle skulker in the cemetery, and may in fact be original to the design of the monument.[81]

If however they were inscribed by a later hand and had no germane association with the original plan of the monument, by far the most likely motivation for their inscription is that which frequently saw simple lists of names incised on (lead) tablets as *defixiones* – namely to curse and control.[82] This would give us another reason to connect this group, under the leadership of 'Heart-throb', with the world of agonistic choral performance. They may be a team of some dozen performers, one of whose rivals sought to enlist the aid of the powers of the dead against them by attaching their names to this tomb.

CHORAL NAMES

David Jordan has commented to me (*per litteras*) that Eunikos is aptly named for a would-be victor active in the world of choral contest.[83] If this is a name given at birth, it may suggest that he came from a family conscious of its status (we might compare the names of the Spartan élite who performed in choruses under Alkman's

---

[79] Gentili (1946) 13 thought of *nomina devotorum*. He describes the inscription of such names as an anticipation of the practice (known from other sites in Sicily) whereby such names are inscribed on *defixiones* with the intention of granting immunity to the tomb—'dare l'immunità alla tomba'.

[80] Cf. e.g. Dubois (1989) nos. 74–6, 88.

[81] This seems the more likely if Gentili (1946: 13) is right to read the words on the right-hand side as Δεῖνος Γελοῖος ἐ[ποίει], or ἐ[γράφει]—'Deinos the Geloan made (or wrote) this'.

[82] See n. 74 above. Examples of such lists from Attic *defixiones* include *CIA App.* 5–13, 19–31. I note in passing that a Eunikos appears on one such list (*CIA App.* 8), dating from the third century.

[83] Cf. also Faraone (1991) 28 n. 50: 'the hereditary nature of the curse and the significant name of Eunikos ("Good at Winning") may suggest a professional actor'.

direction such as Hagesikhora, Agesidamos, Agido[84]); if a 'nick name', Jordan suggests, it may have been won from past victories. However that may be, I would suggest that Apellis delicately draws on the magical potential of his friend's name in the closing phrases of the curse where, despite the illegible opening of line 13, the prayer that Eunikos be always victorious enforces a link between Εὐνίκοι ('for Eunikos') and ἀὲ νικᾶν ('always to be victorious').

This document shows us a context in which choral groups may have been formed at least in part by association through the male family line (and across three generations). It therefore seems more likely that Eunikos was named at birth with an eye to his hoped-for future agonistic career—whether that be taken to imply professionalism or the aspirations of a leisured élite conscious of its status, and of the need to assert and maintain it. Onomastics may be able to take this a little further, or at least to broaden the question. It is a striking coincidence that Eunikos was also the name of one of the choreuts on that most intriguing item of visual evidence for Classical theatrical practice, the Pronomos vase. He is in fact the 'first' choreut on that vase, in so far as he is at the far left-hand side in the top row of the overtly theatrical image. Very probably made in Athens in the late fifth century though found in a western context (Ruvo di Puglia), this krater evidently bears some quite close relation to a (successful) performance of the satyr-play, and so probably of tragedy, in Classical Athens. In addition to Eunikos, others among the named chorus-members on this vase include a Euagon and a Nikoleos. The case has recently been put (by Junker 2003) that these 'sprechenden Namen' serve to reflect the agonistic nature of the theatrical event, with at least a strong implication that Euagon in particular and Eunikos in all likelihood were not the names of actual choreuts involved in the performance that gave rise to the vase, and were probably not 'real' Attic names at all. They are, rather, included simply to evoke the world of agonistic performance.[85] The argument

---

[84] For Agesidamos as a choral leader, explicitly described in a fragment of Alkman as a *khoragos*, see Alkm. fr. 10, b.10ff., with Calame (1983) 277, 459, 463.

[85] Junker (2003: 331) distinguishes this small group of 'agonistic' names from a larger group of common Attic names among the choreuts on the vase. The latter are: Kharias, Kallias, Nikomakhos, Dorotheos, Dion, Philinos. See Wilson (forthcoming) further on Pronomos and his vase.

as it relates to the Pronomos vase is to my mind quite inadequate. Volume 7 of Traill's *PAA* (1998) names a definite Athenian Euagon (no. 425655), an *epimeletes* of the Boule *c.* 130–120, along with well over thirty Attic Eunikoi, among whom there are some very clear Classical examples.[86] Eunikos is thus a perfectly possible—if not common—Attic name, and there is no reason to regard Eunikos the choreut on the Pronomos vase as an invention.

Our ability to identify Eunikoi in Athenian and Geloan choruses in the fifth century implies that such family traditions or aspirations were shared across the Greek world (though it is worth pointing out that the name 'Eunikos' helpfully leaves open the possibility of success in *any* agonistic sphere.) We should not underestimate the inordinate importance of agonistic success to political supremacy and ideological needs among the élite of late Archaic Greek Sicily,[87] as also, under different conditions, in Classical Athens.[88] That importance was amply reflected in practices of naming. A full study of such names is beyond the scope of this book, but would be an invaluable pathway into the sociology of the musical arts in Greece. One name that must surely figure in such a study is an Athenian not mentioned thus far—Khoregos the comic poet.[89] Another is that of the man who appears on another financial document on lead from Sicily (Kamarina, *c.* 300), who is currently known as Koragos, but whom we should very probably call Khoragos.[90]

---

[86] These include a comic poet of *c.* 400 (*PCG* 5, 278); a late fifth-century demesman from Aixone (*PAA* 5850); a fourth-century member of the Pandionid tribe (*PAA* 5854); and a demesman from Kholargai (cf. D. 57.43; *APF* 3126).

[87] Luraghi (1994) 127 writes of 'lo stretto legame tra vittoria agonistica e supremezia politica che percorre tutta la storia greca arcaica, e che proprio in Sicilia, nei primi decenni del V secolo, diviene un fenomeno di importanza cruciale'. That the agonisitic culture of Greek cities in Sicily itself in turn became a subject of theatrical attention is clear from e.g. Epikharmos' comedy *Epinik[i]os*: *PCG* I, 33.

[88] Cf. Osborne (1993).

[89] On whom see Luppe (1971) 126. Note also the choreut [E]pinikos on the Attic bell-krater of *c.* 425, thought to represent a dithyrambic chorus: Copenhagen 13817; for the name and full discussion see Johansen (1959) esp. 9–10.

[90] The document (reference to which I owe to David Jordan) is Dubois (1989) no. 125. The name Κοράγου appears as the buyer in the contract (fragment 2a). Dubois (1989) 136 associates the name, which is otherwise unknown, to the title given to Arkadian priests, Κοραγοί (*IG* V 2, 265 and 266). This is improbable in the extreme, and the first letter of the name is easily and more plausibly read as a khi, not a kappa.

ENODIAI ?

What were the forces upon whose aid Apellis called to promote the appeal and success of his friend Eunikos? Chthonic deities are *prima facie* the most likely candidates, even in a prayer that is as much a *charitesion* as a curse. With no knowledge of the archaeological context in which this tablet was found we are thrown back on the enigmatic document itself. I conclude with a tentative and speculative suggestion.

In the first place, the fact that the document is inscribed on lead already efficacious in a financial transaction should perhaps not be neglected, even though such reuse of lead (as of ostraka) is fairly common and unexceptional. The proven efficacy of the object for Apellis may thereby be implicitly—or perhaps, quite explicitly (see below)—adduced in the second use to which it was put. We could have here an example of the activation of the power of an object already successful that is comparable to the more spectacular reuse of tripods dedicated at Olympia—already markers of élite success and authentic adjudication—as the material on which the Eleans chose to inscribe their laws.[91]

Both texts on this tablet share a concern with τιμά (*tima*).[92] In the case of the financial transaction on Side *A*, τιμά—the 'value' of the cattle (l. 5)—is the essential matter at stake in the record. And, whatever the precise nature of the interaction between Apellis, Myskon, Demokritos, and Empedokles, it seems that Apellis successfully relied on this material record of his having handed over that τιμά (as a monetary sum) in order to draw it back again. The tablet was more than a handy piece of writing material that had outlived its initial usefulness: it had a proven power to draw τιμά.

On Side *B*, τιμά appears in the frustratingly damaged line 13, in Jordan's section VII:

ὃς οὗτος <ὁ> βόλιμος, τὸς *TE-*/[- *c.* 5 -]*OΔIAITIMAN* ἐρύσαιντο
Εὐνίκοι ἀὲ νικᾶν παντὲ.

---

[91] My thanks to Ben Brown for this point. On the Olympic laws: Siewart (1992).

[92] For what follows—including the suggested reading of ll. 12–13—I am greatly indebted to Archibald McKenzie.

The formula of sympathetic magic here that sees the correlation of ὅς and τός appears to extend to οὗτος, suggesting that the *TE-/* of lines 13–14 ought to be a form of τῆνος. A possible restoration becomes:

Ὅς οὗτος <ὁ> βόλιμος, τὸς τή/[νων Ἐν]ọ́διαι τιμὰν ἐρύσαιντο. Εὐνίκοι ἀὲ νικᾶν παντέ.

The meaning would be: 'Just as this lead (*sc.* effectively drew the *tima* of the guarantee), so may the *Enodiai* draw out the *tima* of those men (*sc.* the rival *khoragoi* and their supporters listed in the tablet by ἀπογράφω)'. Εὐνίκοι ἀὲ νικᾶν παντέ becomes a free-standing wish: 'For Eunikos may there be victory always, everywhere.'

Enodiai is not otherwise attested as a collective name or epithet, though the word is used in the singular of Hekate in particular, but also of Persephone, by Sophokles among others.[93] In Thessaly and Macedonia, *Enodia* frequently stands alone as a divine name, and she is a powerful religious presence in many places.[94] It is therefore just possible that this was a way of referring to the 'pair' of chthonic goddesses who so dominated the religious and civic life of early Gela, and in whose cult these choruses may have been performing—

---

[93] Soph. *Ant.* 1199 (ἐνοδίαν θεόν): Hekate is probably intended, though Persephone is also a possibility: Kamerbeek (1978) 194. In fr. 535.2 R (τῆς εἰνοδίας Ἑκάτης), Hekate *einodia* is in attendance on another deity, who should be Artemis, Demeter, or Persephone. In the *Homeric Hymn to Demeter* (440), Hekate is the πρόπολος of Persephone; identified with Artemis at Eleusis, she serves there as 'intermediary between [the Great Goddesses] and mankind': Richardson (1974) 295. At Eur. *Ion* 1048 (Εἰνοδία θύγατερ Δάματρος) the chorus prays to *Einodia* to direct the attack on Ion. It is difficult to decide whether Hekate or Persephone is meant: cf. *Hel.* 569–70 with Kannicht (1969) II.160–1; Owen (1939) 138. Hekate also has this epiclesis in many magical papyri: cf. e.g. Preisendanz no. 4, ll. 1434, 2559, 2609, 2720, 2857. 'Kore' is given as the explanatory gloss for the epiclesis *Hodia* by Hesychius, s.v.: Ὁδία· ἡ κόρη θεός.

[94] Thessaly: e.g. *BCH* 7, 60 (Pherai); *BCH* 13, 392 (Larissa: a dedication 'to Zeus Meilikhios and *Enodia* and the city'), *SEG* 35, 590 (*c.* 450–425); *SEG* 34, 572, 574 (Phthiotic Thebes, *c.* 300: dedications to *Ennodia*); cf. Polyainetos 8.43. A Thessalian (from Phakion) makes a dedication to Artemis or Hekate [*E]nodia* in Euboea: *BCH* 15, 412. Macedonia: e.g. *SEG* 27, 1291 (= *SEG* 30, 579) (Pella, early fourth century, funerary epigram for a priestess of *Enodia*); *SEG* 31, 625 (Beroia, *c.* 275–250, dedication to *Enodia*). On the Thessalian cult and its spread into Macedon see Chrysostomou (1998); Morgan (2003) 135–40.

Demeter and Kore. Or perhaps this was the title of an otherwise unattested pair of avatars of the goddesses, or attendant forces who served as their intermediaries with the world of men—'watchers of the way' between this world and theirs.

Bibliography

Alemdar, S. (2000). 'Le monument de Lysicrate et son trépied', *Ktema* 25: 199–206.

Allan, W. (2001). 'Euripides in Megale Hellas: some aspects of the early reception of tragedy', *G&R* 48: 67–83.

Allen, R. (1983). *The Attalid Kingdom: A Constitutional History*. Oxford.

Aloni, A. (2000). 'Anacreonte ad Atene: datazione e significato di alcune iscrizioni tiranniche', *ZPE* 130: 81–94.

Amandry, P. (1976). 'Trépieds d'Athènes: I. Dionysies', *BCH* 100: 15–93.

—— (1977). 'Trépieds d'Athènes: II. Thargélies', *BCH* 101: 165–202.

—— (1997). 'Monument chorégiques d'Athènes', *BCH* 121: 445–487.

Amandry, P. and Ducat, J. (1973). 'Trépieds déliens', *Études déliennes. BCH Suppl.* 1: 17–64.

Amandry, P. and Spyropoulos, T. (1974). 'Monuments chorégiques d'Orchomène de Béotie', *BCH* 98: 171–246.

Amelotti, M. (1955). 'La posizione degli atleti di fronte al diritto romano', *SDHI* 21: 123–56.

Aneziri, S. (1997). 'Les synagonistes du théâtre grec aux époques hellénistique et romaine: une question de terminologie et de fonction, in B. Le Guen (ed.), *De la scène aux gradins. Pallas* 47: 51–71.

—— (2001–2). 'A different guild of artists: τὸ Κοινὸν τῶν περὶ τὴν Ἱλαρὰν Ἀφροδίτην τεχνιτῶν', Ἀρχαιογνωσία 11: 47–56.

—— (2003). *Die Vereine der dionysischen Techniten im Kontext der hellenistischen Gesellschaft. Untersuchungen zur Geschichte, Organisation und Wirkung der hellenistischen Technitenvereine. Historia Einzelschriften 163.* Stuttgart.

Angiolillo, S. (1997). *Arte e cultura nell'Atene di Pisistrato e dei Pisistratidi: Ὁ ἐπὶ Κρόνου βίος.* Bari.

Arena, R. (1992). *Iscrizioni greche arcaiche di Sicilia e Magna Grecia*, vol. II: *Iscrizioni di Sicilia. Iscrizioni di Gela e Agrigento.* Milan.

Arnush, M. (1995). 'The career of Peisistratos, son of Hippias', *Hesperia* 64: 135–62.

Auffarth, C. (1991). *Der drohende Untergang. Religiöse Versuche und Vorarbeiten 39.* Berlin.

Bacchielli, L. (1993). 'Pittura funeraria antica in Cirenaica', *LibStud* 24: 77–116.

Baran, M. and Petzl, G. (1977–8). 'Beobachtungen im nordöstlichen Hinterland von Teos', *IstMitt* 27–8: 301–8.

Barbantani, S. (2000). 'Competizioni poetiche tespiesi e mecenatismo tolemaico: un gemellaggio tra l'antica e la nuova sede delle Muse nella seconda metà del III secolo A.C. ipotesi su *SH* 959', *Lexis* 18: 127–72.

Barron, J. (1980). 'Bakchylides, Theseus and a woolly cloak', *BICS* 27: 1–8.

Battaglia, R. (1957). 'Eschilo e il teatro greco di Gela', *Archivo storico per la Sicilia orientale* 53: 168–73.

Baudot, A. (1973). *Musiciens romains de l'antiquité.* Montreal.

Bauer, H. (1977). 'Lysikratesdenkmal, Baubestand und Rekonstruktion', *MDAI(A)* 92: 197–227.

Bean, G. (1966). *Aegean Turkey: An Archaeological Guide.* London.

Bechtel, F. (1917). *Die historischen Personennamen des Griechischen bis zur Kaiserzeit.* Halle, repr. Hildesheim 1982.

Béquignon, Y. and Laumonier, A. (1925). 'Fouilles de Téos (1924)', *BCH* 49: 281–321.

Behrend, D. (1970). *Attische Pachturkunden.* Munich.

Bélis, A. (1988). 'Les termes grecs et latins désignant des spécialités musicales', *RPh* 62.2: 227–50.

—— (1995). 'Cithare, citharistes et citharodes', *CRAI* 1995: 1025–65.

—— (1999). *Les musiciens dans l'antiquité.* Paris.

Bergemann, J. (1997). *Demos und Thanatos.* Munich.

Berger, E. (1983). 'Dreiseitiges Relief mit Dionysos und Niken', *Antike Kunst* 26: 114–16.

Berger, S. (1989). 'Democracy in the Greek West and the Athenian example', *Hermes* 117: 303–16.

Bergmans, M. (1979). 'Théores argiens au Fayoum (*P. Lond.* VII 1973)', *ChrÉg* 54: 127–30.

Berneker, E. (1967a). ' Ἐγγύη', *KlP* 22: 267–8.

—— (1967b). ' Ἐγγύησις', *KlP* 2: 268.

Beschi, L. (1969). 'Una base triangolare dell'Asklepieion di Atene', *RivArchCl* 21: 216–27.

Bevan, E. (1987). 'The goddess Artemis and the dedication of bears in sanctuaries', *ABSA* 82: 17–21.

Bieber, M. (1961). *History of Greek and Roman Theater,* 2nd revised and enlarged edn., Princeton.

Biers, W. and Boyd, T. (1982). 'Ikarion in Attica: 1888–1988', *Hesperia* 51: 1–18.

Biraschi, A. (1999). 'La fondazione di Iasos fra mito e storia: a proposito di Polibio XVI.12.2', *PdP* 54.4/6: 250–60.

Bizard, L. and Leroux, G. (1907). 'Fouilles de Délos', BCH 31: 498–511.

Blümel, W. (1994). 'Über die chronologische und geographische Verteilung einheimischer Personennamen in griechischen Inschriften aus Karien', in M. Giannotta et al. (eds.), *La decifrazione del Cario. Atti del 1º simposio internazionale Roma, 3–4 maggio 1993.* Rome, 65–86.

Bodensteiner, E. (1891). 'Über choregische Weihinschriften', *Commentationes philologicae conventui philologorum Monachii congregatorum oblatae.* Munich, 38–92.

Boeckh, A. (1828). *Économie politique des Athéniens.* Paris (translation by A. Lalignant of *Die Staatshaushaltung der Athener,* 1st edn., Berlin, 1817).

Bonacasa, N. and Ensoli, S. (eds.) (2000). *Cirene.* Milan.

Bookidis, N. and Stroud, R. (1997). *Corinth XVIII,* vol. III: *The Sanctuary of Demeter and Kore: Topography and Architecture.* Princeton.

Bosher, K. (2006). 'Theater on the periphery: a social and political history of theater in early Sicily', Ph.D. dissertation, University of Michigan.

Bousquet, J. (1952). *Le trésor de Cyrène. Fouilles de Delphes,* vol. II, 1. Paris.

Bouvier, H. (1985). 'Hommes de lettres dans les inscriptions delphiques', *ZPE* 58: 119–35.

Bowersock, G. (1999). 'Les *euhemerioi* et les confréries joyeuses', *CRAI:* 1241–56.

Bowie, A. (1993). *Aristophanes: Myth, Ritual and Comedy.* Cambridge.

Bravo, B. (1980). 'Sulân: représailles et justice privée contre des étrangers dans les cités grecques', *ASNP* 3.10: 675–987.

Briant, P. (1998). 'Droaphernès et la statue de Sardes', in M. Brosius and A. Kuhrt (eds.), *Studies in Persian History: Essays in Memory of David Lewis.* Leiden, 205–26.

Brinck, A. (1886). *Inscriptiones graecae ad choregiam pertinentes.* Halle.

Bringmann, K. (2000). *Geben und Nehmen. Monarchische Wohltätigkeit und Selbstdarstellung im Zeitalter des Hellenismus. Schenkungen hellenisticher Herrscher an griechische Städte und Heiligtümer,* vol. II, 1. Berlin.

Bringmann, K., Ameling, W. and Schmidt-Dounas, B. (1995). *Schenkungen hellenistischer Herrscher an griechische Städte und Heiligtümer,* vol. I. Berlin.

Broneer, O. (1973). *Isthmia III: Topography and Architecture.* Princeton.

Bruneau, P. (1970). *Recherches sur les cultes de Délos à l'époque hellénistique et à l'époque impériale.* Paris.

Buchanan, J. (1962). *Theorika.* Locust Valley (N.Y.).

Buck, C. D. and Petersen, W. (1948). *A Reverse Index of Greek Nouns and Adjectives.* Chicago.

—— (1955). *The Greek Dialects.* Chicago.

Buraselis, K. (1982). *Das hellenistische Makedonien und die Ägäis.* Munich.

—— (1993). 'Ambivalent roles of centre and periphery', in P. Bilde and T. Engberg-Pedersen (eds.), *Centre and Periphery in the Hellenistic World: Studies in Hellenistic Civilization*, vol. IV. Aarhus, 251–70.

Burford, A. (1966). 'Notes on the Epidaurian building inscriptions', *ABSA* 61: 296–300.

—— (1969). *The Greek Temple Builders at Epidauros*. Liverpool.

Burkert, W. (1987). 'The making of Homer in the sixth century BC: rhapsodes versus Stesichoros', *Papers on the Amasis Painter and his World*. Malibu, 43–62.

—— (1993). 'Bacchic *Teletai* in the Hellenistic age', in T. Carpenter and C. Faraone (eds.), *Masks of Dionysos*. Ithaca, 259–75.

Burnett, A. (1988). 'Jocasta in the west: the Lille Stesichorus', *CA* 7: 107–54.

Burrell, B. (2003). *Neokoroi*. Leiden and New York.

Buschor, E. (1928). 'Ein choregisches Denkmal', *MDAI(A)* 53: 96–108.

Byrne, S. (1995). '*IG* II² 1095 and the Delia of 98/97 BC', *ZPE* 109: 55–61.

—— (2003). *Roman Citizens of Athens*. Leuven, Dudley (Mass.).

Caillemer, E. (1877). 'II. Ἀρχιτέκτων', in C. Daremberg and E. Saglio (eds.), *Dictionnaire des antiquités grecques et romaines*, vol. I. Paris, 382.

Calame, C. (1977). *Les choeurs de jeunes filles en Grèce archaïque*. Rome.

—— (1983). *Alcman*. Rome.

—— (1990). *Thésée et l'imaginaire Athénien: légende et culte en Grèce antique*. Lausanne.

—— (*forthcoming*). 'Apollo in Delphi and in Delos: Poetic performances between paean and dithyramb'.

Caldelli, M. (1993). *L'Agon Capitolinus*. Rome.

—— (1995). 'Considerazioni sulla cronologia dei Chrysanthina di Sardis', *ZPE* 109: 62–9.

—— (1997). 'Gli Agoni alla greca nelle regioni occidentali dell'impero. La Gallia Narbonensis', *Acc. Naz. dei Lincei: Memorie* 9. 4: 387–481.

—— (1998). 'Varia agonistica ostiensia', in G. Paci (ed.), *Epigrafia Romana in area adriatica*. Macerata, 225–47.

Callot, J.-J. (1999). *Recherches sur les cultes en Cyrénaïque durant le haut-empire romain*. Nancy.

Calvet, M. and Roesch, P. (1966). 'Les Sarapieia de Tanagra', *RA*: 297–332.

Cameron, A. (1965). 'Wandering poets: a literary movement in Byzantine Egypt', *Historia* 14: 470–509.

—— (1995). *Callimachus and his Critics*. New York.

Camp, J. (1986). *The Athenian Agora: Excavations in the Heart of Athens*. London.

—— (2001). *The Archaeology of Athens*. New Haven and London.

Caputo, V. (ed.) (2004). *Iasos tra VI e IV sec. a. C.: miscellanea storico-archeologica*. Ferrara.

Cardinali, G. (1906). *Il regno di Pergamo*. Rome.

Caskey, L. and Beazley, J. (1954). *Attic Vase Paintings in the Museum of Fine Arts, Boston*. London.

Cassio, A. (1994). 'Giavellotti contro frecce: nuova lettura di una tessera dal tempio di Atena a Camarina e Hom. *Od.* 8, 229', *RFIC* 122: 5–20.

Catucci, M. (2003). 'Tempi e modi di diffusione di temi teatrali in Italia attraverso la ceramica di importazione', in Todisco (ed.), 1–97.

Cawkwell, G. (1995). 'Early Greek tyranny and the people', *CQ* 45: 73–86.

Ceccarelli, P. (1995). 'Le dithyrambe et la pyrrhique: à propos de la nouvelle liste de vainqueurs aux Dionysies de Cos (Segre, ED 234)', *ZPE* 108: 287–305.

—— (2004). 'Dancing the *Pyrrhiche* at Athens', in Murray and Wilson (eds.), 91–117.

—— (*forthcoming*). 'The dithyramb in the Hellenistic period'.

Chamoux, F. (1953). *Cyrène sous la monarchie des Battiades*. Paris.

—— (1988). 'Les comptes des démiurges à Cyrène', in D. Knoepfler (ed.), *Comptes et inventaires dans la cité grecque*. Neuchâtel and Geneva, 143–54.

Chandezon, C. (2000). 'Foires et panégyries dans le monde grec classique et hellénistique', *REG* 113: 70–100.

—— (2003). *L'élevage en Grèce (fin Ve–fin Ier s. A.C.): l'apport des sources épigraphiques*. Bordeaux.

Chandler, R. (1775). *Travels in Asia Minor*. Oxford

—— (1817). *Travels in Asia Minor and Greece: or, An Account of a Tour Made at the Expense of the Society of Dilettanti*. London.

Chaniotis, A. (1988a). 'Als die Diplomaten noch tanzten und sangen. Zu zwei Dekreten kretischer Städte in Mylasa', *ZPE* 71: 154–56.

—— (1988b). *Historie und Historiker in den griechischen Inschriften: epigraphische Beiträge zur griechischen Historiographie*. Wiesbaden.

—— (1990). 'Zur Frage des Spezialisierung im griechischen Theater des Hellenismus und der Kaiserzeit auf der Grundlage der neuen Prosopographie der dionysischen Techniten', *Ktema* 15: 89–108.

—— (1995). 'Sich selbst feiern? Die städtischen Feste des Hellenismus im Spannungsfeld zwischen Religion und Politik', in M. Wörrle and P. Zanker (eds.), *Stadtbild und Bürgerbild im Hellenismus*. Munich, 147–72.

—— (1997). 'Theatricality beyond the theater: staging public life in the Hellenistic world', in B. Le Guen (ed.), *De la scène aux gradins*. *Pallas* 47: 219–59.

—— (1999). 'Empfängerformular und Urkundenfälschung: Bemerkungen zum Inschriftendossier von Magnesia am Mäander', in R. Khoury (ed.), *Urkunden und Urkundenformulare im klassischen Altertum und in den orientalischen Kulturen.* Heidelberg, 51–69.

—— (2003). 'Der Kaiserkult im Osten des römischen Reiches im Kontext der zeitgenossischen Ritualpraxis', in *Die Praxis der Herrschaftsverehrung in Rom und seinen Provinzen.* Tübingen, 3–28.

—— (2005). 'Ritual dynamics in the eastern Mediterranean: case studies in ancient Greece and Asia Minor', in W. V. Harris (ed.), *Rethinking the Mediterranean.* Oxford, 141–66.

Chapouthier, F., Salac, A. and Salviat, F. (1956). 'Le théâtre de Samothrace', *BCH* 80: 118–46.

Choremi-Spetsieri, A. (1994). 'Ή οδός των Τριπόδων και τα χορηγικά μνημεία στην αρχαία Αθήνα', in W. Coulson et al. (eds.), *The Archaeology of Athens and Attica under the Democracy. Proceedings of an International Conference celebrating 2,500 years since the birth of democracy in Greece, held at the American School of Classical Studies at Athens, December 4–6, 1992,* 31–42.

Chrysostomou, P. (1998). *Η Θεσσαλική Θεά Εν[ν]οδία ή Φεραία Θεά.* Athens.

Clay, D. (2004). *Archilochos Heros: The Cult of Poets in the Greek Polis.* Cambridge (Mass.) and London.

Clinton, K. (1971). 'Inscriptions from Eleusis', *AE*: 81–136.

Cole, S. G. (1984). *Theoi Megaloi: The Cult of the Great Gods at Samothrace.* Leiden.

—— (1989). 'Mysteries of Samothrace during the Roman period', *ANRW* II Prinzipat 18.2: 1564–98.

—— (1993). 'Procession and celebration at the Dionysia', in R. Scodel (ed.), *Theater and Society in the Classical World.* Michigan, 25–38.

Colin, G. (1905). *Le culte d'Apollon Pythien à Athènes.* Paris.

Connor, W. (1968). *Theopompus and Fifth-Century Athens.* Cambridge (Mass.).

—— (1987). 'Tribes, festivals, and processions: civic ceremonial and political manipulation in Archaic Greece', *JHS* 107: 40–50.

—— (1993). 'The Ionian era of Athenian civic identity', *PAPHS* 137: 194–206.

Cordano, F. (1980). 'I Messeni dello stretto di Pausania', *PdP* 35: 436–40.

—— (1992). *Le tessere pubbliche dal Tempio di Atena a Camarina.* Rome.

Crowther, C. (1989). 'Iasos in the early second century B.C.: a note on *OGIS* 237', *BICS* 36: 136–8.

—— (1990). 'Iasos in the second century II: the chronology of the theatre lists', *BICS* 37: 143–51.

—— (1994). 'Lord Dufferin's Grand Tour and the collection of Greek inscriptions at Clandeboye', *JAC* 9: 14–32.

—— (1995a). 'Iasos in the second century III: foreign judges from Priene', *BICS* 40: 91–138.

—— (1995b). 'The chronology of the Iasian theatre lists: again', *Chiron* 25: 225–34.

—— (2007). 'Foreign judges and regional variations in Asia Minor', in G. Reger and H. Elton (eds.), *Regionalism in Asia Minor*. Bordeaux, 11–16.

Csapo, E. (1997). 'Riding the phallos for Dionysos', *Phoenix* 51: 253–95.

—— (2004a). 'The politics of the New Music', in Murray and Wilson (eds.), 207–48.

—— (2004b). 'Some social and economic conditions behind the rise of the acting profession in the fifth and fourth centuries BC', in C. Hugoniot, F. Hurlet, and S. Milanezi (eds.), *Le statut de l'acteur dans l'antiquité grecque et romaine*. Tours, 53–76.

Csapo, E. and Slater, W. (1994). *The Context of Ancient Drama*. Ann Arbor.

Csapo, E. and Wilson, P. (*forthcoming*). 'Timotheus the New Musician', in F. Budelmann (ed.), *The Cambridge Companion to Greek Lyric*. Cambridge.

Curbera, J. (1999). 'Defixiones', *ASNP* ser. 4, *Quaderni* 4.1: 159–85. Pisa.

Curty, O. (1995). *Les parentés légendaires entres cités grecques*. Geneva.

Dale, A. (1954). *Euripides: Alcestis*. Oxford.

d'Alessio, G. (*forthcoming*). 'The name of the dithyramb'.

d'Angour, A. (1997). 'How the dithyramb got its shape', *CQ* 47: 331–51.

Daux, G. (1935). 'Craton, Eumène II et Attale II', *BCH* 59: 210–30.

—— (1967). *Guide de Thasos*. Paris.

Dawson, S. (1997). 'The theatrical audience in fifth-century Athens: numbers and status', *Prudentia* 29: 1–14.

Dearden, C. (1990). 'Fourth-century tragedy in Sicily: Athenian or Sicilian?', in J.-P. Descoeudres (ed.), *Greek Colonists and Native Populations*. Oxford, 231–42.

—— (1999). 'Plays for export', *Phoenix* 53: 222–48.

Debord, P. (1982). *Aspects sociaux et économiques de la vie religieuse dans l'Anatolie gréco-romaine*. Leiden.

Delrieux, F. (1996). 'Remarques sur l'ordre de succession des contributions financières d'Iasos au IIe siècle av. J.-C.', *REA* 98: 371–88.

Demangel, R. and Laumonier, A. (1922). 'Inscriptions d'Ionie', *BCH* 46: 307–55.

Denoyelle, M. (2002). 'Style individuel, style local et centres de production: retour sur le cratère des "Karneia"', *MEFRA* 114: 587–609.

de Schutter, X. (1987). 'Le culte d'Apollon Patrôos à Athènes', *AC* 56: 103–29.

Deubner, L. (1932). *Attische Feste.* Berlin.

Devambez, P. (1962). *Bas-relief de Téos.* Paris.

Dignas, B. (2002). *Economy of the Sacred in Hellenistic and Roman Asia Minor.* Oxford.

Dillery, J. (2002). 'Ephebes in the stadium (not the theatre): *Ath. Pol.* 42.4 and *IG* II²351', *CQ* 52: 462–70.

Dillon, M. (2000). 'Did *parthenoi* attend the Olympic Games? Girls and women competing, spectating and carrying out cult roles at religious festivals', *Hermes* 128: 457–80.

Dinsmoor, W. (1951). 'The Athenian theater of the fifth century', in G. Mylonas (ed.), *Studies Presented to David Moore Robinson,* vol. I. St Louis, 309–30.

Dobias-Lalou, C. (1993). 'Les dépenses engagées par les démiurges de Cyrène pour les cultes', *REG* 106: 24–38.

—— (2000). *Le dialecte des inscriptions grecques de Cyrène.* Paris.

Dörpfeld, W. and Reisch, E. (1896). *Das griechische Theater.* Athens.

Dougherty, C. (1993). *The Poetics of Colonization: from City to Text in Archaic Greece.* Oxford and New York.

Dougherty, C. and Kurke, L. (eds.) (1993). *Cultural Poetics in Archaic Greece.* Cambridge.

—— (eds.) (2003). *The Cultures within Greek Culture: Contact, Conflict, Collaboration.* Cambridge.

Drögenmüller, H.-P. (1969). 'Leontinoi', *KlP* 3: 570–2.

Dubois, L. (1989). *Inscriptions grecques dialectales de Sicile.* Paris and Rome.

Dunand, F. (1986). 'Les associations dionysiaques au service du pouvoir lagide (IIIe s. av. J.-C.)', in *L'association dionysiaque dans les sociétés anciennes.* Rome, 85–104.

Dunbabin, T. (1948). *The Western Greeks: The History of Sicily and South Italy from the Foundation of the Greek Colonies to 480 BC.* Oxford.

Dunbar, N. (1995). *Aristophanes. Birds.* Oxford.

Durrbach, F. (1923). *Choix d'inscriptions de Délos.* Paris.

Easterling, P. (1994). 'Euripides outside Athens: a speculative note', *ICS* 19: 73–80.

—— (ed.) (1997). *The Cambridge Companion to Greek Tragedy.* Cambridge.

Easterling, P. and Hall, E. (eds.) (2002). *Greek and Roman Actors: Aspects of an Ancient Profession.* Cambridge.

Ebert, J. (1982). 'Zur Stiftungsurkunde der Leukophryena in Magnesia am Mäander', *Philologus* 126: 198–216.

Effenterre, H. van and Ruzé, F. (1995). *Nomima: recueil d'inscriptions politiques et juridiques de l'archaïsme grec*, vol. II. Rome.

Ehrhardt, N. (1997). 'Die Phyleninschriften vom Rundbau am Theater in Kaunos', *Archäologischer Anzeiger.* 45–50.

Elrashedy, F. (1985). 'Attic imported pottery in Classical Cyrenaica', in G. Barker, J. Lloyd and J. Reynolds (eds.) *Cyrenaica in Antiquity.* Oxford, 205–17.

Erkelenz, D. (1999). 'Cicero, *Pro Flacco* 55–59. Zur Finanzierung von Statthalterfesten in der Frühphase des Koinon von Asia', *Chiron* 29: 43–57.

Erskine, A. (2001). *Troy between Greece and Rome: Local Tradition and Imperial Power.* Oxford.

Fant, E. (1989). '*Poikiloi Lithoi*: the anomalous economics of the Roman imperial marble quarry at Teos', in S. Walker and A. Cameron (eds.), *The Greek Renaissance in the Roman Empire. Papers from the Xth British Museum Classical Colloquium* (*BICS Supplement* 55). London, 206–18.

Faraone, C. (1991). 'The agonistic context of early Greek binding spells', in C. Faraone and D. Obbink (eds.), *Magika Hiera: Ancient Greek Magic and Religion.* New York and Oxford, 3–32.

—— (1999). *Ancient Greek Love Magic.* Cambridge (Mass.).

—— (2004). 'Hipponax fragment 128W: epic parody or expulsive incantation?', *CA* 23: 209–45.

Farrington, A. (1997). 'Olympic victors and the popularity of the Olympic games in the imperial period', *Tyche* 12: 15–46.

Fearn, D. (2003). *Bacchylides: Politics and Poetic Tradition.* D.Phil. thesis, Oxford.

Felten, F. (1997). 'Antike Architekturkopien', in G. Erarth, M. Lehner and G. Schwarz (eds.), *Komos. Festschrift für Th. Lorenz.* Vienna, 61–9.

Ferrary, J.-L. (2001). 'Rome et la géographie de l'Hellénisme, réflexions sur "hellènes" et "panhellènes" dans les inscriptions de l'époque romaine', in Salomies (ed.), 19–35.

Feyel, M. (1942). *Contribution à l'épigraphie béotienne.* Publications de la Faculté des Lettres de l'Université de Strasbourg 95. Le Puy.

Ferguson, W. (1934). 'Polyeuktos and the Soteria', *AJPh* 55: 318–36.

Fischer-Hansen, T., Nielsen, T. and Ampolo, C. (2004). 'Sikelia', in *Inventory*, 172–248.

Flacelière, R. (1937). *Les Aitoliens à Delphes: contribution à l'histoire de la Grèce centrale au IIIe siècle av. J.-C.* Paris.

Flashar, M. (1999). 'Panhellenische Feste und Asyl: Parameter lokaler Identitätstiftung in Klaros und Kolophon', *Klio* 81: 412–36.

Follet, S. and Peppas-Delmousou, D. (2001). 'Les dedicaces chorégiques d'époque flavienne et antonine à Athènes', in Salomies (ed.), 95–117.

Forbes, C. (1955). 'Ancient athletic guilds', *CPh* 50: 238–52.

Fountoulakis, A. (2000). 'The artists of Aphrodite', *AC* 69: 133–47.

Fraenkel, M. (1890). *Die Inschriften von Pergamon*. Berlin.

Frazer, J. (1913). *The Golden Bough: Part VI, The Scapegoat*, 3rd edn., London.

Frederiksen, M. (1959). 'Republican Capua: a social and economic study', *PBSR* 27: 80–130.

French, D. (1988). *Roman Roads and Milestones of Asia Minor. Fasc. 2: An Interim Catalogue of Milestones*. Oxford.

Frisch, P. (1986). *Zehn agonistische Papyri*. Cologne.

—— (1991). 'Der erste vollkommene Periodonike', *EA* 18: 71–3.

Gager, J. (1992). *Curse tablets and Binding Spells from the Ancient World*. New York and Oxford.

Gantz, T. (1993). *Early Greek Myth*. Baltimore and London.

Garlan, Y. and Masson, O. (1982). 'Les acclamations pédérastiques de Kalami (Thasos)', *BCH* 106: 3–22.

Gauthier, P. (1972). *Symbola. Les étrangers et la justice dans les cités grecques*. Nancy.

—— (1985). *Les cités grecques et leurs bienfaiteurs: IVe–Ier siècle avant J.-C.*, *BCH* Suppl. 12. Athens and Paris.

—— (1989). *Nouvelles inscriptions de Sardes*. Geneva.

—— (1990). 'L'inscription d'Iasos relative à l'*ekklesiastikon* (*I.Iasos 20*)', *BCH* 114: 417–43.

—— (1999). 'Nouvelles inscriptions de Claros', *REG* 112: 1–17.

Gebhard, E. (1973). *Theater at Isthmia*. Chicago.

—— (1988). 'Ruler's use of theaters in the Greek and Roman world', in Πρακτικὰ τοῦ 12ου Διεθνοῦς Συνεδρίου Κλασσικῆς Ἀρχαιολογίας, *4–10 Σεπτεμβρίου 1983*, IV. Athens, 65–9.

—— (1996). 'The theater and the city', in W. Slater (ed.), *Roman Theater and Society*. Michigan, 113–27.

Gebhard, V. (1934). 'Thargelia', *RE* 5A2, cols. 1287–1304.

Gentile, L. (1999). 'L'epiteto ΚΑΤΑΓΩΓΙΣ e l'uso del verbo ΚΑΤΑΓΩ in ambito religioso', *RFIC* 127: 334–43.

Gentili, B. (1979). *Theatrical Performances in the Ancient World. Hellenistic and Early Roman Theatre*. Amsterdam.

—— (1995). *Pindaro. Le Pitiche*. With the collaboration of P. Angeli Bernardini, E. Cingano and P. Giannini. Milan.

Gentili, G. (1946). 'Iscrizione arcaica sul coronamento di cippo gelese del Museo di Siracusa', *Epigraphica* 8: 11–18.

Gernet, L. (1932). *Le génie grec*. Paris.

Gernet, L. and Bizos, M. (1924–6). *Lysias, discours*. Paris.

Geus, K. (2002). *Eratosthenes von Kyrene. Studien zur hellenistischen Kultur- und Wissenschaftsgeschichte.* Munich.

Ghiron-Bistagne, P. (1976). *Recherches sur les acteurs dans la Grèce antique.* Paris.

Giesekam, G. (1976). 'The portrayal of Minos in Bakkhylides 17', *PLLP* 1: 237–52.

Gilula, D. (1995). 'The *Khoregoi* vase – comic yes, but angels?', *ZPE* 109: 5–10.

—— (1996). 'Khoragium and Khoragos', *Athenaeum* 84: 479–92.

Goette, H. R. (1989). 'Ein dorischer Architrav im Kerameikos von Athen', *MDAI(A)* 104: 83–103.

—— (1995a). 'Griechische Theaterbauten der Klassik—Forschungsstand und Fragestellungen', in E. Pöhlmann (ed.), *Studien zur Bühnendichtung und zum Theaterbau der Antike. Studien zur klassischen Philologie* 93. Frankfurt, 9–48.

—— (1995b). 'Studien zur historischen Landeskunde Attikas V: Beobachtungen im Theater des Amphiareion von Oropos', *AM* 110: 253–60.

—— (1999). 'Die Basis des Astydamas im sogenannten lykurgischen Dionysos-Theater zu Athen', *AntK* 42: 21–5.

—— (2001). *Athens, Attica, and the Megarid.* London and New York.

—— (2004). 'Mausoleum oder choregisches Weihgeschenk? Zum Friesfragment Inv. 1688 im Athener Nationalmuseum', in M. Fano Santi (ed.), *Studi di archeologia in onore di Gustavo Traversari.* Rome, I: 463–76.

Goette, H. R. and Hammerstaedt, J. (2004). *Das antike Athen. Ein literarischer Stadtführer.* Munich.

Goff, B. (ed.) (1995). *History, Tragedy, Theory: Dialogues on Athenian Drama.* Austin.

Goldhill, S. (1986). *Reading Greek Tragedy.* Cambridge.

—— (1987). 'The Great Dionysia and civic ideology', *JHS* 107: 58–76.

Goldhill, S. and Osborne, R. (eds.) (1999). *Performance Culture and Athenian Democracy.* Cambridge.

Greco, E. (2001). 'Tripodes: appunti sullo sviluppo urbano di Atene', *Annali di archeologia e storia antica.* Univ. degli studi di Napoli 'L'Orientale' N.S. 8: 25–38.

Green, R. (1998). 'Theatre production: 1987–1995', *Lustrum* 37: 7–202.

Griffith, M. (1978). 'Aeschylus, Sicily, and Prometheus', in R. Dawe et al. (eds.), *Dionysiaca: Nine studies ... presented to Sir Denys Page.* Cambridge, 105–39.

—— (1995). 'Brilliant dynasts: power and politics in Aeschylus' *Oresteia*', *CA* 14: 62–129.

Gruen, E. (1990). *Studies in Greek Culture and Roman Policy.* Leiden.

Guarducci, M. (1929). *Poeti vaganti e conferenzieri dell' età ellenistica: ricerche di epigrafia greca nel campo della letteratura e del costume* (Memorie della R. Accademia nazionale dei lincei. Classe di scienze morali, storiche e filologiche, ser. 5: vol. II, fasc. IX). Rome.

—— (1949–51). 'Note di epigrafia siceliota arcaica', *Annuario* 27–9: 103–16.

Guarisco, D. (2001). '"Comparare il comparabile". Artemide e i riti di passaggio: *Brauronia, Mounichia, Orthia*', in D. M. Cosi (ed.), *L'arkteia di Brauron e i culti femminili*. Bologna, 65–87.

Habicht, C. (1970). *Gottmenschentum und griechische Städte*, 2nd, augmented edn. Munich.

—— (1988). 'Xenokles of Sphettos', *Hesperia* 57: 323–7.

—— (1994). 'Iasos und Samothrake in der Mitte des 3. Jahrhundert v. Chr.', *Chiron* 24: 69–74.

—— (2001). 'Späte Wiederaufzeichnung eines athenischen Proxenie-dekrets', *ZPE* 137: 113–16.

Hall, E. (1989). *Inventing the Barbarian: Greek Self-definition through Tragedy*. Oxford.

Hallof, L. and K. and Habicht, C. (1998). 'Aus der Arbeit der *Inscriptiones Graecae* II. Ehrendekrete aus dem Asklepieion von Kos', *Chiron* 28: 101–42.

Hamilton, R. (1996). 'Panathenaic amphoras: the other side', in J. Neils (ed.), *Worshipping Athena*. Madison, 137–62.

Hansen, E. (1971). *The Attalids of Pergamon*, 2nd edn., corrected and augmented; 1st edn., 1946. Ithaca and London.

Hansen, M. (1991). *The Athenian Democracy in the Age of Demosthenes*. Oxford.

Hansen, M. and Fischer-Hansen, T. (1994). 'Monumental political architecture in Archaic and Classical Greek *Poleis*: evidence and historical significance', in D. Whitehead (ed.), *From Political Architecture to Stephanus Byzantius*. Stuttgart, 23–90.

Harrell, S. (2002). 'King or private citizen?: fifth-century Sicilian tyrants at Olympia and Delphi', *Mnemosyne* 55: 439–64.

Harrison, J. (1903). *Prolegomena to the Study of Greek Religion*. Cambridge.

Hatzopoulos, M. (1991), 'Un prêtre d'Amphipolis dans la grande liste des théarodoques de Delphes', *BCH* 115: 345–7.

Hauvette-Besnault, A. and Pottier, E. (1880). 'Inscriptions d'Érythrées et de Téos', *BCH* 4: 146–53.

Hayward, C. (1998). 'Les grand-prêtresses du culte impérial provincial en Asie Mineure: état de la question', in R. Frei-Stolba and A. Bielman (eds.), *Femmes et vie politique dans l'antiquité gréco-romaine*. Lausanne, 117–30.

Heberdey, R. (1912). *Forschungen in Ephesos II: Das Theater*. Vienna.

Hedrick, C. (1988). 'The temple and cult of Apollo Patroos in Athens', *AJA* 92: 185–210.

Heisserer, A. and Moysey, R. (1986). 'An Athenian decree honoring foreigners', *Hesperia* 55: 177–82.

Hellmann, M.-C. (1992). *Recherches sur le vocabulaire de l'architecture grecque, d'après les inscriptions de Délos*. Paris.

Helms, M. (1988). *Ulysses' Sail: An Ethnographic Odyssey of Power, Knowledge, and Geographical Distance*. Princeton.

Hennig, D. (1997). 'Die Beherbergung von "Staatsgästen" in den hellenistischen Poleis', *Chiron* 27: 355–68.

Henry, A. (1983). *Honours and Privileges in Athenian Decrees*. Hildesheim.

Herington, J. (1967). 'Aeschylus in Sicily', *JHS* 87: 74–85.

Herrmann, P. (1965) 'Antiochos der Grosse und Teos', *Anadolu* 9: 29–159.

—— (1971). 'Zwei Inschriften von Kaunos und Baba Dag', *OAth* 10: 36–9.

—— (1979). 'Die Stadt Temnos und ihre auswärtigen Beziehungen in hellenistischer Zeit', *Ist. Mitt.* 29: 239–71.

Herz, P. (1992). 'Asiarchen und Archieriai', *Tyche* 7: 93–115.

Hicks, E. L. (1887). 'Iasos', *JHS* 8: 83–118.

Higbie, C. (1997). 'The bones of a hero, the ashes of a politician: Athens, Salamis, and the usable past', *CA* 16: 279–308.

Hiller von Gaertringen, F. (1906). *Inschriften von Priene*. Berlin.

Hintzen-Bohlen, B. (1977). *Die Kulturpolitik des Eubulos und des Lykurg*. Berlin.

Hinz, V. (1998). *Der Kult von Demeter und Kore auf Sizilien und in Magna Graecia*. Palilia 4. Wiesbaden.

Hölkeskamp, K.-J. (1993). 'Demonax und die Neuordnung der Bürgerschaft von Kyrene', *Hermes* 121: 404–21.

Holleaux, M. (1952). 'Trois décrets de Rhodes', in M. Holleaux (ed.), *Études d'épigraphie et d'histoire grecques*, vol. IV. Paris, 146–62.

Homolle, T. (1890). 'Comptes et inventaires des temples déliens en l'année 279', *BCH* 14: 389–511.

—— (1895). 'Inscriptions de Delphes: réglements de la phratrie des ΛΑΒΥΑΔΑΓ', *BCH* 19: 5–69.

Hordern, J. (2004). *Sophron's Mimes*. Oxford.

Hornblower, S. (1991). *A Commentary on Thucydides, Vol. 1, Books 1–3*. Oxford.

—— (1992). 'The religious dimension to the Peloponnesian War, or what Thucydides does not tell us', *HSCP* 94: 169–97.

Humphries, S. (2004). *The Strangeness of Gods*. Oxford.

Hunter, R. and Rutherford, I. (eds.) (*forthcoming*). '*Poeti Vaganti': Travelling Poets in Ancient Greece*. Cambridge.

Ieranò, G. (1989). 'Il ditirambo XVII di Bacchilide e le feste apollinee di Delo', *QS* 30: 157–83.

—— (1997). *Il ditirambo di Dioniso*. Pisa and Rome.

Jacottet, A. (2003). *Choisir Dionysos*. Zürich.

Jacquemin, A. (1990). 'Architekton—Ergolabos/Ergones', *Ktema* 15: 81–8.

Jamot, P. (1895). 'Fouilles de Thespies: les jeux en l'honneur des Muses', *BCH* 19: 311–85.

Jebb, R. (1905). *Bacchylides: The Poems and Fragments*. Cambridge.

Jeffrey, L. (1990). *The Local Scripts of Archaic Greece*, rev. edn. Oxford.

Johansen, K. (1959). *Eine Dithyrambos—Aufführung*. Copenhagen.

Jones, C. (1999). *Kinship Diplomacy in the Ancient World*. Cambridge (Mass.).

—— (2001). 'A statuette of Nemesis', *EA* 33: 45–8.

—— (2004). 'Events surrounding the bequest of Pergamon to Rome and the revolt of Aristonicos: new inscriptions from Metropolis', *JRA* 17: 469–85.

Jones, J. W. (1956). *The Law and Legal Theory of the Greeks*. Oxford.

Jones, N. (1999). *The Associations of Classical Athens*. New York and Oxford.

—— (2004). *Rural Athens Under the Democracy*. Philadelphia.

Jordan, D. (1997). '*Πρώιμη γραφή ως μαγεία*', in A.-P. Christidis and D. Jordan (eds.), *Γλώσσα και μαγεία. Κείμενα από την αρχαιότητα*. Athens, 65–74.

Junker, K. (2003). 'Namen auf dem Pronomoskrater', *MDAIA* 118: 317–35.

—— (2004). 'Vom Theatron zum Theater', *AntK* 47: 10–33.

Kahrstedt, U. (1937). 'Zu den delphischen Soterienurkunden', *Hermes* 72: 369–403.

—— (1969) *Untersuchungen zur Magistratur in Athen: Studien zum öffentlichen Recht Athens, Teil II*. Darmstadt (1st edn. Stuttgart, 1936).

Kajava, K. (2002). 'When did the Isthmian Games return to the Isthmus?', *CPh* 97: 168–71.

Kalligas, P. (1963). '*Ἐργασίαι τοῦ ἱεροῦ Διονύσου Ἐλευθερέως τῆς νοτίου κλιτύος Ἀκροπόλεως* (1961–62)', *ADelt* 18, B1, Chron.: 12–18.

Kaltsas, N. (2002). *Sculpture in the National Archaeological Museum, Athens. Catalogue*. Athens.

Kamerbeek, J. (1978). *The Plays of Sophocles. Part III: The Antigone*. Leiden.

Kannicht, R. (1969). *Euripides: Helena*, 2 vols. Heidelberg.

Käppel, L. (1992). *Paian: Studien zur Geschichte einer Gattung.* Berlin and New York.

—— (2000). 'Bakchylides und das System der chorlyrischen Gattungen im 5. Jh. v. Chr.', in A. Bagordo and B. Zimmermann (eds.), *Bakchylides: 100 Jahre nach seiner Wiederentdeckung. Zetemata* 106. Munich, 11–27.

Karadima-Matsa, C. and Clinton, K. (2002). 'Korrane, a sacred woman in Samothrace', *ZPE* 138: 87–92.

Karouzou, S. (1954). *Corpus Vasorum Antiquorum: Grèce Fasc. 2, Athènes— Musée National Fasc. 2.* Paris.

Kavoulaki, A. (1999). 'Processional performance and the democratic polis', in Goldhill and Osborne (eds.), 293–320.

Kayser, F. (2000). 'La gladiature en Egypte', *REA* 102: 459–78.

Kennel, N. (1999). 'Age categories', *Phoenix* 53: 249–62.

Kent, J. (1948). 'The temple estates of Delos, Rheneia, and Mykonos', *Hesperia* 17: 243–338.

Kerkhof, R. (2001). *Dorische Posse, Epicharm und attische Komödie.* Munich.

Kern, O. (1896). *RE* 2 s.v. 'Attaleion', col. 2156.

Kiepert, R. (1908). *Karte von Kleinasien* (1:400 000, in 24 sheets). Berlin.

Klaffenbach, G. (1914). *Symbolae ad historiam collegiorum artificum Bacchiorum.* Diss. Berlin.

—— (1960): 'Bemerkungen zum griechischen Urkundenwesen', *Deutsche Akademie der Wissenschaften zu Berlin, Klasse für Sprachen, Literatur und Kunst, SB* 6: 5–42.

Kleiner, D. (1983). *The Monument of Philopappos in Athens.* Rome.

Klimov, O. (1986). 'Attalists' Associations in the kingdom of Pergamum' (in Russian), *VDI* 4: 102–8.

Knell, H. (2000). *Athen im 4. Jahrhundert v.Chr. – eine Stadt verändert ihr Gesicht.* Darmstadt.

Knoepfler, D. (1996). 'La réorganisation du concours des Mouseia à l'époque hellénistique: esquisse d'une solution nouvelle', in A. Hurst and A. Schachter (eds.), *La montagne des Muses.* Genf, 141–67.

—— (1997). '*Cupido ille propter quem Thespiae visuntur.* Une mésaventure insoupçonnée de l'Eros de Praxitèle et l'institution du concours des Erôtideia', in D. Knoepfler et al. (eds.), *Nomen Latinum. Mélanges de langue, de littérature et de civilisation latines offerts au professeur André Schneider à l'occasion de son départ à la retraite.* Neuchâtel, 17–39.

—— (2001). *Décrets érétriens de proxénie et de citoyenneté.* Lausanne.

Köhler, J. (1996). *Pompai. Untersuchungen zur hellenistischen Festkultur.* Frankfurt, Bern, New York and Paris.

Kolb, F. (1981). *Agora und Theater, Volks- und Festversammlung.* Berlin.

Kolonnas, L. (ed.) (2003). Μουσῶν δῶρα: Μουσικοὶ και χορευτικοὶ ἀποέχοι ἀπὸ την αρχαία Ἑλλάδα. Athens.

Kornemann, E. (1924). *RE Suppl.* 4 s.v. 'κοινόν', 914–41.

Korres, M. (1980). 'Εργασίες στα μνημεία: Ιερό του Διονύσου', *ArchDelt* 35: 16–18.

—— (1983). 'Εργασίες στα μνημεία: Διονυσιακό θέατρο (χορηγικό μνημείο IG II² 3073)', *ArchDelt* 38: 10 pl. 15a.

—— (1996). 'Ein Beitrag zur Kenntnis der attisch-ionischen Architektur', in E.-L. Schwandner (ed.), *Säule und Gebälk. Bauforscherkolloquium Berlin 16.–18.6.1994.* Mainz, 103–33.

—— (2000). 'Κλασική Αθηναϊκή Αρχιτεκτονική', in C. Bouras et al. (eds.), *Αθήναι. Από την Κλασική Εποχή έως Σήμερα (5ος αι. π.Χ. / 2000 μ.Χ.).* Athens, 2–45.

—— (2002). 'Modell des Dionysos-Theaters', in *Die griechische Klassik— Idee oder Wirklichkeit. Exhibition Berlin March 1st–June 2nd 2002.* Mainz, 540–1.

Kossatz-Deissmann, A. (1978). *Dramen des Aischylos auf westgriechischen Vasen.* Mainz am Rhein.

Kotansky, R. (1994). 'θωβαρραβαυ = "the deposit is good",' *HThR* 87: 367–9.

Kourouniotes, K. and Thompson, H. (1932). 'The Pnyx in Athens', *Hesperia* 1: 90–217.

Kowalzig, B. (2005). 'Mapping out *communitas*: performances of *theoria* in their sacred and political context', in J. Elsner and I. Rutherford (eds.), *Pilgrimage in Graeco-Roman and Early Christian Antiquity. Seeing the Gods.* Oxford, 41–72.

—— (2006) 'An Empire of Heroes', in P. Wilson, F. Muecke and J. Davidson (eds.), *Drama III: Studies in Honour of Kevin Lee, Bulletin of the Institute of Classical Studies Suppl.* 87. London, 79–98.

Krummen, E. (1990). *Pyrsos Hymnon. Festliche Gegenwart und mythisch-rituelle Tradition bei Pindar.* Berlin and New York.

Kurke, L. (2007). 'Visualizing the choral: epichoric poetry, ritual, and élite negotiation in fifth-century Thebes', in J. Elsner, H. Foley, S. Goldhill, and C. Kraus (eds.), *Visualizing the Tragic.* Oxford, 63–101.

Lacroix, M. (1914). 'Architectes et entrepreneurs à Délos de 314 à 240', *Revue de Philologie* 38: 303–30.

Lambert, S. (1993). *The Phratries of Attica.* Ann Arbor.

—— (1998). 'The Attic *genos* Bakchiadai and the City Dionysia', *Historia* 47: 394–403.

—— (2000). 'The Greek inscriptions on stone in the British School at Athens', *ABSA* 95: 485–516.

—— (2002). 'The sacrificial calendar of Athens', *ABSA* 97: 353–99.

—— (2003). 'The first Athenian agonothetai', *ΗΟΡΟΣ* (2000–3) 14–16: 99–105.

—— (2005). 'Athenian state laws and decrees 352/1–322/1: II. Religious regulations', *ZPE* 154: 125–59.

Lämmer, M. (1967). *Olympien und Hadrianeen im antiken Ephesos.* Cologne.

Landels, J. (1999). *Music in ancient Greece and Rome.* London and New York.

Laroche, E. (1949). *Histoire de la racine 'nem-' en grec ancien.* Paris.

Laronde, A. (1987). *Cyrène et la Libye hellénistique. Libykai Historiai.* Paris.

Latini, A. (2003). 'Coregia: la riforma di Demetrio Falereo', in Martina (ed.), 305–24.

Laum, B. (1964). *Stiftungen in der griechischen und römischen Antike,* 2nd edn., Berlin (1st edn., 1914).

Laumonier, A. (1958). *Les cultes indigènes en Carie.* Paris.

Lauter, H. and Lauter, H. (1988). '"A-A": Ein Beitrag zur Baugeschichte des athenischen Dionysostheaters', in H. Büsing and F. Hiller (eds.), *Bathron. Beiträge zur Architektur und verwandten Künsten für Heinrich Drerup zu seinem 80. Geburtstag.* Saarbrücken, 287–99.

Lavecchia, S. (2000). *Pindaro: I ditirambi. Introduzione, testo critico, traduzione e commento.* Pisa and Rome.

Lawall, M. (2003). 'In the sanctuary of the Samothracian gods: myth, politics and mystery cult at Ilion', in M. Cosmopoulos (ed.), *Greek Mysteries: The Archaeology and Ritual of Ancient Greek Secret Cults.* London, 79–111.

Leduc, C. (2001). 'En quoi cela concerne-t-il l'archonte? (*A.P.*, LVI, 2–5)', *Pallas* 56: 15–44.

Lefèvre, F. (1998). *L'amphictionie pyléo-delphique: histoire et institutions.* Paris.

Legras, B. (1999). *Néotes: recherches sur les jeunes Grecs dans l'Egypte ptolémaique et romaine.* Geneva.

Le Guen, B. (1995). 'Théâtre et cités à l'époque hellénistique: "Mort de la cité—mort du théâtre"?', *REG* 108: 59–90.

—— (1997). 'Tribulations d'artistes pergaméniens', in B. Le Guen (ed.), *De la scène aux gradins. Pallas* 47: 73–96.

—— (2001a). *Les associations de Technites dionysiaques à l'époque hellénistique,* 2 vols. Nancy and Paris.

—— (2001b). 'L'activité dramatique dans les îles grecques à l'époque hellénistique', *REA* 103.1/2: 261–98.

—— (2003). 'Théâtre, cités et royaumes en Anatolie et au Proche-Orient de la mort d'Alexandre le Grand aux conquêtes de Pompée', in F. Prost (ed.), *L'Orient méditerranéen de la mort d'Alexandre aux campagnes de Pompée. Pallas* 62: 329–55.

—— (2004a). 'Le statut professionel des acteurs grecs à l'époque hellénistique', in C. Hugoniot, F. Hurlet, and S. Milanezi (eds.), *Le statut de l'acteur dans l'antiquité grecque et romaine*. Tours, 77–106.

—— (2004b). 'Remarques sur les associations de l'époque hellénistique. A propos de l'ouvrage de Sophia Aneziri . . .', *Nikephoros* 17: 279–99.

Lenschau, T. (1933). 'Myskon', *RE* 16.1: 1191.

Leppin, H. (1992). *Histrionen*. Bonn.

Leschorn, W. (1998). 'Die Verbreitung von Agonen in den östlichen Provinzen des römischen Reiches', in W. Orth (ed.), *Colloquium 'Agonistik in der römischen Kaiserzeit' Stadion* XXIV, 1. Sankt Augustin: 31–58.

—— (2002). *Lexikon der Aufschriften auf griechischen Münzen*, vol. I. Vienna.

Lévêque, P. and Séchan, L. (1990). *Les grandes divinités de la Grèce*, 2nd edn. Paris.

Levi, D. (1963). 'Le due prime campagne di scavi a Iasos (1960–1)', *Annuario della Scuola Archeologica Italiana de Atene*, N.S. 23–4 (1961–2): 505–71.

Lewis, D. (1960). 'Apollo Delios', *ABSA* 55: 190–4; reprinted in D. Lewis (1997), *Selected Papers in Greek and Near Eastern History*, ed. P. Rhodes. Cambridge.

Leyerle, B. (2001). *Theatrical Shows and Ascetic Lives: John Chrysostom's Attack on Spiritual Marriage*. Berkeley.

Liefferinge, C. van (2000). 'Auditions et conférences à Delphes', *AntCl* 69: 149–64.

Lightfoot, J. (2002). 'Nothing to do with the *technitai* of Dionysos?', in Easterling and Hall (eds.), 208–24.

Lohmann, H. (1998). 'Zur baugeschichtlichen Entwicklung des antiken Theaters: Ein Überblick', in G. Binder (ed.), *Das antike Theater: Aspekte seiner Geschichte, Rezeption und Aktualität*. Trier, 191–249.

López-Jimeno, M. del A. (1991). *Las* tabellae defixionis *de la Sicilia griega*. Amsterdam.

Lorber, C. and Hoover, O. (2003). 'An unpublished tetradrachm issued by the artists of Dionysos', *Numismatic Chronicle* 163: 59–68.

Loucas, I. and Loucas-Durie, E. (1990). 'Delphinion ou Daphnéphorion? Sur la localisation de la scène de la face principale du cratère en cloche no. 3760 de Copenhague', *AC* 59: 70–8.

Lüders, O. (1873). *Die dionysischen Künstler*. Berlin.

Luni, M. (2002). 'Nuove anfore panatenaiche da Cirene', *QAL* 18: 97–113.

—— (2006a). 'Attività recente a Cirene della missione archeologica dell' Università di Urbino', in E. Fabbricotti and O. Menozzi (eds.), *Cirenaica:*

studi, scavi e scoperte, Atti del X Convegno di Archeologia Cirenaica, Chieti 24–26 Novembre 2003, British Archaeological Reports. International Series. Oxford 2006, 469–74.

—— (2006b). 'Il nuovo santuario di Demetra a Cirene', in M. Luni (ed.), *Cirene: Atene d'Africa*. Roma, 147–53.

Luppe, W. (1971). 'Zu den griechischen Didaskalischen Inschriften in Rom', *ZPE* 8: 123–8.

Lupu, E. (2005). *Greek Sacred Law: A Collection of New Documents*. Leiden and Boston.

Luraghi, N. (1994). *Tirannidi arcaiche in Sicilia e Magna Grecia: da Panezio di Leontini all' caduta dei Dinomenidi*. Florence.

Lynch, J. (1984). 'Hipparchos' wall in the Academy at Athens: a closer look at the tradition', in *Studies Presented to Sterling Dow on his Eightieth Birthday. GRBM* 10: 173–9.

Ma, J. (1999). *Antiochus III and the Cities of Western Asia Minor*. Oxford.

—— (2000). *Antiochus III and the Cities of Western Asia Minor*, 2nd edn., with new preface and selection of addenda. Oxford.

Maass, P. (1972). *Die Prohedrie des Dionysostheaters in Athen. Vestigia* 15. Munich.

MacDowell, D. (1990). *Demosthenes 21: 'Against Meidias'*. Oxford.

Maddoli, G. (1995). 'Vicende e prospettive delle iscrizioni di Iasos', in *Iasos di Caria. Un contributo ferrarese alla archeologia microasiatica. Progetti e lavori di restauro*. Ferrara, 65–81.

—— (2000). 'Nuovi testi da Iasos', *PdP* 316–17: 15–32.

Maddoli, G. and Saladino, V. (1995). *Pausania: Guida della Grecia: libro V: L'Elide e Olimpia*. Milan.

Maehler, H. (1997). *Die Lieder des Bakchylides, II: Die Dithyramben und Fragmente*. Leiden, New York, and Cologne.

Maffre, J.-J. (2001a). 'Amphores panathénaïques découvertes en Cyrénaïque', in M. Bentz and N. Esschbach (eds.), *Panathenaïka. Symposion zu den Panathenäischen Preisamphoren*. Mainz, 25–32 and pls. 8–12.

—— (2001b). 'Céramique attique récemment découverte à Apollonia de Cyrénaïque', *CRAI*: 1066–79.

Mahaffy, J. (1897). 'Greek inscriptions at Clandeboye', *The Athenaeum* 3630: 688–9.

Makres, A. (1994). 'The institution of "choregia" in Classical Athens.' D.Phil. thesis, Oxford.

Malay, H. (1999). *Researches in Lydia, Mysia and Aeolis. Ergänzungsbände zu den TAM* 23. Vienna.

Malkin, I. (1994). *Myth and Territory in the Spartan Mediterranean*. Cambridge.

Manganaro, G. (1977). 'Tavolette di piombo inscritte della Sicilia greca', *ASNP* 7: 1329–49.

—— (1989). 'Case e terra a Kamarina e Morgantina nel II–III sec. A.C.,' *PdP* 94: 189–216.

—— (2004). 'Anagrafe di Leontinoi nel V secolo', *ZPE* 149: 55–67.

Marengo, S. (1991). *Lessico delle iscrizioni greche della Cirenaica.* Roma.

Marengo, S. and Paci, G. (1998). 'Nuovi frammenti dei conti dei damiurghi', in E. Catani and S. Marengo (eds.), *La Cirenaica in età antica. Atti del convegno internazionale di studi, Macerata 18–20 Maggio 1995.* Pisa and Rome, 373–92.

Marshall, C. and van Willigenburg, S. (2004). 'Judging Athenian dramatic competitions', *JHS* 124: 90–107.

Martin, R. (1951). *Recherches sur l'agora grecque. BÉFAR* 174. Paris.

—— (1957). 'Sur deux expressions techniques', *RPhil* 31: 66–81.

Martin, R. P. (1992). 'Hesiod's metanastic poetics', *Ramus* 21: 11–33.

Martina, A. (ed.) (2003). *Teatro greco postclassico e teatro latino: teorie e prassi drammatica.* Rome.

Massimillia, G. (1993). 'Callimaco fr.115', *ZPE* 95: 33–44.

Masson, E. (1967). *Recherches sur les plus anciens emprunts sémitiques en grec.* Paris.

Masson, O. (1989). 'Myskellos, fondateur de Crotone, et le nom Μύσκελ-(λ)ος', *RPhil* ser. 3.63: 59–65 (= L. Dubois and C. Dobias (eds.), *Onomastica graeca selecta* III, Geneva (2000), 55–61).

Masson, O. and Mitford, T. (1986). *Les inscriptions syllabiques de Kouklia-Paphos.* Konstanz.

Mastrocinque, A. (1979). *La Caria e la Ionia meridionale in Epoca Ellenistica (323–188 A.C.).* Rome.

Matthaiou, A. (2003a). 'Ἀπόλλων Δήλιος ἐν Ἀθήναις', in D. Jordan and J. Traill (eds.), *Lettered Attica: A Day of Attic Epigraphy.* Athens and Toronto, 85–93.

—— (2003b). 'Εἰς *IG* I³ 130', *ΗΟΡΟΣ* 14–16: 45–9.

Maurizio, L. (1998). 'The Panathenaic procession: Athens' participatory democracy on display?', in D. Boedeker and K. Raaflaub (eds.), *Democracy, Empire, and the Arts in Fifth-century Athens.* Harvard, 297–317.

Maurizi, M. (2000). 'A proposito dei nuovi testi di coregia da Iasos', *PdP* 316–17: 42–68.

McCabe, D. and Plunkett, M. (1985). *Teos Inscriptions: Texts and List.* Princeton.

McCredie, J. (1974). 'A Samothracian enigma', *Hesperia* 43: 454–9.

McPhee, I. (1997). *The Extramural Sanctuary of Demeter and Persephone in Cyrene, Libya. Final Reports*, vol. VI, part II: *Attic Pottery*. Philadelphia.

Meadows, A. (1996). 'Four Rhodian decrees: Rhodes, Iasos and Philip V', *Chiron* 26: 251–66.

Meier, C. (1993). *The Political Art of Greek Tragedy*. Oxford (German edn., Munich, 1988).

Meinhardt, E. (1957). *Perikles bei Plutarch*. Frankfurt.

Meriani, A. (2003). *Sulla musica greca antica: studi e ricerche*. Salerno.

Merkelbach, R. (1973). 'Der Theseus des Bakkhylides (Gedicht für ein attisches Ephebenfest)', *ZPE* 12: 56–62.

—— (1995). 'I. Priene 70 + 69', *EA* 25: 70.

Merkelbach, R. and Stauber, J. (2002). *Steinepigramme aus dem griechischen Osten. Band 4. Die Südküste Kleinasiens, Syrien und Palaestina*. Leipzig.

Meritt, B. (1963). 'Greek inscriptions', *Hesperia* 32: 1–56.

Mette, H. (1977). *Urkunden dramatischer Aufführungen in Griechenland*. Berlin.

Meyer, M. (1989). *Die griechischen Urkundenreliefs*. Berlin.

Migeotte, L. (1992). *Les souscriptions publiques dans les cités grecques*. Quebec and Geneva.

—— (1993). 'De la liturgie à la contribution obligatoire: le financement des Dionysies et des travaux du théâtre à Iasos au IIe siècle avant J.-C.', *Chiron* 23: 269–94.

Mikalson, J. (1982). 'The heorte of heortology', *GRBS* 23: 213–21.

—— (1998). *Religion in Hellenistic Athens*. California.

Milanezi, S. (2004). 'Mémoire civique et mémoire comique des concours en l'honneur de Dionysos à Athènes (Ve–IIIe siècles av. J.-C.)'. Thèse d'habilitation, Paris.

Miller, A. (1973). 'Studies in early Sicilian epigraphy: an opisthographic lead tablet'. Diss., University of North Carolina, Chapel Hill.

Miller, E. (1868). *Mélanges de litterature grecque*. Paris.

Miller, S. (1970). 'Old discoveries from Old Athens', *Hesperia* 39: 223–31.

Mills, S. (1997). *Theseus, Tragedy and the Athenian Empire*. Oxford.

Mitchell, S. (1990) 'Archaeology in Asia Minor 1985–1989', *Archaeological Reports* 36 (1989–90): 83–131.

—— (2000). 'Archaeology in Asia Minor 1990–1998', *Archaeological Reports* 45 (1998–9): 125–92.

Mitsos, M. (1965). 'Χορηγικὴ ἐπιγραφή ἐκ Βαρκίζης', *ArchEphem* 163–7, pls. 45–6.

—— (1970). 'Ἀττικαὶ ἐπιγραφαί' *AAA* 3: 393.

Moore, M. (1987). *The Extramural Sanctuary of Demeter and Persephone in*

Cyrene, Libya. Final Reports, vol. III, part II: *Attic Black Figure and Black Glazed Pottery*. Philadelphia.

Moret, J.-M. (1982). 'L' "apollinisation" de l'imagerie légendaire à Athènes dans la seconde moitié du Vième siècle', *Révue Archéologique* 1: 109–36.

Moretti, J.-C. (1999–2000). 'The theater in the sanctuary of Dionysus Eleuthereus in late fifth-century Athens', *ICS* 24–5: 377–98.

—— (2001). *Théâtre et société dans la Grèce antique*. Paris.

Moretti, L. (1953). *Iscrizioni agonistiche greche*. Rome.

—— (1963). 'I *technitai* di Siracusa', *RFil* 91: 38–45.

Morgan, C. (2003). *Early Greek States beyond the Polis*. London and New York.

Mosino, F. (1977). 'Lirica corale di Reggio: una notizia trascurata', *QUCC* 26: 117–19.

Müller, H. (1989). 'Ein neues hellenistisches Weihepigramm aus Pergamon', *Chiron* 19: 499–553.

Müller, H. and Wörrle, M. (2002). 'Ein Verein im Hinterland Pergamons zur Zeit Eumenes II', *Chiron* 32: 191–235.

Murray, P. and Wilson, P. (eds.) (2004). *Music and the Muses: The Culture of 'mousike' in the Classical Athenian City*. Oxford.

Musti, D. (1986). 'Il dionisismo degli Attalidi: antecedenti, modelli, svillupi', in *L'association dionysiaque dans les sociétés anciennes*. Rome, 105–28.

—— (2002). '*Isopythios, Isolympios* e dintorni', *RIFC* 130: 129–48.

Musti, D. and Beschi, L. (1982). *Pausania: Guida della Grecia: libro 1: L'Attica*. Milan.

Nachtergael, G. (1977). *Les Galates en Grèce et les Sôtéria de Delphes. Mémoires de la classe des lettres de l'Académie Royale de Belgique* 73. Brussels.

Nafissi, M. (1985). 'Battiadi ed Aigeidai: per la storia dei Rapporti fra Cirene e Sparta in età arcaica', in G. Barker, J. Lloyd and J. Reynolds (eds.), *Cyrenaica in Antiquity*. Oxford, 375–86.

—— (2001). 'L'iscrizione di Laodice (*IvIasos* 4): revisione del testo e nuove osservazioni', *PdP* 56: 101–46.

Negri, M. (2004). *Pindaro ad Alessandria: le edizioni e gli editori*. Brescia.

Neils, J. (ed.) (1992). *Goddess and Polis: The Panathenaic Festival in Ancient Athens*. Princeton.

—— (1994). 'The Panathenaia and Kleisthenic ideology', in W. Coulson, O. Palagia, T. Shear, H. Shapiro and F. Frost (eds.), *The Archaeology of Athens and Attica under the Democracy*. Oxford, 151–60.

—— (ed.) (1996). *Worshipping Athena: Panathenaia and Parthenon*. Wisconsin.

Nicolai, R. (1992). 'La fondazione di Cirene e i *Karneia* cirenaici nell'*Inno ad Apollo* di Callimaco', *MD* 28: 153–73.

Nicolucci, V. (2003). 'Il drama satiresco alla corte di Attalo I: fonti letterarie e documenti archeologici', in Martina (ed.), 325–42.

Nielsen, I. (2002). *Cultic Theatres and Ritual Drama: Study in Regional Development and Religious Interchange between East and West in Antiquity*. Aarhus.

Nijf, O. M. van (2001). 'Local heroes: athletics, festivals and elite self-fashioning in the Roman East', in S. Goldhill (ed.), *Being Greek under Rome*. Cambridge, 306–34.

Nilsson, M. (1957). *Griechische Feste von religiöser Bedeutung mit Ausschluss der Attischen*. Stuttgart (1st edn., Leipzig, 1906).

Nollé, J. (1998). '*Εὐτυχοῖς τοῖς κυρίοις—feliciter dominis!* Akklamationsmünzen des griechischen Ostens unter Septimius Severus und städtische Mentalitäten', *Chiron* 28: 323–54.

—— (2001). *Side im Altertum II*. Bonn.

—— (2003). 'Ein ephesischer Kult der *Victoria Romanorum* und das sogenannte Parthermonument', *Chiron* 33: 459–84.

Nordquist, G. (1994). 'Some notes on musicians in Greek cult', in R. Hägg (ed.), *Ancient Greek Cult Practice from the Epigraphical Evidence. Proceedings of the second international seminar of ancient Greek cult, organized by the Swedish Institute at Athens, 22–4 Nov. 1991*. Stockholm, 81–93.

O'Connor, G. (1908). *Chapters in the History of Acting*. Chicago.

Ohlemutz, E. (1940). *Die Kulte und Heiligtümer der Götter in Pergamon*. Darmstadt.

Oliver, J. (1971). 'Epaminondas of Acraephia', *GRBS* 12: 221–37.

Oliverio, A. (1933). *I conti dei demiurgi. Documenti antichi dell'Africa italiana*, vol. II. Bergamo.

Orlandos, A. and Travlos, I. (1986). *Λεξικὸν Ἀρχαίων Ἀρχιτεκτονικῶν Ὅρων*. Athens.

Osborne, R. (1993). 'Competitive festivals and the polis: the emergence of the dramatic festivals at Athens', in S. Halliwell et al. (eds.), *Tragedy, Comedy and the Polis*. Bari, 21–38.

Owen, A. (1939). *Euripides 'Ion'*. Oxford.

Palles, G. (2003). '*Εἰς* IG II² 3057', *ΗΟΡΟΣ* 14–16: 95–7.

Palyvou, C. (2001). 'Notes on the geometry of the ancient theatre of Thorikos', *AA* 45–58.

Papazarkadas, N. (2004). 'Sacred and public land in ancient Athens (*c*. 500–200 BC)'. D.Phil. thesis, Oxford.

Parke, H. (1977). *Festivals of the Athenians*. Ithaca.

Parker, R. (1983). *Miasma: Pollution and Purification in Early Greek Religion.* Oxford.

—— (1988). 'Demeter, Dionysos and the Spartan pantheon', in R. Hägg, N. Marinatos and G. Nordquist (eds.), *Early Greek Cult Practice.* Stockholm, 99–103.

—— (1994). 'Athenian religion abroad', in R. Osborne and S. Hornblower (eds.), *Ritual, Finance, Politics: Athenian Democratic Accounts presented to David Lewis.* Oxford, 339–46.

—— (1996). *Athenian Religion: A History.* Oxford.

—— (2005). *Polytheism and Society at Athens.* Oxford.

Parker, R. and Obbink, D. (2000). 'Sales of priesthoods on Cos I', *Chiron* 30: 415–49.

—— (2001a). 'Sales of priesthoods on Cos II', *Chiron* 31: 229–52.

—— (2001b). 'Three further inscriptions concerning Coan cults', *Chiron* 31: 253–75.

Pearl, O. (1978). 'Rules for musical contests', *ICS* 3: 132–9.

Peek, W. (1970–2). *Neue Inschriften aus Epidauros. AbhLeip.* 63.5. Leipzig.

Pelling, C. (ed.) (1997). *Greek Tragedy and the Historian.* Oxford.

Peppas-Delmousou, D. (1988). 'Autour des inventaires de Brauron', in D. Knoepfler (ed.), *Comptes et inventaires dans la cité grecque.* Neuchâtel and Geneva, 323–46.

Perlman, P. (2000). *City and Sanctuary in Ancient Greece: The Theorodokia in the Peloponnese.* Göttingen.

Perpillou-Thomas, F. (1993). *Fêtes d'Égypte.* Louvain.

Perrin, E. (1997). 'Propagande et culture théâtrale à Athènes à l'époque hellénistique', in B. Le Guen (ed.), *De la scène aux gradins. Pallas* 47: 201–18.

Petrakos, V. (1997). Οἱ ἐπιγραφὲς τοῦ Ὠρωποῦ. Βιβλιοθήκη τῆς ἐν Ἀθήναις Ἀρχαιολογικῆς Ἑταιρείας 170. Athens.

—— (1999). Ὁ δῆμος τοῦ Ραμνοῦντος. II. Οἱ ἐπιγραφές. Athens.

Petzl, G. (1978). 'Inschriften aus der Umgebung von Saittai (I)', *ZPE* 30: 249–76.

Philippson, A. (1911). *Reisen und Forschungen im westlichen Kleinasien,* Heft 2. Gotha.

Pickard-Cambridge, A. (1946). *The Theatre of Dionysus in Athens.* Oxford.

—— (1962). *Dithyramb, Tragedy and Comedy,* rev. 2nd edn. by T. Webster (1st edn., 1927). Oxford.

—— (1988). *The Dramatic Festivals of Athens,* rev. 2nd edn. with supplement by J. Gould and D. Lewis (1st edn., 1968). Oxford.

Pipili, M. (1987). *Laconian Iconography of the Sixth Century BC.* Oxford.

Piranomonte, M. (2002). *Il Santuario della Musica e il bosco sacro di Anna Perenna*. Milan.

Pittakis, K. (1835). *L'ancienne Athènes*. Paris.

Plassart, A. (1921). 'Inscriptions de Delphes: la liste des Théorodoques', *BCH* 45: 1–85.

Pleket, H. (1973). 'Some aspects of the history of the athletic guilds', *ZPE* 10: 197–227.

—— (1975). 'Games, prizes, athletes, and ideology', *Stadion* 1: 49–89.

—— (2001). 'Zur Soziologie des antiken Sports', *Nikephoros* 14: 157–212.

Pöhlmann, E. (1981). 'Die Proedrie des Dionysos-Theaters im 5. Jh. und das Bühnenspiel in der Klassik', *MusHelv* 38: 129–46.

Poland, F. (1895). *De collegiis artificum Dionysiacorum*. Dresden.

—— (1909). *Geschichte des griechischen Vereinswesens*, 3 vols. Leipzig.

—— (1932). *RE* IV² 2, s.v. 'σύνοδος', 1415–34.

—— (1934). *RE* V² 2, s.v. '*Technitaí*', 2473–558.

Polacco, L. and Anti, C. (1990). *Il teatro di Siracusa. Pars altera*. Padua.

Pomtow, H. (1897). 'Fasti Delphici II 2', *Jb. f. Klass. Philol.* 43: 737–848.

—— (1918). 'Neue delphische Inschriften', *Klio* 15: 1–77.

Pottier, E. and Hauvette-Besnault, A.-M. (1880). 'Inscriptions d'Erythrées et de Téos', *BCH* 4: 153–82.

Pounder, R. and Dimitrova, N. (2003). 'Dedication by the Thessalian League to the great gods in Samothrace', *Hesperia* 72: 31–40.

Powell, B. (1991). *Homer and the Origin of the Greek Alphabet*. Cambridge.

Préaux, C. (1987). *Le monde hellénistique*, 2nd edn. Paris.

Preisendanz, K. et al. (1973–4). *Die griechischen Zauberpapyri (Papyri graecae magicae)*, 2 vols. Stuttgart.

Prêtre, C. (2000). 'La Tabula Délienne de 168 av. J.-C.', *BCH* 124: 261–71.

Preuner, E. (1924). 'Σαμιακά', *AM* 49: 26–49.

Prinz, F. (1979). *Gründungsmythen und Sagenchronologie. Zetemata, Heft* 72. Munich.

Privitera, G. (1980). 'Politica religiosa dei Dinomenidi', in *Perennitas. Studi in onore di A. Brelich*. Rome, 393–411.

Prott, H. von (1902). 'Dionysos Kathegemon', *AM* 27: 161–88.

Prott, H. von and Ziehen, L. (1906). *Leges Graecorum Sacrae*. Leipzig.

Pugliese Carratelli, G. (1961–2). 'Nuove iscrizioni di Iasos', *ASAA* 39–40, N.S. 23–4: 536–602.

—— (1967–8). 'Supplemento epigrafico di Iasos', *ASAA* 45–6, N.S. 29–30: 437–85.

—— (1989). 'Decreti di Iasos in onore di giudici stranieri', *Rendiconti dell'Academia Nazionale dei Lincei* 48: 261–9.

Quattrocelli, L. (2006). 'Il mito de Alcesti a Cirene: due rilievi dalla necropoli est', in E. Fabbricotti and O. Menozzi (eds.), *Cirenaica: Studi, scavi e scoperte, Atti del X Convegno di Archeologia Cirenaica, Chieti 24–26 Novembre 2003*, British Archaeological Reports. International Series. Oxford 2006, 373–84.

Queyrel, F. (2001). 'Inscriptions et scènes figurées peintes sur le mur de fond du xyste de Delphes', *BCH* 125: 333–87.

Radt, W. (1999). *Pergamon: Geschichte und Bauten, Funde und Erforschung einer antiken Metropole*. Cologne.

Rehm, R. (2002). *The Play of Space: Spatial Transformation in Greek Tragedy*. Princeton.

Reisch, E. (1890). *Griechische Weihgeschenke*. Vienna.

Revermann, M. (1999–2000). 'Euripides, tragedy and Macedon: some conditions of reception', in M. Cropp, K. Lee and D. Sansone (eds.), *Euripides and Tragic Theatre in the Late Fifth Century*. *ICS* 24–5: 451–67.

Reynolds, J. (1977). 'Inscriptions', in *Excavations at Sidi Khrebish*, vol. I: *Suppl. Libya Antiqua* V. Tripoli, 233–54.

—— (1991). 'Epigraphic evidence for the construction of the theatre: 1st c. b.c. to mid 3rd c. a.d.', in R. Smith and K. Erim (eds.), *Aphrodisias Papers 2: The Theatre, a Sculptor's Workshop, Philosophers, and Coin-types (JRA Suppl. 2)*. Ann Arbor, 15–28.

—— (2000). 'New letters of Hadrian to Aphrodisias', *JRA* 13: 5–20.

Rhodes, P. (1972). *The Athenian Boule*. Oxford.

—— (1981). *A Commentary on the Aristotelian Athenaion Politeia*. Oxford, repr. with addenda, 1993.

—— (2003). 'Nothing to do with democracy', *JHS* 123: 104–19.

Rhodes, P. and Lewis, D. (1997). *The Decrees of the Greek States*. Oxford.

Richardson, N. (1974). *The Homeric Hymn to Demeter*. Oxford.

Rigsby, K. (1987). 'A decree of Haliartus on cult', *AJPh* 108: 729–40.

—— (1996a). *Asylia: Territorial Inviolability in the Hellenistic World*. Berkeley and London.

—— (1996b). 'Craton's legacy', *EA* 26: 137–9.

Ritti, T. (1970). *Sigle ed emblemi sui decreti onorari greci*. Rome.

Robert, L. (1926). 'Notes d'épigraphie hellénistique', *BCH* 50: 497–501 (= *OMS* I.61–5).

—— (1929). 'Décrets de Delphes', *BCH* 53, 34–41 (= *OMS* I.247–54).

—— (1930). 'Sur les Nikephoria de Pergame', *BCH* 54: 332–46.

—— (1936a). *Collection Froehner 1. Inscriptions Grecques*. Paris.

—— (1936b). Recherches épigraphiques, *REA* 38: 5–28 (= *OMS* II.768–91).

—— (1937). *Études anatoliennes. Recherches sur les inscriptions grecques de l'Asie Mineure. Études Orientales V*. Paris.

—— (1938). *Études épigraphiques et philologiques*. Paris.

—— (1940). 'Epigramme de Cyrène', *Hellenica. Recueil d'épigraphie, de numismatique et d'antiquités grecques*. Limoges.

—— (1945). *Le sanctuaire de Sinuri*. Paris.

—— (1966a). *Documents de l'Asie mineure méridionale*. Geneva and Paris.

—— (1966b). *Monnaies antiques en Troade*. Geneva and Paris.

—— (1967). 'Sur des inscriptions d'Éphèse', *Rev. Phil* 1967: 7–84 (=*OMS* V.347–424).

—— (1980). 'Deux poètes grecs à l'époque impériale', in *ΣΤΗΛΗ. ΤΟΜΟΣ ΕΙΣ ΜΝΗΜΗΝ ΝΙΚΟΛΑΟΥ ΚΟΝΤΟΛΕΟΝΤΟΣ*. Athens, 1–20.

—— (1984a). 'Discours d'ouverture', in *Πρακτικὰ τοῦ Η' Διεθνοῦς Συνεδρίου Ἑλληνικῆς καὶ Λατινικῆς Ἐπιγραφικῆς, Ἀθήνα, 3–9 Ὀκτωβρίου 1982*. Athens, 35–45 (=*OMS* VI.709–19).

—— (1984b). 'Un décret d'Elaia', *BCH* 108: 489–96.

—— (1989). *Claros I*. Paris.

Robert, J. and Robert, L. (1976). 'Une inscription grecque de Téos en Ionie: l'union de Téos et de Kyrbissos', *Journal des Savants* 1976: 152–235 (=*OMS* VII.297–379).

—— (1983). *Fouilles d'Amyzon en Carie. Tome 1, Exploration, histoire, monnaies et inscriptions*. Paris.

Robertson, N. (2002). 'The religious criterion in Greek ethnicity: the Dorians and the festival Carneia', *American Journal of Ancient History* 1: 5–74.

Roesch, P. (1975). 'Les Herakleia de Thèbes', *ZPE* 17: 1–7.

—— (1982). *Études béotiennes*. Paris.

—— (1989). 'Les cultes égyptiens en Béotie', in L. Criscuolo and G. Geraci (eds.), *Egitto e storia antica dall' ellenismo all' età araba*. Bologna, 621–9.

Rogers, G. (1991). *The Sacred Identity of Ephesos. Foundation Myths of a Roman City*. London and New York.

Rose, B. (1998). 'The 1997 post-Bronze Age excavations at Troia', *Studia Troica* 8: 71–113.

Ross, L. (1850). *Kleinasien und Deutschland*. Halle.

Rostovtzeff, M. (1930). '*Pergamum*', *CAH* VIII, 1. Cambridge.

—— (1989). *Histoire économique et sociale du monde hellénistique*. Paris (1st edn., 1941).

Roueché, C. (1993). *Performers and Partisans at Aphrodisias*. London.

Rougemont, G. (1977). *Corpus des inscriptions de Delphes*, vol. I: *Lois sacrées et réglements religieux*. Paris.

Ruge, W. (1934). *RE* s.v. 'Teos', 539–70.

Rüpke, G. (2002). '*Collegia Sacerdotum*', in U. Egelhaaf-Gaiser and A. Schäfer (eds.), *Religiöse Vereine in der römischen Antike*. Tübingen, 41–67.

Russo, C. (1984[1962]). *Aristophanes: An Author for the Stage*. London.

Rutherford, I. (1990). 'Paeans by Simonides', *HSCP* 93: 169–209.

—— (1995). 'Apollo's other genre: Proclus on *nomos* and his source', *CP* 90.4: 354–61.

—— (2001). *Pindar's Paeans: A Reading of the Fragments with a Survey of the Genre*. Oxford.

—— (2004). 'χορὸς εἷς ἐκ τῆσδε τῆς πόλεως (Xen. *Mem.* 3.3.12): song-dance and state-pilgrimage at Athens', in Murray and Wilson (eds.), 67–90.

Sahin, S. (1994). 'Piratenüberfall auf Teos: Volksbeschluß über die Finanzierung der Erpressungsgelder', *EA* 23: 1–40.

Salomies, O. (ed.) (2001). *The Greek East in the Roman Context. Proceedings of a colloquium organised by the Finnish Institute at Athens May 21 and 22, 1999*. Helsinki.

Santucci, M. (2002). 'I tempi del sacro in atti pubblici, interstatali e amministrativi del mondo greco', *RIFC* 130: 149–69.

Scafuro, A. (2004). 'The role of the prosecutor and Athenian legal procedure (Dem. 21.10)', *Dike* 7: 113–33.

Schachter, A. (1981–94). *Cults of Boiotia*, 4 vols. *BICS Suppl.* 38. London.

Schäfer, T. (1989). *Imperii Insignia. MDAI(R)* 29. Ergh. Mainz.

Schaus, G. (1985). *The Extramural Sanctuary of Demeter and Persephone in Cyrene, Libya. Final Reports*, vol. II: *The East Greek, Island and Laconian Pottery*. Philadelphia.

Scheid, J. (1985). 'Sacrifice et banquet à Rome: quelques problèmes', *MEFRA* 97: 193–206.

Scheithauer, A. (1997). 'Les aulètes dans le théâtre grec de l'époque hellénistique', in Le Guen (ed.), 107–27.

Schneider, A. (1889). 'Vase des Xenokles und Kleisophos', *AM* 14: 329–33.

Schneidewin, F. (1832). *Diana Phacelitis et Orestes apud Rheginos et Siculos*. Göttingen.

Schnurr, C. (1995). 'Zur Topographie der Theaterstätten und der Tripodenstraße in Athen', *ZPE* 105: 139–53.

Scholl, A. (1994). '*Polytalanta mnemeia*', *JdI* 109: 239–71.

—— (1995). 'Nicht Aristophanes, sondern Epigenes', *JdI* 110: 213–238.

—— (2002). 'Denkmäler der Choregen, Dichter und Schauspieler', in *Die griechische Klassik–Idee oder Wirklichkeit. Exhibition Berlin March 1st–June 2nd 2002*. Mainz, 546–54.

Scholl, A. and Vierneisel, K. (2002). 'Reliefdenkmäler dramatischer Choregen im klassischen Athen. Das Münchner Maskenrelief für Artemis und Dionysos', *Münchner Jahrbuch der bildenden Kunst LIII*. Munich, 20–55.

Schönert-Geiss, E. (1987). *Griechisches Münzwerk: die Münzprägung von Maroneia.* Berlin.

Schröder, B., Schrader, H., Kolbe, W. (1904). 'Die Arbeiten zu Pergamon 1902–1903: Die Inschriften', *AM* 29: 152–78.

Schwarzer, H. (1999). 'Untersuchungen zum hellenistischen Herrscherkult in Pergamon', *Istanbuler Mitteilungen* 49: 249–300.

—— (2002). 'Vereinslokale im hellenistischen und römischen Pergamon', in U. Egelhaaf-Gaiser and A. Schäfer (eds.), *Religiöse Vereine in der römischen Antike.* Tübingen, 221–46.

Scullion, S. (1994). *Three Studies in Athenian Dramaturgy.* Beiträge zur Altertumskunde 25. Stuttgart and Leipzig.

—— (2002). '"Nothing to do with Dionysus": tragedy misconceived as ritual', *CQ* 52: 102–37.

Seaford, R. (1994). *Reciprocity and Ritual: Homer and Tragedy in the Developing City-State.* Oxford.

Shapiro, H. (1992). '*Mousikoi Agones*', in J. Neils (ed.), 53–75.

—— (1996). 'Athena, Apollo, and the religious propaganda of the Athenian empire', *Boreas* 24: 101–13.

Shear, J. (2001). 'Polis and Panathenaia: the history and development of Athena's festival'. Ph.D. thesis, University of Pennsylvania.

—— (2003a). 'Atarbos' base and the Panathenaia', *JHS* 123: 164–80.

—— (2003b). 'Prizes from Athens: the list of Panathenaic prizes and the sacred oil', *ZPE* 142: 87–105.

Shear, L. T. (1978). *Kallias of Sphettos and the Revolt of Athens in 286 BC.* Hesperia Suppl. 17. Princeton.

Shepherd, G. (1995). 'The pride of most colonials: burial and religion in the Sicilian colonies', in T. Fischer-Hansen (ed.), *Ancient Sicily: Acta Hyperborea 6.* Copenhagen, 51–82.

Sherk, R. (1967). *Roman Documents from the Greek East.* Baltimore.

—— (1991). 'The eponymous officials of Greek cities, III', *ZPE* 88: 225–60.

Siewert, P. (1992). 'The Olympic rules', in W. Coulson and H. Kyrileis (eds.), *Proceedings of an international symposium on the Olympic games 5–9 September 1988.* Athens, 113–17.

Sifakis, G. (1967). *Studies in the History of Hellenistic Drama.* London.

Simon, E. (1983). *Festivals of Attica.* Madison.

Slater, W. (1993). 'Three questions on the history of drama', *Phoenix* 47: 189–212.

—— (1995). 'The pantomime Tiberius Iulius Apolaustus', *GRBS* 36: 263–92.

—— (1996). 'Inschriften von Magnesia 192 revisited', *GRBS* 37: 196–204.

—— (1997). 'L'hégemôn dans les fêtes hellénistiques', in B. Le Guen (ed.), *De la scène aux gradins. Pallas* 47: 97–106.

Smith, A. (1892). *Catalogue of Sculpture in the British Museum* I. London.

Sokolowski, F. (1962). *Lois sacrés des cités grecques: supplément.* Paris.

Sommerstein, A. H. (1997). 'The theatre audience, the *Demos,* and the *Suppliants* of Aeschylus', in Pelling (ed.), 63–79.

Sonnabend, H. (1996). *Die Freundschaften der Gelehrten und die zwischenstaatliche Politik im klassischen und hellenistischen Griechenland.* Hildesheim.

Sourvinou-Inwood, C. (1994). 'Something to do with Athens: tragedy and ritual', in R. Osborne and S. Hornblower (eds.), *Ritual, Finance, Politics: Athenian Democratic Accounts presented to David Lewis.* Oxford, 269–90.

Spawforth, A. (1989). 'Agonistic Festivals in Roman Greece', in S. Walker and A. Cameron, *The Greek Renaissance in the Roman Empire. BICS Suppl.* 55. London, 193–7.

Stadter, P. (1989). *A Commentary on Plutarch's 'Pericles'.* Chapel Hill and London.

Stehle, E. (1997). *Performance and Gender in Ancient Greece.* Princeton.

Steinhauer, G. (1992). 'Δύο δημοτικὰ ψηφίσματα τῶν Ἀχαρνέων', *AE* 131: 179–93.

—— (2001). *Το Αρχαιολογικό Μουσείο Πειραιώς.* Athens.

Stephanis, I. (1981). 'Αuletai kuklioî', *Hellenika* 33: 397–402.

—— (1984). 'Ο Ευβοϊκός νόμος για τη μίσθωση των Διονυσιακών τεχνιτών', *EEThess* 22: 499–564.

—— (1988). Διονυσιακοὶ Τεχνῖται. Συμβολὲς στὴν προσωπογραφία τοῦ θεάτρου καὶ τῆς μουσικῆς τῶν ἀρχαίων Ἑλλήνων. Herakleion.

Stewart, A. (1982). 'Dionysos at Delphi: the pediments of the sixth temple of Apollo and religious reform in the age of Alexander', in B. Barr-Sharrar and E. Borza (eds.), *Macedonia and Greece in Late Classical and Early Hellenistic Times. Studies in the History of Art volume 10. National Gallery of Art, Washington.* Washington, 205–27.

Storey, I. (2003). *Eupolis: Poet of Old Comedy.* Oxford.

Strasser, J.-Y. (2002). 'Choraules et pythaules d'époque impériale: à propos d'inscriptions de Delphes', *BCH* 126: 97–142.

Stroud, R. (1968). 'The Sanctuary of Demeter and Kore on Acrocorinth, preliminary report II, 1964–1965', *Hesperia* 37: 299–330.

—— (1974). 'Three Attic decrees', *CSCA* 7: 290–8.

Stucchi, S. (1975). *Architettura cirenaica.* Roma.

Summa, D. (2003a). 'Le *Didascalie* e il teatro postclassico', in Martina (ed.), 293–303.

—— (2003b). 'Dalla coregia all'agonotesia attraverso i documenti epigrafici', in Martina (ed.), 510–32.

—— (2004). 'Una dedica coregica inedita', *ZPE* 150: 147–8.

Susanetti, D. (2001). *Euripide 'Alcesti'*. Venice.

Sutton, D. (1987). 'The theatrical families of Athens', *AJPh* 108: 9–26.

—— (1989). *Dithyrambographi Graeci*. Munich and Zürich.

Svenson-Evers, H. (1996). *Die griechischen Architekten archaischer und klassischer Zeit. Archäologische Studien* 11. Frankfurt.

Szanto, E. (1896). *RE* II, s.v. ᾽Αρχιτέκτων', 552.

Tanoglu, A. et al. (1961). *Türkiye Atlası*. Istanbul.

Taplin, O. (1977). *The Stagecraft of Aeschylus*. Oxford.

—— (1993). *Comic Angels*. Oxford.

—— (1999). 'Spreading the word through performance', in Goldhill and Osborne (eds.), 33–57.

Tedeschi, G. (2003). 'Lo spettacolo in età ellenistica e tardo antica nella documentazione epigrafica e papirace', *Papyrologica Lupiensia* 1: 87–187.

Texier, C. (1849). *Description de l'Asie Mineure faite par ordre du gouvernement français, de 1833 à 1837*, vol. III. Paris.

Thonemann, P. (2003). 'Hellenistic inscriptions from Lydia', *EA* 36: 95–108.

Todisco, L. (2002). *Teatro e spettacolo in Magna Grecia e in Sicilia: testi, immagini, architettura*. Milan.

—— (ed.) (2003). *La ceramica figurata a soggetto tragico in Magna Grecia e Sicilia*. Rome.

Townsend, R. (1985). 'A newly discovered capital from the Thrasyllos monument', *AJA* 89: 676–80.

Tracy, S. (1975). *The Lettering of an Athenian Mason. Hesperia Suppl.* 15. Princeton.

Tracy, S. and Habicht, C. (1991). 'New and old Panathenaic victor lists', *Hesperia* 60: 187–236.

Travlos, J. (1971). *Pictorial Dictionary of Ancient Athens*. London and New York.

Tréheux, J. (1984). 'Les Cosmes à Latô', in Centre G. Glotz, *Aux origines de l'Hellénisme. La Crète et la Grèce*. Paris, 329–42.

Tzachou-Alexandri, O. (1999). 'The original plan of the Greek theater reconsidered: the theater of Euonymon of Attica', in R. Docter and E. Moormann (eds.), *Proceedings of the XVth International Congress of Classical Archaeology, Amsterdam, July 12–17, 1998*. Amsterdam, 420–3.

Vallois, R. (1944). *L'architecture hellénique et hellénistique à Délos jusqu'à l'éviction des Déliens (166 av. J.C.)*. Rome and Paris.

Vandoni, M. (1964). *Feste pubbliche e private nei documenti greci*. Milan.

Vernant, J.-P. and Vidal-Naquet, P. (1988). *Myth and Tragedy in Ancient Greece*. New York (French edns., Paris, 1972, 1986).

Veyne, P. (1985). 'Une inscription dionysiaque peu commune', *BCH* 109: 621–4.

Vial, C. (1984). *Délos indépendante (314–167 avant J.-C.: étude d'une communauté civique et de ses institutions*. Paris.

—— (2003). 'À propos des concours de l'Orient méditerranéen à l'époque hellénistique', in F. Prost (ed.), *L'Orient méditerranéen de la mort d'Alexandre aux campagnes de Pompée. Pallas* 62: 311–28.

Virgilio, B. (1993). *Gli Attalidi di Pergamo*. Pisa.

Vogt, E. (1964). 'Aischylos 1', *KlP* 1: 192–8.

Vollgraff, W. (1901). 'Inscriptions de Béotie, no.19 (Livadie)', *BCH* 25: 365–75.

Voutiras, E. (1991–2). 'Παίδων χορός', *Egnatia* 3: 29–55.

Wade-Gery, H. (1958). *Essays in Greek History*. Oxford.

Walbank, M. (1991). 'Leases of public lands: L13, decree of Peiraieus: construction and lease of a theater', *Agora* 19, *Inscriptions*. Princeton, 194–5.

Wallner, C. (1997). *Soldatenkaiser und Sport*. Frankfurt am Main.

—— (2001). 'Zur Agonistik von Gaza', *ZPE* 135: 125–35.

Walter, O. (1923). *Beschreibung der Reliefs im kleinen Acropolismuseum in Athen*. Vienna.

Walton, J. (1977). 'Financial arrangements for the Athenian dramatic festivals', *Theatre Research International* 2: 79–86.

—— (1980). *Greek Theatre Practice*. London.

Weber, L. (1930). *Euripides 'Alkestis'*. Leipzig and Berlin.

Weiler, I. (1997). 'Olympia—jenseits der Agonistik', *Nikephoros* 10: 191–213.

Weiss, P. (1990). 'Mythen, Dichter and Münzen von Lykaonien', *Chiron* 20: 221–37.

Welles, C. (1934). *Royal Correspondence in the Hellenistic Period. A Study in Greek Epigraphy*. New Haven.

Wensler, A. (1989). 'Zur Datierung des Temenos für den Herrscherkult in Pergamon', *AA*: 33–42.

West, M. (1971). 'Further light on Stesichorus' *Iliou persis*', *ZPE* 7: 262–4.

—— (1983). 'Tragica V', *BICS* 30: 61–78.

West, W. (1997). 'New light on an opisthographic lead tablet in Chapel Hill', *Preatti. XI Congresso internazionale di epigrafia greca e latina, Roma 18–24 settembre 1997*. Rome, 71–8.

Wiegand, T. (1958). *Didyma. Zweiter Teil, Die Inschriften, von Albert Rehm, herausgegeben von Richard Harder*. Berlin.

Wiles, D. (1997). *Tragedy in Athens: Performance Space and Theatrical Meaning.* Cambridge.

Wilhelm, A. (1900). 'Nachlese zu griechischen Inschriften', *JÖAI* 3: 40–62.

—— (1906). *Urkunden dramatischer Aufführungen in Athen.* Vienna.

—— (1909). *Beiträge zur griechischen Inschriftenkunde.* Vienna.

—— (1923). 'Zu Inschriften aus Kleinasien', in W. Buckler, and W. Calder, (eds.), *Anatolian Studies presented to W. M. Ramsay.* Manchester, 415–39.

—— (1951). 'Griechische Inschriften rechtlichen Inhalts', *Πραγματεῖαι τῆς Ἀκαδημίας Ἀθηνῶν* 17.1: 1–112 (= Wilhelm A. (1974). *Akademieschriften zur griechischen Inschriftenkunde (1895–1951)* 3. Leipzig, 391–501).

—— (2002). *Kleine Schriften Teile IV.* Vienna, 145–56 (= 'Parerga', *Wiener Eranos* (1909) 125–36).

Williams, H. and Schaus, G. (2001). 'The sanctuary of Athena at ancient Stymphalos', in S. Deacy and A. Villing (eds.), *Athena in the Classical World.* Leiden, Boston and Cologne, 75–94.

Wilson, P. (1991). 'Demosthenes 21, *Against Meidias*: democratic abuse', *PCPS* 37: 164–95.

—— (1997a). 'Amymon of Sikyon: a first victory in Athens and a first tragic khoregic dedication in the city? (*SEG* 23, 103b)', *ZPE* 118: 174–8.

—— (1997b). 'Leading the tragic chorus', in Pelling (ed.), 81–108.

—— (1999). 'The aulos in Athens', in Goldhill and Osborne (eds.), 58–95.

—— (2000). *The Athenian Institution of the 'Khoregia': The Chorus, the City, and the Stage.* Cambridge.

—— (2002). 'The musicians among the actors', in Easterling and Hall (eds.), 41–70.

—— (2003). 'The politics of dance: dithyrambic contest and social order in ancient Greece', in D. Phillips and D. Pritchard (eds.), *Sport and Festival in the Ancient Greek World.* Swansea, 163–96.

—— (*forthcoming*). 'The musical world of Pronomos'.

Winkler, J. and Zeitlin, F. (eds.) (1990). *Nothing to do with Dionysos?: Athenian Drama in its Social Context.* Princeton.

Wohl, V. (1996). 'Hegemony and democracy at the Panathenaia', *Classica et mediaevalia* 47: 25–88.

Woodward, A. (1924–5). 'Excavations at Sparta, 1924–25: the inscriptions', *ABSA* 26: 159–239.

Wörrle, M. (1988). *Stadt und Fest im kaiserzeitlichen Kleinasien. Studien zu einer agonistischen Stiftung aus Oinoanda.* Munich.

Wycherley, R. (1963). 'The Pythion at Athens', *AJA* 67: 75–9.

Ziegler, K. (1919). *RE* 11, s.v. 'Kamarina', cols. 1801–7.

—— (1925). *RE* 12, s.v. 'Leontinoi', cols. 2042–7.

—— (1967). 'Gela', *KlP* 2: 719–22.

Ziegler, R. (1985). *Städtisches Prestige und kaiserzeitliche Politik.* Düsseldorf.

Zimmermann, B. (1992). *Dithyrambos: Geschichte einer Gattung.* Göttingen.

Zimmermann, K. (2000). 'Späthellenistische Kultpraxis in einer karischen Kleinstadt', *Chiron* 30: 451–85.

Zoumbaki, S. (2001). *Elis und Olympia in der Kaiserzeit. Meletemata* 32. Paris and Athens.

Zwicker, J. (1933). *RE* 16.1, s.v. 'Myskellos', cols. 1189–91.

General Index

solo artists 245
Sopatros, son of Epikrates 299, 308
Sophokles 202, 376
Sophron 363
Sosias 369–70
Soteria, at Delphi 27, 29, 46, 68–9, 72–4,
    75–6, 197, 210
Sparta 51, 201, 202, 204, 206, 211 n. 58,
    302 n. 43, 367, 368
Stratonikeia 25
Stuart and Revett 133
Syracuse 361, 362

Tekhnitai (Dionysiac artists) 5–7, 25,
    32–4, 35, 67–84, 220–45, 246–78
  Anatolian association 249, 259, 261,
    273 *see also* Asia Minor association
  Asia Minor association 30, 70, 77,
    246, 259, 285–6
  Athenian association 68, 70, 75, 76,
    80, 287 n. 30
  contracts 81–2
  of Dionysos Kathegemon 256, 258
  Egyptian association 25, 77–8
  Ionian-Hellespontine association 30,
    68, 220, 231, 241
  Isthmian-Nemean association 69–84,
    248, 259
  synagonists 260–1
  at Syracuse 354 n. 17
  Teian association, *see* Ionian-
    Hellespontine association
  unification of associations 261
Teos:
  geography 216–20
  victor-lists 220–32
Thargelia 8–9, 150–82, 198 n. 27
  choral contests at 156–8
  location of cult 163
  purification rites 172
  see also *khoregoi*; khoregic dedications
thargelos 151, 169–71, **170**
theatre:
  admission charges 92, 97, 100–3, 111,
    303–4
  at Akharnai (Attic deme) 95
  at Anagyrous (Attic deme) 126
  assemblies held in 107, 163
  at Cyrene 197–8
  at Delos 112–13, 197–8

entrepreneurship 93–4, 100
  at Epidauros 113
  fighting in 101
  at Gela 357–8
  at Halai Aixonides (Attic deme) 126
  heel-banging in 98
  honours announced in 55–8
  at Ikarion (Attic deme) 106 n. 37,
    123, 125, 126, 145
  leasing of 90–6, 104, 113, 114–15
  machinery (*periaktriai*) 190–1, 209
  order in 59–60
  at Peiraieus (Attic deme) 89, 92, 95,
    100, 107
  prohedria 61–2, 92–3, 94, 95, 99, 106
    n. 37, 110, 113, 116–18, 120–1,
    125
  at Rhamnous (Attic deme) 106 n. 37
  at Samothrace 287
  seating capacity of 97, 99–100
  seating reservations for 60–1, 101,
    111
  shape of 99, 106
  stone construction of 98
  at Syracuse 106 n. 37, 198, 361, 363
  at Thorikos (Attic deme) 106 n. 37
  wooden construction of 95, 98,
    103–8, 163
Theatre of Dionysos (Athens) 96–100,
    116–20, **131**
  Classical 98–9, 116–21, **117**, **121**
  Lykourgan 95, 98–9, 106, 112, 116,
    117, 118, 120
  seating capacity of 97, 99–100
  shape of, *see* theatre
  Thargelian contests held in 163
theatron:
  meaning of term 89–90
theatronai / theatropolai 88–90, 96–7
Themistokles 124
Theodotos (singer) 76 n. 45
theorikon (festival fund) 100–3
theoroi / theoria 77, 79, 82–3, 282–4,
    286, 288 n. 34
Theseus 172–4, 181
Theseus (*kithara* player) 240–1
Thrasippos (*aulos* player / *khoregos*) 124
Thrason (poet) 240–1, 285
Thrasyllos (*khoregos*), *see* khoregic
    monuments

Index Locorum

Epigraphical Index

---

[1] See 246 n. 3. For a concordance to the TE references see Le Guen (2001a) II. 217–19.